중학영어듣기 만점 솔루션

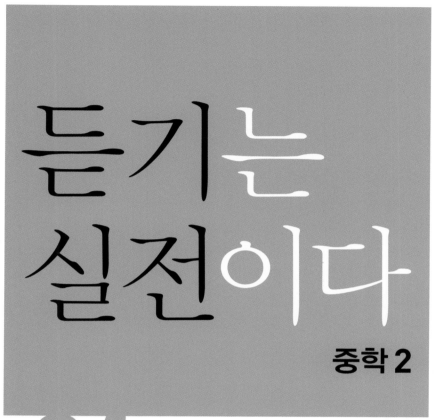

듣기는 실전이다

중학 2

24회

듣기는 실전이다 중학2 24회

저자 강보배, 김대성, 서성용, 소원석, 육상태, 윤진섭, 이수윤, 장정근, 전광훈

펴낸날 [초판 6쇄] 2024년 2월 1일

펴낸이 이기열

펴낸곳 (주)디딤돌 교육

주소 (03972) 서울특별시 마포구 월드컵북로 122 청원선와이즈타워

대표전화 02-3142-9000

구입문의 02-322-8451

내용문의 02-325-3224

팩시밀리 02-335-6038

홈페이지 www.didimdol.co.kr

등록번호 제10-718호

출간 이후 발견되는 오류는 "디딤돌 홈페이지 ⇨ 영어 ⇨ 정오표"를 통해
알려드리고 있습니다.

중학영어듣기 만점 솔루션

듣기는
실전이다

중학 2

24회

딤돌

듣기만점 실전공부법

1단계
나를 진단한다!

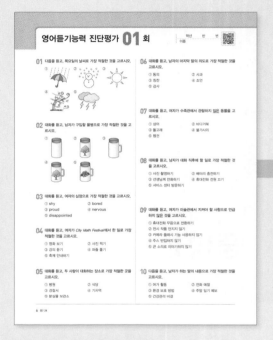

최근 3개년 기출 문제로
나만의 듣기실력 진단!

2단계
듣기는 실전이다!

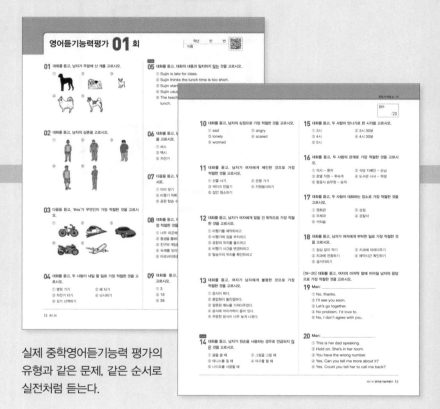

실제 중학영어듣기능력 평가의
유형과 같은 문제, 같은 순서로
실전처럼 듣는다.

만점 듣기전략

교육과정 성취 기준에 맞춰 듣기능력평가 출제 유형을 제시, 각각의 유형을 잘 드러내는
기출문제로 유형별 실전 솔루션을 익힌다.

3 단계 만점 듣기 PLUS BOOK

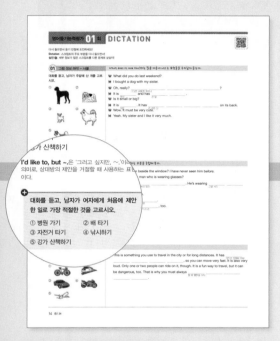

- ## 듣기 만점으로 가는 DICTATION과 실전 PLUS!

  DICTATION 스크립트의 주요 부분을 다시 들으면세!

  실전 Plus 세부 정보가 많은 스크립트를 다른 문제로 샅샅이!

- ## 말할 수 있으면 들린다!

  회별 주요 표현을
  우리말을 보면서
  영어로 듣고 또 듣고
  영어를 보면서 듣고
  따라 말하고

- ## 주요 어휘 및 표현

  회별, 문항별 주요 어휘와 표현을
  시간 날 때마다 반복, 또 반복! 사진처럼 저장한다.

꼼꼼한 해설로 듣기 만점에 도전!

유형 안내부터 스크립트, 해석, 만점 솔루션, 어휘와 표현으로 이어지는 꼼꼼 해설로 듣기 만점에
도전하세요!

중학영어듣기능력 평가

계획을 세워 매일 정해진 양을 공부하고,
공부가 끝나면 공부한 날과 맞힌 문항 수를 체크해 보세요.

만점 듣기전략

01 다음을 듣고, 목요일의 날씨로 가장 적절한 것을 고르시오.

02 대화를 듣고, 남자가 구입할 물병으로 가장 적절한 것을 고르시오.

03 대화를 듣고, 여자의 심정으로 가장 적절한 것을 고르시오.

① shy　　　　　　　② bored
③ proud　　　　　　④ nervous
⑤ disappointed

04 대화를 듣고, 여자가 *City Math Festival*에서 한 일로 가장 적절한 것을 고르시오.

① 영화 보기　　　　　② 사진 찍기
③ 강의 듣기　　　　　④ 퍼즐 풀기
⑤ 축제 안내하기

05 대화를 듣고, 두 사람이 대화하는 장소로 가장 적절한 곳을 고르시오.

① 병원　　　　　　　② 식당
③ 경찰서　　　　　　④ 기차역
⑤ 분실물 보관소

06 대화를 듣고, 남자의 마지막 말의 의도로 가장 적절한 것을 고르시오.

① 동의　　　　　　　② 사과
③ 칭찬　　　　　　　④ 조언
⑤ 감사

07 대화를 듣고, 여자가 수족관에서 관람하지 않은 동물을 고르시오.

① 상어　　　　　　　② 바다거북
③ 돌고래　　　　　　④ 불가사리
⑤ 펭귄

08 대화를 듣고, 남자가 대화 직후에 할 일로 가장 적절한 것을 고르시오.

① 사진 촬영하기　　　② 배터리 충전하기
③ 선생님께 전화하기　　④ 휴대전화 전원 끄기
⑤ 서비스 센터 방문하기

09 대화를 듣고, 여자가 미술관에서 지켜야 할 사항으로 언급하지 않은 것을 고르시오.

① 휴대전화 무음으로 전환하기
② 전시 작품 만지지 않기
③ 카메라 플래시 기능 사용하지 않기
④ 주스 반입하지 않기
⑤ 큰 소리로 이야기하지 않기

10 다음을 듣고, 남자가 하는 말의 내용으로 가장 적절한 것을 고르시오.

① 여가 활동　　　　　② 전화 예절
③ 환경 보호 방법　　　④ 주말 일기 예보
⑤ 건강관리 비결

점수

/20

11 다음을 듣고, 벼룩시장에 대한 내용과 일치하지 <u>않는</u> 것을 고르시오.

① 금요일에 실시된다.
② 아픈 아이들을 돕기 위한 행사이다.
③ 중고품을 판매한다.
④ 학교 강당에서 열린다.
⑤ 수요일까지 참가 신청이 가능하다.

12 대화를 듣고, 여자가 전화를 건 목적으로 가장 적절한 것을 고르시오.

① 분실물을 찾기 위해서
② 모임 불참을 알려주기 위해서
③ 숙소를 예약하기 위해서
④ 비행 일정을 변경하기 위해서
⑤ 식당 예약을 취소하기 위해서

13 대화를 듣고, 두 사람이 만날 시각을 고르시오.

① 3:30 p.m.　　② 4:00 p.m.
③ 4:30 p.m.　　④ 5:00 p.m.
⑤ 5:30 p.m.

14 대화를 듣고, 두 사람의 관계로 가장 적절한 것을 고르시오.

① 교사 – 학생　　② 택배기사 – 고객
③ 경찰관 – 시민　　④ 수의사 – 손님
⑤ 승무원 – 탑승객

15 대화를 듣고, 남자가 여자에게 부탁한 일로 가장 적절한 것을 고르시오.

① 가방 들어주기　　② 숙제 도와주기
③ 병원 함께 가기　　④ 청소 같이 하기
⑤ 계단에서 부축해주기

16 대화를 듣고, 여자가 남자의 제안을 거절한 이유로 가장 적절한 것을 고르시오.

① 감기에 걸려서　　② 숙제를 해야 해서
③ 봉사활동을 해야 해서　　④ 병문안을 가야 해서
⑤ 결혼식에 참석해야 해서

17 다음 그림의 상황에 가장 적절한 대화를 고르시오.

①　　②　　③　　④　　⑤

18 다음을 듣고, 여자가 학교 버스에 대해 언급하지 <u>않은</u> 것을 고르시오.

① 노선 수　　② 승강장 확인 방법
③ 운영 시간　　④ 이용 요금
⑤ 이용 신청 방법

【19~20】대화를 듣고, 남자의 마지막 말에 이어질 여자의 말로 가장 적절한 것을 고르시오.

19 Woman: _____

① No, it doesn't.　　② That's perfect.
③ Can you spell it?　　④ Long time no see.
⑤ I'm taller than you.

20 Woman: _____

① I have a fever.
② It took 40 minutes by bus.
③ I play the piano very well.
④ My favorite food is spaghetti.
⑤ They're blue with white stripes.

01 다음을 듣고, 예상되는 런던의 날씨로 가장 적절한 것을 고르시오.

02 대화를 듣고, 테이블 매트 위의 물건 배치로 가장 적절한 것을 고르시오.

03 대화를 듣고, 여자의 심정으로 가장 적절한 것을 고르시오.

① shy ② bored
③ upset ④ excited
⑤ worried

04 대화를 듣고, 여자가 지난 일요일에 한 일로 가장 적절한 것을 고르시오.

① 자원 봉사 ② 사진 정리
③ 과학 공부 ④ 집안 청소
⑤ 캠핑 용품 구입

05 대화를 듣고, 두 사람이 대화하는 장소로 가장 적절한 곳을 고르시오.

① 교실 ② 실험실
③ 은행 ④ 가방 판매점
⑤ 공원 분실물 센터

06 대화를 듣고, 여자의 마지막 말의 의도로 가장 적절한 것을 고르시오.

① 감사 ② 거절
③ 격려 ④ 허락
⑤ 충고

07 대화를 듣고, 여자가 밴드에서 연주할 악기를 고르시오.

① drum ② guitar
③ piano ④ bass guitar
⑤ saxophone

08 대화를 듣고, 남자가 대화 직후에 할 일로 가장 적절한 것을 고르시오.

① 편지 보내기 ② 설거지 하기
③ 블로그 방문하기 ④ 삼촌댁 방문하기
⑤ 저녁 식사 초대하기

09 다음을 듣고, 여자가 *Nara Public Library* 이용에 대해 언급하지 <u>않은</u> 것을 고르시오.

① 이용 가능 시간 ② 휴관일 안내
③ 무료 수업 ④ 대출 가능 권수
⑤ 휴일 도서 반납 방법

10 다음을 듣고, 남자가 하는 말의 내용으로 가장 적절한 것을 고르시오.

① 다양한 통신 수단 ② 대중교통의 장점
③ 인터넷 쇼핑의 장점 ④ 인터넷 중독의 심각성
⑤ 올바른 휴대전화 사용방법

점수
/20

11 대화를 듣고, 여자가 언급한 내용과 일치하지 <u>않는</u> 것을 고르시오.

① 뮤지컬을 볼 것이다.
② 런던에 갈 것이다.
③ 여행 기간은 일주일이다.
④ 유명한 곳들을 방문할 것이다.
⑤ 사진을 많이 찍을 것이다.

12 대화를 듣고, 여자가 한국을 방문한 목적으로 가장 적절한 것을 고르시오.

① 좋아하는 배우를 만나기 위해서
② 친척 집을 방문하기 위해서
③ 한국 요리를 배우기 위해서
④ K-pop 콘서트에 가기 위해서
⑤ 드라마 촬영장을 구경하기 위해서

13 대화를 듣고, 여자가 지불해야 할 금액으로 가장 적절한 것을 고르시오.

① $1   ② $2
③ $3   ④ $4
⑤ $5

14 대화를 듣고, 두 사람의 관계로 가장 적절한 것을 고르시오.

① 은행원– 고객   ② 사진 작가–모델
③ 문구점 직원– 고객   ④ 인쇄소 사장–직원
⑤ 시험 감독 교사–응시 학생

15 대화를 듣고, 남자가 여자에게 요청한 일로 가장 적절한 것을 고르시오.

① 쿠키 전해주기   ② 숟가락 가져오기
③ 딸기잼 만들기   ④ 땅콩잼 사오기
⑤ 사진 찍어주기

16 대화를 듣고, 여자가 상을 받게 된 이유로 가장 적절한 것을 고르시오.

① 청소를 잘해서   ② 노래를 잘해서
③ 시험성적이 좋아서   ④ 퀴즈쇼에서 우승해서
⑤ 친구들을 도와줘서

17 다음 그림의 상황에 가장 적절한 대화를 고르시오.

①   ②   ③   ④   ⑤

18 대화를 듣고, 두 사람이 여행에 관해 언급하지 <u>않은</u> 것을 고르시오.

① 여름 옷   ② 현지 날씨
③ 여행 목적지   ④ 식사 메뉴
⑤ 숙소 이름

【19~20】대화를 듣고, 남자의 마지막 말에 이어질 여자의 응답으로 가장 적절한 것을 고르시오.

19 Woman: _____

① Okay, let's go together.
② Maybe he can help you.
③ That is my pencil case.
④ Go straight for one block.
⑤ I think that was your problem.

20 Woman: _____

① They hunt only at night.
② They live in South Africa.
③ They eat deer and buffalos.
④ They can run about 100 km per hour.
⑤ They have black spots on their bodies.

01 다음을 듣고, 부산의 오늘 날씨로 가장 적절한 것을 고르시오.

02 대화를 듣고, 남자가 가져와야 할 쟁반으로 가장 적절한 것을 고르시오.

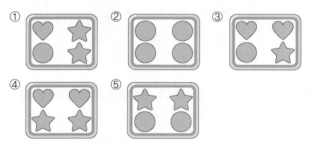

03 대화를 듣고, 남자의 심정으로 가장 적절한 것을 고르시오.

① bored　　　　　② happy
③ nervous　　　　④ proud
⑤ satisfied

04 대화를 듣고, 여자가 과학의 날에 한 일로 가장 적절한 것을 고르시오.

① 3D 영화 보기　　　　② 물 폭탄 만들기
③ 자석 원리 실험하기　④ 에너지 절약 포스터 그리기
⑤ 나무젓가락 비행기 만들기

05 대화를 듣고, 두 사람이 대화하는 장소로 가장 적절한 것을 고르시오.

① 은행　　　　　　② 병원
③ 학교　　　　　　④ 체육관
⑤ 관광 안내소

06 대화를 듣고, 남자의 마지막 말의 의도로 가장 적절한 것을 고르시오.

① 사과　　　　　　② 충고
③ 동의　　　　　　④ 비난
⑤ 감사

07 대화를 듣고, 남자가 *Space Camp*에 대해 언급하지 않은 것을 고르시오.

① 주최 기관　　　　② 개최 기간
③ 참가 대상　　　　④ 활동 내용
⑤ 참가 비용

08 대화를 듣고, 두 사람이 대화 직후에 할 일로 가장 적절한 것을 고르시오.

① 책 구입하기　　　② 교무실 가기
③ 도서관 가기　　　④ 인터넷 검색하기
⑤ 친구에게 전화하기

09 다음을 듣고, 남자가 *Job Experience Day*에 대해 언급하지 않은 것을 고르시오.

① 체험 가능 직업　　② 행사 시작 시간
③ 신청 마감일　　　④ 체험 소요 시간
⑤ 행사 장소

10 다음을 듣고, 여자가 하는 말의 내용으로 가장 적절한 것을 고르시오.

① 감사하는 삶의 자세　　② 다양한 문화의 이해
③ 가족 여행의 즐거움　　④ 신속한 지진 대피 요령
⑤ 규칙적인 생활의 중요성

점수

/20

11 다음을 듣고, *Highlands Zoo*에 대한 내용으로 일치하지 <u>않는</u> 것을 고르시오.

① 전 세계에서 온 많은 종류의 동물들이 있다.
② 중국에서 온 판다 두 마리가 있다.
③ 오늘 판다를 볼 수 있다.
④ 동물들에게 약간의 먹이를 줄 수 있다.
⑤ 동물 우리에 물건을 던지면 안 된다.

12 대화를 듣고, 여자가 전화를 건 목적으로 가장 적절한 것을 고르시오.

① 도서관에 가기 위해서
② 티켓을 구입하기 위해서
③ 공연을 연습하기 위해서
④ 숙제를 확인하기 위해서
⑤ 영화를 함께 보러 가기 위해서

13 대화를 듣고, 밴드가 공연할 날짜를 고르시오.

① 5월 8일
② 5월 9일
③ 5월 10일
④ 5월 11일
⑤ 5월 12일

14 대화를 듣고, 두 사람의 관계로 가장 적절한 것을 고르시오.

① 요리사 – 고객
② 미용사 – 고객
③ 소설가 – 독자
④ 은행원 – 고객
⑤ 미술 교사 – 학생

15 대화를 듣고, 남자가 여자에게 부탁한 일로 가장 적절한 것을 고르시오.

① 버스표 구입하기
② 입장료 알아보기
③ 식사 장소 알아보기
④ 미술 작품 알아보기
⑤ 미술관 위치 확인하기

16 대화를 듣고, 남자가 마스크를 써야 하는 이유로 가장 적절한 것을 고르시오.

① 황사가 있어서
② 햇빛이 강해서
③ 감기에 걸려서
④ 얼굴을 다쳐서
⑤ 청소를 해야 해서

17 다음 그림의 상황에 가장 적절한 대화를 고르시오.

①   ②   ③   ④   ⑤

18 다음을 듣고, 여자가 하는 일로 언급되지 <u>않은</u> 것을 고르시오.

① 외국 관광객들의 언어 소통을 도와준다.
② 외국 관광객에게 한국 전통 의상 만드는 법을 가르친다.
③ 외국 관광객들이 고적지와 박물관 등을 방문하는 것을 돕는다.
④ 외국 관광객들을 데리고 축제에 간다.
⑤ 외국 관광객들에게 한국 음식을 체험하게 한다.

【19~20】 대화를 듣고, 여자의 마지막 말에 이어질 남자의 응답으로 가장 적절한 것을 고르시오.

19 Man: _____

① That sounds good.
② Please forgive me.
③ Thank you for coming.
④ Let me introduce myself.
⑤ That looks too big for you.

20 Man: _____

① Enjoy your meal.
② See you next time.
③ Have a wonderful time.
④ Text him that you are sorry.
⑤ Of course, I'll be there on time.

영어듣기능력평가 **01** 회

01 대화를 듣고, 남자가 주말에 산 개를 고르시오.

02 대화를 듣고, 남자의 삼촌을 고르시오.

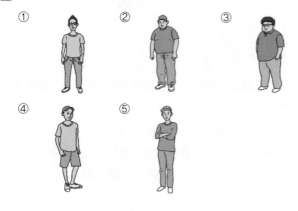

03 다음을 듣고, 'this'가 무엇인지 가장 적절한 것을 고르시오.

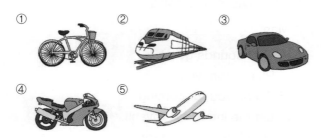

04 대화를 듣고, 두 사람이 내일 할 일로 가장 적절한 것을 고르시오.

① 병원 가기　　　　② 배 타기
③ 자전거 타기　　　④ 낚시하기
⑤ 강가 산책하기

05 대화를 듣고, 대화의 내용과 일치하지 <u>않는</u> 것을 고르시오.

① Sujin is late for class.
② Sujin thinks the lunch time is too short.
③ Sujin stands in line for lunch for a long time.
④ Sujin usually eats fast.
⑤ The teacher suggests Sujin bring her own lunch.

06 대화를 듣고, 남자가 이용할 교통 수단으로 가장 적절한 것을 고르시오.

① 버스　　　　　　② 도보
③ 택시　　　　　　④ 지하철
⑤ 자전거

07 다음을 듣고, 무엇에 관한 안내인지 가장 적절한 것을 고르시오.

① 미아 찾기　　　　② 비행기 연착
③ 비행기 착륙　　　④ 비행기 이륙
⑤ 공항 탑승 수속

08 대화를 듣고, 여자가 영어 에세이를 마치지 <u>못한</u> 이유로 가장 적절한 것을 고르시오.

① 너무 피곤해서
② 동생을 돌봐야 해서
③ 친구와 게임을 해서
④ 숙제를 잊어버려서
⑤ 아르바이트를 해야 해서

09 대화를 듣고, 여자가 학교에서 판매할 책의 권수를 고르시오.

① 3　　　　　　　② 15
③ 18　　　　　　④ 20
⑤ 38

10 대화를 듣고, 남자의 심정으로 가장 적절한 것을 고르시오.

① sad   ② angry
③ lonely   ④ scared
⑤ worried

11 대화를 듣고, 남자가 여자에게 제안한 것으로 가장 적절한 것을 고르시오.

① 선물 사기   ② 은행 가기
③ 케이크 만들기   ④ 자원봉사하기
⑤ 집안 청소하기

12 대화를 듣고, 남자가 여자에게 말을 건 목적으로 가장 적절한 것을 고르시오.

① 비행기를 예약하려고
② 비행기에 짐을 부치려고
③ 공항의 위치를 물으려고
④ 비행기 시간을 변경하려고
⑤ 탑승구의 위치를 확인하려고

13 대화를 듣고, 여자가 남자에게 불평한 것으로 가장 적절한 것을 고르시오.

① 음식이 짜다.
② 종업원이 불친절하다.
③ 잘못된 메뉴를 가져다주었다.
④ 음식에 머리카락이 들어 있다.
⑤ 주문한 음식이 너무 늦게 나왔다.

고난도
14 대화를 듣고, 남자가 왼손을 사용하는 경우로 언급되지 않은 것을 고르시오.

① 글을 쓸 때   ② 그림을 그릴 때
③ 테니스를 칠 때   ④ 야구를 할 때
⑤ 나이프를 사용할 때

15 대화를 듣고, 두 사람이 만나기로 한 시각을 고르시오.

① 3시   ② 3시 30분
③ 4시   ④ 4시 30분
⑤ 5시

16 대화를 듣고, 두 사람의 관계로 가장 적절한 것을 고르시오.

① 의사 – 환자   ② 식당 지배인 – 손님
③ 호텔 직원 – 투숙객   ④ 도서관 사서 – 학생
⑤ 항공사 승무원 – 승객

17 대화를 듣고, 두 사람이 대화하는 장소로 가장 적절한 것을 고르시오.

① 영화관   ② 상점
③ 우체국   ④ 경찰서
⑤ 커피숍

18 대화를 듣고, 여자가 남자에게 부탁한 일로 가장 적절한 것을 고르시오.

① 점심 같이 먹기   ② 치과에 데려다주기
③ 치과에 전화하기   ④ 예약시간 확인하기
⑤ 설거지하기

[19~20] 대화를 듣고, 여자의 마지막 말에 이어질 남자의 응답으로 가장 적절한 것을 고르시오.

19 Man: _____

① No, thanks.
② I'll see you soon.
③ Let's go together.
④ No problem. I'd love to.
⑤ No, I don't agree with you.

20 Man: _____

① This is her dad speaking.
② Hold on. She's in her room.
③ You have the wrong number.
④ Yes. Can you tell me more about it?
⑤ Yes. Could you tell her to call me back?

영어듣기능력평가 01 회 DICTATION

다시 들으면서 듣기 만점에 도전하세요!

Dictation: 스크립트의 주요 부분을 다시 들으면서!

실전 ⊕: 세부 정보가 많은 스크립트를 다른 문제로 샅샅이!

01 그림 정보 파악 – 사물

What does it look like?라는 질문 다음에 나오는 표현들을 주의깊게 듣는다.

대화를 듣고, 남자가 주말에 산 개를 고르시오.

① 
② 
③ 
④ 
⑤ 

W What did you do last weekend?

M I bought a dog with my sister.

W Oh, really? __________ __________ __________ __________? (그것은 어떻게 생겼니)

M It is __________ (흰색) and has __________ __________ (긴 털).

W Is it small or big?

M It is __________ (작은). It has __________ __________ __________ __________ (큰 검은 점) on its back.

W Wow. It must be very cute.

M Yeah. My sister and I like it very much.

What does it look like?는 '그것은 어떻게 생겼니?'라는 의미로, 생김새를 묻는 표현이다.

02 그림 정보 파악 – 인물

삼촌의 생김새를 말하는 부분을 종합해 본다.

대화를 듣고, 남자의 삼촌을 고르시오.

① 
② 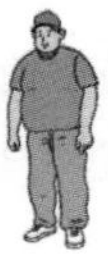
③ 
④ 
⑤ 

고난도

W Who is the man beside the window? I have never seen him before.

M Which one? The man who is wearing glasses?

M No, the man __________ __________ __________ (모자를 쓰고 있는). He's wearing __________ __________ __________ (긴팔 셔츠).

M Oh, that's my uncle.

W Really? He's very __________ (마른).

M Yes, and he's very __________ (키가 큰), too.

03 그림 정보 파악 – 사물

다음을 듣고, 'this'가 무엇인지 가장 적절한 것을 고르시오.

① 
② 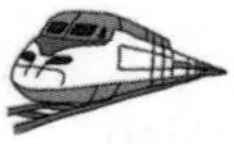
③ 
④ 
⑤ 

M This is something you use to travel in the city or for long distances. It has __________ __________ __________ __________ __________ (작지만 강력한 모터), so you can move very fast. It is also very loud. Only one or two people can ride on it, though. It is a fun way to travel, but it can be dangerous, too. That is why you must always __________ __________ __________ __________ __________ (탈 때 헬멧을 쓰다).

04 할 일 파악

Shall we ~? 이후에 나오는 부분을 주의깊게 듣는다.

대화를 듣고, 두 사람이 내일 할 일로 가장 적절한 것을 고르시오.

① 병원 가기
② 배 타기 go boating
③ 자전거 타기 go bicycling, riding a bike
④ 낚시하기
⑤ 강가 산책하기

I'd like to, but ~.은 '그러고 싶지만, ~.'이라는 의미로, 상대방의 제안을 거절할 때 사용하는 표현이다.

➕ 대화를 듣고, 남자가 여자에게 처음에 제안한 일로 가장 적절한 것을 고르시오.

① 병원 가기　② 배 타기
③ 자전거 타기　④ 낚시하기
⑤ 강가 산책하기

M Are you free tomorrow?

W I am not doing anything special.

M Shall we _____ _____ on the Han River?
호수에서 수영하다

W Well.... I'd like to, but I _____ _____ when I go boating.
멀미가 나다

M Oh, do you? I didn't know that. Do you get motion-sickness when you ride a bike?

W No, it's OK.

M Then shall we _____ instead?
자전거를 타러 가다

W Sounds good . I _____ _____ _____ very much.
자전거 타기를 좋아하다

고난도

05 내용 일치 파악

선택지를 미리 읽어 대화 내용을 짐작해 본다.

대화를 듣고, 대화의 내용과 일치하지 <u>않는</u> 것을 고르시오.

① Sujin is late for class.
② Sujin thinks the lunch time is too short.
③ Sujin stands in line for lunch for a long time.
④ Sujin usually eats fast.
⑤ The teacher suggests Sujin bring her own lunch.

M Why are you so _____ _____ _____, Sujin?
수업에 늦은

W Oh, I'm sorry, Mr. Kim. Our lunch time _____ _____ _____.
너무 짧다

M You have 50 minutes for lunch.

W But I usually have to _____ _____ _____ minutes at the cafeteria.
20분 이상을 기다리다

M Then you still have more than 30 minutes to eat?

W Yes, I do, but I'm _____. It's hard for me to have lunch in such short time.
밥을 천천히 먹는 사람

M How about _____ _____ _____?
네 점심을 가져오는 것

W That's a good idea, Mr. Kim.

---

06 특정 정보 파악

대화를 듣고, 남자가 이용할 교통 수단으로 가장 적절한 것을 고르시오.

① 버스　② 도보
③ 택시　④ 지하철
⑤ 자전거

M Is the Seoul World Cup Stadium around here?

W Oh, it's _____ _____ _____.
여기서 먼

M How long does it take to _____?
거기까지 걸어가다

W It takes around 30 minutes. So take the bus number 30 right here.

M Thanks, but I'd like to _____ _____ _____. Where is the nearest subway station?
지하철을 타다

W It is ten minutes' walk.

M Oh, it's far from here. I'll _____ _____ _____. Thank you.
버스를 타다

핵심 어휘 land, stop, get off 등을 단서로 이용한다.

다음을 듣고, 무엇에 관한 안내인지 가장 적절한 것을 고르시오.

① 미아 찾기
② 비행기 연착
③ 비행기 착륙
④ 비행기 이륙
⑤ 공항 탑승 수속

May I have your attention, please?는 안내 방송 첫머리에 자주 나오는 말로, 주의를 끌기 위한 표현이다.

W Ladies and gentlemen! May I have your attention, please? We _____ ~에 착륙할 것이다
_____ _____ Incheon International Airport in 10 minutes. Please remain seated
and keep your seat belt fastened until the plane _____ _____ _____ 완전히 멈췄다
_____ _____. Please keep your Cellphone turned off until you enter the terminal.
And make sure you _____ _____ _____. Don't forget to have 귀중품을 두고 내리지 않다
your passports ready when you get off. We hope you have a nice trip. Thank you.

Why not? 이후에 나오는 부분을 집중해서 듣는다.

대화를 듣고, 여자가 영어 에세이를 마치지 **못한** 이유로 가장 적절한 것을 고르시오.

① 너무 피곤해서
② 동생을 돌봐야 해서
③ 친구와 게임을 해서
④ 숙제를 잊어버려서
⑤ 아르바이트를 해야 해서

M Did you finish your English essay last night?

W No, I couldn't do it.

M Why not? Were you busy with something?

W I had to _____ _____ _____ _____. 저녁 내내 남동생을 돌보다

M Why didn't you write it after he went to bed?

W He _____ _____ _____. He played with his toys all night. 늦게까지 깨어 있었다

M Well, don't worry. You'll be able to finish it tonight.

학교에서 판매할 책의 종류를 파악한다.

대화를 듣고, 여자가 학교에서 판매할 책의 권수를 고르시오.

① 3 ② 15
③ 18 ④ 20
⑤ 38

W I want to sell some of my old books.

M What kind of books are you selling? Novels are the easiest to get rid of.

W I have 20 novels, but I have some other books as well.

M What about textbooks? Do you have any?

W Yes, I have _____ _____. And 3 travel books as well. 15권의 교과서

M Maybe you should _____ _____ _____ _____ _____. 학교에서 교과서를 팔다

W That's a good idea. I'll do that.

대화를 듣고, 남자의 심정으로 가장 적절한 것을 고르시오.

① sad 슬픈
② angry 화가 난
③ lonely 외로운
④ scared 무서운
⑤ worried 걱정되는

Why don't you ~?는 '~하는 게 어때?'라는 의미로, 상대방에게 제안하는 표현이다.

M I can't believe it!

W What's wrong? Did something happen?

M My phone _____ _____! 작동이 안 되다

W Did you drop it or something?

M No, it just seems to be broken. I can't make phone calls.

W Then you _____ _____ _____. 그것을 수리 받아야 한다

M I already did, last week. _____ _____ _____ it's broken again! 나는 정말 화가 난다

W Why don't you return it and get your money back?

M Yeah, I'll get another phone. This one is terrible.

---

11 특정 정보 파악

대화를 듣고, 남자가 여자에게 제안한 것으로 가장 적절한 것을 고르시오.

① 선물 사기 buy a present
② 은행 가기
③ 케이크 만들기 bake a cake
④ 자원봉사하기
⑤ 집안 청소하기

M What's up, Jane? You look worried.

W Tomorrow's my mother's birthday. I want to _____ _____ _____ for her.
선물을 사다
But I _____ _____ _____.
돈이 충분하지 않다

M Oh, that's too bad. But I have an idea. It doesn't take a lot of money.

W What is it?

M You can _____ _____ _____ for her. I'll help you.
케이크를 만들다

W That's a great idea. It's kind of you!

12 특정 정보 파악

I'd like to ~. 이후에 나오는 부분을 주의깊게 듣는다.

대화를 듣고, 남자가 여자에게 말을 건 목적으로 가장 적절한 것을 고르시오.

① 비행기를 예약하려고
② 비행기에 짐을 부치려고
③ 공항의 위치를 물으려고
④ 비행기 시간을 변경하려고
⑤ 탑승구의 위치를 확인하려고

M Excuse me.

W Yes, may I help you?

M I'd like to _____ _____ to Chicago.
비행기를 예약하다

W When are you going to leave?

M April the fourth.

W Let me see. Oh, sorry, sir. We don't have _____ _____ _____ on that day.
예약 가능한 비행기
We have a flight at 2 p.m. the next day.

M OK, I'll _____ _____ _____ for it.
예약하다

W May I have your name?

M Thomas Edison.

13 특정 정보 파악

대화를 듣고, 여자가 남자에게 불평한 것으로 가장 적절한 것을 고르시오.

① 음식이 짜다.
② 종업원이 불친절하다.
③ 잘못된 메뉴를 가져다주었다.
④ 음식에 머리카락이 들어 있다.
⑤ 주문한 음식이 너무 늦게 나왔다.

That's all right.은 '괜찮아.'라는 의미로, 사과에 대한 용서의 표현이다.

W Oh, my! Excuse me!

M Yes, ma'am. What can I do for you?

W Look at this! _____ _____ _____ in this food!
머리카락이 들어있다

M Oh, we're really sorry about this.

W I know this is an expensive restaurant. So I am _____ _____
이것에 대해 불쾌한
_____.

M So we'll bring you a new one soon. And you _____ _____
값을 지불할 필요가 없다
_____ for your food today. We're really sorry again.

W That's all right.

고난도

14 언급 및 비언급 파악

남자가 오른손을 사용하는 경우를 파악한다.

대화를 듣고, 남자가 왼손을 사용하는 경우로 언급되지 <u>않은</u> 것을 고르시오.

① 글을 쓸 때
② 그림을 그릴 때
③ 테니스를 칠 때
④ 야구를 할 때
⑤ 나이프를 사용할 때

M Are you left-handed?

W Yes, I am. What about you?

M Well, I use both hands. I _____ _____ or _____ _____
글을 쓰다   왼손으로 그림을 그리다
_____ and I usually use my right hand for sports.

W Do you use your right hand when you play baseball or tennis?

M I use _____ _____ _____ _____ _____ _____, but
테니스를 칠 때는 오른손
_____ _____ _____.
야구는 아니다

W Can you use either hand when you eat?

M Yes, I can. But I usually use my right hand for forks or chopsticks and
_____ _____ _____ _____ _____.
나이프는 왼손

15 숫자 파악 – 시각

Shall we ~? 이후에 나오는 부분을 주의깊게 듣는다.

대화를 듣고, 두 사람이 만나기로 한 시각을 고르시오.

① 3시   ② 3시 30분
③ 4시   ④ 4시 30분
⑤ 5시

Shall we ~?는 상대방에게 제안하는 표현으로, '~ 할까요?'라는 의미이며 Let's ~.로 바꿔 말할 수 있다.

W Yeram and I are going to see a movie tomorrow afternoon. Would you like to join us?

M That sounds wonderful. What time does the movie start?

W It _____ _____ _____.
<u>4시에 시작하다</u>

M Oh, it's too early. My school _____ _____ _____. Is there a movie that
<u>3시에 끝나다</u>
starts a little later?

W Sure. One _____ _____ _____.
<u>4시 30분에 시작하다</u>

M That's possible for me.

W Shall we _____ _____ _____ at the bus station?
<u>3시 30분에 만나다</u>

M Sure. See you then.

[고난도]

16 관계 추론

핵심 어구 check in, two nights, room 1201등을 단서로 이용한다.

대화를 듣고, 두 사람의 관계로 가장 적절한 것을 고르시오.

① 의사 – 환자
② 식당 지배인 – 손님
③ 호텔 직원 – 투숙객
④ 도서관 사서 – 학생
⑤ 항공사 승무원 – 승객

M May I help you?

W I'd like to _____ _____.
<u>입실하다</u>

M Do you have a reservation?

W Yes, I have a reservation for two nights.

M May I have your name, please?

W Theresa Baker.

M Let me see.... Ah, yes, please _____ _____ _____.
<u>이 양식에 서명하다</u>

W OK. Here you are.

M You're _____ _____ _____. Here's your key. Have a nice stay at the A-1.
<u>1201호실에</u>

W Thank you.

---

17 대화 장소 파악

대화를 듣고, 두 사람이 대화하는 장소로 가장 적절한 것을 고르시오.

① 영화관   ② 상점
③ 우체국   ④ 경찰서
⑤ 커피숍

M How may I help you?

W I'd like to _____ _____.
<u>잃어버린 지갑을 신고하다</u>

M Do you know where you lost it?

W No. I just realized that it wasn't in my bag.

M When did you last use it?

W Hmm... I think it was at a coffee shop. I bought a coffee.

M Okay. Why don't you _____ _____ _____ for me and leave
<u>이 양식을 작성하다</u>
your contact number? I'll give you a call if it turns up.

W Thank you.

18 부탁한 일 파악

대화를 듣고, 여자가 남자에게 부탁한 일로 가장 적절한 것을 고르시오.

① 점심 같이 먹기
② 치과에 데려다주기
③ 치과에 전화하기
④ 예약시간 확인하기
⑤ 설거지하기

➕ 대화를 듣고, 여자가 치과를 예약한 시각을 고르시오.

① 2:00 pm   ② 2:10 pm
③ 2:20 pm   ④ 2:30 pm
⑤ 3:00 pm

W Oh, no. It's already 2 o'clock. I'm going to be late.

M Where are you going? It's your _____ _____, isn't it?
쉬는 날

W Yes, but I have a dentist appointment at 2:30.

M Well, you can get there in 20 minutes, so if you leave now, you can make your appointment.

W Yes, but I was going to _____ _____ _____ before I go. Could you do
설거지하다
them for me?

M Sure, I'll take care of them. Don't worry.

W Thank you. See you later.

19 알맞은 응답 찾기

[19~20] 대화를 듣고, 여자의 마지막 말에 이어질 남자의 응답으로 가장 적절한 것을 고르시오.

Man: _____

① No, thanks.
② I'll see you soon.
③ Let's go together.
④ No problem. I'd love to.
⑤ No, I don't agree with you.

I can't believe it.은 '그럴 수가.. 믿을 수 없어.'라는 의미로, 놀람을 나타내는 표현이다.

마지막 부탁의 말로 보아이에 대한 승낙이나 거절의 표현이 와야한다.

W _____ _____ _____ it is! It looks expensive. John, how much
정말 멋진 그림이다
was it?

M I didn't buy it. I painted it myself.

W Really? I can't believe it. I thought it was a famous painter's work.

M Thank you. Painting is one of my favorite hobbies.

W How long have you been painting pictures?

M It's been three years. I learned from my uncle.

W John, can you _____ _____ _____ _____ this Saturday?
내가 그림 그리는 것을 도와주다

M _____

20 알맞은 응답 찾기

Man: _____

① This is her dad speaking.
② Hold on. She's in her room.
③ You have the wrong number.
④ Yes. Can you tell me more about it?
⑤ Yes. Could you tell her to call me back?

[Telephone rings.]

W Hello.

M Hello. May I speak to Jennifer, please?

W She _____ _____. _____ _____, please?
집에 없다   누구세요

M This is Tim. I'm Jennifer's classmate.

W Hi, Tim. This is Jennifer's mother.

M How are you, Mrs. Lee?

W I'm fine. Would you like to _____ _____?
메시지를 남기다

M _____

01 대화를 듣고, 남자가 구입한 선물을 고르시오.

① 　② 　③

④ 　⑤

02 대화를 듣고, 두 사람이 배우려는 운동으로 가장 적절한 것을 고르시오.

① 　②

③ 　④

⑤

03 대화를 듣고, 여자의 심정으로 가장 적절한 것을 고르시오.

① angry　　　　　② excited
③ surprised　　　 ④ indifferent
⑤ disappointed

04 대화를 듣고, Scott이 사는 거리로 가장 적절한 것을 고르시오.

① Markwood　　　② Crescent
③ Decker　　　　 ④ Benton
⑤ Chesnutt

05 다음을 듣고, 무엇에 관한 내용인지 가장 적절한 것을 고르시오.

① 연구소 초대　　　② 연구 지원 감사
③ 연구직 추천　　　④ 연구소 위치 확인
⑤ 연구소 지원 거절

06 대화를 듣고, 두 사람이 대화하고 있는 장소로 가장 적절한 곳을 고르시오.

① 면세점　　　　　② 택시 안
③ 비행기 안　　　　④ 공항 세관
⑤ 공항 체크인 센터

07 대화를 듣고, 두 사람의 관계로 가장 적절한 것을 고르시오.

① 학생 – 교사　　　② 비서 – 사장
③ 구직자 – 면접관　 ④ 학생 – 도서관 사서
⑤ 수강생 – 어학원 직원

고난도
08 대화를 듣고, 남자가 지불할 금액을 고르시오.

① $50　　　　　　②$100
③ $150　　　　　 ④$200
⑤ $250

09 대화를 듣고, 여자가 대화 직후에 할 일로 가장 적절한 것을 고르시오.

① 소풍 가기
② 학교 방문하기
③ 기상청에 전화하기
④ 강당 이용 문의하기
⑤ 동창회 모임 참석하기

고난도
10 다음을 듣고, 초기 공룡에 대한 설명으로 일치하는 것을 고르시오.

① 다른 동물들보다 월등히 컸다.
② 곤충을 먹고 살았다.
③ 4개의 다리로 움직였다.
④ 뛰어 오를 수 없었다.
⑤ 쉽게 먹이를 구할 수 없었다.

점수
/20

11 대화를 듣고, 남자의 여행에 대해 언급되지 <u>않은</u> 것을 고르시오.

① 여행 기간
② 여행 지역
③ 여행 중 가장 좋았던 것
④ 여행 중 가장 싫었던 것
⑤ 여행지의 날씨

12 다음 메모를 보면서 대화를 듣고, 대화의 내용과 일치하지 <u>않는</u> 것을 고르시오.

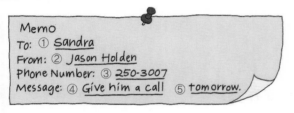

Memo
To: ① Sandra
From: ② Jason Holden
Phone Number: ③ 250-3007
Message: ④ Give him a call ⑤ tomorrow.

13 대화를 듣고, 남자가 전화를 건 목적으로 가장 적절한 것을 고르시오.

① 책을 대출하려고
② 책의 주문을 취소하려고
③ 서점 위치를 확인하려고
④ 작가에 대해 문의하려고
⑤ 찾는 책이 있는지 물어보려고

14 대화를 듣고, 남자가 집들이에 가져가기로 한 선물로 가장 적절한 것을 고르시오.

① 꽃   ② 세제
③ 케이크   ④ 화장지
⑤ 포도주

15 다음 그림의 상황에 가장 적절한 대화를 고르시오.

①   ②   ③   ④   ⑤

16 대화를 듣고, 남자가 늦게 온 이유로 가장 적절한 것을 고르시오.

① 길을 잘못 들어서
② 교통 체증에 걸려서
③ 대중교통을 이용할 수 없어서
④ 교통 위반 딱지를 받게 되어서
⑤ 오는 도중에 자동차가 고장 나서

17 대화를 듣고, 여자가 남자에게 부탁한 일로 가장 적절한 것을 고르시오.

① TV 같이 보기   ② TV 볼륨 줄이기
③ TV 전원 끄기   ④ 친구 초대하기
⑤ 시간되면 알려주기

18 대화를 듣고, 남자가 오늘 한 일로 가장 적절한 것을 고르시오.

① 그림 그리기   ② 도자기 만들기
③ 예술작품 감상하기   ④ 다도회 참하하기
⑤ 머그컵 구입하기

[19~20] 대화를 듣고, 남자의 마지막 말에 이어질 여자의 응답으로 가장 적절한 것을 고르시오.

19 Woman: _____

① Will you? Thanks a lot.
② No. I'm glad you like it.
③ Right. I have a headache.
④ This? This is my favorite one.
⑤ Yes. I hope to see you again.

20 Woman: _____

① Sure. You're so kind to say that.
② Yeah. You look really nice today.
③ Me, too. It's been nice talking to you.
④ That's right. I need to go to the store.
⑤ Not bad. But I think I need more practice.

다시 들으면서 듣기 만점에 도전하세요!
Dictation: 스크립트의 주요 부분을 다시 들으면서!
실전 ⊕: 세부 정보가 많은 스크립트를 다른 문제로 샅샅이!

---

01 그림 정보 파악 – 사물

여자의 마지막 질문을 놓치지 않는다. 포장지나 가방과 혼동하지 않도록 유의한다.

대화를 듣고, 남자가 구입한 선물을 고르시오.

① ② ③ ④ ⑤

M I'd like you to wrap it. It's a gift.

W Okay. What kind of _____ _____ would you like?
　　　　　　　　　　　　　　포장지

M I'll take that one with the kittens and puppies. And I want this pink ribbon on it.

W That's really cute.

M Would you put it in a red bag, please?

W All right. By the way, _____
　　　　　　　　　　　　　　　　　　이 예쁜 치마는 누구 거예요
_____ ?

M It's _____ _____ _____ .
　　　　내 딸을 위한

---

02 그림 정보 파악 – 사물

How about ~? 이후에 나오는 부분을 주의깊게 듣는다.

대화를 듣고, 두 사람이 배우려는 운동으로 가장 적절한 것을 고르시오.

① jogging ② swimming ③ tennis ④ badminton ⑤

고난도

W Do you ever get any exercise?

M Not regularly. And I'm tired of jogging and swimming.

W Well, why don't you do something else?

M Actually, I want to _____ _____ play tennis.
　　　　　　　　　　　　~하는 법을 배우다

W Tennis? I heard it is very difficult to learn. How about _____
　　　　　　　　　　　　　　　　　　　　　　　　　　　　　배드민턴 동아리에 가입하는 것
_____ with me?

M Badminton?

W Yes. It is _____ than tennis.
　　　　　　배우기가 더 쉬운

M Hmm.... Okay.

---

03 심정 추론

대화를 듣고, 여자의 심정으로 가장 적절한 것을 고르시오.

① angry 화가 난
② excited 흥분한
③ surprised 놀란
④ indifferent 무관심한
⑤ disappointed 실망한

⊕

대화를 듣고, 여자가 여름 방학에 할 일로 가장 적절한 것을 고르시오.

① 퀴즈쇼 출연하기　② 보충수업 받기
③ 하와이 여행가기　④ 경품 응모하기
⑤ 휴식 취하기

M Hi, Jessica. How are you?

W I'm great. I _____ at a quiz show
　　　　　　　　하와이행 여행 상품을 탔다
on TV.

M What? A trip to Hawaii? That's amazing.

W Yeah, it really is.

M When are you going? Are you going in July?

W Yeah. Summer vacation in Hawaii!

M _____ _____ _____ .
　　　　　　　그것은 멋질 것이다
_____ _____ to Hawaii. I envy you a lot.
너의 여행을 즐겨라

Scott이 이사한 곳을 파악한다.

대화를 듣고, Scott이 사는 거리로 가장 적절한 것을 고르시오.

① Markwood ② Crescent
③ Decker ④ Benton
⑤ Chesnutt

대화를 듣고, Don이 사는 거리를 고르시오.

① Markwood ② Crescent
③ Decker ④ Benton
⑤ Chesnutt

W Who do we have to pick up today?
M Four people: Meg, Jane, Scott, and Don.
W Does Jane still live on Markwood Street?
M Yes, and I think Scott lives there, too.
W No, he _____ _____ _____, near Meg's on Decker.
　　　　　　　　Crescent 거리로 이사 갔다
M I hope Don lives _____ _____.
　　　　　　　　근처 어디에
W Yes, he lives on Benton Street, between Crescent Street and Chesnutt Street.

I'd like to ~. 이후에 나오는 부분을 주의 깊게 듣는다.

다음을 듣고, 무엇에 관한 내용인지 가장 적절한 것을 고르시오.

① 연구소 초대
② 연구 지원 감사
③ 연구직 추천
④ 연구소 위치 확인
⑤ 연구소 지원 거절

M _____ _____ _____ you to visit Lawrence Research Center.
　　　나는 초대하고 싶다
You and other scientists _____ _____ _____
　　　　　　　　　　　　　　　　　　　　우리를 도와달라고 요청되고 있다
_____ with "Project Alpha." Your ideas may help us greatly. We will provide you with work-related support if you need it. Please _____ _____.
　　　　　　　　　　　　　　　　　　　　　　　　　　　　　　　우리의 초대를 받아주다
If you have any questions about the opportunity, please contact us at 510-486-1234 or by email.

대화를 듣고, 두 사람이 대화하고 있는 장소로 가장 적절한 곳을 고르시오.

① 면세점
② 택시 안
③ 비행기 안
④ 공항 세관
⑤ 공항 체크인 센터

How much do I owe?는 '얼마를 내야 하죠?'라는 의미로, 지불 금액을 묻는 표현이다.

W Do you _____ _____ _____ _____?
　　　　　양식을 기입하다
M Yes, it's right here.
W It says you bought a $200 vase overseas. Is that correct?
M Yes, I have it here. Is there a problem?
W You have to _____ _____ _____ _____.
　　　　　　100달러 이상의 물건에는 관세를 지불하다
M How much do I owe?
W $20. You can pay it at the window by the exit.

대화를 듣고, 두 사람의 관계로 가장 적절한 것을 고르시오.

① 학생 – 교사
② 비서 – 사장
③ 구직자 – 면접관
④ 학생 – 도서관 사서
⑤ 수강생 – 어학원 직원

M Good afternoon, Mrs. Park. My name is Kim Jinho. I'm _____
　　　　　　　　　　　　　　　　　　　　　　　　　　　　　당신의 중국어 수업을 듣고 있다
_____ _____.
W Yes, I've seen you _____ _____ _____. How's the class, then?
M Honestly, listening is difficult. You speak too fast for me.
　　　　　　　　　수업 시간에
W That's too bad. But I hope you'll keep trying.
M I'm trying hard these days.
W I'm happy to hear that. Well, I'll _____ _____
　　　　　　　　　　　　　　　　　　　수업 시간에 너를 보다
_____.
M Okay. See you later.

08 숫자 파악 – 금액

요금(fifty dollars), 예약일수(four nights)를 잘 듣고 계산한다.

대화를 듣고, 남자가 지불할 금액을 고르시오.

① $50   ② $100
③ $150   ④ $200
⑤ $250

How long ~?은 '얼마나 오래(긴)~?'라는 의미로, 소요 시간이나 길이를 묻는 표현이다.

M I'd like to book a room at your hotel.
W Okay. What type of room do you want?
M I'd like _____ _____ _____. How much is that?
        2인실
W It's _____ _____ _____. How long are you going to stay?
     하룻밤에 50달러
M I'll be staying _____ _____ _____.
              4일 밤 동안
W All right. When are you arriving here?
M I'm coming on April 21.

09 할 일 파악

I should ~. 이후에 나오는 부분을 주의깊게 듣는다.

대화를 듣고, 여자가 대화 직후에 할 일로 가장 적절한 것을 고르시오.

① 소풍 가기
② 학교 방문하기
③ 기상청에 전화하기
④ 강당 이용 문의하기
⑤ 동창회 모임 참석하기

M Any plans for the weekend?
W My fellow students were planning a picnic in the park, but it might rain.
M It's supposed to rain on Sunday.
W That's the problem. It's _____ _____ _____.
                          동창회 모임
M So you can't change it. What about changing a meeting place?
W But where? Do you know of a place?
M _____ _____ _____ might do.
   학교 강당
W That's a good idea. I should call the school and _____ _____
                                     그곳이 이용 가능한지 확인하다
_____.

10 내용 일치 파악

다음을 듣고, 초기 공룡에 대한 설명으로 일치하는 것을 고르시오.

① 다른 동물들보다 월등히 컸다.
② 곤충을 먹고 살았다.
③ 4개의 다리로 움직였다.
④ 뛰어 오를 수 없었다.
⑤ 쉽게 먹이를 구할 수 없었다.

W The earliest dinosaurs had an advantage over other creatures. Surprisingly, the advantage was not their size. The first dinosaurs _____ _____
                                            아주 크지는 않았다
_____. In fact, they were quite small and _____ _____.
                                       곤충을 먹고 살았다
However, those dinosaurs were able to _____ _____
                              그들의 뒷다리로 달리고 뛰어 오르다
_____ _____ _____. Their amazing legs allowed them to easily access food.

11 언급 및 비언급 파악

대화를 듣고, 남자의 여행에 대해 언급되지 않은 것을 고르시오.

① 여행 기간
② 여행 지역 the east coast
③ 여행 중 가장 좋았던 것
    scenery along the coast
④ 여행 중 가장 싫었던 것 paying tax
⑤ 여행지의 날씨 really nice

W Tell me some more about your trip to _____ _____ of the United States.
                                     동부 해안
M Okay. What would you like to know?
W What was _____ _____ _____ of your trip?
                         가장 좋았던 부분
M Well, the scenery along the coast was fantastic!
W What was _____ _____ _____?
                 최악의 부분
M I didn't like paying tax whenever I bought something.
W _____ _____ _____ there?
  날씨는 어땠나요
M The weather was really nice.

12 실용문 정보 파악

메모와 대화 내용을 하나씩 대조해 가면서 대화를 듣는다.

다음 메모를 보면서 대화를 듣고, 대화의 내용과 일치하지 <u>않는</u> 것을 고르시오.

Memo
To: ① Sandra
From: ② Jason Holden
Phone Number: ③ 250-3007
Message: ④ Give him a call ⑤ tomorrow.

[*Telephone rings.*]

M Hi, is Sandra there, please?

W No, she isn't. She's out now, but she'll be back at 3:30 in the afternoon.

M Oh, okay. Can I _____ _____ ?
_{메시지를 남기다}

W Sure.

M My name is Jason Holden. Could you please ask her to give me a call _____
_____ _____ _____ ? _{그녀가 돌아오는 대로}

W All right, Jason.

M My phone number is _____ - _____ .

W 250-3007? Okay, I'll give her the message. ₂₅₀₋₃₀₀₇

M Thank you.

---

13 전화 목적 파악

I'm trying to ~. 이후에 나오는 부분을 주의깊게 듣는다.

대화를 듣고, 남자가 전화를 건 목적으로 가장 적절한 것을 고르시오.

① 책을 대출하려고
② 책의 주문을 취소하려고
③ 서점 위치를 확인하려고
④ 작가에 대해 문의하려고
⑤ 찾는 책이 있는지 물어보려고

Go ahead.는 '그렇게 하세요.'라는 의미로, 승낙 또는 허락을 나타내는 표현이다.

[*Telephone rings.*]

W Hello. May I help you?

M Yes, I'm trying to _____ _____ _____ . It's called *The Old Man and The Sea* by Ernest Hemingway. _{책을 찾다}

W I'll _____ _____ _____ for you. _{컴퓨터로 확인해 보다}

M Thank you.

W Well, it's _____ _____ _____ . We can order the book for you. _{재고가 없는}

M Okay. Go ahead, please.

W No problem.

---

14 특정 정보 파악

대화를 듣고, 남자가 집들이에 가져가기로 한 선물로 가장 적절한 것을 고르시오.

① 꽃 flower
② 세제
③ 케이크 cake
④ 화장지 toilet paper
⑤ 포도주 wine

M I have been invited to _____ _____ _____ next week. What should I bring? _{집들이}

W We usually bring _____ _____ to a housewarming party in Korea. _{화장지}

M Oh, that's very practical. How about cake or wine? In America, those are pretty common.

W Yes, we can bring those types of gifts when we have dinner at someone's house. But not a *jipdeuri*.

M *Jipdeuri*? What's that?

W *Jipdeuri* is a party held when you move to a new place. Well, have you decided what you'll bring?

M I'll _____ _____ because I'm here in Korea. _{화장지를 가져가다}

W Sounds good.

15 그림 상황 대화 찾기

다음 그림의 상황에 가장 적절한 대화를 고르시오.

① ② ③ ④ ⑤

① M I'm really sorry I'm late.

    W It's okay. We can still watch the movie.

② M Which movie would you like to watch?

    W What about this one? I like _____ _____.
                                      과학 공상 영화

③ M What kind of movies do you like best?

    W I like romantic comedies. _____ _____ _____?
                            너는 어때?

④ M Wow, it was a really good movie.

    W Yes, it was. Would you like to get a snack now?

⑤ M The sky is so beautiful. Look at all those stars!

    W Wow, it is. I've never seen the sky like this.

고난도

16 이유 파악

Why ~?에 대한 대답 부분을 주의깊게 듣는다.

대화를 듣고, 남자가 늦게 온 이유로 가장 적절한 것을 고르시오.

① 길을 잘못 들어서
② 교통 체증에 걸려서
③ 대중교통을 이용할 수 없어서
④ 교통 위반 딱지를 받게 되어서
⑤ 오는 도중에 자동차가 고장 나서

「give ~ a ticket」은 '~에게 교통 위반 딱지를 발급하다'라는 의미이다.

W You're late again, Jason.

M I'm so sorry.

W _____ _____ _____ _____ this time?
   너는 왜 늦었니

M I _____ _____ _____ on the way here.
   교통 위반 딱지를 받다

W What did you do?

M I _____ _____ _____ _____. A police officer _____
   정지 신호에서 달렸다   내 차를 세웠다
   _____, and he gave me a ticket.

W I'm sorry to hear that. Hey, Jason! I told you to take the subway.

M First of all, I should have been more careful.

---

17 부탁한 일 파악

대화를 듣고, 여자가 남자에게 부탁한 일로 가장 적절한 것을 고르시오.

① TV 같이 보기　② TV 볼륨 줄이기
③ TV 전원 끄기　④ 친구 초대하기
⑤ 시간되면 알려주기

W Jinho, are you watching TV?

M _____ _____ _____, but I'm waiting for the next program.
   지금 당장은 아니다

W What program is it?

M It's a new entertainment show with my favorite singer.

W What time does it start?

M At 5:30.

W Well, you've still got an hour. Can you turn it off for now? I need to _____
   _____ _____ _____. I'll let you know when I'm finished.
   중요한 전화를 걸다

M Okay, but please don't forget in case I fall asleep on the sofa.

W Don't worry, I won't.

18 한 일 파악

대화를 듣고, 남자가 오늘 한 일로 가장 적절한 것을 고르시오.

① 그림 그리기
② 도자기 만들기
③ 예술작품 감상하기
④ 다도회 참가하기
⑤ 머그컵 구입하기

W Jaehoon, how was your day today? Was the field trip good?

M Yes, Mom. We went to the art center. And here, look at this.

W What is this? A mug?

M Yes, I made it myself. ＿＿＿＿＿＿＿ ＿＿＿＿ ＿＿＿＿ ＿＿＿＿ it?
　　　　　　　　　　　　　　~을, 어떻게 생각해?

W Wow, it's really good. Did you really make this yourself?

M Yes, we had a pottery class there. So everyone made their own.

W This is great. I think you ＿＿＿＿＿ ＿＿＿＿＿.
　　　　　　　　　　　　　　　　재능이 있다

19 알맞은 응답 찾기

[19~20] 대화를 듣고, 남자의 마지막 말에 이어질 여자의 응답으로 가장 적절한 것을 고르시오.

Woman: ＿＿＿＿＿＿＿＿＿＿＿＿

① Will you? Thanks a lot.
② No. I'm glad you like it.
③ Right. I have a headache.
④ This? This is my favorite one.
⑤ Yes. I hope to see you again.

M Rosalita? That's a nice name. Is it Spanish?

W Yes. Thank you.

M Then are you from Spain?

W No, I was born in Mexico, but moved to Los Angeles when I was about two years old.

M Really? By the way, it's ＿＿＿＿＿＿＿ ＿＿＿＿＿ in the airport.
　　　　　　　　　　　　　　여기는 아주 붐비는

W That's right.

M Your luggage ＿＿＿＿＿＿＿ ＿＿＿＿＿. I'll ＿＿＿＿＿ ＿＿＿＿.
　　　　　　　　아주 무거워 보이다　　　　　　　　당신이 옮기는 것을 도와주다

W ＿＿＿＿＿＿＿＿＿＿＿＿＿＿＿＿

20 알맞은 응답 찾기

Woman: ＿＿＿＿＿＿＿＿＿＿＿＿

① Sure. You're so kind to say that.
② Yeah. You look really nice today.
③ Me, too. It's been nice talking to you.
④ That's right. I need to go to the store.
⑤ Not bad. But I think I need more practice.

What have you been up to lately?는 '요즘 어떻게 지내니?'라는 의미로, 안부를 묻는 표현이다.

How's it going?의 의미를 파악한다.

M Hi, Susan. How are you this morning?

W Very good, and you?

M Not bad. Susan, what have you been up to lately?

W I've been ＿＿＿＿＿＿＿ ＿＿＿＿ in an after-school class.
　　　　　　　웹 디자인을 배우고 있다

M Web design? How interesting! How long have you been learning it?

W For about three months.

M ＿＿＿＿ ＿＿＿＿ ＿＿＿＿?
　　잘 되어가니

W ＿＿＿＿＿＿＿＿＿＿＿＿＿＿＿

그림 정보 파악/그림 상황에 적절한 대화 찾기

무엇을 평가하는가?	일상생활이나 친숙한 일반적 주제에 관한 그림, 사진에 관한 말이나 대화를 듣고 세부 정보를 파악할 수 있는지를 평가한다.
어떻게 출제되는가?	• 다음을 듣고, 목요일의 날씨로 가장 적절한 것을 고르시오. • 대화를 듣고, 남자가 구입할 물병으로 가장 적절한 것을 고르시오. • 다음 그림의 상황에 가장 적절한 대화를 고르시오.

key solution

❶ 보기의 그림을 살펴보고 그림과 관련된 어휘들에 주위해서 듣는다.

❷ 사물을 묻는 문제는 모양이나 위치 등을 나타내는 어휘에 귀 기울인다.

❸ 인물이나 상황을 묻는 문제는 배경이나 동작 등을 나타내는 어휘나 표현에 주의한다.

[기출로 전략 확인]

대화를 듣고, 남자가 가져와야 할 쟁반으로 가장 적절한 것을 고르시오. [2018 기출]

①   ②   ③   ④   ⑤

❶ 쟁반을 보고 'heart', 'star', 'circle' 등의 어휘들을 예상해 볼 수 있다.

W David, can you help me for a second?
M No problem. What can I do for you?
W Bring me the tray in the kitchen, please.
M All right.
W Did you find it? It's on the shelf.
M Do you mean the tray with the circles?
W Not that one. It has two stars and two hearts.
M Okay, I see the one you're talking about.

❷ 'tray with the circles'를 듣고 섣부르게 답은 선택하지 않도록 주의한다.

여 David, 잠깐 도와줄 수 있어?
남 문제 없어. 뭘 해줄까?
여 부엌에서 쟁반 좀 갖고 와 줄래?
남 알겠어.
여 찾았어? 선반 위에 있어.
남 동그라미들이 있는 쟁반 말하는 거야?
여 그거 말고. 별 두 개랑 하트 두 개가 있는 쟁반.
남 응. 뭐 말하는 지 알겠어.

그림 정보 파악/그림 상황에 적절한 대화 찾기 유형의 발문과 보기

대화를 듣고, 남자가 가져와야 할 쟁반으로 가장 적절한 것을 고르시오.　[2015 기출]

① 　② 　③ 　④ 　⑤

만점 잡는 문장　**W** Wow! You are riding a horse. Weren't you scared?

⋮

W Who is this man standing next to the horse?

대화를 듣고, 여자가 찾고 있는 휴대전화의 위치로 가장 적절한 것을 고르시오.　[2016 기출]

①　②　③　④　⑤

만점 잡는 문장　**M** What do you think of this cap?

W It just looks perfect on you! I really like the star on it!

그림 정보 파악에 쓰이는 어휘 및 표현

● **모양/위치**

rectangle 직사각형　　triangle 삼각형　　circle 원형　　square 정사각형

next to ~옆에　　on the top 맨 위에　　on your left[right] 너의 왼쪽[오른쪽]에

● **상황**

(식당에서 음식을 주문하는 상황)

A Can I take your order? 주문 하시겠어요?

B Sure. I'd like a chicken burger and a soda. 네. 치킨 버거 하나와 음료수 하나요.

(매표소에서 표를 사는 상황)

A How much is the ticket for this museum? 박물관 표가 얼마인가요?

B It's ten dollars per person. 인 당 10달러 입니다.

영어듣기능력평가 **03**회

01 다음 그림의 상황에 가장 적절한 대화를 고르시오.

① ② ③ ④ ⑤

02 대화를 듣고, 신문이 있는 곳을 고르시오.

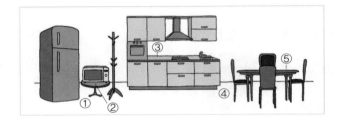

03 대화를 듣고, 두 사람의 관계로 가장 적절한 것을 고르시오.

① 수의사 – 애완동물 주인　② 의사 – 환자
③ 식당주인 – 손님　　　④ 식료품점 직원 – 고객
⑤ 경찰 – 시민

04 다음 표를 보면서 대화를 듣고, 대화의 내용과 일치하지 <u>않</u>는 것을 고르시오.

①	**Product**	Shoes
②	**Size**	9
③	**Color**	Brown
④	**Price**	$ 40
⑤	**Payment**	Credit card

05 대화를 듣고, 두 사람이 이용할 교통 수단으로 가장 적절한 것을 고르시오.

① bus　　　　② boat
③ train　　　④ bicycle
⑤ airplane

06 대화를 듣고, 두 사람이 대화하고 있는 장소로 가장 적절한 곳을 고르시오.

① 학교　　　　② 서점
③ 체육관　　　④ 도서관
⑤ 사무실

07 다음을 듣고, 남자가 안내하는 말의 내용으로 가장 적절한 것을 고르시오.

① 지하철 이용방법　　② 사고 상황 보고
③ 지하철 운행시간　　④ 서비스 변경 사항
⑤ 안전 유의 사항

08 대화를 듣고, 남자의 마지막 말의 의도로 가장 적절한 것을 고르시오.

① 동의　　　　② 사과
③ 거절　　　　④ 의심
⑤ 격려

09 대화를 듣고, 여자가 가리키는 표지판으로 가장 적절한 것을 고르시오.

① No Littering!　　② No Photos!
③ No Parking!　　④ No Smoking!
⑤ No Swimming!

10 대화를 듣고, 여자가 휴가가 필요하다고 말한 이유로 가장 적절한 것을 고르시오.

① 몸이 아파서
② 직장이 바빠서
③ 산에 가고 싶어서
④ 집안일이 하기 싫어서
⑤ 휴가 때 편히 쉬지 못해서

점수
/20

고난도

11 대화를 듣고, 여자에 대한 설명으로 일치하지 <u>않는</u> 것을 고르시오.

① 교장선생님으로부터 전화를 받았다.
② 학교 교사로 일할 것이다.
③ 아들의 학년을 가르칠 것이다.
④ 두 학년을 담당할 것이다.
⑤ 영어를 가르칠 것이다.

12 대화를 듣고, 여자의 장래 희망으로 가장 적절한 것을 고르시오.

① 가수   ② 화가
③ 교사   ④ 간호사
⑤ 의사

13 대화를 듣고, 여자가 전화를 건 목적으로 가장 적절한 것을 고르시오.

① 영화를 함께 보려고
② 영화 예매를 부탁하려고
③ 컴퓨터 게임을 함께 하려고
④ 컴퓨터 프로그램을 빌리려고
⑤ 컴퓨터 수리를 부탁하려고

14 대화를 듣고, 남자가 할 일로 가장 적절한 것을 고르시오.

① 쇼핑 가기   ② 외식하기
③ 붓 사오기   ④ 페인트칠 하기
⑤ 정원 손질하기

15 대화를 듣고, 여자의 마지막 말의 의도로 가장 적절한 것을 고르시오.

① 축하   ② 비난
③ 감사   ④ 위로
⑤ 제안

고난도

16 대화를 듣고, 현재 시각을 고르시오.

① 12:00 p.m.   ② 1:00 p.m.
③ 2:00 p.m.   ④ 3:00 p.m.
⑤ 4:00 p.m.

17 대화를 듣고, 여자의 심정으로 가장 적절한 것을 고르시오.

① 슬픔   ② 걱정됨
③ 외로움   ④ 행복함
⑤ 피곤함

18 대화를 듣고, 대화의 내용과 일치하지 <u>않는</u> 것을 고르시오.

① Sally is calling John.
② Sally has to go to her parents'.
③ Sally can't start her car.
④ Sally is angry at John.
⑤ Sally is in front of her house.

[19~20] 대화를 듣고, 여자의 마지막 말에 이어질 남자의 응답으로 가장 적절한 것을 고르시오.

19 Man: _____

① We'd better not.
② Of course, she is.
③ I won't do it again.
④ I don't know for sure.
⑤ That was nice of you.

고난도

20 Man: _____

① Fine, I'll put it away a little later.
② I can run the polisher by myself.
③ OK, let's try it your way this time.
④ That's why I need you to move it.
⑤ But I already put everything away.

다시 들으면서 듣기 만점에 도전하세요!
Dictation: 스크립트의 주요 부분을 다시 들으면서!
실전 ⊕: 세부 정보가 많은 스크립트를 다른 문제로 샅샅이!

---

01 그림 상황 대화 찾기

다음 그림의 상황에 가장 적절한 대화를 고르시오.

① ② ③ ④ ⑤

① **W** Don't try to lift the stone alone.

　 M I know it's very heavy.

② **W** Look at the fish in the tank.

　 M Yeah. They ＿＿＿＿＿＿＿＿＿＿ Thailand.
　　　　　　　　　 ~에서 오다

③ **W** Hey, pull the rod now.

　 M Wow! It feels like a big fish.

④ **W** Be careful ＿＿＿＿＿ ＿＿＿＿＿.
　　　　　　　　 뛸 때

　 M I will, but I know ＿＿＿＿ ＿＿＿＿ ＿＿＿＿.
　　　　　　　　　　　　 물이 깊지 않다

⑤ **W** Let's race to the river.

　 M Sure. I can beat you this time.

---

02 그림 정보 파악 – 위치

대화를 듣고, 신문이 있는 곳을 고르시오.

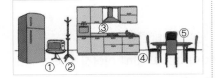

M Was the newspaper delivered?

W Yes, I brought it inside.

M Did you leave it on the kitchen table?

W Sorry, no. I ＿＿＿＿＿ ＿＿＿＿＿ ＿＿＿＿＿ ＿＿＿＿＿.
　　　　　　 냉장고 옆에 그것을 두었다.

M It's not on the floor, is it?

W Don't worry. I ＿＿＿＿＿ ＿＿＿＿＿ ＿＿＿＿＿.
　　　　　　　　　 협탁 위에 그것을 두었다

M Oh, there it is, next to the coat rack.

---

03 관계 파악

대화를 듣고, 두 사람의 관계로 가장 적절한 것을 고르시오.

① 수의사 – 애완동물 주인
② 의사 – 환자
③ 식당주인 – 손님
④ 식료품점 직원 – 고객
⑤ 경찰 – 시민

W So... what seems to be the problem?

M He won't eat, and when he does, he throws up.

W Did you feed him anything unusual?

M No, but I ＿＿＿＿＿ him ＿＿＿＿＿ ＿＿＿＿＿ ＿＿＿＿＿ yesterday. And
　　　　　　 ~를 긴 산책에 데리고 가다
he could have eaten something on the street.

W It's possible. Well, it's been only one day. I think ＿＿＿＿＿ ＿＿＿＿＿
　　　　　　　　　　　　　　　　　　　　　~하는 것이 최선이다
watch him for now.

M Will he be okay?

W I think so. But we can take an X-ray if you're really worried.

품목, 치수, 색깔, 금액, 지불 방법 등을 주의깊게 듣는다.

다음 표를 보면서 대화를 듣고, 대화의 내용과 일치하지 <u>않는</u> 것을 고르시오.

①	**Product**	Shoes
②	**Size**	9
③	**Color**	Brown
④	**Price**	$ 40
⑤	**Payment**	Credit card

shoes, glasses, pants, socks 등은 a pair of(한 쌍의 ~)를 이용하여 수를 센다.

W Can I help you?

M Yes. I want to buy _____.
<small>구두 한 켤레</small>

W What size do you want?

M Size 9.

W How do you like this brown pair? It's very popular with young adults.

M Sorry, but _____. How much is it?
<small>나는 저 검정색이 마음에 든다</small>

W Forty dollars.

M All right. Here is my credit card.

대화를 듣고, 두 사람이 이용할 교통 수단으로 가장 적절한 것을 고르시오.

① bus 버스
② boat 배
③ train 기차
④ bicycle 자전거
⑤ airplane 비행기

W Our hiking is going to be lots of fun.

M I know. I'm so excited about our trip!

W But first we have to decide whether to go _____ _____ or _____
<small>기차로</small>　<small>버스로</small>
_____.

M Good point. Shall we go by bus?

W Well, I like _____ _____ _____.
<small>기차로 여행하는 것</small>

M Okay. Let's buy our tickets online right now.

---

books, semester, overdue charge 등과 관련된 장소를 추론해본다.

대화를 듣고, 두 사람이 대화하고 있는 장소로 가장 적절한 곳을 고르시오.

① 학교　　　　② 서점
③ 체육관　　　④ 도서관
⑤ 사무실

W Did you find everything you were looking for?

M Yes, I have five books here.

W I'll run them through. Can I have your card?

M Sure. How long can I keep them?

W Students are allowed to _____ _____ _____ _____
<small>한 달간 책을 빌리다</small>
during the semester.

M What's _____ _____ _____?
<small>연체료</small>

W It's fifty cents per day. You can check the due date online.

M Great, thanks.

다음을 듣고, 남자가 안내하는 말의 내용으로 가장 적절한 것을 고르시오.

① 지하철 이용방법
② 사고 상황 보고
③ 지하철 운행시간
④ 서비스 변경 사항
⑤ 안전 유의 사항

M This is a public service announcement for everyone. These days, there are many reports of small accidents in our subway station. You can help prevent this. Please _____ _____ _____ while walking. It can put you and everyone around
<small>스마트폰을 사용하지 말아라</small>
you in danger. Also, please don't rush to _____ _____ _____.
<small>지하철을 타다</small>
It can cause serious harm to you or others. Thank you for your cooperation.

대화를 듣고, 남자의 마지막 말의 의도로 가장 적절한 것을 고르시오.

① 동의
② 사과
③ 거절
④ 의심
⑤ 격려

M Hi, Juhee, how was your weekend?

W It was great. I went to the art exhibition on Sunday, and _____
아주 마음에 들었다
_____.

M You did? What was the theme?

W Nature and landscapes. They had famous paintings from major cities around the world.

M That sounds great. I'd love to go see them, too!

W I could _____ _____ _____ _____ if you want. I liked it that much.
너와 다시 가다

M Really? I'd love that. I'll gladly take you up on your offer.

핵심 어휘 water, swimming 등을 단서로 이용한다.

대화를 듣고, 여자가 가리키는 표지판으로 가장 적절한 것을 고르시오.

① **No Littering!** 쓰레기 투입 금지!
② **No Photos!** 사진 촬영 금지!
③ **No Parking!** 주차 금지!
④ **No Smoking!** 흡연 금지!
⑤ **No Swimming!** 수영 금지!

➕ 대화를 듣고, 남자가 실망한 이유로 가장 적절한 것을 고르시오.

① 너무 조용해서
② 카메라를 가져오지 않아서
③ 경치가 기대에 못 미쳐서
④ 수영을 할 수 없어서
⑤ 주위가 지저분해서

W This place is so quiet.

M Even the water is flowing quietly.

W It's too bad that we left the camera at home! The scenery is so wonderful.

M Do you _____ _____ _____ ? The water looks perfect for swimming.
수영하고 싶다

W You are not allowed to do that. Didn't you _____ _____ _____ over
표지판을 보다
there?

M _____ _____ _____ !
정말 실망이야

대화를 듣고, 여자가 휴가가 필요하다고 말한 이유로 가장 적절한 것을 고르시오.

① 몸이 아파서
② 직장이 바빠서
③ 산에 가고 싶어서
④ 집안일이 하기 싫어서
⑤ 휴가 때 편히 쉬지 못해서

W I need a vacation.

M What do you mean? We just had one.

W But I _____ _____ _____ very much.
그것을 즐기지 못했다

M I thought you liked the mountains.

W I do, but I had to cook and clean up.

M I guess you do those things every day.

W Exactly. I _____ _____ _____ _____ to tell you the truth.
쉰 적이 전혀 없다

M Then let's try an all-inclusive holiday resorts package next time.

W That's a great idea!

11 내용 일치 파악

대화를 듣고, 여자에 대한 설명으로 일치하지 않는 것을 고르시오.

① 교장선생님으로부터 전화를 받았다.
② 학교 교사로 일할 것이다.
③ 아들의 학년을 가르칠 것이다.
④ 두 학년을 담당할 것이다.
⑤ 영어를 가르칠 것이다.

M Who was that, Mom?

W _____ _____ .
　　　너의 교장선생님

M What? Why did the principal call you?

W I'm going to _____ _____ _____ at your school next semester.
　　　　　　　　　선생님이 되다

M You're kidding!

W No, I'm not kidding. But don't worry, I _____
　　　　　　　　　　　　　　　　　　　너를 가르치지 않을 것이다
_____ . I'm teaching _____ _____ _____ .
　　　　　　　　　　　　　　8학년과 9학년 영어

M Oh, good.

12 특정 정보 파악

대화를 듣고, 여자의 장래 희망으로 가장 적절한 것을 고르시오.

① 가수　　　　② 화가
③ 교사　　　　④ 간호사
⑤ 의사

What do you want to be in the future? 는 장래 희망을 묻는 표현이다.

➕ 대화를 듣고, 남자의 장래 희망으로 가장 적절한 것을 고르시오.

① 가수　　　　② 화가
③ 교사　　　　④ 간호사
⑤ 의사

W Wow, you sing very well. Do you love singing?

M Yeah. I wanted to be a singer when I was young, but I hope to _____
_____ _____ in the future.
　　　　　　　화가가 되다

W A painter? I think the job would be good for you, too.

M Thanks. How about you? What do you want to be in the future?

W My parents want me to be a teacher, but I want to _____
　　　　　　　　　　　　　　　　　　　　　　　　　　간호사가 되다
_____ .

M You love _____ _____ _____ _____ . I'm
　　　　　　아픈 사람들을 돌보는 것
sure you'll be a good nurse.

W Thank you.

13 전화 목적 파악

대화를 듣고, 여자가 전화를 건 목적으로 가장 적절한 것을 고르시오.

① 영화를 함께 보려고
② 영화 예매를 부탁하려고
③ 컴퓨터 게임을 함께 하려고
④ 컴퓨터 프로그램을 빌리려고
⑤ 컴퓨터 수리를 부탁하려고

[Telephone rings.]

W Hello. This is Lucy. May I speak to Mike, please?

M Speaking.

W Hi, Mike. What are you doing now?

M I'm watching a movie. What's up?

W Well, there's _____ _____ _____ _____ . Will you
　　　　　　　　　내 컴퓨터에 문제
_____ _____ _____ ?
나를 도와주다

M Sure. I'm free at the moment. I'll be over soon.

W Thanks.

14 할 일 파악

남자가 할 일과 여자가 할 일을 구분해서 듣는다.

대화를 듣고, 남자가 할 일로 가장 적절한 것을 고르시오.

① 쇼핑 가기 go shopping
② 외식하기
③ 붓 사오기 buy some brushes
④ 페인트칠 하기 paint the fence
⑤ 정원 손질하기

W Are you going shopping with me today?

M Well, I don't feel like going out today.

W Why not?

M I want to _____ _____ in the garden.
담장에 페인트칠을 하다

W But that's _____ _____ _____ _____. Do you need a hand?
큰 일

M I _____ _____ _____ _____ _____ me paint. But, will you buy
당신이 도울 필요는 없다
some brushes and white paint? I need more.

W Sure.

15 의도 추론

대화를 듣고, 여자의 마지막 말의 의도로 가장 적절한 것을 고르시오.

① 축하   ② 비난
③ 감사   ④ 위로
⑤ 제안

W What's wrong with you, Jerry? You look sad.

M Monica, I'm afraid I gave wrong answers for the last three questions.

W _____ _____. You can't change your answers now.
그것을 잊어버려라

M I'm afraid I won't pass the test.

W Come on, Jerry. Don't you think it's _____ _____ _____
걱정하기에는 너무 늦은
about it now? You'll _____ _____ _____ _____.
다음 번에 더 잘하다

고난도

16 숫자 파악 – 시각

떠날 시각과 현재 시각과의 연관성을 파악한다.

대화를 듣고, 현재 시각을 고르시오.

① 12:00 p.m.
② 1:00 p.m.
③ 2:00 p.m.
④ 3:00 p.m.
⑤ 4:00 p.m.

What time shall we ~?는 만날 시간을 정할 때 사용하는 표현이다.

M Hi, Linda.

W Hi, Frank.

M Linda, how about going to the Hankuk art gallery this afternoon?

W Sounds great. What time shall we leave?

M Let's see.... Let's meet at the entrance of the library, and _____
3시에 떠나다
_____ _____.

W Okay. That's _____ _____ from now.
정확히 2시간

M Please don't be late.

W I won't. See you then.

17 심정 추론

반복되는 어휘 bad를 단서로 이용한다.

대화를 듣고, 여자의 심정으로 가장 적절한 것을 고르시오.

① 슬픔   ② 걱정됨
③ 외로움   ④ 행복함
⑤ 피곤함

I am truly sorry for your loss.는 '삼가 고인의 명복을 빕니다'라는 의미로, 돌아가신 분에 대해 위로의 뜻을 나타낼 때 사용하는 표현이다.

M Are you feeling OK? You don't look good.

W I've just heard some bad news.

M What happened?

W My uncle _____ _____.
돌아가셨다

M I am truly sorry for your loss. Were you close?

W Yes. We spent lots of time together when I was little. Oh, I _____ _____
너무 안되셨다
_____ for my aunt.

M Will you go back home, then?

W For a few days. _____ _____ I have to go home for this.
너무 안좋은

18 내용 일치 파악

선택지 내용을 먼저 파악하고, 대화를 들으면서 일치 여부를 확인한다.

대화를 듣고, 대화의 내용과 일치하지 <u>않는</u> 것을 고르시오.

① Sally is calling John.
② Sally has to go to her parents'.
③ Sally can't start her car.
④ Sally is angry at John.
⑤ Sally is in front of her house.

[Telephone rings.]

W Can I talk to John? This is Sally.

M Speaking.

W John, I must ＿＿＿＿＿＿＿＿＿ ＿＿＿＿＿ ＿＿＿＿＿ but I
　　　　　　내 부모님 댁에 가다　　　　　　　　시동이 안 걸리다
　　＿＿＿＿＿ my car.

M That's too bad. What's the matter with your car?

W I don't know. I think something is wrong with the engine. Could you come over and take a look at it?

M Okay. I'll be there in a minute. Where are you?

W I'm ＿＿＿＿＿ ＿＿＿＿＿ ＿＿＿＿＿ my house. Thanks.
　　～ 앞에

---

19 알맞은 응답 찾기

[19~20] 대화를 듣고, 여자의 마지막 말에 이어질 남자의 응답으로 가장 적절한 것을 고르시오.

Man: ＿＿＿＿＿＿＿＿＿＿＿＿＿＿

① We'd better not.
② Of course, she is.
③ I won't do it again.
④ I don't know for sure.
⑤ That was nice of you.

She must be ~.는 '그녀는 틀림없이 ～할 것이다.'라는 뜻으로 강한 추측을 나타내는 표현이다.

M Are you surprised that my sister has finally passed the test?

W No. I was sure that she would succeed.

M You know she had already ＿＿＿＿＿＿＿＿＿ ＿＿＿＿＿.
　　　　　　　　　　　　　　그것에 두 번이나 떨어졌다

W I know. You told me about that. It makes me happy to hear ＿＿＿＿＿
　　＿＿＿＿＿＿＿＿＿＿.
　　그녀가 그것에 통과했다

M Me, too.

W She ＿＿＿＿＿ ＿＿＿＿＿ ＿＿＿＿＿.
　　　　분명 매우 기뻐할 것이다

M ＿＿＿＿＿＿＿＿＿＿＿＿＿＿

고난도

20 알맞은 응답 찾기

Man: ＿＿＿＿＿＿＿＿＿＿＿＿＿＿

① Fine, I'll put it away a little later.
② I can run the polisher by myself.
③ OK, let's try it your way this time.
④ That's why I need you to move it.
⑤ But I already put everything away.

M I need your help to move furniture. I want to polish the floor.

W OK. What should I do?

M ＿＿＿＿＿＿＿＿＿ ＿＿＿＿ ＿＿＿＿ ＿＿＿＿ and move it all back later.
　　모든 것을 한쪽으로 옮겨라

W Isn't that a lot of extra work?

M What would you suggest?

W Just move each thing over a little bit, ＿＿＿＿＿ ＿＿＿＿ ＿＿＿＿, and then
　　　　　　　　　　　　　　　　　　그곳을 닦다
　　put it back right away.

M ＿＿＿＿＿＿＿＿＿＿＿＿＿＿

학년　　　　반　　　　번
이름

01 대화를 듣고, 남자가 그린 그림을 고르시오.

① ② ③

④ ⑤

02 대화를 듣고, 철물점을 고르시오.

03 대화를 듣고, 여자의 심정으로 가장 적절한 것을 고르시오.

① 슬픔　　　　　　② 실망
③ 당황　　　　　　④ 긴장
⑤ 행복

04 대화를 듣고, 남자가 제일 좋아하는 색깔로 가장 적절한 것을 고르시오.

① 노란색　　　　　② 빨간색
③ 하얀색　　　　　④ 파란색
⑤ 초록색

고난도
05 다음을 듣고, 무엇에 관한 내용인지 가장 적절한 것을 고르시오.

① 응급 처치법　　　② 난로 사용법
③ 안전의 중요성　　④ 컴퓨터 수리법
⑤ 유용한 문구류

06 대화를 듣고, 두 사람이 대화하고 있는 장소로 가장 적절한 곳을 고르시오.

① 식당　　　　　　② 은행
③ 공항　　　　　　④ 약국
⑤ 커피숍

07 대화를 듣고, 두 사람의 관계로 가장 적절한 것을 고르시오.

① 교사 – 학생　　　② 의사 – 환자
③ 경찰관 – 범인　　④ 옷가게 점원 – 고객
⑤ 커피숍 주인 – 손님

08 대화를 듣고, 여자가 전화를 건 목적으로 가장 적절한 것을 고르시오.

① 안부를 물으려고
② 약속을 취소하려고
③ 입원한 병원을 물어보려고
④ 병원의 위치를 확인하려고
⑤ 병문안을 가자고 제안하려고

고난도
09 대화를 듣고, 두 사람이 점심 가격으로 지불할 금액을 고르시오.

① $125　　　　　　② $155
③ $165　　　　　　④ $175
⑤ $195

10 다음을 듣고, 무엇에 관한 안내인지 가장 적절한 것을 고르시오.

① 분실물 신고　　　② 할인 판매
③ 수학 경시대회　　④ 컴퓨터 강좌
⑤ 시험 결과 발표

점수
/20

고난도
11 다음 이메일을 보면서 대화를 듣고, 대화의 내용과 일치하지 <u>않는</u> 것을 고르시오.

> from : ① paulhong@gmail.com
> to : prettie@hanmail.net (Kim Bora)
> date : ② Mon, Nov 16, 2010 at 11:40 a.m.
> subject : ③ Information about the English teacher
> Dear Prettie,
> I have some information about the English teacher your school are looking for. He is Sam Samuel from Canada. ④ He graduated from university last year. He is looking for a job as an English teacher in Korea. ⑤ He is 23 years old. Bye.

12 대화를 듣고, 상품이 배달될 시각을 고르시오.

① 10:00 a.m.   ② 11:00 a.m.
③ 12:00 p.m.   ④ 1:00 p.m.
⑤ 2:00 p.m.

13 대화를 듣고, 여자가 주문한 것으로 언급되지 <u>않은</u> 것을 고르시오.

① 토마토 소스   ② 그린 샐러드
③ 치킨 샐러드   ④ 해산물 파스타
⑤ 햄버거 스테이크

14 대화를 듣고, 호텔에 있는 시설로 언급되지 않은 것을 고르시오.

① 수영장   ② 헬스클럽
③ 보석 가게   ④ 선물 가게
⑤ 현금 인출기

15 대화를 듣고, 남자가 매년 결혼기념일에 하는 일로 가장 적절한 것을 고르시오.

① 아내와 쇼핑하기   ② 아내와 여행하기
③ 아내와 영화 보기   ④ 아내와 식사하기
⑤ 아내에게 줄 꽃 사기

16 대화를 듣고, 남자가 포스터를 가지고 있는 이유로 가장 적절한 것을 고르시오.

① 사무실에 잘 어울려서
② 유년기를 떠올리게 해서
③ 가장 좋은 액자에 있어서
④ 비싼 돈을 주고 구입한 것이라서
⑤ 가장 좋아하는 밴드의 포스터라서

17 다음 그림의 상황에 가장 적절한 대화를 고르시오.

①   ②   ③   ④   ⑤

18 대화를 듣고, 남자가 여자에게 부탁한 일로 가장 적절한 것을 고르시오.

① 책 빌려다주기   ② 책 반납하기
③ 도서관 데려다주기   ④ 축구 시합 보러오기
⑤ 학교로 데리러오기

[19~20] 대화를 듣고, 남자의 마지막 말에 이어질 여자의 응답으로 가장 적절한 것을 고르시오.

19 Woman: _____

① Don't be afraid.
② I'm supposed to meet him.
③ It's nice of you to think so.
④ You'd better do some exercise.
⑤ Don't forget to bring your dinner.

20 Woman: _____

① I'm sorry, I must be going now.
② There is something you have to do.
③ Please give my regards to your parents.
④ You'll have problems if you are late again.
⑤ You'd better stay home until you're better.

다시 들으면서 듣기 만점에 도전하세요!
Dictation: 스크립트의 주요 부분을 다시 들으면서!
실전 ⊕: 세부 정보가 많은 스크립트를 다른 문제로 샅샅이!

---

01 그림 정보 파악 – 사물 　　　　　　사물의 모습을 묘사한 마지막 부분을 잘 듣는다.

대화를 듣고, 남자가 그린 그림을 고르시오.

① ②

③ ④

⑤

W Wow! There are a lot of pictures here.

M We are ＿＿＿＿＿ ＿＿＿＿＿ ＿＿＿＿＿. Look at that picture. That's
　　　 그림 전시회를 가지다
＿＿＿＿＿ ＿＿＿＿＿ ＿＿＿＿＿.
내가 그린 그림

W What picture is it? Is it the picture of a statue in the middle of a garden?

M No, I mean the picture of ＿＿＿＿ ＿＿＿＿ ＿＿＿＿ ＿＿＿＿ on
　　　　　　　　　　　　　　　　 휘날리는 태극기
a pole on the top of a building.

---

02 그림 정보 파악 – 지도 　　　　　위치를 나타내는 전치사를 주의깊게 듣는다.

대화를 듣고, 철물점을 고르시오.

W I need a light bulb. Where's the hardware store?

M There's one on the main street, just ＿＿＿＿ ＿＿＿＿ ＿＿＿＿.
　　　　　　　　　　　　　　　　　　　　 약국 지나서

W Which pharmacy? The one across the street from the grocery store?

M No, the pharmacy ＿＿＿＿ ＿＿＿＿ ＿＿＿＿ ＿＿＿＿.
　　　　　　　　　　 백화점 근처에

W Is it ＿＿＿＿ ＿＿＿＿ ＿＿＿＿, then?
　　 도서관 가까이에

M Yeah, it's around that area.

W OK, then I think I know where it is. Thanks.

---

03 심정 추론

대화를 듣고, 여자의 심정으로 가장 적절한 것을 고르시오.

① 슬픔　　　　② 실망
③ 당황　　　　④ 긴장
⑤ 행복

「**congratulate A on B**」는 'A에게 B를 축하하다' 라는 의미이다.

W I can't believe I did that!

M What happened?

W I just said something I shouldn't have.

M What did you say?

W I congratulated Betty on ＿＿＿＿ ＿＿＿＿ ＿＿＿＿.
　　　　　　　　　　　　　 성적 우수상을 탄 것

M So? What's wrong with that?

W She didn't win, ＿＿＿＿ ＿＿＿＿ ＿＿＿＿. Now I feel bad.
　　　　　　　　 그녀의 여동생이 탔다

M It was an honest mistake. I'm sure Betty isn't angry.

04 특정 정보 파악

대화를 듣고, 남자가 제일 좋아하는 색깔로 가장 적절한 것을 고르시오.

① 노란색   ② 빨간색
③ 하얀색   ④ 파란색
⑤ 초록색

➕ 대화를 듣고, 여자가 좋아하는 색깔로 가장 적절한 것을 고르시오.

① 노란색   ② 빨간색
③ 하얀색   ④ 파란색
⑤ 초록색

W I love spring! All plants begin to bloom into beautiful flowers!

M What's your favorite flower?

W I love roses. I like their _____ _____ _____ (진한 빨간색). It's my favorite color. Do you like spring?

M Yes, but I like _____ _____ (봄보다 가을을 더). I like the yellow and red leaves of trees.

W What's your favorite color?

M I like yellow, but I _____ _____ _____ (노란색보다는 빨간색을 더 좋아하다), just like you.

`고난도`

05 특정 정보 파악

반복되는 어휘 accident, careful 등을 단서로 이용한다.

다음을 듣고, 무엇에 관한 내용이지 가장 적절한 것을 고르시오.

① 응급 처치법
② 난로 사용법
③ 안전의 중요성
④ 컴퓨터 수리법
⑤ 유용한 문구류

W Accidents always happen in our lives. Electricity makes our lives very comfortable, but it is _____ _____ (항상 위험한). If you push something into a socket, you will be shocked and go to the hospital. When you use sharp knives and scissors, you should be careful. If children play with them, they might be cut by them. You should always _____ (조심하다) when you do something. _____ _____ (사고가 일어나다) when you are not careful.

---

06 장소 추론

medicine, vitamins, prescription 등과 같은 특정 상황에 많이 사용되는 어휘들에서 단서를 얻는다.

대화를 듣고, 두 사람이 대화하고 있는 장소로 가장 적절한 곳을 고르시오.

① 식당   ② 은행
③ 공항   ④ 약국
⑤ 커피숍

➕ 대화를 듣고, 여자가 대화 직후에 할 일로 가장 적절한 것을 고르시오.

① 제조약 받아가기   ② 비타민 구입하기
③ 은행일 보러가기   ④ 커피숍 가기
⑤ 병원 진료 예약하기

M Are you _____ _____ (약을 복용하고 있다)?
W No, I am not.
M Then, do you take vitamins?
W Oh, yes. I _____ (종합비타민을 복용하다) every morning.
M Oh, I see. It will take thirty minutes to _____ _____ (당신의 처방전 대로 조제하다).
W Okay. I'll go have a cup of coffee. Is there a coffee shop near here?
M Yes, there's a nice coffee shop across from the bank.
W Thank you. I'll be back in thirty minutes.

---

07 관계 파악

대화를 듣고, 두 사람의 관계로 가장 적절한 것을 고르시오.

① 교사 – 학생
② 의사 – 환자
③ 경찰관 – 범인
④ 옷가게 점원 – 고객
⑤ 커피숍 주인 – 손님

headache: 두통
stomachache: 복통
toothache: 치통
earache: 귀앓이

W What's the matter?
M I just _____ _____ (잠을 잘 수 없다).
W How long have you had this problem?
M For about two weeks now.
W Do you drink coffee?
M No, I don't drink any coffee.
W Do you _____ _____ _____ (두통이 있다)?
M Yes, sometimes.
W Can you lift up your shirt? Let me _____ _____ _____ (당신의 심장 박동을 확인하다).

대화를 듣고, 여자가 전화를 건 목적으로 가장 적절한 것을 고르시오.

① 안부를 물으려고
② 약속을 취소하려고
③ 입원한 병원을 물어보려고
④ 병원의 위치를 확인하려고
⑤ 병문안을 가자고 제안하려고

How awful!은 '저런, 정말 안되셨네요.'라는 의미로, That's too bad. / What a shame! 등으로 바꿔 말할 수 있다.

[Telephone rings.]

M Hello.

W Hello, may I speak to Bob? This is Cathy speaking.

M Hello, Cathy. This is Bob. What's up?

W Tomorrow is Teacher's Day. Let's visit Ms. Song.

M Oh, I was planning to do so. Let's meet in front of the school.

W No, _____ _____ _____ _____. She is in hospital _____
그녀는 학교에 안 계신다   팔이 부러져서
_____ _____ _____.

M Really? How awful! Is she OK?

W Yes, she'll _____ _____ _____ _____ next week. Let's meet at the
        퇴원하다
hospital.

M OK, see you there.

고난도

각 품목의 개당 가격과 사려는 갯수를 정확히 듣고 계산한다.

대화를 듣고, 두 사람이 점심 가격으로 지불할 금액을 고르시오.

① $125   ② $155
③ $165   ④ $175
⑤ $195

W We have to buy lunch for the field trip.

M OK. What should we get?

W The teacher said sandwiches for students and one or two cakes.

M How many sandwiches do we need?

W We need _____. They _____ _____ _____.
            25   개당 5달러이다
M And how much is the cake?

W We can get one big cake for $30, and _____ _____ _____
                                            작은 케이크 하나는 20달러
_____.

M Let's get _____ _____ _____.
            2개의 작은 케이크

W OK.

반복되는 어휘 competition, math, exam 등을 단서로 이용한다.

다음을 듣고, 무엇에 관한 안내인지 가장 적절한 것을 고르시오.

① 분실물 신고
② 할인 판매
③ 수학 경시대회
④ 컴퓨터 강좌
⑤ 시험 결과 발표

M May I have your attention, please? Tomorrow there will be _____ _____
                                                            수학 경시대회
_____ in Room 501. The competition will start at four o'clock after class. The

things you have to bring with you for the exam are black and red felt pens and

correction tapes. The students who _____ _____ _____ it
                                        이미 지원하다
should show up on time. We hope you _____ _____ _____
                                        시험을 잘 보다
_____.

11 실용문 정보 파악

이메일의 내용을 먼저 파악하고, 대화의 내용을 예상해 본다.

다음 이메일을 보면서 대화를 듣고, 대화의 내용과 일치하지 <u>않는</u> 것을 고르시오.

from : ① paulhong@gmail.com
to : prettie@hanmail.net (Kim Bora)
date : ② Mon, Nov 16, 2010 at
      11:40 a.m.
subject : ③ Information about the
          English teacher
Dear Prettie,
I have some information about the
English teacher your school are
looking for. He is Sam Samuel from
Canada. ④ He graduated from
university last year. He is looking
for a job as an English teacher in
Korea. ⑤ He is 23 years old. Bye.

M Ms. Kim, do you know anything about the new English teacher?

W Yes, I do. My Canadian friend, Paul Hong, _____ 나에게 이메일을 보냈다 on November 16. The mail _____ 밤 늦게 도착했다 , so I could open it the next morning.

M What did he say about him?

W He wrote about his age, nationality, and his major.

M Where is the new English teacher from?

W He's from Canada. It's been _____ 그가 ~을 졸업한 지 1년 _____ university. He is looking for a job as an English teacher in Korea. He is _____ 20대 초반인 _____ .

12 숫자 파악 – 시각

대화를 듣고, 상품이 배달될 시각을 고르시오.

① 10:00 a.m.
② 11:00 a.m.
③ 12:00 p.m.
④ 1:00 p.m.
⑤ 2:00 p.m.

M That's one of the best selling products this year.

W OK, I will take it. Can you deliver it to my home? How much do you _____ 배달하는 데 드는 비용 _____ ?

M If you live in Seoul, the delivery is free.

W Good! How soon can it _____ 배달되다 _____ ?

M It will be delivered by 2 p.m. tomorrow.

W Can you make it earlier? Is it possible in the morning?

M OK, I will _____ 오전 11시까지 그것이 배달되도록 하다 _____ tomorrow.

13 특정 정보 파악

여자가 음식을 주문할 때 집중해서 듣는다.

대화를 듣고, 여자가 주문한 것으로 언급되지 <u>않은</u> 것을 고르시오.

① 토마토 소스
② 그린 샐러드
③ 치킨 샐러드
④ 해산물 파스타
⑤ 햄버거 스테이크

I'll order ~. / I'll have ~. 는 음식을 주문할 때 사용하는 표현이다.

M What can I get for you, ma'am?

W What would you recommend?

M Our special is _____ 그린 샐러드를 곁들인 햄버거 스테이크 _____ .

W Do you have anything lighter?

M The chicken or Caesar salad is popular. Or the seafood pasta.

W Is the pasta in cream or tomato sauce?

M You can choose.

W Then I'll _____ 특별 메뉴로 주문하다 _____ for my husband, and I'll have _____ 해산물 파스타 _____ in tomato sauce.

M OK. It'll be ready soon.

14 언급 및 비언급 파악

장소나 찾는 것에 관련된 말을 집중해서 듣고, 선택지에서 언급된 것을 지워나간다.

대화를 듣고, 호텔에 있는 시설로 언급되지 <u>않은</u> 것을 고르시오.

① 수영장 swimming pool
② 헬스클럽 fitness center
③ 보석 가게
④ 선물 가게 gift shop
⑤ 현금 인출기 cash machine

Is there ~?는 대상의 존재 유무를 물을 때 사용하는 표현이다.

W Excuse me. Is the swimming pool still open?

M Yes, but it closes at 9. You have only 30 minutes left.

W Oh, no! Where can I _____ _____ then?
   _{운동하다}

M There's _____ _____ on the fifth floor.
   _{헬스클럽}

W Great. And is there a gift shop in the hotel?

M Yes. Take the elevator to the first floor.

W One more thing, please. Is there _____ _____ _____?
   _{현금 인출기}

M Yes. It's _____ _____ _____ _____ _____.
   _{선물 가게 옆에}

W Thank you.

M You're welcome.

15 특정 정보 파악

대화를 듣고, 남자가 매년 결혼기념일에 하는 일로 가장 적절한 것을 고르시오.

① 아내와 쇼핑하기
② 아내와 여행하기
③ 아내와 영화 보기
④ 아내와 식사하기
⑤ 아내에게 줄 꽃 사기

W Can I ask you a personal question?

M Sure, go ahead.

W What's _____ _____ of the year?
   _{당신이 가장 좋아하는 날}

M It's May 1st.

W Why do you like that day the most?

M Well, I _____ _____ _____ _____.
   _{그 날 결혼했다}

W Do you do anything special then?

M I _____ _____ _____ _____
   _{항상 좋은 식당을 예약하다}
   for a nice dinner with my wife.

W That sounds nice.

16 이유 파악

Why ~? 이후에 나오는 대답을 집중해서 듣는다.

대화를 듣고, 남자가 포스터를 가지고 있는 이유로 가장 적절한 것을 고르시오.

① 사무실에 잘 어울려서
② 유년기를 떠올리게 해서
③ 가장 좋은 액자에 있어서
④ 비싼 돈을 주고 구입한 것이라서
⑤ 가장 좋아하는 밴드의 포스터라서

W What's this?

M It's a poster I had when I was a kid.

W Why do you still have it?

M I got it from the first concert I went to. It _____ _____
   _{나에게 내 유년기를 떠올리게 해 주다}
   _____.

W Oh, I see. You should _____ _____ _____.
   _{그것을 액자로 만들다}

M Good thinking. Then I can hang it in this room.

W No way!

M But I want to put it up somewhere.

W In your office. It will look much nicer there.

17 그림 상황 대화 찾기

다음 그림의 상황에 가장 적절한 대화를 고르시오.

① ② ③ ④ ⑤

① **W** Can you tell me how to get to the Royal Palace?
   M Go straight over there, and turn right.
② **W** How did you like the trip?
   M It was really great. I saw lots of interesting things.
③ **W** Where would you like to go next?
   M I'd like to go have _____ _____ _____ . I'm hungry.
        먹을 것
④ **W** Can we go inside the palace?
   M Yes, but we have to buy a ticket first.
⑤ **W** Could you take a picture of me in front of this door, please?
   M Sure, do I just _____ _____ ?
        이 버튼을 누르다

18 부탁한 일 파악

대화를 듣고, 남자가 여자에게 부탁한 일로 가장 적절한 것을 고르시오.

① 책 빌려다주기
② 책 반납하기
③ 도서관 데려다주기
④ 축구 시합 보러오기
⑤ 학교로 데리러오기

M Mom, what are you doing today?
W I have a meeting in the morning, and I'm free after that. Why?
M I forgot to _____ _____ to the library, and they are due today.
       이 책들을 반납하다
W I reminded you about them last week.
M Yes, I know. I'm sorry. Could you do me this favor, please?
W What about after school? The library closes at 6.
M I _____ _____ this afternoon. I can't miss it!
   축구 연습이 있다
W Okay, but this is the last time.

19 알맞은 응답 찾기

[19~20] 대화를 듣고, 남자의 마지막 말에 이어질 여자의 응답으로 가장 적절한 것을 고르시오.

Woman: _____

① Don't be afraid.
② I'm supposed to meet him.
③ It's nice of you to think so.
④ You'd better do some exercise.
⑤ Don't forget to bring your dinner.

남자의 마지막 말은 여자의 고민을 덜어주려는 의도임을 파악한다.

M Let's _____ _____ .
   저녁을 먹으러 나가다
W I don't want to go out for dinner.
M Aren't you hungry?
W I just want to stay home and have some fruit and salad for dinner.
M Is that all?
W I want to _____ _____ _____ .
       살을 좀 빼다
M You _____ _____ you need to lose weight.
   ~처럼 안 보인다
W _____

20 알맞은 응답 찾기

Woman: _____

① I'm sorry, I must be going now.
② There is something you have to do.
③ Please give my regards to your parents.
④ You'll have problems if you are late again.
⑤ You'd better stay home until you're better.

W You look sick today.
M This cold is killing me.
W I'm sorry to hear that.
M Atchoo!
W Don't sneeze _____ _____ _____ . I don't want to _____ .
       내 쪽으로   감기에 걸리다
   _____ .
M OK, OK. I'll _____ _____ .
       내 거리를 유지하다
W Did you go to see a doctor?
M Yes, but the medicine _____ _____ . Oh, I feel dizzy. I'm afraid I
       별로 효과가 없다
   can't work anymore today.
W _____

말의 내용 파악

무엇을 평가하는가?	일상생활이나 친숙한 일반적 주제에 관한 말이나 대화를 듣고 주제, 요지를 파악할 수 있는지를 평가한다.
어떻게 출제되는가?	• 다음을 듣고, 남자가 안내하는 말의 내용으로 가장 적절한 것을 고르시오. • 다음을 듣고, 여자가 하는 말의 내용으로 가장 적절한 것을 고르시오.

key solution

❶ 한 두 문장의 특징만으로 섣부르게 답을 고르지 않도록 주의하며, 전체적인 내용을 포함하고 있는 답을 찾는다.

[기출로 전략 확인]

다음을 듣고, 남자가 하는 말의 내용으로 가장 적절한 것을 고르시오.　　　[2018 기출]

① 다양한 통신 수단　　　　　　② 대중교통의 장점
③ 인터넷 쇼핑의 장점　　　　　④ 인터넷 중독의 심각성
⑤ 올바른 휴대전화 사용방법

- -

M Hello, students! Let me tell you how to use your cell phone wisely. First, you should not talk too loudly on the phone while using public transportation. Second, you should not send text messages while you are walking. Lastly, when you are at a movie theater, you need to turn off your cell phone.

❶ 남자가 처음부터 학생들에게 휴대전화를 현명하게 사용하는 법을 알려주겠다고 말하며, 3가지 방법을 제시하고 있다.

남 학생 여러분 안녕하세요! 휴대전화를 현명하게 사용하는 법을 알려드리겠습니다. 첫번째, 대중교통을 이용할 때는 통화를 너무 시끄럽게 하지 않는 것이 좋습니다. 두번째, 걷는 동안에는 문자를 보내지 않도록 합니다. 마지막으로, 영화관에 있을 때는 휴대전화의 전화를 끄도록 합니다.

**말의 내용 파악 유형의
발문과 보기**

다음을 듣고, 남자가 하는 말의 내용으로 가장 적절한 것을 고르시오.   [2018 기출]

① 여가 활동   ② 전화 예절   ③ 환경 보호 방법
④ 주말 일기 예보   ⑤ 건강관리 비결

만점 잡는 문장   ① We should turn off the lights when we don't use them.
② Let's use cups while we brush our teeth
③ We should recycle paper, cans and plastics.
④ We should try to reduce food waste.

다음을 듣고, 남자가 안내하는 말의 내용으로 가장 적절한 것을 고르시오. 2016 기출   [2016 기출]

① 할인상품   ② 폐장 시간   ③ 층별 매장
④ 제품 수선   ⑤ 분실물 습득

만점 잡는 문장   ① We have found a coat and a scarf in the women's restroom on the fifth floor.
② If you have lost a coat and a scarf, please come to the customer service
center.

**말의 내용 파악에
쓰이는 표현**

● **규칙**

Please do not run around the pool. 수영장 주변에서 뛰지 마세요.
Don't forget to stretch before you enter the pool.
수영장에 들어가기 전 준비운동 하는 것을 잊지 마세요.

● **모집**

We're looking for new members of our volunteer club.
봉사활동 클럽에서 새로운 멤버를 찾고 있습니다.
If you're interested, please tell your homeroom teacher. 관심이 있다면 담임선생님께 말해주세요.

● **인기도**

Among those books, novels are the most popular books. 책 들 중, 소설이 가장 인기있습니다.
The second most popular books are comic books, and then magazines.
두 번째로 인기 있는 책은 만화책이고 그 다음은 잡지입니다.

● **일정**

Now, we're going to the Eiffel Tower. 이제 우리는 에펠 타워에 갈 것입니다.
After that, we'll come back here to have dinner. 그 다음 우리는 여기로 돌아와서 저녁을 먹을 겁니다.

01 대화를 듣고, 오늘의 날씨로 가장 적절한 것을 고르시오.

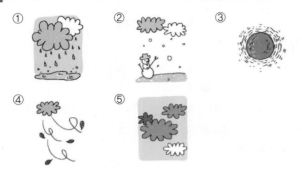

① ② ③ ④ ⑤

02 대화를 듣고, Steve가 하고 있는 일을 고르시오.

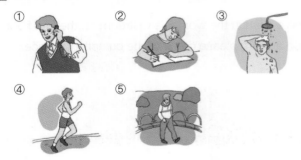

① ② ③ ④ ⑤

고난도
03 대화를 듣고, 송금 절차에 대한 설명으로 일치하지 <u>않는</u> 것을 고르시오.

① Press the "SEND" button.
② Put the card into the slot.
③ Select the amount to send.
④ Report the lost credit card.
⑤ Enter your password.

04 대화를 듣고, 두 사람이 오늘 오후에 할 일로 가장 적절한 것을 고르시오.

① 숙제하기　　　　② 농구 시합하기
③ 배구 시합하기　　④ 영화 관람하기
⑤ 컴퓨터 게임하기

05 다음 그림의 상황에 가장 적절한 대화를 고르시오.

① ② ③ ④ ⑤

06 대화를 듣고, 남자가 이용할 교통 수단으로 가장 적절한 것을 고르시오.

① 택시　　　　　　② 버스
③ 지하철　　　　　④ 기차
⑤ 비행기

고난도
07 다음을 듣고, 무엇에 관한 안내인지 가장 적절한 것을 고르시오.

① 컴퓨터 강좌
② 다이어트 방법
③ 인터넷 접속법
④ 건강 상담 웹사이트
⑤ 새로 출시된 컴퓨터

08 대화를 듣고, 남자가 제일 좋아한 나라로 가장 적절한 것을 고르시오.

① Italy　　　　　　② France
③ Germany　　　　④ Switzerland
⑤ England

09 대화를 듣고, 남자가 여자에게 부탁한 일로 가장 적절한 것을 고르시오.

① 영어 공부 같이 하기
② 영어캠프 신청해주기
③ 부모님께 연락하기
④ 영어캠프 정보 알려주기
⑤ 책자 배포하기

점수

/20

10 대화를 듣고, 여자의 심정 변화로 가장 적절한 것을 고르시오.

① 분노 → 슬픔
② 걱정 → 안도
③ 행복 → 걱정
④ 슬픔 → 행복
⑤ 흥분 → 실망

11 대화를 듣고, 여자가 가입하게 될 동아리로 가장 적절한 것을 고르시오.

① 사진반
② 연극반
③ 운동반
④ 미술반
⑤ 합창반

12 대화를 듣고, 남자가 전화를 건 목적으로 가장 적절한 것을 고르시오.

① 병문안을 함께 가려고
② 친구를 소개시켜 주려고
③ 병원의 위치를 확인하려고
④ 친구의 안부를 물어보려고
⑤ 도서관에서 함께 공부하려고

13 대화를 듣고, 여자가 놀이 공원에 가지 <u>않으려는</u> 이유로 가장 적절한 것을 고르시오.

① 날씨가 너무 더워서
② 도서관에 가야 해서
③ 집에서 너무 멀어서
④ 친구와 약속이 있어서
⑤ 사람들이 많은 것을 싫어해서

14 대화를 듣고, 남자가 오늘 밤에 할 일로 가장 적절한 것을 고르시오.

① 학교 가기
② 영화 보기
③ 데이트하기
④ 숙제 끝내기
⑤ 아르바이트 하기

15 대화를 듣고, 남자가 지불할 금액을 고르시오.

① $35
② $40
③ $45
④ $50
⑤ $55

16 대화를 듣고, 두 사람의 관계로 가장 적절한 것을 고르시오.

① 남편 – 아내
② 제과점 점원 – 손님
③ 식당 주인 – 종업원
④ 야구 선수 – 기자
⑤ 제과점 주인 – 제빵사

17 대화를 듣고, 두 사람이 대화하고 있는 장소로 가장 적절한 곳을 고르시오.

① 해변
② 수영장
③ 등산로
④ 스키장
⑤ 나비 전시관

18 대화를 듣고, 남자가 Shopping Mall에서 한 일로 가장 적절한 것을 고르시오.

① 쇼핑하기
② 볼링 치기
③ 영화보기
④ 저녁 먹기
⑤ 친구 기다리기

[19~20] 대화를 듣고, 여자의 마지막 말에 이어질 남자의 응답으로 가장 적절한 것을 고르시오.

고난도

19 Man: _____

① I hope she gets better soon.
② Maybe she needs medicine.
③ Next time, tell him the truth.
④ Get your mom to call him, then.
⑤ You should have finished on time.

20 Man: _____

① I like playing baseball.
② I made many mistakes today.
③ The game was really exciting.
④ Let's play baseball this afternoon.
⑤ He's the best pitcher in the world.

다시 들으면서 듣기 만점에 도전하세요!
Dictation: 스크립트의 주요 부분을 다시 들으면세!
실전 ➕: 세부 정보가 많은 스크립트를 다른 문제로 샅샅이!

---

01 날씨 파악   today라는 표현이 언급된 부분을 주의깊게 듣는다.

대화를 듣고, 오늘의 날씨로 가장 적절한 것을 고르시오.

① ② ③ ④ ⑤

M Is it going to be rainy again tomorrow?
W No. I heard it's going to _____ _____ tomorrow.
　　　　　　　　　　　　　　　　　　　맑다
M Then I can take my son to Central Park and play there tomorrow.
W Sounds great. By the way, _____ _____ _____ these days.
　　　　　　　　　　　　　　　비가 많이 온다
M Because it's the rainy season.
W I hate the rainy season.
M Look on the bright side. At least, _____ _____ and it'll be sunny
　　　　　　　　　　　　　　　　　오늘은 흐리다
tomorrow.
W You're right.

---

02 그림 정보 파악 – 인물   현재 하고 있는 일은 「am / are / is + -ing」로 표현함에 유의한다.

대화를 듣고, Steve가 하고 있는 일을 고르시오.

① ② ③ ④ ⑤

[Telephone rings.]
W Hello. Can I talk to Steve, please?
M May I ask who's calling?
W This is Mary. I've tried calling his Cellphone, but _____ _____ _____
　　　　　　　　　　　　　　　　　　　　　　　　　　　　　　　　받지 않았다
_____ .
M He's _____ _____ _____ now.
　　　　샤워하고 있다
W I promised to take a walk in the park with him in an hour, but I can't keep my promise.
M Okay. I'll tell Steve to _____ _____ anyway.
　　　　　　　　　　　　　당신에게 다시 전화하다
W Thank you. Bye.

May I ask who's calling?은 '누구세요?'라는 의미로, 전화를 건 사람이 누구인지 물을 때 사용하는 표현이다.

[고난도]

---

03 내용 일치 파악   사물의 사용 절차나 순서에 대한 대화는 그 내용들을 순서대로 확인해야 한다.

대화를 듣고, 송금 절차에 대한 설명으로 일치하지 <u>않는</u> 것을 고르시오.

① Press the "SEND" button.
② Put the card into the slot.
③ Select the amount to send.
④ Report the lost credit card.
⑤ Enter your password.

Could you tell me how to ~?는 '~하는 법을 알려 주시겠어요?'라는 의미로, 어떤 사물의 사용 절차 또는 어떤 장소로 가는 방법을 물을 때 사용하는 표현이다.

W I'll send some money to my grandson. Could you tell me how to use this cash machine?
M Sure. _____ _____ _____ first. And now _____
　　　　　'송금' 버튼을 눌러라　　　　　　　　　　　　　　　~에 카드를 집어넣어라
_____ _____ this slot.
W Like this?
M Yes. Now _____ _____ _____ that you want to send him.
　　　　　액수를 선택하라
W I see. I'll send 50,000 won.
M Okay. And now enter your grandson's account number.
W Oh, wait a minute.... Is that all?
M No. Now, finally, _____ _____ _____ .
　　　　　　　　　　　　당신의 비밀번호를 입력하라

대화를 듣고, 두 사람이 오늘 오후에 할 일로 가장 적절한 것을 고르시오.

① 숙제하기
② 농구 시합하기 play basketball
③ 배구 시합하기
④ 영화 관람하기 go to a movie
⑤ 컴퓨터 게임하기 play computer games

That's a good idea. / That sounds great. / Sounds good.은 제안에 대해 긍정적으로 대답할 때 사용하는 표현이다.

M Didn't you have fun _____ _____ yesterday?
       농구 하는 것

W To be honest, I don't like to play sports very much.

M Oh, really?

W Yes! And yesterday it was too hot, too.

M What do you like to do when you have free time then?

W I like to _____ _____ or go to a movie.
      컴퓨터 게임을 하다

M I like to play computer games, too. How about _____
                                              게임을 좀 하는 것
    together this afternoon?

W That's a good idea.

다음 그림의 상황에 가장 적절한 대화를 고르시오.

① **W** Would you like _____ _____ ?
           마실 것
   M No, thanks. I'm okay.

② **W** Hello, how can I help you?
   M I'd like to buy those flowers for my girlfriend's birthday.

③ **W** Congratulations. These are for you.
   M Oh, thank you so much. These are really nice flowers.

④ **W** What's your _____ ?
         가장 좋아하는 꽃
   M I like little wild flowers in the open field.

⑤ **W** Excuse me, is there a flower shop near here?
   M Sorry, I don't know, either. I'm a stranger here.

① ② ③ ④ ⑤

대화를 듣고, 남자가 이용할 교통 수단으로 가장 적절한 것을 고르시오.

① 택시   ② 버스
③ 지하철   ④ 기차
⑤ 비행기

M Can I take a bus to the airport from here?

W Yes. You can take a bus from here, but _____ _____ _____
                                             버스가 아주 빠르지는 않다
    _____ .

M Really? Then could you tell me how to get to the airport _____
                                                    가능한 한 빨리
    _____ _____ ?

W Sure. _____ _____ _____ at the station there.
        지하철을 타라

M Does it go directly to the airport?

W No. You _____ _____ to the Green Line at City Hall.
      갈아타야 하다

M Okay. I'll take the subway. Thanks a lot.

고난도

다음을 듣고, 무엇에 관한 안내인지 가장 적절한 것을 고르시오.

① 컴퓨터 강좌
② 다이어트 방법
③ 인터넷 접속법
④ 건강 상담 웹사이트
⑤ 새로 출시된 컴퓨터

W You wonder whether you are _____ _____ . But you're not a
                                 건강한지 안 한지
    doctor. Now you can _____ _____ _____ _____ that you
                  의사에게 어떤 질문이든지 하다
    want. It's so easy to see the doctor anytime you want. Email your questions to Dr.
    e-Health _____ _____ . Just turn on your computer and ask Dr.
            인터넷을 통해서
    e-Health. The service is free. The address of our website is www.e-health.com. If you
    have any questions about your health, please _____ _____ .
                                              우리 웹사이트를 방문하다

08 특정 정보 파악

대화를 듣고, 남자가 제일 좋아한 나라로 가장 적절한 것을 고르시오.

① Italy
② France
③ Germany
④ Switzerland
⑤ England

Like what?은 '예를 들면?'이라는 의미로, 예를 들어 설명해 줄 것을 부탁할 때 사용하는 표현이다.

W Have you ever been to Europe?

M Once. I toured France, Germany, Switzerland, and Italy.

W What did you think?

M They're all nice. I enjoyed the food above all.

W Like what?

M In France, crepes are famous street food. And there are many sausage in Germany.

W How about the scenery? I'll bet the Alps in Switzerland were beautiful.

M Yes, but Italy also _____, _____, _____
      놀라운 경치, 음식, 그리고 예술이 있었다
_____ .

W Did you like it better than Switzerland?

M Yes, _____ _____ _____ of the four countries.
      이탈리아가 가장 좋았다

---

09 부탁한 일

대화를 듣고, 남자가 여자에게 부탁한 일로 가장 적절한 것을 고르시오.

① 영어 공부 같이 하기
② 영어캠프 신청해주기
③ 부모님께 연락하기
④ 영어캠프 정보 알려주기
⑤ 책자 배포하기

W Minho, do you know about the English camp?

M No, tell me about it.

W It's a program for the summer vacation. There is this theme park, where you have to speak only English. If you _____ _____ _____ the program, you can stay
      ~에 등록하다
there for a week.

M It sounds like a good chance to practice English!

W That's right. Would you like to go?

M I'm interested. But do you have more information? I'll have to _____
                                                                    부모님께 물어보다
_____ first.

W Sure, I'll bring you the brochure tomorrow.

---

10 심정 추론

대화를 듣고, 여자의 심정 변화로 가장 적절한 것을 고르시오.

① 분노 → 슬픔
② 걱정 → 안도
③ 행복 → 걱정
④ 슬픔 → 행복
⑤ 흥분 → 실망

M You _____. Having a good day?
      기분이 좋아 보이다
W I am now.

M You weren't before?

W No. Yesterday my best friend said she's moving.

M That's too bad.

W I _____ _____ . Then she called today.
    정말 마음이 울적했다
M Did she say when she will leave?

W No. That's the good news. Her parents decided to stay here!

M Then things _____ _____ _____ after all.
      일이 잘 풀렸다

여자가 무엇이 되고 싶어 하는지를 파악한다.

대화를 듣고, 여자가 가입하게 될 동아리로 가장 적절한 것을 고르시오.

① 사진반 photo club
② 연극반 drama club
③ 운동반 sports club
④ 미술반
⑤ 합창반

대화를 듣고, 남자가 가입한 동아리로 가장 적절한 것을 고르시오.

① 사진반　　② 연극반
③ 운동반　　④ 미술반
⑤ 합창반

M Have you decided which club you are going to join?

W No, not yet, but I'm thinking about ＿＿＿＿＿＿＿ or the drama
　　사진반
club.

M I've already joined the sports club.

W What do you do in the club?

M We get together twice a week after school and play various sports. Why don't you join our club?

W I'd like to join the club, but I hope to ＿＿＿＿＿＿＿ in the
　　사진작가가 되다
future.

M Then you should ＿＿＿ ＿＿＿ ＿＿＿.
　　　　　　　　　사진반에 가입하다

W Yeah, you're right.

대화를 듣고, 남자가 전화를 건 목적으로 가장 적절한 것을 고르시오.

① 병문안을 함께 가려고
② 친구를 소개시켜 주려고
③ 병원의 위치를 확인하려고
④ 친구의 안부를 물어보려고
⑤ 도서관에서 함께 공부하려고

How's it going?은 '어떻게 지내니?'라는 의미로, 안부를 묻는 표현이다.

[Telephone rings.]

M Hi, Jane. This is Ted.

W Hi, Ted. How's it going?

M Fine. Did you hear that our classmate John ＿＿＿ ＿＿＿
　　　　　　　　　　　　　　　　　　　　　　　　　　　　입원에 있다
＿＿＿ ＿＿＿ since Thursday?

W Oh, really?

M ＿＿＿ ＿＿＿ ＿＿＿ ＿＿＿ this afternoon. Can you
　　나는 그를 보러 갈 것이다
＿＿＿ ＿＿＿ ＿＿＿?
나와 함께 가다

W Sure. Let's meet in front of the library at 3:30.

M All right. See you then.

전반부에 여자가 놀이 공원에 가지 않으려는 이유가 나와 있다.

대화를 듣고, 여자가 놀이 공원에 가지 않으려는 이유로 가장 적절한 것을 고르시오.

① 날씨가 너무 더워서
② 도서관에 가야 해서
③ 집에서 너무 멀어서
④ 친구와 약속이 있어서
⑤ 사람들이 많은 것을 싫어해서

대화를 듣고, 남자가 대화 후에 할 일로 가장 적절한 것을 고르시오.

① 놀이공원 가기　　② 공원에 가기
③ 집에서 쉬기　　　④ 도서관 가기
⑤ 책 구입하기

M Why don't we go to the amusement park?

W You know ＿＿＿＿＿＿＿ ＿＿＿. I'm sure the park will be ＿＿＿
　　　　　나는 붐비는 건 질색이다　　　　　　　　　　　　　　　　　매우 붐비는
＿＿＿ today.

M Then, what do you want to do?

W The weather is nice, but....

M You want to ＿＿＿ ＿＿＿, don't you?
　　　　　　실내에 있다

W That's right. I'd like to stay inside today. Let's just go to the library and read books.

M Good idea.

W Let's go there now.

14 할 일 파악

I have to ~. 이후에 나오는 부분을 주의깊게 듣는다.

대화를 듣고, 남자가 오늘 밤에 할 일로 가장 적절한 것을 고르시오.

① 학교 가기
② 영화 보기
③ 데이트하기
④ 숙제 끝내기
⑤ 아르바이트 하기

No wonder ~.는 '~은 조금도 놀랍지 않다.' 또는 '~하는 것도 당연하다.'라는 의미이다.

W Are you going to ＿＿＿＿ ＿＿＿＿ ＿＿＿＿?
　　　오늘 밤에 네 숙제를 끝내다

M I can't. I have too much to do.

W Are you ＿＿＿＿ ＿＿＿＿ ＿＿＿＿ with your girlfriend?
　　　데이트하러 가다

M Unfortunately, I can't. I have to ＿＿＿＿ ＿＿＿＿ ＿＿＿＿
　　　　　　　　　　　　　아르바이트 일을 하다
again.

W That's the third night! No wonder you can't finish your homework.

M I know. Maybe I should quit soon.

W You'd better, before you fall behind in school.

15 숫자 파악 – 금액

대화를 듣고, 남자가 지불할 금액을 고르시오.

① $35　　② $40
③ $45　　④ $50
⑤ $55

M Wow, this sweater is really nice.

W It is. And no one else in the market has this sweater.

M How much is it?

W 50 dollars. You can try it on.

M Thank you. Yes, it fits well. But it's a little expensive.

W I can ＿＿＿＿ ＿＿＿＿ ＿＿＿＿ ＿＿＿＿, 45 dollars.
　　　할인해 주다

M It's still too expensive. How about 40 dollars?

W Yes, but ＿＿＿＿ ＿＿＿＿ ＿＿＿＿ ＿＿＿＿ I can
　　　　　40달러가 최저 가격이다
give you.

M Okay. I'll take it.

16 관계 추론

반복되는 어휘 bread, delicious 등을 단서로 이용한다.

대화를 듣고, 두 사람의 관계로 가장 적절한 것을 고르시오.

① 남편 – 아내
② 제과점 점원 – 손님
③ 식당 주인 – 종업원
④ 야구 선수 – 기자
⑤ 제과점 주인 – 제빵사

W Good afternoon. How can I help you?

M I want to ＿＿＿＿ ＿＿＿＿ ＿＿＿＿ for my children.
　　　　　빵을 좀 사다

W ＿＿＿＿ ＿＿＿＿ ＿＿＿＿ do you want?
　　어떤 종류의 빵

M I can't remember the name. It's long and looks like a baseball bat.

W What? A baseball bat?

M Yes. ＿＿＿＿ ＿＿＿＿ ＿＿＿＿ last week. It was very delicious, and
　　　나는 그것을 여기서 샀다
its inner part was soft.

W Oh, I see. This way, please.

17 장소 추론

핵심 어휘 diving, swim, butterfly stroke 등을 단서로 이용한다.

대화를 듣고, 두 사람이 대화하고 있는 장소로 가장 적절한 곳을 고르시오.

① 해변　　② 수영장
③ 등산로　　④ 스키장
⑤ 나비 전시관

W Hey, come on. There is nothing to be afraid of.

M Mom, I don't want to go up there.

W Look up the kids on the board. They ＿＿＿＿ ＿＿＿＿ very much. And you're
　　　　　　　　　　　　　　　　　다이빙하는 것을 즐기다
almost a man.

M No, I'm just twelve years old. I'd ＿＿＿＿ ＿＿＿＿ ＿＿＿＿ in the
　　　　　　　　　　　　　　　그냥 수영만 하고 싶다
water.

W Okay, okay. Have fun. I'll watch you carefully.

M Now, I'll practice ＿＿＿＿ ＿＿＿＿ ＿＿＿＿.
　　　　　　　접영

18 한 일 파악

대화를 듣고, 남자가 Shopping Mall에서 한 일로 가장 적절한 것을 고르시오.

① 쇼핑하기 ② 볼링 치기
③ 영화보기 ④ 저녁 먹기
⑤ 친구 기다리기

M Eunji, you're _____ _____ _____. Is it new?
_{멋진 모자를 쓰고 있는}
W Yes, I bought it when I went shopping with my sister last Sunday.
M That's nice. Where did you buy it?
W I got it at Avalon Shopping Mall.
M Really? I was there last Sunday, too. Chris and I went bowling downtown, and then we went to the mall to _____ _____ _____.
_{영화를 보다}
W Oh, we ate in the food court next to the theater. We could have passed each other somewhere.

---

19 알맞은 응답 찾기

선생님이 여자의 말을 믿게 할 방법을 생각해 본다.

[19~20] 대화를 듣고, 여자의 마지막 말에 이어질 남자의 응답으로 가장 적절한 것을 고르시오.

Man: _____

① I hope she gets better soon.
② Maybe she needs medicine.
③ Next time, tell him the truth.
④ Get your mom to call him, then.
⑤ You should have finished on time.

W I have to talk to the teacher, but I'm worried.
M Why? Is something wrong?
W I couldn't finish my report.
M You mean the history report?
W Yes. _____ _____.
_{그것은 내일이 마감이다}
M Have you been very busy?
W Actually, my mom has been sick lately, so I had to _____
_{집에서 더 많이 도와드리다}
_____ _____.
M Did you tell the teacher?
W I want to, but I'm afraid he'll think I'm lying.
M _____

---

20 알맞은 응답 찾기

Man: _____

① I like playing baseball.
② I made many mistakes today.
③ The game was really exciting.
④ Let's play baseball this afternoon.
⑤ He's the best pitcher in the world.

W Good evening. I'm Susan Arnold from Channel 20 News.
M Good evening, Susan.
W I'd like to interview you right here. Is it possible?
M Okay. Go ahead, please.
W Thank you. Please tell us about the baseball game in Chicago.
M As you know, _____ _____ _____. The score was 3 to 9. It's too bad, but
_{오늘 우리는 졌다}
I _____ _____ today.
_{잘 던지지 못했다}
W _____ _____ _____ _____?
_{왜 그렇게 생각하세요}
M _____

01 대화를 듣고, 내일의 날씨로 가장 적절한 것을 고르시오.

02 대화를 듣고, 두 사람이 구입할 물건을 고르시오.

03 대화를 듣고, 남자에 대한 설명으로 일치하지 않는 것을 고르시오.

① 나이는 22살이다.
② 직업은 미용사이다.
③ 혼자서 연습을 한다.
④ 자전거를 기증받았다.
⑤ 사이클 경주 대회에서 우승했다.

04 대화를 듣고, 두 사람이 이번 주 토요일에 할 일로 가장 적절한 것을 고르시오.

① 영화관 가기   ② 정원일 돕기
③ 음악회 가기   ④ 도서관 가기
⑤ 춤 축제 가기

05 대화를 듣고, 남자가 도시를 다시 방문하지 않으려는 이유로 가장 적절한 것을 고르시오.

① 물가가 비싸서
② 공해가 심해서
③ 교통이 불편해서
④ 사람들이 불친절해서
⑤ 밤에 안전하지 않아서

06 대화를 듣고, 남자가 이용할 교통 수단으로 가장 적절한 것을 고르시오.

① 기차   ② 버스
③ 택시   ④ 자동차
⑤ 지하철

07 다음을 듣고, 두 사람의 대화가 어색한 것을 고르시오.

①   ②   ③   ④   ⑤

08 대화를 듣고, 두 사람이 살 담요의 색깔로 가장 적절한 것을 고르시오.

① red   ② blue
③ yellow   ④ orange
⑤ green

09 대화를 듣고, 두 사람이 대화하고 있는 장소로 가장 적절한 곳을 고르시오.

① 공원   ② 병원
③ 약국   ④ 꽃가게
⑤ 운동장

10 대화를 듣고, 여자의 심정으로 가장 적절한 것을 고르시오.

① sad   ② relieved
③ pleased   ④ surprised
⑤ disappointed

점수
/20

11 대화를 듣고, 남자가 가입하게 될 동아리로 가장 적절한 것을 고르시오.

① 발명반   ② 기타반
③ 수학반   ④ 축구반
⑤ 방송반

12 대화를 듣고, 여자가 전화를 건 목적으로 가장 적절한 것을 고르시오.

① 카풀을 제안하려고
② 운전을 부탁하려고
③ 자동차를 빌리려고
④ 약속 시간을 정하려고
⑤ 자동차에 관해 문의하려고

13 대화를 듣고, 남자가 대화 직후에 할 일로 가장 적절한 것을 고르시오.

① 인터넷 검색하기
② 카탈로그 확인하기
③ 중고 제품 알아보기
④ 제품 수리 신청하기
⑤ 전자 대리점 확인하기

14 다음을 듣고, 무엇에 관한 안내인지 가장 적절한 것을 고르시오.

① 방과 후 수업
② 영어 공부 방법
③ 실험 실습 시간
④ 어학 실습실 이용
⑤ 어학 기계 사용법

고난도
15 대화를 듣고, 여자가 거스름돈으로 받은 금액을 고르시오.

① $ 1   ② $ 2
③ $ 3   ④ $ 5
⑤ $ 7

16 대화를 듣고, 남자가 여자에게 부탁한 일로 가장 적절한 것을 고르시오.

① 우산 구입하기   ② 학교로 데리러 오기
③ 친구에게 전화하기   ④ 일기예보 확인하기
⑤ 버스정류장으로 마중나오기

17 대화를 듣고, 두 사람의 관계로 가장 적절한 것을 고르시오.

① 점원 – 고객   ② 의사 – 환자
③ 코치 – 운동 선수   ④ 사장 – 종업원
⑤ 영화 감독 – 여배우

18 대화를 듣고, 남자가 주말에 한 일로 가장 적절한 것을 고르시오.

① 일광욕 하기   ② 집에 있기
③ 여행 가기   ④ 나무 심기
⑤ 운동하기

[19~20] 대화를 듣고, 여자의 마지막 말에 이어질 남자의 응답으로 가장 적절한 것을 고르시오.

19 Man: _____

① Not at all.
② Sounds great.
③ Good for you.
④ I have no idea.
⑤ I don't agree with you.

20 Man: _____

① The library is closed.
② The subway was late.
③ Don't forget to bring it.
④ I usually take the subway.
⑤ Hmm, I guess I made a mistake.

다시 들으면서 듣기 만점에 도전하세요!
Dictation: 스크립트의 주요 부분을 다시 들으면서!
실전 ➕: 세부 정보가 많은 스크립트를 다른 문제로 샅샅이!

---

01 날씨 파악

tomorrow가 언급된 부분을 주의깊게 듣는다.

대화를 듣고, 내일의 날씨로 가장 적절한 것을 고르시오.

① ② ③ ④ ⑤

W Did you hear tomorrow's weather report?

M Yes, I did. It's going to be _____ _____ .
   화창하고 따뜻한

W Really? But it seems like this heavy rain is never going to stop.

M Oh, don't worry. They said that it would _____ _____ _____ .
   내일은 맑다

W I hope so.

M And they also said that there would be no wind.

W Oh, _____ _____ _____ _____ then.
   좋은 날이 될 것이다

---

02 그림 정보 파악 – 사물

대화를 듣고, 두 사람이 구입할 물건을 고르시오.

① ② ③ ④ ⑤

W Honey, we need a desk for Jenny.

M I don't think so. She is only three years old.

W Umm. You're right.

M But _____ _____ for the dining table _____ _____ , you know?
   의자 한 개   망가지다

W I know, but you can fix the chair.

M No. I'm afraid I can't.

W Then, how about _____ _____ ?
   하나 사는 것

M Good. Let's _____ _____ .
   둘러보다

고난도

03 내용 일치 파악

여자의 다양한 질문에 대한 남자의 응답을 정확히 듣고 선택지와 하나씩 비교해 나간다.

대화를 듣고, 남자에 대한 설명으로 일치하지 않는 것을 고르시오.

① 나이는 22살이다. twenty-two
② 직업은 미용사이다. hairdresser
③ 혼자서 연습을 한다. ride alone
④ 자전거를 기증받았다.
⑤ 사이클 경주 대회에서 우승했다.
   winning the championship

W Now, can you tell us something about yourself?

M I'm _____ and I am _____ _____ .
   22살   미용사

W A hairdresser! Wow! Now you're a sports champion! Who do you go riding with?

M Umm... I _____ _____ . I have no coach.
   혼자서 타다

W And who bought that beautiful racing bicycle for you?

M I _____ _____ _____ . I saved some money every month for it.
   내가 직접 그것을 샀다

W Congratulations on _____ _____ again.
   선수권 대회에서 우승한 것

M Thank you.

---

04 할 일 파악

Can you ~? 이후에 나오는 부분을 주의깊게 듣는다.

대화를 듣고, 두 사람이 이번 주 토요일에 할 일로 가장 적절한 것을 고르시오.

① 영화관 가기
② 정원일 돕기
③ 음악회 가기
④ 도서관 가기
⑤ 춤 축제 가기

Can(Could) you ~?는 상대방에게 부탁할 때 사용하는 표현이다.

M Where are you going, Jane?
W Hi, Tommy. I'm going to the library to return these books.
M Jane, do you have _____ _____ _____ this Saturday?
어떤 특별한 계획
W No. I'm going to watch movies at home. How about you?
M I have _____ _____ _____ _____
B-boy 춤 축제를 위한 두 장의 표
_____.
W Really?
나를 그곳에 데리고 갈 수 있니
_____ _____ _____ _____?
M Yes, I'd love to.

05 이유 파악

남자가 방문한 도시에서 느꼈던 좋은 점과 나쁜 점을 구분해서 듣는다.

대화를 듣고, 남자가 도시를 다시 방문하지 <u>않으려는</u> 이유로 가장 적절한 것을 고르시오.

① 물가가 비싸서
② 공해가 심해서
③ 교통이 불편해서
④ 사람들이 불친절해서
⑤ 밤에 안전하지 않아서

How did you like ~?는 '~는 어땠니?'라는 의미로, 소감이나 의견을 물을 때 사용하는 표현이다.

W How did you like the city?
M Well, it was exciting and there was always something to do. But we _____
거리를 돌아다닐 수 없었다
_____ _____ _____ at night.
W Why? Were the people in the city unkind to foreigners?
M No, they were very kind. But sometimes _____ at night.
강도 사건이 발생했다
W Do you want to visit the city again?
M My snswer is _____.
아니

06 특정 정보 파악

대화를 듣고, 남자가 이용할 교통 수단으로 가장 적절한 것을 고르시오.

① 기차   ② 버스
③ 택시   ④ 자동차
⑤ 지하철

Are you going to ~?는 가까운 미래에 대한 계획을 묻는 표현이다.

W Are you going to drive to the concert hall?
M No, the traffic is very heavy at this hour. I'll take a subway.
W But the concert hall is too far from the subway station. How about _____
버스를 타는 것
_____ _____?
M Is there a bus stop right in front of the concert hall?
W Sure. You should _____ _____ _____.
16번 버스를 타다
M Okay, _____ _____ _____.
나는 그것을 탈 것이다

07 어색한 대화 찾기

play가 '연극'과 '운동하다'라는 두 가지 의미로 쓰인 것에 유의한다.

다음을 듣고, 두 사람의 대화가 <u>어색한</u> 것을 고르시오.

①   ②   ③   ④   ⑤

① **W** Would you like another sandwich?
   M No, thank you. I'm full.
② **W** Jack says that he likes dancing.
   M But he doesn't do it often.
③ **W** How do you feel today?
   M I'm afraid I don't feel any better.
④ **W** I think it is _____ _____ _____.
   좋은 연극
   M No. I don't _____ very well.
   축구를 하다
⑤ **W** What can I do for you?
   M I'd like to _____ _____ _____.
   이 필름을 현상하다

대화를 듣고, 두 사람이 살 담요의 색깔로 가장 적절한 것을 고르시오.

① red 빨간색
② blue 파란색
③ yellow 노란색
④ orange 오렌지색
⑤ green 초록색

➕ 대화를 듣고, 남자가 파란색 담요를 선택하지 않은 이유로 가장 적절한 것을 고르시오.

① 너무 커서　　② 너무 작아서
③ 색이 너무 밝아서　④ 너무 두꺼워서
⑤ 너무 얇아서

Let's ~. 이후에 나오는 부분을 주의깊게 듣는다.

W What kind of blanket do you want for your bed?
M I'd like a nice thick one for the winter.
W How about this blue one?
M It's not thick enough. _____ _____ _____ _____.
　　　　　　　　　이 빨간색이 더 좋다
W It's a bit short, isn't it? The orange or yellow ones would fit.
M They're so bright. Let's _____ _____ _____ _____.
　　　　　　　　　그냥 빨간색으로 사다
W OK, that's fine.

대화를 듣고, 두 사람이 대화하고 있는 장소로 가장 적절한 곳을 고르시오.

① 공원　　　② 병원
③ 약국　　　④ 꽃가게
⑤ 운동장

핵심 어구 hurt your [my] leg, The doctor said ~. 등을 단서로 이용한다.

W How did you _____ _____ _____?
　　　　　　네 다리를 다치다
M I hurt my leg while I was playing basketball in the park yesterday.
W How are you feeling today?
M Much better, thank you.
W These flowers are for you.
M Oh! How beautiful! You are so kind.
W _____ _____ _____ you a lot?
　간호사들이 도와주고 있니
M Yes, but my mom stayed here last night, too. _____ _____ I must
　　　　　　　　　　　　　　　　　의사 선생님이 말씀하셨다
just _____ _____ for a few days.
　이곳에 있다

대화를 듣고, 여자의 심정으로 가장 적절한 것을 고르시오.

① sad 슬픈
② relieved 안도하는
③ pleased 기쁜
④ surprised 놀란
⑤ disappointed 실망한

I'm sure ~.는 자신이 확신을 갖고 의견을 말할 때 사용하는 표현이다.

M Kate, what a beautiful *hanbok* you are wearing!
W Do you like it? My mom _____ _____ for me.
　　　　　　　　특별히, 그것을 만들었다
M That's wonderful! Are you going to wear it to the school festival tomorrow?
W Yes, I will. I'm _____ _____ _____.
　　　　　이것이 정말 자랑스러운
M I'm sure you'll be loved by all the students and teachers.
W _____ _____ _____ _____.
　그렇게 말해 주니 고맙다

남자가 현재 관심이 있거나 좋아하는 것에 집중한다.

대화를 듣고, 남자가 가입하게 될 동아리로 가장 적절한 것을 고르시오.

① 발명반 invention club
② 기타반 guitar club
③ 수학반
④ 축구반
⑤ 방송반

M Which club do you want to join, Mary?

W I'd like to join the invention club. How about you? You like playing football, don't you?

M Yeah, I was a football player. But I'm more _____
_____ . 클래식 기타에 관심이 있는

W So, do you want to _____ _____ _____ ? 기타반에 가입하다

M Yes. I saw a guitar show the other day. It was fantastic.

➕ 대화를 듣고, 여자가 가입하게 될 동아리로 가장 적절한 것을 고르시오.

① 발명반   ② 기타반
③ 수학반   ④ 축구반
⑤ 방송반

대화를 듣고, 여자가 전화를 건 목적으로 가장 적절한 것을 고르시오.

① 카풀을 제안하려고
② 운전을 부탁하려고
③ 자동차를 빌리려고
④ 약속 시간을 정하려고
⑤ 자동차에 관해 문의하려고

[Telephone rings.]

M Hello.

W Hi, Tim? It's June.

M Hi, June. What's up?

W I wonder if you're _____ _____ _____ . 아직 자동차를 팔고 있다

M Are you interested?

W Not me, my brother is. _____ _____ _____ ? 그가 그것을 볼 수 있을까

M Sure. Would _____ _____ _____ ? 그가 그것을 시험 운전해 보기를 원한다

W If possible. Is tomorrow afternoon OK?

M Sure. Come after 2, OK?

W Sounds good. See you then.

I'll ~. 이후에 나오는 부분을 주의깊게 듣는다.

대화를 듣고, 남자가 대화 직후에 할 일로 가장 적절한 것을 고르시오.

① 인터넷 검색하기
② 카탈로그 확인하기
③ 중고 제품 알아보기
④ 제품 수리 신청하기
⑤ 전자 대리점 확인하기

W What are you looking at in the catalogue?

M I'm _____ _____ _____ . 스테레오 음향 시스템을 보고 있다

W Is your old one broken?

M It's all right, but I'd like better sound.

W It might cost a lot more money.

M Yeah, but I've been saving up for it.

W Maybe you can get something on sale on the Internet.

M You're right. I'll have to _____ _____ . 인터넷으로 그것들을 알아보다

I'll ~. 이후에 나오는 부분을 주의깊게 듣는다.

다음을 듣고, 무엇에 관한 안내인지 가장 적절한 것을 고르시오.

① 방과 후 수업
② 영어 공부 방법
③ 실험 실습 시간
④ 어학 실습실 이용
⑤ 어학 기계 사용법

W Hello, everyone. I have a few things to tell you. When you have class in the language lab, please _____ _____ _____ . _____
조금 더 일찍 이곳에 와라
before you enter the lab. Don't bring anything here _____
여러분의 신발을 갈아 신어라
. In class you can only speak English, not Korean. _____
여러분의 교과서를 제외하고
_____ _____ , turn off your machines and leave the lab one by
수업이 끝나면
one. Thank you.

15 숫자 파악 – 금액

대화를 듣고, 여자가 거스름돈으로 받은 금액을 고르시오.

① $1 ② $2
③ $3 ④ $5
⑤ $7

Here is your change.에서 change는 '잔돈, 거스름돈'을 뜻하며, 잔돈을 거슬러 줄 때 사용하는 표현이다.

W How much are the apples?

M They are _____ _____ _____. How many do you want?
_{한 개당 1달러}

W I _____ _____. And I'd like to buy a watermelon, too.
_{7개를 원하다}

M The big one is 10 dollars, and the small one is 7 dollars.

W I'll _____ _____ _____.
_{큰 것으로 사다}

M Do you need anything else?

W No. _____ _____ _____.
_{여기 20달러가 있다}

M Thank you. Here is your change.

16 부탁한 일 파악

대화를 듣고, 남자가 여자에게 부탁한 일로 가장 적절한 것을 고르시오.

① 우산 구입하기
② 학교로 데리러 오기
③ 친구에게 전화하기
④ 일기예보 확인하기
⑤ 버스정류장으로 마중나오기

[Cellphone rings.]

M Hello, Mom. What's up?

W It's raining. Do you have an umbrella with you?

M No. The weather forecast didn't say it would rain today.

W Yeah, I know. But it was wrong. It seems it's going to rain for a while.

M Hmm.. can you _____ _____ to the bus stop near home then?
_{우산을 가져오다}

W Of course, I can, but what about from school?

M I will try to find a friend with an umbrella and _____ _____
_{버스 정류장에 가다}
_____ _____ with him.

17 관계 추론

대화가 일어나고 있는 장소를 파악하여 관계를 추론한다.

대화를 듣고, 두 사람의 관계로 가장 적절한 것을 고르시오.

① 점원 – 고객
② 의사 – 환자
③ 코치 – 운동 선수
④ 사장 – 종업원
⑤ 영화 감독 – 여배우

You're a really fast learner.는 You learn very fast.와 같은 의미이다.

M Judy, wait. You're throwing the ball the wrong way.

W The wrong way? Yesterday _____ _____ _____ it
_{당신이 나에게 하라고 가르쳐 주셨다}
this way.

M No. Your left foot must be in front of your right one.

W I see.

M Can you _____ _____ _____ again?
_{공을 던지다}

W Sure. Like this?

M Great! You're a really fast learner. I'll _____ _____ _____
_{너에게 공 치는 법을 가르쳐 주다}
_____ tomorrow.

W Thank you very much, sir.

대화를 듣고, 남자가 주말에 한 일로 가장 적절한 것을 고르시오.

① 일광욕 하기　　② 집에 있기
③ 여행 가기　　④ 나무 심기
⑤ 운동하기

W Woojin, you got a tan. You look good.

M Thanks, Mary. The weather was really nice over the weekend, wasn't it?

W Yes, but I ＿＿＿＿＿ ＿＿＿＿＿ ＿＿＿＿＿. Did you do something
　종일 집에 있었다
outside?

M Yes, it was Arbor Day, so I ＿＿＿＿＿ ＿＿＿＿＿ with my family.
　　　　　　　　　　　　　나무를 심었다

W Oh, I forgot about it. Do you do that every year?

M No, actually it was our first time, but it was really fun. I want to do it again.

W It sounds really healthy, not only for you but also for the environment.

[19~20] 대화를 듣고, 여자의 마지막 말에 이어질 남자의 응답으로 가장 적절한 것을 고르시오.

Man: ＿＿＿＿＿＿＿＿＿＿

① Not at all.
② Sounds great.
③ Good for you.
④ I have no idea.
⑤ I don't agree with you.

W Well, what do you think?

M The style is ＿＿＿＿＿ ＿＿＿＿＿ ＿＿＿＿＿.
　　　　　　당신에게 완벽한

W What about the color?

M It's a very popular color among teens.

W How does it look on me?

M It ＿＿＿＿＿ ＿＿＿＿＿ ＿＿＿＿＿.
　　당신에게 잘 어울리다

W You ＿＿＿＿＿ ＿＿＿＿＿ I look funny in it?
　　　생각하지 않다

M ＿＿＿＿＿＿＿＿＿＿

Man: ＿＿＿＿＿＿＿＿＿＿

① The library is closed.
② The subway was late.
③ Don't forget to bring it.
④ I usually take the subway.
⑤ Hmm, I guess I made a mistake.

M I saw you yesterday, but you didn't see me.

W Really? When?

M It was at about six o'clock in the evening. You were ＿＿＿＿＿
　　　　　　　　　　　　　　　　　　　　　　　　　지하철에서 내리고 있다
＿＿＿＿＿ at the City Hall station.

W No, ＿＿＿＿＿ ＿＿＿＿＿. Yesterday I was ＿＿＿＿＿
　　　그것은 내가 아니었다　　　　　　　　　　　　보고서를 작성하고 있다
＿＿＿＿＿ at the library at that time.

M ＿＿＿＿＿＿＿＿＿＿

목적 · 이유 · 의도 파악

무엇을 평가하는가?	일상생활이나 친숙한 일반적 주제에 관한 말이나 대화를 듣고 화자의 의도나 목적 또는 사건의 원인과 결과를 추론할 수 있는 지를 평가한다.
어떻게 출제되는가?	• 대화를 듣고, 여자가 전화를 건 목적으로 가장 적절한 것을 고르시오. • 대화를 듣고, 남자의 마지막 말의 의도로 가장 적절한 것을 고르시오. • 대화를 듣고, 여자의 마지막 말의 의도로 가장 적절한 것을 고르시오.

**key
solution**

❶ 목적을 묻는 경우, 대화 초반에 목적이 드러나는 경우가 많으나 전제적인 대화의 내용 안에 간접적으로 제시되는 경우도 있으므로 주의를 기울이며 듣는다.

❷ 이유를 묻는 경우, 제안이나 부탁을 거절한 후 언급되는 경우가 많으므로 그 부분에 집중한다.

❸ 의도를 묻는 경우, 전체적인 상황을 인지하고 마지막 말의 원인을 정확하게 파악한다.

[기출로 전략 확인]

대화를 듣고, 여자가 남자의 제안을 거절한 이유로 가장 적절한 것을 고르시오.   [2018 기출]

① 감기에 걸려서   ② 숙제를 해야 해서   ③ 봉사활동을 해야 해서

④ 병문안을 가야 해서   ⑤ 결혼식에 참석해야 해서

. . . .

M Yuna, why don't we go to the movies tomorrow?

W I'd love to, but I can't. ─────────

M Really? Do you have any special plans?

W Yes. I need to go to Mokpo with my family.

M Oh, why are you going there?

W Tomorrow is my uncle's wedding. ─────────

M Wow, that is cool. Have a great time.

W Thank you. Let's go see a movie next weekend.

❷ 영화를 보러 가자는 남자의 제안을 거절한 후, 가족과 함께 삼촌의 결혼식에 참석해야 한다고 말하고 있다.

남 Yuna, 내일 영화 보러 갈래?

여 그러고 싶은데 안돼.

남 진짜? 뭐 특별한 계획이라고 있어?

여 응. 나 가족들과 목포에 가야 해.

남 아, 거긴 왜 가는 거야?

여 내일이 삼촌 결혼식이거든.

남 왜! 멋진데. 좋은 시간 보내.

여 고마워. 영화는 다음 주에 보러 가자.

목적·의도 파악 유형의 발문과 보기

대화를 듣고, 여자가 전화를 건 목적으로 가장 적절한 것을 고르시오. [2018 기출]

① 분실물을 찾기 위해서
② 모임 불참을 알려주기 위해서
③ 숙소를 예약하기 위해서
④ 비행 일정을 변경하기 위해서
⑤ 식당 예약을 취소하기 위해서

만점 잡는 문장 **W** Hi, I'd like to change my flight schedule, please.

대화를 듣고, 여자의 마지막 말의 의도로 가장 적절한 것을 고르시오. [2017 기출]

① 감사
② 거절
③ 격려
④ 허락
⑤ 충고

만점 잡는 문장 **M** How about Saturday then? (제안)
W I'm really sorry. Every Saturday I have to take a violin lesson.

목적·이유·의도 파악 파악하기에 쓰이는 표현

● 목적

(방문) I went there to meet my favorite cartoonist. 나는 거기에 내가 제일 좋아하는 만화가를 만나러 갈 거야.

(제안) I have tickets for a movie. Can you go with me? 나에게 영화표가 있는데 같이 갈래?

(예약 변경) I'd like to change my flight schedule, please. 비행편을 변경하고 싶습니다.

(부탁) Can you return it to the store on your way home? 집에 가는 길에 가게에 반납 해 줄래?

● 이유

A Do you want to come with me? 나랑 같이 갈래?
B I'd really love to. But I have to go to my dance lesson now. 정말 그러고 싶은데 지금 춤 레슨을 가야만 해.

A Do you know why they chose me? 그들이 왜 날 선택했는지 아니?
B Because you always volunteered to help your friends. 네가 항상 자진해서 친구들을 돕기 때문이야.

A Are you going on a trip? 여행가는 거야?
B No. My grandma will visit us today, so I'm going to meet her at the station.
아니. 할머니가 오늘 우리를 보러 오셔서 역에 마중 나가는 거야.

● 의도

(칭찬) That's my boy! You did a great job! 역시나! 훌륭하게 잘 했어!

(충고) You should not give our snacks to animals. 동물에게 과자를 주면 안돼.

(격려) I'm sure you'll get on the team next time. Cheer up! 다음엔 팀에 합류할 수 있을 거야. 힘내!

(동의) You're right. I agree with you. 네가 맞아. 네 말에 동의해.

(거절) I'm really sorry. Every Saturday I have to take a violin lesson.
진짜 미안해. 매주 토요일마다 바이올린 레슨을 들어야 해.

01 대화를 듣고, 오늘 오후의 날씨로 가장 적절한 것을 고르시오.

02 다음을 듣고, 각 그림에 대한 설명이 <u>잘못된</u> 것을 고르시오.

03 대화를 듣고, 여자의 증상으로 언급되지 <u>않은</u> 것을 고르시오.

① 두통 　　　　② 어지러움
③ 열 　　　　　④ 기침
⑤ 콧물

04 대화를 듣고, 여자가 하게 될 운동으로 가장 적절한 것을 고르시오.

① 농구 　　　　② 수영
③ 조깅 　　　　④ 배드민턴
⑤ 자전거 타기

05 대화를 듣고, Tom의 숙제로 가장 적절한 것을 고르시오.

① 자연에 관한 시 쓰기
② 절수에 관한 글쓰기
③ 절전에 관한 글쓰기
④ 수질오염에 관한 글쓰기
⑤ 환경오염에 관한 그림 그리기

06 대화를 듣고, 남자의 마지막 말의 의도로 가장 적절한 것을 고르시오.

① 기원 　　　　② 명령
③ 감사 　　　　④ 동의
⑤ 칭찬

07 대화를 듣고, 여자의 심정으로 가장 적절한 것을 고르시오.

① 슬픔 　　　　② 흥분됨
③ 초조함 　　　④ 두려움
⑤ 자신감

08 대화를 듣고, 두 사람이 언급하지 <u>않은</u> 것을 고르시오.

① Jane이 간 장소
② Jane이 돌아올 시각
③ 전화 건 이유
④ 전화 건 사람의 이름
⑤ 전화 건 사람의 전화번호

고난도
09 대화를 듣고, 남자가 여자 친구와 연락할 방법으로 가장 적절한 것을 고르시오.

① 온라인 채팅
② 비디오 채팅
③ 휴대전화 통화
④ 인터넷 음성 통화
⑤ 휴대전화 문자 메시지

10 대화를 듣고, 여자가 남자에게 부탁한 일로 가장 적절한 것을 고르시오.

① 편지 쓰기
② 컴퓨터 고치기
③ 파일 복구하기
④ 함께 영어 공부하기
⑤ 컴퓨터 싸게 구입하기

점수 /20

11 대화를 듣고, 남자가 예약한 비행기의 출발 시각을 고르시오.

① 10:40 a.m.　　　② 11:40 a.m.
③ 4:40 p.m.　　　④ 4:50 p.m.
⑤ 5:40 p.m.

고난도
12 다음 카드를 보면서 대화를 듣고, 내용과 일치하지 않는 대화를 고르시오.

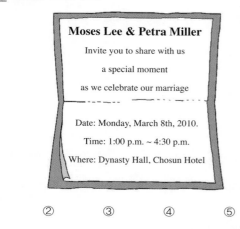

Moses Lee & Petra Miller

Invite you to share with us

a special moment

as we celebrate our marriage

- - - - - - - - - - - - - -

Date: Monday, March 8th, 2010.

Time: 1:00 p.m. ~ 4:30 p.m.

Where: Dynasty Hall, Chosun Hotel

①　　②　　③　　④　　⑤

13 대화를 듣고, 두 사람의 관계로 가장 적절한 것을 고르시오.

① 역무원 – 승객　　　② 여행 가이드 – 여행객
③ 가게 점원 – 손님　　④ 티켓 판매원 – 관광객
⑤ 경찰 – 시민

고난도
14 대화를 듣고, 남자가 현장 학습을 위해 예약할 버스의 수를 고르시오.

① 3　　　　　② 4
③ 5　　　　　④ 6
⑤ 7

15 대화를 듣고, 두 사람이 대화하고 있는 장소로 가장 적절한 곳을 고르시오.

① 공항　　　　② 호텔
③ 도서관　　　④ 우체국
⑤ 비행기 안

16 대화를 듣고, 남자가 방과 후에 할 일로 가장 적절한 것을 고르시오.

① 집에서 쉬기　　　② 친구와 화해하기
③ 친구에게 전화하기　④ 분실물 보관소 방문하기
⑤ 미아 보호소 방문하기

17 대화를 듣고, 대화의 내용과 일치하지 않는 것을 고르시오.

① 여자는 창가 쪽 자리를 원했다.
② 남자는 창가 쪽으로 자리를 안내했다.
③ 여자는 스테이크 2인분을 주문했다.
④ 여자는 특별 샐러드를 함께 주문했다.
⑤ 여자는 식사 후에 커피를 마시기를 원했다.

18 대화를 듣고, 남자가 화가 난 이유로 가장 적절한 것을 고르시오.

① 친구가 놀려서
② 물건을 잃어버려서
③ 좋은 성적을 받지 못해서
④ 친구가 돈을 갚지 않아서
⑤ 어머니가 용돈을 주지 않아서

[19~20] 대화를 듣고, 남자의 마지막 말에 이어질 여자의 응답으로 가장 적절한 것을 고르시오.

19 Woman: _____

① You should be careful.
② I'll take them to the hospital.
③ I'm sorry, I have to leave now.
④ I hope they get along with our kids.
⑤ The bus will come in a few minutes.

20 Woman: _____

① But they've only one left.
② In that case, I'll take the bus.
③ It wasn't raining when I got up.
④ I guess I'll have to do that, then.
⑤ I haven't gone out so I don't know.

다시 들으면서 듣기 만점에 도전하세요!
Dictation: 스크립트의 주요 부분을 다시 들으면서!
실전 ⊕: 세부 정보가 많은 스크립트를 다른 문제로 살살이!

---

01 날씨 파악

afternoon이 언급된 부분을 주의깊게 듣는다.

대화를 듣고, 오늘 오후의 날씨로 가장 적절한 것을 고르시오.

① ② ③ ④ ⑤

W Is it still raining?

M Yes, it is. Did you hear the thunder last night?

W Yes, I did. And I've never seen such heavy rain like this.

M Yeah, it is awful. _____ _____ _____ _____ later today?

W I just heard the forecast from the news. It said that it would _____ and

날씨가 어떻게 될까   비가 그치다
_____ _____ in the afternoon.

맑다

M I hope it is right.

---

02 그림 정보 파악 – 토익형

인물의 동작을 나타내는 동사의 진행형과 전치사의 쓰임에 유의해서 듣는다.

다음을 듣고, 각 그림에 대한 설명이 <u>잘못된</u> 것을 고르시오.

① ② ③ ④ ⑤

W ① I am singing a song with a microphone.

② My big sister is smiling and _____ _____ _____ .

두 손을 위로 치켜세우고 있다

③ My little brother is sitting on a bicycle _____ _____ _____ .

팔짱을 낀 채로

④ My father is _____ _____ the giraffe's face.

~을 쳐다보고 있다

⑤ My mother is pointing her finger at the monkey _____ _____

모자와 선글라스를 쓰고
_____ _____ _____ .

---

03 언급 및 비언급 파악

대화를 듣고, 여자의 증상으로 언급되지 <u>않은</u> 것을 고르시오.

① 두통 headache
② 어지러움 dizzy
③ 열 fever
④ 기침 cough
⑤ 콧물 runny nose

⊕ 대화를 듣고, 두 사람이 대화하고 있는 장소로 가장 적절한 것을 고르시오.

① 병원   ② 학교
③ 수퍼마켓   ④ 호텔
⑤ 앰뷸런스

M Good morning! May I help you?

W Yes, I _____ _____ _____ _____ . And I _____ .

두통이 심하다   어지러움을 느끼다

M Let me take your temperature. You _____ _____ _____ . Do you have a

열이 있다
cough? Or a runny nose?

W I _____ _____ _____ , but I _____

콧물은 나지 않는다
_____ _____ .

기침을 하다

M OK, try these pills. Take two pills 30 minutes after each meal for two days. Visit me again in two days.

W Thank you.

---

04 특정 정보 파악

대화를 듣고, 여자가 하게 될 운동으로 가장 적절한 것을 고르시오.

① 농구
② 수영 swimming
③ 조깅
④ 배드민턴
⑤ 자전거 타기 riding a bike

What should I do?는 '어떻게 해야 할까요?'라는 의미로, 조언을 구할 때 사용하는 표현이다.

M You look tired these days.

W I can't sleep soundly these days. I have many things to worry about.

M Why don't you _____ _____?
  운동을 좀 하다

W You've got a point. Exercising might help me sleep better. But my knees are not good. What should I do?

M How about _____ _____? I heard it's good for knees.
  자전거를 타는 것

W It's too cold outside.

M Then you'd _____ _____.
  수영을 하러 가는 게 낫다

W That would be better.

05 특정 정보 파악

핵심 어휘 essay, pollution, water pollution 등을 단서로 이용한다.

대화를 듣고, Tom의 숙제로 가장 적절한 것을 고르시오.

① 자연에 관한 시 쓰기
② 절수에 관한 글쓰기
③ 절전에 관한 글쓰기
④ 수질오염에 관한 글쓰기
⑤ 환경오염에 관한 그림 그리기

W Tom, turn off the TV and go _____ _____ _____.

M Mom, I'm doing my homework.
  네, 숙제를 하다

W What is your homework?

M _____ _____ _____.
  환경오염에 관한 글

W But this is a cartoon, isn't it?

M Yes, it is, but it is _____ _____.
  수질오염에 관한

W Don't lie.

M I'm not lying. I'm going to _____ _____ _____ the story.
  ~에 관한 글을 쓰다

06 의도 추론

I hope ~.는 희망 또는 기원을 나타낸다.

대화를 듣고, 남자의 마지막 말의 의도로 가장 적절한 것을 고르시오.

① 기원
② 명령
③ 감사
④ 동의
⑤ 칭찬

➕ 대화를 듣고, 여자가 볼링을 치러 갈 수 없는 이유로 가장 적절한 것을 고르시오.

① 어깨를 다쳐서
② 배드민턴을 쳐야 해서
③ 준비운동을 하지 않아서
④ 시간이 없어서
⑤ 잘 치지 못해서

M Let's go bowling this afternoon.

W Sorry, I can't. I hurt my right shoulder while playing badminton.

M That's too bad. When did you _____ _____?
  다치다

W I got hurt last Friday.

M Didn't you _____ before playing?
  준비 운동을 하다

W No, I didn't.

M You should always warm up before playing sports.

W OK, I will. I won't forget it.

M _____ _____ _____ _____ _____ soon.
  네가 좋아지기를 바라다

07 심정 추론

I hope ~.는 희망 또는 기원을 나타낸다.

대화를 듣고, 여자의 심정으로 가장 적절한 것을 고르시오.

① 슬픔
② 흥분됨
③ 초조함
④ 두려움
⑤ 자신감

I bet ~.은 '틀림없이 ~하다.'라는 의미로, 확신을 나타내는 표현이다.

M Are you nervous about your piano recital?

W Not really. I _____ _____.
  기분이 아주 좋다

M How do you do it? I'd _____ _____.
  겁이 나다

W I've been _____ _____ _____. I know my songs.
  연습을 많이 하고 있다

M Doesn't the audience frighten you, though?

W A bit. But I like performing for people.

M I bet you will become a professional piano player someday.

08 언급 및 비언급 파악

대화를 듣고, 두 사람이 언급하지 <u>않은</u> 것을 고르시오.

① Jane이 간 장소
② Jane이 돌아올 시각 Around five
③ 전화 건 이유 today's meeting has been canceled
④ 전화 건 사람의 이름 John Terry
⑤ 전화 건 사람의 전화번호 432-0218

Can I leave a message?는 전화 통화 시 통화하는 사람이 없어 메시지를 남길 때 사용하는 표현이다.

[Telephone rings.]

M Hello. May I speak to Jane, please?

W I'm sorry, but she's not in right now.

M Where did she go?

W I don't know.

M What time will she _____ _____?
 돌아오다

W Around five.

M Can I leave a message?

W Sure.

M Can you tell her today's _____ _____ _____?
 모임이 취소되었다

W OK. May I have your name and phone number, please?

M John Terry. _____ _____ _____ 432-0218.
 내 전화번호는 ~이다

고난도

09 특정 정보 파악

여자의 마지막 말을 단서로 이용한다

대화를 듣고, 남자가 여자 친구와 연락할 방법으로 가장 적절한 것을 고르시오.

① 온라인 채팅
② 비디오 채팅
③ 휴대전화 통화
④ 인터넷 음성 통화
⑤ 휴대전화 문자 메시지

W What's wrong?

M My parents are mad because I call my girlfriend too often.

W Are you wasting too much study time?

M They said _____ _____ _____.
 휴대전화 요금이 너무 많이 나오다

W Then you should _____.
 온라인에서 채팅을 하다

M But my typing is too slow.

W How about a video chat, then?

M I don't have a camera. But we _____ _____ _____, I guess.
 적어도 이야기는 할 수 있다

W Right. You can _____ _____ _____ _____.
 인터넷을 통한 음성 통화를 이용하다

---

10 부탁 파악

Can you ~? 이후에 나오는 부분을 주의깊게 듣는다.

대화를 듣고, 여자가 남자에게 부탁한 일로 가장 적절한 것을 고르시오.

① 편지 쓰기
② 컴퓨터 고치기
③ 파일 복구하기
④ 함께 영어 공부하기
⑤ 컴퓨터 싸게 구입하기

W Excuse me, could you help me?

M Sure, my pleasure. How can I help you?

W I was typing a letter when _____ _____ _____.
 내 컴퓨터가 작동을 멈췄다

M Did you _____ _____?
 당신이 작업한 것을 저장하다

W I don't think I saved all of it. Can you _____ _____?
 그 파일을 복구하다

M It's probably not possible, but I'll try.

11 숫자 파악 – 시각

대화를 듣고, 남자가 예약한 비행기의 출발 시각을 고르시오.

① 10:40 a.m.
② 11:40 a.m.
③ 4:40 p.m.
④ 4:50 p.m.
⑤ 5:40 p.m.

I'd like to ~.는 '나는 ~하고 싶다.'라는 의미로 원하는 것을 말할 때 사용하는 표현이다.

M Excuse me. I'd like to make a reservation.

W Where are you going?

M I'm going to New York.

W When are you going to leave?

M June 4th. It's next Tuesday.

W Yeah, there's _____ _____ _____ _____ : _____ _____
오전 10시 40분 항공편
on Tuesday the 4th.

M Do you have _____ _____ _____ _____ _____ _____ ?
오후 항공편

W Yes, it's at 5:40 p.m.

M OK, I'd like to _____ _____ _____ .
그 항공편으로 하다

고난도

12 실용문 정보 파악

청첩장을 보면서 대화에서 언급한 내용을 확인하되, 특히 숫자에 유의해서 듣는다.

다음 카드를 보면서 대화를 듣고, 내용과 일치하지 **않는** 대화를 고르시오.

Moses Lee & Petra Miller

Invite you to share with us

a special moment

as we celebrate our marriage

Date: Monday, March 8th, 2010.

Time: 1:00 p.m. ~ 4:30 p.m.

Where: Dynasty Hall, Chosun Hotel

① ② ③ ④ ⑤

① W Who is going to _____ _____ ?
결혼하다
M Moses Lee and Petra Miller are going to get married.

② W Where is the wedding going to _____ _____ ?
열리다
M It will _____ _____ at the Chosun Hotel.
열리다

③ W When is the wedding going to happen?
M It's going to be held _____ _____ _____ .
3월 18일에

④ W What day is _____ _____ _____ ?
결혼식
M It's Monday.

⑤ W What time is the wedding ceremony going to finish?
M It's going to finish at 4:30 p.m.

---

13 관계 파악

대화를 듣고, 두 사람의 관계로 가장 적절한 것을 고르시오.

① 역무원 – 승객
② 여행 가이드 – 여행객
③ 가게 점원 – 손님
④ 티켓 판매원 – 관광객
⑤ 경찰 – 시민

W Excuse me, sir, is this platform number 4?

M No, I'm afraid not. It's platform 2. Platform 4 is the other side.

W Can you tell me _____ _____ _____ ?
거기에 어떻게 가는지

M Go up the stairs over there, and you will see signs. By the way, where are you going?

W I want to _____ _____ _____ to Daegu.
기차를 타다

M Oh, then, the platform has just changed. Actually, you are on the right one.

W Oh, really? That's great news. Thank you very much.

14 숫자 파악

총 인원 수와 버스 한 대당 수용 가능 인원 수를 파악한다.

대화를 듣고, 남자가 현장 학습을 위해 예약할 버스의 수를 고르시오.

① 3　　　　② 4
③ 5　　　　④ 6
⑤ 7

M　How many people will go on the field trip?
W　About ＿＿＿＿ ＿＿＿＿ and ＿＿＿＿ ＿＿＿＿. Why?
　　　　학생 130명　　　　　　　　성인 50명
M　The school has to book enough buses.
W　How many people can fit in one bus?
M　＿＿＿＿ ＿＿＿＿ ＿＿＿＿ ＿＿＿＿.
　　버스 한 대당 40명
W　There might be ＿＿＿＿ ＿＿＿＿ ＿＿＿＿. We'll know tomorrow.
　　　　　　20명 더
M　I have to book buses today. Then, I'll just count them in.

15 장소 추론

핵심 어구 check out, room number, charge 등을 단서로 이용한다.

대화를 듣고, 두 사람이 대화하고 있는 장소로 가장 적절한 곳을 고르시오.

① 공항　　　　② 호텔
③ 도서관　　　④ 우체국
⑤ 비행기 안

W　I'd like to ＿＿＿＿ ＿＿＿＿, please.
　　　　　　퇴실하다
M　What was your room number?
W　I ＿＿＿＿ ＿＿＿＿ ＿＿＿＿.
　　415호실에 묵었다
M　You made two international phone calls, didn't you?
W　Yes, I did.
M　Just a moment while I ＿＿＿＿ ＿＿＿＿ for the calls.
　　　　　　　요금을 확인하다
W　What time does the bus leave for the airport?
M　The next one leaves in ten minutes.

16 할 일 파악

대화를 듣고, 남자가 방과 후에 할 일로 가장 적절한 것을 고르시오.

① 집에서 쉬기
② 친구와 화해하기
③ 친구에게 전화하기
④ 분실물 보관소 방문하기
⑤ 미아 보호소 방문하기

W　What's wrong? Did you quarrel with your friend?
M　No, I didn't.
W　Are you sick now?
M　No, I'm not. I ＿＿＿＿ ＿＿＿＿ ＿＿＿＿.
　　　　　　　내, 휴대전화를 잃어버렸다
W　Where did you lose it?
M　On the way to school. I came here by subway.
W　Why don't you visit the subway's "＿＿＿＿ ＿＿＿＿ ＿＿＿＿"?
　　　　　　　　　　　　　　분실물 보관소
M　Good idea. I think I'll do that after school.

17 내용 일치 파악

대화를 듣고, 대화의 내용과 일치하지 <u>않는</u> 것을 고르시오.

① 여자는 창가 쪽 자리를 원했다.
② 남자는 창가 쪽으로 자리를 안내했다.
③ 여자는 스테이크 2인분을 주문했다.
④ 여자는 특별 샐러드를 함께 주문했다.
⑤ 여자는 식사 후에 커피를 마시기를 원했다.

W　Can we have ＿＿＿＿ ＿＿＿＿?
　　　　　　창가 쪽 자리
M　We have one left. ＿＿＿＿ ＿＿＿＿.
　　　　　　　　이쪽으로 오세요
W　This is perfect.
M　May I take your order?
W　We'd like ＿＿＿＿ ＿＿＿＿ with your special salad and coffee.
　　　　　스테이크 2인분
M　Would you like your coffee now or with your meal?
W　＿＿＿＿, ＿＿＿＿.
　　지금 주세요

대화를 듣고, 남자가 화가 난 이유로 가장
적절한 것을 고르시오.

① 친구가 놀려서
② 물건을 잃어버려서
③ 좋은 성적을 받지 못해서
④ 친구가 돈을 갚지 않아서
⑤ 어머니가 용돈을 주지 않아서

What happened to ~?는 '~에게 무슨 일이니?'
라는 의미로, 안부를 묻거나 이유를 물을 때 사용하
는 표현이다.

W What happened to you and Jack?

M I don't want to see him anymore.

W I thought you were good friends.

M Yes, we were, but he _____ _____ _____ _____ he
　　　　　　　　　　　　돈을 절대 갚지 않는다
borrows from me. That _____ _____.
　　　　　　　　　　　　나를 화나게 만들다

W Why don't you tell him about it frankly?

M It's too late. I _____ _____ _____ from now
　　　　　　그에게 어떠한 돈도 빌려 주지 않을 것이다
on. He isn't my friend anymore.

[19~20] 대화를 듣고, 남자의 마지막 말에
이어질 여자의 응답으로 가장 적절한 것을
고르시오.

Woman: _____

① You should be careful.
② I'll take them to the hospital.
③ I'm sorry, I have to leave now.
④ I hope they get along with our kids.
⑤ The bus will come in a few minutes.

같은 또래의 아이들이 있다는 마지막 대화를 단서로 이용한다.

M A family is _____ _____ the house across the street.
　　　　　　　　~로 이사오다
W Yeah. It was empty for a long time.

M Where are they from?

W I heard _____ _____.
　　　　　그들은 캐나다에서 온다
M How many children do they have?

W They have two boys _____ _____ _____.
　　　　　　　　　　　우리 아이들과 같은 또래의
M It's nice that they have children _____ _____ _____ ours.
　　　　　　　　　　　　　　　　　~와 같은 나이
W _____

Woman: _____

① But they've only one left.
② In that case, I'll take the bus.
③ It wasn't raining when I got up.
④ I guess I'll have to do that, then.
⑤ I haven't gone out so I don't know.

남자가 여자에게 제안하는 것을 주의 깊게 듣는다.

W Is it going to rain today?

M That's what the weather report said.

W Maybe I should wear my rain coat.

M But it's so hot outside. You'll sweat. Just bring an umbrella. It's easier.

W I don't have one, though. _____ _____.
　　　　　　　　　　　　　　　내 것이 고장 났다
M You can stop at the store and _____ _____ _____ _____.
　　　　　　　　　　　　　　　　가는 길에 하나 사다
W _____

학년　　　반　　　번
이름

01 다음 그림의 상황에 가장 적절한 대화를 고르시오.

①　　②　　③　　④　　⑤

02 다음을 듣고, 'I'가 무엇인지 가장 적절한 것을 고르시오.

03 대화를 듣고, 여자가 토요일 오후에 할 일로 가장 적절한 것을 고르시오.

① 여행 떠나기　　② 영화 보러 가기
③ 볼링 치러 가기　　④ 아버지 마중 나가기
⑤ 테니스 치러 가기

04 대화를 듣고, 여자의 심정으로 가장 적절한 것을 고르시오.

① 분노　　　　② 안도
③ 걱정　　　　④ 슬픔
⑤ 좌절

05 대화를 듣고, 두 사람의 관계로 가장 적절한 것을 고르시오.

① 옷가게 점원 – 고객　　② 호텔 직원 – 투숙객
③ 보석가게 점원 – 고객　　④ 관광안내원 – 관광객
⑤ 미용사 – 고객

06 대화를 듣고, 남자가 이용할 교통 수단으로 가장 적절한 것을 고르시오.

① by taxi　　　　② on foot
③ by plane　　　④ by subway
⑤ by shuttle bus

07 대화를 듣고, 두 사람이 대화하고 있는 장소로 가장 적절한 곳을 고르시오.

① 공항　　　　② 은행
③ 여행사　　　④ 백화점
⑤ 음식점

08 대화를 듣고, 대화의 내용과 일치하지 <u>않는</u> 것을 고르시오.

① Yumi likes *kimchi* best.
② Harry likes pizza best.
③ Yumi knows how to make *kimchi*.
④ Yumi can make fried rice with *kimchi*.
⑤ Harry will visit Yumi's house on Saturday.

고난도
09 대화를 듣고, 남자가 보낼 문자 메시지로 가장 적절한 것을 고르시오.

① Happy New Year!
② Welcome home, honey!
③ Happy Birthday to You!
④ Thank you for teaching me.
⑤ Please take care of my child.

10 대화를 듣고, 여자가 남자에게 부탁한 일로 가장 적절한 것을 고르시오.

① 우체국 위치 알려주기　　② 집에 초대하기
③ 집에 데려다주기　　　　④ 소포 보내기
⑤ 돈 빌려주기

점수
/20

11 대화를 듣고, Louis에 대한 설명으로 일치하지 <u>않는</u> 것을 고르시오.

① 잘생긴 외모이다.
② 갈색 머리이다.
③ 백화점에서 근무한다.
④ 축구를 좋아한다.
⑤ 피아노를 칠 수 있다.

12 대화를 듣고, 남자가 배우려고 하는 악기로 가장 적절한 것을 고르시오.

① guitar   ② piano
③ violin   ④ flute
⑤ drum

13 대화를 듣고, 남자가 전화를 건 목적으로 가장 적절한 것을 고르시오.

① 방충망 설치 기사가 와서
② 비가 온다는 것을 알려 주려고
③ 여자의 개가 밖에 나와 있어서
④ 여자의 집 창문이 열려 있어서
⑤ 여자가 차의 문을 닫지 않아서

14 대화를 듣고, 여자가 할 일로 가장 적절한 것을 고르시오.

① 미술 대회 참가하기
② Tom에게 이메일 보내기
③ Tom에게 축하 전화하기
④ 미술부의 축제 계획 세우기
⑤ Tom의 고등학교 방문하기

15 대화를 듣고, 여자가 하는 말의 의도로 가장 적절한 것을 고르시오.

① 사과   ② 감사
③ 조언   ④ 칭찬
⑤ 축하

고난도
16 대화를 듣고, 두 사람이 만나기로 한 날짜와 시각을 고르시오.

① 5월 27일 – 2시   ② 5월 27일 – 2시 30분
③ 5월 28일 – 2시   ④ 5월 28일 – 2시 30분
⑤ 5월 28일 – 3시

17 대화를 듣고, 남자가 어젯밤에 한 일로 가장 적절한 것을 고르시오.

① 과학 발표 준비하기   ② 달 관측하기
③ 동아리 친구들 사진찍기   ④ 별 사진 찍기
⑤ 동아리 발표회 하기

고난도
18 다음을 듣고, 여자가 주장하는 바로 가장 적절한 것을 고르시오.

① 우리는 모든 동물을 보호해야 한다.
② 사람들은 유기동물을 입양해야 한다.
③ 멸종 위기 동물은 특별 보호가 필요하다.
④ 일부 동물들의 멸종 위기를 걱정해야 한다.
⑤ 동물을 이용한 화장품 실험을 자제해야 한다.

[19~20] 대화를 듣고, 남자의 마지막 말에 이어질 여자의 응답으로 가장 적절한 것을 고르시오.

19 Woman: _____

① Yes. See you then.
② No. You can pay later.
③ That'll be ten dollars more.
④ Thank you. I'll be back on Thursday.
⑤ Please give me my shirt tomorrow.

20 Woman: _____

① No, I've never tried it.
② Yes, I got your text message.
③ Yes, I'll feel more comfortable.
④ No, I'd like to leave a message.
⑤ Yes, she's talking on the phone.

다시 들으면서 듣기 만점에 도전하세요!

Dictation: 스크립트의 주요 부분을 다시 들으면서!

실전 ⊕: 세부 정보가 많은 스크립트를 다른 문제로 샅샅이!

---

01 그림 상황 대화 찾기

다음 그림의 상황에 가장 적절한 대화를 고르시오.

① ② ③ ④ ⑤

옷가게에서 여자 점원과 남자 손님이 할 수 있는 대화를 찾는다.

① W What kind of TV program do you like?

  M I like sports program.

② W How much are these notebooks?

  M They are three dollars each.

③ W Good afternoon. _____?
  도와드릴까요

  M Yes. I'm looking for _____.
  바지 한 벌

④ W Do you have an English dictionary?

  M Yes. It's right over there.

⑤ W Do you like _____?

  M No, I hate washing the dishes.
  설거지하는 것

---

02 그림 정보 파악 – 사물

다음을 듣고, 'I'가 무엇인지 가장 적절한 것을 고르시오.

① ② ③ ④ ⑤

핵심 어휘 feet, cold, footwear 등을 단서로 이용한다.

M I am something you probably use every day, especially in the winter. That's because, without me, _____.
  당신의 발이 추울 것이다
You can even wear two of me if your feet are really cold. And without me, your feet would _____. You can wear me with _____. I protect your feet from getting rubbed too hard.
  훨씬 더 축축해지다
  거의 모든 종류의 신발

That's because ~. 는 '그것은 ~이기 때문이다.'라는 의미로, 이유를 나타내는 표현이다.

---

03 할 일 파악

대화를 듣고, 여자가 토요일 오후에 할 일로 가장 적절한 것을 고르시오.

① 여행 떠나기
② 영화 보러 가기 go to the movie
③ 볼링 치러 가기 go bowling
④ 아버지 마중 나가기 meet my father
⑤ 테니스 치러 가기 play tennis

⊕

대화를 듣고, 남자가 토요일 오후에 할 일로 가장 적절한 것을 고르시오

① 여행 떠나기
② 영화 보러 가기
③ 볼링 치러 가기
④ 아버지 마중 나가기
⑤ 테니스 치러 가기

남자와 여자가 각각 언제 무엇을 하는지 구분해서 듣는다.

W Do you have any plans this weekend?

M Yes. On Saturday morning, I have to meet my father at the airport.

W _____?
  토요일 오후는 어때

M I'll go bowling with my sister in the afternoon. How about you?

W I'll _____ on Saturday morning and _____ with my brother in the afternoon.
  집에 있다
  영화 보러 가다

M And on Sunday morning?

W I plan to play tennis with Susan.

---

04 심정 추론

대화를 듣고, 여자의 심정으로 가장 적절한 것을 고르시오.

① 분노   ② 안도
③ 걱정   ④ 슬픔
⑤ 좌절

M I heard you had bad news yesterday.

W Yeah. I thought I failed my test!

M What? But you studied so hard!

W Yeach. I was shocked when I saw the result.

M You must be very upset, then.

W No. It was _____ (선생님의 실수) _____ _____. She wrote my score down wrong.

M So _____ (넌 떨어진 게 아니다) _____ _____?

W No. In fact, I got an A!

05 관계 파악

대화를 듣고, 두 사람의 관계로 가장 적절한 것을 고르시오.

① 옷가게 점원 – 고객
② 호텔 직원 – 투숙객
③ 보석가게 점원 – 고객
④ 관광안내원 – 관광객
⑤ 미용사 – 고객

W Hi, do you need any help?

M Yes, please. I _____ (특별한 것을 원하다) _____ for my girlfriend, but I'm not sure what's good.

W What kind of design does she like?

M I think she _____ (간단한 것을 좋아하다) _____, not too colorful.

W Then, what about this? It's made of real silver, with a heart pendant.

M It looks very cute. I think she will like it.

W Or there is this one, too, with a moon and a star pendant.

M Hmm, that looks good as well.

06 특정 정보 파악

대화를 듣고, 남자가 이용할 교통 수단으로 가장 적절한 것을 고르시오.

① by taxi 택시로
② on foot 도보로
③ by plane 비행기로
④ by subway 지하철로
⑤ by shuttle bus 셔틀 버스로

「either A or B」는 양자택일할 때 사용하는 표현으로, 'A나 B 둘 중의 하나'라고 해석한다.

M Excuse me, but what's _____ (~하는 가장 좋은 방법) _____ _____ get to Rainbow Department Store?

W You can either walk or take the subway.

M How far is it from here?

W Not that far. You can walk to the department store in fifteen minutes.

M _____ (셔틀 버스는 없나요) _____ _____ _____ to go there from here?

W Oh, you're right. You can _____ (셔틀 버스를 타다) _____ _____ _____ in front of the Paradise Hotel.

M Then, I'll take that.

07 장소 추론

핵심 어휘 cash, money, account 등을 단서로 이용한다.

대화를 듣고, 두 사람이 대화하고 있는 장소로 가장 적절한 곳을 고르시오.

① 공항   ② 은행
③ 여행사   ④ 백화점
⑤ 음식점

W Hi, what can I do for you?

M Hi, I _____ (미국 달러가 좀 필요하다) _____.

W How much do you want?

M 1,500 US dollars _____ _____.

W One second. Hmm. Okay. 1,500 US dollars will be 1,734,000 Korean won.

M Please _____ (현금으로) _____ _____ _____ (이 계좌에서 돈을 인출하다) _____ _____.

W Okay. And can I see your passport, too?

M Yes, here it is.

08 내용 일치 파악

대화를 듣고, 대화의 내용과 일치하지 <u>않는</u> 것을 고르시오.

① Yumi likes *kimchi* best.
② Harry likes pizza best.
③ Yumi knows how to make *kimchi*.
④ Yumi can make fried rice with *kimchi*.
⑤ Harry will visit Yumi's house on Saturday.

I can't wait to ~. 는 '몹시 ~하고 싶다.'는 의미로, 기대를 나타내는 표현이다.

M What's your favorite Korean food, Yumi?

W I _____. How about you, Harry?
_{김치를 제일 좋아하다}

M I like *kimchi*, too. But I like pizza best. Can you _____ _____?
_{김치를 담그다}

W _____, _____, but I can cook with kimchi.
_{아니,} _{할 수 없어}

M Can you show me how?

W Sure. I'm going to make fried rice with *kimchi* this weekend. Come to my house at 6 o'clock on Saturday.

M Okay. I can't wait to _____ _____.
_{김치로 요리하다}

09 특정 정보 파악

스승의 날(Teacher's Day)을 맞아 중학교 때 선생님께 보낼 수 있는 문자 메시지를 찾는다.

대화를 듣고, 남자가 보낼 문자 메시지로 가장 적절한 것을 고르시오.

① Happy New Year!
② Welcome home, honey!
③ Happy Birthday to You!
④ Thank you for teaching me.
⑤ Please take care of my child.

Teacher's Day: 스승의 날

Parents' Day: 어버이 날

Children's Day: 어린이 날

Coming-of-Age Day: 성년의 날

M Tomorrow is _____ _____.
_{스승의 날}

W It has been about five months since we graduated from middle school.

M Yes. I _____ _____ _____ _____ _____ in middle school. He really took care of our class.
_{우리 수학 선생님을 뵙고 싶다}

W He was a nice teacher. I'll go and see him tomorrow. How about you?

M I have to go to the library to write a science report with Scott.

W Then, why don't you _____ _____ _____ _____? He'll be happy to see your message.
_{그에게 문자 메시지를 보내다}

M Oh, you're right. I'll do that right now.

10 부탁한 일 파악

대화를 듣고, 여자가 남자에게 부탁한 일로 가장 적절한 것을 고르시오.

① 우체국 위치 알려주기
② 집에 초대하기
③ 집에 데려다주기
④ 소포 보내기
⑤ 돈 빌려주기

W Junhee, you live on Pleasant Street, don't you?

M Yes, I do. Why?

W And there's a post office on your street, right?

M Yes, I live _____ _____ _____ the post office.
_{~와 매우 가까운}

W Great. Can I ask you a big favor? I need to send this package to my friend in China, but there aren't any post offices near me.

M Do you want me to send it for you?

W Yes, that would be great. Could you, please?

M Okay, but _____ _____.
_{너 나에게 빚졌어}

11 내용 일치 파악

Louis에 대한 내용을 하나씩 정확히 확인하고 부정어(not, never)가 나오는 부분에 집중한다.

대화를 듣고, Louis에 대한 설명으로 일치하지 <u>않는</u> 것을 고르시오.

① 잘생긴 외모이다. good-looking
② 갈색 머리이다. brown hair
③ 백화점에서 근무한다. works for a department store
④ 축구를 좋아한다.
⑤ 피아노를 칠 수 있다. played the piano

M My French friend Louis is coming to my house next week. I think you might like him.

W Tell me about him. You said he was very good-looking, right?

M Sure. He has brown hair and green eyes. He works for a department store in Paris.

W That's nice. Maybe he could go with us to _____ _____ .
_{축구 경기를 보다}

M I don't think so. He loves playing tennis and _____ _____ , _____ .
_{축구가 아니라 테니스 구경하는 것}

W What else does he like?

M He likes music and dancing. He's played the piano for years.

12 특정 정보 파악

남자가 현재 연주하고 있는 것과 앞으로 배울 것을 구분해서 듣는다.

대화를 듣고, 남자가 배우려고 하는 악기로 가장 적절한 것을 고르시오.

① guitar 기타
② piano 피아노
③ violin 바이올린
④ flute 플루트
⑤ drum 드럼

W What are you doing?

M I'm playing the guitar. I've been playing the guitar since I was an elementary school boy.

W Oh, really? That sounds great!

M I heard that you played the violin.

W Yes. I learned how to play the violin when I was young. I often play the violin.

M I'm planning to _____ _____ _____ .
_{드럼 수업을 받다}

W Why? Do you have any special plan?

M Yes. I _____ _____ _____ _____ in our school band.
_{드럼 연주자가 되고 싶다}

13 전화 목적 파악

대화를 듣고, 남자가 전화를 건 목적으로 가장 적절한 것을 고르시오.

① 방충망 설치 기사가 와서
② 비가 온다는 것을 알려 주려고
③ 여자의 개가 밖에 나와 있어서
④ 여자의 집 창문이 열려 있어서
⑤ 여자가 차의 문을 닫지 않아서

Any time.은 '천만에요.' 또는 '괜찮아요.'라는 의미로, You're welcome.으로 바꿔 말할 수 있다.

[Telephone rings.]

W Hello.

M Hi, Susan?

W Yeah, is this Peter?

M Yes, I saw _____ _____ _____ .
_{네 창문이 열려 있다}

W Oh, is it going to rain?

M No, but I _____ _____ _____ _____ .
_{네 개들이 걱정이 되었다}

W I didn't think of that. I'd better close it. Thanks.

M Any time. Maybe you should _____ _____ _____ _____ .
_{그것에 철망을 달다}

W That's a good idea. That will keep the bugs out, too.

14 할 일 파악

I'm going to ~. 이후에 나오는 부분을 주의깊게 듣는다.

대화를 듣고, 여자가 할 일로 가장 적절한 것을 고르시오.

① 미술 대회 참가하기
② Tom에게 이메일 보내기
③ Tom에게 축하 전화하기
④ 미술부의 축제 계획 세우기
⑤ Tom의 고등학교 방문하기

➕ 대화를 듣고, Tom에 대한 설명으로 일치하지 않는 것을 고르시오.

① 전국 그림대회에서 상을 탔다.
② 작년에 같은 반 친구였다.
③ 작년 11월에 이사를 갔다.
④ 지금은 시카고에서 학교를 다닌다.
⑤ 최근에 여자에게 이메일을 보냈다.

W Did you hear Tom _____ _____ _____ _____ at the National Painting Contest? (1등상을 탔다)

M Tom who?

W Tom Gerald.

M Oh, the guy in our class last year?

W Yes, he moved to Chicago last November. He goes to Redwood High School in Chicago.

M He got the first prize? Oh, that's amazing!

W Yes. I think he's going to be a great artist. I'm going to _____ (그에게 이메일을 보내다) _____ _____.

M That's a good idea! _____ (그에게 말해 줘) _____ _____ I say congratulations to him.

15 의도 추론

First of all과 Second의 바로 뒤에 나오는 명령문 형태의 내용은 충고 또는 조언인 경우가 많다.

대화를 듣고, 여자가 하는 말의 의도로 가장 적절한 것을 고르시오.

① 사과   ② 감사
③ 조언   ④ 칭찬
⑤ 축하

W What's the problem with you, John?

M I can't sleep well at night these days. _____ (무엇을 추천해 줄래) _____ _____ I do?

W Try to maintain a regular lifestyle. First of all, _____ (일찍 일어나라) _____ _____ in the morning and _____ (밤에 늦게까지 깨어 있지 말라) _____ _____.

M I see. I'll try to change my lifestyle.

W Second, _____ (매일 운동을 하라) _____. Exercise like jogging would be good for you.

M Okay. I can do that.

고난도

16 숫자 파악 – 날짜, 시각

대화 과정에서 날짜와 시각이 변경되는 것을 정확히 파악한다.

대화를 듣고, 두 사람이 만나기로 한 날짜와 시각을 고르시오.

① 5월 27일 – 2시
② 5월 27일 – 2시 30분
③ 5월 28일 – 2시
④ 5월 28일 – 2시 30분
⑤ 5월 28일 – 3시

M I'm going to a great new movie on Saturday. Would you like to come?

W Saturday? It's May 27th. I can't. It's my mom's birthday. _____ (일요일은 어때) _____ ?

M Okay. Sunday is fine. Hmm.... Let me check.... _____ (5월 28일에) _____ _____, the movie starts at 3.

W Then let's meet in front of the Universal Cinema at 2:30.

M All right, but how about _____ (30분 일찍 만나는 것) _____ ? Then we can eat something first.

W Sounds great. See you then.

17 한 일 파악

대화를 듣고, 남자가 어젯밤에 한 일로 가장 적절한 것을 고르시오.

① 과학 발표 준비하기
② 달 관측하기
③ 동아리 친구들 사진찍기
④ 별 사진 찍기
⑤ 동아리 발표회 하기

W Jack, you look very tired this morning.
M Yes, I didn't sleep much, but I'll be okay. It was worth it.
W What did you do?
M Oh, we went to _____ _____ _____ last night.
　　　　　　　　　　　　　　　별을 관찰하다
W The stars in the night sky?
M Yes. You know I'm in an astronomy club. We wanted to take some pictures of the stars because it was a special night. We _____ _____ _____
_____ _____ _____.
많은 유성을 봤다
W That sounds great. Can you show me the pictures later?
M Sure.

고난도

18 특정 정보 파악

but 이후에 나오는 부분을 주의깊게 듣는다.

다음을 듣고, 여자가 주장하는 바로 가장 적절한 것을 고르시오.

① 우리는 모든 동물을 보호해야 한다.
② 사람들은 유기동물을 입양해야 한다.
③ 멸종 위기 동물은 특별 보호가 필요하다.
④ 일부 동물들의 멸종 위기를 걱정해야 한다.
⑤ 동물을 이용한 화장품 실험을 자제해야 한다.

W We must _____ _____ _____ _____
모든 동물들을 보호하기 위해 더 많은 것을 하다
_____. Now, we focus mainly on the endangered animals. Of course, these are important, but there are _____ _____ _____
나쁜 대접을 받고 있는 많은 일반 동물들
_____ _____ _____ every day. Companies use animals to test things like cosmetics and medications. These animals are common animals, like rabbits, cats, and dogs. Many of them suffer. Don't they deserve our protection?

---

19 알맞은 응답 찾기

[19~20] 대화를 듣고, 남자의 마지막 말에 이어질 여자의 응답으로 가장 적절한 것을 고르시오.

Woman: _____

① Yes. See you then.
② No. You can pay later.
③ That'll be ten dollars more.
④ Thank you. I'll be back on Thursday.
⑤ Please give me my shirt tomorrow.

W Good morning. May I help you?
M Yes. I _____ _____ _____
이 코트를 드라이 클리닝하고 싶다
W All right.
M When can I pick it up? I have to wear it this Friday.
W Don't worry about it. This will _____ _____ _____.
목요일에는 준비되다
M Okay. How much will it cost?
W It's ten dollars.
M Oh, that's not so expensive. Do I _____ _____ _____?
지금 돈을 지불해야 한다
W _____

---

20 알맞은 응답 찾기

Woman: _____

① No, I've never tried it.
② Yes, I got your text message.
③ Yes, I'll feel more comfortable.
④ No, I'd like to leave a message.
⑤ Yes, she's talking on the phone.

Guess what?은 '있잖아.' 또는 '알아맞혀 봐.'라는 의미로, 상대가 놀랄 것 같은 일을 알려 줄 때 사용하는 표현이다.

[Telephone rings.]

W Hello, is Frank there?
M Speaking.
W Hi, Frank. This is Susie. Guess what?
M What? Did something special happen?
W I just _____ _____ _____.
내 휴대전화를 샀다
M Great. Christine got a cell phone, too. Have you _____ _____
문자 메시지 보내는 것을 해 보다
_____ _____?
W _____

숫자 정보·심정 파악

무엇을 평가하는가?	일상생활 관련 대상이나 친숙한 일반적 주제에 관한 말이나 대화를 듣고 세부 정 보를 파악하고 화자의 심정이나 태도를 추론 할 수 있는지를 평가한다.
어떻게 출제되는가?	• 대화를 듣고, 여자가 지불해야 할 금액으로 가장 적절한 것을 고르시오. • 대화를 듣고, 여자가 지불해야 할 금액을 고르시오. • 대화를 듣고, 남자가 지불한 금액을 고르시오. • 대화를 듣고, 남자의 심정으로 가장 적절한 것을 고르시오.

key
solution

❶ 금액을 묻는 경우, 물건의 가격, 구입할 물건, 개수, 할인율 등의 정보에 주의해서 듣는다.

❷ 심정을 묻는 경우, 전체적인 대화의 분위기와 화자의 어조에 주의를 기울인다.

[기출로 전략 확인]

대화를 듣고, 여자가 지불해야 할 금액으로 가장 적절한 것을 고르시오.　　　　[2017 기출]

① $1　　　　　　② $2　　　　　　③ $3

④ $4　　　　　　⑤ $5

....

W Excuse me, I'd like to print out this picture.

M Okay. How many do you need?

W I need two copies. How much will it cost?

M Well, our photo shop offers two options.

W All right, what are they?

M One dollar each for black and white or two dollars each for color.　　❶ 물건의 정가와 개수의 정보를 들

W Then, I'd like two copies in black and white.　　　　　　　　　　　　을 수 있다.

M Sure. One moment, please.

　

여 실례합니다. 이 사진을 프린트하고 싶은데요.

남 네. 얼마나 필요하시죠?

여 2장이요. 얼마인가요?

남 음, 우리 사진관은 2가지 옵션이 있습니다.

여 알겠습니다. 뭔가요?

남 흑백사진은 장 당 1달러이고 컬러사진은 장 당 2달러입니다.

여 그럼 흑백으로 두 장 부탁드려요.

남 알겠습니다. 잠시만 기다려 주세요.

대화를 듣고, 여자가 지불할 금액을 고르시오.   [2014 기출]

① $2   ② $3   ③ $4
④ $5   ⑤ $6

만점 잡는 문장   ① The cookies are one dollar each.
                  ② A cup of coffee is two dollars.
                  ③ I'll take two cookies and a cup of coffee.

대화를 듣고, 남자의 심정으로 가장 적절한 것을 고르시오.   [2017 기출]

① bored   ② happy   ③ nervous
④ proud   ⑤ satisfied

만점 잡는 문장   **M** I <u>get afraid</u> when I speak in front of many people.
                  W You should take a deep breath before you start. You can do it.
                  M I will try my best, but <u>this contest makes me uncomfortable</u>.

● 가격

The one with the rainbow is 2 dollars. The one with the clover is 3 dollars.
무지개가 있는 것은 2달러이고 클로버가 있는 것은 3달러입니다.
The cookies are one dollar each. 쿠키는 개 당 1달러입니다.
The total is fifteen dollars. 전부해서 15달러입니다.
It'll be 20 dollars for the book and 3 dollars for the bookmark. 책은 20달러이고 책갈피는 3달러입니다.

● 할인

We give a one dollar discount per ticket after six o'clock. 6시 이후에는 티켓 당 1달러씩 할인해 드립니다.
If you buy two, we will give you a 10% discount. 두 개를 사면 10% 할인해 드립니다.
We're giving a 10% discount on the item. 그 물품은 10% 할인해 드리고 있습니다.

● 심정

excited 신이 난	proud 자랑스러워 하는	relaxed 여유 있는	satisfied 만족하는
moved 감동한	relieved 안도한	pleased 기쁜	thankful 고맙게 생각하는
bored 지루해 하는	nervous 불안한	frustrated 좌절한	scared 무서워하는
annoyed 짜증 난	worried 걱정하는	regretful 후회되는	embarrassed 당황한

학년   반   번
이름

01 다음 그림의 상황에 가장 적절한 대화를 고르시오.

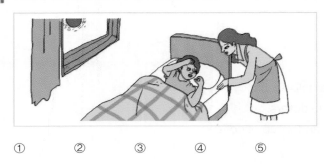

① ② ③ ④ ⑤

02 대화를 듣고, 남자가 구입할 셔츠를 고르시오.

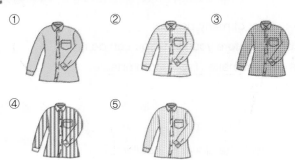

03 다음을 듣고, 무엇에 관한 내용인지 가장 적절한 것을 고르시오.

① 최신 유행 패션
② 천연 염료 제조법
③ 저렴하게 옷을 구입하는 방법
④ 오래된 옷을 새롭게 만드는 방법
⑤ 새 옷보다 오래된 옷이 좋은 이유

04 대화를 듣고, 두 사람이 대화 직후에 할 일로 가장 적절한 것을 고르시오.

① 샤워하기   ② 창문 열기
③ 에어컨 켜기   ④ 선풍기 가져오기
⑤ 도서관에 가기

05 다음 그림의 상황에 가장 적절한 대화를 고르시오.

① ② ③ ④ ⑤

고난도
06 대화를 듣고, 여자의 마지막 말의 의도로 가장 적절한 것을 고르시오.

① 숙제를 끝마쳐라.
② 꽃에 물을 주어라.
③ 학교에 빨리 가거라.
④ 침대에 가서 쉬어라.
⑤ 정원의 풀을 뽑아라.

07 대화를 듣고, 두 사람의 관계로 가장 적절한 것을 고르시오.

① 식당 주인 – 종업원   ② 요리사 – 식당 직원
③ 식당 직원 – 손님   ④ 식료품점 직원 – 고객
⑤ 식당 직원 – 택배 직원

08 대화를 듣고, 창문 옆에 위치할 물건으로 가장 적절한 것을 고르시오.

① 소파   ② 책상
③ 탁자   ④ 의자
⑤ 서류함

09 대화를 듣고, 남자가 전화를 건 목적으로 가장 적절한 것을 고르시오.

① 관광 예약 확인   ② 버스 예약 문의
③ 관광 예약 취소   ④ 신문 광고 접수
⑤ 버스 기사 취업 문의

점수
/20

10 대화를 듣고, 여자가 남자에게 부탁한 일로 가장 적절한 것을 고르시오.

① 과학 과제 끝내기　　② 조용히 공부하기
③ 간식 준비하기　　④ 식료품 배달 받기
⑤ 물건 전달해주기

11 대화를 듣고, 여자가 준비한 음식으로 언급되지 않은 것을 고르시오.

① 주스　　② 수프
③ 샐러드　　④ 스테이크
⑤ 아이스크림

12 대화를 듣고, 남자가 한 일로 가장 적절한 것을 고르시오.

① 병원 가기　　② 건강검진 받기
③ 감기약 먹기　　④ 체력 기르기
⑤ 휴식 취하기

13 대화를 듣고, 남자가 지불할 금액을 고르시오.

① $2　　② $2.50
③ $3　　④ $3.50
⑤ $4.50

14 대화를 듣고, 두 사람이 대화하고 있는 장소로 가장 적절한 곳을 고르시오.

① 경기장　　② 음식점
③ 도서관　　④ 영화관
⑤ 박물관

고난도
15 대화를 듣고, 현재 시각을 고르시오.

① 6:00　　② 7:00
③ 8:00　　④ 9:00
⑤ 10:00

16 다음을 듣고, Bill Smith에 대해 언급되지 않은 것을 고르시오.

① 직업　　② 국적
③ 동아리 가입 동기　　④ 취미
⑤ 자녀 수

17 다음을 듣고, 포스터의 내용과 일치하지 않는 것을 고르시오.

Felix Band
Concert
to help poor children
Date : Oct. 12th. 5 p.m. ~ 7 p.m.
Place : School Gym
Fee : $20.00 each student (a Free T-shirt)

①　　②　　③　　④　　⑤

18 대화를 듣고, 여자의 심정으로 가장 적절한 것을 고르시오.

① happy　　② angry
③ scared　　④ delighted
⑤ surprised

[19~20] 대화를 듣고, 남자의 마지막 말에 이어질 여자의 응답으로 가장 적절한 것을 고르시오.

19 Woman: _____

① You'll get well soon.
② That's really too bad.
③ I must be going home.
④ Oh, it's very kind of you.
⑤ I hope everything goes well.

고난도
20 Woman: _____

① I like my current job better.
② Unfortunately, I must take classes.
③ I didn't know you changed careers.
④ They're usually too expensive to hire.
⑤ I often take pictures at special events.

다시 들으면서 듣기 만점에 도전하세요!
Dictation: 스크립트의 주요 부분을 다시 들으면서!
실전 ⊕: 세부 정보가 많은 스크립트를 다른 문제로 샅샅이!

---

01 그림 상황 대화 찾기

머리가 아파서 침대에 누워 있는 남자와 여자가 할 수 있는 대화를 찾는다.

다음 그림의 상황에 가장 적절한 대화를 고르시오.

① ② ③ ④ ⑤

① **W** May I open the windows, please?

　 M Certainly. It's hot in here!

② **W** Hey! Look at the birds in the sky.

　 M Oh, yeah! It's a very lovely day.

③ **W** Why can't you ＿＿＿＿＿ ＿＿＿＿＿ ＿＿＿＿＿?
　　　　　　　　　　혼자서 일어나다

　 M I ＿＿＿＿＿ ＿＿＿＿＿ ＿＿＿＿＿ this morning.
　　　두통이 심하다

④ **W** How long are you going to stay?

　 M I'd like to stay for three days.

⑤ **W** How much is the bed over there?

　 M Sorry, ma'am. It's ＿＿＿＿＿ ＿＿＿＿＿ ＿＿＿＿＿.
　　　　　　　　　　　　판매용이 아닌

---

02 그림 정보 파악 – 사물

대화를 듣고, 남자가 구입할 셔츠를 고르시오.

① ②

③ ④

⑤

M I need a shirt for my new suit.

W For your black suit?

M Yeah. How about ＿＿＿＿＿ ＿＿＿＿＿ ＿＿＿＿＿?
　　　　　　　　　이 작은 점무늬 셔츠

W I think it would probably look weird.

M Then, would this thick striped shirt be good?

W It might, ＿＿＿＿＿ ＿＿＿＿＿ ＿＿＿＿＿ ＿＿＿＿＿ ＿＿＿＿＿.
　　　　　　만약 줄무늬가 아주 얇다면

M How about this shirt? It looks like what you suggested.

W Yep, that is what I meant.

M OK. I will get this. Thanks.

---

03 주제 파악

다음을 듣고, 무엇에 관한 내용인지 가장 적절한 것을 고르시오.

① 최신 유행 패션
② 천연 염료 제조법
③ 저렴하게 옷을 구입하는 방법
④ 오래된 옷을 새롭게 만드는 방법
⑤ 새 옷보다 오래된 옷이 좋은 이유

M Tired of your old clothes, but can't afford new ones? ＿＿＿＿＿ ＿＿＿＿＿.
　　　　　　　　　　　　　　　　　　　　　　　　　　　　　그것들을 한번 바꿔 보라
The easiest way is to ＿＿＿＿＿ ＿＿＿＿＿. This works best on light-
　　　　　　　　　당신의 옷들을 염색하다
colored clothes. Use special paints or stickers to decorate dark clothes. Another option
is to cut them. For example, an old pair of pants ＿＿＿＿＿ ＿＿＿＿＿
　　　　　　　　　　　　　　　　　　　　　　　그것을 잘라서 새로운 반바지가 되다
＿＿＿＿＿ ＿＿＿＿＿ ＿＿＿＿＿.

남자의 마지막 말에서 that이 의미하는 바를 파악한다.

대화를 듣고, 두 사람이 대화 직후에 할 일로 가장 적절한 것을 고르시오.

① 샤워하기
② 창문 열기
③ 에어컨 켜기
④ 선풍기 가져오기
⑤ 도서관에 가기

That's ridiculus. 는 '말도 안 돼.'라는 의미로, 부당함을 나타낼 때 사용하는 표현이다.

M   It's so hot. Why can't we _____ _____ _____ _____ ?
　　　　　　　　　　　　　　　　　에어컨을 켜다
W   The school wants to save money.
M   That's ridiculous. I can't study in this heat.
W   We could open the window.
M   That won't help. I wish _____ _____ _____ _____ .
　　　　　　　　　　　　　　　　　선풍기가 있다
W   There's _____ _____ _____ _____
　　　　다른 교실에 작은 선풍기 하나
　　　_____ we can use.
M   Well, it seems that is all we've got.

다음 그림의 상황에 가장 적절한 대화를 고르시오.

① ② ③ ④ ⑤

① M   Excuse me, you're not allowed to _____ _____ here.
　　　　　　　　　　　　　　　　　　　　동물에게 먹이를 주다
　 W   Oops, I'm sorry. I didn't see the sign.
② M   I really like rabbits. They are so cute.
　 W   So do I. I like how they eat the grass.
③ M   Mom, can we get a dog, please?
　 W   I wish we could, but you're allergic to fur.
④ M   It was a really good idea to _____ _____ _____ some
　　　　　　　　　　　　　　　　　　　밖에 나와서
　　　_____ .
　　　신선한 공기를 마시다
　 W   Yes, indeed, thank you for asking me.
⑤ M   What is your favorite thing to do on the weekend?
　 W   I like going to the zoo and watching the animals.

고난도

대화를 듣고, 여자의 마지막 말의 의도로 가장 적절한 것을 고르시오.

① 숙제를 끝마쳐라.
② 꽃에 물을 주어라.
③ 학교에 빨리 가거라.
④ 침대에 가서 쉬어라.
⑤ 정원의 풀을 뽑아라.

W   What are you doing here, David?
M   I'm watering the garden. The flowers are dry.
W   Take care of yourself. You should _____ _____
　　　　　　　　　　　　　　　　　　침대에서 휴식을 취하다
　　_____ .
M   But it's so boring.
W   If you don't rest more, you _____ _____ enough to go to school
　　　　　　　　　　　　　　　　회복되지 못할 것이다
　　tomorrow.
M   Mom, I'm well enough to water the flowers.
W   David, you _____ _____ _____ .
　　　　　　　나중에 그것을 할 수 있다
M   Yes, Mom.

대화를 듣고, 두 사람의 관계로 가장 적절한 것을 고르시오.

① 식당 주인 – 종업원
② 요리사 – 식당 직원
③ 식당 직원 – 손님
④ 식료품점 직원 – 고객
⑤ 식당 직원 – 택배 직원

M Is everything all right? Do you need anything?

W Yes, actually, could we _____ _____ _____, please?
　　　　　　　　　　　물을 마시다

M Sure, would you like it cold or warm?

W Cold would be great. Thank you. And we'd like to _____ _____.
　　　　　　　　　　　　　　　　　　　　　　　　　　　　다른 음식을 주문하다
Could you bring us the menu again?

M Of course, I'll be right back with your water and the menu.

W Thanks, oh, and this salad is delicious. What dressing is this?

M In fact, it's our chef's secret dressing, so I can't tell you. But I'm glad you like it.

window가 언급된 부분을 주의깊게 듣는다.

대화를 듣고, 창문 옆에 위치할 물건으로 가장 적절한 것을 고르시오.

① 소파　　　　② 책상
③ 탁자　　　　④ 의자
⑤ 서류함

W How do you want to rearrange your office?

M Let's move _____ _____ _____ _____.
　　　　　　　책상을 창문에 더 가깝게

W And your file cabinet?

M That should go by the door.

W Do you want the sofa by the file cabinet?

M Sure, and the table _____ _____ _____ _____ _____
　　　　　　　　　　　　　방 가운데
_____.

W Won't it be crowded?

M Maybe. Let's put it against the wall.

대화를 듣고, 남자가 전화를 건 목적으로 가장 적절한 것을 고르시오.

① 관광 예약 확인
② 버스 예약 문의
③ 관광 예약 취소
④ 신문 광고 접수
⑤ 버스 기사 취업 문의

[Telephone rings.]

W Hello, Global Tour. This is Yuna Lee.

M Hello, this is Chris Baker.

W Hello, Chris Baker. How can I help you?

M Well, I'm calling about _____ _____ _____
　　　　　　　　　　　　　어제 신문에 난 광고
_____.

W Do you mean _____ _____ _____ _____?
　　　　　　　　　버스 기사를 찾는 광고

M Yes. That's right.

W I'm sorry. _____ _____ _____ _____.
　　　　　　그 자리는 이미 충원되었다

M I see. Thank you anyway.

대화를 듣고, 여자가 남자에게 부탁한 일로 가장 적절한 것을 고르시오.

① 과학 과제 끝내기 ② 조용히 공부하기
③ 간식 준비하기 ④ 식료품 배달 받기
⑤ 물건 전달해주

W Kevin, are you going to stay home this afternoon?

M I'm not sure. I need to work on the science project with Sungho.

W Then, why not invite him here? I'm leaving right now, so you can _____ _____.
<u>조용히 작업하다</u>

M That sounds good. Can we have some food if we get hungry?

W Oh, there's not much food now. Actually, I _____ _____ _____, and
<u>식료품을 주문했다</u>
they'll be delivered soon. Can you make sure you get them?

M Sure, what time is the delivery guy supposed to come?

<u>By the way 이후에 나오는 부분을 주의깊게 듣는다.</u>

대화를 듣고, 여자가 준비한 음식으로 언급되지 <u>않은</u> 것을 고르시오.

① 주스 juice
② 수프 soup
③ 샐러드 salad
④ 스테이크 steak
⑤ 아이스크림 ice cream

➕ 대화를 듣고, 여자가 남자에게 부탁한 일로 가장 적절한 것을 고르시오.

① 저녁 준비하기 ② 식탁 차리기
③ 스테이크 굽기 ④ 수프 끓이기
⑤ 후식 사오기

M Is supper ready? I'm hungry.

W Almost ready. Could you set the table?

M Okay. What are we having?

W We'll _____ _____ _____ and the steak.
<u>샐러드로 시작해서 먹다</u>

M I'll have my steak well-done, please. By the way, _____ _____
<u>수프는 없나요</u>
_____ tonight?

W I _____ _____ _____, but we have some juice to drink and some ice
<u>하나도 준비하지 않았다</u>
cream for dessert.

M That sounds fine. Thanks.

대화를 듣고, 남자가 한 일로 가장 적절한 것을 고르시오.

① 병원 가기 ② 건강검진 받기
③ 감기약 먹기 ④ 체력 기르기
⑤ 휴식 취하기

W Hi, Adam, how are you? I heard you were sick a couple of days ago.

M I'm feeling better now, thanks.

W Did you have a cold?

M I don't know, but probably. I _____ _____ bad _____ and felt very weak.
<u>두통이 있었다</u>

W Didn't you go to see a doctor?

M No, I just rested at home. I drank a lot of orange juice and slept a lot.

W Well, I'm glad you're better. But maybe you should go to the doctor and _____
_____ _____.
<u>진찰을 받다</u>

13 숫자 파악 – 금액

대화를 듣고, 남자가 지불할 금액을 고르시오.

① $2   ② $2.50
③ $3   ④ $3.50
⑤ $4.50

juice, milk, water 등은 a glass of(한 잔의 ~)를 이용하여 수를 센다.

W May I help you?
M Yes, I'd like a cheese sandwich. How much is it?
W _____ _____ _____ _____. Do you want
   2달러 50센트이다
anything to drink with that?
M Yes, I'll have a glass of orange juice.
W _____ _____ _____.
   1달러이다
M Here you are.
W Thank you. Your food _____ _____ in a moment.
                준비될 것이다
M Thank you.

14 장소 추론

핵심 어구 save a seat, score, The ball is flying towards us! 등을 통해 장소를 파악한다.

대화를 듣고, 두 사람이 대화하고 있는 장소로 가장 적절한 곳을 고르시오.

① 경기장   ② 음식점
③ 도서관   ④ 영화관
⑤ 박물관

Look out!은 '조심해!'라는 의미로, 주의나 경고를 나타내는 표현이다.

➕
대화를 듣고, 여자의 마지막 말의 의도로 가장 적절한 것을 고르시오.

① 칭찬   ② 거절
③ 요청   ④ 동의
⑤ 경고

M Sorry I'm late. How is it going?
W Sit down. I _____ _____ _____ for you. You've missed a really exciting
        자리를 잡아 두었다
part.
M Really? What's the score now?
W Three to nothing.
M Who has three?
W The Korean team. They _____ _____ _____ in the
            3점 홈런을 쳤다
bottom of the third inning.
M Oh, that's too bad I missed it.
W Look out! _____ _____ towards us!
      공이 날아오고 있다

고난도

15 숫자 파악 – 시각

오늘 문을 닫는 시각(at nine)과 남은 시간(an hour more)을 파악한다.

대화를 듣고, 현재 시각을 고르시오.

① 6:00   ② 7:00
③ 8:00   ④ 9:00
⑤ 10:00

W Hurry up. _____ _____ _____.
      곧 가게가 문을 닫는다
M Don't worry. I saw the sign telling closing times.
W But they usually close the store at eight.
M Right. But today they are going to _____ _____ _____.
                     9시에 문을 닫다
W Are you sure?
M Of course. Before I came here I saw the sign clearly.
W Then, _____ _____ _____ _____.
       우리는 1시간이 더 남아있다
M So, take it easy.

16 언급 및 비언급 파악

다음을 듣고, Bill Smith에 대해 언급되지 않은 것을 고르시오.

① 직업 animal doctor
② 국적 Canada
③ 동아리 가입 동기
   helping lost and deserted dogs
④ 취미
⑤ 자녀 수 three

W Hello, everyone. Today we have a new member, Bill Smith, in our PET club. He is
_____ _____ _____. He is very interested in
  캐나다 출신의 수의사
helping _____ _____ _____ so he is joining our club. He
        잃어버리고 버려진 개들
_____, a daughter and two sons. Let's welcome our new
세 명의 자녀가 있다
member, Bill Smith. Thank you.

17 실용문 정보 파악
포스터의 내용을 미리 읽어보고 하나씩 확인한다.

다음을 듣고, 포스터의 내용과 일치하지 않는 것을 고르시오.

Felta Band
Concert
to help poor children
Date : Oct. 12th. 5 p.m. ~ 7 p.m.
Place : School Gym
Fee : $20.00 each student (a Free T-shirt)

① ② ③ ④ ⑤

W ① The purpose of the concert is to _____ .
　　　　　　　　　　　　　　　　가난한 아이들을 돕다
② The concert will be on October 12th.
③ The concert will _____ _____ .
　　　　　　　　3시간 동안 계속되다
④ The concert will be held in the school gym.
⑤ They will give a free T-shirt to every student who pays for the concert.

18 심정 추론

대화를 듣고, 여자의 심정으로 가장 적절한것을 고르시오.
① happy 행복한
② angry 화가 난
③ scared 겁먹은
④ delighted 기쁜
⑤ surprised 놀란

M Hurry up, Sally! You're _____ _____ _____ in 20 minutes.
　　　　　　　　　　　　　　무대 위에
W Where is my dress? I'm sure I hung it here.
M Maybe it's in the other room. Some kids were looking at it this afternoon.
W Oh, here it is. Look! _____ _____ .
　　　　　　　　그것은 너무 더럽다
M You're right. It has a lot of spots on it.
W How could this happen? I _____ _____ .
　　　　　　　　　　그 아이들을 용서하지 않을 것이다

19 알맞은 응답 찾기
두 사람이 말하는 친구가 처한 상황을 파악한다.

[19~20] 대화를 듣고, 남자의 마지막 말에 이어질 여자의 응답으로 가장 적절한 것을 고르시오.

Woman: _____

① You'll get well soon.
② That's really too bad.
③ I must be going home.
④ Oh, it's very kind of you.
⑤ I hope everything goes well.

M Did you hear that Ron is _____ _____ ?
　　　　　　　　　　　　병원에
W Oh, really? What's the matter with him?
M He's very ill. Probably _____ _____ .
　　　　　　　　　　　그는 돼지 독감에 걸렸다
W Swine flu! _____ _____ _____ ?
　　　그는 어떻게 하다 그게 걸렸데
M He's just come back from Mexico. It is certain that he got it while he was there.
W _____

고난도
20 알맞은 응답 찾기

Woman: _____

① I like my current job better.
② Unfortunately, I must take classes.
③ I didn't know you changed careers.
④ They're usually too expensive to hire.
⑤ I often take pictures at special events.

M Did you take this picture?
W Yes, on my last vacation.
M It's good. Do you take a lot of pictures?
W Sometimes. _____ _____ _____ at special occasions and things.
　　　　　　　그냥 재미로
M You mean birthdays and graduations?
W Yeah, it's _____ _____ _____ _____ .
　　　　　부업으로 하는 일
M Did you take photography classes?
W Actually, when I was at university, photography was my minor.
M Wow, I didn't know that. Why didn't you _____ _____ _____ ?
　　　　　　　　　　　전문 사진작가가 되다
W _____

01 다음을 듣고, 날씨가 잘못 짝지어진 것을 고르시오.

①	Tomorrow morning	
②	Saturday morning	
③	Saturday afternoon	
④	Sunday morning	
⑤	Sunday afternoon	

02 대화를 듣고, Jim Thacker를 고르시오.

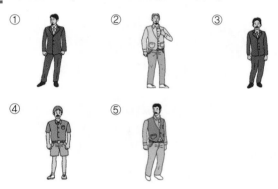

03 대화를 듣고, 대화가 이루어지는 상황으로 가장 적절한 것을 고르시오.

① 길 묻기   ② 손님 접대
③ 취업 면접   ④ 환자 진료
⑤ 물건 판매

04 대화를 듣고, 남자가 한 일로 가장 적절한 것을 고르시오.

① 쿠키 만들기   ② 액자 만들기
③ 그림 그리기   ④ 케이크 만들기
⑤ 쿠키 장식하기

05 다음을 듣고, 무엇에 관한 안내인지 가장 적절한 것을 고르시오.

① 휴점일   ② 신상품
③ 폐점 시간   ④ 할인 행사
⑤ 안전 수칙

06 대화를 듣고, 여자가 파티에 갈 수 <u>없는</u> 이유로 가장 적절한 것을 고르시오.

① 너무 피곤해서
② 초대받지 않아서
③ 해야 할 숙제가 많아서
④ 시험 준비를 해야 해서
⑤ 다른 파티에 가야 해서

07 대화를 듣고, 두 사람이 대화하고 있는 장소로 가장 적절한 것을 고르시오.

① 기차역   ② 연주회장
③ 공원   ④ 미술관
⑤ 공항

08 대화를 듣고, 여자가 오늘 밤에 외출할 수 <u>없는</u> 이유로 가장 적절한 것을 고르시오.

① 쇼핑을 해야 해서
② 숙제를 해야 해서
③ 부모님을 만나야 해서
④ 친구와 영화를 보기로 해서
⑤ 부모님의 전화를 받아야 해서

09 대화를 듣고, 여자의 마지막 말의 의도로 가장 적절한 것을 고르시오.

① 감사   ② 허락   ③ 변명
④ 용서   ⑤ 후회

10 대화를 듣고, 여자가 남자에게 충고한 것으로 가장 적절한 것을 고르시오.

① 병원에 가 봐라.
② 충분히 연습해라.
③ 급하게 서두르지 마라.
④ 준비 운동을 충분히 해라.
⑤ 공을 너무 많이 던지지 마라.

11 대화를 듣고, 여자가 여름 방학에 한 일로 언급되지 <u>않은</u> 것을 고르시오.

① TV 시청하기   ② 비치발리볼하기
③ 수영하기   ④ 사원 방문하기
⑤ 미술관 방문하기

12 대화를 듣고, 남자가 전화를 건 목적으로 가장 적절한 것을 고르시오.

① 상품을 교환하려고
② 상품을 수리하려고
③ 상품에 대해 문의하려고
④ 상품의 품질에 대해 항의하려고
⑤ 상품 배달 가능 여부를 확인하려고

13 대화를 듣고, 여자의 현재 심정으로 가장 적절한 것을 고르시오.

① angry
② nervous
③ afraid
④ bored
⑤ disappointed

14 다음을 듣고, 광고문의 내용과 일치하지 <u>않는</u> 것을 고르시오.

SEOUL ELECTRONICS PLAZA
THE CHEAPEST PRICES IN TOWN

Open : from 10 a.m. – 8 p.m.
on weekdays
from 10 a.m. – 6 p.m.
on Saturdays
Not open on Sundays
12 Yongsan, Seoul
☎ 419-530-4514

①   ②   ③   ④   ⑤

고난도
15 대화를 듣고, 현재 시각을 고르시오.

① 1:20   ② 2:20   ③ 3:20
④ 4:20   ⑤ 5:20

16 대화를 듣고, 여자가 남자에게 부탁한 일로 가장 적절한 것을 고르시오.

① 휴식 시간 갖기   ② 푸드코트 위치 찾기
③ 메뉴 가져오기   ④ 음식 사오기
⑤ 테이블 잡기

17 대화를 듣고, 두 사람의 관계로 가장 적절한 것을 고르시오.

① 교사 – 학생   ② 소설가 – 독자
③ 심사위원 – 참가자   ④ 기자 – 대회 참자가
⑤ 가이드 – 여행객

18 다음 그림의 상황에 가장 적절한 대화를 고르시오.

①   ②   ③   ④   ⑤

[19~20] 대화를 듣고, 여자의 마지막 말에 이어질 남자의 응답으로 가장 적절한 것을 고르시오.

19 Man: _____

① I'm sorry. Next time I'll remember.
② Fine, if you think it will be enough.
③ Good idea. We can do it tomorrow.
④ Thanks. I appreciate your doing that.
⑤ That's OK. Everyone makes mistakes.

20 Man: _____

① It looks brand new.
② I'll let you know about that later.
③ Mom! What would you like me to do?
④ Oh, there are so many choices I can do.
⑤ Oh, Mom! I need some coffee to wake me up.

다시 들으면서 듣기 만점에 도전하세요!
Dictation: 스크립트의 주요 부분을 다시 들으면서!
실전 ⊕: 세부 정보가 많은 스크립트를 다른 문제로 샅샅이!

---

01 날씨 파악

다음을 듣고, 날씨가 <u>잘못</u> 짝지어진 것을 고르시오.

①	Tomorrow morning	☀
②	Saturday morning	⛅
③	Saturday afternoon	☂
④	Sunday morning	☀
⑤	Sunday afternoon	⛅

W Good morning. This is the KBC weather forecast. It will _____ _____ tomorrow for all parts of Korea. It will be cloudy on Saturday morning and it will begin to (맑다) rain Saturday afternoon for most parts of the nation. A storm will come in from the South Sea. You can see _____ _____ again on Sunday. The weather on (맑은 하늘) Sunday will be _____ _____ _____ all day long. (야외 활동에 적합한)

---

02 그림 정보 파악 – 인물

대화를 듣고, Jim Thacker를 고르시오.

① ② ③
④ ⑤

W Who am I supposed to meet at the airport?

M Jim Thacker. He's _____ _____ _____. (초청 연설자)

W What does he look like?

M He's quite tall and has _____ _____ _____ _____. (짙은색 머리와 콧수염)

W Will he be wearing a suit?

M No, he said he'll wear _____ _____ _____. (청바지와 조끼)

W And where should I wait for him?

M Outside Gate 7B.

W All right. Tell him I'll pick him up.

---

03 특정 정보 파악

대화를 듣고, 대화가 이루어지는 상황으로 가장 적절한 것을 고르시오.

① 길 묻기
② 손님 접대
③ 취업 면접
④ 환자 진료
⑤ 물건 판매

Don't mention it.은 '천만에요.'라는 의미로, 감사의 말에 대한 응답의 표현이다.

W Thank you for _____. (나를 초대해 준 것)

M Don't mention it. I'm glad you can visit my home.

W You have a very nice home.

W Thanks. We _____ _____ for a long time. (여기서 살아왔다)

W When will everyone else arrive?

M They'll arrive in a few minutes. Would you like a drink?

W Yes, please. I'd like a glass of orange juice.

M OK, hold on. _____ _____ _____. (편안히 계세요)

---

04 한 일 파악

But 이후에 나오는 부분을 주의깊게 듣는다.

대화를 듣고, 남자가 한 일로 가장 적절한 것을 고르시오.

① 쿠키 만들기
② 액자 만들기
③ 그림 그리기
④ 케이크 만들기
⑤ 쿠키 장식하기

W Did you _____ _____ _____ _____ at the bazaar today? (팔 것을 가져오다)

M Yes, I brought some cookies.

W Really? Did you make them yourself?

M No, my mom did. But _____ _____ _____. (내가 그것들을 장식했다)

W They look better than my pictures.

M You _____ _____ _____. You made them in art class, didn't you? (그것들을 액자에 넣었다)

W Yes, but I only have two that are good enough to sell.

---

05 주제 파악

개점 시간 및 폐점 시간이 반복됨에 유의한다.

다음을 듣고, 무엇에 관한 안내인지 가장 적절한 것을 고르시오.

① 휴점일 ② 신상품
③ 폐점 시간 ④ 할인 행사
⑤ 안전 수칙

W Good evening, ladies and gentlemen! Thank you _____ _____ at K-mart. Our store will _____ _____ _____. Shopping hours are from 11 a.m. to 9 p.m. on weekdays, and from 11 a.m. to 6 p.m. on weekends. I hope you will _____ _____ at 11 a.m. tomorrow morning. Thank you. Good-bye.
(쇼핑 오신 것을 / 30분 후면 문을 닫는다 / 다시 방문하다)

06 이유 파악

대화를 듣고, 여자가 파티에 갈 수 없는 이유로 가장 적절한 것을 고르시오.

① 너무 피곤해서
② 초대받지 않아서
③ 해야 할 숙제가 많아서
④ 시험 준비를 해야 해서
⑤ 다른 파티에 가야 해서

The reason is (that) ~.는 '그 이유는 ~이다.'라는 의미로, 이유를 나타내는 표현이다.

W What are you going to do this weekend, Alex?

M Well, my friend is going to have a party. I will go there.

W Sounds great!

M How about you? Can you _____ _____ _____? (나와 같이 가다)

W Thank you, but I can't.

M Why not? Do you _____ _____? (무슨 계획이 있다)

W _____. The reason is _____ _____ to the party.
(특별한 건 없다 / 나는 초대받지 않았다)

07 대화 장소 파악

대화를 듣고, 두 사람이 대화하고 있는 장소로 가장 적절한 것을 고르시오.

① 기차역 ② 연주회장
③ 공원 ④ 미술관
⑤ 공항

M Excuse me, is it okay if I take some pictures?

W Yes, but you can't take any pictures in the special exhibition room.

M The special exhibition room? Where is it?

W It's in the right wing of the building. Currently, the exhibition "Realistic Paintings of Our Time" _____ _____ _____ there. (전시 중이다)

M I see, thank you.

W Oh, and one more thing. Please don't use your flash because it can _____ _____. (다른 방문객을 방해하다)

M Okay, no problem.

08 이유 파악

거절의 말 뒤에 이어진 이유를 말하는 부분을 주의깊게 듣는다.

대화를 듣고, 여자가 오늘 밤에 외출할 수 없는 이유로 가장 적절한 것을 고르시오.

① 쇼핑을 해야 해서
② 숙제를 해야 해서
③ 부모님을 만나야 해서
④ 친구와 영화를 보기로 해서
⑤ 부모님의 전화를 받아야 해서

M I wonder if you can go out to see a movie tonight.

W Probably not. I don't have time for a movie.

M You have to do your homework or something?

W Actually not. I've done already.

M Then, how about going for dinner instead?

W Sorry, I really can't. My parents are _____ _____. (내게 집으로 전화하시다)

M We could go to the nice restaurant _____ _____. (전화를 받은 후에)

W The problem is, I'm not sure _____ _____ _____. (언제 그분들이 내게 전화하실지)

M I see. You have to wait for a while then.

09 의도 추론

대화를 듣고, 여자의 마지막 말의 의도로
가장 적절한 것을 고르시오.

① 감사　　　　② 허락
③ 변명　　　　④ 용서
⑤ 후회

「should have p.p.」는 '~했어야 했는데'라는 의
미로, 과거에 하지 않은 일에 대한 후회나 유감을 나
타내는 표현이다.

➕ 대화를 듣고, 여자가 정시에 퇴근하지 못한
이유로 가장 적절한 것을 고르시오.

① 일이 많아서
② 회의가 길어져서
③ 전화기 충전을 해야 해서
④ 업무 전화가 와서
⑤ 저녁식사를 해야 해서

M　Where have you been? You're late.
W　I'm sorry. I couldn't ＿＿＿＿ ＿＿＿＿ ＿＿＿＿.
　　　　　　　제 때 직장에서 나오다
M　Were you working on something?
W　Kind of. We had a meeting, which lasted forever.
M　Why didn't you call?
W　My phone battery went dead. It's my mistake. I ＿＿＿＿ ＿＿＿＿
　　　　　　　　　　　　　　　　　　　　　미리 그것을 충전했어야 했다
　　＿＿＿＿ ＿＿＿＿ ＿＿＿＿.
M　That's all right. The dinner is on you.

10 특정 정보 파악

대화를 듣고, 여자가 남자에게 충고한 것으로
가장 적절한 것을 고르시오.

① 병원에 가 봐라.
② 충분히 연습해라.
③ 급하게 서두르지 마라.
④ 준비 운동을 충분히 해라.
⑤ 공을 너무 많이 던지지 마라.

M　Don't touch me. My arm is killing me.
W　Is there anything ＿＿＿＿ ＿＿＿＿ ＿＿＿＿?
　　　　　　　　　　네 팔에 문제가 있다
M　Yeah, I have ＿＿＿＿ ＿＿＿＿ in my arm and shoulder.
　　　　　　　　근육통
W　What did you do?
M　I played baseball yesterday. I pitched a long game.
W　You are a pitcher? Oh, I didn't know that.
M　I threw the baseball too many times.
W　Be careful. If you ＿＿＿＿ ＿＿＿＿ ＿＿＿＿ too much, you'll hurt yourself.
　　　　　　　　　　공을 던지다

11 언급 및 비언급 파악

질문 뒤에 나오는 대답을 잘 들으면서 언급된 것은 선택지에서 지워나간다.

대화를 듣고, 여자가 여름 방학에 한 일로
언급되지 않은 것을 고르시오.

① TV 시청하기
② 비치발리볼하기 played beach volley
　ball
③ 수영하기 swam
④ 사원 방문하기 temple
⑤ 미술관 방문하기 small art museum

M　What did you do during this summer vacation?
W　My family went to the beach.
M　Were there a lot of people at the beach?
W　No, we found a quiet beach. We ＿＿＿＿ ＿＿＿＿ ＿＿＿＿ and
　　　　　　　　　　　　　　　　비치발리볼을 했다　　　　　　　　바다에서 수영을 했다
　　＿＿＿＿ ＿＿＿＿ ＿＿＿＿.
M　What else did you do?
W　We ＿＿＿＿ ＿＿＿＿ ＿＿＿＿ and ＿＿＿＿ ＿＿＿＿
　　　아름다운 절을 방문했다　　　　　　　　　　　　　　작은 미술관
　　＿＿＿＿ on the way home. How about you?
M　I just stayed home and watched TV.

12 전화 목적 파악

Can you ~? 이후에 나오는 부분을 주의깊게 듣는다.

대화를 듣고, 남자가 전화를 건 목적으로 가장 적절한 것을 고르시오.

① 상품을 교환하려고
② 상품을 수리하려고
③ 상품에 대해 문의하려고
④ 상품의 품질에 대해 항의하려고
⑤ 상품 배달 가능 여부를 확인하려고

[Telephone rings.]

W Hello, Yunjin Electronics. May I help you?

M Hello. I _____ _____ _____ there yesterday.
　LCD 모니터를 샀다

W Yes, is this Mr. Harrison?

M Yes, speaking.

W What's wrong with it?

M When I opened the package, I found the LCD panel _____. Can you _____
　　　　　　　　　　　　　　　　　　　　　　　　깨진　　　　　　　　그것을 교환하다
　_____ ?

W I'm sorry it was broken. I'll send a new one right now. Please _____
　_____ _____ back to us.
　깨진 것을 보내라

M That's great. Thank you.

13 심정 추론

대화를 듣고, 여자의 현재 심정으로 가장 적절한 것을 고르시오.

① angry 화가 난
② nervous 긴장한
③ afraid 두려운
④ bored 지루한
⑤ disappointed 실망한

I'm looking forward to ~.는 '나는 ~을 고대한다.'라는 의미로, 몹시 기대하는 것을 나타내는 표현이다.

M I'm glad we have a long holiday.

W Me too. _____ _____ _____ seeing my family.
　나는 ~이 기대가 된다

M Are you going to your hometown?

W Yes, my parents still live there. How about you?

M I'm going to stay in Seoul. I live with my parents.

W _____ _____ _____ this holiday to begin.
　나는 ~을 기다릴 수 없다

M But next year's Chusok is on Sunday. That means next year's Chusok holiday
　_____ _____ _____ .
　더 짧아질 것이다

W Oh, that sounds sad. I won't be able to go to my hometown next year.

14 실용문 정보 파악

요일과 시각에 주의해서 듣는다.

다음을 듣고, 광고문의 내용과 일치하지 <u>않는</u> 것을 고르시오.

SEOUL ELECTRONICS PLAZA
THE CHEAPEST PRICES IN TOWN

Open : from 10 a.m. – 8 p.m.
　　on weekdays
　　from 10 a.m. – 6 p.m.
　　on Saturdays
　　Not open on Sundays
12 Yongsan, Seoul
☎ 419-530-4514

① ② ③ ④ ⑤

W ① The store sells electronic devices like TVs and computers.

② The store has _____ _____ _____ .
　　　　　　　　　　가장 싼 가격

③ The store closes at 8 p.m. on Fridays.

④ The store opens at 10 a.m. on Saturdays.

⑤ The store _____ _____ _____ on Sundays.
　　　　　오후 6시에 문을 닫는다

15 숫자 파악 – 시각

비행기가 이륙할 시각(3:20)과 기다려온 시각, 앞으로 기다릴 시간(an hour)을 파악하여 계산한다.

대화를 듣고, 현재 시각을 고르시오.

① 1:20　　　　② 2:20
③ 3:20　　　　④ 4:20
⑤ 5:20

+

대화를 듣고, 이륙 시간이 지연된 이유로 가장 적절한 것을 고르시오.

① 기체 결함　　② 연결편 문제
③ 기상 상황　　④ 점검시간 지연
⑤ 미탑승 승객

W What time does the plane take off?

M It _____ _____ _____ : _____ .
　　　3시 20분에 이륙하다

W Really? We've been here for an hour! Do we have to _____
　　　한 시간 더 기다리다
?

M I'm really sorry. _____ _____ _____ _____
　　　항공편이 한 시간 지연되었다
because of the rain.

W This is terrible. I'm going to be late for tonight's meeting.

M I'm very sorry, ma'am.

W That's all right. There is no other way.

16 부탁한 일 파악

대화를 듣고, 여자가 남자에게 부탁한 일로 가장 적절한 것을 고르시오.

① 휴식 시간 갖기
② 푸드코트 위치 찾기
③ 메뉴 가져오기
④ 음식 사오기
⑤ 테이블 잡기

M I'm getting tired. Can we have a little break?

W Sure. I was actually getting hungry. Why don't we _____ _____ to
　　　　　　　　　　　　　　　　　간단히 한 입 먹다
eat?

M Great idea. The food court is just around the corner.

W That's convenient. What do you feel like?

M I'll have a hamburger and French fries. What about you?

W I'm not sure. Could you go get us a table? I want to _____ quick
　　　　　　　　　　　　　　　　　　　　　주위를 둘러보다
_____ _____ the different restaurants first.

M Sounds like a plan.

17 관계 파악

대화를 듣고, 두 사람의 관계로 가장 적절한 것을 고르시오.

① 교사 – 학생
② 소설가 – 독자
③ 심사위원 – 참가자
④ 기자 – 대회 참가가
⑤ 가이드 – 여행객

W Congratulations, Dan. You did a wonderful job.

M It's all thanks to you, Ms. Tailor. Even entering this speech competition was all your idea. If it weren't for you, I never would have joined.

W Not at all. You always _____ _____ my _____ .
　　　　　　　　　학교생활을 잘하다

M Thank you, but I still have a long way to go.

W Don't be so humble, Dan. You're allowed to feel proud today. I _____
_____ share this good news with our school.
　빨리, ~하고 싶다

M Neither can I.

다음 그림의 상황에 가장 적절한 대화를 고르시오.

① ② ③ ④ ⑤

① W Can I talk to the manager, please?

   M He is not in today. Can I help you with anything?

② W I think I've _____ _____ . I can't find it in my bag.
   휴대 전화를 잃어버리다

   M Do you want me to call your number?

③ W Okay, I found these. Is one of them yours?

   M Yes, the blue jacket is mine. My ID card is in the pocket.

④ W I bought this new jacket. What do you think of it?

   M It's really cool. Where did you buy it?

⑤ W Can you _____ _____ and contact information?
   당신 이름을 남겨라

   M Yes, sure. Please let me know if you find it.

[19~20] 대화를 듣고, 여자의 마지막 말에 이어질 남자의 응답으로 가장 적절한 것을 고르시오.

Man: _____

① I'm sorry. Next time I'll remember.

② Fine, if you think it will be enough.

③ Good idea. We can do it tomorrow.

④ Thanks. I appreciate your doing that.

⑤ That's OK. Everyone makes mistakes.

W Did you put gas in the car yesterday?

M I'm sorry, I forgot.

W What? You said you would put gas. Hmm.... Then let's stop for gas before we go to dinner.

M It's fine. There's _____ _____ _____ .
   통에 충분한

W I don't want to take a risk.

M OK. If we hurry up and leave now, we will have time to stop and get some gas.

W I wish you _____ _____ yesterday like you said you
   기름을 가득 채워 두었다
   would.

M _____

Man: _____

① It looks brand new.

② I'll let you know about that later.

③ Mom! What would you like me to do?

④ Oh, there are so many choices I can do.

⑤ Oh, Mom! I need some coffee to wake me up.

You'd better ~.는 '~하는 게 좋겠다.'는 의미로, 충고나 조언을 나타내는 표현이다.

알겠다는 긍정의 반응이나 거절하고 다시 커피를 부탁하는 반응이 올 수 있다.

W Tom, you'd better go to bed early.

M I have a big test tomorrow, Mom. I have to _____ _____
   시험을 잘 보다
   _____ _____ tomorrow.

W I'm sure you'll _____ _____ _____ this time.
   좋은 결과를 얻다

M I hope so, Mom.

W Do you want something to drink?

M Could I have some coffee?

W Coffee is not good for you. I'll _____ _____ _____ .
   너에게 오렌지 주스를 갖다주다

M _____

어색한 대화 찾기

무엇을 평가하는가?	일상생활이나 친숙한 일반적 주제에 관한 말이나 대화를 듣고 화자의 의도나 목 적을 추론할 수 있는지를 평가한다.
어떻게 출제되는가?	• 대화를 듣고, 어색한 것을 고르시오. • 대화를 듣고, 두 사람의 대화가 어색한 것을 고르시오.

key solution

❶ 의문사로 시작하는 의문문은 Yes/No의 답변을 취할 수 없고, 의문사가 답변의 단서가 되므로 집중하며 듣는다.

❷ 비슷한 뜻이나 발음의 어휘가 반복되어 나오는 경우 오답일 확률이 높으므로 주의한다.

[기출로 전략 확인]

대화를 듣고, 어색한 것을 고르시오.　　　　　　　　　　　　　[2017 기출]

① 　　　　② 　　　　③ 　　　　④ 　　　　⑤

. . . .

① **W** Why are you late?

　M I'm sorry. I missed the bus.

② **W** What are you going to do this Saturday?

　M I went to America three years ago.

③ **W** Sam, have you ever met Jenny?

　M No, I haven't.

④ **W** Watch out! There is a car coming!

　M Oh, my! Thank you.

⑤ **W** Tony! I lost my bag. What should I do?

　M Don't worry. Let's find it together.

❶ 'What are you going to do ~?'라는 계획을 묻는 질문에 'went'라는 과거 동사와 함께 'three years ago'라는 과거 시점을 나타내는 표현을 사용하여 대답하고 있다.

① **여** 왜 늦었어?

　남 미안. 버스를 놓쳤어.

② **여** 이번 토요일에 뭐 할 거야?

　남 나 3년 전에 미국에 갔었어.

③ **여** Sam, Jenny 만난 적 있어?

　남 아니, 없어.

④ **여** 조심해! 차가 오고 있어!

　남 이런! 고마워.

⑤ **여** Tony! 나 가방을 잃어버렸어. 어떻게 해야 하지?

　남 걱정마. 같이 찾아 보자.

| 어색한 대화 찾기
유형의 발문과 보기 | 다음을 듣고, 두 사람의 대화가 <u>어색한</u> 것을 고르시오. [2014 기출]

① ② ③ ④ ⑤ |

만점 잡는 문장　③ **W** Are you <u>good</u> at singing?

　　　　　　　　　M <u>Good</u> job!

| | 다음을 듣고, 두 사람의 대화가 <u>어색한</u> 것을 고르시오. [2014 기출]

① ② ③ ④ ⑤ |

만점 잡는 문장　① **W** <u>What time</u> do you usually get up?

　　　　　　　　　M It was <u>last Saturday</u>.

**자연스러운 대화에
쓰이는 표현**

● 질문(의문사)

A Why are you late? 왜 늦었어?

B I'm sorry. I missed the bus. 미안. 버스를 놓쳤어.

A What time shall we meet? 몇 시에 만날까?

B How about at 5? 5시 어때?

A How much is this hat? 이 모자는 얼만가요?

B It's $15. 15달러입니다.

● 질문(조동사/일반동사)

A Will you do me a favor? 부탁 좀 해도 될까요?

B Sure. What is it? 물론이죠. 뭔 가요?

A Sam, have you ever met Jenny? Sam. Jenny를 만난 적 있어?

B No, I haven't. 아니, 없어.

A Did you see the TV show, Quiz King, last night? 어젯밤 TV쇼 Quiz King 봤어?

B Yes, it was great! 응, 굉장했어!

● 평서문

A Watch out! There is a car coming! 조심해! 차가 오고 있어!

B Oh, my! Thank you. 이럴 수가! 고마워.

A Tony! I lost my bag. What should I do? Tony! 나 가방을 잃어버렸어. 어떻게 하지?

B Don't worry. Let's find it together. 걱정 마. 같이 찾아보자.

A Long time no see. 오랜만이야.

B I've been out of town for a month. 한달 간 마을을 떠나 있었어.

학년   반   번

이름

01 대화를 듣고, 남자가 찾는 곳을 고르시오.

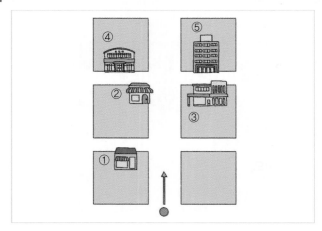

02 대화를 듣고, 남자가 아들에게 줄 선물을 고르시오.

03 대화를 듣고, 여자가 말한 내용이 <u>아닌</u> 것을 고르시오.

① Don't be late for class.
② Don't chew gum.
③ Don't run in the halls.
④ Take good care of library books.
⑤ Raise your hand to ask a question in class.

04 대화를 듣고, 여자가 여행지를 선택한 가장 우선적인 조건을 고르시오.

① 물가   ② 거리
③ 기후   ④ 숙소
⑤ 교통수단

05 다음을 듣고, 무엇에 관한 내용인지 가장 적절한 것을 고르시오.

① 대학 공부의 어려움
② 캠퍼스 생활의 장점
③ 대학 졸업 후의 진로
④ 경제적 독립의 필요성
⑤ 캠퍼스 시설의 중요성

06 대화를 듣고, 여자가 직장을 선택할 때 가장 중요하게 여기는 것을 고르시오.

① 연봉   ② 승진 기회
③ 전임제 일   ④ 근무 시간
⑤ 휴가 기간

07 대화를 듣고, 남자가 대화 직후에 할 일로 가장 적절한 것을 고르시오.

① 책을 빌린다.   ② 책을 반납한다.
③ 연체료를 낸다.   ④ 아래층으로 내려간다.
⑤ 선생님을 만나러 간다.

08 다음 그림의 상황에 가장 적절한 대화를 고르시오.

①   ②   ③   ④   ⑤

09 다음 안내문을 보면서 대화를 듣고, 내용과 일치하지 <u>않는</u> 것을 고르시오.

Come and Join Us
for ① Susan McKenzie's birthday party
at ② Pirate Ship Restaurant
on ③ Friday   ④ May 17
at ⑤ 7 : 30 in the evening

Look forward to seeing you....

R.S.V.P. Tel : 223.768. 2897

10 대화를 듣고, 남자의 심정으로 가장 적절한 것을 고르시오.

① bored   ② happy
③ surprised   ④ disappointed
⑤ excited

점수

/20

11 대화를 듣고, 남자가 선생님과 면담 후 장래희망으로 선택한 직업을 고르시오.

① 의사 ② 변호사
③ 생물학자 ④ 약사
⑤ 화학자

12 대화를 듣고, 남자가 전화를 건 목적으로 가장 적절한 것을 고르시오.

① 집 전화번호를 바꾸려고
② 집 전화에 문제가 생겨서
③ 전화 요금에 대해 물어보려고
④ 기사의 전화번호를 물어보려고
⑤ 휴대 전화의 수리를 신청하려고

13 대화를 듣고, 남자가 주문한 제품이 도착하지 <u>않은</u> 이유로 가장 적절한 것을 고르시오.

① 생산에 차질이 빚어져서
② 판매자가 주문을 누락하여서
③ 수취인이 없어 반송되었기 때문에
④ 판매자가 주소를 잘못 기입해서
⑤ 고객이 신청한 주소가 잘못되어서

14 대화를 듣고, 남자가 목적지로 가는 데 사용하지 <u>않은</u> 방법을 고르시오.

① 비행기 ② 택시
③ 버스 ④ 도보
⑤ 자전거

15 대화를 듣고, 남자가 예약한 시각을 고르시오.

① 6:00 p.m. ② 6:30 p.m.
③ 7:00 p.m. ④ 7:30 p.m.
⑤ 8:00 p.m.

16 대화를 듣고, 두 사람이 대화하는 장소로 가장 적절한 곳을 고르시오.

① 기숙사 ② 병원
③ 요양원 ④ 경찰서
⑤ 약국

17 대화를 듣고, 두 사람의 관계로 가장 적절한 것을 고르시오.

① 보행자 – 관광객 ② 여행사 직원 – 고객
③ 버스기사 – 승객 ④ 수족관 직원 – 관람객
⑤ 경찰 – 시민

18 대화를 듣고, 남자가 여자에게 부탁한 일로 가장 적절한 것을 고르시오.

① 잃어버린 물건 찾기 ② 판매할 물건 찾기
③ 운동화 사이즈 교환하기 ④ 운동화 빨기
⑤ 벼룩시장 구경오기

[19~20] 대화를 듣고, 여자의 마지막 말에 이어질 남자의 응답으로 가장 적절한 것을 고르시오.

19 Man: _____

① What are you going to buy?
② May I have your name, please?
③ Okay, where is the fitting room?
④ Could you bring me some cake?
⑤ Do you want to make a reservation?

고난도
20 Man: _____

① Sure. We have cold drinks.
② Yes, please. I'd like the steak.
③ No. The fish doesn't taste fresh.
④ Sorry about that. Let me check.
⑤ Yes. I'd like to try something else.

다시 들으면서 듣기 만점에 도전하세요!
Dictation: 스크립트의 주요 부분을 다시 들으면서!
실전 ⊕: 세부 정보가 많은 스크립트를 다른 문제로 샅샅이!

---

01 그림 정보 파악 – 위치　　　위치를 표현하는 부사어에 유의하여 듣는다.

대화를 듣고, 남자가 찾는 곳을 고르시오.

M　Excuse me. Can you tell me ＿＿＿ ＿＿＿ ＿＿＿ ?
　　　　　　　　　　　　　　　　　　　약국이 어디 있는지
W　Go straight two blocks, and turn right. It's ＿＿＿ ＿＿＿ .
　　　　　　　　　　　　　　　　　　　　　　　당신 오른 편에
M　Is there any big building near there?
W　Yes, there is a department store ＿＿＿ ＿＿＿ ＿＿＿ from it.
　　　　　　　　　　　　　　　　　맞은 편에
M　What's the name of it?
W　It's Hankuk Department Store.
M　Thank you very much.

---

02 그림 정보 파악 – 사물　　　세발자전거(tricycle)에 대한 남자의 반응의 변화에 주목한다.

대화를 듣고, 남자가 아들에게 줄 선물을
고르시오.

① ② ③ ④ ⑤

M　I'm looking for a birthday present for my three-year-old son.
W　We have many nice toys. How about a train, a plane or a car?
M　I bought all of those for him last year.
W　＿＿＿ ＿＿＿ ＿＿＿ , then?
　　세발자전거는요
M　I guess he might be too young for that.
W　No, a three-year-old boy can ＿＿＿ ＿＿＿ ＿＿＿ . It's really fun.
　　　　　　　　　　　　　　　　　　쉽게 타다
M　Okay. My son will love it. ＿＿＿ ＿＿＿ ＿＿＿ .
　　　　　　　　　　　　　　그걸로 살게요

---

03 내용 일치 파악

대화를 듣고, 여자가 말한 내용이 <u>아닌</u> 것
을 고르시오.

① Don't be late for class.
② Don't chew gum.
③ Don't run in the halls.
④ Take good care of library books.
⑤ Raise your hand to ask a question
　 in class.

W　There are some rules you have to follow at school, Steve.
M　What are they, Mrs. Kim?
W　First of all, you should ＿＿＿ ＿＿＿ ＿＿＿ ＿＿＿ .
　　　　　　　　　　　　　　　　수업 시간에 지각하지 않다
M　Okay. I won't be late for class again.
W　Next, you ＿＿＿ ＿＿＿ ＿＿＿ , and you're ＿＿＿
　　　　　　　　껌을 씹을 수 없다　　　　　　　　　　　　뛰는 것이 허용되지 않다
　　＿＿＿ ＿＿＿ in the halls.
M　Okay. I promise to follow those rules.
W　Finally, you must ＿＿＿ ＿＿＿ ＿＿＿ to ask me a question in class.
　　　　　　　　　　손을 들다
M　I will, Mrs. Kim.

최상급으로 표현된 부분에 주의해야 한다.

대화를 듣고, 여자가 여행지를 선택한 가장 우선적인 조건을 고르시오.

① 물가 price
② 거리 distance
③ 기후 climate
④ 숙소 hotel
⑤ 교통수단 transportation

+

대화를 듣고, 여자의 심정으로 가장 적절한 것을 고르시오.

① 초조   ② 설렘
③ 수줍음   ④ 안도
⑤ 걱정

M Wow, Christmas is coming!

W Yeah. I can't wait for Christmas holidays. I'm going to Phuket in Thailand.

M What made you choose that place? Was it because Phuket is _____? Or, are prices low?
선탠을 하기에 좋은

W Do you want to know? The most attractive thing about it is _____ _____ _____.
여기서부터의 거리

M How long does it take to get there by plane?

W It takes _____ _____ _____. Imagine! In three hours, I can be on an emerald beach.
3시간밖에

다음을 듣고, 무엇에 관한 내용인지 가장 적절한 것을 고르시오.

① 대학 공부의 어려움
② 캠퍼스 생활의 장점
③ 대학 졸업 후의 진로
④ 경제적 독립의 필요성
⑤ 캠퍼스 시설의 중요성

W This is the first time I've lived on campus, but I enjoy campus life. I can _____ _____ here and discuss with them the problems in my studies. So, I _____ _____ . Here it's _____ for me to use the library, the sports center, and all the other facilities.
더 많은 친구를 사귀다
이곳에서의 생활이 즐겁다
좀 더 편리한

대화를 듣고, 여자가 직장을 선택할 때 가장 중요하게 여기는 것을 고르시오.

① 연봉
② 승진 기회
③ 전임제 일
④ 근무 시간
⑤ 휴가 기간

M Here's an ad. Let's take a look at it.

W Let's see.... It's a nice job.

M It is. You finished college three years ago, right?

W Yes, and I've worked in several companies since then.

M _____ _____ _____ for you in finding jobs? Money?
가장 중요한 게 뭐니

W No. I'm tired of part-time work. I really _____ _____ _____.
전임제 일자리를 원하다

M Then, this is a good job for you.

대화를 듣고, 남자가 대화 직후에 할 일로 가장 적절한 것을 고르시오.

① 책을 빌린다.
② 책을 반납한다.
③ 연체료를 낸다.
④ 아래층으로 내려간다.
⑤ 선생님을 만나러 간다.

M I'm looking for a book, but I can't find it.

W What's the title of the book?

M I'm sorry I forgot it. It is about President Lincoln's _____ _____.
종교생활

W Oh, I know _____ _____ _____.
무엇을 찾고 있는지

M Do you have a copy here?

W No, go downstairs, you can find one.

M Thanks a lot, ma'am.

08 그림 상황 대화 찾기

다음 그림의 상황에 가장 적절한 대화를 고르시오.

① ② ③ ④ ⑤

① M What time does the concert begin?

　W It begins at eight. We still have some time.

② M The concert was really good, wasn't it?

　W I don't know. I thought it was ＿＿＿＿＿ ＿＿＿＿＿ ＿＿＿＿＿.
　　　　　　　　　　　　　　　　　　　　　　조금 지루한

③ M Can I get two tickets for the 7 o'clock show?

　W Sure, that will be $40.

④ M These are great seats. Thank you.

　W You're welcome. I got them ＿＿＿＿＿ ＿＿＿＿＿ ＿＿＿＿＿ the ticket sales
　　　　　　　　　　　　　　　　　　　~하자마자
　　opened.

⑤ M Excuse me, but I think you're in my seat.

　W Oh, really? I'm so sorry. Isn't this 10D?

09 내용 일치 파악

다음 안내문을 보면서 대화를 듣고, 내용과 일치하지 <u>않는</u> 것을 고르시오.

Come and Join Us
for ① Susan McKenzie's birthday party
at ② Pirate Ship Restaurant
on ③ Friday　　④ May 17
at ⑤ 7 : 30 in the evening

Look forward to seeing you....

R.S.V.P. Tel : 223.768. 2897

숫자 표현에 주의하여 듣는다.

M ＿＿＿＿＿ ＿＿＿＿＿ ＿＿＿＿＿ this Friday night?
　　시간이 있어요

W Sure, I am. What date is it?

M It's ＿＿＿＿＿ ＿＿＿＿＿.
　　　5월 27일

W Oh, it's Susan's birthday!

M It is. Come to Pirate Ship Restaurant at 7 : 30 in the evening.

W OK. I'll be there.

M Here's ＿＿＿＿＿ ＿＿＿＿＿ ＿＿＿＿＿. See you then.
　　　　초청장

10 심정 추론

대화를 듣고, 남자의 심정으로 가장 적절한 것을 고르시오.

① bored 지루한
② happy 행복한
③ surprised 놀란
④ disappointed 실망한
⑤ excited 흥분한

Look on the bright side.는 상대방의 슬픔이나 기분을 위로해 줄 때 쓰는 표현이다.

M Today has been a long day.

W ＿＿＿＿＿ ＿＿＿＿＿ ＿＿＿＿＿ ?
　　피곤하니

M Yes. I have to ＿＿＿＿＿ ＿＿＿＿＿ ＿＿＿＿＿ every day.
　　　　　　　　똑같은 일을 하다

W I understand you, but....

M Look at those people. They seem to be tired of the same thing every day, too.

W Hey, David. Look on the bright side of life.

M I don't know. ＿＿＿＿＿ ＿＿＿＿＿ in this work any more.
　　　　　　　　나는 흥미가 없다

11 특정 정보 파악

대화를 듣고, 남자가 선생님과 면담 후 장래희망으로 선택한 직업을 고르시오.

① 의사　　　　② 변호사
③ 생물학자　　④ 약사
⑤ 화학자

➕
대화를 듣고, 남자가 면담 전에 희망하던 장래 희망으로 가장 적절한 것을 고르시오.

① 의사　　　　② 변호사
③ 생물학자　　④ 약사
⑤ 화학자

M Ms. Lee, I want to become a doctor. What should I do?

W It is not easy to become a doctor. It ＿＿＿＿＿ ＿＿＿＿＿.
　　　　　　　　　　　　　　　　　　　오랜 세월이 걸리다

M Tell me about it in detail.

W You need to ＿＿＿＿＿ ＿＿＿＿＿ biology or chemistry when you go to university. It
　　　　　　　~을 전공하다
　　takes four years, followed by four years of medical school and four years of medical
　　practice.

M It takes too long. I don't think I will be able to do it.

W ＿＿＿＿＿ ＿＿＿＿＿ ＿＿＿＿＿ the saying, "No pain, no gain?"
　　~에 대해 들어 본 적이 없니

M I know, ma'am, but ＿＿＿＿＿ become a pharmacist.
　　　　　　　　　~하는 것이 차라리 낫다

앞부분에 나와 있는 남자가 전화를 건 이유를 파악한다.

대화를 듣고, 남자가 전화를 건 목적으로 가장 적절한 것을 고르시오.

① 집의 전화번호를 바꾸려고
② 집의 전화에 문제가 생겨서
③ 전화 요금에 대해 물어보려고
④ 기사의 전화번호를 물어보려고
⑤ 휴대 전화의 수리를 신청하려고

[Telephone rings.]

W Good morning. This is Julia Miller speaking. How can I help you?

M I've been trying to call my house, but I _____ <u>연결할 수 없다</u> _____ .

W You can't get through?

M Yes. _____ <u>전화가 불통이다</u> _____ _____ _____ . I've tried it at least ten times already.

W What's your home phone number, sir?

M It's 765-3876.

W Hold on, please. *[pause]* It seems like we're having _____ <u>당신의 지역에 문제</u> _____ . Our engineers are fixing it now. It'll be fixed soon.

M Thank you.

대화를 듣고, 남자가 주문한 제품이 도착하지 <u>않은</u> 이유로 가장 적절한 것을 고르시오.

① 생산에 차질이 빚어져서
② 판매자가 주문을 누락하여서
③ 수취인이 없어 반송되었기 때문에
④ 판매자가가 주소를 잘못 기입해서
⑤ 고객이 신청한 주소가 잘못되어서

[Telephone rings.]

W Micro Electronics. May I help you?

M I _____ <u>주문을 받지 못했다</u> _____ _____ yet. It's been already five days!

W We're really sorry. _____ <u>~가 있음에 틀림없다</u> _____ a mistake. Can you tell me your name and address?

M My name is Bill Smith, 614 Maple Street, Pittsburgh, Pennsylvania.

W The address you told us was 410 Presley.

M Oh, I'm sorry, I _____ <u>실수했군요</u> _____ _____ . It is my old address.

W Don't worry. I will _____ <u>다른 것을 보내다</u> _____ _____ to your new address.

M Thank you.

남자가 목적지에 가는데 이용한 교통 수단을 순서대로 파악한다.

대화를 듣고, 남자가 목적지로 가는 데 사용하지 <u>않은</u> 방법을 고르시오.

① 비행기 airplane
② 택시 taxi
③ 버스 bus
④ 도보 walk
⑤ 자전거 bike

W Hi, Tom! Welcome home! How was your trip?

M It was fantastic, mom!

W How did you get to Mt. Halla?

M After I _____ <u>공항에 도착했다</u> _____ _____ _____ , I _____ <u>택시를 탔다</u> _____ _____ to the bus terminal. Then I _____ <u>버스를 탔다</u> _____ _____ and arrived at the mountain.

W Then you walked?

M Yes. I _____ <u>정상까지 걸었다</u> _____ _____ _____ of the mountain.

W No bike?

M No, _____ <u>자전거는 타지 않았다</u> _____ . I just walked, mom.

대화를 듣고, 남자가 예약한 시각을 고르시오.

① 6:00 p.m. ② 6:30 p.m.
③ 7:00 p.m. ④ 7:30 p.m.
⑤ 8:00 p.m.

대화 중에 나오는 여러 가지 숫자가 무엇에 해당하는지 정확히 파악한다.

W Can I help you?

M Yes. I want to _____ _____ on Friday evening.
　　　　　　　　　　　　자리를 예약하다

W This coming Friday?

M Yes. _____ _____ Is that possible?
　　　금요일 저녁 7시

W Sure. How many people are in your party?

M Eight.

W Okay, party of eight, this Friday at 7 p.m. Anything else?

M Some of them will _____ _____ _____ _____. Is it okay?
　　　　　　　　　　　　6시 30분쯤에 여기에 도착하다

W Oh, that's no problem.

16 장소 추론

대화를 듣고, 두 사람이 대화하는 장소로 가장 적절한 곳을 고르시오.

① 기숙사
② 병원
③ 요양원
④ 경찰서
⑤ 약국

M Hello, Mrs. Miller. What _____ _____ _____ the problem?

W When I went to bed yesterday, I had chest pain and _____.
　　　　　　　　　　　　　　　　　　　　　　　　　　　　～인 것 같다　　　　　　　어지러움을 느끼다

M Did you have dinner yesterday?

W Yes, I _____ _____ _____. After that, I felt sick in my stomach and my
　　　　　회를 먹었다
heart began to hurt.

M I think you have an _____ _____. Stomachache can go with a chest pain. I'll
　　　　　　　　　　　　　　체하다
prescribe the medicine.

W Thank you, sir.

17 관계 파악

대화를 듣고, 두 사람의 관계로 가장 적절한 것을 고르시오.

① 보행자 – 관광객
② 여행사 직원 – 고객
③ 버스기사 – 승객
④ 수족관 직원 – 관람객
⑤ 경찰 – 시민

W Excuse me. We are going to city hall, right?

M No, I'm afraid not. This goes in the Marine Aquarium direction.

W Oh, I have to _____ _____ then. I'm sorry, but could you tell me which
　　　　　　　　　　～에서 내리다
number I should take?

M You should take 970 or 971. I think 970 takes the quicker route.

W And can I take it from the stop when I can get off?

M No, you should _____ _____ _____ _____. City hall is in
　　　　　　　　　　반대 쪽으로 건너다
the opposite direction.

W I see. Thank you very much!

대화를 듣고, 남자가 여자에게 부탁한 일로
가장 적절한 것을 고르시오.

① 잃어버린 물건 찾기
② 판매할 물건 찾기
③ 운동화 사이즈 교환하기
④ 운동화 빨기
⑤ 벼룩시장 구경오기

W Andy, what are you doing? Are you looking for something?

M Yes, I need some _____ _____ _____ at the school flea market.
팔 것

W What kind of things do you need?

M Anything still useful, like books, clothes, bags, sneakers...

W Oh, what about your white sneakers? They're almost new, but you can't wear them because they're _____ _____ now.
너무 작은

M That's a good idea! But can you wash them, please? There's _____ _____ _____ on one of them.
작은 자국

W Sure, when do you need them by?

[19~20] 대화를 듣고, 여자의 마지막 말
에 이어질 남자의 응답으로 가장 적절한 것
을 고르시오.

Man: _____

① What are you going to buy?
② May I have your name, please?
③ Okay, where is the fitting room?
④ Could you bring me some cake?
⑤ Do you want to make a reservation?

Here it is.는 상대방에게 '여기 있어요.'라며 물건을
건넬 때 쓰는 표현이다.

M Can I _____ _____, please?
이 셔츠를 교환하다

W What's wrong with it? Is there something wrong with it?

M No, but I think it's too large for me. Do you have something smaller?

W Of course, but do you _____ _____?
영수증을 가지고 있다

M Yes, here it is.

W Okay. This one is a smaller size. Why don't you _____ _____?
그것을 입어 보다

M _____

식당에서 손님이 계산서에 잘못이 있다고 말했을 때, 종업원이 할 수 있는 말에 주목해야 한다.

Man: _____

① Sure. We have cold drinks.
② Yes, please. I'd like the steak.
③ No. The fish doesn't taste fresh.
④ Sorry about that. Let me check.
⑤ Yes. I'd like to try something else.

M _____ _____, ma'am?
모든 게 어땠는지요

W The sandwich and pasta were good, but the soup was a bit salty.

M Oh, I'm sorry about that. Do you want me to bring you your bill?

W Yes, please. [pause]

M _____ _____.
여기 있습니다

W Let's see.... This can't be our bill. I'm sure _____ _____ _____.
네가 실수를 했다

M _____

학년　　반　　번
이름

01 대화를 듣고, 두 사람이 만들 방석으로 가장 적절한 것을 고르시오.

① 　② 　③

④ 　⑤

02 대화를 듣고, 여자의 직업으로 가장 적절한 것을 고르시오.

① 　② 　③

④ 　⑤

03 대화를 듣고, 여자의 심정으로 가장 적절한 것을 고르시오.

① relieved　　　② nervous
③ excited　　　④ lonely
⑤ disappointed

04 대화를 듣고, 남자가 잘하는 운동을 고르시오.

① 수영　　　　② 축구
③ 농구　　　　④ 야구
⑤ 볼링

05 대화를 듣고, 두 사람의 관계로 가장 적절한 것을 고르시오.

① 점원 - 고객　　② 은행원 - 고객
③ 감독 - 선수　　④ 면접관 - 지원자
⑤ 경찰관 - 목격자

06 대화를 듣고, 두 사람이 대화하는 장소로 가장 적절한 곳을 고르시오.

① bank　　　　② library
③ airport　　　④ museum
⑤ bookstore

07 다음 그림의 상황에 가장 적절한 대화를 고르시오.

①　　　②　　　③　　　④　　　⑤

08 대화를 듣고, 현재 시각을 고르시오.

① 4:40　　　　② 5:00
③ 5:10　　　　④ 5:20
⑤ 5:30

09 대화를 듣고, 여자가 태어난 곳을 고르시오.

① Italy　　　　② Spain
③ Canada　　　④ America
⑤ Australia

10 다음을 듣고, 무엇에 관한 안내인지 가장 적절한 것을 고르시오.

① 경품 행사　　② 노래 경연
③ 할인 판매　　④ 성금 모금
⑤ 신상품 소개

점수 /20

11 대화를 듣고, 여자가 화가 난 이유로 가장 적절한 것을 고르시오.

① 자기를 말로 무시해서
② 선물을 안 주어서
③ 물건을 빌려주지 않아서
④ 약속을 지키지 않아서
⑤ 돈을 갚지 않아서

12 대화를 듣고, 남자가 여자를 방문한 목적으로 가장 적절한 것을 고르시오.

① 제품을 판매하려고
② 우편물을 배달하려고
③ 친구를 병문안 하려고
④ 주문 상품을 배달하려고
⑤ 습득물을 되돌려 주려고

13 대화를 듣고, 두 사람이 다음 약속한 때를 고르시오.

① 월요일 오후 4시
② 수요일 오전 9시
③ 수요일 오후 4시
④ 목요일 오전 9시
⑤ 목요일 오후 4시

14 대화를 듣고, Sarah에 관해 알 수 없는 것을 고르시오.

① 외모
② 나이
③ 직업
④ 취미
⑤ 근무처

고난도
15 대화를 듣고, 남자가 여자에게 하는 충고로 가장 적절한 것을 고르시오.

① 공공장소에서 인터넷 사용에 유의하라.
② 인터넷 비밀번호는 자주 바꾸어야 한다.
③ 노트북 컴퓨터보다 데스크탑을 사라.
④ 인터넷에서 노트북을 구입하지 마라.
⑤ 인터넷에서 물건을 구입하는 것이 훨씬 저렴하다.

16 다음 메모를 보면서 대화를 듣고, 내용과 일치하지 않는 것을 고르시오.

> **Memo**
>
> To : ① Mr. Parker
> From : ② Dean Martin
> Message : ③ Car repair will have been finished
> ④ at 5 p.m.
> Charge : ⑤ 113 dollars

17 대화를 듣고, 남자가 여자에게 요청한 일로 가장 적절한 것을 고르시오.

① 예약 확인하기
② 예약 취소하기
③ 인원수 추가하기
④ 시간 변경하기
⑤ 음식 주문하기

18 대화를 듣고, 여자가 대화 직후에 할 일로 가장 적절한 것을 고르시오.

① 시청 찾아가기
② 도서관 가기
③ 신문 구입하기
④ 역사 다큐멘터리 보기
⑤ 인터넷 검색하기

[19~20] 대화를 듣고, 여자의 마지막 말에 이어질 남자의 응답으로 가장 적절한 것을 고르시오.

19 Man: _____

① That's fine with me.
② Sorry for being late.
③ We'll have a great time.
④ You can finish it in time.
⑤ It doesn't take a long time.

20 Man: _____

① Maybe next time.
② I know how you feel.
③ What are friends for?
④ That's easier said than done.
⑤ Keep my fingers crossed for you.

다시 들으면서 듣기 만점에 도전하세요!
Dictation: 스크립트의 주요 부분을 다시 들으면서!
실전 ➕: 세부 정보가 많은 스크립트를 다른 문제로 샅샅이!

---

01 그림 정보 파악 – 사물

방석의 모양과 그 안에 들어갈 말이 있다는 것을 파악한다.

대화를 듣고, 두 사람이 만들 방석으로 가장 적절한 것을 고르시오.

① ② ③ ④ ⑤

M Jenny, ＿＿＿＿＿＿ ＿＿＿＿＿ ＿＿＿＿＿ ＿＿＿＿ for mom as a birthday present?
　　　방석을 만드는 것이 어때

W Sounds great. What kind of cushion do you have in mind?

M I'd like a square one with a heart in the middle of it.

W Well, how about ＿＿＿＿＿ ＿＿＿＿＿＿ one with ＿＿＿＿＿ ＿＿＿＿＿,
　　　　　　　　　　하트 모양의
"＿＿＿＿＿＿＿＿＿＿" on it?
　"Love Mom"이라는 말

M Great! That would be ＿＿＿＿ ＿＿＿＿ ＿＿＿＿ ＿＿＿＿ ＿＿＿＿.
　　　　　　　　　　　네모난 것보다 더 좋다

W Okay. Let's make it.

---

02 직업 추론

여자는 운전과 관련 있는 일을 한다는 것을 파악한다.

대화를 듣고, 여자의 직업으로 가장 적절한 것을 고르시오.

① ② ③ ④ ⑤

W Would you ＿＿＿＿＿＿＿＿ ＿＿＿＿＿＿＿?
　　　　　안전벨트를 착용하다

M No, I don't want to.

W Well, put it on please.

M Why do I have to? You ＿＿＿＿＿＿ ＿＿＿＿＿.
　　　　　　　　　　절대 빨리 운전하지 않는다

W I know I don't drive fast, but it's much safer with your seatbelt on.

M Okay, I'll put it on.

W I hate this road. It's a very dangerous road. There are a lot of curves.

M I believe you ＿＿＿＿＿＿＿ ＿＿＿＿＿.
　　　　　　매우 안전하게 운전하다

---

03 심정 추론

여자가 응원하는 팀이 경기에서 진 것을 파악한다.

대화를 듣고, 여자의 심정으로 가장 적절한 것을 고르시오.

① relieved 안도한
② nervous 긴장된
③ excited 흥분한
④ lonely 외로운
⑤ disappointed 실망한

➕ 대화를 듣고, 남자의 마지막 말의 의도로 가장 적절한 것을 고르시오.

① 동의 ② 사과
③ 반대 ④ 의심
⑤ 비난

M Did you see the Champions league semi-final?

W Sure, I did. In fact, I supported Barcelona, but the result ＿＿＿＿＿＿
　　　　　　　　　　　　　　　　　　　　　　　　　　나를 몹시 실망시키다
＿＿＿＿＿ ＿＿＿＿＿.

M As for me, I can't tell how excited I was to see that match. It was fantastic.

W Frankly speaking, Munich players were ＿＿＿＿＿ ＿＿＿＿＿ ＿＿＿＿＿
　　　　　　　　　　　　　　　　　　　　　　더 활력이 있고 힘이 있는
than those of Barcelona.

M ＿＿＿＿＿ ＿＿＿＿＿ ＿＿＿＿＿.
　전적으로 동감이야

축구와 야구는 보는 것을 좋아하고 볼링은 여자가 좋아하는 운동임을 파악한다.

대화를 듣고, 남자가 잘하는 운동을 고르시오.

① 수영 swimming
② 축구 soccer
③ 농구 basketball
④ 야구 baseball
⑤ 볼링 bowling

➕ 대화를 듣고, 여자가 좋아하는 운동을 고르시오.

① 수영　　　② 축구
③ 농구　　　④ 야구
⑤ 볼링

W What are you reading, Allan?
M A sports magazine.
W You like sports?
M Sure. Almost every man likes sports.
W _____ _____ _____ _____?
　　어떤 운동들을 좋아하니
M Basketball, soccer, and baseball, I'd say.
W Are you good at them?
M I'm _____ _____. As for soccer and baseball, I
　　　농구는 아주 잘하다
_____ _____ _____. How about you?
단지 경기를 보는 것을 좋아하다
W Well! I don't like rough sports, so I like to go bowling.

대화를 듣고, 두 사람의 관계로 가장 적절한 것을 고르시오.

① 점원-고객 clerk-customer
② 은행원-고객 bank clerk-customer
③ 감독-선수 manager-player
④ 면접관-지원자 interviewer-interviewee
⑤ 경찰관-목격자 police-witness

M Now, Miss Baker. Look at the shoes on the table.
W Yes, they're the same shoes the man was wearing.
M And the bag?
W Yes, I saw him carrying it _____ _____
그가 은행 밖으로 나오고 있을 때
_____ _____.
M And _____ _____ _____ _____?
그밖의 다른 것을 기억하세요
W Hmm... Ah! He was wearing a white hat.
M Thank you for your help.
W I hope _____ _____ _____ as soon as possible.
당신은 그 남자를 잡을 수 있다

looking for books, borrow this book 등의 표현을 보고 장소를 추론한다.

대화를 듣고, 두 사람이 대화하는 장소로 가장 적절한 곳을 고르시오.

① bank 은행
② library 도서관
③ airport 공항
④ museum 박물관
⑤ bookstore 서점

I beg your pardon?는 '다시 한 번 말씀해 주시겠어요?'라는 뜻으로 상대방의 말을 되묻는 표현이다.

M Is this your first time here?
W Yes. I'm _____ _____. I'm looking for books about computers.
　　　　　신입생
M Come over here, please.
W _____ _____ _____ _____?
이 책을 빌릴 수 있나요
M Yes, you may. Please _____ _____ _____.
이 카드를 작성하다
W I beg your pardon?
M Write your name and student ID number on this card.

다음 그림의 상황에 가장 적절한 대화를 고르시오.

① W How did you get here? Did you take the train?
　 M No, I _____ _____ _____. It's a lot faster.
여기에 비행기로 왔다
② W I'll send you something nice for your birthday.
　 M Really? Thank you. That's so nice of you.
③ W How much is it for two people to go to Seoul?
　 M It is 50,000 won, but if you buy the tickets online, it's cheaper.
④ W How would you like to send this package to Canada?
　 M How much would it cost by air?
⑤ W I have _____ _____ _____ to you. Are you home now?
배달할 소포 하나
　 M Yes, I am. What time are you coming

①　　②　　③　　④　　⑤

08 시각 파악

영화가 시작되는 시간에 남아 있는 시간을 빼면 현재 시각이 나온다.

대화를 듣고, 현재 시각을 고르시오.

① 4:40
② 5:00
③ 5:10
④ 5:20
⑤ 5:30

W Look at the crowd. Do you think we'll still be able to get tickets?

M Come on! We're already here. Besides, I want to see this movie.

W All right! _____ _____ _____ _____ ?
영화가 언제 시작하니

M _____.
5시 30분에

W Five-thirty? There's only _____ _____ _____. But look at the long line
20분 남다
and it's moving so slowly.

M Let's see the next movie.

W Sorry, but I have to be home before nine.

09 특정 정보 파악

대화를 듣고, 여자가 태어난 곳을 고르시오.

① Italy 이탈리아
② Spain 스페인
③ Canada 캐나다
④ America 미국
⑤ Australia 오스트레일리아, 호주

M Do you live around here?

W No. Actually, _____ _____, _____.
나는 캐나다 몬트리올 출신이다

M Were you born there?

W Well, I _____ _____ _____, but my family moved to Canada
스페인에서 태어났다
when I was eight.

M _____ _____ _____ _____ ?
스페인 어를 말할 수 있니

W Sure, how about you? Are you American?

M No, I'm Australian, from Sydney.

10 주제 파악

다음을 듣고, 무엇에 관한 안내인지 가장 적절한 것을 고르시오.

① 경품 행사
② 노래 경연
③ 할인 판매
④ 성금 모금
⑤ 신상품 소개

W Welcome to JB Music Store. Today we _____ _____ _____
for you. 특별행사를 하다 $1,000 worth of CDs here. If you
~의 기회를 잡다 _____ _____ _____
just buy any two CDs, your name will go into competition. _____
_____ _____ from many different kinds of rock, pop, jazz, and classical
당신 자신의 상품을 골라라
music. Good luck to you. Thank you.

11 이유 파악

마지막 부분에서 이유를 파악할 수 있다.

대화를 듣고, 여자가 화가 난 이유로 가장 적절한 것을 고르시오.

① 자기를 말로 무시해서
② 선물을 안 주어서
③ 물건을 빌려주지 않아서
④ 약속을 지키지 않아서
⑤ 돈을 갚지 않아서

M What's wrong with you? You look upset.

W I'm upset with what you have said to me.

M What did I say?

W You belittled me.

M I don't know what you are talking about.

W Yesterday when you told me to email you the file, I _____ _____
_____ because I didn't know how to do that. Then, you said shouting on the
몹시 당황했다
phone, "You don't even know that?"

M I'm sorry I _____ _____ _____. I won't do so next time.
감정을 상하게 하다

12 목적 파악

대화를 듣고, 남자가 여자를 방문한 목적으로 가장 적절한 것을 고르시오.

① 제품을 판매하려고
② 우편물을 배달하려고
③ 친구를 병문안 하려고
④ 주문 상품을 배달하려고
⑤ 습득물을 되돌려 주려고

How do you do?는 처음 만난 사이에 하는 인사말 표현이다.

[Someone knocks the door.]

M Hello. Does Mr. Raymond live here?

W Yes. He's my husband.

M I'm Jimmy Douglas at SMS Taxi Company. How do you do?

W How do you do? Is there a problem?

M Your husband _____ _____ _____ _____
　　　　　　　　　그의 가방을 내 택시에 놓고 내렸다
this morning.

W Oh, thank you! This is very nice of you.

M Don't mention it. This is only _____ _____ _____ .
　　　　　　　　　　　　　　　　　　　내 임무들 중 하나

---

13 특정 정보 파악

마지막에 바뀐 요일과 시각에 유의한다.

대화를 듣고, 두 사람이 다음 약속한 때를 고르시오.

① 월요일 오후 4시
② 수요일 오전 9시
③ 수요일 오후 4시
④ 목요일 오전 9시
⑤ 목요일 오후 4시

M Hello, what problem do you have?

W For about six months, whenever I work on the computer, I've been feeling pain on the back.

M How long do you work on the computer every day?

W All day long. _____ _____ _____ it because of my job.
　　　　　　　어쩔 수가 없다

M From now on, you have to exercise every day _____ _____ _____
_____ on the leaflet I will give you. See you at 9 next Wednesday.
　　　　　　　　　　　　　　　지시에 따라

W Sorry, I can't. How about Thursday afternoon?

M OK. I can make it by 4.

W Thank you. I'll see you then.

---

14 내용 일치 파악

beautiful and tall, a nurse, works at, 28 years old를 듣고 Sarah에 대해 언급되지 않은 것을 찾는다.

대화를 듣고, Sarah에 관해 알 수 **없는** 것을 고르시오.

① 외모
② 나이
③ 직업
④ 취미
⑤ 근무처

What does she do?는 직업을 묻는 표현으로 뒤에 for a living이 생략되어 있다.

M Who is that girl over there?

W Oh, that's Sarah. _____ _____ _____ _____ ?
　　　　　　　　　　　그녀는 예쁘고 키가 크지 않니

M Yes, she is. What does she do?

W She is _____ _____ . She works at the Grand Central Hospital in New York
　　　　　　　간호사
City.

M Um. She is young, isn't she?

W Yeah. She looks very young, but _____ _____ _____ . And
　　　　　　　　　　　　　　　　　　　그녀는 28살이다
she went to high school with me.

15

대화를 듣고, 남자가 여자에게 하는 충고로 가장 적절한 것을 고르시오.

① 공공장소에서 인터넷 사용에 유의하라.
② 인터넷 비밀번호는 자주 바꾸어야 한다.
③ 노트북 컴퓨터보다 데스크탑을 사라.
④ 인터넷에서 노트북을 구입하지 마라.
⑤ 인터넷에서 물건을 구입하는 것이 훨씬 저렴하다.

M Oh, you bought a new laptop! It _____ _____ _____.
_{얇고 가벼워 보이다}

W This is the latest model. Now, I can use the Internet _____
_{그들이 제공하는 곳은 어디든지}
free wireless Internet access, like coffee shops and libraries.

M Just so you know, you need to be careful when you use the Internet in free public Wifi areas. Hackers can easily _____ _____ such as your passwords,
_{모든 것을 들여다 보다}
your bank accounts.

W Really?

M Yes, I'm serious. It is not safe to use the Internet like here at the cafe. But I think it will be okay to check your mails, or _____ _____.
_{인터넷을 검색하다}

W Thanks for your advice.

16 실용문 정보 파악

다음 메모를 보면서 대화를 듣고, 내용과 일치하지 <u>않는</u> 것을 고르시오.

Memo

To : ① Mr. Parker
From : ② Dean Martin
Message : ③ Car repair will have been finished
④ at 5 p.m.
Charge : ⑤ 113 dollars

[Telephone rings.]

M Hello. May I speak to Mr. Parker?

W I'm afraid he isn't here right now. Can I _____ _____?
_{메시지를 받아 두다}

M Yes. This is Dean Martin from _____ _____ _____ _____.
_{BMB 자동차 수리점}

W Dean Martin from the repair shop?

M Yes. I'm calling to tell him his car will be ready at five this afternoon. _____ _____ _____.
_{수리비는 130달러이다}

W Okay. I'll give him the message.

M Thanks.

17 부탁한 일 파악

대화를 듣고, 남자가 여자에게 요청한 일로 가장 적절한 것을 고르시오.

① 예약 확인하기   ② 예약 취소하기
③ 인원수 추가하기   ④ 시간 변경하기
⑤ 음식 주문하기

[Telephone rings.]

W Napoli Bistro, how may I help you?

M Hi, my name is Nick, and I made a reservation for tonight.

W Hold on. Yes, here it is. Your reservation is for four people at seven, right?

M Yes, that's correct. But I'd like to _____ _____ _____.
_{변경하다}

W What would you like to change?

M Can I add two more people? Is there a table for six?

W Let me check, please. *[pause]* Yes, luckily, there is one available.

M Awesome, thanks.

W Great, I'll _____ _____ _____ _____ this evening then.
_{7시에 보다}

대화를 듣고, 여자가 대화 직후에 할 일로 가장 적절한 것을 고르시오.

① 시청 찾아가기
② 도서관 가기
③ 신문 구입하기
④ 역사 다큐멘터리 보기
⑤ 인터넷 검색하기

W Hi, Mr. Jackson, can I ask you for some advice?

M Of course, what is it about?

W It's about my new project. You know, I'm researching _____ _____ _____ _____, but I can't get much information after the 1970s.

우리 마을의 역사

M Why don't you check out the library? They keep all the old newspapers there.

W That's a great idea. Why didn't I think of that?

M Maybe you _____ _____ _____ the Internet?

~에 너무 많이 의존하다

W That's true. Thank you. I think I'll go check right away.

독감으로 누워 있는 친구의 병문안을 가기로 하고 시간을 제안하고 있음을 파악한다.

[19~20] 대화를 듣고, 여자의 마지막 말에 이어질 남자의 응답으로 가장 적절한 것을 고르시오.

Man: _____

① That's fine with me.
② Sorry for being late.
③ We'll have a great time.
④ You can finish it in time.
⑤ It doesn't take a long time.

W I haven't seen Clark in class for a few days.

M I heard he's _____ _____ with the flu.

아파서 침대에 누워 있다

W Really? Should we _____ _____ and _____ _____ _____?

잠깐 들르다   그가 어떤지 보다

M Okay. When do you want to go?

W How about today, after school?

M _____

Man: _____

① Maybe next time.
② I know how you feel.
③ What are friends for?
④ That's easier said than done.
⑤ Keep my fingers crossed for you.

M It's not so easy for me to _____ _____ _____ together with Jane.

프로젝트를 수행하다

W Is that so?

M I don't know what she is so busy with. I can't even get to see her easily.

W But there's no other way. You guys _____ _____ _____ _____, but you still have to work together to finish the project before the deadline.

잘 지내지 못하다

W She isn't answering my phone, so that drives me crazy.

W Still, you need to calm down and _____ _____ _____ _____ with smile.

도움을 구하다

M _____

언급 유무 / 내용 불일치

무엇을 평가하는가?	일상생활 관련 대상이나 친숙한 일반적 주제에 관한 말이나 대화를 듣고 세부 정보를 파악할 수 있는지를 평가한다.

어떻게 출제되는가?	• 대화를 듣고, 여자가 미술관에서 지켜야 할 사항으로 언급하지 않은 것을 고르시오. • 다음을 듣고, 벼룩시장에 대한 내용과 일치하지 않는 것을 고르시오.

key solution

❶ 선택지를 통해 주의해서 들어야 할 내용을 숙지한 뒤, 선택지를 지워가며 정답을 찾는다.

❷ 대화의 경우, 질문과 대답을 통해 선택지의 내용이 제시됨으로 집중하며 듣는다.

[기출로 전략 확인]

대화를 듣고, 두 사람이 여행에 관해 언급하지 <u>않은</u> 것을 고르시오.　　　　　[2017 기출]

① 여름 옷　　　　　② 현지 날씨　　　　　③ 여행 목적지
④ 식사 메뉴　　　　　⑤ 숙소 이름

....

W Hi, Dad.
M Hi, Jihee. Are you excited about the family trip?
W Sure, I can't wait to go to the Philippines.
M Yeah, I just got information from the travel agency.
W Cool. Did they say anything about the weather?
M Yes, it'll be very hot.
W Okay, then I should bring summer clothes.
M Right. They also told us we would stay at the Star Hotel.
W It looks like we're ready for the trip then.

❷ 질문과 대답을 통해 여행 목적지, 현지 날씨, 여름 옷, 숙소 이름이 언급되었다.

여 안녕하세요, 아빠.
남 안녕, Jihee. 가족 여행 기대하고 있니?
여 물론이죠. 필리핀에 가는 게 너무 기다려져요.
남 그래. 여행사에서 방금 정보를 받았단다.
여 잘됐네요. 거기 날씨에 대한 정보도 있나요?
남 그래. 아주 덥다고 하는 구나.
여 알겠어요. 그럼 여름 옷을 챙겨야 겠네요
남 그래. 그리고 우리가 Star Hotel에서 묵을 거라고 했단다.
여 여행을 위한 준비가 다 된 거 같네요.

언급 유무·내용 불일치 파악의 발문과 보기

다음을 듣고, 여자가 학교 축제에 대해 언급하지 <u>않은</u> 것을 고르시오. [2016 기출]

① 장소   ② 공연 내용   ③ 점심시간
④ 축제 시작 시간   ⑤ 복장

만점 잡는 문장

① It will be held in the gym tomorrow.
② There will be performances such as dancing, singing, and a magic show.
③ The festival will start at 10:00 a.m.
④ Don't forget to wear your school uniform.

다음을 듣고, 여자의 말에 대한 내용으로 일치하지 <u>않는</u> 것을 고르시오. [2016 기출]

① Dream Resort에서 머물 예정이다.
② 4일 동안 지금 도착한 숙소에 머물 것이다.
③ 오늘은 얼음낚시를 할 예정이다.
④ 오늘 저녁에는 비프 스테이크를 먹을 것이다.
⑤ 내일은 수영장을 무료로 이용할 수 있다.

만점 잡는 문장   W We're going to stay here for 2 days.

언급 유무·내용 불일치 파악하기에 쓰이는 표현

● 장소

A Where are we going to meet this Saturday? 토요일에 어디서 볼까?
B The meeting will be in classroom 203. 회의는 203호에서 열릴 거야.

The event will be held on the school playground. 행사는 학교 운동장에서 열립니다.
Our cafeteria is on the first floor of the building. 우리 카페는 빌딩 일층에 있습니다.

● 시간/기간

We're going to stay here for 2 days. 우린 여기서 이틀 간 머물 거야.
We are open from 9 a.m. to 6 p.m. 우리는 9시부터 6시까지 엽니다.

A When does it start? 그건 언제 시작하나요?
B It starts next week. 다음 주에 시작해요.

Lunch starts at 12:30, and it's open for one hour.
점심은 12시 반에 시작하고 한 시간 동안 엽니다.

A How long did you stay there? 그곳에서 얼마나 머물렀니?
B For four days. 나흘 동안.

01 다음 그림의 상황에 가장 적절한 대화를 고르시오.

① ② ③ ④ ⑤

고난도
02 대화를 듣고, 내용과 일치하는 그림을 고르시오.

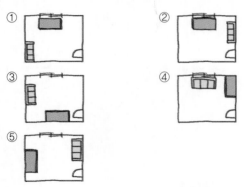

03 대화를 듣고, 두 사람이 먼저 할 일로 가장 적절한 것을 고르시오.

① 모노레일 타기 ② 롤러코스터 타기
③ 풍선 타기 ④ 스케이트 타기
⑤ 볼링 치기

04 대화를 듣고, 내용과 일치하지 <u>않는</u> 것을 고르시오.

① Product – Sweater ② Size – Large
③ Color – Black ④ Price – $ 9
⑤ Change – $ 2

05 대화를 듣고, 여자가 이용할 교통수단으로 가장 적절한 것을 고르시오.

① 버스 ② 자동차
③ 지하철 ④ 자전거
⑤ 택시

06 대화를 듣고, 내용에 가장 알맞은 안내 표지판을 고르시오.

① ②

③ ④

⑤

07 대화를 듣고, 두 사람의 관계로 가장 적절한 것을 고르시오.

① 경찰 – 시민 ② 서점 직원 – 손님
③ 여행사 직원 – 고객 ④ 여행안내소 직원 – 관광객
⑤ 도서관 사서 – 이용객

08 대화를 듣고, 두 사람이 대화하는 장소로 가장 적절한 곳을 고르시오.

① 병원 ② 쇼핑몰
③ 주차장 ④ 지하철역
⑤ 자동차 수리소

09 다음을 듣고, 남자가 하는 말의 내용으로 가장 적절한 것을 고르시오.

① 안전 예방 수칙 ② 재활용 방법
③ 미래 기후 변화 ④ 지구 환경 변화
⑤ 환경 보호 방법

10 대화를 듣고, 여자가 대화 직후에 할 일로 가장 적절한 것을 고르시오.

① 목욕
② 준비운동
③ 병원 진찰
④ 클럽 가입
⑤ 마무리 스트레칭

11 대화를 듣고, 여자가 남자에게 부탁한 일로 가장 적절한 것을 고르시오.

① 경기 응원하러 오기　② 간식 준비해주기
③ 샌드위치 사다주기　④ 외식하러 나가기
⑤ 저녁식사 요리하기

12 대화를 듣고, 남자가 여자에게 말을 건 목적으로 가장 적절한 것을 고르시오.

① 내일 결석하려고
② 과제를 연기하려고
③ 과제의 주제를 바꾸려고
④ 과제 제출 방식을 문의하려고
⑤ 좋은 점수를 달라고 부탁하려고

13 대화를 듣고, Mr. Lee에 관한 내용과 일치하지 <u>않는</u> 것을 고르시오.

① 여행을 많이 한다.
② 국립 오페라단에서 일한다.
③ 일하지 않을 때에는 친구들과 함께 시간을 보낸다.
④ 비싼 음식을 사먹는 것을 좋아한다.
⑤ Susan의 옆집에 살고 있다.

14 대화를 듣고, 여자의 마지막 말의 의도로 가장 적절한 것을 고르시오.

① 사과　　② 동의　　③ 축하
④ 불평　　⑤ 반대

고난도
15 대화를 듣고, 내용과 일치하지 <u>않는</u> 것을 고르시오.

① Sarah has around ten pen pals.
② Sarah writes letters on weekends.
③ Sarah writes letters in English and French.
④ Sarah has been to France.
⑤ Sarah has learned French for two years.

16 대화를 듣고, 두 사람의 심정으로 가장 적절한 것을 고르시오.

① worried　　② satisfied
③ lonely　　④ bored
⑤ scared

17 대화를 듣고, 두 사람이 만날 시각을 고르시오.

① 12시　　② 1시
③ 2시　　④ 2시 30분
⑤ 3시

18 대화를 듣고, 남자가 주말에 한 일로 가장 적절한 것을 고르시오.

① 숙제하기　　② 이웃집 일손 돕기
③ 집안 청소하기　　④ 음식 준비하기
⑤ 설거지하기

[19~20] 대화를 듣고, 여자의 마지막 말에 이어질 남자의 응답으로 가장 적절한 것을 고르시오.

고난도
19 Man: _____

① I guess there's only one left.
② I'm afraid it will be expensive.
③ I hope you will have a good time.
④ Hurry up, or you'll be late.
⑤ Sure. I'm strong enough to lift it by myself.

20 Man: _____

① I'm just joking.
② I'll be there soon.
③ I'm a stranger here, too.
④ Sorry, I can't join you.
⑤ I hope not. Take care.

다시 들으면서 듣기 만점에 도전하세요!
Dictation: 스크립트의 주요 부분을 다시 들으면서!
실전 ⊕: 세부 정보가 많은 스크립트를 다른 문제로 샅샅이!

---

01 그림 상황 대화 찾기

다음 그림의 상황에 가장 적절한 대화를 고르시오.

① ② ③ ④ ⑤

① **M** Do you see her?

　W Oh, yes.... She's sitting at the table at the back of the coffee shop.

② **M** We can't park here. Look at the sign.

　W No problem. I'll be back in a moment.

③ **M** Are there any coffee shops around here?

　W Oh, yeah, lots. There's one ＿＿＿＿＿ ＿＿＿＿＿ ＿＿＿＿＿.
　　　　　　　　　　　　　　　　　　저기 저쪽에

④ **M** Can you show me how?

　W Sure. Look at me. You place your hands behind your back.

⑤ **M** You ＿＿＿＿＿ ＿＿＿＿＿ ＿＿＿＿＿ by yourself.
　　　　　테이블을 옮겨서는 안 된다

　W Maybe you're right. ＿＿＿＿＿ ＿＿＿＿＿ ＿＿＿＿＿ ＿＿＿＿＿ a
　　　　　　　　　　　　　내 등이 아픈 것 같다
little.

고난도

02 내용 일치 파악

대화를 듣고, 내용과 일치하는 그림을 고르시오.

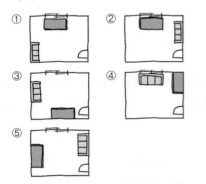

① ② ③ ④ ⑤

Can you give me a hand?는 '저를 좀 도와주시겠어요?'라는 뜻의 상대방에게 도움을 요청하는 표현이다.

next to, in front of 라는 표현에 주의해서 듣는다

W I'd like to ＿＿＿＿＿ ＿＿＿＿＿. Can you give me a hand?
　　　　　　　　이 방을 재배치하다

M Sure. What can I do for you?

W OK. Put the sofa ＿＿＿＿＿ ＿＿＿＿＿ ＿＿＿＿＿.
　　　　　　　　　　　　문 옆에

M Next to the door?

W Yes, please.

M And where do you want the desk?

W I'd like it ＿＿＿＿＿ ＿＿＿＿＿ the window.
　　　　　　　　　~ 앞에

M Are you sure?

W Yeah. That looks good.

---

03 할 일 파악

대화를 듣고, 두 사람이 먼저 할 일로 가장 적절한 것을 고르시오.

① 모노레일 타기
② 롤러코스터 타기
③ 풍선 타기
④ 스케이트 타기
⑤ 볼링 치기

M Wow! This is ＿＿＿＿＿ ＿＿＿＿＿ ＿＿＿＿＿ theme park in the world.
　　　　　　　　가장 큰 실내의

W Really? It would be terrific! I really enjoy riding a roller-coaster and balloons.

M In addition to the rides here, we can ice-skate in the center field.

W Why don't we ＿＿＿＿＿ ＿＿＿＿＿? After that, let's ride the most exciting
　　　　　　　　　　먼저 스케이트 타러 가다
thing—roller-coaster! OK?

M Sure. I don't mind either way.

04 내용 일치 파악

숫자, 색깔, 지불 방법 등의 표현들에 유의한다.

대화를 듣고, 내용과 일치하지 <u>않는</u> 것을 고르시오.

① Product – Sweater
② Size – Large
③ Color – Black
④ Price – $ 9
⑤ Change – $ 2

M Excuse me. I'm _____ _____ _____ .
<small>스웨터를 찾고 있는</small>

W What size do you want?

M Medium.

W I don't think medium _____ _____ _____ .
<small>당신에게 맞다</small>

M Okay, give me large one.

W And what color do you want? We have white, black, and red.

M Black is good. How much is it?

W _____ _____ _____ .
<small>9달러이다</small>

M Here's _____ _____ _____ .
<small>10달러짜리 지폐</small>

W Here's your change. Thank you.

---

05 특정 정보 파악

대화를 듣고, 여자가 이용할 교통수단으로 가장 적절한 것을 고르시오.

① 버스 bus
② 자동차 car
③ 지하철 subway
④ 자전거 bicycle
⑤ 택시 taxi

➕ 대화를 듣고, 남자가 처음에 제안한 교통수단으로 가장 적절한 것을 고르시오

① 버스   ② 자동차 car
③ 지하철   ④ 자전거
⑤ 택시

W Excuse me, how long does it take to go from here to the National Museum?

M Oh, it's _____ _____ _____ . You'd better take a bus at this
<small>걷기에는 너무 먼</small>
stop.

W OK. What number bus do I have to take?

M Take bus number 150. It will take 15 minutes.

W Is there a subway station near here?

M There's one _____ _____ _____ . That will take longer.
<small>2블록 떨어진</small>

W I'm a stranger here in Korea. So using _____ _____ _____
<small>지하철이 더 편하다</small>
_____ for me.

---

06 실용문 정보 파악

run out of gas 라는 표현을 이해하면 쉽게 답을 찾을 수 있다.

대화를 듣고, 내용에 가장 알맞은 안내 표지판을 고르시오.

① ② ③ ④ ⑤

W What seems to be the problem?

M I'm afraid we are about to _____ _____ _____ _____ . We need to
<small>기름이 떨어지다</small>
get some.

W We're in a remote village. We _____ _____ _____ around here. How
<small>기름을 얻을 수 없다</small>
much further can we go in the car?

M Around 25 kilometers. Look at the sign!

W Oh, we're _____ _____ _____ in this remote place.
<small>한 군데 있다니 다행이다</small>

07 관계 파악

대화를 듣고, 두 사람의 관계로 가장 적절한 것을 고르시오.

① 경찰 – 시민
② 서점 직원 – 손님
③ 여행사 직원 – 고객
④ 여행안내소 직원 – 관광객
⑤ 도서관 사서 – 이용객

M Hi, do you need any help?

W No, thanks. *[pause]* Actually, it would be nice if you can help me.

M Sure, what are you looking for?

W I'm going to Thailand, and I want to buy _____ _____ _____
여행 계획을 위한 책
_____ _____.

M What about this one? This series is very popular nowadays.

W I already checked it, but I want something with more maps and detailed information.

M Oh, then, I think this one is perfect for you. The writer _____ _____
~로 알려져 있다
_____ _____ very thorough.

08 장소 추론

대화를 듣고, 두 사람이 대화하는 장소로 가장 적절한 곳을 고르시오.

① 병원 hospital
② 쇼핑몰 shopping mall
③ 주차장 parking lot
④ 지하철역 subway station
⑤ 자동차 수리소 car repair shop

W Will you _____ _____ _____ _____ my car, please?
살펴보다

M What's the problem?

W Well, I'm not sure. But it's not running very well. It is making _____ _____
많은 소음
_____ _____.

M I'll _____ _____ _____ for you and find out what the trouble is.
엔진을 점검하다

W When will the work be finished?

M Let me see, the day after tomorrow.

09 말의 내용 파악(담화)

다음을 듣고, 남자가 하는 말의 내용으로 가장 적절한 것을 고르시오.

① 안전 예방 수칙
② 재활용 방법
③ 미래 기후 변화
④ 지구 환경 변화
⑤ 환경 보호 방법

M Hello, students! Our earth is getting more and more crowded, and many people aren't taking good care of it. If we keep going like this, it will _____
보호하기 힘들다
_____ _____ our planet. Do you want to help? First, recycling is good, but there is a step you can do before that. See if you can use those things again first. Second, don't waste resources. When you aren't using water or electricity, turn them off. Please remember that little things can _____ _____ _____
큰 차이를 만들다
_____.

10 할 일 파악

마지막 부분에서 남자가 한 말에 유의한다.

대화를 듣고, 여자가 대화 직후에 할 일로 가장 적절한 것을 고르시오.

① 목욕
② 준비운동
③ 병원 진찰
④ 클럽 가입
⑤ 마무리 스트레칭

M How are you today?

W My whole body aches. Yesterday I played badminton. It was really fun.

M Why don't you join the badminton club _____ _____ _____? I bet lots of
내가 속한
boys will happily help you out.

W _____ _____ _____! I heard you get shoulder and back injuries playing
농담하지 마
badminton.

M It could happen. So you need to do enough warm-up beforehand.

W How could I relieve my sore muscles?

M You can just _____ _____ _____ _____ for a little while.
뜨거운 욕조에 앉아 있다
That helps you feel better.

W That sounds good.

대화를 듣고, 여자가 남자에게 부탁한 일로 가장 적절한 것을 고르시오.

① 경기 응원하러 오기
② 간식 준비해주기
③ 샌드위치 사다주기
④ 외식하러 나가기
⑤ 저녁식사 요리하기

➕ 대화를 듣고, 여자의 기분이 좋은 이유로 가장 적절한 것을 고르시오.

① 학교가 끝나서   ② 숙제를 다 끝내서
③ 푹 쉬어서   ④ 배구 시합을 이겨서
⑤ 배가 불러서

W Hi, Dad. I'm home.

M Hi, Minyoung. Did you have a good day at school?

W Yes, it was a busy day. But I feel good because we _____ _____ .
배구 시합에서 이겼다

M That's great news. I know how hard you practiced. You must be very tired, though.

W Yes, and I'm very hungry. Is there anything to eat?

M Hmm, is a sandwich okay? I don't have _____ _____ _____ , but I can
요리할 시간
quickly make you a sandwich.

W That's just what I want, thanks! I want to have dinner later, too!

대화의 첫 부분에서 목적을 파악할 수 있다.

대화를 듣고, 남자가 여자에게 말을 건 목적으로 가장 적절한 것을 고르시오.

① 내일 결석하려고
② 과제를 연기하려고
③ 과제의 주제를 바꾸려고
④ 과제 제출 방식을 문의하려고
⑤ 좋은 점수를 달라고 부탁하려고

W What's up, Tom?

M I know the report is due today. But I'd like to ask you if I _____
그것을 제출할 수 있다
_____ _____ until tomorrow.

W Is there any problem with you?

M I'd like to have enough time to get a better report. So could you extend _____
마감기한
_____ _____ ?

W It wouldn't be fair if I gave you more time than other students. I suggest you finish up your assignment and hand it in today.

M I see. Thank you.

대화를 듣고, Mr. Lee에 관한 내용과 일치하지 <u>않는</u> 것을 고르시오.

① 여행을 많이 한다.
② 국립 오페라단에서 일한다.
③ 일하지 않을 때에는 친구들과 함께 시간을 보낸다.
④ 비싼 음식을 사먹는 것을 좋아한다.
⑤ Susan의 옆집에 살고 있다.

M What does Mr. Lee do, Susan?

W He works for the National Opera Company.

M Does he travel a lot?

W Yes. He does _____ _____ _____ for his work.
여행을 많이 하다

M What does he like to do when he's not working?

W He _____ _____ _____ with his friends. He _____ and
시간 보내는 것을 좋아하다   요리를 좋아하다
he likes to make dinner for his friends. He often _____
나를 저녁 식사에 초대한다
_____ .

M Does he live next door?

W Yes, he does. He sometimes visits my house with big gifts.

14 의도 추론

여자의 마지막 말 'I'm against ~.'에서 남자의 의견에 반대하고 있음을 알 수 있다.

대화를 듣고, 여자의 마지막 말의 의도로 가장 적절한 것을 고르시오.

① 사과
② 동의
③ 축하
④ 불평
⑤ 반대

M Oh, you look like _____ _____ _____.
　　　　　　　　　　　　　　　　살이 빠지다
W I exercise as often as I can. And I don't eat anything at night.
M I often do exercise, but I like eating snacks at night. It's difficult to keep from eating them.
W What time do you go to bed?
M I go to bed very late. I do a lot of things late at night.
W You should go to bed early. That's the best way to lose weight.
M What do you think of taking diet medicine?
W Well, I'm _____ diet medicine. It is _____ _____ _____
　　　　　먹는 것을 반대하다　　　　　　　　　　　　　　~에 좋지 않다
your health.

[고난도]

15 내용 일치 파악

선택지의 내용을 미리 읽고, 일치하는 내용들을 지워 나간다.

대화를 듣고, 내용과 일치하지 <u>않는</u> 것을 고르시오.

① Sarah has around ten pen pals.
② Sarah writes letters on weekends.
③ Sarah writes letters in English and French.
④ Sarah has been to France.
⑤ Sarah has learned French for two years.

M Do you collect stamps, Sarah?
W No, I collect postcards. I _____ _____ _____ around the
　　　　　　　　　　　　　　　펜팔 친구들이 많이 있다
world. They send them to me.
M Wow! Amazing! How many pen pals do you have?
W Around 10.
M That's great! When do you usually write letters?
W I usually write on weekends. I _____ _____ _____.
　　　　　　　　　　　　　　　　　　영어와 불어로 편지를 쓰다
M Do you speak French, too?
W Yes, a little bit. I've _____ _____ for two years.
　　　그것을 배워오다

---

16 심정 추론

대화를 듣고, 두 사람의 심정으로 가장 적절한 것을 고르시오.

① worried 걱정하는
② satisfied 만족하는
③ lonely 외로운
④ bored 지루한
⑤ scared 겁먹은

Neither do I.는 부정문에 동의하는 표현이다. 긍정문에 동의할 때는 So do I.라고 표현한다.

M Have you heard the news?
W What news?
M The city is planning to build tall apartment buildings near the river.
W _____ _____! The river is beautiful now.
　　　심각하네
M I agree. If apartments are built, water pollution will get worse.
W How are the citizens feeling about it?
M Some of them are _____ _____ _____ the city's plan, and others are
　　　　　　　　　　　　　　찬성하다
against it.
W I _____ _____ _____ are in favor of it.
　　~하는 사람들을 이해할 수 없다
M _____.
　　나도 그래

17 시각 파악

대화를 듣고, 두 사람이 만날 시각을 고르시오.

① 12시　　② 1시
③ 2시　　④ 2시 30분
⑤ 3시

make it은 '시간을 맞추다'라는 말로 약속 시간을 정할 때 쓰는 표현이다.

W The movie starts at three. How about meeting ____ ____ ____ <u>점심시간 정도에</u> and having lunch before the movie?

M I don't think I can make it then. I have to ____ ____ ____ <u>장을 보러 가다</u> at lunch time with my mom.

W Anyway, you will have lunch, won't you?

M Right. I'm going to have lunch with my mom at a fast food restaurant. Can you ____ ____ ____ ____ <u>2시에 만나다</u> ?

W Sure. See you then. Let's meet at the subway station.

18 한 일 파악

대화를 듣고, 남자가 주말에 한 일로 가장 적절한 것을 고르시오.

① 숙제하기
② 이웃집 일손 돕기
③ 집안 청소하기
④ 음식 준비하기
⑤ 설거지하기

W Hi, Jamie. Did you have a good weekend?

M Yes, I did. I'm a little tired, but that's OK.

W Why are you tired? There was no homework on the weekend. I thought you'd ____ ____ ____ <u>휴식을 취하다</u> .

M I know, but my parents invited some neighbors over, and I ____ ____ ____ <u>그들이 준비하는 걸 도왔다</u> .

W What did you do?

M I cleaned the house with my dad, while my mom was cooking.

W What about your sister?

M Oh, she helped mom with the cooking and washed the dishes.

고난도

19 알맞은 응답 찾기

부탁에 대한 응답으로 기꺼이 승낙한다는 표현(Sure, Of course 등)이 와야 한다.

[19~20] 대화를 듣고, 여자의 마지막 말에 이어질 남자의 응답으로 가장 적절한 것을 고르시오.

Man: _____

① I guess there's only one left.
② I'm afraid it will be expensive.
③ I hope you will have a good time.
④ Hurry up, or you'll be late.
⑤ Sure. I'm strong enough to lift it by myself.

W I've decided to throw away this sofa.

M How long ____ ____ ____ <u>너는 그것을 사용했다</u> ?

W I have had it for five years.

M That's not a long time. Why do you want to ____ ____ ____ <u>그것을 버리다</u> ?

W Tom gave me a better sofa. Could you give me a hand? I'd like to ____ ____ ____ <u>이것을 밖으로 옮기다</u> .

M _____

20 알맞은 응답 찾기

Man: _____

① I'm just joking.
② I'll be there soon.
③ I'm a stranger here, too.
④ Sorry, I can't join you.
⑤ I hope not. Take care.

M It's raining again.

W Again? I hate this weather. It was sunny about half an hour ago. I can't stand this weather.

M Don't you have an umbrella?

W No, I don't. I'll have to get one at the grocery store.

M You have to ____ ____ ____ <u>우산을 가지고 다니다</u> with you all the time in this type of weather.

W OK, I will. Oh, ____ ____ <u>날씨가 점점 추워지다</u> . I'm afraid I am ____ <u>감기에 걸리는</u> ____ now.

M _____

01 다음을 듣고, 어떤 운동 경기에 대한 설명인지 가장 적절한 것을 고르시오.

02 대화를 듣고, 남자가 갖게 될 물건으로 가장 적절한 것을 고르시오.

03 다음 그림의 상황에 가장 적절한 대화를 고르시오.

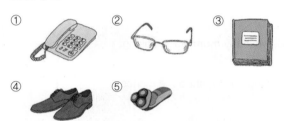

① ② ③ ④ ⑤

04 대화를 듣고, 두 사람의 관계로 가장 적절한 것을 고르시오.

① 치과의사 – 환자 ② 약사 – 손님
③ 병원 접수직원 – 고객 ④ 교사 – 학생
⑤ 사진작가 – 모델

05 대화를 듣고, 남자가 하는 말의 의도로 가장 적절한 것을 고르시오.

① 사과 ② 축하
③ 경고 ④ 조언
⑤ 칭찬

06 대화를 듣고, 두 사람이 그림을 걸 곳을 고르시오.

07 대화를 듣고, 남자가 체중 감량을 위해 섭취하지 않은 것을 고르시오.

① 콩 ② 돼지고기
③ 닭고기 ④ 녹차
⑤ 아이스크림

08 대화를 듣고, 남자가 전화를 건 목적으로 가장 적절한 것을 고르시오.

① Jane의 안부를 물어보려고
② 전화 메시지를 확인하려고
③ 파티 시간에 대해 물어보려고
④ 파티에 못 가는 것을 알려주려고
⑤ 파티 장소가 변경된 것을 알려주려고

고난도
09 대화를 듣고, 두 사람이 만날 시각을 고르시오.

① 7:00 ② 7:10
③ 7:20 ④ 7:30
⑤ 7:40

10 다음을 듣고, 전화 메모의 내용과 일치하지 않는 것을 고르시오.

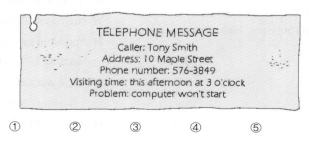

① ② ③ ④ ⑤

점수

/20

11 다음을 듣고, 남자에 관해 알 수 <u>없는</u> 것을 고르시오.

① 이름
② 기상 시간
③ 근무하는 동물원 이름
④ 동물들에게 아침 식사를 주는 시간
⑤ 오후에 하는 일

12 대화를 듣고, 내일 오후의 날씨로 가장 적절한 것을 고르시오.

① sunny   ② snowy
③ cloudy   ④ windy
⑤ rainy

고난도
13 대화를 듣고, 여자가 목표로 하고 있는 체중을 고르시오.

① 55kg   ② 60kg
③ 63kg   ④ 67kg
⑤ 70kg

14 대화를 듣고, 두 사람이 대화하는 장소로 가장 적절한 곳을 고르시오.

① 호텔   ② 음식점
③ 가구점   ④ 회의장
⑤ 음악회장

15 대화를 듣고, 두 사람이 오후에 함께 할 일로 가장 적절한 것을 고르시오.

① 공부하기
② 보고서 제출하기
③ 방학 계획 세우기
④ 서점에서 책 사기
⑤ 도서관에서 책 빌리기

16 다음을 듣고, 여자가 하는 말의 내용으로 가장 적절한 것을 고르시오.

① 근면한 생활습관의 중요성
② 하루를 알차게 보내는 법
③ 건강한 뇌를 위한 생활 습관
④ 충분한 수면의 중요성
⑤ 학습 능률 향상을 위한 방법

고난도
17 대화를 듣고, Mark에 관한 내용과 일치하지 <u>않는</u> 것을 고르시오.

① 오렌지 주스를 들고 있다.
② 안경을 쓰고 있다.
③ 피아노를 치고 있다.
④ 긴 머리를 하고 있다.
⑤ 흰 양복을 입고 있다.

18 대화를 듣고, 남자의 심정으로 가장 적절한 것을 고르시오.

① angry
② bored
③ excited
④ satisfied
⑤ frightened

[19~20] 대화를 듣고, 남자의 마지막 말에 이어질 여자의 응답으로 가장 적절한 것을 고르시오.

19 Woman: _____

① I will stop it.
② Because I have to.
③ I will keep that in mind.
④ I run in the park every evening.
⑤ Losing weight is not easy at all.

20 Woman: _____

① That's fine with me.
② I think I'm getting old.
③ Thank you for giving me a tip.
④ Action speak louder than words.
⑤ Don't worry. It's not too late yet.

영어듣기능력평가 **14** 회 DICTATION

다시 들으면서 듣기 만점에 도전하세요!
Dictation: 스크립트의 주요 부분을 다시 들으면서!
실전 ➊: 세부 정보가 많은 스크립트를 다른 문제로 살살이!

---

01 그림 정보 파악 – 사물

다음을 듣고, 어떤 운동 경기에 대한 설명인지 가장 적절한 것을 고르시오.

① ② ③ ④ ⑤

W When you play this, you need ＿＿＿＿ ＿＿＿＿ ＿＿＿＿ ＿＿＿＿
_{라켓과 가벼운 공}
＿＿＿＿ . You can't play this alone. You need a partner. You and your partner play this
game on a hard table, and it is ＿＿＿＿ ＿＿＿＿ ＿＿＿＿ . The ball
_{네트로 나뉘어져}
must bounce on your side only once. Then you ＿＿＿＿ ＿＿＿＿
_{그것을 쳐서 넘기다}
＿＿＿＿ ＿＿＿＿ to the other opposite side.

---

02 특정 정보 파악

대화를 듣고, 남자가 갖게 될 물건으로 가장 적절한 것을 고르시오.

① ② ③ ④ ⑤

vision, eyeglasses store 등에서 정답을 알 수 있다.

M I can't read books these days. My vision gets blurry.

W Oh, dad. It proves that you are getting older. You ＿＿＿＿＿＿ ＿＿＿＿ .
_{원시임에 틀림없다}
You need to go to the eyeglasses store.

M That's what I need to do.

W I know one of the stores. It's not far from our house.

M OK. Let's go there together.

---

03 그림 상황 대화 찾기

다음 그림의 상황에 가장 적절한 대화를 고르시오.

① ② ③ ④ ⑤

관광 안내소(TOURIST INFORMATION)에서 나눌 수 있는 대화를 찾는다.

① M Do you go to the movies very often?
　 W Yes. I go to the movies every weekend.

② M Could you give me a copy of this photo?
　 W Okay. Do you want it in the same size?

③ M Would you suggest ＿＿＿＿＿＿ ＿＿＿＿ in this city?
　　　　　　　　　　　　　_{흥미로운 장소 몇 군데}
　 W Sure. First of all, ＿＿＿＿ ＿＿＿＿ Seoul Tower.
　　　　　　　　　　_{놓치지 마라}

④ M Did you buy this tour guide book?
　 W Yes, I bought it in ABC Bookstore yesterday.

⑤ M Would you please ＿＿＿＿ ＿＿＿＿ ＿＿＿＿ for me?
　　　　　　　　　　　_{사진을 찍다}
　 W Sure. Where would you like to stand?

대화를 듣고, 두 사람의 관계로 가장 적절한 것을 고르시오.

① 치과의사 – 환자
② 약사 – 손님
③ 병원 접수직원 – 고객
④ 교사 – 학생
⑤ 사진작가 – 모델

M Okay, let me see. Open your mouth, please.

W Sure. *[pause]* Do I have any cavities?

M I'm afraid so. There's one. You will have to get it treated.

W Is it bad? I didn't know, because it didn't hurt.

M No, it's not too bad, but we should take care of it ＿＿＿＿＿ ＿＿＿＿＿ ＿＿＿＿＿
가능한 한 빨리
＿＿＿＿＿ .

W What about today? I have time.

M Today, you will just get your teeth cleaned. I'll take care of the cavity ＿＿＿＿＿
＿＿＿＿＿ ＿＿＿＿＿ ＿＿＿＿＿ .
다음 방문 시에

W Oh, okay. I will make another appointment.

대화를 듣고, 남자가 하는 말의 의도로 가장 적절한 것을 고르시오.

① 사과
② 축하
③ 경고
④ 조언
⑤ 칭찬

Why don't you ~?는 '~하는 게 어때?'라는 뜻으로 상대방에게 제안을 할 때 쓰는 표현이다.

➕
대화를 듣고, 여자가 대화 후에 할 일로 가장 적절한 것을 고르시오.

① Jessica와 얘기하기
② 휴대폰 숨기기
③ 이메일 쓰기
④ 사무실에 전화하기
⑤ 상사와 상담하기

M What's wrong? You look angry.

W Jessica really makes me angry in the office. She sometimes uses my Cellphone without my permission.

M Really? If I were you, I would ＿＿＿＿＿ ＿＿＿＿＿ ＿＿＿＿＿ .
그녀에게 그만하라고 말하다

W I've tried that, but she just keeps doing it.

M Why don't you ＿＿＿＿＿ ＿＿＿＿＿ about her?
사장에게 말하다

W I'm not sure I have to do that.

M Maybe ＿＿＿＿＿ ＿＿＿＿＿ ＿＿＿＿＿ to change her bad behavior.
그게 유일한 방법이다

W Okay. I'll do that right now.

대화를 듣고, 두 사람이 그림을 걸 곳을 고르시오.

W Could you please help me ＿＿＿＿＿ ＿＿＿＿＿ ＿＿＿＿＿ ?
이 그림을 옮기다

M Sure I can. Are you going to put it over your desk?

W I don't know. It would ＿＿＿＿＿ ＿＿＿＿＿ on my study. I thought I'd
집중력을 혼란스럽게 하다
hang it above the door.

M Who likes putting such a picture above the door? And the picture is too big.

W Then where do you think is the right place for it?

M I think it would be nice to ＿＿＿＿＿ ＿＿＿＿＿ ＿＿＿＿＿ ＿＿＿＿＿ .
책상 위에 두다
There is no other space for it.

W OK. Let's do that.

남자가 체중 감량을 위해 먹은 것들을 순서대로 정확히 파악한다.

대화를 듣고, 남자가 체중 감량을 위해 섭취하지 <u>않은</u> 것을 고르시오.

① 콩 bean
② 돼지고기 pork
③ 닭고기 chicken
④ 녹차 green tea
⑤ 아이스크림 ice cream

W You've changed a lot. You look very slim.

M I've lost ten kilograms in the last three months.

W How did you lose that much weight? Did you eat only vegetables?

M No, but I had lots of them, _____ _____ . And I
특히 콩   녹차를 마셨다
_____ whenever I felt hungry.

W Did you stop eating meat?

M No, but I _____ _____ _____ , not pork.
닭고기만 먹었다

W What about ice cream?

M I ate only _____ _____ _____ . That's okay.
무가당 아이스크림

대화를 듣고, 남자가 전화를 건 목적으로 가장 적절한 것을 고르시오.

① Jane의 안부를 물어보려고
② 전화 메시지를 확인하려고
③ 파티 시간에 대해 물어보려고
④ 파티에 못 가는 것을 알려주려고
⑤ 파티 장소가 변경된 것을 알려주려고

Can I take a message?는 전화 대화에서 상대방에게 메시지를 남길 것인지 물을 때 쓰는 표현이다.

[Telephone rings.]

W Hello.

M Hello. Could I speak to Jane, please?

W I'm afraid she isn't here right now. Can I take a message?

M Yes, please. This is Richard.

W Oh, hello, Richard. This is Jane's mother.

M I _____ _____ her party this Saturday. But tell her that I'm very
파티에 초대받았다
sorry _____ _____ _____ . I have to _____ _____
나는 갈 수 없다   건강검진을 받다
_____ that day.

W Oh, that's too bad. I'll give her the message.

M Thank you. Good-bye.

대화 중에 나오는 3개의 시각이 각각 무슨 시간인지 파악한다.

대화를 듣고, 두 사람이 만날 시각을 고르시오.

① 7:00   ② 7:10
③ 7:20   ④ 7:30
⑤ 7:40

W Hi, George. How are you doing?

M I'm fine. How about getting together tonight, Laura?

W Good. I'm free tonight.

M I'll be at the office until 7 in the evening.

W Let's meet at the restaurant in front of your office. How about 7:30?

M Could we _____ _____ _____ ?
조금 더 일찍 만나다

W No problem. Then, _____ _____ _____ ?
7시 10분은 어때

M Great. _____ _____ _____ at the restaurant.
그때 보자

10 실용문 정보 파악

메모의 내용과 여자가 하는 말을 순서대로 정확히 확인한다.

다음을 듣고, 전화 메모의 내용과 일치하지 <u>않는</u> 것을 고르시오.

TELEPHONE MESSAGE
Caller: Tony Smith
Address: 10 Maple Street
Phone number: 576-3849
Visiting time: this afternoon at 3 o'clock
Problem: computer won't start

① ② ③ ④ ⑤

W ① Tony Smith called.
② Tony Smith lives at 10 Maple Street.
③ Tony Smith's phone number is 576-3849.
④ _____ _____ _____ _____ at 3 o'clock this afternoon.
　　누군가 Tony를 방문할 것이다
⑤ Tony Smith's _____ _____ _____ .
　　컴퓨터에서 소음이 나다

---

11 내용 일치 파악

담화 중에 나오는 것들을 순서대로 정확히 확인해야 한다.

다음을 듣고, 남자에 관해 알 수 <u>없는</u> 것을 고르시오.

① 이름
② 기상 시간
③ 근무하는 동물원 이름
④ 동물들에게 아침 식사를 주는 시간
⑤ 오후에 하는 일

M I'm an animal trainer, Michael Taylor. Our zoo is in Redwood Forest. I usually _____ _____ _____ _____ in the morning every day. I have to
　　　　　　　　　　　　　　　　　　　　　　　　　　　　　　　　5시에 일어나다
_____ _____ _____ their breakfast at around six o'clock. After that, I visit all of the
　　　　　　　동물들에게 먹이를 주다
animals and check if they're in good health. In the afternoon, I spend about four hours
_____ _____ .
동물들을 조련시키는 데

---

12 날씨 파악

대화를 듣고, 내일 오후의 날씨로 가장 적절한 것을 고르시오.

① sunny 화창한
② snowy 눈 오는
③ cloudy 구름 낀
④ windy 바람부는
⑤ rainy 비 오는

➕ 대화를 듣고, 오늘 오후의 날씨로 가장 적절한 것을 고르시오.

① sunny　　② snowy
③ cloudy　　④ windy
⑤ rainy

M What's the weather forecast for this afternoon?
W It'll rain, so we can't go to the beach this afternoon.
M That's too bad. _____ _____ _____ ?
　　　　　　　　　　　　내일은 어때
W The weather forecast said it would be cloudy in the morning and _____
　　　　　　　　　　　　　　　　　　　　　　　　　　　　　　　　　　　오후에는 해가 비치는
_____ _____ .
M Then, let's _____ _____ _____ _____ tomorrow afternoon.
　　　　　　　　해변에 가다
W Sounds good.

고난도

13 특정 정보 파악

여러 숫자들에 유의하여 듣는다.

대화를 듣고, 여자가 목표로 하고 있는 체중을 고르시오.

① 55kg　　② 60kg
③ 63kg　　④ 67kg
⑤ 70kg

M How's your diet these days, Rachel?
W Fine. I've already lost three kilograms.
M No kidding? That's great!
W Yeah, my clothes are starting to feel loose.
M How much do you _____ _____ _____ ?
　　　　　　　　　　　　　　체중을 빼고 싶다
W _____ _____ _____ .
　　7kg 더
M Then how much do you weigh now, Rachel?
W I _____ _____ _____ now.
　　70kg 나가다

14 장소 추론

대화를 듣고, 두 사람이 대화하는 장소로 가장 적절한 곳을 고르시오.

① 호텔
② 음식점
③ 가구점
④ 회의장
⑤ 음악회장

M Good evening. Do you have a reservation?

W Yes. My name is Jennifer Williams.

M Ah, yes, Miss Williams. You _____ _____ _____ _____
3인용 테이블을 예약했다
at seven o'clock.

W That's right.

M _____ _____ _____ _____ now. Please come this way.
테이블이 준비되다

W All right. *[pause]* Could we have the menu, please?

M Here you are, ma'am.

---

15 할 일 파악

대화를 듣고, 두 사람이 오후에 함께 할 일로 가장 적절한 것을 고르시오.

① 공부하기
② 보고서 제출하기
③ 방학 계획 세우기
④ 서점에서 책 사기
⑤ 도서관에서 책 빌리기

W Hi, John. Long time no see.

M Beth! It's been so long since we last saw each other.

W You're right. I'm at home for the summer vacation. Would you like to get together this afternoon?

M I'd love to.

W Well, I'm going to _____ _____ _____ _____ at half past 4. I'll
도서관에 있다
_____ _____ for my report.
약간의 책을 빌리다

M I _____ _____ _____, too. We can meet at the library.
약간의 책이 필요하다

W Great. See you there.

---

16 말의 내용 파악(담화)

다음을 듣고, 여자가 하는 말의 내용으로 가장 적절한 것을 고르시오.

① 근면한 생활습관의 중요성
② 하루를 알차게 보내는 법
③ 건강한 뇌를 위한 생활 습관
④ 충분한 수면의 중요성
⑤ 학습 능률 향상을 위한 방법

W Hello, listeners! Welcome back to Your Health Partner. I'm Dolly Sharp. A few months ago, I didn't sleep much because I was very busy. I got a lot of work done, so I thought I was being productive. But more research is saying that doing that is _____ _____ _____ _____ and brain activity. We need to
우리 건강에 아주 나쁜
_____ _____ _____ _____ a day to work well the next
최소 일곱 시간을 자다
day. And for young students, it's even more important. Let's talk about it today.

고난도

17 내용 일치 파악

대화 중에 순서대로 나오는 Mark에 대한 인상착의나 설명에 주의한다.

대화를 듣고, Mark에 관한 내용과 일치하지 <u>않는</u> 것을 고르시오.

① 오렌지 주스를 들고 있다.
② 안경을 쓰고 있다.
③ 피아노를 치고 있다.
④ 긴 머리를 하고 있다.
⑤ 흰 양복을 입고 있다.

M Wow, there are so many people here.

W Oh, look over there! That's Mark, the famous singer.

M Which one are you talking about?

W The man holding a glass of orange juice. He's _____ _____ _____.
안경을 쓰고 있다

M The man _____ _____ _____? He's got long hair?
피아노 옆에

W Yes. He's _____ _____ _____. Let's go say hello.
흰색 양복을 입고 있다

M Really? Do you know him?

W Yes. He's one of my friends.

대화를 듣고, 남자의 심정으로 가장 적절한 것을 고르시오.

① angry 화난
② bored 지루한
③ excited 흥분한
④ satisfied 만족한
⑤ frightened 무서운

M Do you believe there are _____ _____ in the lake?
_{날아다니는 괴물}
W No, I don't. Look at it. It's so peaceful. Why are you asking me?
M I saw something flying last night. I'm really serious.
W Go ahead.
M As I was walking by the lake, I _____ _____ straight up into the air
_{뭔가 날아다니는 것을 보다}
from behind the trees by the lake. It _____ _____ _____ and flew east.
_{날개를 펼치다}
W Wasn't it a bird?
M It was not a bird. It was just too big. I'd say it was about 10 ft long and had wings like a bat.
W I think you _____ _____ _____ a flying monster. Take it easy.
_{박쥐를 ~로 착각하다}

남자의 마지막 질문을 잘 파악해 본다.

[19~20] 대화를 듣고, 남자의 마지막 말에 이어질 여자의 응답으로 가장 적절한 것을 고르시오.

Woman: _____

① I will stop it.
② Because I have to.
③ I will keep that in mind.
④ I run in the park every evening.
⑤ Losing weight is not easy at all.

M Have some French fries. Aren't you eating at all?
W No, thank you. I'm on a diet.
M Oh, come on. You can eat a few.
W No, thank you. I'd really like to _____ _____.
_{몸무게를 줄이다}
M Well, then _____ _____ _____ _____ to lose weight?
_{다른 어떤 것을 하니}
W _____

Woman: _____

① That's fine with me.
② I think I'm getting old.
③ Thank you for giving me a tip.
④ Action speak louder than words.
⑤ Don't worry. It's not too late yet.

W What should we cook for today's dinner party?
M I think I'm going to make the Indian chicken we had on Jane's birthday.
W Sounds good. _____ _____ 'Tandoori Chicken'?
_{그것은 ~라고 하지?}
M Right. That's the food we had at the Indian restaurant.
W Do you have _____ _____ _____?
_{그것에 대한 조리법}
M Of course. I _____ _____ _____ the recipe that day.
_{요리사에게 ~을 부탁하다}
W But Linda doesn't eat chicken, does she?
M Linda? Oh, my Gosh! I forgot to invite her! She'll be mad at me. It just _____
_{깜빡했다}
_____ _____.
W _____

장소·관계 파악

무엇을 평가하는가?	일상생활이나 친숙한 일반적 주제에 관한 말이나 대화를 듣고 상황 및 화자 간의 관계를 추론할 수 있는지를 평가한다.
어떻게 출제되는가?	• 대화를 듣고, 두 사람이 대화하는 장소로 가장 적절한 곳을 고르시오. • 대화를 듣고, 두 사람의 관계로 가장 적절한 것을 고르시오.

key solution

❶ 전체적인 상황을 파악하면서, 특정 장소나 관계에 자주 쓰이는 표현에 집중한다.

[기출로 전략 확인]

대화를 듣고, 두 사람이 대화하는 장소로 가장 적절한 곳을 고르시오.   [2018 기출]

① 병원   ② 식당   ③ 경찰서
④ 기차역   ⑤ 분실물 보관소

- -

W Good afternoon, sir. Where are you going?

M I'm going to Daejeon. How much is the train ticket?

W It's 25,000 won. Howwmany tickets do you need?

M Just one ticket, please. Here's my credit card.

W Okay. [*Pause*] This is your ticket.

M Good. How long will it take to Daejeon Station?

W It will take about one hour. Your train leaves in 10 minutes.

M Thank you very much.

W Have a nice trip.

❶ 기차표를 사려는 남자와 기차표를 발급해 주는 여자의 대화를 보고 두 사람이 대화하는 장소를 유추할 수 있다.

여 안녕하세요. 어디로 가시나요?

남 대전이요. 기차표가 얼마죠?

여 2만 5천원입니다. 표는 몇 장이 필요하시죠?

남 한 장이요. [*멈춤*] 여기 신용카드요.

여 알겠습니다. 여기 표요.

남 대전역까지 얼마나 걸릴까요?

여 1시간 정도 걸릴 거에요. 기차는 10분 후 떠납니다.

남 고맙습니다.

여 즐거운 여행 되세요.

대화를 듣고, 두 사람이 대화하는 장소로 가장 적절한 곳을 고르시오. [2017 기출]

① 교실   ② 실험실   ③ 은행
④ 가방 판매점   ⑤ 공원 분실물 센터

만점 잡는 문장   **W** I lost my bag here in this park.

                   ⋮

             M I see. We'll contact you when we find it.

대화를 듣고, 두 사람의 관계로 가장 적절한 것을 고르시오. [2017 기출]

① 은행원 – 고객   ② 사진 작가 – 모델
③ 문구점 직원 – 고객   ④ 인쇄소 사장 – 직원
⑤ 시험 감독 교사 – 응시 학생

만점 잡는 문장   **W** Don't forget to write your name and student number on the answer sheet.
             M How long will the test take, ma'am?
             W The test will take 45 minutes.

● 장소

(햄버거 가게)

A I ordered a chicken burger, but this is a cheese burger. 치킨 버거를 시켰는데 치즈 버거네요.
B Sorry about that. Can I get you a new one? 죄송합니다. 새로 드릴까요?

(관광 안내소)

A Hi! I'd like to look around the city today. 안녕하세요. 오늘 도시를 둘러보고 싶은데요.
B Okay, do you need a city tour map? 네, 도시 관광 지도가 필요하신가요?

(영화관)

A Our seats are D9 and D10. Right here. 우리자리는 D9이랑 D10이야. 바로 여기야.
B Did you know this movie was filmed in China? 이 영화 중국에서 촬영한 거 알고 있어?

● 관계

(택배기사 – 고객)

A Your package will be delivered around 3 p.m. 택배가 3시쯤에 도착할 겁니다.
B Really? That's sooner than I expected. 정말요? 예상보다 빠르네요.

(도서관 사서 – 이용객)

A Hi, I'd like to return these books. 이 책을 반납하고 싶은데요.
B Okay. You want to return five books, right? 알겠습니다. 5권을 반납하시려는 거 맞죠?

(미용사 – 고객)

A I'd like to get a haircut, please. How much will it cost? 머리를 자르려고 하는데 얼마가요?
B It's 10 dollars. 10달러입니다.

영어듣기능력평가 **15**회

학년　　　반　　　번
이름

01 다음을 듣고, 그림을 바르게 설명한 것을 고르시오.

① ② ③ ④ ⑤

02 다음을 듣고, 세계 대도시별 날씨가 잘못 짝지어진 것을 고르시오.

① 서울 – sunny
② 베이징 – foggy
③ 동경 – windy
④ 모스크바 – cloudy
⑤ 뉴욕 – rainy

03 대화를 듣고, 남자가 지난 주말에 한 일로 가장 적절한 것을 고르시오.

① 하이킹 가기
② 집안 청소하기
③ 정원일 돕기
④ 페인트칠하기
⑤ 이삿짐 싸기

04 다음을 듣고, 무엇에 관한 안내인지 가장 적절한 것을 고르시오.

① 불편 사항 신고
② 건물 보수 공사
③ 엘리베이터 고장
④ 계단 이용 방법
⑤ 화재 시 대피 요령

05 대화를 듣고, 여자가 약국에서 구입한 것이 아닌 것을 고르시오.

① 기침약
② 피부 로션
③ 소화제
④ 복합 비타민
⑤ 오메가3

06 대화를 듣고, 두 사람이 대화하는 장소로 가장 적절한 곳을 고르시오.

① 기차역
② 자동차 안
③ 도로 위
④ 공항
⑤ 비행기 안

07 대화를 듣고, 두 사람의 관계로 가장 적절한 것을 고르시오.

① 경찰 – 시민
② 기자 – 목격자
③ 드라마 감독 – 연기자
④ 자동차 정비소 직원 – 고객
⑤ 토크쇼 호스트 – 게스트

08 대화를 듣고, 남자가 여자에게 전화를 건 목적으로 가장 적절한 것을 고르시오.

① 자전거를 빌리려고
② 병문안을 함께 가려고
③ 자전거를 함께 타려고
④ 전화를 대신해 달라고
⑤ 집에 데려다 달라고

09 대화를 듣고, 여자가 남자에게 부탁한 일로 가장 적절한 것을 고르시오.

① 집안 정돈하기
② 장 봐오기
③ 화장실 청소하기
④ 공부 열심히 하기
⑤ 청소용품 사오기

10 대화를 듣고, 여자가 대화 직후에 할 일로 가장 적절한 것을 고르시오.

① 컴퓨터 수리공을 부르는 일
② 전화번호를 알아내는 일
③ 접속되지 않는 사이트에 전화하는 일
④ 컴퓨터 전원을 끄는 일
⑤ 인터넷 선이 연결되었는지 확인하는 일

11
다음 그림의 상황에 가장 적절한 대화를 고르시오.

①   ②   ③   ④   ⑤

12
다음을 듣고, 실험실에서 지켜야 할 내용으로 언급되지 않은 것을 고르시오.

① 음식물을 갖고 들어오지 말 것
② 선생님이 없으면 들어오지 말 것
③ 선반에 있는 물건을 만지지 말 것
④ 병 속에 있는 것을 맛보지 말 것
⑤ 실험 후 도구 정리를 잘할 것

13
대화를 듣고, 남자의 심정으로 가장 적절한 것을 고르시오.

① sad   ② excited
③ worried   ④ nervous
⑤ disappointed

14
다음을 듣고, 광고문의 내용과 일치하지 않는 것을 고르시오.

Library Bistro
Italian Food
92 Madison Street, Seattle
Open Monday - Friday : 10 a.m. to 11 p.m.
Saturday - Sunday : 10 a.m. to midnight
Reservation : 624-3646

①   ②   ③   ④   ⑤

15
대화를 듣고, 뮤지컬이 시작되는 시각을 고르시오.

① 6:10   ② 6:20
③ 6:30   ④ 6:40
⑤ 6:50

16
대화를 듣고, 여자가 하는 말의 의도로 가장 적절한 것을 고르시오.

① 사과   ② 변명
③ 제안   ④ 충고
⑤ 칭찬

17
대화를 듣고, 여자의 마지막 말의 의도로 가장 적절한 것을 고르시오.

① 거절   ② 허락
③ 동의   ④ 비난
⑤ 감사

18
대화를 듣고, 여자가 소파를 배달 받을 날짜를 고르시오.

① July 15   ② July 16
③ July 17   ④ July 18
⑤ July 19

[19~20] 대화를 듣고, 남자의 마지막 말에 이어질 여자의 응답으로 가장 적절한 것을 고르시오.

19
Woman: _____

① That sounds strange.
② It was a waste of time.
③ Here's your key, sir.
④ I've never thought of that.
⑤ It doesn't matter at all.

20
Woman: _____

① Yes. There's one near here.
② Yes. I will wait for you here.
③ Yes. Your order won't be long.
④ No. I don't like to eat out today.
⑤ No. I don't want to eat this food.

다시 들으면서 듣기 만점에 도전하세요!
Dictation: 스크립트의 주요 부분을 다시 들으면서!
실전 ⊕: 세부 정보가 많은 스크립트를 다른 문제로 샅샅이!

---

01 그림 정보 파악 – 토익형

무대 위에서 노래를 부르고 있는 모습을 묘사한 내용을 찾는다.

다음을 듣고, 그림을 바르게 설명한 것을 고르시오.

W ① Two students _____ _____ _____ _____.
　　　　　　　　　　　　　　도로를 건너고 있다
② Two students are answering quizzes.
③ Two students _____ _____ _____ _____.
　　　　　　　　　　　　　무대 위에서 노래를 하고 있다
④ Two students are helping an old woman.
⑤ Two students _____ _____ _____ _____.
　　　　　　　　　　　　모형 비행기를 만들고 있다

① ② ③ ④ ⑤

---

02 날씨 파악

언급된 도시들 중에서 구름 낀 날씨의 도시는 없다는 것을 파악한다.

다음을 듣고, 세계 대도시별 날씨가 <u>잘못</u> 짝지어진 것을 고르시오.

① 서울 – sunny
② 베이징 – foggy
③ 동경 – windy
④ 모스크바 – cloudy
⑤ 뉴욕 – rainy

M Good morning. This is Peter Lee. Here is a radio report of the weather for some big cities in the world. Let's start with Seoul. It will be warm and sunny in Seoul, so today will be a perfect time _____ _____. Beijing will be
　　　　　　　　　　　　　　　　　　　　　　　　　　외부활동을 위한
_____ _____ _____, but Tokyo will be windy. There _____
　　　　　　　　　　하루 종일 안개가 가득　　　　　　　　　　　　　　　　　　　　　　모스크바에는 눈이 올 것이다
_____ _____ _____ _____ with a low temperature. New York is going to have heavy rain today. That's all. Thank you.

---

03 한 일 파악

대화를 듣고, 남자가 지난 주말에 한 일로 가장 적절한 것을 고르시오.

① 하이킹 가기
② 집안 청소하기
③ 정원일 돕기
④ 페인트칠하기
⑤ 이삿짐 싸기

Not really.는 '그렇지도 않아.'라는 뜻으로 말하기 곤란할 때 쓰는 표현이다.

W Do you _____ _____ _____ _____ this weekend?
　　　　　특별한 계획을 가지다
M Not really. How about you?
W I'm going hiking with my friends. Would you like to come with us?
M I'd like to, but I have to help my father paint my room.
W But you _____ _____ _____ _____ last weekend, right?
　　　어머니가 집안 청소하는 것을 도와드렸다
M Yes. We have just _____ _____ _____ _____, you know.
　　　　　　　　　　　새 집으로 이사했다
We have a lot of work to do.

⊕ 대화를 듣고, 여자가 남자에게 제안한 일로 가장 적절한 것을 고르시오

① 하이킹 가기　　② 집안 청소하기
③ 정원일 돕기　　④ 페인트칠하기
⑤ 이삿짐 싸기

---

04 주제 파악

다음을 듣고, 무엇에 관한 안내인지 가장 적절한 것을 고르시오.

① 불편 사항 신고
② 건물 보수 공사
③ 엘리베이터 고장
④ 계단 이용 방법
⑤ 화재 시 대피 요령

M May I have your attention, please? I'm sorry to bother you again. As you know, our building is very old, and _____ _____ _____ _____. Unfortunately,
　　　　　　　　　　　　　　　　엘리베이터도 그렇다
the elevator is _____ _____ _____ again. Our repairmen
　　　　　　　　　고장난　　　　　　　　　　　　　　　　　　　　　　　고치려고 노력하고 있다
_____ _____ it, but it will take about an hour. Please take the stairs. Thank you for your understanding.

05 특정 정보 파악

대화를 듣고, 여자가 약국에서 구입한 것이
아닌 것을 고르시오.

① 기침약
② 피부 로션
③ 소화제
④ 복합 비타민
⑤ 오메가 3

W Could I have _____ _____ _____ _____? I think I'm coming down
    기침에 좋은 것
    with a cold.

M Well, I suggest a box of _____ _____ _____.
    이 기침 물약

W Thank you. And what do you suggest for dry skin?

M Try this new lotion. It's very moisturizing.

W OK. And one more thing. My husband has no energy these days. Can you suggest
    anything?

M He should try taking multivitamins. They're excellent.

W And could you suggest something good for my _____ _____ as well?
    작은 두통

M How about omega 3 pills? It helps blood circulation.

W Great! May I have _____ _____ _____ _____ multivitamins and one
    ~의 큰 병으로 세 병
    bottle of omega 3, please?

M Sure. I'll be right back with you.

06 대화 장소 파악

대화를 듣고, 두 사람이 대화하는 장소로
가장 적절한 곳을 고르시오.

① 기차역   ② 자동차 안
③ 도로 위   ④ 공항
⑤ 비행기 안

W We finally got here. The traffic was so bad.

M I know, I've never experienced anything like that. Anyway, we really _____

    _____ _____.
    서둘러야 한다

W What time is our boarding time?

M I think it'll be 12:45 p.m., as our flight time is 1:15 p.m.

W Oh, no, then we have only an hour and a half.

M Yes, so we can't waste any time. Let's find the check-in counter, first. Then we need to
    go straight to the security check.

W I hope the line is _____ _____ _____.
    너무 길지 않은

07 관계 파악

대화를 듣고, 두 사람의 관계로 가장 적절
한 것을 고르시오.

① 경찰 – 시민
② 기자 – 목격자
③ 드라마 감독 – 연기자
④ 자동차 정비소 직원 – 고객
⑤ 토크쇼 호스트 – 게스트

M You were here when the accident happened. Could you tell me about it?

W It happened very fast, so I _____ _____ _____. But there was something
    모든 것을 보지 못했다
    wrong with the driver of the white car.

M What do you mean?

W Well, the driver was switching lanes a lot and then he _____ _____ _____
    갑자기 더 빠르게 갔다
    before he hit the blue car.

M Maybe he had a medical emergency. Can I use this interview on TV? It will help viewers
    understand what happened.

W Will I be on the news? Yes, you can use it.

남자가 다리를 다친 상황에서 여자에게 전화를 건 것임을 파악한다.

대화를 듣고, 남자가 여자에게 전화를 건 목적으로 가장 적절한 것을 고르시오.

① 자전거를 빌리려고
② 병문안을 함께 가려고
③ 자전거를 함께 타려고
④ 전화를 대신해 달라고
⑤ 집에 데려다 달라고

➕ 대화를 듣고, 남자가 혼자 집에 갈 수 없는 이유로 가장 적절한 것은?

① 자전거를 잃어버려서
② 다리를 다쳐서
③ 엄마에게 일이 생겨서
④ 자전거가 고장나서
⑤ 시간이 너무 늦어서

[Telephone rings.]

M Hello, Cathy. This is Mark.

W Hi, Mark. What happened? Your voice sounds strange.

M I've _____ _____ _____ .
　　　　　자전거에서 떨어진

W Are you hurt?

M Yes. I've hurt my leg. I can't walk any more, so can you _____
　　　　　　　　　　　　　　　　　　　　　　　　　　　　　　나를 집으로 데려다 주다
_____ _____ _____ ?

W Oh, heavens! Why don't you call your mom?

M I did, but she _____ _____ _____ .
　　　　　　　　　　　전화를 받지 않았다

W Wait! I'll come and take you home.

대화를 듣고, 여자가 남자에게 부탁한 일로 가장 적절한 것을 고르시오.

① 집안 정돈하기　② 장 봐오기
③ 화장실 청소하기　④ 공부 열심히 하기
⑤ 청소용품 사오기

M Mom, you look tired. Are you okay?

W I'm just very tired. I've been so busy at work lately, and there's so much housework to do.

M I can help you with the housework. What can I do?

W _____ _____ _____ _____ _____ . The bathroom really needs
　　아주 친절하구나
cleaning.

M Sure, I can do that. Do you want me to do that now?

W No, I need to _____ some _____ _____ first. How about tomorrow?
　　　　　　　　　청소 용품을 사다

M No problem.

대화를 듣고, 여자가 대화 직후에 할 일로 가장 적절한 것을 고르시오.

① 컴퓨터 수리공을 부르는 일
② 전화번호를 알아내는 일
③ 접속되지 않는 사이트에 전화하는 일
④ 컴퓨터 전원을 끄는 일
⑤ 인터넷 선이 연결되었는지 확인하는 일

W I need somebody to come over and fix my Internet connection.

M What's wrong with it?

W For some reason I _____ _____ _____ _____ the site I want.
　　　　　　　　　　　접속할 수 없다

M Well, the Internet isn't down, so _____ _____ _____ _____
　　　　　　　　　　　　　　　　　　　　　　　　　　　뭔가 잘못된 것이 틀림없다
_____ with the site.

W What should I do? I need to download a file right now.

M The fastest solution is _____ _____ _____ _____ to the site.
　　　　　　　　　　　　　　　　전화하다

W I don't know the phone number.

M Why don't you call 114?

W Oh, that's it. I didn't think of that.

다음 그림의 상황에 가장 적절한 대화를 고르시오.

① ② ③ ④ ⑤

① W Would you like something to drink?

M Yes, please. Can I have some water, please?

② W So... _____ _____ _____ this place?
　〜을 어떻게 생각해?

M I think it's very nice. We should take it.

③ W Are you ready to order now?

M No, sorry, can I have some more time, please?

④ W Excuse me, sir, can I see your ticket, please?

M Sure, I have it in my bag. _____ _____ _____ _____.
　　　　　　　　　　　　　　　　　잠시만요

⑤ W Excuse me, if you're not using this chair would you mind if I take it?

M Not at all. Take it if you need it.

실험실 규칙을 언급할 때마다 일치하는 것을 지워나간다.

다음을 듣고, 실험실에서 지켜야 할 내용으로 언급되지 <u>않은</u> 것을 고르시오.

① 음식물을 갖고 들어오지 말 것
② 선생님이 없으면 들어오지 말 것
③ 선반에 있는 물건을 만지지 말 것
④ 병 속에 있는 것을 맛보지 말 것
⑤ 실험 후 도구 정리를 잘할 것

W I'm so glad that you've chosen chemistry. Now I'd like to talk about lab rules to you. First, you can't bring any food or drinks into the lab. Second, _____ _____ _____ without a teacher. Third, please _____ on the shelves. Fourth, never taste anything in the bottles. Lastly, when doing experiments, _____ _____ _____ attentively. Thank you for listening to me.
(실험실에 들어오지 않는다 / 아무것도 만지지 않는다 / 선생님의 말씀을 듣는다)

대화를 듣고, 남자의 심정으로 가장 적절한 것을 고르시오.

① sad 슬픈
② excited 흥분한
③ worried 걱정하는
④ nervous 긴장한, 초조한
⑤ disappointed 실망한

I can't believe it!은 '그럴 수가!, 믿을 수가 없어!'라는 뜻으로 놀람을 나타내는 말이다.

W Here's a letter for you, Alex.

M Thanks. *[opens it]* _____ _____ _____ _____!
　　　　　　　　　　　　믿을 수 없어

W Why?

M This letter says I _____ _____ _____ _____!
　　　　　　　　　　　　　　공짜 여행에 당첨됐다

W Really? To where?

M The letter says _____ _____ _____ in Europe or Asia.
　　　　　　　　나는 어디든지 갈 수 있다

W Are you sure the trip is really free?

M That's what it says. Here, you can read it.

시각과 관련된 두 가지 정보를 이용하여 파악한다.

다음을 듣고, 광고문의 내용과 일치하지 <u>않는</u> 것을 고르시오.

Library Bistro
Italian Food
92 Madison Street, Seattle
Open Monday - Friday : 10 a.m. to 11 p.m.
Saturday - Sunday : 10 a.m. to midnight
Reservation : 624-3646

① ② ③ ④ ⑤

W ① People can eat Italian food at Library Bistro.

② Library Bistro is at 92 Madison Street, Seattle.

③ Library Bistro opens every day at 10 a.m.

④ Library Bistro _____ _____ _____
　　　　　　　　매일 오후 11시에 문을 닫는다

⑤ People can _____ _____ _____ at 624-3646.
　　　　　　예약을 하다

먼저 현재 시각을 알아낸다.

대화를 듣고, 뮤지컬이 시작되는 시각을 고르시오.

① 6:10
② 6:20
③ 6:30
④ 6:40
⑤ 6:50

W Jim, I'm sorry to have kept you waiting for so long.

M Oh, I don't mind. ＿＿＿＿＿ ＿＿＿＿＿ .
6시밖에 되지 않았다

W Thank you for saying so. When does the musical start?

M We've ＿＿＿＿＿ ＿＿＿＿＿ ＿＿＿＿＿ .
아직 50분 남다

W But, we must enter the concert hall 10 minutes before the musical starts.

M Yes, but don't worry. It takes only 20 minutes to walk there.

W Okay. Let's go.

대화를 듣고, 여자가 하는 말의 의도로 가장 적절한 것을 고르시오.

① 초대
② 변명
③ 제안
④ 충고
⑤ 칭찬

W Hi, Jason.

M Hi, Carol. What's up?

W You want to ＿＿＿＿＿ ＿＿＿＿＿ ＿＿＿＿＿ , don't you?
자원봉사일을 하다

M Yes, I do. I want to help people in need.

W Well, Central Hospital needs volunteers. ＿＿＿＿＿ ＿＿＿＿＿ ＿＿＿＿＿ ？
함께 가는 게 어때

M Sounds interesting. When do they need volunteers?

W Anytime. But ＿＿＿＿＿ ＿＿＿＿＿ ＿＿＿＿＿ ＿＿＿＿＿ .
대부분 주말에

M Good. That's perfect for me.

대화를 듣고, 여자의 마지막 말의 의도로 가장 적절한 것을 고르시오.

① 거절 ② 허락
③ 동의 ④ 비난
⑤ 감사

M Youngmi, what are you doing tonight?

W Nothing much. Why?

M Would you like to go to a concert? I have free tickets.

W Really? It sounds interesting. What time is it?

M It starts at 7 p.m. Maybe, we can ＿＿＿＿＿ ＿＿＿＿＿ ＿＿＿＿＿ before the concert.
만나서 저녁을 먹자

W What kind of concert is it?

M It's classical music. They're going to play Mozart and Mendelssohn.

W Oh, well..., I'm not a big fan of ＿＿＿＿＿ ＿＿＿＿＿ ＿＿＿＿＿ . Thanks for inviting me, but I'll pass.
그런 종류의 음악

18 특정 정보 파악 – 날짜

대화를 듣고, 여자가 소파를 배달 받을 날짜를 고르시오.

① July 15   ② July 16
③ July 17   ④ July 18
⑤ July 19

[Cellphone rings.]

W Hello?

M Hello. This is Comfy Furniture. _____ _____ _____ Ms. Kim?
~와 통화할 수 있을까요?

W Speaking.

M Hi, we'd like to _____ _____ this week. Is it okay?
당신의 소파를 배달하다

W Yes, I've been waiting. Hmm..., today is July 15. How about tomorrow?

M Sorry, we're booked with deliveries for tomorrow. But we can deliver it any day from Tuesday, July 17.

W I'll be away for the day this Tuesday. So, it'll have to be the next day.

M Sure, no problem. Do you prefer any particular time?

W No, anytime in the afternoon is fine.

19 알맞은 응답 찾기

호텔에서 체크인 하는 상황임을 파악한다.

[19~20] 대화를 듣고, 남자의 마지막 말에 이어질 여자의 응답으로 가장 적절한 것을 고르시오.

Woman: _____

① That sounds strange.
② It was a waste of time.
③ Here's your key, sir.
④ I've never thought of that.
⑤ It doesn't matter at all.

M I have a reservation. My name is John Stevens.

W Okay. You're in room 507. It's _____ _____ _____ , spacious.
퀸사이즈의 싱글 침대

M It's that a smoking room?

W I'm sorry, but every room here is non-smoking.

M Okay. Thank you. And does that _____ _____ ?
해변이 내려다 보이다

W Yes, it does.

M It sounds like everything I expected.

W _____

20 알맞은 응답 찾기

Woman: _____

① Yes. There's one near here.
② Yes. I will wait for you here.
③ Yes. Your order won't be long.
④ No. I don't like to eat out today.
⑤ No. I don't want to eat this food.

W I really enjoyed the movie. How about you?

M I liked it too. The last part was really exciting.

W Yes, it was. And now _____ _____ . Let's have something to eat.
나는 정말 배고프다

M Okay. _____ _____ _____ _____ ?
너는 무엇을 먹고 싶니

W Anything is okay with me. Do you like Chinese food?

M Sure, but do you know _____ _____ _____ around here?
중국 음식점

W _____

영어듣기능력평가 **16**회

학년　　　반　　　번
이름

01 대화를 듣고, 그림에서 Cathy를 고르시오.

02 대화를 듣고, 내일 날씨로 가장 적절한 것을 고르시오.

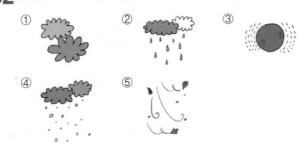

03 대화를 듣고, 두 사람이 오늘 저녁에 할 일로 가장 적절한 것을 고르시오.

① 쇼핑
② 병문안
③ 영화 감상
④ 저녁 식사
⑤ 운동 경기 관람

고난도
04 대화를 듣고, 내용과 일치하지 <u>않는</u> 것을 고르시오.

① 남자는 예약을 하고 있다.
② 남자는 호텔에서 체크인을 하고 있다.
③ 남자의 방은 7층에 있다.
④ 남자는 오른쪽 엘리베이터를 탈 것이다.
⑤ 남자의 방에서는 바다를 볼 수 없다.

05 대화를 듣고, 여자가 이용할 교통수단으로 가장 적절한 것을 고르시오.

① 비행기
② 지하철
③ 택시
④ 셔틀버스
⑤ 자전거

06 다음 그림의 상황에 가장 적절한 대화를 고르시오.

①　　　　②　　　　③　　　　④　　　　⑤

07 대화를 듣고, 두 사람이 현장학습을 가는 날짜를 고르시오.

① 5월 1일
② 5월 2일
③ 5월 8일
④ 5월 10일
⑤ 5월 15일

08 대화를 듣고, 두 사람이 대화하는 장소로 가장 적절한 곳을 고르시오.

① 공항
② 호텔
③ 주유소
④ 렌터카 사무실
⑤ 운전면허 시험장

09 대화를 듣고, 남자가 여자에게 제안한 것으로 가장 적절한 것을 고르시오.

① 문법보다는 표현에 집중하라.
② 많은 어휘를 공부하도록 하라.
③ 규칙을 반복적으로 연습하라.
④ 시간 투자와 연습이 지름길이다.
⑤ 말할 때 긴장을 풀고 천천히 하라.

10 대화를 듣고, 여자의 심정으로 가장 적절한 것을 고르시오

① excited
② surprised
③ worried
④ disappointed
⑤ lonely

점수

/20

11 대화를 듣고, 여자가 하게 될 봉사활동으로 가장 적절한 것을 고르시오.

① 청소하기   ② 요리하기
③ 책 읽어주기   ④ 숙제 도와주기
⑤ 관광 안내하기

12 대화를 듣고, 남자가 전화를 건 목적으로 가장 적절한 것을 고르시오.

① 길을 물어보려고
② 안부를 물으려고
③ 이사한 위치를 알려주려고
④ 치과 예약을 하려고
⑤ 위치를 문의하려고

13 대화를 듣고, 여자가 방문한 곳을 좋아하는 이유로 언급되지 않은 것을 고르시오.

① 조용했다.
② 사람들이 친절했다.
③ 호텔의 시설이 매우 좋았다.
④ 음식이 맛있었다.
⑤ 비가 왔다.

14 대화를 듣고, 남자가 사울 물건이 아닌 것을 고르시오.

① 양파   ② 햄
③ 토마토   ④ 오렌지 주스
⑤ 오렌지

15 대화를 듣고, 남자가 지불한 금액을 고르시오.

① $4   ② $14
③ $20   ④ $30
⑤ $40

16 대화를 듣고, 두 사람의 관계로 가장 적절한 것을 고르시오.

① 의사 – 환자   ② 운전사 – 승객
③ 교사 – 학생   ④ 가게 주인 – 손님
⑤ 교사 – 학부모

17 다음을 듣고, 무엇에 관한 안내인지 가장 적절한 것을 고르시오.

① 기차 예매권 매진
② 기차표 예매 일정
③ 기차 승강장 변경
④ 기차 출발 시각 연기
⑤ 기차 도착 시각 연기

18 대화를 듣고, 남자가 여자에게 부탁한 일로 가장 적절한 것을 고르시오.

① 함께 시험공부 하기   ② 비밀 지켜주기
③ 공부 방법 알려주기   ④ 선배 소개시켜 주기
⑤ 과학 과외해주기

[19~20] 대화를 듣고, 여자의 마지막 말에 이어질 남자의 응답으로 가장 적절한 것을 고르시오.

고난도

19 Man: _____

① Here's your change.
② How long does it take?
③ Sorry, I'll do it tomorrow.
④ You need more time to do it.
⑤ I hope you'll have a good time.

20 Man: _____

① Much better, thank you.
② You'd better choose this.
③ I'll be back soon with that.
④ Let's see. I'll have a glass of milk.
⑤ Do you have a bigger one?

다시 들으면서 듣기 만점에 도전하세요!
Dictation: 스크립트의 주요 부분을 다시 들으면서!
실전 ➕: 세부 정보가 많은 스크립트를 다른 문제로 샅샅이!

---

01 그림 정보 파악 – 인물 | short hair, jeans, T-shirt, glasses 등의 모습을 나타내는 단어들을 익혀두도록 한다.

대화를 듣고, 그림에서 Cathy를 고르시오.

M Did you come here alone?

W No, I came here with my friend Cathy.

M Where is she?

W She's sitting on the grass.

M You mean the one _____ _____ _____?
    긴 머리를 가진

W No, she _____ _____ . She's _____ and
    짧은 머리를 하다   청바지를 입고 있다
    _____ .
    티셔츠

M Oh, I see, _____ _____ _____ _____ .
    안경 쓴 사람

W That's right.

---

02 날씨 파악 | 오늘의 날씨와 내일의 날씨를 혼동하지 않도록 한다.

대화를 듣고, 내일 날씨로 가장 적절한 것을 고르시오.

① ② ③ ④ ⑤

M Oh, it's raining!

W Why does it rain every weekend? We were supposed to go on a picnic today.

M The weather forecast said it would be sunny this weekend. So I was looking forward to the picnic.

W Sometimes weather forecasts are wrong.

M But most forecasts are right. I think _____ _____ _____
    이번 비는 곧 그칠 것이다
    soon.

W Oh, it's _____ _____ . As you said, it was a shower.
    비가 멈추다

M The weather forecast was right. It says tomorrow _____
    날씨는 맑을 것이다
    _____ , too.

W Let's go on a picnic after lunch.

---

03 할 일 파악

대화를 듣고, 두 사람이 오늘 저녁에 할 일로 가장 적절한 것을 고르시오.

① 쇼핑
② 병문안
③ 영화 감상
④ 저녁 식사
⑤ 운동 경기 관람

W Did you get our tickets?

M No, tickets _____ _____ _____ .
    매진되다

W Really? Then what are we going to do? That's the movie we _____
    놓치고 싶지 않았다
    _____ _____ .

M That's right. We came a long way to see this movie. So we have to do something else.

W Let's make a reservation for tomorrow evening first and then _____ _____ .
    저녁 식사를 하다

M OK, sounds good.

04 내용 일치 파악

대화를 듣고, 내용과 일치하지 <u>않는</u> 것을 고르시오.

① 남자는 예약을 하고 있다.
② 남자는 호텔에서 체크인을 하고 있다.
③ 남자의 방은 7층에 있다.
④ 남자는 오른쪽 엘리베이터를 탈 것이다.
⑤ 남자의 방에서는 바다를 볼 수 없다.

W May I help you, sir?

M Yes, I _____ _____ here. My name is Kim Chiwon.
<u>예약을 했다</u>

W Just moment, please. OK, your room number is 702 on the 7th floor.

M Does the room _____ _____ of the sea?
<u>풍경을 가지다</u>

W I'm sorry, it doesn't.

M OK, I see.

W Take the elevator to your right, and you'll easily get to your room.

M Thank you very much.

05 특정 정보 파악

대화를 듣고, 여자가 이용할 교통수단으로 가장 적절한 것을 고르시오.

① 비행기 airplane
② 지하철 subway
③ 택시 taxi
④ 셔틀버스 shuttle bus
⑤ 자전거 bicycle

➕ 대화를 듣고, 여자가 남자를 방문한 목적으로 가장 적절한 것을 고르시오.

① 스쿠버다이빙을 예약하러
② 호텔 예약을 알아보러
③ 셔틀버스를 예약하러
④ 여행 상품을 문의하러
⑤ 보트 탑승권을 구입하러

M Hi. Can I help you?

W Yes, please. I'd like to go scuba diving. How much does it cost?

M It's $ 70 per person.

W I see. And what time _____ _____ _____ _____?
<u>배가 떠나니</u>

M It leaves each morning at 8.

W Oh, that's quite early. How do I get here from my hotel?

M Just _____ _____ _____. It will stop in front of the hotel. The
<u>셔틀버스를 타다</u>
buses drop by here.

W OK, great. I'd like to _____ _____ _____ for tomorrow morning.
<u>여행을 예약하다</u>

06 그림 상황 대화 찾기

다음 그림의 상황에 가장 적절한 대화를 고르시오.

① ② ③ ④ ⑤

① **W** Wow, look at that. What a nice view!

   M You're right. It's really nice. Let's take a picture!

② **W** Excuse me, could you please _____ _____ _____
<u>우리 사진을 찍다</u>
_____?

   M Sure, which button should I press?

③ **W** Is that a new Cellphone? It looks really nice!

   M Yes, I bought it last week because it was on sale.

④ **W** How should we _____ _____ from here?
<u>집으로 돌아가다</u>
   M We can take the bus, can't we?

⑤ **W** Excuse me, you're not allowed to take pictures here.

   M Oh, I'm sorry. I'll put the camera back in my bag.

다음 주 토요일이 5월 8일이므로 현장학습 가는 날짜는 일주일 앞선 날짜이다.

대화를 듣고, 두 사람이 현장학습을 가는 날짜를 고르시오.

① 5월 1일 　　② 5월 2일
③ 5월 8일 　　④ 5월 10일
⑤ 5월 15일

➕ 대화를 듣고, 두 사람이 영화를 보러 갈 날짜를 고르시오.

① 5월 1일 　　② 5월 2일
③ 5월 8일 　　④ 5월 10일
⑤ 5월 15일

M Would you like to go to the movies this Saturday?

W Don't you know that's the day we go on _____ _____ _____ ?
　　　　　　　　　　　　　　　　　　　　　　　　　현장학습

M Really? Is it next Saturday?

W No, it isn't. We're _____ _____ this Saturday.
　　　　　　　　　　　　　가기로 되어 있다

M Oh, I'm sorry, I forgot. Then let's go to the movies next Saturday.

W What date is it next Saturday?

M It's _____ _____ .
　　　　5월 8일

W That's fine with me.

insurance, return the car 등의 표현에서 정답을 유추할 수 있다.

대화를 듣고, 두 사람이 대화하는 장소로 가장 적절한 곳을 고르시오.

① 공항
② 호텔
③ 주유소
④ 렌터카 사무실
⑤ 운전면허 시험장

W Would you like insurance on the car?

M How much is the insurance?

W It's $15 a day. Who is going to be the driver?

M My wife and me.

W Can I _____ _____ _____ ?
　　　　운전면허증을 보다

M Sure. Here you are.

W Thank you. OK. Now I will tell you some rules. The gas tank is full. You
　　　　　　　　　　　　　　　　　　　　　　　　　　　　가득 채워야 한다
_____ _____ _____ before you return the car. Otherwise, we charge $3 a
gallon. You can _____ _____ _____ downstairs.
　　　　　　당신의 차를 인수받다

M Thank you.

대화를 듣고, 남자가 여자에게 제안한 것으로 가장 적절한 것을 고르시오.

① 문법보다는 표현에 집중하라.
② 많은 어휘를 공부하도록 하라.
③ 규칙을 반복적으로 연습하라.
④ 시간 투자와 연습이 지름길이다.
⑤ 말할 때 긴장을 풀고 천천히 하라.

W Mr. Smith, I _____ _____ in English. What should I do?
　　　　　　　말하는 데 어려움이 있다

M If you want to become fluent in English, you should try to learn English
　　　　　　　　　　　　　　　　　　　　　　　　　　　　　　　　문법을 공부하지 않고
_____ _____ .

W I don't understand what you are saying.

M Studying grammar will _____ _____ and confuse you. You will
　　　　　　　　　　　당신을 느리게 하다
think about the rules when creating sentences.

W It makes sense. I'm worried too much about making grammatical mistakes when
speaking English.

M So I want you to _____ what you want to express. Enjoy
　　　　　　~에 초점을 맞추다
communication.

W Thank you for good advice.

10 심정 추론

여자의 부모님이 안 계신 상황임을 파악한다.

대화를 듣고, 여자의 심정으로 가장 적절한 것을 고르시오

① excited 흥분된
② surprised 놀란
③ worried 걱정하는
④ disappointed 실망한
⑤ lonely 외로운

M What's up?

W Nothing special. My parents _____ _____ _____ for about a
   month to celebrate their 20th wedding anniversary.
   [멀리 휴가 중에 있다]

M Do you have any brothers or sisters?

W I have an older brother. He is a university student, so he _____
   _____ _____ . So I'm home alone after school.
   [기숙사에 머물다]

M What do you do in the evening?

W I read books for an hour or two until it gets dark. Then I turn on TV, watch it for a while,
   and fall asleep on the couch.

M I know how you feel.

W I'm just waiting for my parents to come back.

11 특정 정보 파악

대화를 듣고, 여자가 하게 될 봉사활동으로 가장 적절한 것을 고르시오.

① 청소하기
② 요리하기
③ 책 읽어주기
④ 숙제 도와주기
⑤ 관광 안내하기

W Are you _____ _____ ?
   [관광안내원을 찾고 있다]

M Yes, we need people _____ _____ _____ _____ each
   piece of art.
   [그룹을 이끌고 설명할]

W Well, I was a history teacher. I retired last year. I'm looking for some ways to spend a few
   hours volunteering _____ _____ _____ .
   [관광안내원으로서]

M Then you're the person we've been looking for.

W Great! When do I start?

M Can you come next Monday, please?

12 전화 목적 파악

대화를 듣고, 남자가 전화를 건 목적으로 가장 적절한 것을 고르시오.

① 길을 물어보려고
② 안부를 물으려고
③ 이사한 위치를 알려주려고
④ 치과 예약을 하려고
⑤ 위치를 문의하려고

[Telephone rings]

W Thank you for calling Maple Dental Clinic. How can I help you?

M It's John Woods calling. How are you today?

W I'm fine, Mr. Woods. How are you?

M Well, actually, I have _____ _____ . I was hoping Dr. Morris would have some
   time to see me.
   [약간의 치통]

W OK. I can _____ _____ for 2 p.m tomorrow. How does that sound?
   [오후 2시에 당신을 끼워 넣다]

M That would be great.

W I'll have to give you the new address of our new office.

M Oh, you moved.

W Yes, we moved across the road from the Business Bank.

M I think I know where it is. I'll see you tomorrow.

W Okay. Thanks for calling. See you then.

13 언급 및 비언급 파악

대화를 듣고, 여자가 방문한 곳을 좋아하는 이유로 언급되지 <u>않은</u> 것을 고르시오.

① 조용했다.
② 사람들이 친절했다.
③ 호텔의 시설이 매우 좋았다.
④ 음식이 맛있었다.
⑤ 비가 왔다.

방문한 곳에 대한 내용을 잘 듣고 선택지의 내용과 비교해 본다.

W Hi, John.

M Hi, Jane. Did you have a nice vacation?

W It was wonderful. I went to Japan.

M Japan? How was your trip?

W It was fantastic! I stayed in a small town. It was _____ _____ , and the sights
매우 조용한
were so beautiful. _____ _____ to me and _____
사람들은 매우 친절했다 음식은 맛있었다
_____ , too.

M What was the weather like?

W It _____ _____ _____ . But I like rainy weather. The foggy scenes looked
대부분 비가 왔다
like paintings.

14 특정 정보 파악

대화를 듣고, 남자가 사올 물건이 <u>아닌</u> 것을 고르시오.

① 양파 onion
② 햄 ham
③ 토마토 tomato
④ 오렌지 주스 orange juice
⑤ 오렌지 orange

오렌지 주스와 오렌지가 혼동되지 않도록 주의한다.

[On the telephone.]

W John, why aren't you home from school yet?

M Soccer practice was _____ _____ _____ . I'm leaving now.
평소보다 더 긴

W I'm going to make soup and sandwiches for dinner. Can you buy _____
약간의 양파, 햄 그리고 토마토
, _____ _____ _____ on the way home?

M OK. Is there anything to drink?

W Yes, we have plenty of orange juice. And _____ _____ _____
오렌지 좀 사와라
for me.

M OK, mom.

15 금액 파악

대화를 듣고, 남자가 지불한 금액을 고르시오.

① $ 4
② $ 14
③ $ 20
④ $ 30
⑤ $ 40

M I'd like to _____ _____ _____ .
이 시계를 사다

W OK. That's twenty dollars.

M Excuse me, but isn't this watch on sale this week?

W Oh, I'm sorry. You're right. It's _____ _____ _____ .
30% 할인된

M That's okay.

W That'll be fourteen dollars.

M _____ _____ .
여기 14달러 있습니다

W Thanks.

16 관계 추론

대화를 듣고, 두 사람의 관계로 가장 적절한 것을 고르시오.

① 의사 – 환자
② 운전사 – 승객
③ 교사 – 학생
④ 가게 주인 – 손님
⑤ 교사 – 학부모

Who's speaking?은 전화 대화에서 상대방이 누구인지 물을 때 쓰는 표현으로 '누구세요'라는 뜻이다.

'I want to know how ~' 뒤에 나오는 내용을 잘 듣도록 한다.

[Telephone rings.]

W Hello. Can I speak to Mr. Adams?

M This is he speaking. Who's speaking, please?

W This is Jenny's mother. I want to know _____ _____ _____
제 딸이 어떻게 생활하는지
_____ in school.

M She's doing fine. Her behavior is excellent, and she _____ _____
그녀의 학교 생활을 좋아하다
_____ . But her spelling is not good.

W I already know that. Can you help her _____ _____ _____ ?
그녀의 맞춤법을

M Yes, I can. And I want you to help her at home, too.

W OK, I will.

17 주제 파악

다음을 듣고, 무엇에 관한 안내인지 가장 적절한 것을 고르시오.

① 기차 예매권 매진
② 기차표 예매 일정
③ 기차 승강장 변경
④ 기차 출발 시각 연기
⑤ 기차 도착 시각 연기

W Good afternoon, ladies and gentlemen. This is for _____ for the 5
   _{기다리고 계신 승객들}
o'clock train to Busan. The 5 o'clock train to Busan _____ _____ because of
   _{지연되다}
heavy snow. _____ _____ _____ here at 7 o'clock. The train
   _{기차는 떠날 것이다}
will arrive in Busan at 10:20. We're very sorry for the delay. Thank you for your patience.

18 부탁한 일 파악

대화를 듣고, 남자가 여자에게 부탁한 일로 가장 적절한 것을 고르시오.

① 함께 시험공부 하기
② 비밀 지켜주기
③ 공부방법 알려주기
④ 선배 소개시켜 주기
⑤ 과학 과외해주기

W Hi, Matt. How was the exam?

M Don't ask. It was bad.

W But you _____ _____. I was sure you'd do well.
   _{정말 열심히 공부했다}

M Well, I hoped so, too. But maybe, my studying style wasn't right.

W That's too bad. Why don't you use the school's tutoring program? They find a senior
student who can help you.

M Maybe... but you're _____ _____ _____ science, too. Why don't you be
   _{~을 아주 잘하는}
my tutor?

W I can, but do you really think I can help you?

M Of course!

고난도

19 알맞은 응답 찾기

[19~20] 대화를 듣고, 여자의 마지막 말에 이어질 남자의 응답으로 가장 적절한 것을 고르시오.

Man: _____

① Here's your change.
② How long does it take?
③ Sorry, I'll do it tomorrow.
④ You need more time to do it.
⑤ I hope you'll have a good time.

W Where can I find a toy?

M Come this way, please. This is _____ _____. Is there anything you
   _{장난감 구역이다}
want?

W These are not the toys I'm looking for. Do you have anything bigger?

M How about this section? Here are some _____ _____ _____.
   _{좀 더 비싼 것들}

W How much is this?

M The robot is 90 dollars.

W I'll take it. Here's _____ _____ _____.
   _{100달러 지폐}

M _____

20 알맞은 응답 찾기

마실 것을 묻는 질문에 대해 마실 것을 주문하는 말이 와야한다.

Man: _____

① Much better, thank you.
② You'd better choose this.
③ I'll be back soon with that.
④ Let's see. I'll have a glass of milk.
⑤ Do you have a bigger one?

W What would you like to order?

M I'd _____ _____ _____ _____ galbi.
   _{1인분 주세요}

W All right. And what would you like with that, rice or _____ _____ _____ ?
   _{구운 감자}

M I'd like a baked potato.

W And would you like _____ _____ _____ ?
   _{마실 것}

M _____

무엇을 평가하는가?	일상생활이나 친숙한 일반적 주제에 관한 말이나 대화를 듣고 상황 및 대화의 흐름을 추론할 수 있는지 평가한다.
어떻게 출제되는가?	• 대화를 듣고, 남자의 마지막 말에 이어질 여자의 말로 가장 적절한 것을 고르시오. • 대화를 듣고, 여자의 마지막 말에 이어질 남자의 응답으로 가장 적절한 것을 고르시오.

key solution

❶ 적절한 응답을 고르는 경우. 전반적인 내용을 이해하면서 마지막 말에 집중한다.

[기출로 전략 확인]

대화를 듣고, 남자의 마지막 말에 이어질 여자의 말로 가장 적절한 것을 고르시오. [2018 기출]

Woman: _____

① No, it doesn't.　　② That's perfect.　　③ Can you spell it?

④ Long time no see.　　⑤ I'm taller than you.

···

W Paul, did you hear that our English teacher is going back to the U.S.?

M Oh, really? When is he leaving?

W Next week. So, I'd like to have a goodbye party for him.

M That sounds great. How about asking other classmates to join the party?

W All right. I'll ask the mto join us.

M Good. Why don't we have the party this Wednesday?

❶ 송별회 날짜를 제안하고 있다. 제안에 반대하거나 찬성하는 답변이 올 수 있다.

여 Paul, 우리 영어 선생님이 미국으로 돌아가신 다는 소식 들었어?

남 진짜? 언제 떠나신대?

여 다음 주에. 그래서 선생님을 위한 송별회를 하고 싶어.

남 좋은 생각이야. 다른 반 학생들한테 송별회에 함께하자고 하는 거 어때?

여 그래. 내가 물어볼게.

남 좋아. 이번 수요일에 파티를 하는 게 어떨까?

적절한 응답의 발문과 보기

대화를 듣고, 남자의 마지막 말에 이어질 여자의 말로 가장 적절한 것을 고르시오.

[2018 기출]

Woman: _____

① I have a fever.

② It took 40 minutes by bus.

③ I play the piano very well.

④ My favorite food is spaghetti.

⑤ They're blue with white stripes.

만점 잡는 문장　**W** I think I lost my new running shoes.

⋮

M Okay. I'll help you to find them. <u>What do your shoes look like?</u>

대화를 듣고, 남자의 마지막 말에 이어질 여자의 응답으로 가장 적절한 것을 고르시오.

[2017 기출]

① Okay, let's go together.　② Maybe he can help you.

③ That is my pencil case.　④ Go straight for one block.

⑤ I think that was your problem.

만점 잡는 문장　**M** <u>Why don't we visit there this Sunday?</u>

적절한 응답에 쓰이는 어휘 및 표현

● **동의 / 감사**

That sounds good. 좋은 생각이에요.

That's perfect. 완벽해.

Thank you for coming. 와 주셔서 감사해요.

● **충고/기대**

You should not run here. 여기서는 뛰면 안됩니다.

Text him that you are sorry. 그에게 미안하다고 문자를 보내.

I'm looking forward to meeting you. 만나는 걸 기대하고 있습니다.

● **제안/격려**

Let me help you. 도와줄게.

Please help yourself. 마음껏 드세요.

Don't worry. You can do it. 걱정 마. 넌 할 수 있어.

I'm sorry to hear that. 안됐다.

학년   반   번
이름

01 대화를 듣고, 여자가 선택한 캐릭터를 고르시오.

①   ②   ③

④   ⑤

02 다음을 듣고, 그림을 <u>잘못</u> 설명한 것을 고르시오.

①   ②   ③   ④   ⑤

03 다음을 듣고, 여자의 심정 변화로 가장 적절한 것을 고르시오.

① sad → happy
② lonely → angry
③ excited → upset
④ angry → peaceful
⑤ terrified → relieved

고난도
04 대화를 듣고, 대화의 결론으로 가장 적절한 것을 고르시오.

① 고양이가 개보다 더 영리하다.
② 개가 고양이보다 더 영리하다.
③ 사회성이 좋을수록 지능이 높다.
④ 고등동물일수록 두뇌의 크기가 크다.
⑤ 지능의 정도는 두뇌의 크기와 직접적인 관련이 없다.

05 대화를 듣고, 무엇에 관한 내용인지 가장 적절한 것을 고르시오.

① 월세 비용   ② 새로운 거처
③ 장학금   ④ 주차 문제
⑤ 이직 문제

06 대화를 듣고, 두 사람이 대화하는 장소로 가장 적절한 곳을 고르시오.

① 영화관   ② 동물원
③ 음식점   ④ 백화점
⑤ 미술관

07 대화를 듣고, 두 사람의 관계로 가장 적절한 것을 고르시오.

① 경찰 – 증인   ② 점원 – 고객
③ 약사 – 환자   ④ 교사 – 학부모
⑤ 의사 – 간호사

08 대화를 듣고, 두 사람이 버스터미널에 도착할 시각을 고르시오.

① 4:30   ② 4:50
③ 5:10   ④ 5:30
⑤ 5:40

고난도
09 대화를 듣고, 마늘의 효능에 대해 언급한 내용이 <u>아닌</u> 것을 고르시오.

① 피를 맑게 해 준다.
② 혈압을 낮추어 준다.
③ 질병을 예방해 준다.
④ 음식을 맛있게 해 준다.
⑤ 심장마비를 예방해 준다.

10 대화를 듣고, 남자가 여자에게 전화를 건 목적으로 가장 적절한 것을 고르시오.

① 신문 원고를 부탁하려고
② 대회 일정을 연기하려고
③ 여행 일정을 문의하려고
④ 신문 광고를 문의하려고
⑤ 경연 대회 참가를 제안하려고

점수

/20

11 다음 그림의 상황에 가장 적절한 대화를 고르시오.

①   ②   ③   ④   ⑤

12 다음 메모를 보면서 대화를 듣고, 내용과 일치하지 <u>않는</u> 것을 고르시오.

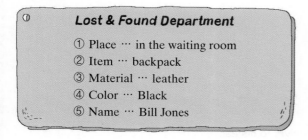

Lost & Found Department

① Place … in the waiting room
② Item … backpack
③ Material … leather
④ Color … Black
⑤ Name … Bill Jones

13 대화를 듣고, Lily의 생일선물로 두 사람이 사기로 한 것을 고르시오.

① book   ② purse
③ flower   ④ jacket
⑤ chocolate

14 대화를 듣고, Joanna에 관해 알 수 <u>없는</u> 것을 고르시오.

① 연령   ② 직업
③ 자녀 수   ④ 운동 장소
⑤ 운동 시간

15 대화를 듣고, 여자가 이용할 교통수단으로 가장 적절한 것을 고르시오.

① bus   ② car
③ taxi   ④ train
⑤ subway

16 대화를 듣고, 남자가 샌프란시스코에 가려는 이유로 가장 적절한 것을 고르시오.

① 뉴스 취재   ② 친척 방문
③ 구직 면접   ④ 대학 진학
⑤ 결혼식 참여

17 대화를 듣고, 여자가 남자에게 부탁한 일로 가장 적절한 것을 고르시오.

① 연극 관람 와주기   ② 함께 연극하기
③ 새로운 사람 찾아주기   ④ 함께 친구 설득해주기
⑤ 경찰에 신고해주기

18 대화를 듣고, 남자가 방학 동안 한 일로 가장 적절한 것을 고르시오.

① 수영 배우기   ② 축구 연습하기
③ 체육관 다니기   ④ 요가 배우기
⑤ 아르바이트 하기

[19~20] 대화를 듣고, 여자의 마지막 말에 이어질 남자의 응답으로 가장 적절한 것을 고르시오.

19 Man: _____

① We should study math more.
② I promise to keep it a secret.
③ You'd better call him back later.
④ Okay, I'd like to buy you dinner.
⑤ You should be very proud of him.

20 Man: _____

① I'll buy some flowers.
② That's a problem at all.
③ I don't use it any more.
④ That would look better.
⑤ I'd like to, but I am too busy.

다시 들으면서 듣기 만점에 도전하세요!
Dictation: 스크립트의 주요 부분을 다시 들으면서!
실전 ⊕: 세부 정보가 많은 스크립트를 다른 문제로 샅샅이!

---

01 그림 정보 파악 – 사물　여자는 처음에 원한 호랑이를 계속 원한다는 것을 파악해야한다.

대화를 듣고, 여자가 선택한 캐릭터를 고르시오.

① ② ③ ④ ⑤

W　Yeah. These characters are so cute. Did you make them all?
M　Sure. Choose one, and I'll give it to you.
W　Really? Hmm... I'll _____ _____ _____.
　　　　　　　　　　　　　호랑이를 고르다
M　You mean the one with a ball on his head?
W　Well, no. The one _____ _____ _____.
　　　　　　　　　　　공을 차고 있는
M　But I think the teddy bear playing the guitar is better.
W　I _____ _____ _____.
　　여전히 그 호랑이를 원하다

---

02 그림 정보 파악 – 토익형　receiver는 전화 수화기이다.

다음을 듣고, 그림을 잘못 설명한 것을 고르시오.

① ② ③ ④ ⑤

W　①　The boy is holding a receiver to his ear.
　　②　The man is _____ _____ the ladder to fix the light.
　　　　　　　　　　올라가다
　　③　The curtains have been pulled shut.
　　④　Boxes are stacked in the room.
　　⑤　Some tools _____ _____ on the floor.
　　　　　　　　　　흩어져 있다

---

03 심정 추론

다음을 듣고, 여자의 심정 변화로 가장 적절한 것을 고르시오.

① sad → happy
② lonely → angry
③ excited → upset
④ angry → peaceful
⑤ terrified → relieved

W　An old woman was walking down a street at night carrying two bags full of potatoes.
One man _____ _____ _____. She had
　　　　　　　　뒤에서 바싹 다가오다　　　　　　　　　　　　　　　　많은 양의 현금
_____ _____ _____ in her handbag. No one else was around
and it looked like she was going _____ _____ _____. Suddenly she had
　　　　　　　　　　　　　　　　　　강도를 당하다
an idea that she would give up her two bags of potatoes and run. She dropped them on
the ground and started to run. Then the man said, "Mom, it's me! Your son, Tommy.
What's wrong with you?" The man _____ _____ _____, and
　　　　　　　　　　　　　　　　　봉지를 집어들다
walked towards his mom.

04 특정 정보 파악

대화를 듣고, 대화의 결론으로 가장 적절한 것을 고르시오.

① 고양이가 개보다 더 영리하다.
② 개가 고양이보다 더 영리하다.
③ 사회성이 좋을수록 지능이 높다.
④ 고등동물일수록 두뇌의 크기가 크다.
⑤ 지능의 정도는 두뇌의 크기와 직접적인 관련이 없다.

M Which do you think are smarter, dogs or cats?

W I think dogs are smarter. I think dogs _____ _____ . And dogs are
　　더 큰 두뇌를 갖고 있다
_____ _____ .
고양이보다 더 사교적이다

M Then I am smarter than you, because I have a bigger head than you.

W You are kidding. That doesn't make sense.

M Right. Most scientists still question whether the size of the brain _____
_____ _____ the intelligence level.
　　직접적인 관련이 있다

W That means cats _____ _____ _____ smarter than dogs.
　　　　혹시 ~할지도 모른다

M They might possibly be indeed.

05 주제 파악

대화를 듣고, 무엇에 관한 내용인지 가장 적절한 것을 고르시오.

① 월세 비용
② 새로운 거처
③ 장학금
④ 주차 문제
⑤ 이직 문제

➕ 대화를 듣고, 여자가 새 집을 구하려고 하는 이유로 가장 적절한 것을 고르시오.

① 새 집에서 살고 싶어서
② 더 넓은 집에 살고 싶어서
③ 집세를 아끼고 싶어서
④ 학교에서 가까이 살고 싶어서
⑤ 더 높은 층에 살고 싶어서

여자는 사는 곳과 학교가 너무 멀어서 이사가려고 하는 상황이다.

M Hi, Ann. How's it going? How is your new apartment?

W That's _____ _____ _____ to you. I'm looking for a new place.
　　내가 말하는 바

M Why? What's the problem with your apartment? I thought you liked the apartment.

W I liked it because It's cheap and spacious, but the problem is that it is _____
_____ from the school. It takes too long to get there.
너무 먼

M Well, I know there's an apartment complex around the corner near my place. I'll
_____ _____ _____ on my way to class today.
거기에 들르다

W Thanks a lot.

06 장소 추론

대화를 듣고, 두 사람이 대화하는 장소로 가장 적절한 곳을 고르시오.

① 영화관 theater
② 동물원 zoo
③ 음식점 restaurant
④ 백화점 department store
⑤ 미술관 art museum

동물과 관련된 곳에서 이루어지는 대화임을 파악한다.

W Look at this poster, Dad. The birds are so beautiful.

M Yeah. They are all from Africa.

W Look around and _____ _____ _____ .
　　　　　　동물들을 구경하다

M Janet, I'm very hungry. Let's eat something before going around.

W After lunch, I'd like to _____ _____ _____ _____ , too. The third
　　　　　　　　돌고래 쇼를 보다
show starts at 2 o'clock.

M Wait a moment. I'll go to _____ _____ _____ and some food.
　　　　　　표를 사다

07 관계 추론

대화를 듣고, 두 사람의 관계로 가장 적절한 것을 고르시오.

① 경찰 – 증인
② 점원 – 고객
③ 약사 – 환자
④ 교사 – 학부모
⑤ 의사 – 간호사

M Hello, how can I help you?

W I think _____ _____ _____ .
　　감기에 걸리려고 하다

M Well, we have many _____ _____ _____ .
　　　　　　　의사의 처방 없이 복용할 수 있는 약

W Could I have something for a runny nose?

M Yes. This works for _____ _____ _____ _____ .
　　　　콧물을 흘리거나 기침에

W Thank you. And what do you have for dry skin?

M Try some of this new lotion. It's very good.

W Okay. Thanks a lot.

대화를 듣고, 두 사람이 버스터미널에 도착할 시각을 고르시오.

① 4:30   ② 4:50
③ 5:10   ④ 5:30
⑤ 5:40

➕ 대화를 듣고, 여자가 타려고 하는 버스의 출발 시간을 고르시오.

① 4:30   ② 4:50
③ 5:10   ④ 5:30
⑤ 5:40

W David, can I ask a favor?

M What is it?

W Could you _____ _____ _____ to the Express Bus Terminal this afternoon?
_{나를 태워주다}

M I think so. What time do you need to be there?

W Well, my plan is to take the 5:40 bus to Vancouver.

M Then, I'll _____ _____ _____ _____.
_{5시에 차로 태우러 가다}
It _____ _____ _____ to the terminal.
_{단지 30분 걸리다}

W Good. Thank you.

대화를 듣고, 마늘의 효능에 대해 언급한 내용이 <u>아닌</u> 것을 고르시오.

① 피를 맑게 해 준다.
② 혈압을 낮추어 준다.
③ 질병을 예방해 준다.
④ 음식을 맛있게 해 준다.
⑤ 심장마비를 예방해 준다.

W Do you like eating garlic?

M Actually I don't like it. It smells bad and tastes strong.

W That's the reason people don't like it. But it is very good for health.

M I know. Garlic doesn't smell good, but it _____ _____ _____.
_{음식을 더 맛있게 해 준다}
What is garlic good for?

W It prevents many different diseases. It _____ _____
_{혈압을 낮추는 데 도움이 되다}
and prevent heart attack.

M That is why people in the world _____ _____ _____ in Kimchi.
_{더 관심을 갖다}

W That's right. Kimchi has been popular in the world these days. They know Kimchi has lots of garlic, so it is healthy food.

광고에 난 내용에 대하여 남자가 한 말을 잘 파악해야 한다.

대화를 듣고, 남자가 여자에게 전화를 건 목적으로 가장 적절한 것을 고르시오.

① 신문 원고를 부탁하려고
② 대회 일정을 연기하려고
③ 여행 일정을 문의하려고
④ 신문 광고를 문의하려고
⑤ 경연 대회 참가를 제안하려고

[Telephone rings.]

M Hello, I'd like to speak to Cara.

W Oh, hi, Bill. What's up?

M Did you ever _____ _____ in the school newspaper?
_{광고를 보다}

W Which one do you mean?

M I mean the ad _____ _____ _____.
_{노래 부르기 경연 대회에 관한}

W No, I haven't seen it. When is it?

M November the 20th. Why don't _____ _____ _____?
_{우리 함께 참여하다}

W That sounds great.

다음 그림의 상황에 가장 적절한 대화를 고르시오.

① ② ③ ④ ⑤

① W You look nice. Is that a new jacket?

  M Yes, my parents bought it for me for my birthday.

② W I will take this jacket and _____ _____ _____.
  이 바지 한 벌

  M Great. How would you like to pay?

③ W What do you think? Does it fit you?

  M I think it's too big. _____ _____ _____ a smaller size,
  ~을 입어봐도 되나요?
     please?

④ W What do you think of my new jacket?

  M I like it, especially the pattern on the shoulders.

⑤ W Where can I try on these clothes?

  M The fitting room is over there, around the corner.

다음 메모를 보면서 대화를 듣고, 내용과 일치하지 않는 것을 고르시오.

Lost & Found Department
① Place … in the waiting room
② Item … backpack
③ Material … leather
④ Color … Black
⑤ Name … Bill Jones

M I've _____ _____ in the waiting room. Could you help me find it?
   배낭을 잃어버리다

W Of course. Could you tell me _____ _____ _____ _____?
   그것이 어떻게 생겼는지

M Let me see. It's _____ _____ _____.
   천으로 된 작은 배낭

W What color is it?

M Black. And my name is printed on the top.

W Oh, yes. What's your name then?

M Bill Jones.

W All right.

대화를 듣고, Lily의 생일선물로 두 사람이 사기로 한 것을 고르시오.

① book 책
② purse 지갑
③ flower 꽃
④ jacket 재킷
⑤ chocolate 초콜릿

W It's Lily's birthday tomorrow.

M Well, let me see. Should we buy her a present?

W Certainly. _____ _____ _____ _____?
   그녀에게 무엇을 사줘야 할까?

M How about a box of chocolates? She likes it very much.

W I hear she's on a diet. How about flowers? Most girls like flowers.

M But Peter will send her lots of flowers.

W Yeah. _____ _____ _____ _____?
   지갑은 어때   그녀의 것이 좋아 보이지 않는다
   _____ _____.

M That's a good idea.

여자에 관한 내용을 순서대로 파악하여 일치하지 않는 것을 찾아야 한다.

대화를 듣고, Joanna에 관해 알 수 없는 것을 고르시오.

① 연령
② 직업
③ 자녀 수
④ 운동 장소
⑤ 운동 시간

M Thanks for coming, Joanna.

W Don't mention it. I'm glad to be here.

M We all know that you are in _____ _____ and _____
   40대 중반   두 자녀를 두고 있다
   _____ _____. Do you exercise a lot?

W Yes, I _____ _____ _____ regularly.
   체육관에 간다

M How often do you go there?

W Almost every day, except when I have to visit my mother.

M How long do you usually work out for each day?

W _____ _____ _____ a day.
   약 두 시간

15 특정 정보 파악

대화를 듣고, 여자가 이용할 교통수단으로 가장 적절한 것을 고르시오.

① bus 버스
② car 차
③ taxi 택시
④ train 기차
⑤ subway 지하철

M Honey, I'm going to work. Don't be late for today's meeting.
W Okay, but I don't know ＿＿＿＿＿＿ ＿＿＿＿＿ ＿＿＿＿＿.
　그곳에 빨리 가는 방법
M You'd better not use your car. You don't know the way.
W Then should I go there by taxi?
M No. ＿＿＿＿＿ ＿＿＿＿＿ ＿＿＿＿ at that time. And it's too expensive.
　붐비는 시간이다
W But there is no subway station around it.
M You'd better ＿＿＿＿＿ ＿＿＿＿. There is a bus-only lane to the hotel.
　버스를 이용하다
W Okay. That's good.

16 이유 파악

대화를 듣고, 남자가 샌프란시스코에 가려는 이유로 가장 적절한 것을 고르시오.

① 뉴스 취재
② 친척 방문
③ 구직 면접
④ 대학 진학
⑤ 결혼식 참여

What's new with you?는 '뭐 새로운 일 있니?, 좋은 일 있니?'라고 상대방의 안부를 묻는 말이다.

M Hi, Linda. How are you today?
W Fine. You look very good. What's new with you?
M Well, I'm going to San Francisco tomorrow.
W Going to San Francisco? ＿＿＿＿＿ ＿＿＿＿?
　무엇 때문에
M Yeah, I have an aunt there and ＿＿＿＿＿＿＿＿＿. ＿＿＿＿＿ ＿＿＿＿
　　　　　　　　　　　　　그녀가 나를 초대하셨다　　　　나는 그곳에 머물 것이다
for about a month.
W That's great. Have a good time there.
M Thank you.

17 부탁한 일 파악

대화를 듣고, 여자가 남자에게 부탁한 일로 가장 적절한 것을 고르시오.

① 연극 관람 와주기
② 함께 연극하기
③ 새로운 사람 찾아주기
④ 함께 친구 설득해주기
⑤ 경찰에 신고해주기

M Hi, Jenny, I heard you're performing a play in the school festival. How's it going?
W To be honest, we're in trouble. We need a new actor.
M Why? What happened?
W Jaehun ＿＿＿＿＿ ＿＿＿＿. He didn't like his role.
　갑자기 도중하차하다
M That's too bad. What's the role?
W It's a police officer role. [pause] Wait, are you interested, Woobin?
M Maybe. I've always wanted to try acting.
W Really? Can you do it, please? I think you'll be good at it.
M Hmm... okay. I'll ＿＿＿＿ ＿＿＿＿ ＿＿＿＿.
　한번 해 보다

18 한 일 파악

대화를 듣고, 남자가 방학 동안 한 일로 가장 적절한 것을 고르시오.

① 수영 배우기　　② 축구 연습하기
③ 체육관 다니기　④ 요가 배우기
⑤ 아르바이트 하기

W Hi, Minho, did you do anything interesting over the summer vacation?

M Well, I wanted to ＿＿＿＿＿＿＿ ＿＿＿＿ ＿＿＿＿, but I didn't get the chance.
　　　　　　　　수영하는 법을 배우다

W Oh, no. Were you too busy with your soccer practice?

M No, I couldn't find a good swimming pool in my neighborhood.

W That's too bad. I heard a new gym will open soon. I hope they will have a pool there.

M Yes, but it's okay. I ＿＿＿＿＿＿＿ ＿＿＿＿, and I really liked it.
　　　　　　　　대신 요가를 배웠다

W Wow, really? Tell me more about it.

19 알맞은 응답 찾기

엄마가 아들의 수학 성적이 우수하다는 말을 듣고 기뻐할 때 선생님이 할 수 있는 말을 생각해 본다.

[19~20] 대화를 듣고, 여자의 마지막 말에 이어질 남자의 응답으로 가장 적절한 것을 고르시오.

Man: ＿＿＿＿＿＿＿＿＿＿＿

① We should study math more.
② I promise to keep it a secret.
③ You'd better call him back later.
④ Okay, I'd like to buy you dinner.
⑤ You should be very proud of him.

W Hello. I'm Mrs. Carter, David's mother.

M Oh! Mrs. Carter! I'm pleased to meet you.

W I'm glad to meet you, too. Please tell me, ＿＿＿＿＿＿＿ ＿＿＿
　＿＿＿＿ ＿＿＿＿ this year?　David가 수학에서 어떻게 하고 있는지

M He's doing very well. He works very hard, and ＿＿＿＿＿＿ ＿＿＿
　＿＿＿＿. He's already a top student in my class.　그의 성적들은 우수하다

W I'm glad to hear that.

M ＿＿＿＿＿＿＿＿＿＿＿＿

20 알맞은 응답 찾기

Man: ＿＿＿＿＿＿＿＿＿＿

① I'll buy some flowers.
② That's a problem at all.
③ I don't use it any more.
④ That would look better.
⑤ I'd like to, but I am too busy.

W How do you like my new dress? I bought it yesterday.

M It looks very fashionable.

W Thank you. I'm going to wear it to my friend's party tomorrow. What do you think?

M Not a bad idea. But I don't think ＿＿＿＿＿＿ ＿＿＿＿ ＿＿＿＿ ＿＿＿＿
　＿＿＿＿ matches the dress.　왼쪽의 꽃

W I don't like it, either. I'll ＿＿＿＿＿ ＿＿＿＿ ＿＿＿＿.
　　　　　　　　　떼어버리다

M ＿＿＿＿＿＿＿＿＿＿＿

01 대화를 듣고, 여자가 속한 동아리를 고르시오.

02 다음 그림의 상황에 가장 적절한 대화를 고르시오.

①   ②   ③   ④   ⑤

03 대화를 듣고, 남자가 지금 할 일로 가장 적절한 것을 고르시오.

① 숙제   ② 쇼핑
③ TV 시청   ④ 거실 청소
⑤ 농구 시합

04 대화를 듣고, 여자가 지불할 금액을 고르시오.

① $20   ② $30   ③ $35   ④ $40   ⑤ $60

05 대화를 듣고, 두 사람이 이용할 교통수단으로 가장 적절한 것을 고르시오.

① bus   ② car
③ taxi   ④ train
⑤ subway

06 대화를 듣고, 남자가 하는 말의 의도로 가장 적절한 것을 고르시오.

① 칭찬   ② 경고
③ 사과   ④ 조언
⑤ 축하

07 대화를 듣고, 남자가 가장 좋아했던 관광지를 고르시오.

① 왕궁   ② 해변
③ 박물관   ④ 불교사원
⑤ 코끼리 농장

08 대화를 듣고, 내용을 가장 잘 나타낸 안내문을 고르시오.

① SLOW
② NO PARKING
③ ONE-WAY ONLY
④ DO NOT ENTER
⑤ DO NOT PASS

09 대화를 듣고, 여자의 장래희망으로 가장 적절한 것을 고르시오.

① 화가   ② 요리사
③ 디자이너   ④ 가수
⑤ 교사

고난도
10 대화를 듣고, Sally에 관한 내용과 일치하지 <u>않는</u> 것을 고르시오.

① Baker 선생님의 초등학교 제자이다.
② Harry와 초등학교 동창이다.
③ Baker 선생님의 병문안을 갈 예정이다.
④ 3개월 동안 병원에 입원한 적이 있다.
⑤ 토요일 오전에 Harry를 만날 예정이다.

11 대화를 듣고, 두 사람이 확인하지 않은 물품을 고르시오.

① 여권 ② 비행기 표
③ 수영복 ④ 콘텍트렌즈
⑤ 안내 책자

12 대화를 듣고, 남자가 여자에게 전화를 건 목적으로 가장 적절한 것을 고르시오.

① 캠핑 장비를 주문하려고
② 내일 날씨를 물어보려고
③ 캠핑 약속을 취소하려고
④ 캠핑 일정을 변경하려고
⑤ 일기예보가 틀린 것을 항의하려고

13 대화를 듣고, 남자가 기분이 언짢은 이유로 가장 적절한 것을 고르시오.

① 딸이 집에 늦게 들어와서
② 딸이 물을 낭비하기 때문에
③ 윗층의 물소리 때문에 잠이 깨서
④ 날씨가 더워 잠을 이룰 수 없어서
⑤ 이웃집에서 시끄럽게 한다고 항의해서

14 대화를 듣고, 두 사람이 대화하는 장소로 가장 적절한 곳을 고르시오.

① 서점 ② 교실
③ 도서관 ④ 백화점
⑤ 사무실

15 대화를 듣고, 두 사람의 관계로 가장 적절한 것을 고르시오.

① 여행사 직원 – 고객 ② 공항 직원 – 여행객
③ 교사 – 학생 ④ 은행 직원 – 고객
⑤ 경찰 – 시민

16 대화를 듣고, 남자의 심정 변화로 가장 적절한 것을 고르시오.

① upset → relieved
② nervous → disappointed
③ amused → frightened
④ angry → interested
⑤ thankful → angry

17 다음을 듣고, 여자가 하는 말의 내용으로 가장 적절한 것을 고르시오.

① 캠핑 회원 모집 ② 캠핑 일정 변경
③ 캠핑 주의사항 ④ 캠핑 장소 소개
⑤ 캠핑 후기

18 다음을 듣고, 요일과 날씨가 바르게 연결된 것을 고르시오.

① 월요일 오전 – cloudy
② 월요일 오후 – snowy
③ 화요일 오후 – rainy
④ 수요일 오전 – rainy
⑤ 수요일 오후 – snowy

[19~20] 대화를 듣고, 여자의 마지막 말에 이어질 남자의 응답으로 가장 적절한 것을 고르시오.

고난도
19 Man: _____

① I mean I really love you.
② Would you do me a favor?
③ What? What did I do wrong?
④ Do you want to look at them?
⑤ It's good. I'd like to try some more.

20 Man: _____

① You're kidding.
② You're welcome.
③ Enjoy your visit there.
④ That's fine with me.
⑤ OK, take care of yourself.

다시 들으면서 듣기 만점에 도전하세요!
Dictation: 스크립트의 주요 부분을 다시 들으면서!
실전 ⊕: 세부 정보가 많은 스크립트를 다른 문제로 샅샅이!

---

01 특정 정보 파악

대화를 듣고, 여자가 속한 동아리를 고르시오.

①   ②

③   ④

⑤

M Can I use your computer for a moment, Susie?

W Sure, but is it okay if I ask why?

M I need to check some information about a dance club.

W Oh, I didn't know you're interested in dance.

M I heard that you're a member of the school band, right?

W Yes, I was last year, but I _____ _____ this year.
　　　　　　　　　　　　　동아리를 바꿨다

M You're _____. So, you _____ _____
　　　　　그림에 관심이 있는　　　　　　　　　　　　　　　미술부에 가입했다
_____?

W That's right.

---

02 그림 상황 대화 찾기

다음 그림의 상황에 가장 적절한 대화를 고르시오.

①　②　③　④　⑤

남자가 한쪽 무릎을 꿇고, 서 있는 여자에게 장미 한 다발을 주면서 할 수 있는 말에 주목한다.

① **M** I'm _____ _____.
　　　　　　약간의 꽃을 찾고 있다
　W How about these?

② **M** Do you have a boyfriend?
　W Yes. His name is Richard.

③ **M** Happy birthday, Nancy. _____ _____ _____ _____.
　W Oh, _____ _____. Thank you.
　　　　나는 정말로 행복하다　이것은 당신을 위한 것이다

④ **M** I'm sorry. I'm too cold.
　W Really? Then I'll close the window.

⑤ **M** The room was filled with the smell of roses.
　W Yeah, they smell good.

고난도

03 할 일 파악

대화를 듣고, 남자가 지금 할 일로 가장 적절한 것을 고르시오.

① 숙제
② 쇼핑
③ TV 시청
④ 거실 청소
⑤ 농구 시합

어머니인 여자가 아들인 남자에게 요청하는 것이 무엇인지 파악한다.

M Mom! Can I watch the basketball game on TV now?

W No, you can't. I want you to _____ _____ _____ now.
　　　　　　　　　　　　　　　　　거실을 청소하다

M Oh, mom! I'll do it tomorrow morning. I promise.

W Mr. and Mrs. Conway are _____ _____ _____.
　　　　　　　　　　　　　　　저녁 식사를 하러 올

M But the basketball game starts now. Please, mom.

W No. I'm going shopping now and I need _____ _____ _____.
　　　　　　　　　　　　　　　　　　　　네가 도와주다
So, please clean the living room now.

M Oh, alright.

50% 세일 중인 상품이라는 것에 유의한다.

대화를 듣고, 여자가 지불할 금액을 고르시오.

① $20
② $30
③ $35
④ $40
⑤ $60

➕

대화를 듣고, 두 사람의 관계로 가장 적절한 것을 고르시오.

① 옷가게 점원 – 손님
② 디자이너 – 모델
③ 영화 감독 – 배우
④ 옷수선점 직원 – 손님
⑤ 미용사 – 고객

M Can I help you?

W Yes, how much is that skirt?

M It's $40.

W Can I _____ _____ _____?
   입어보다

M Yes, you can. The changing room is over there.

W It feels like it's a bit small for me and I don't like the color. How much is that pink skirt?

M It was 60 dollars, but it's on sale for _____ _____ _____.
   50% 할인

W I like it. It looks luxurious and high-quality. Is that size 11?

M Yes, it will perfectly fit you.

W OK. I'll take it.

대화를 듣고, 두 사람이 이용할 교통수단으로 가장 적절한 것을 고르시오.

① bus 버스
② car 자동차
③ taxi 택시
④ train 기차
⑤ subway 지하철

How about -ing?는 '~하는 게 어때?'라는 의미로 상대방에게 제안하는 말이다.

M It's a quarter past six. The movie starts at 7:00. We should hurry.

W How should we get there?

M Let's take the subway. The subway is always the fastest way.

W But this isn't rush hour. How about taking a taxi? A taxi will be faster than the subway now.

M How about going by bus? They use _____ _____ _____ _____, and
   버스 전용차선
   it's not so easy to _____ _____ _____ here.
   택시를 잡다

W I guess you're right. Oh, _____ _____ _____.
   저기 버스가 온다

M Okay.

여자가 어떤 상황에 처해 있고, 그런 여자에게 남자가 뭐라고 말하는지를 파악한다.

대화를 듣고, 남자가 하는 말의 의도로 가장 적절한 것을 고르시오.

① 칭찬
② 경고
③ 사과
④ 조언
⑤ 축하

M You look upset. Is there anything wrong?

W My best friend won't talk to me.

M What happened?

W I don't know, but she _____ _____ _____ me.
   쳐다보려고 하지도 않는다

M Maybe you can _____ _____ _____ _____. Then she
   그녀에게 편지를 보내다
   will like you again.

W Send a letter to her? That's a good idea. I'll write a letter right now.

M That's good. I'm sure _____ _____ _____ again.
   너희들의 우정이 좋아지다

W Thank you, Jason.

대화를 듣고, 남자가 가장 좋아했던 관광지를 고르시오.

① 왕궁 royal palace
② 해변 beach
③ 박물관 museum
④ 불교사원 Buddhist temple
⑤ 코끼리 농장 elephant farm

W Hi, Andy! You've got a suntan!

M Yes, I _____ _____ _____ on holiday.
   태국에 다녀왔다

W I'm sure you saw many beautiful things.

M Well, Bangkok is really beautiful.

W I heard the city is like a great, big museum.

M Sure. There are many palaces and Buddhist temples.

W What is _____ _____ _____ you saw in Thailand?
   가장 흥미로웠던 것

M I enjoyed visiting an elephant farm, but _____ _____ _____ in Bangkok is
   왕궁
   _____ _____ I saw.
   가장 흥미로운 것

대화를 듣고, 내용을 가장 잘 나타낸 안내문을 고르시오.

① SLOW 천천히
② NO PARKING 주차 금지
③ ONE-WAY ONLY 일방통행
④ DO NOT ENTER 진입 금지
⑤ DO NOT PASS 추월 금지

M You can't turn here.

W Oh, I'm so sorry. Can I park over there near the subway station?

M No, you can't. There's a police officer in front of the drugstore.

W But there's _____ _____ _____ .
   주차에 관한 표지판은 없다

M There it is. You see _____ _____ _____ _____ ?
   저쪽에 저 표지판

W Where? Oh, thanks for telling me. I had better _____ _____ .
   여기에는 주차하지 않는다

M Sure. You had better find a parking lot over there.

남자와 여자의 희망 사항을 구별할 수 있어야 한다.

대화를 듣고, 여자의 장래희망으로 가장 적절한 것을 고르시오.

① 화가 painter
② 요리사 cook
③ 디자이너 designer
④ 가수 singer
⑤ 교사 teacher

W What are you going to do after you graduate?

M I'm planning to get a job as a designer.

W Good for you. I know that you're really gifted in that area.

M Thanks. I wanted to be a painter when I was young, but now I want to be one of the best designers.

W I'd like _____ _____ _____ .
   선생님이 되는 것

M Oh, really?

W Yeah, I want to _____ _____ _____ .
   초등학교에서 가르치다

M I'm sure you'll be _____ _____ .
   훌륭한 선생님

10 내용 일치 파악

대화 중에 나오는 내용들을 정확히 듣고 순서대로 일치 여부를 판단한다.

대화를 듣고, Sally에 관한 내용과 일치하지 <u>않는</u> 것을 고르시오.

① Baker 선생님의 초등학교 제자이다.
② Harry와 초등학교 동창이다.
③ Baker 선생님의 병문안을 갈 예정이다.
④ 3개월 동안 병원에 입원한 적이 있다.
⑤ 토요일 오전에 Harry를 만날 예정이다.

How's it going?은 안부를 묻는 인사말로 '어떻게 지내니?'라는 뜻이다.

[Telephone rings.]

W Hi, Harry. It's Sally. How's it going?

M Good. How about you?

W I'm fine, too. By the way, did you hear that Mr. Baker from our elementary school _____ _____ _____ _____ for three months?
병원에 입원해 있다

M You mean _____ _____ _____ when we were elementary school students?
담임선생님

W Yes. I'm going to see him this Saturday. Do you want to go with me?

M Okay. How about _____ _____ _____ _____ of our school at 9:30 Saturday morning?
정문에서 만나는 것

W All right. See you then.

11 특정 정보 파악

대화 중에 언급된 품목을 정확히 듣고 일치 여부를 파악한다.

대화를 듣고, 두 사람이 확인하지 <u>않은</u> 물품을 고르시오.

① 여권 passport
② 비행기 표 airplane ticket
③ 수영복 swimming suit
④ 콘택트렌즈 contact lenses
⑤ 안내 책자 guide book

M It's already two o'clock. We have to hurry to the airport.

W Yeah, but we should check we have packed everything we need.

M Okay, let's check. Do you _____ _____ _____ ?
목록을 가지다

W Yes, I do. I'll read the list. You check. First of all, our _____ _____ _____ .
여권과 비행기 표

M Yes, they're here.

W Next, _____ _____ _____ .
수영복과 선글라스

M Perfect! And _____ _____ _____ are here too.
안내 책자와 지도

W That's good.

12 전화 목적 파악

대화를 듣고, 남자가 여자에게 전화를 건 목적으로 가장 적절한 것을 고르시오.

① 캠핑 장비를 주문하려고
② 내일 날씨를 물어보려고
③ 캠핑 약속을 취소하려고
④ 캠핑 일정을 변경하려고
⑤ 일기예보가 틀린 것을 항의하려고

[Telephone rings.]

W Good morning. May I help you?

M Yes. My father and I are planning to go camping tomorrow. Could you _____ _____ _____ _____ for tomorrow?
나에게 날씨를 말해 주다

W Sure. It's going to rain tomorrow across the country.

M What? Are you sure it's going to _____ _____ ?
내일 비가 오다

W Yes, I'm sure. Actually, _____ _____ _____ tomorrow.
퍼부을 예정이다

M Oh, no! I was looking forward to going camping tomorrow.

W That's too bad.

13 이유 파악

대화를 듣고, 남자가 기분이 언짢은 이유로 가장 적절한 것을 고르시오.

① 딸이 집에 늦게 들어와서
② 딸이 물을 낭비하기 때문에
③ 윗층의 물소리 때문에 잠이 깨서
④ 날씨가 더워 잠을 이룰 수 없어서
⑤ 이웃집에서 시끄럽게 한다고 항의해서

M Who is taking a shower now? Isn't it Rebecca?

W I'll _____ _____ _____. [pause] It isn't Rebecca. I think somebody else is
  가서 확인한다
  taking a shower upstairs.

M I'll go upstairs and warn them. They are _____ _____ take a
  ~하지 않기로 되어 있다
  shower after 10 p.m.

W Calm down now. If you tell them now, you will hurt their feelings. I'll talk to them about it
  later. The noise will stop before long.

M Even a little noise wakes me up at night. I think I'm sensitive to noise.

고난도

14 장소 추론

library card를 사용할 수 있는 곳에 주목해야한다.

대화를 듣고, 두 사람이 대화하는 장소로 가장 적절한 곳을 고르시오.

① 서점 bookstore
② 교실 classroom
③ 도서관 library
④ 백화점 department store
⑤ 사무실 office

W Do you _____ _____ _____?
  도서관 카드를 가지고 있다
M No, I don't. I just moved here last week.

W Then do you live around here?

M Yes, I do. I live on Maple Street.

W If you live in this town, you can _____ _____. But you have to
  여기서 책을 빌리다
  have a library card. Let's see.... Here's a form for you to _____.
  기입하다

M Thank you very much.

---

15 관계 파악

대화를 듣고, 두 사람의 관계로 가장 적절한 것을 고르시오.

① 여행사 직원 – 고객
② 공항 직원 – 여행객
③ 교사 – 학생
④ 은행 직원–고객
⑤ 경찰 – 시민

W Thank you for waiting. _____ _____ _____. Is this your first time here?
  앉으세요
M Yes, I just moved here.

W Really? Welcome. So, what can I do for you?

M I'd like to open a new account.

W Sure, do you have any ID with you? We need two different photo IDs.

M I have my passport. And..., will my student ID card be okay?

W Yes, it will. Which would you like to open, a savings account or a checking account?

M I'm sorry, but could you _____ _____, please?
  차이점을 설명하다

---

16 심정 추론

예약이 안 된 줄 알고 당황하다가 다시 안도하고 있다.

대화를 듣고, 남자의 심정 변화로 가장 적절한 것을 고르시오.

① upset → relieved
② nervous → disappointed
③ amused → frightened
④ angry → interested
⑤ thankful → angry

➕

대화를 듣고, 남자가 전화를 건 목적으로 가장 적절한 것을 고르시오.

① 비행기 예약을 하려고
② 비행기 예약을 확인하려고
③ 비행기 예약을 변경하려고
④ 비행기 예약을 취소하려고
⑤ 회원 번호를 확인하려고

W Hanguk Airline. How can I help you?

M I want to _____ _____.
  나의 예약을 재확인하다
W Your membership number, please.

M It's 321475.

W Please, wait a moment. [keyboard sound] I'm sorry, but we have no reservation
  _____ _____ _____.
  그런 번호로는
M No way! I reserved it on the Internet a month ago.

W May I have your name and ID number?

M My name is Grey Waston, and my ID number CL23986.

W Wait a moment. [keyboard sound] You _____ _____ for the flight
  두 개의 좌석을 예약했다
  for Singapore at 15:10 on June 27.

W Oh, that's right. I'm relieved to hear that.

17 말의 내용 파악(담화)

다음을 듣고, 여자가 하는 말의 내용으로 가장 적절한 것을 고르시오.

① 캠핑 회원 모집   ② 캠핑 일정 변경
③ 캠핑 주의사항   ④ 캠핑 장소 소개
⑤ 캠핑 후기

W Hello, students! Are you all excited about our camping trip? I'd like to remind you of a few important things. First, we'll meet here at school at 8 o'clock tomorrow morning. Please _____ _____ _____, because our buses will leave on time.
늦지 마라
Second, don't forget to bring warm clothes. It'll be quite cold at night. Lastly, safety comes first. Don't leave your group without telling other members, and _____
_____ _____ _____.
서로를 돌보아라

18 날씨 파악

요일별 날씨를 잘 연결시켜 본다.

다음을 듣고, 요일과 날씨가 바르게 연결된 것을 고르시오.

① 월요일 오전 – cloudy 구름 낀
② 월요일 오후 – snowy 눈 오는
③ 화요일 오후 – rainy 비 오는
④ 수요일 오전 – rainy 비 오는
⑤ 수요일 오후 – snowy 눈 오는

W Monday will be a good day for all you winter holiday skiers. It'll be snowy in the morning and then cloudy in the afternoon. Temperatures will be around two degrees Celsius. But _____ _____, we'll have _____ _____ _____
화요일에는   하루 종일 약간의 비
_____ and it'll be warmer than today. We can expect another wonderful snowy day for the skiers Wednesday morning. But Wednesday afternoon, it'll rain again.

고난도

19 알맞은 응답 찾기

김치 맛이 어떠냐고 물었을 때의 적절한 응답을 찾아야 한다.

[19~20] 대화를 듣고, 여자의 마지막 말에 이어질 남자의 응답으로 가장 적절한 것을 고르시오.

Man: _____

① I mean I really love you.
② Would you do me a favor?
③ What? What did I do wrong?
④ Do you want to look at them?
⑤ It's good. I'd like to try some more.

M I heard that Koreans eat *kimchi* every day.
W That's right. This is _____ _____. Why don't you try a bit?
배추김치
M Is it hot?
W Yes, it's a bit hot, but if you try it once, you'll like it.
M [pause] Oh, it's _____ _____ _____.
그렇게 맵지는 않은
W _____ _____ _____ _____ _____?
어때요
M _____

20 알맞은 응답 찾기

Man: _____

① You're kidding.
② You're welcome.
③ Enjoy your visit there.
④ That's fine with me.
⑤ OK, take care of yourself.

M Hello, Mary. You look tired. What's wrong with you?
W I have a terrible cold.
M Oh, how long have you had it?
W Since _____ _____ _____ _____. I got it from my brother.
그저께
M Really? I think you should go see the doctor.
W It's a good idea. I will go right now.
M _____

특정 정보 파악

무엇을 평가하는가?	일상생활 관련 대상이나 친숙한 일반적 주제에 관한 말이나 대화를 듣고 세부 정보를 파악할 수 있는지를 평가한다.
어떻게 출제되는가?	• 대화를 듣고, 밴드가 공연할 날짜를 고르시오. • 대화를 듣고, 두 사람이 만날 시각을 고르시오. • 대화를 듣고, 여자가 밴드에서 연주할 악기를 고르시오. • 대화를 듣고, 두 사람이 여행 갈 도시를 고르시오.

key solution

❶ 지시문을 보고 어떤 정보를 찾아야 하는지 파악 한 후, 특정 정보에 주의하며 듣는다.

❷ 전체적인 상황보다는 날짜, 시간, 물건, 장소 등 특정 정보를 듣는데 집중한다.

[기출로 전략 확인]

대화를 듣고, 두 사람이 만날 시각을 고르시오.　　　　　　　　　　　[2018 기출]

① 3:30 p.m.　　　　　② 4:00 p.m.　　　　　③ 4:30 p.m.

④ 5:00 p.m.　　　　　⑤ 5:30 p.m.

❶ 두 사람이 만날 시각이므로 남자나 여자가 제안 하는 시간과 두 사람 모두 동의하는 시간이 헷갈리지 않도록 주의한다.

W All right. We've almost finished our science project.

M Yeah. But the presentation is on Friday.

W Yes, you're right. We still need to practice.

M And we have only two days left.

W Why don't we get started today?

M Okay. Let's meet here at 4 o'clock this afternoon.

W Oh, sorry. I have a club meeting at 4.

M How about 5:30?

W Sounds good. See you then.

❷ 남자가 처음에 제안한 4시는 여자의 스케줄과 맞지 않았고, 남자가 두 번째로 제안한 5시 30분에 여자가 동의했다.

여 좋았어. 과학 프로젝트가 거의 끝났어.

남 그래. 하지만 금요일이 발표잖아.

여 그래. 맞아. 연습을 해야 해.

남 그리고 우리에겐 이틀밖에 없어.

여 오늘 시작하는 게 어때?

남 좋아. 오늘 4시에 만나자.

여 미안 나 4시에 클럽 회의가 있어.

남 5시 30분은 어때?

여 좋아. 그때 보자.

특정 정보 파악 유형의 발문과 보기

대화를 듣고, 여자가 밴드에서 연주할 악기를 고르시오. [2017 기출]

① drum　　　　　② guitar　　　　　③ piano
④ bass guitar　　　⑤ saxophone

만점 잡는 문장
M Great. We need both a piano player and a guitarist.
W I'd love to play the piano. Could I?
M Sure, why don't you join our next practice?

대화를 듣고, 밴드가 공연할 날짜를 고르시오. [2017 기출]

① 5월 8일　　　　② 5월 9일　　　　③ 5월 10일
④ 5월 11일　　　⑤ 5월 12일

만점 잡는 문장
W When is the event?
M It's on May 9th.
W Sorry. Only the 11th is possible. Is that okay?
M Let me check. May 11th will be fine.

특정 정보 파악하기에 쓰이는 표현

● 날짜

A When is the event? 행사가 언제죠?
B It's on May 9th. 5월 9일이요.

We only practice on Tuesdays. 우리는 화요일에만 연습해요.

● 시각

I'll pick you up at 3 in front of your school. 3시에 너네 학교 앞에서 태워 줄게.
He arrives at 4:30 p.m. at the airport. 그는 공항에 4시 30분에 도착해.

There are shows at one, four, and seven o'clock. 쇼는 1시, 4시 그리고 7시에 있습니다.

● 장소

A I am in Class C. What about you? 난 C반이야. 너는?
B Wow! We are in the same class this year. 와! 우리 이번 년도에도 같은 반이야.

Namwon sounds good. I've always been interested in history.
남원 괜찮은데. 난 항상 역사에 관심이 많았어.

학년　　반　　번

이름

01 대화를 듣고, 그림에서 여자가 묘사하는 남자를 고르시오.

02 대화를 듣고, 내용과 가장 잘 어울리는 안내판을 고르시오.

① 　② 　③

④ 　⑤

03 대화를 듣고, 여자의 나라의 겨울 날씨의 특징이 <u>아닌</u> 것을 고르시오.

① 낮과 밤의 온도차가 크다.
② 흐린 날이 많다.
③ 눈이 전혀 오지 않는다.
④ 바람이 많이 분다.
⑤ 주로 건조하다.

04 대화를 듣고, 남자가 내일 할 일로 가장 적절한 것을 고르시오.

① 축구하기　　　　　② 데이트하기
③ 콘서트 가기　　　　④ 박물관 관람하기
⑤ 팬클럽 가입하기

05 대화를 듣고, 여자가 남자에게 전화를 건 목적으로 가장 적절한 것을 고르시오.

① 사장님 면담을 알려주려고
② 모임 시간을 물어보려고
③ 회사의 위치를 물어보려고
④ 친구의 소재를 파악하려고
⑤ 회의 취소를 알려주려고

06 대화를 듣고, 남자가 이용할 교통수단으로 가장 적절한 것을 고르시오.

① bus　　　　　　② taxi
③ airplane　　　　④ bicycle
⑤ subway

07 대화를 듣고, 두 사람의 관계로 가장 적절한 것을 고르시오.

① 중고차 매매 직원 – 손님
② 여행 안내원 – 여행객
③ 승무원 – 손님
④ 자동차 수리공 – 손님
⑤ 자동차 보험 사원 – 손님

08 다음 메뉴를 보면서 대화를 듣고, 여자가 지불할 총 금액을 고르시오.

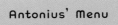

Antonius' Menu

* Today's special: grilled salmon $10
• seafood spaghetti $12　• orange juice $3
• tomato spaghetti $10　• coke $3
• pasta $12　　　　　　　• milk $4

① $13　② $15　③ $20　④ $23　⑤ $25

09 대화를 듣고, 여자의 장래희망으로 가장 적절한 것을 고르시오.

① 캠프 강사　　　　② 음악가
③ TV 드라마 작가　　④ 화가
⑤ 뉴스 기자

10 대화를 듣고, 남자의 심정으로 가장 적절한 것을 고르시오.

① sad　　　　　　② joyful
③ satisfied　　　　④ disappointed
⑤ anxious

점수

/20

11 대화를 듣고, 남자가 이사할 집에 관련된 내용과 일치하지 않는 것을 고르시오.

① It is near the school.

② It may be noisy.

③ It is very cheap.

④ It has a dishwasher.

⑤ Pets are allowed there.

12 대화를 듣고, 두 사람이 대화하는 장소로 가장 적절한 곳을 고르시오.

① 식당   ② 쇼핑몰

③ 자동차 안   ④ 기차 안

⑤ 기차역

13 대화를 듣고, 여자가 남자의 제안을 받아들인 이유로 가장 적절한 것을 고르시오.

① 밥을 사 준다고 해서

② 프린트 비용을 준다고 해서

③ 여자의 과제를 도와준다고 해서

④ 프린트 사용법을 알려준다고 해서

⑤ 새로운 프린트 잉크를 사 준다고 해서

14 다음을 듣고, 무엇에 관한 안내인지 가장 적절한 것을 고르시오.

① 클럽 회장 선출 공고

② 클럽 신입 회원 모집

③ 전임 회장 송별식 안내

④ 도서 전시회 출품 안내

⑤ 인터넷 홈페이지 홍보

15 대화를 듣고, 여자의 질문에 대해 남자가 말한 잘못된 답을 고르시오.

① 3분 30초

② 7분

③ 7분 30초

④ 8분

⑤ 8분 30초

16 대화를 듣고, Jane에 관한 내용과 일치하지 않는 것을 고르시오.

① She is crying now.

② Her dog died this morning.

③ She loved her dog very much.

④ Her dog was very old.

⑤ She will go to see a movie now.

17 다음 그림의 상황에 가장 적절한 대화를 고르시오.

①   ②   ③   ④   ⑤

18 대화를 듣고, 남자가 여자에게 부탁한 일로 가장 적절한 것을 고르시오.

① 아침에 데려다 주기   ② 아침에 깨워 주기

③ 알람 시간 맞추어 주기   ④ 아침식사 준비해 주기

⑤ 준비물 챙겨 주기

[19~20] 대화를 듣고, 여자의 마지막 말에 이어질 남자의 응답으로 가장 적절한 것을 고르시오.

19 Man: _____

① Maybe by then it'll be too late.

② You know him better than me.

③ You can't stay in the heat so long.

④ I wish the weather would just stay the same.

⑤ You had better not stay up late with those things.

20 Man: _____

① What are friends for?

② By the way, who is Kate?

③ You should drive carefully.

④ Sorry, but I'm busy on Monday.

⑤ I'm sorry I don't know how to drive.

다시 들으면서 듣기 만점에 도전하세요!
Dictation: 스크립트의 주요 부분을 다시 들으면서!
실전 ➕: 세부 정보가 많은 스크립트를 다른 문제로 샅샅이!

---

01 그림 정보 파악 – 인물

현재의 모습과 과거의 모습을 구별하여 들어야 한다.

대화를 듣고, 그림에서 여자가 묘사하는 남자를 고르시오.

W Can you show me your album?

M Sure. I was about to show it to you. This is _____ _____
〜할 때 찍은 사진
_____ I was in high school.

W Where are you in the photo? I can't tell who you are. You must have
_____ _____ . Oh, here, this boy with short hair in the front and long hair in the
곱슬머리를 갖고 있다
back, right?

M You got it.

W Then you were _____ _____ _____ , and you were chubby.
그들 중에서 가장 키가 큰
And you didn't wear glasses like you are now.

M At that time I had _____ _____ .
좋은 시력

W Anyway, you are quite different now.

M Yes, I am.

---

02 실용문 정보 파악

대화를 듣고, 내용과 가장 잘 어울리는 안내판을 고르시오.

① ② ③ ④ ⑤

M Look at the bear. It is telling us something.

W I think It's asking us for food.

M Do we have anything to feed? Oh, I have _____ _____
남은 빵 한 조각
_____ .

W Look, it's coming towards us. Hey, it has a funny way of walking, doesn't it?

M Wait, look at that sign. It says, "Don't feed animals."

W Right. I heard that _____ _____ is harmful. That causes many kinds of
동물에게 먹을 것을 주는 것
diseases.

M Let's just go.

W The bear _____ _____ _____ to us for food.
계속해서 표시하고 있다

M Let's go for the animal's health.

---

03 특정 정보 파악

a few와 few의 차이점을 알고 있어야 한다.

대화를 듣고, 여자의 나라의 겨울 날씨의 특징이 <u>아닌</u> 것을 고르시오.

① 낮과 밤의 온도차가 크다.
② 흐린 날이 많다.
③ 눈이 전혀 오지 않는다.
④ 바람이 많이 분다.
⑤ 주로 건조하다.

What's the weather like?는 '날씨가 어떻습니까?'라는 날씨를 묻는 말이다.

M What's the weather like in winter in your country?

W It is hot in the day but turns very cold at night.

M You must live near the desert.

W Exactly. It never snows and _____ _____ throughout the winter. Besides,
바람이 많이 분다
there are _____ _____ .
흐린 날이 거의 없는

M Does it rain much?

W It rains just a little, so _____ _____ _____ .
몹시 건조하다

---

04 할 일 파악

대화를 듣고, 남자가 내일 할 일로 가장 적절한 것을 고르시오.

① 축구하기
② 데이트하기
③ 콘서트 가기
④ 박물관 관람하기
⑤ 팬클럽 가입하기

W You look very excited. Did you play soccer?

M No. Actually, I have a _____.

내일 좀 특별한 계획

W What is it? Do you have a date with your girl friend?

M I had a date with her yesterday. We went to a museum.

W Then what's the special plan?

M I'm going to the _____.

Wonder Girls 콘서트

W How did you get the ticket?

M _____ through a fan club website.

티켓을 구했다

05 전화 목적 파악

전화 용건을 말하는 부분에 집중하여 듣는다.

대화를 듣고, 여자가 남자에게 전화를 건 목적으로 가장 적절한 것을 고르시오.

① 사장님 면담을 알려주려고
② 모임 시간을 물어보려고
③ 회사의 위치를 물어보려고
④ 친구의 소재를 파악하려고
⑤ 회의 취소를 알려주려고

[Telephone rings.]

M Hello.

W Hello. This is Yuna Lee from the ABC company. May I speak to Andrew, please?

M Oh, I'm sorry he is not here. He is in the boss's room.

W Could you take a message for him then?

M Yes, I could. Please go ahead. _____?

메시지가 무엇이죠

W Tomorrow's business meeting with the ABC company _____.

취소되다

M Okay. I will _____.

그에게 메시지를 전하다

06 특정 정보 파악

대화를 듣고, 남자가 이용할 교통수단으로 가장 적절한 것을 고르시오.

① bus 버스
② taxi 택시
③ airplane 비행기
④ bicycle 자전거
⑤ subway 지하철

➕ 대화를 듣고, 두 사람의 관계로 가장 적절한 것을 고르시오.

① 박물관 직원 – 관람객
② 관광객 – 지역 주민
③ 역무원 – 탑승객
④ 운전기사 – 승객
⑤ 경찰 – 시민

M Excuse me, but what's the best way to get to the National Museum?

W You can take a bus, a subway, or a taxi.

M Then, how long does it take to walk there?

W Oh, it's about a thirty-minute walk. But are you a tourist?

M Yes, I'm from Canada.

W Well, you _____ for free in front of any subway

자전거를 빌릴 수 있다
station in this city.

M Good! I'd like to borrow one. Where is the nearest subway station?

W Look over there. _____.

코너를 돌아서

M Thanks for _____.

조언

07 관계 추론

대화를 듣고, 두 사람의 관계로 가장 적절한 것을 고르시오.

① 중고차 매매 직원 – 손님
② 여행 안내원 – 여행객
③ 승무원 – 손님
④ 자동차 수리공 – 손님
⑤ 자동차 보험 사원 – 손님

➕

대화를 듣고, 두 사람의 대화 내용과 일치하지 않는 것을 고르시오.

① 여자는 중형 중고차를 사려고 한다.
② 남자는 3년된 중고차를 추천했다.
③ 남자가 추천한 차의 가격은 $16,000이다.
④ 여자는 가격을 깎아줄 것을 요청했다.
⑤ 남자는 여자가 요구한 가격으로 깎아줬다.

M Hi, ma'am. May I help you?

W I'd like to see ＿＿＿＿＿＿＿＿＿ ＿＿＿＿＿.
　　　　　　　　　　중간 크기의 중고 자동차

M OK. This way. I think this would ＿＿＿＿＿＿＿＿ ＿＿＿＿＿.
　　　　　　　　　　　　　　　　　　당신의 요구 조건에 맞다

W How old is it?

M Well, it's only three years old.

W And what's the mileage?

M Uh, let me check. Oh yes. 75,000 miles.

W What's the price?

M You see, it's $16,000.

W Can you give me ＿＿＿＿＿ ＿＿＿＿＿? How about $14,000?
　　　　　　　　　　　　할인

M Sorry, we can't.

W OK, I think I'll just keep looking around.

08 금액 파악

다음 메뉴를 보면서 대화를 듣고, 여자가 지불할 총 금액을 고르시오.

Antonius' Menu

* Today's special: grilled salmon $10
• seafood spaghetti $12   • orange juice $3
• tomato spaghetti $10   • coke $3
• pasta $12   • milk $4

① $13 ② $15 ③ $20 ④ $23 ⑤ $25

M Welcome to Antonius'. *[pause]* Are you ready to order?

W I'd like the seafood spaghetti and a grilled salmon, today's special.

M Would you like ＿＿＿＿＿ ＿＿＿＿＿ ＿＿＿＿＿?
　　　　　　　　　　마실 것

W I'll have a coke, please.

M OK. That's one seafood spaghetti, one grilled salmon, and one coke. It will take five minutes.

09 특정 정보 파악

여자의 취미와 여자가 장래 희망하는 직업을 구별한다.

대화를 듣고, 여자의 장래희망으로 가장 적절한 것을 고르시오.

① 캠프 강사
② 음악가
③ TV 드라마 작가
④ 화가
⑤ 뉴스 기자

I'll keep my fingers crossed for you.는 '행운을 빌어 줄게.'라는 뜻의 기원을 나타내는 말이다.

W I'm glad to attend this camp with you.

M Me too. ＿＿＿＿＿ ＿＿＿＿＿ ＿＿＿＿＿ ＿＿＿＿＿?
　　　　　취미가 뭔가요

W I am into music, drama, and painting.

M Really? You must be artistic. And then what is your major?

W My major is mass media studies.

M ＿＿＿＿＿ ＿＿＿＿＿ ＿＿＿＿＿ do you want after you graduate?
　　어떤 종류의 일을

W I want to be ＿＿＿＿＿ ＿＿＿＿＿ ＿＿＿＿＿ ＿＿＿＿＿. It is very
　　　　　　　　TV 드라마 작가
difficult, but I'll keep trying.

M I'll keep my fingers crossed for you.

10 심정 추론

남자가 무대에서 처음으로 노래를 부르기 전의 심리 상태를 파악한다.

대화를 듣고, 남자의 심정으로 가장 적절한 것을 고르시오.

① sad 슬픈
② joyful 즐거운
③ satisfied 만족하는
④ disappointed 실망하는
⑤ anxious 걱정하는

M Who is next?

W You are. Are you ready to sing your song?

M Ye....s, I guess so. How much time do I have?

W You have to ＿＿＿＿＿ ＿＿＿＿＿ in five minutes.
　　　　　　　무대에 오르다

M You know, this is my ＿＿＿＿＿ ＿＿＿＿＿ singing in front of an audience.
　　　　　　　　　　　　처음인

W Don't worry. I'm sure you'll do well. Just relax.

M That's easy to say, but ＿＿＿＿＿ ＿＿＿＿＿ ＿＿＿＿＿!
　　　　　　　　　　　　　　　긴장을 풀 수 없다

11 내용 일치 파악

대화 중에 남자가 말하는 부분에 중점을 두어 듣고 순서대로 일치 여부를 판단한다.

대화를 듣고, 남자가 이사할 집에 관련된 내용과 일치하지 <u>않는</u> 것을 고르시오.

① It is near the school.
② It may be noisy.
③ It is very cheap.
④ It has a dishwasher.
⑤ Pets are allowed there.

M I visited my new house today. I'll move there soon.

W Is the house near the school?

M It is between our school and ABC Shopping Center.

W It is so near, but it may be noisy because of the large shopping center.

M It may be, but ＿＿＿ ＿＿＿ ＿＿＿ is so cheap!
_{집세}

W Is there a washing machine, a dryer and a dishwasher?

M Of course, but ＿＿＿ ＿＿＿ ＿＿＿ ＿＿＿.
_{문제는 애완용 동물을 기르는 것이다}

W You ＿＿＿ ＿＿＿ in most apartments!
_{애완동물을 기를 수 없다}

12 대화 장소 파악

대화를 듣고, 두 사람이 대화하는 장소로 가장 적절한 곳을 고르시오.

① 식당   ② 쇼핑몰
③ 자동차 안   ④ 기차 안
⑤ 기차역

W I'm hungry. Did you bring any food?

M No, I thought we could get something at the snack bar.

W Is there a snack bar? That's cool. Which car is it in?

M I think it's car number 4. Shall we go together?

W No, I'll ＿＿＿ ＿＿＿. I want to use the restroom on the way, and I don't want to ＿＿＿ our bags ＿＿＿.
_{혼자 가다} _{지켜보는 사람없이 내버려 두다}

M Okay, can you get me something as well?

W Sure, how long do we have until our destination?

M We just passed Daegu Station, so maybe an hour.

13 이유 파악

대화를 듣고, 여자가 남자의 제안을 받아들인 이유로 가장 적절한 것을 고르시오.

① 밥을 사 준다고 해서
② 프린트 비용을 준다고 해서
③ 여자의 과제를 도와준다고 해서
④ 프린트 사용법을 알려준다고 해서
⑤ 새로운 프린트 잉크를 사 준다고 해서

M Would you print this file for me? My printer ＿＿＿ ＿＿＿.
_{고장나다}

W How many pages is that?

M That'll be about 150 pages.

W 150 pages? That's not going to be possible. That's ＿＿＿ ＿＿＿ ＿＿＿.
_{정말로 엄청난 요청}

M I know. But I must have it right away.

W I'm sorry, but I think ＿＿＿ ＿＿＿ ＿＿＿ to a print shop.
_{가는 것이 좋겠다}

M I went to the shop first, but it's already been closed. If you ＿＿＿ ＿＿＿ ＿＿＿, I'll pay for a new ink cartridge.
_{프린트할 수 있도록 허락하다}

W Really? OK. Which file is it?

14 주제 파악

다음을 듣고, 무엇에 관한 안내인지 가장 적절한 것을 고르시오.

① 클럽 회장 선출 공고
② 클럽 신입 회원 모집
③ 전임 회장 송별식 안내
④ 도서 전시회 출품 안내
⑤ 인터넷 홈페이지 홍보

W Attention, please. Our Book Club was formed five years ago. Through your love and help, our club has progressed. Especially, our club's president, John, has worked hard for us. But he has ＿＿＿ ＿＿＿ because of his business matters. So there will be ＿＿＿ ＿＿＿ ＿＿＿ ＿＿＿ next Thursday night. We hope many members want ＿＿＿ of our club. Please read our website for more information.
_{사퇴를 결심했다} _{새로운 클럽 지도자 선출을 위한 선거} _{회장이 되는 것}

15 특정 정보 파악

대화를 듣고, 여자의 질문에 대해 남자가 말한 잘못된 답을 고르시오.

① 3분 30초
② 7분
③ 7분 30초
④ 8분
⑤ 8분 30초

W John, I'd like to give you some science quizzes and you can guess the answers, ok?

M Fine. I'm quite _____ _____ . Go ahead.
　　　　　　　과학을 좀 잘하는

W How fast does light travel? Number 1, 30,000 km per second, Number 2, 300,000 km per second.

M The answer is number 1.

W Wow, you are great! Next question. How long does it take _____ _____ _____ from the Sun to the Earth? Number 1, 7½ minutes, Number 2, 8½ minutes.
　　　　　　　　　　　　　　　　　　빛이 이동하는데

M Number 1, 7½ minutes.

W This time you _____ _____ _____ _____ . The answer is Number 2, 8½ minutes.
　　　　　답이 틀렸다

M I was confused. I'm not good at numbers.

16 내용 일치 파악

마지막 부분에 언급된 내용에 유의한다.

대화를 듣고, Jane에 관한 내용과 일치하지 않는 것을 고르시오.

① She is crying now.
② Her dog died this morning.
③ She loved her dog very much.
④ Her dog was very old.
⑤ She will go to see a movie now.

M What's the matter, Jane? You're crying.

W It's okay. I'll be all right.

M Why? Did _____ _____ ?
　　　　　안 좋은 일이 생기다

W My dog, Charlie, died this morning. I loved my Charlie very much.

M I'm sorry to hear that. Was it an accident?

W No, it wasn't. He was a very old dog. And he hadn't eaten recently.

M Don't be so sad. Let's _____ _____ _____ _____ .
　　　　　　　　　　　　나가서 영화를 보다

W Thank you, David, but _____ _____ _____ _____ right now.
　　　　　　　　　　　　나는 집에 있고 싶다

17 그림 상황 대화 찾기

다음 그림의 상황에 가장 적절한 대화를 고르시오.

① ② ③ ④ ⑤

① M Can you tell me when your birthday is?

　 W Sure, my birthday is October 13.

② M How was the party? Did you enjoy it?

　 W Yes, a lot of people _____ _____ _____ , and it was fun.
　　　　　　　　　　　축하하러 왔다

③ M Which do you think is better?

　 W I think this one is better. I like the blue color.

④ M What do you want for Christmas, Susie?

　 W I'd love to have the new comic book series, Dad.

⑤ M Happy birthday, Sarah! _____ _____ _____ .

　 W Thank you so much! Can I open it now?
　　이거 널 위한 거야

18 부탁한 일 파악하기

대화를 듣고, 남자가 여자에게 부탁한 일로 가장 적절한 것을 고르시오.

① 아침에 데려다 주기
② 아침에 깨워 주기
③ 알람 시간 맞추어 주기
④ 아침식사 준비해 주기
⑤ 준비물 챙겨 주기

M Mom, what time are we leaving tomorrow?

W If we want to avoid the rush hour, we should _____ _____ . Probably at 7
　　　　　　　　　　　　　　　　　　　　일찍 떠나다
a.m.?

M Wow, that's early. I should go to bed now, then.

W Yes, that's a good idea.

M I set the alarm, but can you still wake me up tomorrow morning? I'm afraid I won't

_____ _____ _____ .
알람을 듣다

W Sure, I will wake you up at 6.

M It takes only 30 minutes for me to get ready, so 6:30 would be fine.

W Okay. Good night, son

19 알맞은 응답 찾기

빨리 자라는 것, 물건을 만드는 재료, 음식이 될 수도 있다는 특징들을 정리한다.

[19~20] 대화를 듣고, 여자의 마지막 말에 이어질 남자의 응답으로 가장 적절한 것을 고르시오.

Man: _____

① Maybe by then it'll be too late.
② You know him better than me.
③ You can't stay in the heat so long.
④ I wish the weather would just stay the same.
⑤ You had better not stay up late with those things.

W Have you ever been to Halla Mountain?

M No, I haven't. How about you?

W Neither have I. I really want to _____ _____ _____
　　　　　　　　　　　　　　　　　　꼭대기에 올라가다
_____ of Halla Mountain. Shall we go to Mt. Halla during the Chusok holidays?

M That sounds fun.

W How is the weather going to be during the holidays?

M I heard that it's going _____ _____ _____ _____ .
　　　　　　　　　따뜻하고 맑다

W It's going to be perfect weather for climbing, isn't it?

M I believe so. But you know that the weather in Jeju-do is unpredictable.

W You're right. One minute it's sunny, and then the next minute it's rainy.

M _____

고난도

20 알맞은 응답 찾기

여자가 남자에게 도와준 것에 대해 고마워 할때 응답할 수 있는 것을 파악한다.

Man: _____

① What are friends for?
② By the way, who is Kate?
③ You should drive carefully.
④ Sorry, but I'm busy on Monday.
⑤ I'm sorry I don't know how to drive.

Will you do me a favor?는 '부탁 하나 들어 줄래?'라는 뜻의 부탁하는 표현이다.

W Andrew, will you _____ _____ _____ ?
　　　　　　　　　　　부탁을 들어주다

M Sure, what is it?

W Can you drive Jane and me to the hospital on Monday?

M I think so. I'll mark it on my calendar _____ _____ _____ .
　　　　　　　　　　　　　　　　　　　잊지 않도록

W It's really kind of you. But I'm sorry to bother you.

M _____ _____ _____ .
그 점에 대해서 걱정하지 마

W Thanks. I haven't forgotten your helping me several times.

M _____

영어듣기능력평가 **20** 회

01 대화를 듣고, 남자가 찾는 개를 고르시오.

① 　② 　③

④ 　⑤

02 다음을 듣고, 그림을 바르게 설명한 것을 고르시오.

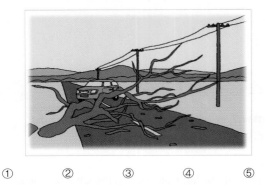

①　　②　　③　　④　　⑤

03 대화를 듣고, 두 사람의 심정 변화로 가장 적절한 것을 고르시오.

① upset → relieved
② excited → disappointed
③ amused → frightened
④ angry → interested
⑤ thankful → angry

04 대화를 듣고, 남자가 가장 좋아하는 두 과목이 바르게 짝지어진 것을 고르시오.

① 음악, 체육　　　② 수학, 화학
③ 지리, 체육　　　④ 역사, 생물
⑤ 음악, 역사

05 다음 그림의 상황에 가장 적절한 대화를 고르시오.

①　　②　　③　　④　　⑤

06 대화를 듣고, 두 사람이 대화하는 장소로 가장 적절한 곳을 고르시오.

① 음식점　　　　② 동물원
③ 음악회장　　　④ 음반 가게
⑤ 뮤지컬 공연장

07 대화를 듣고, 두 사람의 관계로 가장 적절한 것을 고르시오.

① 사장 – 비서　　② 교사 – 학생
③ 어머니 – 아들　④ 면접관 – 구직자
⑤ 백화점 종업원 – 손님

08 대화를 듣고, 남자가 집에서 출발할 시각을 고르시오.

① 3:50　　　　② 4:00
③ 5:00　　　　④ 5:10
⑤ 7:30

09 대화를 듣고, 여자가 남자에게 제안한 것으로 가장 적절한 것을 고르시오.

① 직장을 옮기는 것
② 집주인과 친해질 것
③ 걸어서 직장에 다니는 것
④ 운전하면서 음악을 듣는 것
⑤ 자기 아파트 건물로 이사오는 것

10 다음을 듣고, 무엇에 관한 안내인지 가장 적절한 것을 고르시오.

① 분실물　　　　② 경품 추첨
③ 할인 판매　　　④ 신상품 소개
⑤ 슈퍼마켓 개업

점수

/20

11 대화를 듣고, 남자가 여자에게 부탁한 일로 가장 적절한 것을 고르시오.

① 발표 자료 준비하기   ② 남자 대신 발표해주기
③ 시간표 확인하기   ④ 영사기 점검하기
⑤ 발표 자료 복사하기

12 대화를 듣고, 여자가 전화를 건 목적으로 가장 적절한 것을 고르시오.

① 딸의 소식을 물어보려고
② 딸의 취직을 부탁하려고
③ 회사의 위치를 물어보려고
④ 할머니의 사고 소식을 알리려고
⑤ 남편의 사고에 대해 설명하려고

13 대화를 듣고, 여자가 선물하기로 한 것을 고르시오.

① game CD   ② watch
③ book   ④ digital camera
⑤ sweater

고난도
14 대화를 듣고, 남자의 형에 관해 알 수 없는 것을 고르시오.

① 외모   ② 직업
③ 학력   ④ 나이
⑤ 취미

15 대화를 듣고, 여자가 목적지에 가기 위해 이용할 교통수단을 순서대로 나열한 것을 고르시오.

① taxi → bus
② bus → taxi
③ bus → subway
④ subway → bus
⑤ subway → taxi

16 대화를 듣고, 여자가 자전거를 타러 가지 않는 이유로 가장 적절한 것을 고르시오.

① 할머니 댁에 가기로 해서
② 친구들과 다른 약속이 있어서
③ 자전거 타는 것을 좋아하지 않아서
④ 어머니와 함께 공항으로 마중을 나가야 해서
⑤ 자전거 타는 친구들 중에 싫어하는 사람이 있어서

17 대화를 듣고, 여자가 한 일로 가장 적절한 것을 고르시오.

① 야구 경기 관람   ② 공항 견학
③ 손님 접대   ④ 친척 배웅
⑤ 가족 여행

18 대화를 듣고, 남자의 마지막 말의 의도로 가장 적절한 것을 고르시오.

① 의심   ② 동의
③ 비난   ④ 조언
⑤ 감사

[19~20] 대화를 듣고, 남자의 마지막 말에 이어질 여자의 응답으로 가장 적절한 것을 고르시오.
고난도
19 Woman: _____

① Yes, he looks really better.
② I'm glad I left my door open.
③ You'd better talk to him then.
④ My pleasure. Have a safe trip.
⑤ I'm looking forward to seeing you soon.

고난도
20 Woman: _____

① Why don't you study now?
② I can't answer this question.
③ How are you doing in school?
④ I study English hard every day.
⑤ I was worried about only three mistakes.

다시 들으면서 듣기 만점에 도전하세요!

Dictation : 스크립트의 주요 부분을 다시 들으면서!

실전 ⊕ : 세부 정보가 많은 스크립트를 다른 문제로 살살이!

---

01 그림 정보 파악 – 사물 　　　남자의 개를 묘사하는 표현들에 주의한다.

대화를 듣고, 남자가 찾는 개를 고르시오.

① ② ③ ④ ⑤

M　I lost my dog. Have you seen a dog around here?

W　Oh, yes. I saw ＿＿＿＿＿ ＿＿＿＿＿, ＿＿＿＿＿ ＿＿＿＿＿ on the farm.
　　　　　　　　크고, 흰 개

M　Really? It may be my dog. Is there anything that you can remember about it?

W　Yes. I'm certain it had ＿＿＿＿＿ ＿＿＿＿＿ ＿＿＿＿＿.
　　　　　　　　　　　　　　　짧은 꼬리

M　Really? How about its ears? Were they short?

W　Yes, ＿＿＿＿＿ ＿＿＿＿＿ ＿＿＿＿＿.
　　　　그것들은 짧았다

M　Oh, it must be mine. Where was it?

W　Just over there.

---

02 그림 정보 파악 – 토익형 　　　넘어진 나무 때문에 차가 지나가지 못하는 상황이다.

다음을 듣고, 그림을 바르게 설명한 것을 고르시오.

① ② ③
④ ⑤

W　① It is raining cats and dogs.

　　② The car ＿＿＿＿＿ ＿＿＿＿＿ by the tree.
　　　　　　　훼손되다

　　③ The big tree is fallen across the road.

　　④ The car is passing by the ＿＿＿＿＿ ＿＿＿＿＿.
　　　　　　　　　　　　　　　　넘어진, 나무

　　⑤ The rescuers are pulling the injured driver from the car.

---

03 심정 추론

대화를 듣고, 두 사람의 심정 변화로 가장 적절한 것을 고르시오.

① upset → relieved
② excited → disappointed
③ amused → frightened
④ angry → interested
⑤ thankful → angry

W　Wake up! It's four o'clock.

M　Let's hurry up, or we'll ＿＿＿＿＿ ＿＿＿＿＿ ＿＿＿＿＿.
　　　　　　　　　　　　　　　일출을 놓치다

W　Don't forget to take your camera.

M　OK. Oh! I'm looking forward to taking pictures of the beautiful sunrise.

W　Me, too. Is it going to be sunny?

M　Of course, I've already checked the ＿＿＿＿＿ ＿＿＿＿＿.
　　　　　　　　　　　　　　　　　　　　일기 예보

[After a while]

M　Uh, the sky was filled with thick rain clouds.

W　It's very foggy everywhere. Our hope is completely gone.

M　It's been the second time we failed to take photos of a sunrise.

W　Let's go to other places. There are lots of things we can take pictures of.

대화를 듣고, 남자가 가장 좋아하는 두 과목이 바르게 짝지어진 것을 고르시오.

① 음악, 체육
② 수학, 화학
③ 지리, 체육
④ 역사, 생물
⑤ 음악, 역사

M Jessica, what classes are you planning to take?

W History, biology, and geography. How about you?

M I'm planning to take music, math, physical education, and chemistry.

W Do you like physical education?

M Of course. _____ _____ _____ _____ are my two
___음악과 체육___   ___가장 좋아하는 과목들___
_____.

W I took physical education last year. I really had a hard time in the class.

M My physical education teacher is _____ _____ _____ _____.
                                    ___정말 나에게 좋은___

다음 그림의 상황에 가장 적절한 대화를 고르시오.

① ② ③ ④ ⑤

① M How long will it take to get to Seoul?
  W I don't know exactly, but it usually takes two hours.

② M I'd like to buy two tickets. _____ _____ _____ _____?
                                  ___얼마입니까?___
  W Sure, it will be $20 in total.

③ M Can I check your ticket, please?
  W Sure, here are tickets for both of us.

④ M I'm so excited about this trip.
  W So am I. We'll see a lot of new things, and it'll be so fun.

⑤ M _____ _____ _____ _____ Jeju Island?
     ___~에 가본 적 있어?___
  W Yes, once. I went there with my family.

음악이나 뮤지컬에 관한 대화 내용에 현혹 되지 말아야 한다.

대화를 듣고, 두 사람이 대화하는 장소로 가장 적절한 곳을 고르시오.

① 음식점
② 동물원
③ 음악회장
④ 음반 가게
⑤ 뮤지컬 공연장

M Listen to that song! Do you know that song?

W Umm, it sounds familiar. Ah, it's "Memory."

M Right. It's a really beautiful song. Someday I want to see the musical "Cats."

W Anyway, _____ _____ _____, Kevin? Lobster? Steak?
          ___너는 무엇을 먹을 거니___

M I can't decide yet. Why aren't they _____ _____?
                                        ___우리 주문을 받는___

W The waiters _____ _____ tonight.
             ___아주 바쁜 것 같다___

M Yeah. It's very crowded here tonight.

대화를 듣고, 두 사람의 관계로 가장 적절한 것을 고르시오.

① 사장 – 비서
② 교사 – 학생
③ 어머니 – 아들
④ 면접관 – 구직자
⑤ 백화점 종업원 – 손님

W Do you have any _____ _____?
                   ___경력___

M Yes. I had a part-time job at a department store when I was a high school student.

W Why did you _____ _____ _____?
              ___이 일자리에 지원하다___

M I'm interested in fashion.

W Are you interested in working _____ _____ _____?
                                 ___전임제로 아니면 아르바이트로___

M I'd like to work part-time. As you know, I'm still a college student.

W Good.

08 시각 파악

대화 중에 나오는 시간 표현들이 무엇에 관한 시간인지를 정확히 파악한다.

대화를 듣고, 남자가 집에서 출발할 시각을 고르시오.

① 3:50 ② 4:00
③ 5:00 ④ 5:10
⑤ 7:30

➕ 대화를 듣고, 남자가 탈 기차의 출발 시간을 고르시오.

① 3:50 ② 4:00
③ 5:00 ④ 5:10
⑤ 7:30

W Honey, what time does your train leave?

M At 7:30. Why do you ask?

W You have an appointment with Mr. Evans at 5 o'clock, remember?

M Oh, that's right! I nearly forgot about it. Thanks.

W What time are you _____ _____ _____?
(집에서 떠나는)

M About 4 o'clock, I guess.

W All right. _____ _____ _____, I'll call a taxi. It'll
(3시 50분경에)   _____ _____ for a taxi to get here. (10분 정도 걸리다)

M Okay. Thanks, honey.

09 특정 정보 파악

남자가 처한 상황을 잘 파악해 본다.

대화를 듣고, 여자가 남자에게 제안한 것으로 가장 적절한 것을 고르시오.

① 직장을 옮기는 것
② 집주인과 친해질 것
③ 걸어서 직장에 다니는 것
④ 운전하면서 음악을 듣는 것
⑤ 자기 아파트 건물로 이사오는 것

➕ 대화를 듣고, 남자가 이사를 가려고 생각하는 이유로 가장 적절한 것을 고르시오.

① 직장이 너무 멀어서
② 새로운 직장을 구해서
③ 더 큰 집에 살고 싶어서
④ 지금 집이 너무 비싸서
⑤ 차를 사게 되어서

M My office is far from where I live. Driving all those hours is just killing me.

W Yeah, I know what you mean. I _____ _____ _____ two hours to work
(운전하곤 했다)   each day. But now I walk to work. It's great.

M Did you move?

W No, I got a new job near my apartment.

M Well, I don't think I can change my job, but I am thinking about moving.

W How about moving to my apartment building? There is one empty apartment for rent. And I'm sure it _____ _____ _____ to your work than you are now.
(더 가까운)

M Really? Isn't it expensive?

W No, it isn't. It is new and big.

M That sounds great. I'd love to see it.

10 주제 파악

다음을 듣고, 무엇에 관한 안내인지 가장 적절한 것을 고르시오.

① 분실물 ② 경품 추첨
③ 할인 판매 ④ 신상품 소개
⑤ 슈퍼마켓 개업

W Attention, please, shoppers! Thank you for shopping at Super Mart. We're having _____ _____ _____ this week. Our beef is only $8.99 a pound. That's
(대폭 할인 판매)   right, shoppers, only $8.99 a pound. We're also offering chicken on sale. Our chicken is only $2.99 a pound. This sale is _____ _____ _____. Enjoy your
(단지 오늘만)   shopping today here!

11 부탁한 일 파악

대화를 듣고, 남자가 여자에게 부탁한 일로 가장 적절한 것을 고르시오.

① 발표 자료 준비하기
② 남자 대신 발표해주기
③ 시간표 확인하기
④ 영사기 점검하기
⑤ 발표 자료 복사

W We've finally finished all of the preparation work.

M Yes, but now is the real challenge. I hope we will _____ _____ _____ our
(~을 잘하다)   presentation.

W Don't worry. We will do just fine. How long do we have before the class?

M About an hour. I'll _____ _____ _____ to make sure our
(마지막 확인을 하다)   projector works with the computer.

W Thanks. What should I do meanwhile?

M Can you go photocopy these handouts?

W Sure, I can manage that. How many copies do we need?

M I think 40 will be enough.

12 전화 목적 파악

대화를 듣고, 여자가 전화를 건 목적으로 가장 적절한 것을 고르시오.

① 딸의 소식을 물어보려고
② 딸의 취직을 부탁하려고
③ 회사의 위치를 물어보려고
④ 할머니의 사고 소식을 알리려고
⑤ 남편의 사고에 대해 설명하려고

Who's calling, please?는 전화 대화에서 전화를 걸어온 상대방에게 '누구세요?'라고 묻는 표현이다.

[Telephone rings.]

W Hello, can I speak to Susan, please?

M She's not in now. Who's calling, please?

W This is her mother Jane Brown from Los Angeles.

M Oh, Mrs. Brown. May I take a message?

W Yes, please. Tell her that her grandmother _____ _____ _____ this morning.
<u>사고를 당했다</u>

M Oh, no!

W She _____ _____ in the bathroom. It's not serious, but she _____
<u>쓰러졌다</u>   <u>전화하기를 원하다</u>
_____ _____ Susan.

M Oh, that's too bad. I'll give her the message.

13 특정 정보 파악

마지막에 선택한 것이 무엇인지 파악한다.

대화를 듣고, 여자가 선물하기로 한 것을 고르시오.

① game CD 게임 CD
② watch 시계
③ book 책
④ digital camera 디지털 카메라
⑤ sweater 스웨터

W Tomorrow is my boyfriend's birthday, but I don't know what I should get for him.

M Boys like game CDs.

W He doesn't like computer games, so I don't want to give him that kind of present.

M Then, how about a watch or a digital camera?

W Those are too expensive.

M _____ _____ _____ _____ ? It will _____
<u>스웨터는 어때</u>   <u>그를 따뜻하게 해주다</u>
_____ .

W Good idea. I'll _____ _____ _____ .
<u>그에게 그걸 사주다</u>

고난도

14 내용 일치 파악

남자의 형에 관한 내용들을 하나씩 정확히 이해한다.

대화를 듣고, 남자의 형에 관해 알 수 <u>없는</u> 것을 고르시오.

① 외모
② 직업
③ 학력
④ 나이
⑤ 취미

M Laura, I'd like to introduce my brother to your sister.

W That's a good idea! My sister doesn't have a boyfriend.

M My brother is _____ _____ . He _____ _____
<u>키가 크고 잘 생긴</u>   <u>여행사에 근무하다</u>
_____ _____ .

W How old is he?

M He's 28 years old, but he looks very young.

W What are his hobbies?

M He _____ _____ , and he plays tennis very well.
<u>스포츠를 좋아하다</u>

W Wow, my sister also plays tennis. I think they'll like each other.

15 특정 정보 파악

어디에서 어디까지 어떤 교통수단을 이용하는지를 정확히 파악한다.

대화를 듣고, 여자가 목적지에 가기 위해 이용할 교통수단을 순서대로 나열한 것을 고르시오.

① taxi → bus 택시 → 버스
② bus → taxi 버스 → 택시
③ bus → subway 버스 → 지하철
④ subway → bus 지하철 → 버스
⑤ subway → taxi 지하철 → 택시

W I want to go to Charlotte International Airport. How can I get there?

M You can take the express bus, but the bus stop is far from here.

W Oh, no! I have heavy bags, so I can't _____ _____ _____ _____ _____.
먼 길을 걷다

M Then you can take a taxi, but it'll cost a lot. Umm, I have an idea.

W What is it?

M You can go to Hudson Airport _____ _____. From there you can _____
지하철로   버스를 타다
_____ _____ to Charlotte International Airport.

W Okay. I'll do that.

16 이유 파악

대화를 듣고, 여자가 자전거를 타러 가지 않는 이유로 가장 적절한 것을 고르시오.

① 할머니 댁에 가기로 해서
② 친구들과 다른 약속이 있어서
③ 자전거 타는 것을 좋아하지 않아서
④ 어머니와 함께 공항으로 마중을 나가야 해서
⑤ 자전거 타는 친구들 중에 싫어하는 사람이 있어서

What have you been up to lately?는 '최근에 어떻게 지내니?'라는 뜻의 안부를 물을 때 쓰는 표현이다.

M Rachel! How are you doing?

W I'm fine. What have you been up to lately?

M Nothing much. Oh, can you _____ _____ this Saturday? Many of our friends
자전거를 타러 가다
are going.

W Where are you going bicycling?

M We're going to _____ _____ _____.
강을 따라서 타다

W Sounds great, but I'm afraid I can't. I have to go to _____ _____ at
할머니를 마중 나가다
the airport with my Mom. Maybe next time.

M Okay.

17 한 일 파악

대화를 듣고, 여자가 한 일로 가장 적절한 것을 고르시오.

① 야구 경기 관람   ② 공항 견학
③ 손님 접대   ④ 친척 배웅
⑤ 가족 여행

M Sumin, you're late. The baseball game _____ _____ _____.
이미 시작했다

W I'm so sorry. The traffic was really bad on the way back from the airport.

M The airport? Why did you go to the airport?

W Oh, you know my Aunt Sally was visiting us from Australia. She left today, and I
_____ _____ _____ _____ with my parents.
그녀를 배웅하러 갔다

M I see. But you could have texted or called me, you know.

W I know, sorry. I forgot while talking to my parents. I promise I'll call next time.

대화를 듣고, 남자의 마지막 말의 의도로 가장 적절한 것을 고르시오.

① 의심　　② 동의
③ 비난　　④ 조언
⑤ 감사

M　So, what did you think of the movie?

W　Hmm... I don't know. I _____ _____ _____.
　　　　　　　　　　　　　　　복잡한 감정이다

M　What do you mean? I thought it was awesome.

W　I thought it was good at first. The scenes were very colorful and unique, and the acting was pretty good.

M　Then, what changed your mind?

W　Well, the story was too boring, don't you think? It was a simple plot, and there weren't any surprises. The ending was very predictable.

M　Yeah, you certainly _____ _____ _____ there.
　　　　　　　　　　　일리가 있다

[19~20] 대화를 듣고, 남자의 마지막 말에 이어질 여자의 응답으로 가장 적절한 것을 고르시오.

Woman: _____

① Yes, he looks really better.
② I'm glad I left my door open.
③ You'd better talk to him then.
④ My pleasure. Have a safe trip.
⑤ I'm looking forward to seeing you soon.

M　Hello. Is anyone here?

W　Yes, can I help you?

M　I saw your door open and I just wanted to _____ _____ everything was okay.
　　　　　　　　　　　　　　　　　　　　확인하다
　　Are you moving out?

W　Yes, I am. I'm only moving about a mile from here to another apartment.

M　Oh, so you're not moving out of the area.

W　No, I'm not.

M　Can I help you _____ _____ your furniture?
　　　　　　　　　분해하다

W　Really? Are you sure you are able to do that?

M　Sure. Hand me those tools and I'll have it done in no time.

W　_____

Woman: _____

① Why don't you study now?
② I can't answer this question.
③ How are you doing in school?
④ I study English hard every day.
⑤ I was worried about only three mistakes.

M　What happened to you, Judy?

W　I _____ _____ _____.
　　　믿을 수가 없다

M　What's that?

W　I got my math test back this afternoon.

M　And?

W　I thought I would fail, but I _____ _____ after all. In fact, I made _____ _____.
　　　　　　　　　　　　　　　　낙제하지 않았다　　　　　　　　　　　겨우 세 개의 실수

M　That's great!

W　_____

한 일·할 일·부탁한 일 파악

무엇을 평가하는가?	일상생활이나 친숙한 일반적 주제에 관한 말이나 대화를 듣고 일이나 사건의 순서, 전후 관계를 추론할 수 있는지를 평가한다.

어떻게 출제되는가?	• 대화를 듣고, 여자가 지난 일요일에 한 일로 가장 적절한 것을 고르시오. • 대화를 듣고, 남자가 대화 직후에 할 일로 가장 적절한 것을 고르시오. • 대화를 듣고, 남자가 여자에게 요청한 일로 가장 적절한 것을 고르시오.

key solution

❶ 지시문을 읽고, 누가 한 일이고 할 일인지, 누가 누구에게 부탁한 일을 묻는지 확인한다.

❷ 상대방이 한 일이나 할 일이 동시에 언급되는 경우가 많으므로 혼동하지 않도록 주의한다.

❸ 부탁한 일은 'Could you ~?', 'Can you ~?' 같이 직접적인 표현을 사용하는 경우가 많다.

[기출로 전략 확인]

대화를 듣고, 여자가 과학의 날에 한 일로 가장 적절한 것을 고르시오.　　　[2017 기출]

① 3D 영화 보기　　　　　　　　② 물 폭탄 만들기
③ 자석 원리 실험하기　　　　　④ 에너지 절약 포스터 그리기
⑤ 나무젓가락 비행기 만들기

- -

W That was a great science day! Did you have fun?
M Of course. I made water bombs.
W Nice. I wanted to watch a 3D movie but I couldn't.
M That's too bad. What did you do then?
W I built airplanes out of wooden chopsticks instead.
M Did you like it?
W Yeah, it was really fun.
M Great! I'd like to make chopstick airplanes next year.

여 정말 굉장한 과학의 날이었어! 즐거웠니?
남 물론이야. 난 물 폭탄을 만들었어.
여 멋진데. 난 3D영화를 보고싶었는데 못 봤어.
남 안됐다. 그럼 뭐 했어?
여 대신 나무 젓가락으로 비행기를 만들었어.
남 맘에 들었어?
여 응, 아주 재미 있었어.
남 잘됐네! 내년에 나도 나무 젓가락 비행기를 만들고 싶다.

❶ 지시문을 통해 '여자'가 과학의 날에 한 일과 관련된 내용이 나올 것임을 인지한다.

❷ 남자가 한 일로 착각해 ②를 정답으로 체크하지 않도록 주의한다. 여자가 3D영화를 보지 못한 대신에 나무젓가락 비행기를 만들었다고 언급하고 있다.

대화를 듣고, 남자가 대화 직후에 할 일로 가장 적절한 것을 고르시오. **[2018 기출]**

① 사진 촬영하기　　② 배터리 충전하기　　③ 선생님께 전화하기

④ 휴대전화 전원 끄기　　⑤ 서비스 센터 방문하기

만점 잡는 문장　**W** Then, you probably need to visit the service center.

　　　　　　　M Okay. I'll go there now.

대화를 듣고, 남자가 여자에게 부탁한 일로 가장 적절한 것을 고르시오. **[2018 기출]**

① 가방 들어주기　　② 숙제 도와주기　　③ 병원 함께 가기

④ 청소 같이 하기　　⑤ 계단에서 부축해주기

오답 찍는 문장　**W** Do you need help going up the stairs?

만점 잡는 문장　**M** It's okay, thanks. But can you carry my bag to the classroom for me?

한 일·할 일·부탁한
일 파악하기에 쓰이는
표현

● **한 일**

I watched a movie on math history. 수학 역사에 대한 영화를 봤어.

I went to the class farm to water the tomatoes. 토마토에 물을 주기 위해 학급 농장에 갔어.

I bought a new lantern and chairs for camping. 캠핑을 위해 새 손전등과 의자를 샀어.

I drew a scene from my favorite book on a cup. 컵에 내가 제일 좋아하는 책의 한 장면을 그렸어.

● **할 일**

A You probably need to visit the service center. 서비스 센터에 방문할 필요가 있어.

B Okay. I'll go there now. 알겠어. 지금 가야지.

A She runs a blog on Korean food. 그녀는 한국 음식 블로그를 운영해.

B Then I need to visit her blog right now. 지금 바로 그녀의 블로그를 방문해야지.

A You should go and buy some medicine. 가서 약을 좀 사와야겠다.

B Okay. I will go now. 알겠어. 지금 갈게.

A Why don't we ask the teacher for help? 선생님한테 좀 도와 달라고 하는 게 어때?

B Let's go to the teachers' office now. 지금 교무실로 가자.

● **부탁한 일**

Can you check my blue coat? 내 파란 코트 좀 확인 해 줄래?

Could you pass me some more cookies? 쿠키 좀 건네줄래?

Please take an apple pie to her on your way to the library. 도서관 가는 길에 그녀에게 사과파이를 전해줘.

고난도 영어듣기능력평가

01 다음을 듣고, 목요일의 날씨로 가장 적절한 것을 고르시오.

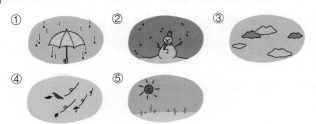

02 대화를 듣고, 여자가 구입할 케이크로 가장 적절한 것을 고르시오.

03 대화를 듣고, 남자의 심정으로 가장 적절한 것을 고르시오.

① proud　　　　　② excited
③ worried　　　　④ relaxed
⑤ bored

04 대화를 듣고, 여자가 주말에 한 일로 가장 적절한 것을 고르시오.

① 쇼핑하기　　　　② 영화보기
③ 수영하기　　　　④ 볼링 치기
⑤ 스케이트 타기

05 대화를 듣고, 두 사람이 대화하는 장소로 가장 적절한 곳을 고르시오.

① 경찰서　　　　　② 서점
③ 교무실　　　　　④ 교실
⑤ 도서관

06 대화를 듣고, 남자의 마지막 말의 의도로 가장 적절한 것을 고르시오.

① 찬성　　　　　　② 실망
③ 거절　　　　　　④ 조언
⑤ 감사

07 대화를 듣고, 여자가 음악회에서 연주한 악기를 고르시오.

① violin　　　　　② piano
③ flute　　　　　④ guitar
⑤ drums

08 대화를 듣고, 남자가 대화 직후에 할 일로 가장 적절한 것을 고르시오.

① 도서관 가기　　　② 친구들 만나기
③ 커피숍 가기　　　④ 방문 열어놓기
⑤ 선풍기 옮기기

09 대화를 듣고, 수영장에서 지켜야 할 사항으로 언급되지 <u>않은</u> 것을 고르시오.

① 음식 반입하지 않기　　② 휴대폰 반입하지 않기
③ 큰 소리로 떠들지 않기　④ 수영 시 수영모 쓰기
⑤ 50분 수영 후 10분 휴식하기

10 다음을 듣고, 여자가 하는 말의 내용으로 가장 적절한 것을 고르시오.

① 공원의 이로운 점　　② 공원 이용 수칙
③ 쓰레기 처리 방법　　④ 동물 보호 방법
⑤ 환경 보호 이유

점수
/20

11 다음을 듣고, The Tree House에 관한 정보로 일치하지 <u>않은</u> 것을 고르시오.

① 2주 전에 개봉했다.
② 지난 주말 가장 인기있는 영화였다.
③ 평론가들에게 많은 비평을 받고 있다.
④ 프랑스에서 만들어진 영화이다.
⑤ 한 가족에 대한 이야기이다.

12 대화를 듣고, 남자가 전화를 건 목적으로 가장 적절한 것을 고르시오.

① 상점 운영시간을 문의하려고
② 식당을 예약하려고
③ 병원 예약을 확인하려고
④ 치과 진료를 예약하려고
⑤ 기록 정정을 요청하려고

13 대화를 듣고, 남자가 물건을 배달할 시간을 고르시오.

① 12시 이전   ② 12시에서 5시 사이
③ 5시에서 6시 사이   ④ 6시에서 7시 사이
⑤ 7시 이후

14 대화를 듣고, 두 사람의 관계로 가장 적절한 것을 고르시오.

① 공항 직원 – 여행객   ② 경찰관 – 시민
③ 역무원 – 승객   ④ 은행 직원 – 고객
⑤ 여행사 직원 – 고객

15 대화를 듣고, 여자가 남자에게 부탁한 일로 가장 적절한 것을 고르시오.

① 집안 청소하기   ② 식탁 차리기
③ 선물 포장하기   ④ 음식 데우기
⑤ 쓰레기 내다 버리기

16 대화를 듣고, 남자가 후식을 사양한 이유로 가장 적절한 것을 고르시오.

① 배가 너무 불러서
② 다이어트 중이라서
③ 알레르기가있어서
④ 단 것을 좋아하지 않아서
⑤ 집에 빨리 돌아가야 해서

17 다음 그림의 상황에 가장 적절한 대화를 고르시오.

①   ②   ③   ④   ⑤

18 다음을 듣고, 여자가 오늘 일정에 대해 언급하지 <u>않은</u> 것을 고르시오.

① 수족관까지 걸리는 시간
② 라벤더 밭에 도착하는 시간
③ 점심 먹는 시간
④ 수족관에 도착하는 시간
⑤ 수족관에서 보내는 시간

[19~20] 대화를 듣고, 남자의 마지막 말에 이어질 여자의 말로 가장 적절한 것을 고르시오.

19 Woman: _____

① Yes, I'd love to.
② I'm sorry to hear that.
③ Congratulations!
④ Please help yourself.
⑤ Don't worry. You can do it.

20 Woman: _____

① I'd like to be an imaginative person.
② Yes, you should to talk to my dad.
③ Right? They're so old and boring.
④ Well, I'm very good at computers.
⑤ No way. It would be so inconvenient.

다시 들으면서 듣기 만점에 도전하세요!
Dictation: 스크립트의 주요 부분을 다시 들으면서!
실전 ➕: 세부 정보가 많은 스크립트를 다른 문제로 샅샅이!

---

01 그림 정보 파악 – 날씨   다른 요일의 날씨와 혼동하지 않도록 집중하여 듣는다.

다음을 듣고, 목요일의 날씨로 가장 적절한 것을 고르시오.

① ② ③ ④ ⑤

W   Good morning! Are you all enjoying the recent good weather? Do you wonder if this weather will continue? Here's the weather forecast for this week. We'll start the week _____ _____ _____ _____ . It'll be sunny and nice on Monday, just
좋은 분위기로
like today. But we'll have some clouds on Tuesday. These clouds will stay with us all day Tuesday. On Wednesday and Thursday, we'll _____ _____ _____ .
폭우가 내리다
On Friday, the sunny weather will return, but the temperature will drop, and it might even snow.

---

02 그림 정보 파악 – 사물

대화를 듣고, 여자가 구입할 케이크로 가장 적절한 것을 고르시오.

① ② ③ ④ ⑤

M   Good afternoon, may I help you?

W   Yes, please. I'd like to _____ _____ _____ for my friend.
생일 케이크를 사다

M   Do you want a message on the cake?

W   Yes, I want "Happy Birthday!" on the cake.

M   Okay. What about this dark chocolate cake? It's very popular.

W   I don't think she likes chocolate. She loves cakes with fresh fruit.

M   Then, we have strawberries, cherries, and blueberries.

W   Oh, she likes strawberries. Do you have one with lots of strawberries?

M   Sure, what about this one? It's _____ _____ lots of strawberries.
~로 덮인

W   Yes! That's the one.

---

03 심정 파악

대화를 듣고, 남자의 심정으로 가장 적절한 것을 고르시오.

① proud   ② excited
③ worried   ④ relaxed
⑤ bored

W   Hi, Minsu, I heard you're busy lately.

M   Yes, I'm organizing the food competition for the school festival.

W   That sounds amazing. Are you cooking something, too?

M   No, I'm just organizing the event. I'd need to _____ _____
텐트를 설치하다
_____ and arrange the chairs.

W   Tents? Is it an outdoor event?

M   Yeah, but I'm not so sure anymore.

W   What do you mean?

M   They are calling for rain that day. So now I have to _____ _____
실내 장소를 찾다
_____ , but it's not going well.

W   What about the auditorium? It would be perfect.

M   It would be good, but it's already fully booked. I don't know what to do.

초반에 outlet mall만 듣고 섣부르게 답을 체크하지 않도록 주의한다.

대화를 듣고, 여자가 주말에 한 일로 가장 적절한 것을 고르시오.

① 쇼핑하기　　② 영화보기
③ 수영하기　　④ 볼링 치기
⑤ 스케이트 타

M Hi, Yerin! Did you have a good weekend?

W Yes, I went to an outlet mall with my family.

M An outlet mall? Did you _____ _____ _____?
　　　　　　　　　많은 새로운 것들을 사다

W No, I didn't have time for shopping.

M Really? Then what did you go there for?

W Oh, there's a lot to do at this mall. There's a movie theater, a swimming pool, a bowling alley, and even a skating rink.

M Wow, that's cool. I know you like skating.

W Yeah, but this time we all _____ _____. It was really fun!
　　　　　　　　　　같이 볼링 치러 갔다

M Cool! Let's see a movie there one day.

대화를 듣고, 두 사람이 대화하는 장소로 가장 적절한 곳을 고르시오.

① 경찰서　　② 서점
③ 교무실　　④ 교실
⑤ 도서관

W Hi, how may I help you?

M I'd like to return these books.

W Okay, let me check. [pause] Oh, they are two days late. That means that you can't borrow any other books for four days.

M Yes, I know. But there's a book I really need today. Isn't there any way I can borrow it today?

W You can _____ _____ _____ _____ instead. It's 50 cents per book
　　　　　연체료를 내다
for each day. Would you like to do that?

M Yes, please. Here's $2.

W Okay, now you can _____ _____ _____ _____.
　　　　　　　　　당신이 원하는 책을 빌리다

대화를 듣고, 남자의 마지막 말의 의도로 가장 적절한 것을 고르시오.

① 찬성　　② 실망
③ 거절　　④ 조언
⑤ 감사

M Hi, Cathy, happy birthday!

W Thank you, Dan. You remembered!

M Of course. I also remember your birthday party last year. It was great.

W You're right. It was a really good party, but it was so _____ _____ _____
　　　　　　　　　　　　　　　청소하기 힘든
_____ afterwards.

M Oh, really? I'm sorry to hear that.

W Don't worry. It wasn't your fault.

M So, what about this year? When are you having the party?

W Actually, there's no party this year. I decided to have a quiet birthday this year.

M Oh, _____ _____ _____. I was looking forward to it.
　　　아쉽다

대화를 듣고, 여자가 음악회에서 연주한 악기를 고르시오.

① violin
② piano
③ flute
④ guitar
⑤ drums

M You did so well. I'm so proud of you, Jihye.

W Thanks, Dad. I'm glad I didn't _____ any _____ this time.
　실수를 하다

M Are you still thinking about the last concert? You should forget about it.

W Yes, I know. But I was so afraid it would happen again.

M You were a beginner with the violin at that time. You are much better at it now.

W Yes, that's true. I feel a lot better with my violin ability.

M So, you _____ _____ _____ _____ _____ so far.
　　피아노와 바이올린을 연주하다
What's the next instrument?

W Actually, I'd like to try the drums.

대화를 듣고, 남자가 대화 직후에 할 일로 가장 적절한 것을 고르시오.

① 도서관 가기
② 친구들 만나기
③ 커피숍 가기
④ 방문 열어놓기
⑤ 선풍기 옮기기

➕ 대화를 듣고, 두 사람이 대화하는 장소로 가장 적절한 것을 고르시오.

① 보도
② 도서관
③ 커피숍
④ 집안
⑤ 학교

M It is so hot. I should study for my exams, but I can't concentrate.

W Why don't you _____ _____ _____ ?
　　　　　　　　도서관에 가다

M If I go to the library and see my friends, I'll end up hanging out with them.

W Hmm, what about a coffee shop?

M I can't study there either. It's too noisy.

W Well, then you have no other choice. You'll have to study in your room.

M But the air is _____ _____ _____ in my room.
　　　　　　　너무 덥고 답답한

W You can take this fan to your room if you want.

M Thanks, I'll do that.

언급된 내용을 보기에서 지워가며 답을 찾는다.

대화를 듣고, 수영장에서 지켜야 할 사항으로 언급되지 <u>않은</u> 것을 고르시오.

① 음식 반입하지 않기
② 휴대폰 반입하지 않기
③ 큰 소리로 떠들지 않기
④ 수영 시 수영모 쓰기
⑤ 50분 수영 후 10분 휴식하기

W Hi, is this your first time to our swimming pool?

M Yes, I just moved to this city.

W Welcome. I'll just go over a few rules first.

M Sure. Let me guess. I can't take any food into the pool area.

W Right. And you can't take your Cellphone, either. Please _____ _____
　그것을 보관함에 두어라
_____ _____ .

M Oh, okay. Anything else?

W You must _____ _____ _____ _____ when you swim. And you
　　　　　　　수영모를 쓰다
should take a 10-minute break after swimming for 50 minutes.

M I see. Luckily, I brought my swimming cap today.

---

rules, follow, park 등의 단어를 보고 답을 유추할 수 있다.

다음을 듣고, 여자가 하는 말의 내용으로 가장 적절한 것을 고르시오.

① 공원의 이로운 점
② 공원 이용 수칙
③ 쓰레기 처리 방법
④ 동물 보호 방법
⑤ 환경 보호 이유

W Welcome to Citizen's Park. This park is for everyone, but please let me remind you of some _____ _____ _____ in our park. First, please don't litter
　　따라야 할 중요한 규칙
in the park. Take any garbage back with you when you leave. Second, don't feed the animals. People food isn't good for animals, and it poses lots of problems. Last, if you're walking your dog, keep your dog on a leash at all times. Respect that some people _____ _____ _____ _____ . Thank you.
　　　　　　개를 무서워하다

11 내용 불일치 파악

다음을 듣고, The Tree House에 관한 정보로 일치하지 않는 것을 고르시오.

① 2주 전에 개봉했다.
② 지난 주말 가장 인기있는 영화였다.
③ 평론가들에게 많은 비평을 받고 있다.
④ 프랑스에서 만들어진 영화이다.
⑤ 한 가족에 대한 이야기이다.

M Hello, everyone. This is Chris from Movie World. I'm going to talk about the movie The Tree House that was ＿＿＿＿＿ ＿＿＿＿＿ ＿＿＿＿＿. It was the most watched movie last weekend, and it's receiving a lot of good reviews from critics. This movie was made in France, and it's a story about a family who moved to a little town in the countryside. Many strange things happen to them, but they work hard and ＿＿＿＿＿ ＿＿＿＿＿.

2주 전에 개봉한

미스터리를 풀다

12 전화한 목적 파악

대화를 듣고, 남자가 전화를 건 목적으로 가장 적절한 것을 고르시오.

① 상점 운영시간을 문의하려고
② 식당을 예약하려고
③ 병원 예약을 확인하려고
④ 치과 진료를 예약하려고
⑤ 기록 정정을 요청하려고

목적이 대화 초반에 등장하므로 남자의 첫 대사를 집중하여 듣는다.

[Telephone rings.]

W Hello, Hugh Dentist Clinic. ＿＿＿＿＿ ＿＿＿＿＿ ＿＿＿＿＿?

무엇을 도와드릴까요?

M Hi, I'd like to make an appointment.

W Okay, sure. Is it your first visit to our clinic?

M Ah, no. It's my second time. I was there six months ago.

W Then we should have your record. Could you ＿＿＿＿＿ ＿＿＿＿＿, please?

이름을 알려주세요

M It's David Kim. I'd like to go on a Saturday, if possible.

W Hold on, Mr. Kim. *[pause]* Ah, here's your record. This Saturday is not possible, but next Saturday at 2 o'clock is open.

M You said 2 p.m., right? That should work.

13 특정 정보 파악

대화를 듣고, 남자가 물건을 배달할 시간을 고르시오.

① 12시 이전
② 12시에서 5시 사이
③ 5시에서 6시 사이
④ 6시에서 7시 사이
⑤ 7시 이후

➕ 대화를 듣고, 남자가 전화한 목적으로 가장 적절한 것을 고르시오.

① 배달 완료를 알리기 위해
② 배달 시간을 정하기 위해
③ 재배달 사실을 알리기 위해
④ 근무 시간을 알려주기 위해
⑤ 본인 여부를 확인하기 위해

시간이 마지막에 결정되므로 섣부르게 답을 고르지 않도록 주의한다.

[Telephone rings.]

W Hello?

M Hello, this is Hana Delivery Service. May I speak to Mina Park?

W This is she speaking.

M Hi, will you ＿＿＿＿＿ ＿＿＿＿＿ ＿＿＿＿＿? I have a package for you.

오늘 집에 있다

W Can you come in the morning? I'm leaving around 12.

M Sorry, but I can't ＿＿＿＿＿ ＿＿＿＿＿ ＿＿＿＿＿ ＿＿＿＿＿. What time will you be back? I'm working until 6 today.

오전에 그곳에 가다

W Oh, I won't be back until after 7, but actually my mom will be home at 5. Can you leave it with her?

M Sure, I can do that.

대화를 듣고, 두 사람의 관계로 가장 적절한 것을 고르시오.

① 공항 직원 – 여행객
② 경찰관 – 시민
③ 역무원 – 승객
④ 은행 직원 – 고객
⑤ 여행사 직원 – 고객

표를 사고 파는 대화만 듣고 답을 체크하지 않도록 주의한다.

M Hi, how may I help you?

W I was wondering if you ＿＿＿＿＿ ＿＿＿＿ ＿＿＿＿ here.
   _{급행열차 표를 팔다}

M Yes, we do. Where are you going?

W I want to go to Amsterdam next Thursday, preferably before 8 a.m. How much will that be?

M ＿＿＿＿＿ ＿＿＿＿, ＿＿＿＿. *[pause]* Okay, for the 7:40 train, it's €82 for 2nd
   _{기다려 주세요}
   class, and €117 for 1st class.

W I'll take 2nd class.

M Okay. Do you need any help with hotel reservations or a car rental? We also have many great sightseeing programs.

W No, that's okay, thanks. I'm staying at a friend's place.

대화를 듣고, 여자가 남자에게 부탁한 일로 가장 적절한 것을 고르시오.

① 집안 청소하기   ② 식탁 차리기
③ 선물 포장하기   ④ 음식 데우기
⑤ 쓰레기 내다 버리기

부탁을 나타내는 표현인 'Can You~?'와 앞뒤 상황으로 답을 유추한다.

W Whew, I think we're finally done. What time is it?

M It's 5:30. Mom and Dad will be back in 30 minutes.

W Okay, let's do one more final check. The house is clean, and ＿＿＿＿＿＿
   _{음식이 준비되다}
   ＿＿＿＿ ＿＿＿＿ to serve for dinner.

M And our presents are wrapped. I can't wait to see them surprised!

W Neither can I. Now, we need to ＿＿＿＿ ＿＿＿＿ ＿＿＿＿. Can you do that
   _{식탁을 차리다}
   while I heat up the food?

M Sure. Is there anything else we need to do?

W I don't think so. We have to take out the garbage, but we can do that after dinner.

대화를 듣고, 남자가 후식을 사양한 이유로 가장 적절한 것을 고르시오.

① 배가 너무 불러서
② 다이어트 중이라서
③ 알레르기가 있어서
④ 단 것을 좋아하지 않아서
⑤ 집에 빨리 돌아가야 해서

M Thank you, Mrs. Brown. The dinner was delicious.

W I'm glad you liked it, Jason. Now, ＿＿＿＿ ＿＿＿＿ ＿＿＿＿ walnut
   _{~하시겠습니까?}
   pie for dessert?

M I'd like to, but I can't.

W Oh, are you allergic to nuts?

M Ah, no, actually, I'm just too full. I ＿＿＿＿ ＿＿＿＿ ＿＿＿＿.
   _{너무 많이 먹었다}

W Then, would you like to take some with you? I can wrap it up for you.

M Really? That's very nice of you. I usually don't like sweet things, but it looks very good.

W Thanks. I'll give you enough so that you can share it with your family.

다음 그림의 상황에 가장 적절한 대화를 고르시오.

① ② ③ ④ ⑤

① W Hi, long time no see! Is this your dog? It's so cute!
  M Thanks. His name is Baily. I'm just walking him. He likes this park.
② W Where did you get the hat? It _____ really _____ you.
      ~에게 잘 어울리다
  M Thank you, Sandy. I actually borrowed it from my dad.
③ W Which scene did you like the best in the movie?
  M I liked the scene when all the people ran across the beach at the same time.
④ W Excuse me, you're not allowed to go in there. _____ _____, _____.
      나오세요
  M Oh, I'm so sorry. I didn't know that.
⑤ W Can I have a look at those pictures, too?
  M Sure, take a look. I think you look really good in this one.

다음을 듣고, 여자가 오늘 일정에 대해 언급하지 <u>않은</u> 것을 고르시오.

① 수족관까지 걸리는 시간
② 라벤더 밭에 도착하는 시간
③ 점심 먹는 시간
④ 수족관에 도착하는 시간
⑤ 수족관에서 보내는 시간

순서대로 언급하는 내용을 보기에서 체크하여 답을 찾는다.

W Let me tell you today's schedule first. It will take us three hours to get to today's main attraction, Blue Aquarium, and we'll stop at two places _____ _____ _____. The first is the lavender field, where you can take pictures with beautiful flowers. We'll _____ _____ _____ at a famous local restaurant. After lunch, we'll take a short tour of the local village. When we finally arrive at the aquarium, it'll be 2:30, and you'll have two hours to spend there.
가는 길에 / 정오에 점심을 먹다

[19~20] 대화를 듣고, 남자의 마지막 말에 이어질 여자의 말로 가장 적절한 것을 고르시오.

Woman: _____

① Yes, I'd love to.
② I'm sorry to hear that.
③ Congratulations!
④ Please help yourself.
⑤ Don't worry. You can do it.

제안하는 남자의 말에 여자는 승낙이나 거절을 할 수 있다.

M Hi, Areum, are you okay? You look worried.
W Hi, Brad, I was just thinking what I should do to lose weight.
M What do you mean? You're _____ _____ _____.
    전혀 뚱뚱하지 않은
W Okay, maybe it's not about losing weight. This summer, I promised to _____ _____ _____ _____ with my cousins. I want to look healthier in my swimsuit.
    워터파크에 가다
M If that's the case, tennis is a very good sport.
W Really? Do you play?
M Yes, I do. Would you like to give it a try?
W _____

Woman: _____

① I'd like to be an imaginative person.
② Yes, you should to talk to my dad.
③ Right? They're so old and boring.
④ Well, I'm very good at computers.
⑤ No way. It would be so inconvenient.

W What are you reading, Dan?
M I'm _____ _____ _____ about technology. It's really interesting.
    책을 읽고 있는
W Can you give me one example?
M It says if cars had been developed as fast as computers, we'd have flying cars now.
W Wow, that is interesting. That means computers were developed very fast, right?
M Yes, exactly. My mom said she didn't have a computer when she was a child.
W Yeah, my dad said the same thing. He didn't have a Cellphone, either.
M It's crazy. Can you imagine _____ _____ _____ or smartphones?
    컴퓨터가 없는 삶
W _____

답안 체크지

실전처럼 문항별 정답을 마킹해서 확인하세요.

틀린 문제는 다시 듣고 확인하세요.

*디딤돌 홈페이지에서 다운로드 받아 교재 안에 수록된 모든 회차의 모의고사 답안 마킹에 활용하세요.

번호	답 란
01	① ② ③ ④ ⑤
02	① ② ③ ④ ⑤
03	① ② ③ ④ ⑤
04	① ② ③ ④ ⑤
05	① ② ③ ④ ⑤
06	① ② ③ ④ ⑤
07	① ② ③ ④ ⑤
08	① ② ③ ④ ⑤
09	① ② ③ ④ ⑤
10	① ② ③ ④ ⑤
11	① ② ③ ④ ⑤
12	① ② ③ ④ ⑤
13	① ② ③ ④ ⑤
14	① ② ③ ④ ⑤
15	① ② ③ ④ ⑤
16	① ② ③ ④ ⑤
17	① ② ③ ④ ⑤
18	① ② ③ ④ ⑤
19	① ② ③ ④ ⑤
20	① ② ③ ④ ⑤
plus ⬚	① ② ③ ④ ⑤
plus ⬚	① ② ③ ④ ⑤

_____회

번호	답 란
01	① ② ③ ④ ⑤
02	① ② ③ ④ ⑤
03	① ② ③ ④ ⑤
04	① ② ③ ④ ⑤
05	① ② ③ ④ ⑤
06	① ② ③ ④ ⑤
07	① ② ③ ④ ⑤
08	① ② ③ ④ ⑤
09	① ② ③ ④ ⑤
10	① ② ③ ④ ⑤
11	① ② ③ ④ ⑤
12	① ② ③ ④ ⑤
13	① ② ③ ④ ⑤
14	① ② ③ ④ ⑤
15	① ② ③ ④ ⑤
16	① ② ③ ④ ⑤
17	① ② ③ ④ ⑤
18	① ② ③ ④ ⑤
19	① ② ③ ④ ⑤
20	① ② ③ ④ ⑤
plus ⬚	① ② ③ ④ ⑤
plus ⬚	① ② ③ ④ ⑤

_____회

번호	답 란
01	① ② ③ ④ ⑤
02	① ② ③ ④ ⑤
03	① ② ③ ④ ⑤
04	① ② ③ ④ ⑤
05	① ② ③ ④ ⑤
06	① ② ③ ④ ⑤
07	① ② ③ ④ ⑤
08	① ② ③ ④ ⑤
09	① ② ③ ④ ⑤
10	① ② ③ ④ ⑤
11	① ② ③ ④ ⑤
12	① ② ③ ④ ⑤
13	① ② ③ ④ ⑤
14	① ② ③ ④ ⑤
15	① ② ③ ④ ⑤
16	① ② ③ ④ ⑤
17	① ② ③ ④ ⑤
18	① ② ③ ④ ⑤
19	① ② ③ ④ ⑤
20	① ② ③ ④ ⑤
plus ⬚	① ② ③ ④ ⑤
plus ⬚	① ② ③ ④ ⑤

_____ 회	
번호	답 란
01	① ② ③ ④ ⑤
02	① ② ③ ④ ⑤
03	① ② ③ ④ ⑤
04	① ② ③ ④ ⑤
05	① ② ③ ④ ⑤
06	① ② ③ ④ ⑤
07	① ② ③ ④ ⑤
08	① ② ③ ④ ⑤
09	① ② ③ ④ ⑤
10	① ② ③ ④ ⑤
11	① ② ③ ④ ⑤
12	① ② ③ ④ ⑤
13	① ② ③ ④ ⑤
14	① ② ③ ④ ⑤
15	① ② ③ ④ ⑤
16	① ② ③ ④ ⑤
17	① ② ③ ④ ⑤
18	① ② ③ ④ ⑤
19	① ② ③ ④ ⑤
20	① ② ③ ④ ⑤
plus □	① ② ③ ④ ⑤
plus □	① ② ③ ④ ⑤

_____ 회	
번호	답 란
01	① ② ③ ④ ⑤
02	① ② ③ ④ ⑤
03	① ② ③ ④ ⑤
04	① ② ③ ④ ⑤
05	① ② ③ ④ ⑤
06	① ② ③ ④ ⑤
07	① ② ③ ④ ⑤
08	① ② ③ ④ ⑤
09	① ② ③ ④ ⑤
10	① ② ③ ④ ⑤
11	① ② ③ ④ ⑤
12	① ② ③ ④ ⑤
13	① ② ③ ④ ⑤
14	① ② ③ ④ ⑤
15	① ② ③ ④ ⑤
16	① ② ③ ④ ⑤
17	① ② ③ ④ ⑤
18	① ② ③ ④ ⑤
19	① ② ③ ④ ⑤
20	① ② ③ ④ ⑤
plus □	① ② ③ ④ ⑤
plus □	① ② ③ ④ ⑤

_____ 회	
번호	답 란
01	① ② ③ ④ ⑤
02	① ② ③ ④ ⑤
03	① ② ③ ④ ⑤
04	① ② ③ ④ ⑤
05	① ② ③ ④ ⑤
06	① ② ③ ④ ⑤
07	① ② ③ ④ ⑤
08	① ② ③ ④ ⑤
09	① ② ③ ④ ⑤
10	① ② ③ ④ ⑤
11	① ② ③ ④ ⑤
12	① ② ③ ④ ⑤
13	① ② ③ ④ ⑤
14	① ② ③ ④ ⑤
15	① ② ③ ④ ⑤
16	① ② ③ ④ ⑤
17	① ② ③ ④ ⑤
18	① ② ③ ④ ⑤
19	① ② ③ ④ ⑤
20	① ② ③ ④ ⑤
plus □	① ② ③ ④ ⑤
plus □	① ② ③ ④ ⑤

번호	답 란
01	① ② ③ ④ ⑤
02	① ② ③ ④ ⑤
03	① ② ③ ④ ⑤
04	① ② ③ ④ ⑤
05	① ② ③ ④ ⑤
06	① ② ③ ④ ⑤
07	① ② ③ ④ ⑤
08	① ② ③ ④ ⑤
09	① ② ③ ④ ⑤
10	① ② ③ ④ ⑤
11	① ② ③ ④ ⑤
12	① ② ③ ④ ⑤
13	① ② ③ ④ ⑤
14	① ② ③ ④ ⑤
15	① ② ③ ④ ⑤
16	① ② ③ ④ ⑤
17	① ② ③ ④ ⑤
18	① ② ③ ④ ⑤
19	① ② ③ ④ ⑤
20	① ② ③ ④ ⑤
plus	① ② ③ ④ ⑤
plus	① ② ③ ④ ⑤

.... 회

번호	답 란
01	① ② ③ ④ ⑤
02	① ② ③ ④ ⑤
03	① ② ③ ④ ⑤
04	① ② ③ ④ ⑤
05	① ② ③ ④ ⑤
06	① ② ③ ④ ⑤
07	① ② ③ ④ ⑤
08	① ② ③ ④ ⑤
09	① ② ③ ④ ⑤
10	① ② ③ ④ ⑤
11	① ② ③ ④ ⑤
12	① ② ③ ④ ⑤
13	① ② ③ ④ ⑤
14	① ② ③ ④ ⑤
15	① ② ③ ④ ⑤
16	① ② ③ ④ ⑤
17	① ② ③ ④ ⑤
18	① ② ③ ④ ⑤
19	① ② ③ ④ ⑤
20	① ② ③ ④ ⑤
plus	① ② ③ ④ ⑤
plus	① ② ③ ④ ⑤

.... 회

번호	답 란
01	① ② ③ ④ ⑤
02	① ② ③ ④ ⑤
03	① ② ③ ④ ⑤
04	① ② ③ ④ ⑤
05	① ② ③ ④ ⑤
06	① ② ③ ④ ⑤
07	① ② ③ ④ ⑤
08	① ② ③ ④ ⑤
09	① ② ③ ④ ⑤
10	① ② ③ ④ ⑤
11	① ② ③ ④ ⑤
12	① ② ③ ④ ⑤
13	① ② ③ ④ ⑤
14	① ② ③ ④ ⑤
15	① ② ③ ④ ⑤
16	① ② ③ ④ ⑤
17	① ② ③ ④ ⑤
18	① ② ③ ④ ⑤
19	① ② ③ ④ ⑤
20	① ② ③ ④ ⑤
plus	① ② ③ ④ ⑤
plus	① ② ③ ④ ⑤

번호	답 란
01	① ② ③ ④ ⑤
02	① ② ③ ④ ⑤
03	① ② ③ ④ ⑤
04	① ② ③ ④ ⑤
05	① ② ③ ④ ⑤
06	① ② ③ ④ ⑤
07	① ② ③ ④ ⑤
08	① ② ③ ④ ⑤
09	① ② ③ ④ ⑤
10	① ② ③ ④ ⑤
11	① ② ③ ④ ⑤
12	① ② ③ ④ ⑤
13	① ② ③ ④ ⑤
14	① ② ③ ④ ⑤
15	① ② ③ ④ ⑤
16	① ② ③ ④ ⑤
17	① ② ③ ④ ⑤
18	① ② ③ ④ ⑤
19	① ② ③ ④ ⑤
20	① ② ③ ④ ⑤
plus	① ② ③ ④ ⑤
plus	① ② ③ ④ ⑤

_____ 회

번호	답 란
01	① ② ③ ④ ⑤
02	① ② ③ ④ ⑤
03	① ② ③ ④ ⑤
04	① ② ③ ④ ⑤
05	① ② ③ ④ ⑤
06	① ② ③ ④ ⑤
07	① ② ③ ④ ⑤
08	① ② ③ ④ ⑤
09	① ② ③ ④ ⑤
10	① ② ③ ④ ⑤
11	① ② ③ ④ ⑤
12	① ② ③ ④ ⑤
13	① ② ③ ④ ⑤
14	① ② ③ ④ ⑤
15	① ② ③ ④ ⑤
16	① ② ③ ④ ⑤
17	① ② ③ ④ ⑤
18	① ② ③ ④ ⑤
19	① ② ③ ④ ⑤
20	① ② ③ ④ ⑤
plus	① ② ③ ④ ⑤
plus	① ② ③ ④ ⑤

_____ 회

번호	답 란
01	① ② ③ ④ ⑤
02	① ② ③ ④ ⑤
03	① ② ③ ④ ⑤
04	① ② ③ ④ ⑤
05	① ② ③ ④ ⑤
06	① ② ③ ④ ⑤
07	① ② ③ ④ ⑤
08	① ② ③ ④ ⑤
09	① ② ③ ④ ⑤
10	① ② ③ ④ ⑤
11	① ② ③ ④ ⑤
12	① ② ③ ④ ⑤
13	① ② ③ ④ ⑤
14	① ② ③ ④ ⑤
15	① ② ③ ④ ⑤
16	① ② ③ ④ ⑤
17	① ② ③ ④ ⑤
18	① ② ③ ④ ⑤
19	① ② ③ ④ ⑤
20	① ② ③ ④ ⑤
plus	① ② ③ ④ ⑤
plus	① ② ③ ④ ⑤

중학영어듣기 만점 솔루션

듣기는
실전이다

중학 2

24회

정답과 해설

딤돌

01 ②

W Let's have a look at the weather for this week. On Monday, it will be sunny all day long. From Tuesday to Wednesday, it will be rainy, so don't forget your umbrella. On Thursday, we will have a lot of snow. It will be getting colder on Friday, but the snow will stop.

W 이번 주 날씨는 봐 봅시다. 월요일에는 하루 종일 맑겠습니다. 화요일부터 수요일까지는 비가 오겠으니 우천을 잊지 마세요. 목요일에는 많은 눈이 내리겠습니다. 금요일에는 더욱 추워질 예정이나 눈은 멈추겠습니다.

02 ③

M Good afternoon.

W Hello. What can I do for you?

M I'm looking for a water bottle.

W Okay. How about this one? It has a handle and a picture of a tree.

M I need the handle, but I don't want any pictures on it.

W Well, here's one with a handle but no picture. Do you like it?

M Great! I'll take it.

M 안녕하세요.

W 안녕하세요. 무엇을 도와드릴까요?

M 물병을 찾고 있습니다.

W 알겠습니다. 이 제품 어떠세요? 손잡이가 있고 나무 그림이 있습니다.

M 손잡이는 필요하지만 어떤 그림도 원하지 않습니다.

W 그럼, 여기 손잡이는 있지만 그림이 없는 제품입니다. 마음에 드세요?

M 좋네요! 그걸로 하겠습니다.

03 ③

M Mom, I have some big news to tell you.

W Big news? What is it?

M I won the first prize in the webtoon contest.

W Wow, congratulations! Your work must be great.

M You know I worked on it for more than two months.

W Right. You worked so hard.

M Yeah. I enjoyed it a lot.

W I'm so happy for you, James.

M 엄마, 엄마에게 말할 약간 중대한 소식이 있어요.

W 중대한 소식? 뭐니?

M 저 웹툰 대회에서 일등상을 탔어요.

W 와, 축하해! 네 작품이 훌륭한 게 분명해.

M 제가 두 달 넘게 작업한 거 아시잖아요.

W 맞아. 넌 정말 열심히 작업했어.

M 맞아요. 많이 즐겼어요.

W 정말 잘 됐다, 제임스.

04 ①

M Sarah, I heard you went to City Math Festival last Saturday.

W Yes, I did. So many people came to enjoy the festival.

M Were there many fun activities?

W Yes. There were many interesting puzzles and games.

M Oh, I like puzzles. Did you do any puzzles?

W Sadly I couldn't, because the line was too long.

M Then what activities did you do?

W I watched a movie on math history.

M 사라, 네가 지난 토요일 시 수학 축제에 갔다고 들었어.

W 맞아, 나갔어. 정말 많은 사람들이 축제를 즐기러 왔어.

M 재미있는 활동들이 많이 있었니?

W 응. 재미있는 퍼즐과 게임들이 많이 있었어.

M 아, 나 퍼즐 좋아해. 어떤 퍼즐이라도 했니?

W 슬프게도 할 수 없었어, 줄이 너무 길었거든.

M 그럼 어떤 활동들을 했어?

W 수학 역사에 대한 영화를 봤어.

05 ④

W Good afternoon, sir. Where are you going?

M I'm going to Daejeon. How much is the train ticket?

W It's 25,000 won. How many tickets do you need?

M Just one ticket, please. Here's my credit card.

W Okay. [Pause] This is your ticket.

M Good. How long will it take to Daejeon Station?

W It will take about one hour. Your train leaves in 10 minutes.

M Thank you very much.

W Have a nice trip.

W 안녕하세요. 어디를 가시나요?

M 대전에 갈 겁니다. 열차표가 얼마인가요?

W 25,000원 입니다. 얼마나 많은 표가 필요하시나요?

M 한 장 부탁드립니다. 여기 제 신용카드 입니다.

W 알겠습니다. [멈춤] 여기 표 입니다.

M 대전역까지 얼마나 걸리나요?

W 약 한 시간이 걸릴 겁니다. 손님 열차는 10분 후에 출발합니다.

M 고맙습니다.

W 즐거운 여행 되세요.

06 ④

W Good morning, Mr. Lee.

M Hi, Mina. Are you ready for the speech contest?

W Yes. I practiced a lot, but I'm still nervous.

M Don't worry. I think you're very talented at speaking.

W Thanks. But how can I make my speech better?

M Well, try to show your points with gestures.

W Okay. I'll keep that in mind.

M Also, you should make eye contact during the speech.

W 안녕하세요, Mr. Lee.

M 안녕, 미나. 웅변대회를 위한 준비가 되었니?

W 네. 많이 연습했지만 아직 떨리네요.

M 걱정 마. 너는 웅변에 아주 재능이 있다고 생각해.

W 고마워요. 하지만 제 연설을 어떻게 더 좋게 할 수 있을까요?

M 글쎄. 너의 핵심을 몸동작과 함께 보여주도록 해.

W 알겠어요. 명심하겠습니다.

M 또, 웅변을 하는 동안 시선을 마주쳐야 해.

07 ⑤

M Today's field trip was great, wasn't it?

W Yeah. The aquarium was fantastic.

M What did you see?

W I saw big sharks and sea turtles.

M I saw them, too. What else did you see?

W Dolphins and starfish. What was your favorite in the aquarium?

M I really liked the penguins. They were so cute.

W Penguins? Where were they?

M They were on the 2nd floor.

W Oh, really? I didn't see them.

M 오늘의 현장 학습 멋졌어, 안 그래?

W 그래. 수족관은 정말 환상적이었어.

M 무엇을 보았니?

W 큰 상어와 바다 거북을 보았어.

M 나도 봤어. 다른 건 무얼 보았어?

W 돌고래와 불가사리. 수족관에서 네가 가장 좋았던 게 뭐야?

M 나는 펭귄이 정말 좋았어. 펭귄들이 너무 귀여웠어.

W 펭귄? 어디에 있었는데?

M 2층에 있었어.

W 아 진짜? 난 못 봤어.

08 ⑤

W Todd, what's the matter?

M I dropped my cell phone in the water.

W Oh, no! Is it okay?

M I tried to turn it on, but it doesn't work at all.

W Um... Did you try drying the phone first?

M I already did, but it still isn't turning on.

W Then, you probably need to visit the service center.

M Okay. I'll go there now.

W 토드, 무슨 일이야?

M 나 내 휴대 전화를 물에 떨어뜨렸어.

W 이럴수가! 괜찮아?

M 전원을 켜보려고 했는데 전혀 작동을 안 해.

W 음... 전화를 우선 말려보려고 했어?

M 이미 했는데 여전히 안 켜져.

W 그럼, 서비스 센터를 방문해야겠다.

M 알겠어. 지금 갈 거야.

09 ②

M Mom, can we go into the art gallery now?

W Sure. Just set your phone to silent mode first.

M I already did. Can we take pictures inside the gallery?

W Of course. But we should not use the flash.

M I see. Wait, Mom. I didn't finish this juice yet.

W Then, finish it now. You can't bring it in.

M Okay. Let's go now.

W Remember, we shouldn't talk loudly in the gallery.

M 엄마, 지금 미술관에 들어갈 수 있나요?

W 물론. 단지 우선 네 전화를 무음 모드로 설정하렴.

M 이미 했어요. 미술관 안에서 사진을 찍을 수 있나요?

W 물론. 하지만 플래시는 터뜨리면 안 된다.

M 알아요. 잠깐만요. 엄마. 아직 이 주스를 다 안 마셨어요.

W 그럼, 지금 다 마시렴. 그걸 가지고 안에 들어갈 수 없어.

M 알겠어요. 이제 들어가요.

W 기억하렴, 미술관 안에서 크게 이야기하면 안 돼.

10 ③

M Okay, class. Thanks for all the great ideas. As you said, we should turn off the lights when we don't use them. Also, to save water, let's use cups while we brush our teeth. Next, we should recycle paper, cans and plastics. Lastly, we should try to reduce food waste. Let's remember these things to protect our environment.

M 자, 반 친구 여러분. 모든 좋은 생각들 고마워요. 여러분이 말한대로, 우리는 전등을 사용하지 않을 때. 그것을 꺼야 합니다. 또, 물을 절약하기 위해서, 양치를 하는 동안 컵을 사용합니다. 다음으로, 우리는 종이, 캔 그리고 플라스틱을 재활용해야 해요. 마지막으로, 우리는 물낭비를 줄이기 위해 노력해야 합니다. 우리 환경을 지키기 위해 이런 것들을 기억하도록 하세요.

11 ④

W Hello, students. We're going to hold a school flea market this Friday. This event is to help the sick children in our town hospital. You can bring your used items to sell such as bags and books. It'll be held on the school playground. If you have any items to sell, please tell Ms. Brown by this Wednesday.

W 안녕하세요, 학생 여러분. 우리는 이번 주 금요일에 학교 벼룩시장을 열

것입니다. 이 행사는 우리 마을 병원의 아픈 어린이들을 돕기 위한 것입니다. 여러분은 가방이나 책처럼 팔 중고 물품을 가져올 수 있습니다. 벼룩시장은 학교 운동장에서 열릴 예정입니다. 여러분이 팔 물건이 있다면, 이번 주 수요일까지 Ms. Brown께 말하세요.

12 ④

[Telephone rings.]

M Hello. Blue Star Tours. May I help you?

W Hi, I'd like to change my flight schedule, please.

M Okay. Can you tell me your reservation number?

W Yes. It's KR1256.

M When would you like to change it to?

W I want to change my flight to next Sunday.

M Okay. But you'll need to pay a service fee of 30 dollars.

W No problem.

[전화벨이 울린다.]

M 안녕하세요. 블루 스타 여행사입니다. 무엇을 도와드릴까요?

W 안녕하세요, 제 항공편 스케줄을 변경하고 싶습니다.

M 네. 당신의 예약 번호를 말씀해 주세요.

W 네. KR1256입니다.

M 날짜를 언제로 바꾸고 싶으신가요?

W 제 항공편을 다음 주 일요일로 바꾸고 싶습니다.

M 알겠습니다. 하지만 30달러 서비스 요금을 내셔야 합니다.

W 문제 없어요.

13 ⑤

W All right. We've almost finished our science project.

M Yeah. But the presentation is on Friday.

W Yes, you're right. We still need to practice.

M And we have only two days left.

W Why don't we get started today?

M Okay. Let's meet here at 4 o'clock this afternoon.

W Oh, sorry. I have a club meeting at 4.

M How about 5:30?

W Sounds good. See you then.

W 좋았어. 우리 과학 프로젝트가 거의 끝나가.

M 그래. 하지만 발표가 금요일이야.

W 그래, 네가 맞아. 우린 아직도 연습해야 해.

M 그리고 이틀밖에 안 남았어.

W 오늘 시작하는 게 어때?

M 그래. 오늘 오후 4시에 여기서 만나자.

W 아, 미안. 나 4시에 동아리 모임이 있어.

M 그럼 5시 30분 어때?

W 좋아. 그때 보자.

14 ②

[Telephone rings.]

W Hello?

M Hello. This is White Rabbit Express. Is this Jiyoung Kim?

W Yes, speaking.

M Your package will be delivered around 3 p.m.

W Really? That's sooner than I expected.

M Will you be at home at that time?

W I'm afraid no one will be at home.

M Then where can I leave the package?

W Could you please leave it in the security office?

M Okay. I will.

[전화벨이 울린다.]

W 여보세요?

M 안녕하세요. 화이트 래빗 택배 회사입니다. 김지영 씨 맞나요?

W 네, 접니다.

M 고객의 소포가 오후 3시쯤 도착할 예정입니다.

W 정말요? 제가 예상한 것보다 빠르네요.

M 그 시간에 집에 계시나요?

W 집에 아무도 없을 거예요.

M 그럼 소포를 어디에 두면 될까요?

W 경비실에 맡겨 주시겠어요?

M 알겠습니다.

15 ①

W James, what's wrong?

M I fell down and hurt my knee yesterday.

W Oh, I'm sorry to hear that. Did you see a doctor?

M Yes, I did. He said it would take three weeks to get better.

W Do you need help going up the stairs?

M It's okay, thanks. But can you carry my bag to the classroom for me?

W Sure. Let me take it.

M Thanks. It's very kind of you.

W 제임스, 무슨 일이야?

M 나 어제 넘어져서 무릎을 다쳤어.

W 오, 안됐다. 병원에 갔어?

M 응, 갔어. 나으려면 삼 주정도 걸릴 거라고 했어.

W 계단 올라가는 데 도움이 필요하니?

M 괜찮아, 고마워. 하지만 나를 위해 내 가방을 교실까지 들어줄 수 있어?

W 물론. 내가 들게.

M 고마워. 너 정말 친절하구나.

16 ⑤

M Yuna, why don't we go to the movies tomorrow?

W I'd love to, but I can't.

M Really? Do you have any special plans?

W Yes. I need to go to Mokpo with my family.

M Oh, why are you going there?

W Tomorrow is my uncle's wedding.

M Wow, that is cool. Have a great time.

W Thank you. Let's go see a movie next weekend.

M 유나, 내일 영화를 보러 갈래?

W 그러고 싶은데, 그럴 수 없어.

M 진짜? 무슨 특별한 계획이라도 있니?

W 응. 가족과 목포에 가야 해.

M 아, 거기는 왜 가는 거야?

W 내일이 삼촌의 결혼식이야.

M 와, 멋지다. 좋은 시간 보내.

W 고마워. 다음 주에 영화 보러 가자.

17 ①

① W Excuse me, sir. You have to wear a swimming cap here.

   M Oh, I'm sorry. I forgot to bring it today.

② W Watch out! There are cars coming.

   M Thanks. I'll be careful.

③ W What time does the movie start?

   M It starts in 10 minutes.

④ W How long does it take?

   M It takes two hours by bus.

⑤ W I like this shirt. How much is it?

   M It's 10 dollars. It's on sale now.

① W 실례합니다. 여기서는 수영모를 쓰여야 합니다.

   M 아, 죄송해요. 오늘 갖고 오는 걸 깜박했어요.

② W 조심해요! 고양이들이 오고 있어요.

   M 고마워요. 조심할게요.

③ W 영화가 몇 시에 시작하지?

   M 10분 후에 시작해.

④ W 얼마나 오래 걸려?

   M 버스로 두 시간 걸려.

⑤ W 이 셔츠에 마음에 드네요. 얼마인가요?

   M 10달러입니다. 지금 세일 중이에요.

18 ③

W Hello, new students. I'd like to tell you about our school bus service. There are six bus lines. You can check the bus stops on our school website. The bus fare is free for our students. If you want to use the bus service, please fill out the form and give it to Mr. Smith by this Friday. Thanks.

W 안녕하세요, 신입생 여러분. 우리 학교 버스 서비스에 대해 말씀드리겠습니다. 여섯 개의 버스 라인이 있습니다. 우리 학교 웹사이트에서 버스 정류장을 확인할 수 있습니다. 버스 요금은 우리 학생들에게는 무료입니다. 버스 서비스를 이용하고 싶다면 양식을 작성해서 이번 주 금요일까지 Mr. Smith께 주세요. 감사합니다.

19 ②

W Paul, did you hear that our English teacher is going back to the U.S.?

M Oh, really? When is he leaving?

W Next week. So, I'd like to have a goodbye party for him.

M That sounds great. How about asking other classmates to join the party?

W All right. I'll ask them to join us.

M Good. Why don't we have the party this Wednesday?

W That's perfect.

W 폴, 우리 영어 선생님이 미국으로 돌아 가신다는 거 들었니?

M 아, 진짜? 언제 떠나신대?

W 다음 주. 그래서, 선생님을 위한 송별회를 열었으면 해.

M 좋은 생각이야. 다른 학생들한테 파티에 참여해 달라고 하는 게 어떨까?

W 좋아. 내가 우리와 함께 하자고 할게.

M 그래. 송별회는 이번 주 수요일에 하는 거 어때?

W 완벽해.

① 안돼.

③ 그거 철자 쓸 수 있어?

④ 오랜만이야.

⑤ 내가 너보다 커.

20 ⑤

M Julia, you look worried. What happened?

W I think I lost my new running shoes.

M Sorry to hear that. Where did you put them last?

W I think I put them in the locker this morning.

M Are you sure?

W Not really. I was in a hurry for the next class.

M Okay. I'll help you to find them. What do your shoes look like?

W They're blue with white stripes.

M 줄리아, 걱정스러워 보인다. 무슨 일이야?

W 나 내 새로운 운동화를 잃어버린 거 같아.

M 안됐다. 마지막으로 그것을 어디에 뒀는데?

W 오늘 아침 보관함에 둔 거 같은데.

M 확실해?

W 확실하지는 않아. 다음 수업 때문에 서둘렀거든.

M 그래. 운동화 찾는 걸 도와줄게. 신발이 어떻게 생겼어?

W 파란 색이고 하얀 끈이야.

① 나 열이 있어.

② 버스로 40분 걸렸어.

③ 나 피아노 잘 쳐.

④ 내가 가장 좋아하는 음식은 스파게티야.

01 ③	02 ②	03 ④	04 ⑤	05 ⑤
06 ②	07 ③	08 ③	09 ④	10 ⑤
11 ①	12 ①	13 ②	14 ⑤	15 ①
16 ⑤	17 ③	18 ④	19 ①	20 ④

01 ③

M Good evening! Here is today's world weather report. Today in Seoul, the rain is expected to continue from last night. In New York, there will be showers and thunderstorms all day long. The forecast for Paris is mostly cloudy. Snow is expected for London. Thank you very much.

M 안녕하세요! 오늘의 세계 일기 예보입니다. 오늘 서울은 지난 밤부터 계속해서 비가 오겠습니다. 뉴욕은 하루 종일 소나기와 뇌우가 있겠습니다. 파리는 대부분 흐리겠습니다. 런던은 눈이 오겠습니다. 감사합니다.

02 ②

M Mom. Can I help you set the table?
W Sure Jake! Could you put the dish on the left side of the mat?
M Okay! What about the spoon?
W You can put it to the right of the dish.
M What about the fork, then?
W Put it to the right of the spoon.
M No problem. Do we also need the knife?
W No, we won't need it tonight.

M 엄마. 식탁 차리는 거 도와드릴까요?
W 물론이지 Jake! 접시를 매트 왼쪽에 두겠니?
M 네! 숟가락은요?
W 숟가락은 접시의 오른 쪽에 두렴.
M 그럼 포크는요?
W 포크는 숟가락의 오른쪽에 두렴.
M 문제 없어요. 나이프도 필요할까요?
W 아니, 오늘 밤은 필요하지 않아.

03 ④

M Yunhee, what will you do during the holidays?
W I'm going to see the Peking Opera again.
M What's the Peking Opera?
W It's the famous traditional Chinese opera, Minsoo.
M What's it like?
W The actors perform while wearing traditional face paint.
M I think I've seen it on TV before. It was very beautiful.

W And their voices are also unique.
M I think so, too.
W I really want to see it. I can't wait.

M Yunhee, 휴일동안 무엇을 할 거야?
W 또 경극을 보러 갈 거야.
M 경극이 뭐야?
W 유명한 중국 전통 오페라야, Minsoo.
M 어떤 거야?
W 배우들이 전통적인 얼굴 분장을 하고 공연을 해.
M 전에 TV에서 봤던 거 같아. 아주 아름다웠어.
W 그리고 그들의 목소리도 독특해.
M 나도 그렇게 생각해.
W 진짜 보고 싶어. 너무 기대돼.

04 ⑤

M Hi, Sujin. How was your weekend?
W I went shopping with my mom last Sunday.
M Nice. What did you buy?
W I bought a new lantern and chairs for camping.
M Oh, are you going camping soon?
W Yes, my family goes camping every month.
M I guess your family has a lot of fun together.

M Hi, Sujin. 주말 어땠어?
W 지난 일요일에 엄마랑 쇼핑을 갔어.
M 좋다. 무엇을 샀어?
W 캠핑을 위한 새로운 손전등과 의자를 샀어.
M 아, 곧 캠핑을 가?
W 응, 우리 가족은 매 달 캠핑을 가.
M 너희 가족은 함께 참 재미있겠다.

05 ⑤

M Welcome. May I help you?
W Yes, I lost my bag here in this park.
M What does it look like?
W It's a red backpack.
M And how big is it?
W It's big enough to hold about 10 books.
M Is there anything else you can tell me about it?
W Uhm... It has a picture of a monkey on the front.
M I see. We'll contact you when we find it.
W Here's my phone number. Thanks.

M 환영합니다. 도와드릴까요?
W 네, 이 공원에서 가방을 분실했어요.
M 어떻게 생겼나요?
W 빨간색 책가방이에요.
M 얼마나 큰가요?
W 책 10권이 들어갈 만큼 커요.
M 그것에 대해 더 말할 게 있나요?
W 음... 앞에 원숭이 그림이 있어요.

M 알겠습니다. 찾으면 연락 드리겠습니다.
W 여기 제 휴대 전화 번호입니다. 감사해요.

06 ②

M Kate, do you like any Korean pop groups?
W Yes. I love the group, "Dreamers". Their music is really fantastic.
M Yeah, then, how about coming with me to a K-pop festival this Friday?
W I'd love to, but I can't. I have a family dinner.
M How about Saturday then?
W I'm really sorry. Every Saturday I have to take a violin lesson.

M Kate, 한국 팝 그룹 좋아하니?
W 응. 난 "Dreamers"를 좋아해. 그들의 음악은 정말 멋져.
M 맞아, 그럼, 나랑 이번 주 금요일에 케이팝 축제에 가지 않을래?
W 가고 싶은데 가족과 저녁을 먹어야 해.
M 그럼 토요일은 어때?
W 진짜 미안. 매주 토요일에는 바이올린 레슨이 있어.

07 ③

M Hi, you must be Katie!
W Yes, it's nice to meet you. I really wanted to join your new band.
M Great. We need both a piano player and a guitarist.
W I'd love to play the piano. Could I?
M Sure, why don't you join our next practice?
W Sounds good. Do you practice every day?
M No, we only practice on Tuesdays.
W That's perfect. I'm free on Tuesdays.

M 안녕, 넌 Katie겠구나!
W 응, 만나서 반가워. 나 정말 너희 새로운 밴드에 가입하고 싶었어.
M 잘됐다. 우리는 피아노 연주자와 기타리스트를 필요로 해.
W 나는 피아노를 연주하고 싶어. 할 수 있을까?
M 물론이야. 다음 연습에 참여하는 거 어때?
W 좋아. 매일 연습해?
M 아니, 화요일에만 해.
W 완벽하다. 나 화요일에 한가하거든.

08 ③

M Hi, Julie. Thank you for inviting me to dinner last night.
W Thank you for coming. I was happy you could visit my house.
M All the food was really delicious. Did you make it all yourself?
W Oh, no. My mom helped me. She's a good cook.
M I'd love to get the recipes from your mom.

W Oh really? She runs a blog on Korean food.
M Then I need to visit her blog right now.

M 안녕, Julie. 어젯밤 저녁식사에 초대해 주어서 고마워.
W 와주어서 고마워. 우리집에 와주어서 즐거웠어.
M 모든 음식이 정말 맛있었어. 다 네가 만든 거야?
W 아니. 엄마가 도와줬어. 엄마는 요리를 잘해.
M 어머니께 요리 방법을 얻고 싶다.
W 진짜? 엄마는 한국 음식에 대한 블로그를 운영하고 있어.
M 그럼 당장 그녀의 블로그에 방문해야지.

09 ④

W Welcome to the Nara Public Library. We are open from 9 a.m. to 6 p.m. We are closed every Monday. There are free children's classes from 10 to 11 a.m. on Wednesdays. If you want to borrow books, make sure to bring your ID. When you return books during a holiday, please put them in the drop box located next to the front door. Thank you.

W Nara 공공 도서관에 오신 걸 환영합니다. 우리는 9시부터 6시까지 운영합니다. 우리는 매주 목요일에 휴관합니다. 수요일마다 10시부터 11시까지 어린이들을 위한 무료 수업이 있습니다. 책을 대출하기를 원하시면 신분증을 가져오세요. 휴일에 책을 반납하기를 원하시면 앞 문 옆에 위치한 투입함에 넣어주세요. 감사합니다.

10 ⑤

M Hello, students! Let me tell you how to use your cell phone wisely. First, you should not talk too loudly on the phone while using public transportation. Second, you should not send text messages while you are walking. Lastly, when you are at a movie theater, you need to turn off your cell phone.

M 안녕하세요. 학생 여러분! 휴대 전화를 현명하게 사용하는 법을 알려드리겠습니다. 첫번째로, 대중교통을 사용할 때 전화 통화를 너무 큰 소리로 하지 않도록 합니다. 두번째, 걸으면서 문자를 보내지 않습니다. 마지막으로. 영화관에 있을 때는 전원을 끕니다.

11 ①

W Guess what, Minho. I'm going to visit London.
M Wow! How long will you stay there?
W I'll be there for a week. I can't wait to visit all of the famous places.
M I hope you can take lots of photos.
W Sure. I'll show them to you when I come back.
M Great. Are you also planning to see a musical?
W No, I don't have enough time.
M I see. Maybe you can see one next time.

W 그거 알아. Minho. 나 런던에 갈 거야.
M 왜! 거기서 얼마나 머물 거야?

W 일주일은 있을 거야. 빨리 모든 유명한 장소들을 방문하고 싶어!

M 사진을 많이 찍어 오길 바랄게.

W 물론이야. 내가 돌아오면 사진을 보여줄게.

M 좋아. 뮤지컬을 볼 계획도 있어?

W 아니, 나 시간이 충분하지 않아.

M 알겠어. 다음에 볼 수 있을 거야.

12 ①

M Welcome back to Korea, Lucy.

W I'm glad to see you again.

M Me, too. What brings you back to Korea?

W I'm here to meet the main actor of the movie, "Great Love".

M Really? When are you going to see him?

W I'm going to his fan meeting this Saturday.

M You must be excited to see your favorite actor.

M 한국에 돌아온 걸 환영해요, Lucy.

W 다시 봐서 기뻐요.

M 저도요. 왜 한국에 다시 왔어요?

W 영화 "Great Love"의 주연 배우를 만나러 왔어요.

M 진짜요? 언제 그를 볼 건가요?

W 이번 주 토요일에 팬미팅에 갈 예정이에요.

M 제일 좋아하는 배우를 볼 생각에 흥분되겠어요.

13 ②

W Excuse me, I'd like to print out this picture.

M Okay. How many do you need?

W I need two copies. How much will it cost?

M Well, our photo shop offers two options.

W All right, what are they?

M One dollar each for black and white or two dollars each for color.

W Then, I'd like two copies in black and white.

M Sure. One moment, please.

W 실례합니다, 이 사진을 뽑고 싶어요.

M 네. 얼마나 많이 필요하시죠?

W 두 장이요. 얼마인가요?

M 저희 사진관은 두 가지 옵션이 있습니다.

W 네, 무엇이죠?

M 흑백사진은 장당 1달러이고 컬러사진은 장당 2달러입니다.

W 그럼, 흑백사진으로 2장이요.

M 알겠습니다. 잠시만 기다려주세요.

14 ⑤

W All right, please be sure to clear off your desk.

M Yes, ma'am.

W And don't forget to write your name and student number on the answer sheet.

M How long will the test take, ma'am?

W The test will take 45 minutes.

M Oh, some pages are missing in my test booklet.

W Let me check. I'll give you a new one.

M Thank you.

W 책상을 깨끗하게 치워주세요.

M 네. 선생님.

W 그리고 정답지에 이름과 번호를 쓰는 것을 잊지 마세요.

M 시험은 얼마나 보나요, 선생님?

W 시험은 45분 봅니다.

M 아, 제 시험지에 빠진 부분이 있어요.

W 봅시다. 새 것을 줄게요.

M 감사합니다.

15 ①

W Wow! Brian, your art project looks wonderful!

M Thank you, ma'am. I am making the Eiffel Tower using cookies.

W How are you putting them together?

M I'm using strawberry jam and peanut butter.

W That's very clever.

M Thank you, ma'am. Could you pass me some more cookies?

W Yes. Here they are.

W 와! Brian, 네 미술 프로젝트 정말 굉장하구나!

M 고맙습니다. 선생님. 쿠키를 이용해서 에펠탑을 만들고 있어요.

W 어떻게 쿠키를 붙였니?

M 딸기잼과 땅콩버터를 사용하고 있어요.

W 아주 영리하구나.

M 감사합니다. 선생님. 쿠키를 좀 건네주시겠어요?

W 그래. 여기 있어.

16 ⑤

M Congratulations, Mary!

W What is this about?

M You're going to get the Student of the Month Award.

W Really? I didn't expect that. I'm so happy to hear the good news.

M Yeah, your classmates chose you.

W Do you know why they chose me?

M Because you always volunteered to help your friends.

W Wow. My mom will be so glad.

M 축하해, Mary!

W 뭐 때문에 그래요?

M 너 이 달의 학생 상을 받게 될 거야.

W 진짜요? 생각도 못했어요. 좋은 소식을 들으니 기쁘네요.

M 그래, 네 반 친구들이 널 선택했어.

W 왜 친구들이 절 선택했을까요?

M 너는 항상 자진해서 친구들을 돕잖니.

W 와. 엄마가 기뻐하실 거예요.

17 ③

① M How was your trip?
　W It was great. I enjoyed going to the beach in Thailand.
② M Can I take your order?
　W Sure. I'd like a chicken burger and a soda.
③ M I'm so sorry. Let me clean that up for you.
　W No worries. Anyone can make a mistake.
④ M May I see your passport?
　W Sure, here you are.
⑤ M Excuse me. You can't park here.
　W Sorry, I didn't know that.

① M 여행 어땠니?
　W 좋았어. 태국 바닷가에 가는 걸 즐겼어.
② M 주문하시겠습니까?
　W 네. 치킨 버거 하나와 소다 한 잔 주세요.
③ M 정말 죄송해요. 닦아 드릴게요.
　W 걱정 마세요. 누구나 실수는 하니까요.
④ M 여권을 볼 수 있을까요?
　W 네, 여기요.
⑤ M 실례합니다. 여기에 주차하실 수 없습니다.
　W 죄송해요, 몰랐어요.

18 ④

W Hi, Dad.
M Hi, Jihee. Are you excited about the family trip?
W Sure, I can't wait to go to the Philippines.
M Yeah, I just got information from the travel agency.
W Cool. Did they say anything about the weather?
M Yes, it'll be very hot.
W Okay, then I should bring summer clothes.
M Right. They also told us we would stay at the Star Hotel.
W It looks like we're ready for the trip then.

W 안녕하세요, 아빠.
M 안녕, Jihee. 가족 여행 기대하고 있니?
W 네, 빨리 필리핀에 가고 싶어요.
M 그래, 여행사에서 막 정보를 받았단다.
W 잘됐네요. 날씨에 대해서 말해줬나요?
M 그래, 아주 뜨거울 거래.
W 알겠어요, 그럼 여름옷을 가져가야 하겠네요.
M 그래. 거기서 우리가 스타 호텔에서 묵을 거라고 했어.
W 그럼 우리 여행 준비가 다 된 거 같네요.

19 ①

M Have you ever been to Daehan Tower?
W Never, but I've heard a lot about it.
M Yeah, the tower is a wonderful place for tourists.

W Really? Can you tell me a little more about it?
M Sure. It has a lovely view and many famous restaurants.
W Sounds like a nice place.
M It is. Why don't we visit there this Sunday?
W Okay, let's go together.

M 대한 타워에 가본 적 있어?
W 아니, 하지만 많이 들어 봤어.
M 그래, 그 타워는 여행객들에게 멋진 곳이야.
W 진짜? 조금 더 말해 줄래?
M 물론이야. 타워는 멋진 경관과 많은 유명한 음식점들이 있어.
W 좋은 곳처럼 들린다.
M 좋은 곳이야. 이번 주 일요일에 방문해보지 않을래?
W 그래, 같이 가자.
② 아마 그게 널 도울 수 있을 거야.
③ 저건 내 필통이야.
④ 한 블록 쭉 가세요.
⑤ 그건 네 문제였다고 생각해.

20 ④

W Hi, Eric. Did you watch the animal documentary on TV yesterday?
M No, what was it about?
W It was about the life of cheetahs.
M Did you find out anything interesting?
W Yeah. They are very fast hunters.
M Are they faster than tigers?
W Yes, they are one of the fastest animals in the world.
M Really? How fast can they run?
W They can run about 100 km per hour.

W 안녕, Eric. 어제 TV에서 동물 다큐멘터리를 봤니?
M 아니, 무엇에 관한 것이었어?
W 치타의 삶에 대한 것이었어
M 흥미로운 걸 발견했니?
W 응. 그들은 정말 빠른 사냥꾼이야.
M 호랑이보다도 빠르니?
W 응, 그들은 세계에서 제일 빠른 동물들 중 하나야.
M 진짜? 얼마나 빨리 달릴 수 있는데?
W 대략 시속 100km를 달릴 수 있어.
① 그들은 오직 밤에만 사냥해.
② 그들은 남아프리카에 살아.
③ 그들은 사슴이나 버팔로를 먹어.
⑤ 그들은 몸에 검은 반점을 가지고 있어.

01 ②	**02** ④	**03** ③	**04** ⑤	**05** ⑤
06 ③	**07** ⑤	**08** ②	**09** ④	**10** ①
11 ④	**12** ⑤	**13** ④	**14** ②	**15** ③
16 ①	**17** ③	**18** ②	**19** ①	**20** ④

01 ②

M Good morning! This is today's weather. In Seoul, it will rain all day long. In Daejeon, it is cloudy this morning but it will snow a lot in the afternoon. In Busan, you will see a sunny sky all day. It will be a good day for a picnic. Thank you very much.

M 안녕하세요! 오늘의 일기 예보입니다. 서울은 하루 종일 비가 오겠습니다. 대전은 아침에는 흐리겠으나 오후에는 눈이 많이 오겠습니다. 부산은 종일 맑은 하늘을 볼 수 있겠습니다. 소풍을 가기에 좋은 날이 되겠습니다. 감사합니다.

02 ④

W David, can you help me for a second?
M No problem. What can I do for you?
W Bring me the tray in the kitchen, please.
M All right.
W Did you find it? It's on the shelf.
M Do you mean the tray with the circles?
W Not that one. It has two stars and two hearts.
M Okay, I see the one you're talking about.

W David, 잠깐 도와줄 수 있겠니?
M 걱정 없어요. 무엇을 도와드릴까요?
W 부엌에서 쟁반을 가져와 주겠니?
M 네.
W 찾았니? 선반 위에 있어.
M 동그라미가 있는 쟁반 맞나요?
W 아니 그거 말고. 별 두 개와 하트 두 개가 있는 것.
M 아, 무엇을 말하는지 알겠어요.

03 ③

W Hi, Junho. You don't look well. What's the matter?
M Well... I have an English speaking contest tomorrow.
W Don't worry! You practiced a lot.
M Yeah... But I get afraid when I speak in front of many people.
W You should take a deep breath before you start. You can do it.

M I will try my best, but this contest makes me uncomfortable.

W 안녕, Junho. 안 좋아 보이는데. 무슨 일 있니?
M 그게...나 내일 영어 말하기 대화가 있어.
W 걱정 마! 많이 연습을 했잖아.
M 응... 하지만 많은 사람들 앞에서 말할 때 두려워.
W 시작하기 전에 심호흡을 크게 해. 할 수 있어.
M 최선을 다 할 거야. 하지만 이 대회가 날 불편하게 해.

04 ⑤

W That was a great science day! Did you have fun?
M Of course. I made water bombs.
W Nice. I wanted to watch a 3D movie but I couldn't.
M That's too bad. What did you do then?
W I built airplanes out of wooden chopsticks instead.
M Did you like it?
W Yeah, it was really fun.
M Great! I'd like to make chopstick airplanes next year.

W 엄청난 과학의 날이었어! 재미있었어?
M 당연하지. 나 물 폭탄을 만들었어.
W 멋지다. 나는 3D영화를 보고 싶었는데 못 봤어.
M 안됐다. 그럼 뭐 했어?
W 대신 나무젓가락으로 비행기를 만들었어.
M 좋았어?
W 응, 진짜 재미있었어.
M 잘됐다! 내년에 나도 나무젓가락 비행기를 만들고 싶다.

05 ⑤

W Welcome! What can I do for you?
M Hi! I'd like to look around the city today.
W Okay, do you need a city tour map?
M Yes, please. Are there any famous places to visit?
W There are Gyeongbokgung Palace and the National Museum nearby.
M I see. Can I also find Korean restaurants on the map?
W Sure. The map has all kinds of useful information.
M Great. Thanks a lot.

W 환영합니다! 무엇을 도와드릴까요?
M 안녕하세요! 오늘 도시를 둘러보고 싶어요
W 알겠습니다. 도시 여행 지도가 필요하신가요?
M 네. 방문할 만한 유명한 장소가 있나요?
W 근처에 경복궁과 국립 박물관이 있습니다.
M 알겠습니다. 지도에서 한식당을 찾을 수 있나요?
W 물론입니다. 지도에는 온갖 종류의 유용한 정보들이 있습니다.
M 잘됐네요. 감사합니다.

06 ③

M Hey, Cathy. How do you like the new community center?

W I love it. It has many fun programs.

M Good. What do they have?

W There are lots of sports programs.

M Really? Like what?

W They have table tennis, badminton and swimming.

M I like swimming. Do you want to go together?

W Sounds great. Let's check the schedule and sign up.

M Yes. Good idea.

M 안녕, Cathy. 새 주민회관 어떠니?

W 좋아. 재미있는 프로그램이 많이 있어.

M 잘됐네. 어떤 것들이 있어?

W 많은 스포츠 프로그램이 있어.

M 진짜? 어떤 거?

W 탁구, 배드민턴 그리고 수영이 있어.

M 나 수영 좋아해. 같이 갈래?

W 좋아. 스케줄을 확인하고 등록하자.

M 그래. 좋은 생각이야.

07 ⑤

M Do you know that Midam University will run a Space Camp?

W No, I don't. When is it?

M It's from July 2nd to the 6th.

W Can we join the camp?

M Sure, it's for middle school students.

W Sounds good. What can we do there?

M We can look at stars through telescopes.

W Cool. What else can we do?

M We can wear spacesuits and try space foods.

M 미담대학이 우주 캠프를 열 거라는 거 알고 있니?

W 아니, 몰랐어. 언제야?

M 7월 2일부터 6일까지

W 우리 캠프에 참가할 수 있나?

M 당연하지, 이건 중학생들을 위한 거야.

W 잘됐다. 거기서 무엇을 할 수 있어?

M 망원경으로 별들을 볼수 있어.

W 멋지다. 다른 거는?

M 우주복을 입을 수 있고 우주 음식을 먹어볼 수 있어.

08 ②

W Brian, did you finish your project about ancient buildings?

M Not yet. It's due next Monday, right? What about you?

W I went to the library, but there was too much information.

M I know. I searched the Internet, but it was difficult to find useful information.

W Hmm... Why don't we ask the teacher for help?

M That's a good idea. Let's go to the teachers' office now.

W Okay.

W Brian, 고대 건물에 대한 네 프로젝트 끝났니?

M 아직. 다음 주 월요일까지 맞지? 너는?

W 나는 도서관에 갔는데 정보가 별로 없었어.

M 알아. 나는 인터넷을 찾아봤는데 유용한 정보를 찾기 힘들었어

W 흠... 선생님한테 도와달라고 할까?

M 좋은 생각이다. 지금 교무실로 가자.

W 그래.

09 ④

M Hello, students. We will have Job Experience Day in the student hall this Friday. There will be job experience zones for cooks, doctors, and producers. The event will start at 9:00 a.m. Please decide which job you will try first. To sign up, fill out the form and give it to your class leader by this Wednesday. Don't forget to bring your name card to the event. Have a good day.

M 안녕하세요. 학생 여러분. 우리는 이번 주 금요일 학생 회관에서 직업 체험날을 엽니다. 요리사, 의사 그리고 프로듀서를 위한 직업 체험존이 있을 것입니다. 행사는 오전 9시에 시작합니다. 어떤 직업을 우선 체험할지 정하세요. 등록을 위해서는 이번 주 수요일까지 반장에게 양식을 채워서 전달하세요. 행사에 당신의 이름표를 갖고 오는 것을 잊지 마세요. 좋은 하루 보내세요.

10 ①

W Let me tell you a story about a girl living in Nepal. She lost her family in an earthquake. At that time many people offered to help her. After that she felt like the luckiest person in the world. I used to complain a lot before I read her story. But the story made me thankful. Now, I try my best to be thankful for everything in my life.

W 네팔에 사는 한 소녀에 대한 이야기를 해드리겠습니다. 그녀는 지진으로 가족을 잃었습니다. 당시 많은 사람들이 그녀에게 도움을 제공했습니다. 그 후 그녀는 세상에서 가장 운 좋은 사람이라고 느꼈습니다. 그녀의 이야기를 읽기 전에 나는 불평하곤 했습니다. 하지만 그 이야기는 나를 고맙게 생각하도록 했습니다. 이제, 저는 내 삶의 모든 것에 감사하기 위해 최선을 다합니다.

11 ④

M Thank you for visiting the Highlands Zoo. We have many kinds of animals from all over the world. Let me tell you some special news before you look around the zoo. Two pandas arrived from China a month ago and you can see them today. Before we start, please remember you must not give any food to the animals. Also, you must not throw anything into the cage. Are you ready? Let's go!

M Highlands Zoo에 오신 걸 환영합니다. 우리는 전세계의 많은 종류의 동물들을 가지고 있습니다. 여러분이 동물원을 둘러보기 전에 특별

한 소식을 알려드리겠습니다. 판다 두 마리가 한 달 전에 중국에서 도착했고 여러분은 그들을 오늘 볼 수 있습니다. 시작하기 전에, 동물들에게 음식을 주어서는 안된다는 걸 기억하세요. 또한, 우리 안으로 어떤 것도 던지면 안됩니다. 준비됐나요? 갑시다!

12 ⑤

[Cellphone rings.]

W Hello! Mike.

M Hi! Jenny! What's up?

W I have tickets for a movie. Can you go with me?

M When is the movie?

W It's at 7 o'clock tonight.

M Sorry, but I can't go. I have to get ready for a presentation tomorrow.

W That's okay. Maybe next time.

[휴대 전화가 울린다.]

W 여보세요! Mike!

M 안녕! Jenny! 무슨 일이야?

W 나 영화표가 있어. 같이 갈래?

M 몇 시 영화인데?

W 오늘 밤 7시 영화.

M 미안하지만 못 가. 내일 발표 준비를 해야 해.

W 알겠어. 다음에 가자.

13 ④

[Telephone rings.]

W Hello, This is Jackie's Rock Band.

M This is the manager of Daehan Culture Center.

W How can I help you?

M Could your band perform for our center?

W When is the event?

M It's on May 9th.

W Sorry. Only the 11th is possible. Is that okay?

M Let me check. May 11th will be fine.

[전화벨이 울린다.]

W 안녕하세요, Jackie's Rock Band입니다.

M 대한문화센터의 관리인입니다.

W 무엇을 도와드릴까요?

M 당신 밴드가 우리 센터에서 공연을 할 수 있을까요?

W 행사가 언제인가요?

M 5월 9일입니다.

W 죄송합니다. 11일만 가능해요. 괜찮나요?

M 확인해 보겠습니다. 5월 11일 괜찮습니다.

14 ②

M How can I help you?

W I'd like to get a haircut, please. How much will it cost?

M It's 10 dollars.

W That's good. And can you change my hair color, too?

M What color do you want?

W Hmm... I can't decide. What color is popular these days?

M Brown is trendy now.

W That'll be nice.

M 무엇을 도와드릴까요?

W 머리를 자르고 싶습니다. 얼마인가요?

M 10달러입니다.

W 좋습니다. 머리 색깔도 바꿀 수 있나요?

M 어떤 색을 원하시나요?

W 흠... 결정을 못하겠네요. 요즘 어떤 색이 인기가 많나요?

M 지금 갈색이 유행입니다.

15 ③

W Junkyu, how about going to the Modern Art Gallery for our field trip?

M How long does it take to get there from the school?

W It takes about one hour by bus.

M Can we have lunch there?

W Hmm... I don't think so. Maybe we need to find a place to eat.

M Can you find a good restaurant nearby?

W All right. I'll look for one.

W Junkyu, 현장 학습으로 현대 미술관에 가는 거 어때?

M 학교에서 거기까지 얼마나 걸려?

W 버스로 한 시간 정도 걸려.

M 거기서 점심을 먹을 수 있어?

W 흠... 안 될 걸. 먹을 장소를 찾아야 할 거야.

M 근처에 괜찮은 식당을 찾을 수 있어?

W 응. 하나 찾아볼게.

16 ①

W Hurry up, Minsu. It's time to go to school.

M Okay, Mom. What time is it?

W It's almost 7:30.

M Is it raining outside?

W No, but it's very cloudy.

M Look! It's really hard to see outside.

W I think it is because of the yellow dust.

M Yeah, I think so, too.

W Make sure you wear a mask before you go out.

W 서둘러라, Minsu. 등교 시간이야.

M 알겠어요, 엄마. 몇 시인가요?

W 거의 7시 반이야.

M 밖에 비가 오나요?

W 아니, 하지만 아주 흐려.

M 봐 보세요! 밖을 보기 진짜 힘들어요.

W 미세먼지 때문인 거 같구나.

M 맞아요. 저도 그렇게 생각해요.

W 나가기 전에 꼭 마스크를 쓰렴.

17 ③

① **W** Where is the bakery?

　M It is near here.

② **W** This Sunday is our family camping trip. Do you remember?

　M Yes, I am so excited to go with Uncle Jim.

③ **W** I want to go to a baseball game this Saturday.

　M Great, let's go together.

④ **W** Can you take off the baseball cap inside?

　M Sorry. I forgot to take it off.

⑤ **W** There are a lot of pop stars on the stage.

　M So that's why it is crowded now.

① **W** 빵집이 어디에 있어?

　M 이 근처에 있어.

② **W** 이번 주 일요일에 우리 가족 캠핑 여행이야. 기억하지?

　M 네, Jim삼촌이랑 가니까 기대돼요.

③ **W** 이번 주 토요일에 야구 경기를 보러 가고 싶어.

　M 좋아, 같이 가자.

④ **W** 안에서는 야구 모자를 벗어 줄래?

　M 미안. 벗는 걸 잊었어.

⑤ **W** 무대 위에 많은 팝 스타들이 있어.

　M 지금 이렇게 붐비는 이유가 그거였구나.

18 ②

W Let me tell you about my job. I am a tour guide. I use English and Chinese to help foreign tourists communicate. I help them to visit historical places, museums and so on. Sometimes we go to the festivals. We try Korean foods like kimchi and bulgogi there together. I love to introduce Korean culture to foreign tourists.

W 제 직업에 대해 이야기하겠습니다. 저는 여행 가이드입니다. 저는 외국인 여행객들이 소통하는 것을 돕기 위해 영어와 중국어를 사용합니다. 저는 그들이 역사적인 장소, 박물관 등을 방문하는 것을 도와줍니다. 가끔 우리는 축제에 갑니다. 우리는 함께 그곳에서 김치나 불고기 같은 한국 음식을 먹어봅니다. 저는 외국인 관광객들에게 한국 문화를 소개하는 것을 좋아합니다.

19 ①

M Sumi, nice to see you.

W Hi! What's up?

M Not much. Do you remember Brian?

W Of course. Your Canadian friend. I remember him.

M He's coming to stay with my family for two weeks.

W Oh! Really?

M He said he'd like to visit famous places in Seoul.

W Then you should take him to Hanok Village.

M That sounds good.

M 수미야. 만나서 반가워.

W 안녕! 무슨 일이야?

M 별거 아니야. Brian 기억해?

W 당연하지. 너의 캐나다인 친구잖아. 기억해.

M 그가 2주동안 우리 가족들과 머물러 올 거야.

W 아! 진짜?

M 그가 서울의 유명한 곳을 방문하고 싶어해.

W 그럼 한옥 마을에 데려가.

M 좋은 의견이야.

② 나를 용서해줘.

③ 와줘서 고마워.

④ 내 소개를 할 게.

⑤ 저에게 너무 커 보이네요.

20 ④

W Chris, I have something to tell you.

M What is it, Mina?

W I had some trouble with Danny.

M What happened?

W I forgot to do my part of the group project, so we couldn't finish it in time.

M Really?

W Yeah, so I think he's angry at me.

M He must be upset. Did you try to call him?

W I did, but he didn't answer my call. What should I do?

M Text him that you are sorry.

W Chris, 나 말할 게 있어.

M 뭐야, Mina?

W 나 Danny와 문제가 있어.

M 무슨 일이야?

W 나 그룹 프로젝트에서 내 부분을 까먹어서 우리가 제 시간에 그걸 끝낼 수 없었어.

M 진짜?

W 어, 그래서 그가 나에게 화난 거 같아.

M 그는 분명히 화났을 거야. 전화해 봤어?

W 했는데 내 전화를 안 받았어. 어떻게 해야할까?

M 미안하다고 그에게 문자를 보내.

① 잘 먹어.

② 다음에 보자.

③ 좋은 시간 보내.

⑤ 물론이야, 정각에 갈

01 ②	02 ⑤	03 ④	04 ③, ❶ ②	05 ④
06 ①	07 ③	08 ②	09 ②	10 ②
11 ③	12 ①	13 ④	14 ③	15 ②
16 ③	17 ④	18 ⑤, ❶ ④	19 ④	20 ⑤

01 ②

W What did you do last weekend?

M I bought a dog with my sister.

W Oh, really? What does it look like?

M It is white and has long hair.

W Is it small or big?

M It is small. It has a big black spot on its back.

W Wow. It must be very cute.

M Yeah. My sister and I like it very much.

W 지난 주말에 무엇을 했니?

M 여동생과 함께 개를 샀어.

W 오, 정말? 그것은 어떻게 생겼니?

M 흰색이고 털이 길어.

W 작은 개야, 아니면 큰 개야?

M 작아. 등에 큰 검은 점이 하나 있어.

W 와. 틀림없이 매우 귀엽겠다.

M 그래. 내 여동생과 나는 그것이 무척 마음에 들어.

만점 솔루션 남자는 흰색에 털이 길며, 크기는 작고, 등에 검은 점이 있는 개를 샀다고 했다.

02 ⑤

W Who is the man beside the window? I have never seen him before.

M Which one? The man who is wearing glasses?

W No, the man wearing a hat. He's wearing a long shirt.

M Oh, that's my uncle.

W Really? He's very thin.

M Yes, and he's very tall, too.

W 창문 옆에 있는 남자는 누구야? 전에 그를 본 적이 전혀 없어.

M 어느 남자? 안경 쓰고 있는 남자?

W 아니, 모자를 쓰고 있는 남자. 그는 긴팔 셔츠를 입고 있어.

M 오, 그 사람은 내 삼촌이야.

W 정말? 아주 마르셨다.

M 맞아, 그리고 키가 매우 크시기도 하지.

03 ④

M This is something you use to travel in the city or for long distances. It has a small but strong motor, so you can move very fast. It is also very loud. Only one or two people can ride on it, though. It is a fun way to travel, but it can be dangerous, too. That is why you must always wear a helmet when riding.

M 이것은 도시 내에서 혹은 먼 거리를 여행하는 데 사용하는 것입니다. 이것은 작지만 강력한 모터를 가지고 있어서, 아주 빨리 움직일 수 있습니다. 또한 소리가 아주 큽니다. 그러나, 겨우 한 사람 혹은 두 사람만 그것에 탈 수 있습니다. 그것을 타고 여행하는 것은 아주 재미있지만, 위험할 수도 있습니다. 그래서 이것을 탈 때 당신은 항상 헬멧을 써야 합니다.

04 ③ | ❶ ②

M Are you free tomorrow?

W I am not doing anything special.

M Shall we go boating on the Han River?

W Well.... I'd like to, but I get motion-sickness when I go boating.

M Oh, do you? I didn't know that. Do you get motion-sickness when you ride a bike?

W No, it's OK.

M Then shall we go bicycling instead?

W Sounds good. I like riding a bike very much.

M 내일 시간이 있니?

W 특별한 일은 없어.

M 한강에 배 타러 갈까?

W 글쎄…. 가고 싶지만, 나는 배를 타면 멀미가 나.

M 오, 그러니? 몰랐는걸. 너는 자전거를 탈 때도 멀미가 나니?

W 아니, 그건 괜찮아.

M 그러면 대신에 자전거를 타러 갈까?

W 좋아. 나는 자전거 타는 것을 매우 좋아해.

05 ④

M Why are you so late for class, Sujin?

W Oh, I'm sorry, Mr. Kim. Our lunch time is very short.

M You have 50 minutes for lunch.

W But I usually have to wait for more than twenty minutes at the cafeteria.

M Then you still have more than 30 minutes to eat?

W Yes, I do, but I'm a slow-eater. It's hard for me to have lunch in such short time.

M How about bringing your own lunch?

W That's a good idea, Mr. Kim.

M 수진아, 너는 왜 수업에 그렇게 늦니?

W 오, 죄송해요, 김 선생님. 점심 시간이 너무 짧아요.

M 점심 시간으로 50분이 있잖아.

W 하지만 저는 식당에서 보통 20분 이상을 기다려야 해요.

M 그래도 너는 여전히 식사할 시간이 30분 이상 있잖니?

W 예, 그래요, 하지만 저는 밥을 천천히 먹어요. 그렇게 짧은 시간에 점심을 먹는 것이 저는 어려워요.

M 네 점심을 가져오는 것은 어떠니?

W 좋은 생각이에요, 김 선생님.

① 수진은 수업 시간에 늦는다.
② 수진은 점심 시간이 너무 짧다고 생각한다.
③ 수진은 오랫동안 점심을 먹기 위해 줄을 선다.
④ 수진은 대개 음식을 빨리 먹는다.
⑤ 선생님은 수진에게 점심을 가져오라고 제안한다.

I'm a slow-eater.에서 수진은 음식을 빨리 먹지 않음을 알 수 있으므로, ④가 일치하지 않는다.

06 ①

M Is the Seoul World Cup Stadium around here?

W Oh, it's far from here.

M How long does it take to walk there?

W It takes around 30 minutes. So take the bus number 30 right here.

M Thanks, but I'd like to take the subway. Where is the nearest subway station?

W It is ten minutes' walk.

M Oh, it's far from here. I'll take the bus. Thank you.

M 이 근처에 서울 월드컵 공원이 있나요?

W 오, 여기서 멀어요.

M 거기까지 걸어가는 데 시간이 얼마나 걸리나요?

W 약 30분 정도 걸립니다. 그러니까 바로 여기서 30번 버스를 타세요.

M 감사합니다, 하지만 저는 지하철을 타고 싶어요. 가장 가까운 지하철역은 어디 있나요?

W 10분 정도 걸어 가셔야 합니다.

M 오, 여기서 멀군요. 버스를 탈게요. 감사합니다.

07 ③

W Ladies and gentlemen! May I have your attention, please? We will be landing at Incheon International Airport in 10 minutes. Please remain seated and keep your seat belt fastened until the plane has made a complete stop. Please keep your Cellphone turned off until you enter the terminal. And make sure you don't leave any valuables. Don't forget to have your passports ready when you get off. We hope you have a nice trip. Thank you.

W 신사 숙녀 여러분! 잠깐 주목해 주시겠습니까? 우리는 10분 후면 인천 국제 공항에 착륙할 것입니다. 비행기가 완전히 멈췄을 때까지 자리에 앉으셔서 안전벨트를 매 주시기 바랍니다. 공항에 들어가실 때까지 휴대 전화는 꺼 두시기 바랍니다. 그리고 귀중품은 두고 내리시지 않도록 확인해 주시기 바랍니다. 내리실 때 여권을 준비해 주시는 것도 잊지 마시기 바랍니다. 즐거운 여행 되십시오. 감사합니다.

비행기가 10분 후면 착륙할 것이라는 안내 방송을 하면서 승객들에게 주의사항을 말하고 있는 담화이다.

08 ②

M Did you finish your English essay last night?

W No, I couldn't do it.

M Why not? Were you busy with something?

W I had to babysit my little brother all evening.

M Why didn't you write it after he went to bed?

W He stayed up late. He played with his toys all night.

M Well, don't worry. You'll be able to finish it tonight.

M 너 어젯밤에 영어 에세이를 끝냈니?

W 아니, 끝내지 못했어.

M 왜 못 끝냈어? 뭔가 바쁜 일이 있었어?

W 저녁 내내 남동생을 돌봐야 했어.

M 그 애가 자고 나서 쓰지 않니?

W 그 애가 늦게까지 깨어 있었어. 밤새 장난감을 가지고 놀았거든.

M 음, 걱정 마. 넌 오늘 밤에 그것을 끝낼 수 있을 거야.

09 ②

W I want to sell some of my old books.

M What kind of books are you selling? Novels are the easiest to get rid of.

W I have 20 novels, but I have some other books as well.

M What about textbooks? Do you have any?

W Yes, I have 15 textbooks. And 3 travel books as well.

M Maybe you should sell the textbooks at school.

W That's a good idea. I'll do that.

W 난 내 오래된 책을 좀 팔고 싶어.

M 어떤 종류의 책을 팔려는 거야? 소설은 처리하기가 가장 쉬운데.

W 소설책은 20권 있어, 하지만 다른 책들도 좀 있어.

M 교과서는? 가진 것이 있어?

W 응, 15권의 교과서가 있어. 그리고 여행서도 3권 있어.

M 학교에서 교과서를 팔아야 할 거야.

W 좋은 생각이야. 그래야겠다.

학교에서 여자가 판매하려는 책은 교과서이며 여자가 가진 교과서는 15권이므로 판매할 책도 15권이다.

10 ②

M I can't believe it!

W What's wrong? Did something happen?

M My phone isn't working!

W Did you drop it or something?

M No, it just seems to be broken. I can't make phone calls.

W Then you should get it fixed.

M I already did, last week. I'm so mad it's broken again!

W Why don't you return it and get your money back?

M Yeah, I'll get another phone. This one is terrible.

M 믿을 수가 없어!

W 뭐가 문제야? 안 좋은 일이 있었어?

M 내 전화기가 작동이 안 돼!

W 그것을 떨어뜨리기라도 한 거야?

M 아니, 그냥 고장 난 거 같아. 전화를 걸 수가 없어.

W 그럼 그것을 수리받아야겠구나.

M 지난주에 이미 그것을 수리받았어. 다시 고장이 나서 나는 정말 화가 나.

W 그것을 반품하고 돈을 환불받는 게 어때?

M 응, 다른 전화기를 사야겠어. 이건 최악이야.

만점 솔루션 남자는 지난주에 수리받은 전화기가 또 다시 고장이 나 매우 화가 난 상태이다.

11 ③

M What's up, Jane? You look worried.

W Tomorrow's my mother's birthday. I want to buy a present for her. But I don't have enough money.

M Oh, that's too bad. But I have an idea. It doesn't take a lot of money.

W What is it?

M You can bake a cake for her. I'll help you.

W That's a great idea. It's kind of you!

M Jane, 무슨 일이니? 걱정스러워 보이네.

W 내일이 엄마 생신이셔. 엄마에게 선물을 사 드리고 싶은데, 돈이 충분하지 않아.

M 오, 정말 안됐다. 하지만 내게 좋은 생각이 있어. 그것은 많은 돈이 필요하지 않아.

W 그게 뭔데?

M 엄마에게 케이크를 만들어 드릴 수 있어. 내가 도와줄게.

W 좋은 생각이야. 넌 친절하구나!

12 ①

M Excuse me.

W Yes, may I help you?

M I'd like to book a flight to Chicago.

W When are you going to leave?

M April the fourth.

W Let me see. Oh, sorry, sir. We don't have an available flight on that day. We have a flight at 2 p.m. the next day.

M OK, I'll make a reservation for it.

W May I have your name?

M Thomas Edison.

M 실례합니다.

W 예, 도와드릴까요?

M Chicago 행 비행기를 예약하고 싶어서요.

W 언제 출발하시죠?

M 4월 4일입니다.

W 잠시만요. 오, 미안합니다, 손님. 그 날 예약 가능한 비행기가 없네요. 그 다음 날 오후 2시에 비행기가 있습니다.

M 좋습니다, 그것으로 예약하죠.

W 성함이 어떻게 되세요?

M Thomas Edison이에요.

13 ④

W Oh, my! Excuse me!

M Yes, ma'am. What can I do for you?

W Look at this! There's a hair in this food!

M Oh, we're really sorry about this.

W I know this is an expensive restaurant. So I am not pleased with this.

M So we'll bring you a new one soon. And you don't have to pay for your food today. We're really sorry again.

W That's all right.

W 오, 이런! 여보세요!

M 예, 손님. 뭘 도와드릴까요?

W 여기 좀 보세요! 이 음식에 머리카락이 들어 있어요!

M 오, 정말 죄송합니다.

W 저는 이곳이 매우 비싼 식당이라고 알고 있어요. 그래서 이것에 대해 불쾌하군요.

M 그럼 곧 새 음식으로 갖다 드리겠습니다. 그리고 오늘 음식에 대한 값은 지불하실 필요가 없습니다. 다시 한 번 정말 죄송합니다.

W 괜찮습니다.

14 ③

M Are you left-handed?

W Yes, I am. What about you?

M Well, I use both hands. I write or draw with my left hand and I usually use my right hand for sports.

W Do you use your right hand when you play baseball or tennis?

M I use my right hand for playing tennis, but not baseball.

W Can you use either hand when you eat?

M Yes, I can. But I usually use my right hand for forks or chopsticks and my left hand for knives.

M 당신은 왼손잡이세요?

W 예, 그렇습니다. 당신은요?

M 음, 저는 두 손을 다 사용합니다. 저는 왼손으로 글을 쓰거나 그림을 그리고 운동을 할 때는 보통 오른손을 사용합니다.

W 야구나 테니스를 칠 때 오른손을 사용하세요?

M 테니스를 칠 때는 오른손을 사용하지만 야구는 아니에요.

W 밥 먹을 때는 어느 손이든 사용할 수 있어요?

M 예, 그럴수 있어요. 하지만 저는 보통 포크나 젓가락은 오른손을, 나이프는 왼손을 사용합니다.

만점 솔루션 남자는 양손잡이로 글을 쓰거나 그림을 그릴 때, 야구를 할 때, 나이프를 쓸 때 왼손을 사용한다. 테니스를 칠 때와 포크나 젓가락을 쓸 때는 오른손을 사용한다.

15 ②

W Yeram and I are going to see a movie tomorrow afternoon. Would you like to join us?

M That sounds wonderful. What time does the movie start?

W It starts at four.

M Oh, it's too early. My school finishes at three. Is there a movie that starts a little later?

W Sure. One starts at four thirty.

M That's possible for me.

W Shall we meet at three thirty at the bus station?

M Sure. See you then.

W 예람과 나는 내일 오후에 영화를 볼 거야. 우리랑 같이 갈래?

M 그거 좋은데. 영화는 몇 시에 시작하니?

W 4시에 시작해.

M 오, 너무 빨라. 우리 학교는 3시에 끝나거든. 좀 더 늦게 시작하는 영화가 있니?

W 물론이지. 4시 30분에 시작하는 게 하나 있어.

M 나에게는 그게 가능하겠다.

W 버스 정류장에서 3시 30분에 만날까?

M 좋아. 그때 보자.

16 ③

M May I help you?

W I'd like to check in.

M Do you have a reservation?

W Yes, I have a reservation for two nights.

M May I have your name, please?

W Theresa Baker.

M Let me see.... Ah, yes, please sign this form.

W OK. Here you are.

M You're in room 1201. Here's your key. Have a nice stay at the A-1.

W Thank you.

M 도와드릴까요?

W 입실하고 싶은데요.

M 예약하셨어요?

W 예, 이틀 밤을 예약했습니다.

M 성함이 어떻게 되시죠?

W Theresa Baker입니다.

M 잠깐만 기다리세요…. 아, 있네요, 이 양식에 서명해 주세요.

W 알겠습니다. 여기 있습니다.

M 당신은 1201호실입니다. 여기 열쇠가 있습니다. A-1에서 좋은 시간 보내세요.

W 감사합니다.

17 ④

M How may I help you?

W I'd like to report a lost wallet.

M Do you know where you lost it?

W No. I just realized that it wasn't in my bag.

M When did you last use it?

W Hmm... I think it was at a coffee shop. I bought a coffee.

M Okay. Why don't you fill in this form for me and leave your contact number? I'll give you a call if it turns up.

W Thank you.

M 도와드릴까요?

W 지갑을 분실해서 신고하려고 합니다.

M 어디서 잃어버렸는지 아시나요?

W 아니요. 가방에 없다는 걸 막 알았습니다.

M 마지막으로 사용한 건 언제 인가요?

W 흠... 커피숍에서 사용했던 거 같아요. 커피를 샀거든요.

M 알겠습니다. 이 양식을 작성해주시고 연락가능한 번호도 남겨주시겠어요? 발견하면 연락 드리겠습니다.

W 감사합니다.

18 ⑤ | ➕ ④

W Oh, no. It's already 2 o'clock. I'm going to be late.

M Where are you going? It's your day off, isn't it?

W Yes, but I have a dentist appointment at 2:30.

M Well, you can get there in 20 minutes, so if you leave now, you can make your appointment.

W Yes, but I was going to do the dishes before I go. Could you do them for me?

M Sure, I'll take care of them. Don't worry.

W Thank you. See you later.

W 안돼. 벌써 2시잖아. 늦겠어.

M 어디 가는데? 오늘 쉬는 날이잖아, 아니야?

W 맞아. 그런데 치과 예약이 2시 30분이야.

M 20분이면 갈 수 있으니까 지금 출발하면 늦지 않을 거야.

W 맞아, 그런데 가기 전에 설거지를 하려고 했거든. 대신 해줄 수 있을까?

M 물론, 내가 해 놓을게. 걱정하지 마.

W 고마워. 나중에 봐.

19 ④

W What a lovely painting it is! It looks expensive. John, how much was it?

M I didn't buy it. I painted it myself.

W Really? I can't believe it. I thought it was a famous painter's work.

M Thank you. Painting is one of my favorite hobbies.

W How long have you been painting pictures?

M It's been three years. I learned from my uncle.

W John, can you help me with my painting this Saturday?

M _____

W 정말 멋진 그림이야! 비싸 보여. John, 저 그림은 얼마였니?

M 나는 그것을 사지 않았어. 내가 직접 그린 거야.

W 정말? 믿을 수가 없어. 나는 그것이 유명한 화가의 작품이라고 생각했어.

M 고마워. 그림 그리기는 내가 가장 좋아하는 취미 중 하나야.

W 너는 얼마 동안 그림을 그려 왔니?

M 3년 되었어. 삼촌한테서 배웠어.

W John, 이번 토요일에 내가 그림 그리는 것을 도와주겠니?
M 물론이지. 그러고 싶어.

① 고맙지만, 됐어.
② 곧 보자.
③ 함께 가자.
⑤ 아니, 네 말에 동의하지 않아.

20 ⑤

[Telephone rings.]
W Hello.
M Hello. May I speak to Jennifer, please?
W She isn't home. Who's calling, please?
M This is Tim. I'm Jennifer's classmate.
W Hi, Tim. This is Jennifer's mother.
M How are you?
W I'm fine. Would you like to leave a message?
M _____

[전화벨이 울린다.]
W 여보세요.
M 여보세요. Jennifer와 통화할 수 있나요?
W 그녀는 집에 없는데요. 누구세요?
M 저 Tim이에요. Jennifer와 같은 반 친구예요.
W 안녕. Tim. 나는 Jennifer의 엄마란다.
M 어떻게 지내세요?
W 잘 지낸단다. 메시지를 남기겠니?
M 예, 저에게 전화해 달라고 말씀해 주시겠어요?

① 저는 그애의 아빠입니다.
② 기다려요. 그 애는 방에 있어요.
③ 전화 잘못 거셨어요.
④ 예. 그것에 대해 좀 더 말씀해 주시겠어요?

영어듣기능력평가 **02**회

01 ③	**02** ④	**03** ②, ➕③	**04** ②, ➕④	**05** ①
06 ④	**07** ①	**08** ④	**09** ④	**10** ②
11 ①	**12** ⑤	**13** ⑤	**14** ④	**15** ②
16 ④	**17** ③	**18** ②	**19** ①	**20** ⑤

01 ③

M I'd like you to wrap it. It's a gift.
W Okay. What kind of wrapping paper would you like?
M I'll take that one with the kittens and puppies. And I want this pink ribbon on it.
W That's really cute.
M Would you put it in a red bag, please?
W All right. By the way, who is this pretty skirt for?
M It's for my daughter.

M 그것을 포장해 주시면 좋겠어요. 선물이거든요.
W 알겠어요. 어떤 종류의 포장지로 하고 싶으세요?
M 새끼고양이와 강아지들이 있는 저것으로 할게요. 그리고 그 위에 이 분홍색 리본을 하고 싶어요.
W 정말 귀엽네요.
M 그것을 빨간색 가방에 넣어 주시겠어요?
W 알겠어요. 그런데, 이 예쁜 치마는 누구 거예요?
M 제 딸을 위한 거예요.

만점 솔루션 마지막 부분에서 남자가 구입한 것은 딸에게 줄 예쁜 치마임을 알 수 있다.

02 ④

W Do you ever get any exercise?
M Not regularly. And I'm tired of jogging and swimming.
W Well, why don't you do something else?
M Actually, I want to learn how to play tennis.
W Tennis? I heard it is very difficult to learn. How about joining the badminton club with me?
M Badminton?
W Yes. It is easier to learn than tennis.
M Hmm... Okay.

W 어떤 운동이라도 하고 있니?
M 규칙적으로는 아냐. 그리고 조깅과 수영은 지겨워.
W 음, 다른 것을 해 보지 그러니?
M 사실, 테니스 치는 법을 배우고 싶어.
W 테니스? 배우기가 아주 어렵다고 들었는데. 나와 함께 배드민턴 동아리에 가입하는 것이 어때?
M 배드민턴?
W 그래. 그것이 테니스보다 배우기가 더 쉬워.
M 흠…. 좋아.

03 ② | ➕ ③

M Hi, Jessica. How are you?

W I'm great. I <u>won a trip to Hawaii</u> at a quiz show on TV.

M What? A trip to Hawaii? That's amazing.

W Yeah, it really is.

M When are you going? Are you going in July?

W Yeah. Summer vacation in Hawaii! <u>That will be wonderful.</u>

M <u>Enjoy your trip</u> to Hawaii. I envy you a lot.

M 안녕, Jessica. 어떻게 지내니?

W 잘 지내. 나는 TV 퀴즈 쇼에서 하와이행 여행 상품을 탔어.

M 뭐라고? 하와이행 여행 상품이라고? 그거 놀라운데.

W 그래. 정말 그렇지.

M 언제 가는데? 7월에 가니?

W 응. 하와이에서 여름 휴가를! 그것은 멋질 거야.

M 하와이행 여행을 즐기렴. 네가 정말 부러운데.

04 ② | ➕ ④

W Who do we have to pick up today?

M Four people: Meg, Jane, Scott, and Don.

W Does Jane still live on Markwood Street?

M Yes, and I think Scott lives there, too.

W No, he <u>moved to Crescent Street</u>, near Meg's on Decker.

M I hope Don lives <u>somewhere near</u>.

W Yes, he lives on Benton Street, between Crescent Street and Chesnutt Street.

W 오늘 누구를 데려와야 하는 거지?

M 네 명이야. Meg, Jane, Scott, 그리고 Don.

W Jane은 아직 Markwood 거리에 살고 있어?

M 응, 그리고 Scott도 아직 거기에 살 거야.

W 아니야. 그는 Crescent 거리로 이사 갔어. Meg이 사는 Decker 근처야.

M Don이 근처 어디에 살았으면 좋겠다.

W 맞아. 그는 Crescent 거리와 Chesnutt 거리 사이인 Benton 거리에 살아.

> **만점 솔루션** 여자의 말에서 Scott이 Crescent 거리로 이사 갔음을 알 수 있다.

05 ①

M I'd like to invite you to visit Lawrence Research Center. You and other scientists <u>are being asked to help us</u> with "Project Alpha." Your ideas may help us greatly. We will provide you with work-related support if you need it. Please <u>accept our invitation</u>. If you have any questions about the opportunity, please contact us at 510-486-1234 or by email.

M 저는 귀하(貴下)를 Lawrence 연구센터에 방문하시도록 초대하고 싶습니다. 귀하와 다른 과학자들께 '프로젝트 알파'와 관련해서 저희를 도와달라고 요청드리는 바입니다. 귀하의 아이디어가 저희에게 큰 힘이 될 것입니다. 귀하께서 필요하시다면 업무와 관련된 지원을 제공해 드리겠습니다. 부디 저희의 초대를 받아주시기 바랍니다. 이 기회에 대해 질문

이 있으시면, 510-486-1234나 이메일로 저희에게 연락을 주시기 바랍니다.

06 ④

W Do you <u>have your form filled out</u>?

M Yes, it's right here.

W It says you bought a $200 vase overseas. Is that correct?

M Yes, I have it here. Is there a problem?

W You have to <u>pay duty on anything over $100</u>.

M How much do I owe?

W $20. You can pay it at the window by the exit.

W 양식을 기입하셨나요?

M 예, 여기 있습니다.

W 200달러짜리 꽃병을 해외에서 구매하셨다고 되어 있네요. 맞나요?

M 예, 여기 있어요. 문제가 있나요?

W 100달러 이상의 물건에는 관세를 지불하셔야 합니다.

M 얼마를 내야 하죠?

W 20달러입니다. 출구 옆의 창구에서 지불하시면 됩니다.

> **만점 솔루션** 해외에서 산 물건을 검사하고 세금을 부과하고 있으므로, '공항 세관'에서의 대화임을 알 수 있다.

07 ①

M Good afternoon, Mrs. Park. My name is Kim Jinho. I'm <u>taking your Chinese class</u>.

W Yes, I've seen you <u>in the class</u>. How's the class, then?

M Honestly, listening is difficult. You speak too fast for me.

W That's too bad. But ! hope you'll keep trying.

M I'm trying hard these days.

W I'm happy to hear that. Well, I'll <u>see you in the class</u>.

M Okay. See you later.

M 안녕하세요, 박 선생님. 제 이름은 김진호입니다. 저는 선생님의 중국어 수업을 듣고 있어요.

W 그래요. 수업 시간에 본 적이 있네요. 그런데 수업은 어때요?

M 솔직히, 듣는 게 어려워요. 저에게는 선생님 말씀이 너무 빠르거든요.

W 안됐군요. 하지만 계속해서 노력하기를 바랍니다.

M 요즘 열심히 노력하고 있습니다.

W 그 말을 들으니 기쁘군요. 그럼, 수업 시간에 봐요.

M 알겠습니다. 나중에 뵙죠.

08 ④

M I'd like to book a room at your hotel.

W Okay. What type of room do you want?

M I'd like <u>a double room</u>. How much is that?

W It's <u>50 dollars per night</u>. How long are you going to stay?

M I'll be staying <u>for 4 nights</u>.

W All right. When are you arriving here?

M I'm coming on April 21.

M 호텔 객실을 하나 예약하고 싶은데요.

W 알겠습니다. 어떤 종류의 객실을 원하시나요?

M 2인실로 주세요. 얼마죠?

W 하룻밤에 50달러예요. 얼마 동안 묵으실 건데요?

M 4일 밤 동안 묵을 예정입니다.

W 알겠습니다. 언제 이곳에 도착하실 예정이세요?

M 4월 21일에 갈 겁니다.

> **만점 솔루션** 남자는 하룻밤에 50달러인 2인실을 4일 밤 사용한다고 했으므로, 총 200달러를 지불해야 한다.

09 ④

M Any plans for the weekend?

W My fellow students were planning a picnic in the park, but it might rain.

M It's supposed to rain on Sunday.

W That's the problem. It's a class reunion.

M So you can't change it. What about changing a meeting place?

W But where? Do you know of a place?

M The school auditorium might do.

W That's a good idea. I should call the school and check if it's available.

M 주말에 무슨 계획 있어?

W 내 동창들이 공원에서의 소풍을 계획하고 있었어. 하지만 비가 올 것 같아.

M 일요일에 비가 올 거야.

W 그건 문제인데. 동창회 모임이거든.

M 그럼 바꿀 수가 없는 거구나. 모임 장소를 바꾸는 건 어때?

W 하지만 어디로? 아는 장소 있어?

M 학교 강당이 괜찮을지도 몰라.

W 좋은 생각이다. 학교에 전화해서 그곳이 이용 가능한지 확인해 봐야겠다.

10 ②

W The earliest dinosaurs had an advantage over other creatures. Surprisingly, the advantage was not their size. The first dinosaurs were not very big. In fact, they were quite small and fed on insects. However, those dinosaurs were able to run and jump on their back legs. Their amazing legs allowed them to easily access food.

W 초기 공룡들은 다른 생명체에 비해 이점이 있었습니다. 놀랍게도, 그 이점은 그들의 크기가 아니었습니다. 초기 공룡들은 아주 크지는 않았습니다. 사실, 그들은 꽤 작았고 곤충을 먹고 살았습니다. 그러나, 그 공룡들은 뒷다리로 달리고 뛰어 오를 수 있었습니다. 그들의 놀라운 다리는 그들이 쉽게 먹이에 접근하게 해 주었습니다.

11 ①

W Tell me some more about your trip to the east coast of the United States.

M Okay. What would you like to know?

W What was the best part of your trip?

M Well, the scenery along the coast was fantastic!

W What was the worst part?

M I didn't like paying tax whenever I bought something.

W What about the weather there?

M The weather was really nice.

W 미국 동부 해안으로 갔던 여행에 대해 좀 더 말씀해 주세요.

M 좋아요. 무엇을 알고 싶은데요?

W 여행 중에 가장 좋았던 부분은 뭐였어요?

M 글쎄요, 해안을 따라서 펼쳐진 경치가 환상적이었어요!

W 최악의 부분은 뭐였어요?

M 뭔가를 살 때마다 세금을 내는 게 싫었어요.

W 거기 날씨는 어땠나요?

M 날씨는 정말 좋았어요.

12 ⑤

[Telephone rings.]

M Hi, is Sandra there, please?

W No, she isn't. She's out now, but she'll be back at 3:30 in the afternoon.

M Oh, okay. Can I leave a message?

W Sure.

M My name is Jason Holden. Could you please ask her to give me a call as soon as she comes back?

W All right, Jason.

M My phone number is 250-3007.

W 250-3007? Okay, I'll give her the message.

M Thank you.

[전화벨이 울린다.]

M 안녕하세요, Sandra 있나요?

W 아니요, 없어요. 그녀는 지금 외출 중인데, 오후 3시 30분에 돌아올 거예요.

M 오, 알겠습니다. 메시지를 남길 수 있을까요?

W 물론이죠.

M 제 이름은 Jason Holden입니다. 그녀가 돌아오는 대로 저에게 전화를 좀 해 달라고 전해 주시겠어요?

W 알겠어요, Jason.

M 제 전화번호는 250-3007입니다.

W 250-3007이라고요? 알겠어요, 그녀에게 메시지를 전해 줄게요.

M 고마워요.

> **만점 솔루션** 남자는 Sandra가 돌아오는 대로 전화를 해 달라는 메시지를 남겼는데 메모에서는 tomorrow라고 되어 있으므로, ⑤가 일치하지 않는다.

13 ⑤

[Telephone rings.]

W Hello. May I help you?

M Yes, I'm trying to find a book. It's called *The Old Man and The Sea* by Ernest Hemingway.

W I'll check on the computer for you.

M Thank you.

W Well, it's not in stock. We can order the book for you.

M Okay. Go ahead, please.

W No problem.

[전화벨이 울린다.]

W 안녕하세요. 도와드릴까요?

M 예, 책을 찾으려고 하는데요. Ernest Hemingway가 쓴 '노인과 바다'라는 책입니다.

W 컴퓨터로 확인해 볼게요.

M 감사합니다.

W 음, 그건 재고가 없네요. 당신을 위해 그 책을 주문해 드릴 수는 있어요.

M 좋아요. 그렇게 해 주세요.

W 문제없습니다.

14 ④

M I have been invited to a housewarming party next week. What should I bring?

W We usually bring toilet paper to a housewarming party in Korea.

M Oh, that's very practical. How about cake or wine? In America, those are pretty common.

W Yes, we can bring those types of gifts when we have dinner at someone's house. But not a jipdeuri.

M Jipdeuri? What's that?

W Jipdeuri is a party held when you move to a new place. Well, have you decided what you'll bring?

M I'll bring toilet paper because I'm here in Korea.

W Sounds good.

M 다음 주에 집들이에 초대받았어요. 무엇을 가져가야 할까요?

W 한국에서는 보통 집들이에 화장지를 가지고 가요.

M 오, 그건 아주 실용적이군요. 케이크나 와인은 어때요? 미국에서는, 그런 것들이 꽤 일반적이거든요.

W 예, 누군가의 집에서 저녁 식사를 할 때는 그런 종류의 선물을 가져갈 수 있어요. 하지만 '집들이' 때는 그렇지 않아요.

M '집들이'요? 그게 뭐예요?

W '집들이'는 새로운 곳으로 이사하면 여는 파티예요. 그런데, 뭘 가져갈지는 결정했어요?

M 이곳 한국에 있으니까 화장지를 가져갈 거예요.

W 좋아요.

15 ②

① **M** I'm really sorry I'm late.

  W It's okay. We can still watch the movie.

② **M** Which movie would you like to watch?

  W What about this one? I like science fiction movies.

③ **M** What kind of movies do you like best?

  W I like romantic comedies. What about you?

④ **M** Wow, it was a really good movie.

  W Yes, it was. Would you like to get a snack now?

⑤ **M** The sky is so beautiful. Look at all those stars!

  W Wow, it is. I've never seen the sky like this.

① **M** 늦어서 정말 미안해.

  W 괜찮아. 아직 영화 볼 수 있어.

② **M** 어떤 영화가 보고 싶어?

  W 이거 어때? 나 과학 공상 영화가 좋아.

③ **M** 어떤 영화가 가장 좋아?

  W 나는 로맨틱 코미디가 좋아. 넌 어때?

④ **M** 와, 정말 좋은 영화였어.

  W 응. 이제 간식 먹으러 갈래?

⑤ **M** 하늘이 정말 아름답다. 저 별들을 봐!

  W 와. 이런 하늘은 본 적이 없어.

16 ④

W You're late again, Jason.

M I'm so sorry.

W Why were you late this time?

M I got a ticket on the way here.

W What did you do?

M I ran a red light. A police officer stopped my car, and he gave me a ticket.

W I'm sorry to hear that. Hey, Jason! I told you to take the subway.

M First of all, I should have been more careful.

W 또 늦었네, Jason.

M 정말 미안해.

W 이번에는 왜 늦었니?

M 여기 오는 길에 교통 위반 딱지를 받았어.

W 어떻게 했는데?

M 정지 신호에서 달렸어. 경찰관이 내 차를 세우더니 나에게 교통 위반 딱지를 발급했어.

W 유감인걸. 이봐. Jason! 내가 너한테 지하철을 타라고 말했잖아.

M 무엇보다도, 나는 좀 더 신중해야 했어.

17 ③

W Jinho, are you watching TV?

M Not at the moment, but I'm waiting for the next program.

W What program is it?

M It's a new entertainment show with my favorite singer.

W What time does it start?

M At 5:30.

W Well, you've still got an hour. Can you turn it off for now? I need to make an important phone call. I'll let you know when I'm finished.

M Okay, but please don't forget in case I fall asleep on the sofa.

W Don't worry, I won't.

W 진호, TV보고 있어?

M 지금은 아닌데 다음 프로그램을 기다리고 있어.

W 무슨 프로그램인데?

M 내가 좋아하는 가수가 나오는 새로운 오락쇼야.

W 언제 시작하는데?

M 5시 30분.

W 그럼 아직 한 시간 남았네. 지금 TV를 꺼줄래? 중요한 통화를 해야 해서 말이야. 통화가 끝나면 말해줄게.

M 알겠어, 하지만 내가 소파에서 잠들 수도 있으니까 잊지 마.

W 걱정하지마, 안 잊을게.

18 ②

W Jaehoon, how was your day today? Was the field trip good?

M Yes, Mom. We went to the art center. And here, look at this.

W What is this? A mug?

M Yes, I made it myself. <u>What do you think of it?</u>

W Wow, it's really good. Did you really make this yourself?

M Yes, we had a pottery class there. So everyone made their own.

W This is great. I think you <u>have talent.</u>

W 재훈, 오늘 어땠니? 현장 학습 좋았니?

M 네, 엄마. 우리는 아트 센터에 갔어요. 그리고 거기서, 이거 보세요.

W 이게 뭐니? 머그컵?

M 네, 제가 만들었어요. 어떻게 생각하세요?

W 와, 정말 잘 만들었네. 정말 이걸 네가 만들었니?

M 네, 거기서 도자기 수업을 들었어요. 그래서 모두 자기 걸 만들었어요.

W 이거 굉장하구나. 너에게 재능이 있다고 생각해.

19 ①

M Rosalita? That's a nice name. Is it Spanish?

W Yes. Thank you.

M Then are you from Spain?

W No, I was born in Mexico, but moved to Los Angeles when I was about two years old.

M Really? By the way, it's <u>very crowded here</u> in the airport.

W That's right.

M Your luggage <u>looks very heavy.</u> I'll <u>help you carry.</u>

W _____

M Rosalita? 멋진 이름인데요. 스페인어입니까?

W 예. 고마워요.

M 그럼 스페인에서 오셨어요?

W 아니요, 멕시코에서 태어났지만, 제가 2살쯤에 로스앤젤레스로 이주했어요.

M 그래요? 그런데, 여기 공항이 아주 붐비는군요.

W 맞아요.

M 짐이 아주 무거워 보이네요. 당신이 옮기는 것을 도와드릴게요.

W <u>그러실래요? 정말 고마워요.</u>

② 아니요. 당신이 그걸 좋아한다니 기쁘군요.

③ 맞아요. 저는 머리가 아파요.

④ 이거요? 이게 제가 가장 좋아하는 거예요.

⑤ 그래요. 당신을 다시 만나기를 바라요.

만점 솔루션 남자가 여자의 짐이 무거워 보인다고 하면서 옮기는 것을 도와주겠다고 말했을 때, 여자는 고맙다는 말을 하는 것이 가장 자연스럽다.

20 ⑤

M Hi, Susan. How are you this morning?

W Very good, and you?

M Not bad. Susan, what have you been up to lately?

W I've been <u>learning web design</u> in an after-school class.

M Web design? How interesting! How long have you been learning it?

W For about three months.

M <u>How's it going?</u>

W _____

M 안녕, Susan. 오늘 아침 어때?

W 아주 좋아, 너는?

M 나쁘진 않아. Susan, 요즘 뭐 하고 지냈니?

W 방과 후 수업에서 웹 디자인을 배우고 있어.

M 웹 디자인이라고? 정말 흥미로운데! 얼마나 오랫동안 그것을 배우고 있는 거야?

W 약 세 달 정도.

M 잘 되어가니?

W <u>나쁘진 않아. 그런데 연습을 좀 더 해야 할 것 같아.</u>

① 물론이지. 그렇게 말하는 것을 보니 너는 참 친절하구나.

② 그래. 너는 오늘 정말 멋져 보인다.

③ 나도 그래. 너와 이야기 하게 되어서 좋았어.

④ 맞아. 나는 가게에 가 봐야 해.

01 ④	02 ②	03 ①	04 ③	05 ③
06 ④	07 ⑤	08 ①	09 ⑤, ❸④	10 ⑤
11 ③	12 ④, ❸②	13 ⑤	14 ④	15 ④
16 ②	17 ①	18 ④	19 ②	20 ③

01 ④

① W Don't try to lift the stone alone.
   M I know it's very heavy.
② W Look at the fish in the tank.
   M Yeah. They are from Thailand.
③ W Hey, pull the rod now.
   M Wow! It feels like a big fish.
④ W Be careful when you hop.
   M I will, but I know the water is not deep.
⑤ W Let's race to the river.
   M Sure. I can beat you this time.

① W 그 돌을 혼자 들려고 하지 마.
   M 그건 매우 무거워.
② W 수족관에 있는 물고기들을 봐.
   M 그래. 그것들은 태국에서 온 거야.
③ W 이봐, 지금 낚싯대를 당겨.
   M 왜! 큰 물고기 같은 느낌이야.
④ W 뛸 때 조심해.
   M 그럴게, 하지만 물이 깊지 않아.
⑤ W 강까지 경주하자.
   M 좋아. 이번에는 내가 널 이길 수 있어.

02 ②

M Was the newspaper delivered?
W Yes, I brought it inside.
M Did you leave it on the kitchen table?
W Sorry, no. I left it by the refrigerator.
M It's not on the floor, is it?
W Don't worry. I put it on the side table.
M Oh, there it is, next to the coat rack.

M 신문이 배달되어 왔어?
W 응, 내가 안으로 가져왔어.
M 그것을 부엌 식탁 위에 두었어?
W 미안, 아니야. 냉장고 옆에 그것을 두었어.
M 바닥에 있는 건 아니지, 그렇지?
W 걱정 마. 협탁 위에 그것을 두었어.
M 오, 여기 있네. 옷걸이 옆에.

03 ①

W So... what seems to be the problem?
M He won't eat, and when he does, he throws up.
W Did you feed him anything unusual?
M No, but I took him for a long walk yesterday. And he could have eaten something on the street.
W It's possible. Well, it's been only one day. I think it's best to watch him for now.
M Will he be okay?
W I think so. But we can take an X-ray if you're really worried.

W 그래서... 뭐가 문제인 거 같나요?
M 먹지도 않고 먹으면 토해요.
W 평소와 다른 걸 먹였나요?
M 아니요, 하지만 어제 산책을 오래 했어요. 길에서 무언가 먹었을 수도 있어요.
W 가능성이 있네요. 하루밖에 안되었으니 지금은 지켜보는게 최선이네요.
M 괜찮을까요?
W 그럴 겁니다. 하지만 정말 걱정된다면 엑스레이를 찍어볼 수 있어요.

04 ③

W Can I help you?
M Yes. I want to buy a pair of shoes.
W What size do you want?
M Size 9.
W How do you like this brown pair? It's very popular with young adults.
M Sorry, but I'd like that black pair. How much is it?
W Forty dollars.
M All right. Here is my credit card.

W 도와드릴까요?
M 예. 구두 한 켤레를 사고 싶습니다.
W 몇 사이즈를 원하세요?
M 9사이즈로 주세요.
W 이 갈색 구두는 어떠세요? 젊은 층에게 매우 인기가 있어요.
M 미안하지만, 저 검정색이 마음에 들어요. 얼마죠?
W 40달러입니다.
M 좋아요. 여기 신용카드 있습니다.

05 ③

W Our hiking is going to be lots of fun.
M I know. I'm so excited about our trip!
W But first we have to decide whether to go by train or by bus.
M Good point. Shall we go by bus?
W Well, I like traveling by train.
M Okay. Let's buy our tickets online right now.

W 우리 하이킹은 매우 재미있을 거야.
M 알아. 나는 우리의 여행에 너무 신이 나!
W 그런데 먼저 기차로 갈 것인지 버스로 갈 것인지 결정해야 해.

M 좋은 지적이야. 버스로 갈까?

W 글쎄, 나는 기차로 여행하는 것이 좋은데.

M 좋았어. 지금 당장 인터넷에서 표를 사자.

06 ④

W Did you find everything you were looking for?

M Yes, I have five books here.

W I'll run them through. Can I have your card?

M Sure. How long can I keep them?

W Students are allowed to keep books for a month during the semester.

M What's the overdue charge?

W It's fifty cents per day. You can check the due date online.

M Great, thanks.

W 찾고 계신 것을 모두 찾으셨나요?

M 예, 여기 5권의 책이 있어요.

W 한번 볼게요. 카드 있으신가요?

M 물론이죠. 얼마나 빌릴 수 있을까요?

W 학생들은 학기 중에 한 달간 책을 빌릴 수 있어요.

M 연체료는 얼마인가요?

W 하루에 50센트에요. 인터넷으로 마감 날짜를 확인할 수 있어요.

M 괜찮네요, 고마워요.

만점 솔루션 책을 대출하고 있는 상황이므로 '도서관'에서의 대화임을 알 수 있다.

07 ⑤

M This is a public service announcement for everyone. These days, there are many reports of small accidents in our subway station. You can help prevent this. Please don't use your smartphone while walking. It can put you and everyone around you in danger. Also, please don't rush to get on the subway. It can cause serious harm to you or others. Thank you for your cooperation.

M 이것은 모두를 위한 공익 광고입니다. 요즘, 우리 지하철역에서 작은 사고들이 많이 접수되었습니다. 여러분은 이것을 예방하도록 도울 수 있습니다. 걸으면서 스마트폰을 사용하지 말아주세요. 이것은 여러분과 여러분 주변 모두를 위험하게 만들 수 있습니다. 또, 지하철을 타기 위해 급하게 달리지 마세요. 여러분과 다른 사람들에게 심각하게 해를 끼칠 수 있습니다. 협조에 감사드립니다.

08 ①

M Hi, Juhee, how was your weekend?

W It was great. I went to the art exhibition on Sunday, and I loved it.

M You did? What was the theme?

W Nature and landscapes. They had famous paintings from major cities around the world.

M That sounds great. I'd love to go see them, too!

W I could go again with you if you want. I liked it that much.

M Really? I'd love that. I'll gladly take you up on your offer.

M 안녕, 준희. 주말 어땠니?

W 좋았어. 일요일에 미술 전시회를 갔는데 아주 마음에 들었어.

M 그래? 주제가 뭐였는데?

W 자연과 풍경. 전세계 주요 도시에서 가져온 유명한 그림들이 있었어.

M 굉장하다. 나도 보고 싶어!

W 네가 원하면 나는 너랑 다시 갈 수 있어. 그만큼 좋았으니까.

M 진짜? 그럼 좋겠다. 기쁘게 네 제안을 받아들일게.

09 ⑤ | ➕ ④

W This place is so quiet.

M Even the water is flowing quietly.

W It's too bad that we left the camera at home! The scenery is so wonderful.

M Do you feel like swimming? The water looks perfect for swimming.

W You are not allowed to do that. Didn't you see the sign over there?

M What a disappointment!

W 이 장소는 정말 조용해.

M 물도 너무 고요하게 흐르고.

W 카메라를 집에 놓고 온 것이 너무 유감이야! 경치가 너무 아름다워.

M 너는 수영하고 싶니? 물이 수영하기에 딱 좋아 보여.

W 그렇게 해서는 안 돼. 저쪽에 있는 표지판 보지 못했어?

M 정말 실망이야!

만점 솔루션 남자의 Do you feel like swimming?이라는 말에 여자가 그렇게 해서는 안 된다며 표지판을 보라고 한 것에서 '수영 금지!' 표지판임을 알 수 있다.

10 ⑤

W I need a vacation.

M What do you mean? We just had one.

W But I did not enjoy it very much.

M I thought you liked the mountains.

W I do, but I had to cook and clean up.

M I guess you do those things every day.

W Exactly. I never got any time off to tell you the truth.

M Then let's try an all-inclusive holiday resorts package next time.

W That's a great idea!

W 난 휴가가 필요해요.

M 무슨 말이에요? 우리 방금 다녀왔잖아요.

W 하지만 나는 별로 그것을 즐기지 못했어요.

M 당신이 산을 좋아한다고 생각했는데요.

W 그래요, 하지만 내가 요리하고 청소해야 했잖아요.

M 당신은 매일 그런 일들을 하죠.

W 맞아요. 난 사실 쉰 적이 전혀 없어요.

M 그럼 다음 번에는 모든 것이 포함된 휴가 리조트 패키지를 한번 시도해 보죠.

W 아주 좋은 생각이에요!

11 ③

M Who was that, Mom?

W <u>Your principal.</u>

M What? Why did the principal call you?

W I'm going to <u>be a teacher</u> at your school next semester.

M You're kidding!

W No, I'm not kidding. But don't worry, I <u>won't be teaching you</u>. I'm teaching <u>eighth and ninth-grade English</u>.

M Oh, good.

M 누구였어요, 엄마?

W 너의 교장선생님.

M 뭐라고요? 교장선생님이 왜 엄마에게 전화하셨어요?

W 내가 다음 학기에 너의 학교 선생님이 될 예정이거든.

M 설마요!

W 아니, 농담 아니야. 하지만, 걱정 마라, 너를 가르치지는 않을 거야. 8학년과 9학년 영어를 가르칠 거야.

M 오, 잘됐네요.

> **만점 솔루션** 여자의 But don't worry, I won't be teaching you.에서 여자가 아들의 학년을 가르치지 않는다는 것을 알 수 있으므로, ③이 일치하지 않는다.

12 ④ | ➋ ②

W Wow, you sing very well. Do you love singing?

M Yeah. I wanted to be a singer when I was young, but I hope to <u>be a painter</u> in the future.

W A painter? I think the job would be good for you, too.

M Thanks. How about you? What do you want to be in the future?

W My parents want me to be a teacher, but I want to <u>be a nurse</u>.

M You love <u>taking care of the sick people</u>. I'm sure you'll be a good nurse.

W Thank you.

W 와, 너는 정말 노래를 잘 부르는구나. 노래 부르는 것을 정말 좋아하니?

M 응. 어렸을 때는 가수가 되고 싶었지만, 장래에는 화가가 되고 싶어.

W 화가라고? 나도 그 직업이 너한테 좋을 거라고 생각해.

M 고마워. 너는 어때? 너는 장래에 뭐가 되고 싶니?

W 부모님께서는 내가 교사가 되기를 바라시는데, 나는 간호사가 되고 싶어.

M 너는 아픈 사람들을 돌보는 것을 정말 좋아하잖아. 나는 네가 훌륭한 간호사가 될 거라고 확신해.

W 고마워.

13 ⑤

[Telephone rings.]

W Hello. This is Lucy. May I speak to Mike, please?

M Speaking.

W Hi, Mike. What are you doing now?

M I'm watching a movie. What's up?

W Well, there's <u>something wrong with my computer</u>. Will you <u>give me a hand</u>?

M Sure. I'm free at the moment. I'll be over soon.

W Thanks.

[전화벨이 울린다.]

W 여보세요. Lucy인데요. Mike와 통화할 수 있나요?

M 나야.

W 안녕, Mike. 지금 뭐 하고 있니?

M 영화를 보고 있어. 무슨 일이야?

W 그게, 내 컴퓨터에 문제가 있어. 나 좀 도와줄래?

M 물론. 난 지금 한가해. 내가 곧 갈게.

W 고마워.

14 ④

W Are you going shopping with me today?

M Well, I don't feel like going out today.

W Why not?

M I want to <u>paint the fence</u> in the garden.

W But that's <u>a lot of work</u>. Do you need a hand?

M I <u>don't need you to help</u> me paint. But, will you buy some brushes and white paint? I need more.

W Sure.

W 오늘 나와 함께 쇼핑 갈래요?

M 글쎄. 오늘은 외출하고 싶지 않아요.

W 왜요?

M 정원에 있는 담장에 페인트칠을 하고 싶어요.

W 하지만 그건 큰 일이에요. 도움이 필요해요?

M 당신이 페인트칠 하는 것을 도울 필요는 없어요. 하지만, 붓 몇 개와 흰색 페인트를 사다 줄래요? 좀 더 필요하거든요.

W 물론이죠.

15 ④

W What's wrong with you, Jerry? You look sad.

M Monica, I'm afraid I gave wrong answers for the last three questions.

W <u>Forget about it</u>. You can't change your answers now.

M I'm afraid I won't pass the test.

W Come on, Jerry. Don't you think it's <u>too late to worry</u> about it now? You'll <u>do better next time</u>.

W 무슨 일이야, Jerry? 슬퍼 보여.

M Monica, 난 마지막 세 개의 문제에 답을 잘못 한 것 같아.

W 그것을 잊어버려. 이제 답을 바꿀 수 없잖아.

M 시험에 통과하지 못할까 봐 두려워.

W 진정해, Jerry. 이제 그것에 대해 걱정하기에는 너무 늦었다고 생각하지 않니? 너는 다음 번에 더 잘할 거야.

16 ②

M Hi, Linda.

W Hi, Frank.

M Linda, how about going to the Hankuk art gallery this afternoon?

W Sounds great. What time shall we leave?

M Let's see.... Let's meet at the entrance of the library, and leave at three o'clock.

W Okay. That's exactly two hours from now.

M Please don't be late.

W I won't. See you then.

M 안녕, Linda.

W 안녕, Frank.

M Linda, 오늘 오후에 한국 미술관에 가는 게 어때?

W 좋아. 몇 시에 출발할까?

M 어디 보자…. 도서관 입구에서 만나서, 3시에 떠나자.

W 좋아. 지금부터 정확히 2시간 후야.

M 제발 늦지 마.

W 늦지 않을게. 그 때 봐.

만점 솔루션 남자가 3시에 떠나자고 말하자, 여자가 지금부터 2시간 후라고 했으므로 현재 시각은 오후 1시가 된다.

17 ①

M Are you feeling OK? You don't look good.

W I've just heard some bad news.

M What happened?

W My uncle passed away.

M I am truly sorry for your loss. Were you close?

W Yes. We spent lots of time together when I was little. Oh, I feel so bad for my aunt.

M Will you go back home, then?

W For a few days. Too bad I have to go home for this.

M 너 괜찮아? 좋아 보이지가 않는다.

W 방금 안 좋은 소식을 들었어.

M 무슨 일이 있었어?

W 삼촌께서 돌아가셨어.

M 고인의 명복을 빌어. 가까운 분이셨어?

W 응. 내가 어렸을 때 함께 많은 시간을 보냈어. 오, 숙모가 너무 안되셨어.

M 그럼, 고향에 갈 거야?

W 며칠 동안. 이런 일로 고향에 가야 한다는 것이 너무 안좋아.

18 ④

[Telephone rings.]

W Can I talk to John? This is Sally.

M Speaking.

W John, I must go to my parents' but I can't start my car.

M That's too bad. What's the matter with your car?

W I don't know. I think something is wrong with the engine. Could you come over and take a look at it?

M Okay. I'll be there in a minute. Where are you?

W I'm in front of my house. Thanks.

[전화벨이 울린다.]

W John과 통화할 수 있나요? 저는 Sally예요.

M 나야.

W John, 부모님 댁에 가야 하는데 내 차가 시동이 안 걸려.

M 그거 안됐구나. 네 차에 무슨 문제가 있니?

W 모르겠어. 엔진에 무엇인가가 잘못된 것 같아. 여기로 와서 차를 봐 줄 수 있겠니?

M 알았어. 금방 갈게. 어디에 있니?

W 집 앞에 있어. 고마워.

① Sally는 John에게 전화를 걸고 있다.
② Sally는 부모님 댁에 가야 한다.
③ Sally는 그녀의 차에 시동이 안 걸린다.
④ Sally는 John에게 화가 나 있다.
⑤ Sally는 그녀의 집 앞에 있다.

19 ②

M Are you surprised that my sister has finally passed the test?

W No. I was sure that she would succeed.

M You know she had already failed it twice.

W I know. You told me about that. It makes me happy to hear she passed it.

M Me, too.

W She must be very happy.

M _____

M 내 여동생이 마침내 그 시험에 합격한 것이 놀랍지?

W 아니. 나는 그녀가 합격할 것을 확신했어.

M 너도 알다시피, 그녀는 이미 그 시험에 두 번이나 떨어졌잖아.

W 알고 있어. 네가 말했잖아. 그녀가 시험에 통과했다는 것을 들으니 기뻐.

M 나도 그래.

W 그녀는 분명 매우 기뻐할 거야.

M 물론, 그렇지.

① 그러지 않는 게 좋아.
③ 다시는 그것을 하지 않을게.
④ 확실히 몰라.
⑤ 그렇게 해 줘서 고마웠어.

만점 솔루션 여동생이 두 번이나 실패한 시험에 마침내 합격하였으므로, '그녀는 분명 매우 기뻐할 거야.'라는 여자의 마지막 말에 남자는 동의의 말을 하는 것이 가장 자연스럽다.

20 ③

M I need your help to move furniture. I want to polish the floor.

W OK. What should I do?

M Move everything to one side and move it all back later.

W Isn't that a lot of extra work?

M What would you suggest?

W Just move each thing over a little bit, polish that area, and then put it back right away.

M _____

M 가구를 옮기는 데 네 도움이 필요해. 난 바닥을 닦고 싶어.

W 좋아. 내가 뭘 하면 되지?

M 모든 것을 한쪽으로 옮겼다가 나중에 다시 모두 옮겨.

W 그건 일을 더 많게 하는 거 아니야?

M 네 생각은 뭔데?

W 그냥 물건들을 약간씩 옮기고, 그곳을 닦은 후에, 바로 다시 옮기는 거야.

M 좋아, 이번에는 네가 말한 대로 해 보자.

① 좋아, 조금 후에 내가 그것을 치울게.

② 청소기를 내가 직접 돌릴 수 있어.

④ 그게 바로 네가 그것을 옮기는 데 필요한 이유야.

⑤ 하지만 난 이미 모든 것을 치웠어.

영어듣기능력평가 **04** 회

01 ④	02 ②	03 ③	04 ②, ➊②	05 ③
06 ④, ➊④	07 ②	08 ⑤	09 ③	10 ③
11 ②	12 ②	13 ③	14 ③	15 ④
16 ②	17 ③	18 ②	19 ③	20 ⑤

01 ④

W Wow! There are a lot of pictures here.

M We are having a picture exhibition. Look at that picture. That's the picture I painted.

W What picture is it? Is it the picture of a statue in the middle of a garden?

M No, I mean the picture of a Korean national flag flying on a pole on the top of a building.

W 와! 여기 그림이 많네.

M 우리는 그림 전시회를 가질 예정이야. 저 그림을 봐. 저것은 내가 그린 그림이야.

W 그게 어떤 그림인데? 정원 가운데 동상을 그린 그림이니?

M 아니. 내가 말하는 것은 건물 꼭대기 깃대에서 휘날리는 태극기를 그린 그림이야.

02 ②

W I need a light bulb. Where's the hardware store?

M There's one on the main street, just past the pharmacy.

W Which pharmacy? The one across the street from the grocery store?

M No, the pharmacy near the department store.

W Is it close to the library, then?

M Yeah, it's around that area.

W OK, then I think I know where it is. Thanks.

W 난 전구가 필요해. 철물점이 어디 있지?

M 시내 중심가에 약국 지나자마자 하나 있어.

W 어떤 약국? 식료품 가게 길 건너편에 있는 거?

M 아니, 백화점 근처에 있는 약국.

W 그럼, 도서관 가까이에 있네?

M 응. 그 지역 주변에 있어.

W 알았어, 그럼 어디 있는지 알 것 같아. 고마워.

만점 솔루션 철물점은 백화점 근처에 있는 약국 지나자마자 있다고 했다.

03 ③

W I can't believe I did that!

M What happened?

W I just said something I shouldn't have.

M What did you say?

W I congratulated Betty on <u>winning an academic award</u>.

M So? What's wrong with that?

W She didn't win, <u>her sister did</u>. Now I feel bad.

M It was an honest mistake. I'm sure Betty isn't angry.

W 내가 그걸 했다니 믿을 수가 없어!

M 무슨 일이야?

W 하지 말았어야 할 말을 내가 방금 했어.

M 뭐라고 말했는데?

W Betty에게 성적 우수상을 탄 것을 축하한다고 했어.

M 그런데? 그게 뭐가 잘못됐어?

W 그녀가 탄 게 아니라, 그녀의 여동생이 탔어. 난 지금 기분이 안좋아.

M 그건 순전히 실수였잖아. 틀림없이 Betty는 화나지 않았을 거야.

<u>만점 솔루션</u> 여자는 성적 우수상을 탄 사람을 Betty로 착각해 축하 인사를 한 뒤 실수한 것을 알고 당황해하고 있는 상황이다.

04 ② | ➕ ②

W I love spring! All plants begin to bloom into beautiful flowers!

M What's your favorite flower?

W I love roses. I like their <u>strong red color</u>. It's my favorite color. Do you like spring?

M Yes, but I like <u>fall better than spring</u>. I like the yellow and red leaves of trees.

W What's your favorite color?

M I like yellow, but I <u>like red more than yellow</u>, just like you.

W 나는 봄이 정말 좋아! 모든 식물들이 아름다운 꽃으로 피어나기 시작하잖아!

M 네가 가장 좋아하는 꽃은 뭐니?

W 나는 장미를 정말 좋아해. 나는 그것의 진한 빨간색을 좋아해. 그것은 내가 가장 좋아하는 색깔이야. 너는 봄을 좋아하니?

M 응, 하지만 봄보다 가을을 더 좋아해. 나는 노랗고 빨간 나뭇잎을 좋아하거든.

W 네가 가장 좋아하는 색깔은 뭐니?

M 나는 노란색을 좋아해. 하지만 너처럼 노란색보다는 빨간색을 더 좋아해.

05 ③

W Accidents always happen in our lives. Electricity makes our lives very comfortable, but it is <u>always dangerous</u>. If you push something into a socket, you will be shocked and go to the hospital. When you use sharp knives and scissors, you should be careful. If children play with them, they might be cut by them. You should always <u>be careful</u> when you do something. <u>Accidents happen</u> when you are not careful.

W 사고는 항상 우리 생활 속에서 일어납니다. 전기는 우리의 생활을 매우 편안하게 해 줍니다. 하지만 그것은 항상 위험합니다. 만약 당신이 뭔가를 소켓에 밀어넣으면, 당신은 쇼크를 받아 병원에 갈 것입니다. 당신은 날카로운 칼이나 가위를 사용할 때, 주의해야 합니다. 만일 어린이들이

그것들을 가지고 놀면, 그들은 그것에 베일 수도 있습니다. 당신은 항상 무언가를 할 때 조심해야 합니다. 주의하지 않을 때 사고가 일어납니다.

<u>만점 솔루션</u> 전기나 칼, 가위 사용을 예로 들면서 안전의 중요성에 대해 설명하고 있는 담화이다.

06 ④ | ➕ ④

M Are you <u>taking any medicine</u>?

W No, I am not.

M Then, do you take vitamins?

W Oh, yes. I <u>take multivitamins</u> every morning.

M Oh, I see. It will take thirty minutes to <u>fill your prescription</u>.

W Okay. I'll go have a cup of coffee. Is there a coffee shop near here?

M Yes, there's a nice coffee shop across from the bank.

W Thank you. I'll be back in thirty minutes.

M 당신은 약을 복용하고 있습니까?

W 아니요, 그렇지 않습니다.

M 그러면, 비타민은 드시고 계세요?

W 예. 매일 아침 종합비타민을 복용하고 있어요.

M 오, 알겠어요. 처방전 대로 조제하는 데 30분 정도 걸립니다.

W 알겠습니다. 커피 한 잔 하러 가야겠어요. 이 근처에 커피숍이 있나요?

M 예, 은행 건너편에 좋은 커피숍이 있습니다.

W 고맙습니다. 30분 후에 다시 오겠습니다.

07 ②

W What's the matter?

M I just <u>can't sleep</u>.

W How long have you had this problem?

M For about two weeks now.

W Do you drink coffee?

M No, I don't drink any coffee.

W Do you <u>have a headache</u>?

M Yes, sometimes.

W Can you lift up your shirt? Let me <u>check your heartbeat</u>.

W 무슨 문제죠?

M 잠을 잘 수가 없어요.

W 이 문제를 가진 지 얼마나 됐어요?

M 지금 약 2주 되었습니다.

W 커피를 마시나요?

M 아니요, 전혀 커피를 마시지 않습니다.

W 두통이 있으세요?

M 예, 가끔씩요.

W 셔츠를 들어 주시겠어요? 심장 박동을 확인하겠습니다.

08 ⑤

[Telephone rings.]

M Hello.

W Hello, may I speak to Bob? This is Cathy speaking.

M Hello, Cathy. This is Bob. What's up?

W Tomorrow is Teacher's Day. Let's visit Ms. Song.

M Oh, I was planning to do so. Let's meet in front of the school.

W No, she isn't at school. She is in hospital with a broken arm.

M Really? How awful! Is she OK?

W Yes, she'll get out of hospital next week. Let's meet at the hospital.

M OK, see you there.

[전화벨이 울린다.]

M 여보세요.

W 여보세요, Bob과 통화할 수 있나요? 저 Cathy인데요.

M 안녕, Cathy. 나 Bob이야. 무슨 일이니?

W 내일이 '스승의 날'이잖아. 송 선생님을 방문하자.

M 오, 나도 그렇게 할 계획이었는데. 학교 앞에서 만나자.

W 아니, 선생님은 학교에 안 계셔. 팔이 부러져서 병원에 계셔.

M 정말? 저런! 선생님은 괜찮으신 거야?

W 응, 다음 주에 퇴원하실 거야. 병원에서 만나자.

M 좋아, 거기서 보자.

09 ③

W We have to buy lunch for the field trip.

M OK. What should we get?

W The teacher said sandwiches for students and one or two cakes.

M How many sandwiches do we need?

W We need 25. They cost $5 each.

M And how much is the cake?

W We can get one big cake for $30, and one small cake for $20.

M Let's get two small cakes.

W OK.

W 우리는 현장 학습에 가져갈 점심 식사를 사야 해.

M 좋아. 무엇을 사야 하지?

W 선생님께서 학생들을 위한 샌드위치와 케이크 한두 개를 말씀하셨어.

M 샌드위치는 몇 개가 필요하지?

W 25개가 필요해. 개당 5달러야.

M 그리고 케이크는 얼마지?

W 큰 케이크 하나는 30달러, 작은 케이크 하나는 20달러에 살 수 있어.

M 2개의 작은 케이크를 사자.

W 좋아.

만점 솔루션 5달러짜리 샌드위치 25개(5×25=125달러)와 20달러짜리 작은 케이크 2개(20×2=40달러)를 사기로 했으므로, 총 165달러를 지불해야 한다.

10 ③

M May I have your attention, please? Tomorrow there will be a math competition in Room 501. The competition will start at four o'clock after class. The things you have to bring with you for the exam are black and red felt pens and correction tapes. The students who have already applied for it should show up on time. We hope you do well on the exam.

M 방송에 귀 기울여 주시기 바랍니다. 내일 501호실에서 수학 경시대회가 있을 예정입니다. 경시대회는 수업이 끝난 후 4시 정각에 시작할 예정입니다. 여러분들이 시험을 위해 가져올 것은 검정색과 붉은색 사인펜과 수정 테이프입니다. 이미 그것을 신청한 학생들은 정시에 오시기 바랍니다. 여러분 모두 시험을 잘 보시길 바랍니다.

만점 솔루션 내일 수학 경시대회가 방과 후 4시에 실시되며 준비할 물건이 무엇인지 알려 주는 안내 방송이다.

11 ②

M Ms. Kim, do you know anything about the new English teacher?

W Yes, I do. My Canadian friend, Paul Hong, sent me an email on November 16. The mail arrived late at night, so I could open it the next morning.

M What did he say about him?

W He wrote about his age, nationality, and his major.

M Where is the new English teacher from?

W He's from Canada. It's been one year since he graduated from university. He is looking for a job as an English teacher in Korea. He is in his early twenties.

M 김 선생님, 새로운 영어 선생님에 관해 아는 것이 있어요?

W 예. 저의 캐나다 친구 Paul Hong이 저에게 11월 16일에 이메일을 보냈습니다. 그 메일이 밤 늦게 도착해서 그 다음날 아침에 메일을 열어 볼 수 있었습니다.

M 그가 그에 관해 뭐라고 말하던가요?

W 그는 그의 나이, 국적, 그리고 전공에 대해 썼습니다.

M 새로운 영어 선생님은 어디 출신인가요?

W 그는 캐나다 출신입니다. 그는 대학을 졸업한 지 1년이 되었습니다. 그는 한국에서 영어 선생님으로 일할 일자리를 찾고 있습니다. 그는 20대 초반입니다.

만점 솔루션 Paul Hong이 보내온 메일은 밤 늦게 도착했다고 했으므로, ②가 일치하지 않는다.

12 ②

M That's one of the best selling products this year.

W OK, I will take it. Can you deliver it to my home? How much do you charge for shipping?

M If you live in Seoul, the delivery is free.

W Good! How soon can it be delivered?

M It will be delivered by 2 p.m. tomorrow.

W Can you make it earlier? Is it possible in the morning?

M OK, I will have it delivered by 11 a.m. tomorrow.

M 그것은 올해 가장 많이 팔리는 상품들 중 하나입니다.

W 좋아요, 그것으로 하죠. 집으로 배달해 주실 수 있어요? 배달하는 데 드는 비용은 얼마죠?

M 서울에 사신다면, 배달은 무료입니다.

W 좋네요! 얼마나 빨리 배달될 수 있죠?

M 내일 오후 2시까지 배달될 겁니다.

W 좀 더 일찍 될까요? 아침에 가능할까요?

M 좋습니다. 내일 오전 11시까지 그것이 배달되도록 하죠.

만점 솔루션 내일 오후 2시까지 배달해 주겠다는 것을 여자가 좀 더 일찍 배달해 달라고 부탁하자 남자는 오전 11시까지 배달해 주겠다고 했다.

13 ③

M What can I get for you, ma'am?

W What would you recommend?

M Our special is hamburger steak with green salad.

W Do you have anything lighter?

M The chicken or Caesar salad is popular. Or the seafood pasta.

W Is the pasta in cream or tomato sauce?

M You can choose.

W Then I'll order the special for my husband, and I'll have the seafood pasta in tomato sauce.

M OK. It'll be ready soon.

M 무엇을 준비해 드릴까요, 손님?

W 추천해 주실 만한 것이 있나요?

M 저희 특별 메뉴는 그린 샐러드를 곁들인 햄버거 스테이크입니다.

W 더 가벼운 것이 있나요?

M 치킨 혹은 시저 샐러드가 인기가 있습니다. 아니면 해산물 파스타도 있습니다.

W 파스타는 크림 소스인가요, 토마토 소스인가요?

M 손님께서 선택하실 수 있습니다.

W 그럼 제 남편은 특별 메뉴로 주문해 주시고요, 전 토마토 소스의 해산물 파스타로 할게요.

M 알겠습니다. 곧 준비될 것입니다.

만점 솔루션 여자는 햄버거 스테이크나 그린 샐러드가 나오는 특별 메뉴와 토마토 소스의 해산물 파스타를 주문했다.

14 ③

W Excuse me. Is the swimming pool still open?

M Yes, but it closes at 9. You have only 30 minutes left.

W Oh, no! Where can I work out then?

M There's a fitness center on the fifth floor.

W Great. And is there a gift shop in the hotel?

M Yes. Take the elevator to the first floor.

W One more thing, please. Is there a cash machine?

M Yes. It's next to the gift shop.

W Thank you.

M You're welcome.

W 실례합니다. 수영장이 아직 열려 있죠?

M 예, 하지만 9시에 문을 닫습니다. 겨우 30분 남았네요.

W 오, 안 되는데! 그러면 어디에서 운동을 할 수 있을까요?

M 5층에 헬스클럽이 있어요.

W 좋습니다. 그리고 호텔에 선물 가게가 있나요?

M 예. 엘리베이터를 타고 1층으로 가세요.

W 한 가지 더 여쭤 볼게요. 현금 인출기가 있나요?

M 있습니다. 선물 가게 옆에 있어요.

W 고맙습니다.

M 천만에요.

15 ④

W Can I ask you a personal question?

M Sure, go ahead.

W What's your favorite day of the year?

M It's May 1st.

W Why do you like that day the most?

M Well, I got married that day.

W Do you do anything special then?

M I always make reservations at a nice restaurant for a nice dinner with my wife.

W That sounds nice.

W 개인적인 질문을 해도 될까요?

M 물론이죠, 어서 하세요.

W 한 해 중에서 당신이 가장 좋아하는 날은 언제죠?

M 5월 1일입니다.

W 왜 그 날을 가장 좋아하세요?

M 음, 그 날 제가 결혼했거든요.

W 그러면 그 날 특별한 일을 하세요?

M 저는 아내와 멋진 저녁 식사를 위해 항상 좋은 식당을 예약합니다.

W 근사하게 들리네요.

16 ②

W What's this?

M It's a poster I had when I was a kid.

W Why do you still have it?

M I got it from the first concert I went to. It reminds me of my childhood.

W Oh, I see. You should get it framed.

M Good thinking. Then I can hang it in this room.

W No way!

M But I want to put it up somewhere.

W In your office. It will look much nicer there.

W 이게 뭐지?

M 내가 어렸을 때 갖고 있던 포스터야.

W 그것을 왜 아직도 가지고 있는 거야?

M 내가 처음으로 갔던 음악회에서 얻은 것이야. 그것은 나에게 내 유년기를 떠올리게 해 주거든.

W 오, 알겠다. 그것을 액자로 만들어야겠네.

M 좋은 생각이야. 그럼 그것을 이 방에 걸 수도 있겠다.

W 안 돼!

M 하지만 난 그것을 어딘가에 걸고 싶어.

W 네 사무실이 좋겠군. 그곳에 훨씬 더 잘 어울릴 거야.

만점 솔루션 남자는 포스터가 유년기를 떠올리게 해 주기 때문에 지금까지 그것을 가지고 있다고 했다.

17 ③

① W Can you tell me how to get to the Royal Palace?

   M Go straight over there, and turn right.

② W How did you like the trip?

   M It was really great. I saw lots of interesting things.

③ W Where would you like to go next?

   M I'd like to go have something to eat. I'm hungry.

④ W Can we go inside the palace?

   M Yes, but we have to buy a ticket first.

⑤ W Could you take a picture of me in front of this door, please?

   M Sure, do I just press this button?

① W 왕궁까지 어떻게 가는지 알려주실 수 있나요?

   M 저기까지 쭉 가신 다음에 오른쪽으로 도세요.

② W 여행은 어땠니?

   M 진짜 좋았어. 많은 흥미로운 것들을 봤어.

③ W 다음은 어디를 가고 싶어?

   M 무언가 먹고 싶어. 나 배고파.

④ W 궁전 안으로 들어갈 수 있나요?

   M 네, 하지만 우선 표를 사야해요.

⑤ W 이 문 앞에서 사진 좀 찍어줄 수 있을까요?

   M 물론이죠, 이 버튼을 누르면 되나요?

18 ②

M Mom, what are you doing today?

W I have a meeting in the morning, and I'm free after that. Why?

M I forgot to return these books to the library, and they are due today.

W I reminded you about them last week.

M Yes, I know. I'm sorry. Could you do me this favor, please?

W What about after school? The library closes at 6.

M I have soccer practice this afternoon. I can't miss it!

W Okay, but this is the last time.

M 엄마, 오늘 뭐하실 거예요?

W 아침에 회의가 있고 그 다음에는 별 일 없어. 왜?

M 이 책들을 도서관에 반납하는 걸 깜빡했는데 오늘이 반납일이거든요.

W 저번주에 내가 말했잖니.

M 네, 알아요. 죄송해요. 대신 반납해주실 수 없나요?

W 방과 후에 어떠니? 도서관은 6시에 닫잖아.

M 오늘 오후에 축구 연습이 있어요. 빠질 수 없어요!

W 알겠다. 하지만 이번이 마지막이야.

19 ③

M Let's go out for dinner.

W I don't want to go out for dinner.

M Aren't you hungry?

W I just want to stay home and have some fruit and salad for dinner.

M Is that all?

W I want to lose some weight.

M You don't look like you need to lose weight.

W _____

M 저녁을 먹으러 나가자.

W 저녁 먹으러 나가고 싶지 않아.

M 배고프지 않니?

W 나는 그냥 집에 있으면서 저녁으로 과일과 샐러드를 좀 먹고 싶어.

M 그게 전부야?

W 난 살을 좀 빼고 싶어.

M 너는 살을 빼야 할 것처럼은 안 보이는데.

W 그렇게 생각한다니 고마워.

① 두려워하지 마.

② 나는 그를 만나기로 되어 있어.

④ 너는 운동을 좀 하는 게 좋겠어.

⑤ 저녁 식사를 가져오는 것을 잊지 마.

20 ⑤

W You look sick today.

M This cold is killing me.

W I'm sorry to hear that.

M Atchoo!

W Don't sneeze in my direction. I don't want to catch a cold.

M OK, OK. I'll keep my distance.

W Did you go to see a doctor?

M Yes, but the medicine doesn't work well. Oh, I feel dizzy. I'm afraid I can't work anymore today.

W _____

W 너 오늘 아파 보인다.

M 감기 때문에 죽겠어.

W 그 말을 들으니 안됐다.

M 에취!

W 내 쪽으로 숨을 쉬지 마. 나는 감기에 걸리고 싶지 않단 말이야.

M 알았어, 알았어. 거리를 유지할게.

W 너는 진찰을 받아 보았니?

M 응, 하지만 약이 별로 효과가 없어. 오, 어지럽네. 나는 오늘 더 이상 일 할 수 없을 것 같아.

W 나을 때까지 너는 집에 있는 게 좋겠다.

① 미안하지만, 지금 가 봐야 해.
② 네가 해야 할 일이 있어.
③ 너의 부모님께 안부 좀 전해 줘.
④ 네가 또 늦으면 너에게 문제가 생길 거야.

만점 솔루션 몸이 아파 더 이상 일할 수 없다는 남자에게 나올 때까지 집에서 쉬라는 조언의 말을 해 주는 것이 가장 자연스럽다.

01 ⑤	**02** ③	**03** ④	**04** ⑤	**05** ②
06 ③	**07** ④	**08** ①	**09** ④	**10** ④
11 ①, ➊ ③	**12** ①	**13** ⑤, ➊ ④	**14** ⑤	**15** ②
16 ②	**17** ②	**18** ③	**19** ④	**20** ②

01 ⑤

M Is it going to be rainy again tomorrow?

W No. I heard it's going to be fine tomorrow.

M Then I can take my son to Central Park and play there tomorrow.

W Sounds great. By the way, it rains a lot these days.

M Because it's the rainy season.

W I hate the rainy season.

M Look on the bright side. At least, it's cloudy today and it'll be sunny tomorrow.

W You're right.

M 내일 또 비가 올 건가?

W 아니. 내일은 날씨가 맑을 거라고 들었어.

M 그럼 내일 중앙 공원으로 아들을 데리고 가서 놀 수 있겠네.

W 아주 멋진데. 그나저나, 요즘 비가 많이 와.

M 장마철이니까 그렇지.

W 나는 장마철이 싫어.

M 긍정적으로 생각해. 적어도, 오늘은 흐리고 내일은 맑을 거야.

W 네 말이 맞아.

02 ③

[Telephone rings.]

W Hello. Can I talk to Steve, please?

M May I ask who's calling?

W This is Mary. I've tried calling his Cellphone, but there was no answer.

M He's taking a shower now.

W I promised to take a walk in the park with him in an hour, but I can't keep my promise.

M Okay. I'll tell Steve to call you back anyway.

W Thank you. Bye.

[전화벨이 울린다.]

W 여보세요. Steve 좀 바꿔 주시겠어요?

M 누구시죠?

W Mary인데요. 그의 휴대 전화로 전화를 걸었는데 받지 않아서요.

M 그는 지금 샤워하고 있어요.

W 그와 함께 한 시간 후에 공원에서 산책을 하기로 약속했는데, 제가 약속을 지킬 수 없어서요.

M 알겠어요. 아무튼 Steve에게 당신에게 다시 전화하라고 할게요.
W 감사합니다. 안녕히 계세요.

만점 솔루션 He's taking a shower now.라는 남자의 말에서 Steve가 샤워 중임을 알 수 있다.

03 ④

W I'll send some money to my grandson. Could you tell me how to use this cash machine?
M Sure. Press the "SEND" button first. And now put your card into this slot.
W Like this?
M Yes. Now select the amount that you want to send him.
W I see. I'll send 50,000 won.
M Okay. And now enter your grandson's account number.
W Oh, wait a minute.... Is that all?
M No. Now, finally, enter your password.

W 손자에게 돈을 좀 보내려고 해요. 이 현금 인출기 사용법을 말씀해 주시겠어요?
M 물론이죠. 먼저 '송금' 버튼을 누르세요. 그리고 이제 이 구멍에 카드를 집어넣으세요.
W 이렇게요?
M 예. 이제 손자분에게 송금하려는 액수를 선택하세요.
W 알겠어요. 5만원을 보낼 거예요.
M 좋아요. 그리고 이제 손자분의 계좌번호를 누르세요.
W 오, 잠깐만요…. 그게 전부인가요?
M 아니요. 이제, 마지막으로, 비밀번호를 입력하세요.

① '송금' 버튼을 누르세요.
② 구멍에 카드를 집어넣으세요.
③ 송금할 액수를 선택하세요.
④ 분실한 신용카드를 신고하세요.
⑤ 비밀번호를 입력하세요.

만점 솔루션 ④ '분실한 신용카드를 신고하세요.'는 송금과 관련된 대화 내용에 언급되어 있지 않다.

04 ⑤

M Didn't you have fun playing basketball yesterday?
W To be honest, I don't like to play sports very much.
M Oh, really?
W Yes! And yesterday it was too hot, too.
M What do you like to do when you have free time then?
W I like to play computer games or go to a movie.
M I like to play computer games, too. How about playing some games together this afternoon?
W That's a good idea.

M 어제 농구하는 것 재미있지 않았니?
W 솔직히 말해서, 나는 운동하는 것을 아주 좋아하지는 않아.
M 오, 그래?
W 응! 그리고 어제는 무척 덥기까지 했잖아.

M 그럼 너는 시간이 나면 뭘 하는 걸 좋아하니?
W 나는 컴퓨터 게임을 하거나 영화를 보러 가는 게 좋아.
M 나도 컴퓨터 게임을 하는 것을 좋아해. 오늘 오후에 나와 함께 게임을 좀 하는 게 어때?
W 좋은 생각이야.

05 ②

① W Would you like something to drink?
  M No, thanks. I'm okay.
② W Hello, how can I help you?
  M I'd like to buy those flowers for my girlfriend's birthday.
③ W Congratulations. These are for you.
  M Oh, thank you so much. These are really nice flowers.
④ W What's your favorite flower?
  M I like little wild flowers in the open field.
⑤ W Excuse me, is there a flower shop near here?
  M Sorry, I don't know, either. I'm a stranger here.

① W 뭐 마실래?
  M 아니, 괜찮아.
② W 안녕하세요. 무엇을 도와드릴까요?
  M 여자친구 생일이라 꽃을 사고 싶어요.
③ W 축하해요. 당신을 위한 거예요.
  M 아, 고맙습니다. 정말 예쁜 꽃이네요.
④ W 가장 좋아하는 꽃이 뭔가요?
  M 넓은 벌판에 작은 야생화를 좋아해요.
⑤ W 실례합니다. 여기 근처에 꽃집이 있나요?
  M 죄송하지만 몰라요. 저도 여기가 처음이라서요.

06 ③

M Can I take a bus to the airport from here?
W Yes. You can take a bus from here, but the bus isn't very fast.
M Really? Then could you tell me how to get to the airport as fast as possible?
W Sure. Take the subway at the station there.
M Does it go directly to the airport?
W No. You have to change to the Green Line at City Hall.
M Okay. I'll take the subway. Thanks a lot.

M 여기서 공항 가는 버스를 탈 수 있나요?
W 예. 여기서 버스를 탈 수 있지만, 버스가 아주 빠르지는 않아요.
M 그래요? 그럼 가능한 한 빨리 공항에 가는 법을 말씀해 주시겠어요?
W 물론이죠. 저기 지하철역에서 지하철을 타세요.
M 지하철이 공항까지 바로 가나요?
W 아니요. 시청에서 녹색 노선으로 갈아타야 해요.
M 알겠어요. 지하철을 타겠어요. 정말 고마워요.

07 ④

W You wonder whether you are healthy or not. But you're

not a doctor. Now you can <u>ask a doctor any question</u> that you want. It's so easy to see the doctor anytime you want. Email your questions to Dr. e-Health <u>through the Internet</u>. Just turn on your computer and ask Dr. e-Health. The service is free. The address of our website is www. e-health.com. If you have any questions about your health, please <u>visit our website</u>.

W 당신은 건강한지 안 한지 궁금해 합니다. 하지만 당신은 의사가 아닙니다. 이제 당신은 의사에게 당신이 원하는 어떤 질문이든지 하실 수 있습니다. 당신이 원할 때는 언제든지 의사를 만나는 것이 아주 쉽습니다. 인터넷을 통해서 당신의 질문을 e-Health 박사님에게 이메일을 보내 주십시오. 단지 컴퓨터를 켜시고, e-Health 박사님에게 물어보십시오. 서비스는 무료입니다. 저희 웹사이트의 주소는 www.e-health.com입니다. 당신의 건강에 대해 어떤 질문이라도 있으시면, 저희 웹사이트를 방문해 주십시오.

08 ①

W Have you ever been to Europe?
M Once. I toured France, Germany, Switzerland, and Italy.
W What did you think?
M They're all nice. I enjoyed the food above all.
W Like what?
M In France, crepes are famous street food. And there are many sausages in Germany.
W How about the scenery? I'll bet the Alps in Switzerland were beautiful.
M Yes, but Italy also <u>had amazing scenery, food, and art</u>.
W Did you like it better than Switzerland?
M Yes, <u>Italy was my favorite</u> of the four countries.

W 유럽에 가 본 적 있어?
M 한 번. 난 프랑스, 독일, 스위스, 그리고 이탈리아를 여행했어.
W 어땠어?
M 모두 좋았어. 나는 무엇보다 음식을 즐겼지.
W 예를 들면?
M 프랑스에서는, 크레페가 유명한 거리 음식이야. 그리고 독일에는 많은 종류의 소시지가 있어.
W 경치는 어땠어? 스위스의 알프스는 틀림없이 아름다웠을 거야.
M 맞아, 하지만 이탈리아에도 놀라운 경치, 음식, 그리고 예술이 있었어.
W 그곳이 스위스보다 더 좋았어?
M 응, 이탈리아가 네 나라 중에 가장 좋았어.

09 ④

W Minho, do you know about the English camp?
M No, tell me about it.
W It's a program for the summer vacation. There is this theme park, where you have to speak only English. If you <u>sign up for</u> the program, you can stay there for a week.
M It sounds like a good chance to practice English!
W That's right. Would you like to go?

M I'm interested. But do you have more information? I'll have to <u>ask my parents</u> first.
W Sure, I'll bring you the brochure tomorrow.

W 민호, 영어캠프에 대해 알아?
M 아니, 말해줘.
W 여름방학 프로그램이야. 영어로만 말해야 하는 테마 파크가 있어. 프로그램에 등록하면 일주일 동안 거기에 머물 수 있어.
M 영어를 익힐 수 있는 좋은 기회인 거 같네!
W 맞아. 가고 싶어?
M 관심있어. 하지만 더 많은 정보 있어? 부모님께 우선 물어봐야 해.
W 물론, 내일 책자 가져다 줄게.

10 ④

M You <u>look cheerful</u>. Having a good day?
W I am now.
M You weren't before?
W No. Yesterday my best friend said she's moving.
M That's too bad.
W <u>I was really down</u>. Then she called today.
M Did she say when she will leave?
W No. That's the good news. Her parents decided to stay here!
M Then things <u>turned out well</u> after all.

M 너 기분이 좋아 보인다. 일진이 좋은가 보구나?
W 지금은 그래.
M 전에는 그렇지 않았다는 거야?
W 맞아. 어제 내 가장 친한 친구가 이사 간다고 말했거든
M 저런.
W 정말 마음이 울적했어. 그런데 오늘 그녀가 전화한 거야.
M 그녀가 언제 떠나는지 말했니?
W 아니. 좋은 소식이었어. 그녀의 부모님이 여기 머무르시기로 결정하셨대!
M 그럼 결국 일이 잘 풀렸구나.

만점 솔루션 여자는 어제 가장 친구가 이사 간다는 말을 들어 슬펐지만 오늘 이사 가지 않기로 했다는 말을 들어 행복한 상태이다.

11 ① | ➕ ③

M Have you decided which club you are going to join?
W No, not yet, but I'm thinking about <u>the photo club</u> or the drama club.
M I've already joined the sports club.
W What do you do in the club?
M We get together twice a week after school and play various sports. Why don't you join our club?
W I'd like to join the club, but I hope to <u>be a photographer</u> in the future.
M Then you should <u>join the photo club</u>.
W Yeah, you're right.

M 어느 동아리에 가입할지 결정했니?

W 아니, 아직 못했는데, 사진반이나 연극반에 대해 생각 중이야.
M 나는 이미 운동반에 가입했어.
W 그 동아리에서는 뭘 하는데?
M 우리는 일주일에 두 번 방과 후에 모여서 다양한 운동을 해. 우리 동아리에 가입하는 건 어때?
W 그 동아리에 가입하고 싶지만, 나는 장래에 사진작가가 되고 싶어.
M 그럼 너는 사진반에 가입해야 하네.
W 그래, 네 말이 맞아.

만점 솔루션 여자는 사진작가가 되고 싶다며 사진반에 가입하기로 했다.

12 ①

[Telephone rings.]
M Hi, Jane. This is Ted.
W Hi, Ted. How's it going?
M Fine. Did you hear that our classmate John has been in the hospital since Thursday?
W Oh, really?
M I'm going to see him this afternoon. Can you go with me?
W Sure. Let's meet in front of the library at 3:30.
M All right. See you then.

[전화벨이 울린다.]
M 안녕, Jane. 나 Ted야.
W 안녕, Ted. 어떻게 지내니?
M 잘 지내. 우리 반 친구인 John이 목요일부터 입원해 있다는 얘기를 들었니?
W 오, 정말이니?
M 나는 오늘 오후에 그를 보러 갈 거야. 너도 나와 함께 갈래?
W 물론이지. 3시 30분에 도서관 앞에서 만나자.
M 알았어. 그 때 봐.

13 ⑤ | ➕ ④

M Why don't we go to the amusement park?
W You know I hate crowds. I'm sure the park will be very crowded today.
M Then, what do you want to do?
W The weather is nice, but....
M You want to stay inside, don't you?
W That's right. I'd like to stay inside today. Let's just go to the library and read books.
M Good idea.
W Let's go there now.

M 놀이 공원에 가는 게 어때?
W 너도 알다시피 나는 붐비는 건 질색이야. 오늘은 놀이 공원이 분명히 매우 붐빌 거야.
M 그럼, 너는 뭘 하고 싶니?
W 날씨는 좋지만, ….
M 너는 실내에 있고 싶구나, 그렇지 않니?
W 맞아. 오늘은 실내에 있고 싶어. 그냥 도서관에 가서 책을 읽자.
M 좋은 생각이야.

W 지금 거기로 가자.

14 ⑤

W Are you going to finish your homework tonight?
M I'm afraid I can't. I have too much to do.
W Are you going out on a date with your girlfriend?
M Unfortunately, I can't. I have to work at my part-time job again.
W That's the third night! No wonder you can't finish your homework.
M I know. Maybe I should quit soon.
W You'd better, before you fall behind in school.

W 오늘 밤에 네 숙제를 끝낼 거야?
M 그럴 수 없을 것 같아. 할 일이 너무 많아.
W 네 여자 친구와 데이트하러 가니?
M 불행히도, 그럴 수 없어. 난 아르바이트 일을 또 해야 해.
W 벌써 3일 밤이야! 네가 숙제를 못 끝내는 게 이해가 간다.
M 나도 알아. 곧 그만두어야 할 것 같아.
W 그러는 게 좋겠다. 학교에서 뒤쳐지기 전에 말이야.

만점 솔루션 남자는 오늘 밤에 아르바이트를 할 예정이라고 했다.

15 ②

M Wow, this sweater is really nice.
W It is. And no one else in the market has this sweater.
M How much is it?
W 50 dollars. You can try it on.
M Thank you. Yes, it fits well. But it's a little expensive.
W I can give you a discount, 45 dollars.
M It's still too expensive. How about 40 dollars?
W Yes, but 40 dollars is the lowest price I can give you.
M Okay. I'll take it.

M 와, 이 스웨터 정말 멋지네요.
W 그렇죠. 시장 어느 곳에서도 이 스웨터를 팔지 않아요.
M 얼마예요?
W 50달러요. 입어 보실 수 있어요.
M 고마워요. 그래요, 잘 맞네요. 하지만 약간 비싸요.
W 할인해서 45달러에 드릴게요.
M 그래도 너무 비싸요. 40달러는 어때요?
W 그래요, 하지만 40달러가 제가 드릴 수 있는 최저 가격이에요.
M 알았어요. 그걸로 할게요.

16 ②

W Good afternoon. How can I help you?
M I want to buy some bread for my children.
W What kind of bread do you want?
M I can't remember the name. It's long and looks like a baseball bat.
W What? A baseball bat?

M Yes. I bought it here last week. It was very delicious, and its inner part was soft.

W Oh, I see. This way, please.

W 안녕하세요. 뭘 도와드릴까요?

M 제 아이들을 위해 빵을 좀 사고 싶은데요.

W 어떤 종류의 빵을 원하세요?

M 이름은 기억이 안 나는데요. 길면서, 야구 방망이처럼 생겼어요.

W 뭐라고요? 야구 방망이라고요?

M 예. 지난주에 여기서 그것을 샀거든요. 빵은 아주 맛있었고, 그것의 안쪽 부분은 부드러웠어요.

W 오, 알겠어요. 이쪽으로 오세요.

17 ②

W Hey, come on. There is nothing to be afraid of.

M Mom, I don't want to go up there.

W Look up at the kids on the board. They enjoy diving very much. And you're almost a man.

M No. I'm just twelve years old. I'd just like to swim in the water.

W Okay, okay. Have fun. I'll watch you carefully.

M Now, I'll practice the butterfly stroke.

W 자, 이리와. 두려워할 것 없어.

M 엄마, 저 위에 올라가고 싶지 않아요.

W 다이빙대에 있는 아이들을 봐. 다이빙하는 것을 매우 즐기고 있잖아. 그리고 이제 너는 남자이고.

M 아니요. 저는 이제 12살이에요. 그냥 물 속에서 수영만 하고 싶어요.

W 좋아. 좋아, 재미있게 놀아라. 내가 잘 지켜볼게.

M 이제, 접영을 연습할게요.

만점 솔루션 diving, swim in the water, practice the butterfly stroke를 통해 '수영장'에서의 대화임을 알 수 있다.

18 ③

M Eunji, you're wearing a nice hat. Is it new?

W Yes, I bought it when I went shopping with my sister last Sunday.

M That's nice. Where did you buy it?

W I got it at Avalon Shopping Mall.

M Really? I was there last Sunday, too. Chris and I went bowling downtown, and then we went to the mall to watch a movie.

W Oh, we ate in the food court next to the theater. We could have passed each other somewhere.

M 은지, 멋진 모자를 쓰고 있네. 새 거야?

W 응, 지난 일요일에 여동생이랑 같이 쇼핑 가서 샀어.

M 멋지다. 어디서 샀어?

W 아발론 쇼핑몰에서 샀어.

M 진짜? 나도 지난 일요일 거기 있었는데. 크리스랑 시내에 볼링 치러 갔다가 영화를 보러 그 몰에 갔어.

W 아, 우리 극장 옆에 있는 푸드코트에서 밥 먹었는데. 어딘가에서 서로 지나쳤을 수도 있겠다.

19 ④

W I have to talk to the teacher, but I'm worried.

M Why? Is something wrong?

W I couldn't finish my report.

M You mean the history report?

W Yes. It's due tomorrow.

M Have you been very busy?

W Actually, my mom has been sick lately, so I had to help out more at home.

M Did you tell the teacher?

W I want to, but I'm afraid he'll think I'm lying.

M _____

W 선생님에게 말을 해야 하는데, 걱정이 돼.

M 왜? 무슨 문제 있어?

W 내 보고서를 끝내지 못했어.

M 역사 보고서 말이야?

W 응. 그것은 내일이 마감이야.

M 너 많이 바쁘니?

W 사실, 엄마가 최근에 아프셨어. 그래서 집에서 더 많이 도와드려야 했거든.

M 선생님께 말씀드렸니?

W 말하고는 싶은데, 내가 거짓말한다고 생각하실까 봐 겁이 나.

M 그럼, 네 어머니께서 선생님께 전화하면 되지.

① 네 어머니께서 곧 회복되시기를 바라.

② 네 어머니는 약이 필요하실 거야.

③ 다음 번에는, 선생님께 사실을 말씀드려.

⑤ 넌 제 시간에 끝냈어야 했어.

20 ②

W Good evening. I'm Susan Arnold from Channel 20 News.

M Good evening, Susan.

W I'd like to interview you right here. Is it possible?

M Okay. Go ahead, please.

W Thank you. Please tell us about the baseball game in Chicago.

M As you know, we lost today. The score was 3 to 9. It's too bad, but I didn't pitch well today.

W Why do you think so?

M _____

W 안녕하세요. 저는 채널 20 뉴스에서 나온 Susan Arnold입니다.

M 안녕하세요, Susan.

W 바로 여기서 인터뷰를 하고 싶은데요. 가능할까요?

M 좋아요. 어서 시작하지요.

W 고마워요. Chicago에서 열린 야구 경기에 대해 말씀해 주세요.

M 아시다시피, 오늘 저희는 졌어요. 점수는 3대 9였어요. 정말 안 됐지만, 제가 오늘 잘 던지지 못했어요.

W 왜 그렇게 생각하세요?

M 제가 오늘 실수를 많이 했어요.

① 저는 야구하는 것을 좋아해요.

③ 경기는 정말로 재미있었어요.

④ 오늘 오후에 야구를 합시다.

⑤ 그는 세계 최고의 투수예요.

만점 솔루션 자기가 잘 던지지 못해서 경기에서 졌다고 말하는 남자에게 여자가 왜 그렇게 생각하는지 물었으므로 그 이유를 말하는 것이 가장 자연스럽다.

영어듣기능력평가 **06**회

01 ①	02 ④	03 ④	04 ⑤	05 ⑤
06 ②	07 ④	08 ①, ➊⑤	09 ②	10 ③
11 ②, ➊①	12 ⑤	13 ①	14 ④	15 ③
16 ⑤	17 ③	18 ④	19 ①	20 ⑤

01 ①

W Did you hear tomorrow's weather report?

M Yes, I did. It's going to be sunny and warm.

W Really? But it seems like this heavy rain is never going to stop.

M Oh, don't worry. They said that it would be fine tomorrow.

W I hope so.

M And they also said that there would be no wind.

W Oh, it'll be a nice day then.

W 내일의 일기 예보 들었니?

M 그래, 들었어. 내일은 화창하고 따뜻할 거래.

W 정말? 그런데 이 폭우는 절대 그칠 것 같지 않아 보이는데.

M 오, 걱정 마. 내일은 맑을 거라고 했어.

W 나도 그러기를 바라.

M 그리고 바람도 없을 거라고 했어.

W 오, 그럼 좋은 날이 되겠네.

02 ④

W Honey, we need a desk for Jenny.

M I don't think so. She is only three years old.

W Umm. You're right.

M But a chair for the dining table is broken, you know?

W I know, but you can fix the chair.

M No. I'm afraid I can't.

W Then, how about buying one?

M Good. Let's look around.

W 여보, Jenny에게 책상이 필요해요.

M 나는 그렇게 생각하지 않아요. 겨우 3살인데요.

W 음. 당신 말이 맞아요.

M 그런데 식탁의 의자 한 개가 망가진 것 알아요?

W 알고 있어요, 하지만 당신이 그 의자를 고칠 수 있어요.

M 아니요. 고칠 수 없을 것 같아요.

W 그럼, 하나 사는 것이 어때요?

M 좋아요. 둘러봅시다.

만점 솔루션 두 사람은 Jenny를 위한 책상 대신 부서진 식탁 의자를 사기로 했다.

03 ④

W Now, can you tell us something about yourself?
M I'm twenty-two and I am a hairdresser.
W A hairdresser! Wow! Now you're a sports champion! Who do you go riding with?
M Umm... I ride alone. I have no coach.
W And who bought that beautiful racing bicycle for you?
M I bought it myself. I saved some money every month for it.
W Congratulations on winning the championship again.
M Thank you.

W 이제, 자신에 대한 것을 말씀해 주시겠어요?
M 저는 22살이고 미용사입니다.
W 미용사! 왜! 이제 당신은 스포츠 우승자입니다! 누구와 같이 타러 갑니까?
M 음… 혼자서 탑니다. 저는 코치가 없습니다.
W 그리고 누가 당신에게 저 멋진 경주용 자전거를 사 주었습니까?
M 제가 직접 그것을 샀습니다. 그것을 위해 매달 약간의 돈을 저축했습니다.
W 다시 한 번 선수권 대회에서 우승한 것을 축하드립니다.
M 감사합니다.

만점 솔루션 자전거는 기증받은 것이 아니라 남자가 직접 샀다고 했으므로, ④가 일치하지 않는다.

04 ⑤

M Where are you going, Jane?
W Hi, Tommy. I'm going to the library to return these books.
M Jane, do you have any special plan this Saturday?
W No. I'm going to watch movies at home. How about you?
M I have two tickets for a B-boy dance festival.
W Really? Can you take me there?
M Yes, I'd love to.

M Jane, 어디에 가고 있니?
W 안녕, Tommy. 이 책들을 반납하러 도서관에 가고 있어.
M Jane, 너 이번 주 토요일에 어떤 특별한 계획 있니?
W 아니. 집에서 영화를 볼 거야. 너는 어때?
M 나에게 B-boy 춤 축제를 위한 두 장의 표가 있는데.
W 정말이야? 나를 그곳에 데리고 갈 수 있니?
M 그래, 기꺼이.

만점 솔루션 B-boy 춤 축제를 위한 표가 두 장 있다는 남자의 말에 여자가 그곳에 데리고 갈 수 있는지 묻자 남자는 그러겠다고 했으므로, 두 사람은 춤 축제에 갈 것이다.

05 ⑤

W How did you like the city?
M Well, it was exciting and there was always something to do. But we couldn't walk the streets at night.
W Why? Were the people in the city unkind to foreigners?

M No, they were very kind. But sometimes robberies happened at night.
W Do you want to visit the city again?
M My answer is no.

W 그 도시는 어땠니?
M 글쎄, 신났었고 항상 할 일이 있었어. 그러나 밤에는 거리를 돌아다닐 수 없었어.
W 왜? 그 도시의 사람들이 외국인들에게 불친절했니?
M 아니, 매우 친절했어. 그러나 때때로 밤에 강도 사건이 발생했어.
W 그 도시를 다시 방문하고 싶니?
M 내 대답은 아니라는 거야.

06 ②

W Are you going to drive to the concert hall?
M No, the traffic is very heavy at this hour. I'll take a subway.
W But the concert hall is too far from the subway station. How about taking a bus?
M Is there a bus stop right in front of the concert hall?
W Sure. You should take number 16 bus.
M Okay, I'll take it.

W 연주회장에 운전해서 갈 예정이에요?
M 아니요, 이 시각에는 교통이 매우 혼잡해요. 지하철을 탈까 해요.
W 하지만 연주회장은 지하철역에서 너무 멀어요. 버스를 타는 것이 어때요?
M 연주회장 바로 앞에 버스 정류장이 있나요?
W 물론이죠. 16번 버스를 타세요.
M 알았어요, 그것을 탈게요.

07 ④

① W Would you like another sandwich?
   M No, thank you. I'm full.
② W Jack says that he likes dancing.
   M But he doesn't do it often.
③ W How do you feel today?
   M I'm afraid I don't feel any better.
④ W I think it is a good play.
   M No. I don't play soccer very well.
⑤ W What can I do for you?
   M I'd like to have this film developed.

① W 샌드위치 한 개 더 드시겠어요?
   M 아니요, 고맙습니다. 배가 불러요.
② W Jack은 춤 추기를 좋아한다고 말해요.
   M 하지만 그는 자주 춤을 추지 않아요.
③ W 오늘은 기분이 어때요?
   M 조금도 더 나아진 것 같지 않아 걱정이에요.
④ W 그것은 좋은 연극인 것 같아요.
   M 아니요, 저는 축구를 아주 잘 하지 못해요.
⑤ W 무엇을 도와드릴까요?
   M 이 필름을 현상하고 싶습니다.

08 ① | ➕ ⑤

W What kind of blanket do you want for your bed?
M I'd like a nice thick one for the winter.
W How about this blue one?
M It's not thick enough. This red one is better.
W It's a bit short, isn't it? The orange or yellow ones would fit.
M They're so bright. Let's just get the red one.
W OK, that's fine.

W 네 침대에 어떤 종류의 담요를 원하니?
M 난 겨울용으로 예쁘고 두꺼운 것을 원해.
W 이 파란색 담요는 어때?
M 그리 두껍지가 않네. 이 빨간색 담요가 더 좋아.
W 그건 조금 짧잖아, 그렇지 않아? 오렌지색이나 노란색 담요가 맞을 것 같아.
M 그것들은 너무 밝아. 그냥 빨간색 담요로 사자.
W 알았어, 좋아.

09 ②

W How did you hurt your leg?
M I hurt my leg while I was playing basketball in the park yesterday.
W How are you feeling today?
M Much better, thank you.
W These flowers are for you.
M Oh! How beautiful! You are so kind.
W Are the nurses helping you a lot?
M Yes, but my mom stayed here last night, too. The doctor said I must just stay here for a few days.

W 어떻게 하다가 네 다리를 다쳤니?
M 어제 공원에서 농구를 하다가 다리를 다쳤어.
W 오늘은 기분이 어떠니?
M 훨씬 더 나아졌어, 고마워.
W 이 꽃들은 너를 위한 것이야.
M 오! 정말 예쁘다! 너는 정말 친절해.
W 간호사들이 너를 많이 도와주고 있니?
M 그래, 하지만 엄마도 어젯밤에 여기 계셨어. 의사 선생님이 며칠 동안 이곳에 있어야 한다고 말씀하셨어.

10 ③

M Kate, what a beautiful *hanbok* you are wearing!
W Do you like it? My mom made it especially for me.
M That's wonderful! Are you going to wear it to the school festival tomorrow?
W Yes, I will. I'm very proud of this.
M I'm sure you'll be loved by all the students and teachers.
W Thank you for saying so.

M Kate, 너 참 아름다운 한복을 입고 있구나!

W 좋아 보이니? 우리 엄마가 나를 위해 특별히 그것을 만드셨어.
M 멋지다! 내일 학교 축제에 그것을 입고 갈 거니?
W 응, 그럴 거야. 나는 이 옷이 정말 자랑스러워.
M 나는 네가 모든 학생들과 선생님들에게 사랑을 받을 것이라고 확신해.
W 그렇게 말해 주니 고마워.

만점 솔루션 very proud of this, Thank you for saying so. 등의 표현을 통해 여자가 기뻐하고 있음을 알 수 있다.

11 ② | ➕ ①

M Which club do you want to join, Mary?
W I'd like to join the invention club. How about you? You like playing football, don't you?
M Yeah, I was a football player. But I'm more interested in the classic guitar.
W So, do you want to join the guitar club?
M Yes. I saw a guitar show the other day. It was fantastic.

M 너는 어느 동아리에 가입하고 싶니, Mary?
W 발명반에 가입하고 싶어. 너는 어때? 너는 축구하는 것을 좋아하지, 그렇지 않니?
M 그래, 난 축구 선수였어. 하지만 난 클래식 기타에 더 관심이 있어.
W 그럼, 기타반에 가입하고 싶니?
M 그래. 나는 며칠 전에 기타 쇼를 봤어. 환상적이었어.

12 ⑤

[Telephone rings.]

M Hello.
W Hi, Tim? It's June.
M Hi, June. What's up?
W I wonder if you're still selling your car.
M Are you interested?
W Not me, my brother is. Could he check it out?
M Sure. Would he like to test-drive it?
W If possible. Is tomorrow afternoon OK?
M Sure. Come after 2, OK?
W Sounds good. See you then.

[전화벨이 울린다.]

M 여보세요.
W 안녕, Tim이니? 나 June이야.
M 안녕, June. 무슨 일이야?
W 네가 아직 자동차를 팔고 있는지 궁금해서.
M 관심이 있니?
W 내가 아니고, 내 남동생이. 그가 그것을 볼 수 있을까?
M 물론이지. 네 남동생이 그것을 시험 운전해 보기를 원하니?
W 가능하면, 내일 오후 괜찮아?
M 물론. 2시 이후에 와, 괜찮지?
W 좋아. 그 때 보자.

만점 솔루션 여자는 자동차를 사려는 남동생을 위해 자동차를 파는 남자에게 전화를 걸어 자동차에 관해 문의하고 있다.

13 ①

W What are you looking at in the catalogue?

M I'm checking out stereo sound systems.

W Is your old one broken?

M It's all right, but I'd like better sound.

W It might cost a lot more money.

M Yeah, but I've been saving up for it.

W Maybe you can get something on sale on the Internet.

M You're right I'll have to check them online.

W 카탈로그에서 무엇을 보고 있는 거야?

M 스테레오 음향 시스템을 보고 있어.

W 예전 것은 고장 났어?

M 괜찮지만, 더 좋은 소리를 듣고 싶어서.

W 돈이 훨씬 더 많이 들지도 몰라.

M 그래, 하지만 난 그것 때문에 돈을 모아 왔어.

W 인터넷에서 할인 판매하는 것을 살 수 있을지도 몰라.

M 네 말이 맞아. 인터넷으로 그것들을 알아봐야겠다.

14 ④

W Hello, everyone. I have a few things to tell you. When you have class in the language lab, please be here a little earlier. Change your shoes before you enter the lab. Don't bring anything here except your textbooks. In class you can only speak English, not Korean. When class is over, turn off your machines and leave the lab one by one. Thank you.

W 안녕하세요, 여러분. 몇 가지 드릴 말씀이 있습니다. 어학 실습실에서 수업을 할 때, 조금 더 일찍 이곳에 오십시오. 실습실에 들어오기 전에 신발을 갈아 신으세요. 교과서를 제외하고 어떤 것도 가져오지 마세요. 수업 시간에 여러분은 한국어가 아니라 영어로만 말할 수 있습니다. 수업이 끝나면, 기계를 끄고 한 명씩 실습실에서 나가세요. 감사합니다.

15 ③

W How much are the apples?

M They are one dollar each. How many do you want?

W I want seven. And I'd like to buy a watermelon, too.

M The big one is 10 dollars, and the small one is 7 dollars.

W I'll take the big one.

M Do you need anything else?

W No. Here is 20 dollars.

M Thank you. Here is your change.

W 이 사과들 얼마죠?

M 한 개당 1달러입니다. 몇 개나 원하세요?

W 7개 주세요. 그리고 수박도 한 개 사고 싶어요.

M 큰 것은 10달러이고, 작은 것은 7달러입니다.

W 큰 것으로 살게요.

M 필요한 다른 것이 있나요?

W 아니요. 여기 20달러가 있어요.

M 감사합니다. 거스름돈 여기 있습니다.

만점 솔루션 한 개에 1달러짜리 사과 7개, 10달러짜리 수박 1개를 사고, 20달러를 지불했으므로, 거스름돈은 3달러가 된다.

16 ⑤

[Cellphone rings.]

M Hello, Mom. What's up?

W It's raining. Do you have an umbrella with you?

M No. The weather forecast didn't say it would rain today.

W Yeah, I know. But it was wrong. It seems it's going to rain for a while.

M Hmm.. can you bring an umbrella to the bus stop near home then?

W Of course, I can, but what about from school?

M I will try to find a friend with an umbrella and go to the bus stop with him.

[휴대 전화가 울린다.]

M 여보세여, 엄마. 무슨 일 있어요?

W 비가 오는구나. 우산 챙겼니?

M 아니요. 일기 예보에서 오늘 비 온다는 말이 없었어요.

W 그래, 알고 있어. 하지만 일기 예보가 틀렸어. 잠시동안 비가 올 거 같아.

M 흠... 그럼 집 근처 버스 정류장에 우산을 갖고 와 주실 수 있어요?

W 물론이지, 하지만 학교에서는 어쩌려고?

M 우산을 같이 써 줄 친구를 찾아보고 버스 정류장까지 친구랑 갈게요.

17 ③

M Judy, wait. You're throwing the ball the wrong way.

W The wrong way? Yesterday you taught me to do it this way.

M No. Your left foot must be in front of your right one.

W I see.

M Can you throw the ball again?

W Sure. Like this?

M Great! You're a really fast learner. I'll teach you how to bat tomorrow.

W Thank you very much, sir.

M Judy, 잠깐만. 너는 공을 잘못된 방법으로 던지고 있어.

W 잘못된 방법이라고요? 어제 선생님께서 저에게 이런 식으로 하라고 가르쳐 주셨어요.

M 아니. 네 왼발이 오른발 앞에 있어야 해.

W 알겠어요.

M 공을 다시 던져 볼 수 있겠니?

W 물론이죠. 이렇게요?

M 잘했다! 넌 정말 빨리 배우는구나. 너에게 내일은 공 치는 법을 가르쳐 줄게.

W 정말 고맙습니다, 선생님.

18 ④

W Woojin, you got a tan. You look good.

M Thanks, Mary. The weather was really nice over the

weekend, wasn't it?

W Yes, but I <u>stayed home all day</u>. Did you do something outside?

M Yes, it was Arbor Day, so I <u>planted trees</u> with my family.

W Oh, I forgot about it. Do you do that every year?

M No, actually it was our first time, but it was really fun. I want to do it again.

W It sounds really healthy, not only for you but also for the environment.

W 우진, 너 탔구나. 보기 좋다.

M 고마워, 메리. 주말내내 날씨가 정말 좋았어, 그렇지?

W 응, 하지만 난 종일 집에 있었어. 밖에서 무언가 했니?

M 응, 식목일이어서 가족들과 나무를 심었어.

W 아, 잊고 있었어. 매년 나무를 심니?

M 아니, 사실 처음이야. 하지만 정말 재미있었어. 다시 해보고 싶어.

W 진짜 건강한 거 같아, 너뿐만 아니라 환경한테도.

19 ①

W Well, what do you think?

M The style is <u>perfect on you</u>.

W What about the color?

M It's a very popular color among teens.

W How does it look on me?

M It <u>looks great on you</u>.

W You <u>don't think</u> I look funny in it?

M _____

W 그런데, 어떻게 생각해요?

M 스타일은 당신에게 완벽해요.

W 색상은 어때요?

M 십대들 사이에서 아주 인기 있는 색상이에요.

W 저에게는 어떻게 보이나요?

M 당신에게 잘 어울려요.

W 제가 그것을 입으면 웃겨 보인다고 생각하지 않는 거죠?

M <u>전혀요.</u>

② 그거 좋은데요.
③ 잘했어요.
④ 모르겠어요.
⑤ 동의하지 않아요.

만점 솔루션 ① Not at all.은 '전혀 아니다.'라는 뜻으로 You don't look funny in it at all.에서 여자의 말과 공통된 부분이 생략된 형태이다.

20 ⑤

M I saw you yesterday, but you didn't see me.

W Really? When?

M It was at about six o'clock in the evening. You were <u>getting off the subway</u> at the City Hall station.

W No, <u>that wasn't me</u>. Yesterday I was <u>writing a report</u> at the library at that time.

M _____

M 나는 어제 너를 보았는데, 너는 나를 알아보지 못했어.

W 정말? 언제?

M 저녁 6시쯤이었어. 너는 시청역 지하철에서 내리고 있었어.

W 아니, 그것은 내가 아니었어. 어제 나는 그 시각에 도서관에서 보고서를 작성하고 있었어.

M <u>흠, 내가 착각한 것 같구나.</u>

① 도서관이 문을 닫았어.
② 지하철이 연착했어.
③ 그것을 가지고 오는 것을 잊지 마.
④ 나는 보통 지하철을 타고 가.

01 ②	**02** ⑤	**03** ⑤, ✚①	**04** ②	**05** ④
06 ①, ✚①	**07** ⑤	**08** ①	**09** ④	**10** ③
11 ⑤	**12** ③	**13** ①	**14** ③	**15** ②
16 ④	**17** ⑤	**18** ④	**19** ④	**20** ④

01 ②

W Is it still raining?

M Yes, it is. Did you hear the thunder last night?

W Yes, I did. And I've never seen such heavy rain like this.

M Yeah, it is awful. How will the weather be later today?

W I just heard the forecast from the news. It said that it would stop raining and be fine in the afternoon.

M I hope it is right.

W 아직도 비가 오고 있니?

M 응, 그래. 너는 어젯밤에 천둥 소리를 들었니?

W 응, 들었어. 그리고 이와 같은 폭우를 본 적이 없어.

M 그래, 끔찍해. 오늘 늦게는 날씨가 어떻게 될까?

W 내가 방금 뉴스에서 일기 예보를 들었어. 오후에는 비가 그치고 맑을 거라고 했어.

M 일기 예보가 맞았으면 좋겠다.

02 ⑤

W ① I am singing a song with a microphone.
② My big sister is smiling and holding her hands up.
③ My little brother is sitting on a bicycle with his arms folded.
④ My father is looking up at the giraffe's face.
⑤ My mother is pointing her finger at the monkey with a hat and sunglasses on.

W ① 나는 마이크를 들고 노래를 부르고 있다.
② 나의 언니는 웃고 있고 두 손을 위로 치켜세우고 있다.
③ 나의 남동생은 팔짱을 낀 채로 자전거에 앉아 있다.
④ 나의 아버지는 기린의 얼굴을 쳐다보고 있다.
⑤ 나의 어머니는 모자와 선글라스를 쓰고 원숭이를 향해 손가락으로 가리키고 있다.

03 ⑤ | ✚①

M Good morning! May I help you?

W Yes, I have a terrible headache. And I feel dizzy.

M Let me take your temperature. You have a fever. Do you have a cough? Or a runny nose?

W I don't have a runny nose, but I have a cough.

M OK, try these pills. Take two pills 30 minutes after each

meal for two days. Visit me again in two days.

W Thank you.

M 안녕하세요! 도와드릴까요?

W 예, 두통이 심해서요. 그리고 어지러워요.

M 체온을 재겠습니다. 열이 있네요. 기침을 하세요? 아니면 콧물이 나나요?

W 콧물은 나지 않지만 기침을 합니다.

M 좋아요, 이 약을 드세요. 이틀 동안 식후 30분마다 두 알씩 드세요. 이틀 후에 저를 다시 방문해 주세요.

W 고맙습니다.

04 ②

M You look tired these days.

W I can't sleep soundly these days. I have many things to worry about.

M Why don't you get some exercise?

W You've got a point. Exercising might help me sleep better. But my knees are not good. What should I do?

M How about riding a bike? I heard it's good for knees.

W It's too cold outside.

M Then you'd better go swimming.

W That would be better.

M 요즘 피곤해 보이네요.

W 요즘 잠을 푹 잘 수가 없어요. 걱정되는 일들이 많이 있어요.

M 운동을 좀 해 보는 게 어때요?

W 좋은 지적이네요. 운동은 잠을 더 잘 자게 도와줄 거예요. 하지만 저는 무릎이 좋지 않아요. 어떻게 하면 좋을까요?

M 자전거를 타는 것은 어때요? 그게 무릎에 좋다고 들었는데.

W 밖의 날씨가 너무 추워서요.

M 그러면 수영을 하러 가는 게 낫겠네요.

W 그게 더 나을 것 같네요.

05 ④

W Tom, turn off the TV and go do your homework.

M Mom, I'm doing my homework.

W What is your homework?

M An essay about pollution.

W But this is a cartoon, isn't it?

M Yes, it is, but it is about water pollution.

W Don't lie.

M I'm not lying. I'm going to write an essay about the story.

W Tom, TV를 끄고 네 숙제를 하러 가라.

M 엄마, 저는 숙제하고 있어요.

W 숙제가 뭔데?

M 환경오염에 관한 글이에요.

W 하지만 이것은 만화잖니, 안 그래?

M 예, 그래요, 하지만 그것은 수질오염에 관한 것이에요.

W 거짓말하지 마라.

M 거짓말하는 게 아니에요. 저는 그 이야기에 관한 글을 쓸 거예요.

Tom은 수질오염에 관한 만화책을 보면서 그것에 관한 글을 쓸 거라고 말하고 있다.

06 ① | ➕ ①

M Let's go bowling this afternoon.

W Sorry, I can't. I hurt my right shoulder while playing badminton.

M That's too bad. When did you get hurt?

W I got hurt last Friday.

M Didn't you warm up before playing?

W No, I didn't.

M You should always warm up before playing sports.

W OK, I will. I won't forget it.

M I hope you will get better soon.

M 오늘 오후에 볼링 치러 가자.

W 미안하지만, 안 될 것 같아. 난 배드민턴을 치다가 오른쪽 어깨를 다쳤 거든.

M 너무 안됐다. 언제 다쳤니?

W 지난 금요일에 다쳤어.

M 경기를 하기 전에 준비 운동을 하지 않았니?

W 응, 하지 않았어.

M 운동을 하기 전에는 항상 준비 운동을 해야 해.

W 알았어, 그렇게 할게. 잊지 않을게.

M 빨리 네가 좋아지기를 바랄게.

남자는 처음에는 운동 전에 준비 운동을 하라는 충고의 말을, 마지막에는 빨리 낫기를 바란다는 기원의 말을 하고 있다.

07 ⑤

M Are you nervous about your piano recital?

W Not really. I feel pretty good.

M How do you do it? I'd be scared.

W I've been practicing a lot. I know my songs well.

M Doesn't the audience frighten you, though?

W A bit. But I like performing for people.

M I bet you will become a professional piano player someday.

M 너는 피아노 연주회 때문에 긴장되니?

W 그렇지는 않아. 난 기분이 아주 좋아.

M 어떻게 그래? 난 겁이 날 거야.

W 연습을 많이 했거든. 난 내 노래를 잘 알아.

M 하지만, 청중이 너를 두렵게 하지는 않니?

W 약간. 하지만 난 사람들을 위해 연주하는 것이 좋아.

M 넌 언젠가 전문 피아노 연주자가 될 거라고 확신해.

여자는 피아노 연주회를 앞두고 있지만 충분한 연습으로 자신 감에 찬 모습을 보여주고 있다.

08 ①

[Telephone rings.]

M Hello. May I speak to Jane, please?

W I'm sorry, but she's not in right now.

M Where did she go?

W I don't know.

M What time will she be back?

W Around five.

M Can I leave a message?

W Sure.

M Can you tell her today's meeting has been canceled?

W OK. May I have your name and phone number, please?

M John Terry. My phone number is 432-0218.

[전화벨이 울린다.]

M 여보세요. Jane과 통화할 수 있나요?

W 미안하지만, 그녀는 지금 집에 없어요.

M 어디 갔죠?

W 잘 모르겠어요.

M 몇 시에 돌아오죠?

W 5시쯤에요.

M 메모 좀 남겨도 될까요?

W 물론이죠.

M 그녀에게 오늘 모임이 취소되었다고 말씀해 주시겠어요?

W 좋아요. 이름과 전화번호가 어떻게 되죠?

M John Terry입니다. 제 전화번호는 432-0218입니다.

09 ④

W What's wrong?

M My parents are mad because I call my girlfriend too often.

W Are you wasting too much study time?

M They said the Cellphone bill is too high.

W Then you should chat online.

M But my typing is too slow.

W How about a video chat, then?

M I don't have a camera. But we could at least talk, I guess.

W Right. You can use voice calls over the Internet.

W 무슨 문제야?

M 내가 여자 친구에게 전화를 너무 자주 해서 부모님께서 화가 나셨어.

W 네 공부 시간을 너무 많이 쓰고 있는 거니?

M 휴대 전화 요금이 너무 많이 나온다고 말씀하셨어.

W 그럼 온라인에서 채팅을 해야겠네.

M 하지만 난 타이핑이 너무 느려.

W 그럼, 비디오 채팅은 어때?

M 난 카메라가 없어. 하지만 적어도 이야기는 할 수 있겠다.

W 맞아. 넌 인터넷을 통한 음성 통화를 이용할 수 있어.

여자가 인터넷을 통한 비디오 채팅을 제안하자, 남자는 카메라 가 없지만 이야기는 할 수 있겠다고 했으므로, 인터넷 음성 통 화를 이용할 것임을 알 수 있다.

10 ③

W Excuse me, could you help me?

M Sure, my pleasure. How can I help you?

W I was typing a letter when <u>my computer stopped working</u>.

M Did you <u>save what you had done</u>?

W I don't think I saved all of it. Can you <u>restore the file</u>?

M It's probably not possible, but I'll try.

W 실례합니다. 좀 도와주시겠어요?

M 물론이죠. 어떻게 도와드릴까요?

W 편지를 타이핑 하고 있었는데 내 컴퓨터가 작동을 멈췄어요.

M 당신이 작업한 것을 저장했나요?

W 모든 파일을 저장하진 못했어요. 그 파일을 복구할 수 있나요?

M 아마도 힘들 것 같지만, 한 번 해 볼게요.

만점 솔루션 컴퓨터로 작업을 하던 여자가 컴퓨터에 문제가 생기자 남자에게 파일 복구를 부탁하고 있는 상황이다.

11 ⑤

M Excuse me. I'd like to make a reservation.

W Where are you going?

M I'm going to New York.

W When are you going to leave?

M June 4th. It's next Tuesday.

W Yeah, there's <u>a flight at 10:40 a.m.</u> on Tuesday the 4th.

M Do you have <u>a flight in the afternoon</u>?

W Yes, it's at 5:40 p.m.

M OK, I'd like to <u>take that flight</u>.

M 실례합니다. 예약을 하고 싶은데요.

W 어디로 가시죠?

M 뉴욕으로 갈 거예요.

W 언제 떠날 예정이시죠?

M 6월 4일입니다. 다음 주 화요일이에요.

W 예, 4일 화요일 오전 10시 40분에 항공편 하나가 있네요.

M 오후 항공편이 있습니까?

W 예, 오후 5시 40분에 있습니다.

M 좋아요, 그 항공편으로 하고 싶네요.

12 ③

① **W** Who is going to <u>get married</u>?

   M Moses Lee and Petra Miller are going to get married.

② **W** Where is the wedding going to <u>take place</u>?

   M It will <u>be held</u> at the Chosun Hotel.

③ **W** When is the wedding going to happen?

   M It's going to be held <u>on March 18th</u>.

④ **W** What day is <u>the wedding ceremony</u>?

   M It's Monday.

⑤ **W** What time is the wedding ceremony going to finish?

   M It's going to finish at 4:30 p.m.

① **W** 누가 결혼할 예정입니까?

   M Moses Lee와 Petra Miller가 결혼할 예정입니다.

② **W** 결혼식은 어디에서 열릴 예정입니까?

M 조선 호텔에서 열릴 예정입니다.

③ **W** 결혼식은 언제 열릴 예정입니까?

   M 3월 18일에 열릴 예정입니다.

④ **W** 결혼식은 무슨 요일입니까?

   M 월요일입니다.

⑤ **W** 결혼식은 몇 시에 끝날 예정입니까?

   M 오후 4시 30분에 끝날 예정입니다.

만점 솔루션 결혼식은 3월 8일(March 8th)에 열릴 예정이므로, ③이 일치하지 않는다.

13 ①

W Excuse me, sir, is this platform number 4?

M No, I'm afraid not. It's platform 2. Platform 4 is the other side.

W Can you tell me <u>how to get there</u>?

M Go up the stairs over there, and you will see signs. By the way, where are you going?

W I want to <u>take the train</u> to Daegu.

M Oh, then, the platform has just changed. Actually, you are on the right one.

W Oh, really? That's great news. Thank you very much.

W 실례합니다, 여기가 4번 승강장인가요?

M 아니요, 2번 승강장입니다. 4번 승강장은 다른 쪽입니다.

W 거기에 어떻게 가는지 말씀해 주실 수 있나요?

M 저기서 위로 올라가면 표지판이 보일 겁니다. 그건 그렇고 어디 가시는 거죠?

W 대구행 기차를 타려고요.

M 아, 그러면 승강장이 막 바뀌었어요. 사실, 맞는 곳에 있는 겁니다.

W 아, 진짜요? 잘됐네요. 감사합니다.

14 ③

M How many people will go on the field trip?

W About <u>130 students</u> and <u>50 adults</u>. Why?

M The school has to book enough buses.

W How many people can fit in one bus?

M <u>40 people in each bus.</u>

W There might be <u>20 more people</u>. We'll know tomorrow.

M I have to book buses today. Then, I'll just count them in.

M 현장 학습에 몇 명이 갈 건가요?

W 학생 130명과 성인 50명이에요. 왜요?

M 학교에서 충분한 버스를 예약해야 하거든요.

W 한 대의 버스에 몇 명이 탈 수 있죠?

M 버스 한 대당 40명이에요.

W 20명 더 있을 수도 있어요. 내일 알게 될 거예요.

M 오늘 버스를 예약해야 해요. 그럼, 그냥 그들도 수에 넣을게요.

만점 솔루션 현장 학습에 가는 사람의 수는 확정된 인원 180명에 미확정된 인원 20명이 더 있고, 마지막에 이들까지 예약 인원 수에 포함

15 ②

W I'd like to check out, please.
M What was your room number?
W I was in room 415.
M You made two international phone calls, didn't you?
W Yes, I did.
M Just a moment while I check the charge for the calls.
W What time does the bus leave for the airport?
M The next one leaves in ten minutes.

W 퇴실하고 싶은데요.
M 몇 호실이십니까?
W 저는 415호실에 묵었어요.
M 당신은 국제 전화 두 통화를 하셨군요, 맞죠?
W 예, 그렇습니다.
M 제가 전화 요금을 확인할 동안 잠시만 기다려 주세요.
W 공항으로 가는 버스는 몇 시에 출발하죠?
M 다음 버스는 10분 후에 출발합니다.

16 ④

W What's wrong? Did you quarrel with your friend?
M No, I didn't.
W Are you sick now?
M No, I'm not. I lost my cell phone.
W Where did you lose it?
M On the way to school. I came here by subway.
W Why don't you visit the subway's "Lost and Found Office"?
M Good idea. I think I'll do that after school.

W 무슨 일이니? 친구와 싸웠어?
M 아니, 그렇지 않아.
W 지금 아프니?
M 아니, 그렇지 않아. 내 휴대 전화를 잃어버렸어.
W 어디서 그것을 잃어버렸니?
M 학교에 오는 길에. 나는 지하철을 타고 여기 왔어.
W 지하철 '분실물 보관소'에 가 보지 그래?
M 좋은 생각이야. 방과 후에 가야 할 것 같아.

17 ⑤

W Can we have a table by the window?
M We have one left. Come this way.
W This is perfect.
M May I take your order?
W We'd like two orders of steak with your special salad and coffee.
M Would you like your coffee now or with your meal?
W Now, please.

W 창가 쪽 자리가 있을까요?
M 한 자리가 남았는데요. 이쪽으로 오세요.
W 완벽하군요.
M 주문하시겠어요?
W 스테이크 2인분에 특별 샐러드와 커피를 함께 주세요.
M 커피를 지금 드릴까요, 아니면 식사와 함께 드릴까요?
W 지금 주세요.

만점 솔루션 여자는 식사가 나오기 전에 커피를 마시기를 원했으므로, ⑤가 일치하지 않는다.

18 ④

W What happened to you and Jack?
M I don't want to see him anymore.
W I thought you were good friends.
M Yes, we were, but he never pays back the money he borrows from me. That makes me crazy.
W Why don't you tell him about it frankly?
M It's too late. I won't lend him any money from now on. He isn't my friend anymore.

W 너와 Jack에게 무슨 일이 생긴 거니?
M 다시는 그를 보고 싶지 않아요.
W 너희들은 좋은 친구라고 생각했는데.
M 그랬죠. 하지만 그는 나에게 빌려간 돈을 절대 갚지 않아요. 그게 저를 화나게 만들어요.
W 그에게 솔직하게 그것에 관해 말해 보지 그러니?
M 너무 늦었어요. 저는 지금부터 그에게 어떠한 돈도 빌려 주지 않을 거예요. 그는 더 이상 제 친구가 아니예요.

19 ④

M A family is moving into the house across the street.
W Yeah. It was empty for a long time.
M Where are they from?
W I heard they're from Canada.
M How many children do they have?
W They have two boys of our kids' age.
M It's nice that they have children the same age as ours.
W _____

M 한 가족이 길 건너 집으로 이사 올 예정이라고 해요.
W 그래요. 그 집은 오랫동안 비어 있었어요.
M 어디서 온대요?
W 캐나다에서 온다고 들었어요.
M 아이들은 몇 명이래요?
W 우리 아이들과 같은 또래의 남자아이들 둘이 있대요.
M 우리 아이들과 같은 나이의 아이들이 있다니 좋네요.
W 그들이 우리 아이들과 잘 지냈으면 좋겠어요.

① 당신은 조심해야 해요.
② 제가 그들을 병원에 데려다 줄게요.
③ 미안해요, 저는 지금 떠나야 해요.
⑤ 그 버스는 몇 분 후면 올 거예요.

20 ④

W Is it going to rain today?

M That's what the weather report said.

W Maybe I should wear my rain coat.

M But it's so hot outside. You'll sweat. Just bring an umbrella. It's easier.

W I don't have one, though. <u>Mine is broken</u>.

M You can stop at the store and <u>get one on the way</u>.

W _____

W 오늘 비가 올 거래?

M 일기 예보에서는 그렇게 말했어.

W 내 우비를 입어야 할 것 같군.

M 하지만 밖은 아주 더워. 땀이 날 거야. 그냥 우산을 가져가. 그게 더 수월해.

W 하지만, 난 가진 것이 없어. 내 우산이 고장 났거든.

M 가는 길에 가게에 들러서 하나 살 수도 있잖아.

W <u>그럼, 그렇게 해야겠다.</u>

① 하지만 거기에 하나만 남아 있어.

② 그런 경우라면, 난 버스를 탈 거야.

③ 내가 일어났을 때 비가 오고 있지 않았어.

⑤ 밖에 나가지 않아서 모르겠어.

만점 솔루션 남자는 여자에게 가게에 들러 우산을 살 것을 제안하고 있으므로 그렇게 하겠다는 말을 하는 것이 가장 자연스럽다.

---

01 ③	02 ①	03 ②, ➍③	04 ②	05 ③
06 ⑤	07 ②	08 ③	09 ④	10 ④
11 ④	12 ⑤	13 ④	14 ②, ➍⑤	15 ③
16 ③	17 ④	18 ①	19 ②	20 ①

01 ③

① **W** What kind of TV program do you like?
  M I like sports program.
② **W** How much are these notebooks?
  M They are three dollars each.
③ **W** Good afternoon. <u>May I help you</u>?
  M Yes. I'm looking for <u>a pair of pants</u>.
④ **W** Do you have an English dictionary?
  M Yes. It's right over there.
⑤ **W** Do you like <u>washing the dishes</u>?
  M No, I hate washing the dishes.

① **W** 너는 어떤 종류의 TV 프로그램을 좋아하니?
  M 나는 스포츠 프로그램을 좋아해.
② **W** 이 공책들은 얼마예요?
  M 한 권에 3달러예요.
③ **W** 안녕하세요. 도와드릴까요?
  M 예. 바지 한 벌을 찾고 있어요.
④ **W** 영어 사전이 있나요?
  M 예. 바로 저기에 있어요.
⑤ **W** 너는 설거지하는 것을 좋아하니?
  M 아니, 설거지하는 것은 정말 싫어.

02 ①

M I am something you probably use every day, especially in the winter. That's because, without me, <u>your feet would be cold</u>. You can even wear two of me if your feet are really cold. And without me, your feet would <u>get a lot wetter</u>. You can wear me with <u>almost any other kind of footwear</u>. I protect your feet from getting rubbed too hard.

M 나는 당신이 아마도 매일, 특히 겨울에 사용하는 물건입니다. 그 이유는 내가 없으면, 당신의 발이 추울 것이기 때문입니다. 만약 당신의 발이 정말로 춥다면 나를 2개를 신을 수도 있습니다. 그리고 내가 없다면, 당신의 발은 훨씬 더 축축해질 것입니다. 당신은 거의 모든 종류의 신발과 함께 나를 신을 수 있습니다. 나는 당신의 발이 너무 심하게 비벼지는 것을 방지합니다.

만점 솔루션 신발과 함께 신는다고 했으므로 신발이 아니라 '양말'이라는 것을 알 수 있다.

---

03 ② | ⊕ ③

W   Do you have any plans this weekend?

M   Yes. On Saturday morning, I have to meet my father at the airport.

W   <u>What about Saturday afternoon</u>?

M   I'll go bowling with my sister in the afternoon. How about you?

W   I'll <u>stay at home</u> on Saturday morning and <u>go to the movies</u> with my brother in the afternoon.

M   And on Sunday morning?

W   I plan to play tennis with Susan.

W   이번 주말에 어떤 계획이라도 있니?

M   응. 토요일 오전에 공항으로 아버지를 마중 나가야 해.

W   토요일 오후는 어때?

M   오후에 누나랑 볼링을 치러 갈 거야. 너는 어때?

W   나는 토요일 오전에는 집에 있을 거고, 오후에는 오빠와 함께 영화 보러 갈 거야.

M   그럼 일요일 오전에는?

W   Susan과 테니스를 치려고 해.

04 ②

M   I heard you had bad news yesterday.

W   Yeah. I thought I failed my test!

M   What? But you studied so hard!

W   Yeah. I was shocked when I saw the result.

M   You must be very upset, then.

W   No. It was <u>the teacher's mistake</u>. She wrote my score down wrong.

M   So <u>you didn't fail</u>?

W   No. In fact, I got an A!

M   어제 너한테 안 좋은 소식이 있었다고 들었어.

W   응. 난 시험에 떨어졌다고 생각했어!

M   뭐라고? 하지만 넌 정말 열심히 공부했잖아!

W   그래. 난 그 결과를 봤을 때 충격을 받았어.

M   그럼, 넌 화가 많이 났겠구나.

W   아니야. 그건 선생님의 실수였어. 내 성적을 잘못 적으셨더라고.

M   그럼 넌 떨어진 게 아니야?

W   아니야. 사실, 나 A 받았어!

> **만점 솔루션** 여자는 처음에는 시험에 떨어져 충격을 받았으나, 선생님의 실수로 밝혀지자 안도하고 있는 상황이다.

05 ③

W   Hi, do you need any help?

M   Yes, please. I <u>want something special</u> for my girlfriend, but I'm not sure what's good.

W   What kind of design does she like?

M   I think she <u>likes something simple</u>, not too colorful.

W   Then, what about this? It's made of real silver, with a heart pendant.

M   It looks very cute. I think she will like it.

W   Or there is this one, too, with a moon and a star pendant.

M   Hmm, that looks good as well.

W   안녕하세요, 도와드릴까요?

M   네. 여자친구를 위한 특별한 무언가를 찾고 있는데 무엇이 좋을지 모르겠네요.

W   여자친구가 어떤 디자인을 좋아하나요?

M   간단하고 너무 다채롭지 않은 걸 좋아할 거예요.

W   그럼 이건 어때세요? 진짜 은으로 만들어진 하트 모양 펜던트예요.

M   아주 귀엽네요. 그녀가 좋아할 거 같아요.

W   아니면 이것도 있어요. 달과 별 모양의 펜던트요.

M   흠, 그거도 좋아 보이네요.

06 ⑤

M   Excuse me, but what's <u>the best way to</u> get to Rainbow Department Store?

W   You can either walk or take the subway.

M   How far is it from here?

W   Not that far. You can walk to the department store in fifteen minutes.

M   <u>Isn't there a shuttle bus</u> to go there from here?

W   Oh, you're right. You can <u>take a shuttle bus</u> in front of the Paradise Hotel.

M   Then, I'll take that.

M   실례하지만, 무지개 백화점에 가는 가장 좋은 방법이 뭔가요?

W   걸어가시거나 아니면 지하철을 타실 수 있어요.

M   여기서 얼마나 먼가요?

W   그렇게 멀지 않아요. 15분이면 백화점까지 걸어가실 수 있어요.

M   여기서 거기에 가는 셔틀 버스는 없나요?

W   오, 맞아요. 파라다이스 호텔 앞에서 셔틀 버스를 타실 수 있어요.

M   그럼, 그걸 타겠어요.

07 ②

W   Hi, what can I do for you?

M   Hi, I <u>need some US dollars</u>.

W   How much do you want?

M   1,500 US dollars <u>in cash</u>.

W   One second. Hmm. Okay. 1,500 US dollars will be 1,734,000 Korean won.

M   Please <u>take the money out of this account</u>.

W   Okay. And can I see your passport, too?

M   Yes, here it is.

W   안녕하세요, 무엇을 도와드릴까요?

M   안녕하세요, 미국 달러가 좀 필요해서요.

W   얼마나 원하시나요?

M   현금으로 미화 1,500달러요.

W   잠깐만요. 흠. 좋아요. 미화 1,500달러는 한국 원화로 173만 4천 원이에요.

M 이 계좌에서 돈을 인출하세요.

W 알겠어요. 그리고 여권도 보여주실 수 있나요?

M 예, 여기 있어요.

08 ③

M What's your favorite Korean food, Yumi?

W I like *kimchi* best. How about you, Harry?

M I like *kimchi*, too. But I like pizza best. Can you make *kimchi*?

W No, I can't, but I can cook with *kimchi*.

M Can you show me how?

W Sure. I'm going to make fried rice with *kimchi* this weekend. Come to my house at 6 o'clock on Saturday.

M Okay. I can't wait to cook with *kimchi*.

M 유미야, 네가 제일 좋아하는 한국 음식이 뭐니?

W 나는 김치를 제일 좋아해. Harry, 너는?

M 나도 김치가 좋아. 하지만 난 피자가 제일 좋아. 너는 김치를 담글 수 있니?

W 아니, 할 수 없어. 하지만 김치로 요리는 할 수 있어.

M 방법을 보여 줄 수 있니?

W 물론이지. 이번 주말에 김치로 볶음밥을 만들려고 해. 토요일 6시에 우리 집으로 와.

M 알았어. 빨리 김치로 요리를 하고 싶은걸.

① 유미는 김치를 제일 좋아한다.

② Harry는 피자를 제일 좋아한다.

③ 유미는 김치 담그는 법을 알고 있다.

④ 유미는 김치로 볶음밥을 만들 수 있다.

⑤ Harry는 토요일에 유미의 집에 갈 것이다.

만점 솔루션 남자의 Can you make *kimchi*?라는 말에 유미는 No, I can't라고 대답했으므로, ③이 일치하지 않는다.

09 ④

M Tomorrow is Teacher's Day.

W It has been about five months since we graduated from middle school.

M Yes. I want to see our math teacher in middle school. He really took care of our class.

W He was a nice teacher. I'll go and see him tomorrow. How about you?

M I have to go to the library to write a science report with Scott.

W Then, why don't you send him a text message? He'll be happy to see your message.

M Oh, you're right. I'll do that right now.

M 내일이 '스승의 날'이야.

W 우리가 중학교를 졸업한 지 약 5달이 됐어.

M 그래. 나는 중학교 때 우리 수학 선생님을 뵙고 싶어. 그는 우리 반을 아주 잘 돌보셨지.

W 그는 멋진 선생님이셨어. 나는 내일 그를 만나러 갈 거야. 너는 어때?

M 나는 Scott과 과학 보고서를 쓰러 도서관에 가야만 해.

W 그럼, 그에게 문자 메시지를 보내는 게 어때? 네 메시지를 보시면 기뻐하실 거야.

M 오, 그렇구나. 지금 당장 그렇게 해야지.

① 새해 복 많이 받으세요!

② 잘 다녀왔어요, 여보!

③ 당신의 생일을 축하합니다!

④ 저를 가르쳐 주셔서 감사합니다.

⑤ 제 아이를 돌봐주세요.

만점 솔루션 중학교 수학 선생님께 스승의 날을 맞아 보낼 수 있는 문자 메시지로는 ④ '저를 가르쳐 주셔서 감사합니다.'가 적절하다.

10 ④

W Junhee, you live on Pleasant Street, don't you?

M Yes, I do. Why?

W And there's a post office on your street, right?

M Yes, I live very close to the post office.

W Great. Can I ask you a big favor? I need to send this package to my friend in China, but there aren't any post offices near me.

M Do you want me to send it for you?

W Yes, that would be great. Could you, please?

M Okay, but you owe me.

W 준희야, 너 플레전트 가에 살지, 맞지?

M 응, 왜?

W 너네 거리에 우체국 하나 있지?

M 응. 우체국이랑 매우 가까운 곳에 살고 있어.

W 잘됐다. 나 큰 부탁 하나만 해도 될까? 이 소포를 중국에 사는 친구에게 보내야 하는데 내 주변에 우체국이 없어.

M 너를 대신해서 소포를 보내주길 바라는 거야?

W 응, 그럼 좋겠어. 해줄 수 있어?

M 알겠어, 하지만 나한테 빚진 거야.

11 ④

M My French friend Louis is coming to my house next week. I think you might like him.

W Tell me about him. You said he was very good-looking, right?

M Sure. He has brown hair and green eyes. He works for a department store in Paris.

W That's nice. Maybe he could go with us to watch a soccer game.

M I don't think so. He loves playing tennis and watching tennis, not soccer.

W What else does he like?

M He likes music and dancing. He's played the piano for years.

M 내 프랑스 친구 Louis가 다음 주에 우리 집에 올 거야. 네가 그를 좋아할 것 같은데.

W 그에 대해서 말해 봐. 그가 아주 멋지게 생겼다고 말했었지, 그렇지?

M 물론이지. 그는 갈색 머리에 초록색 눈동자야. 파리에 있는 백화점에서 근무해.

W 멋지네. 그는 아마도 우리와 함께 축구 경기를 보러 갈 수도 있을 거야.

M 나는 그렇게 생각하지 않아. 그는 축구가 아니라 테니스 치는 것과 테니스 구경하는 것을 정말 좋아해.

W 다른 건 뭘 좋아하는데?

M 그는 음악과 춤 추는 것을 좋아해. 수년 동안 피아노를 치고 있어.

> **만점 솔루션** 함께 축구를 보러 갈 수도 있을 거라는 여자의 말에 남자가 He loves playing tennis and watching tennis, not soccer.라고 말한 것으로 보아 Louis가 축구가 아니라 테니스를 좋아한다는 것을 알 수 있다.

12 ⑤

W What are you doing?

M I'm playing the guitar. I've been playing the guitar since I was an elementary school boy.

W Oh, really? That sounds great!

M I heard that you played the violin.

W Yes. I learned how to play the violin when I was young. I often play the violin.

M I'm planning to take a drum lesson.

W Why? Do you have any special plan?

M Yes. I want to be a drummer in our school band.

W 뭐 하고 있니?

M 기타를 치고 있어. 나는 초등학생 때부터 기타를 치고 있거든.

W 오, 정말이니? 대단한걸!

M 너는 바이올린을 연주했다고 들었는데.

W 응. 어렸을 때 바이올린 연주하는 법을 배웠어. 종종 바이올린을 연주해.

M 나는 드럼 수업을 받으려고 해.

W 왜? 무슨 특별한 계획이라도 있니?

M 응. 나는 우리 학교 밴드부에서 드럼 연주자가 되고 싶어.

13 ④

[Telephone rings.]

W Hello.

M Hi, Susan?

W Yeah, is this Peter?

M Yes, I saw your window is open.

W Oh, is it going to rain?

M No, but I was worried about your dogs.

W I didn't think of that. I'd better close it. Thanks.

M Any time. Maybe you should get a screen on it.

W That's a good idea. That will keep the bugs out, too.

[전화벨이 울린다.]

W 여보세요.

M 안녕, Susan?

W 응, Peter니?

M 응, 네 창문이 열려 있는 것을 봤어.

W 오, 비가 올 거래?

M 아니, 하지만 네 개들이 걱정이 돼서.

W 그 생각은 못했네. 창문을 닫는 게 좋겠어. 고마워.

M 별거 아냐. 넌 창문에 철망을 달아야 할 것 같아.

W 좋은 생각이야. 그러면 벌레도 막아 줄 테니까.

> **만점 솔루션** 남자는 여자의 집 창문이 열려 있다는 것을 알려 주기 위해 전화를 걸었다.

14 ② | ➕ ⑤

W Did you hear Tom got the first prize at the National Painting Contest?

M Tom who?

W Tom Gerald.

M Oh, the guy in our class last year?

W Yes, he moved to Chicago last November. He goes to Redwood High School in Chicago.

M He got the first prize? Oh, that's amazing!

W Yes. I think he's going to be a great artist. I'm going to send him an email.

M That's a good idea! Please tell him I say congratulations to him.

W Tom이 전국 그림 그리기 대회에서 1등상을 탔다는 것을 들었니?

M Tom이 누구야?

W Tom Gerald.

M 오, 작년에 우리 반이었던 친구?

W 응, 그는 작년 11월에 Chicago로 이사 갔잖아. 그는 Chicago에서 Redwood 고등학교에 다니고 있어.

M 그가 1등상을 탔다고? 오, 놀라운데!

W 그래. 나는 그가 훌륭한 화가가 될 거라고 생각해. 나는 그에게 이메일을 보내려고 해.

M 그거 좋은 생각이다! 내가 축하한다고 그에게 말해 줘.

15 ③

W What's the problem with you, John?

M I can't sleep well at night these days. What do you recommend I do?

W Try to maintain a regular lifestyle. First of all, wake up early in the morning and don't stay up late.

M I see. I'll try to change my lifestyle.

W Second, exercise daily. Exercise like jogging would be good for you.

M Okay. I can do that.

W 무슨 문제라도 있니, John?

M 요즘 밤에 잠을 푹 잘 수가 없어. 무엇을 해 보라고 추천해 줄래?

W 규칙적인 생활방식을 유지하도록 노력해. 우선, 아침에 일찍 일어나고 밤에 늦게까지 깨어 있지 마.

M 알았어. 내 생활방식을 바꾸려고 노력할게.

W 둘째, 매일 운동을 해. 조깅과 같은 운동이 너에게 좋을 거야.

M 알았어. 그건 할 수 있어.

16 ③

M I'm going to a great new movie on Saturday. Would you like to come?

W Saturday? It's May 27th. I can't. It's my mom's birthday. How about Sunday?

M Okay. Sunday is fine. Hmm.... Let me check.... On May 28th, the movie starts at 3.

W Then let's meet in front of the Universal Cinema at 2:30.

M All right, but how about meeting half an hour earlier? Then we can eat something first.

W Sounds great. See you then.

M 토요일에 멋진 신작 영화를 보려고 해. 너도 갈래?

W 토요일이라고? 5월 27일이네. 나는 갈 수 없어. 그 날이 엄마 생신이거든. 일요일은 어때?

M 좋아. 일요일도 좋아. 흠…. 확인 좀 해 보고…. 5월 28일에는 영화가 3시에 시작해.

W 그럼 Universal 극장 앞에서 2시 30분에 만나자.

M 좋아, 하지만 30분 일찍 만나는 것은 어때? 그럼 먼저 뭔가를 먹을 수 있잖아.

W 아주 좋아. 그 때 보자.

만점 솔루션 5월 27일이 여자의 엄마의 생신이라 28일에 만나기로 하고, 2시 30분에 만나자는 여자에게 남자가 30분 일찍 만나 함께 뭔가를 좀 먹자고 제안하는 상황이다.

17 ④

W Jack, you look very tired this morning.

M Yes, I didn't sleep much, but I'll be okay. It was worth it.

W What did you do?

M Oh, we went to observe the stars last night.

W The stars in the night sky?

M Yes. You know I'm in an astronomy club. We wanted to take some pictures of the stars because it was a special night. We saw a lot of falling stars.

W That sounds great. Can you show me the pictures later?

M Sure.

W 잭, 오늘 아침 엄청 피곤해 보인다.

M 응, 잘 못 잤는데 괜찮아. 가치가 있었어.

W 뭐 했는데?

M 아, 우리 어젯밤 별을 관찰하러 갔어.

W 밤 하늘의 별?

M 응. 내가 천문학 동아리인지 알지. 특별한 밤이었기 때문에 별 사진을 찍길 원했거든. 우리는 많은 유성을 보았어.

W 멋지다. 나중에 나도 사진을 볼 수 있을까?

M 물론이야.

18 ①

W We must do more to protect all animals. Now, we focus mainly on the endangered animals. Of course, these are important, but there are many common animals that are treated badly every day. Companies use animals to test things like cosmetics and medications. These animals are common animals, like rabbits, cats, and dogs. Many of them suffer. Don't they deserve our protection?

W 우리는 모든 동물들을 보호하기 위해 더 많은 것을 해야 합니다. 지금, 우리는 주로 멸종 위기에 처한 동물에 초점을 맞추고 있습니다. 물론, 이 동물들은 중요하지만, 매일 나쁜 대접을 받고 있는 많은 일반 동물들이 있습니다. 회사들은 화장품과 약품 같은 것들을 시험하는 데 이 동물들을 이용합니다. 이 동물들은 토끼, 고양이, 그리고 개와 같은 일반 동물들입니다. 그들 중 많은 것들이 고통을 받고 있습니다. 그들은 우리 보호를 받을 자격이 없는 건가요?

만점 솔루션 여자는 멸종 위기에 처한 동물들뿐만 아니라 일반 동물들도 보호해야 한다고 주장하고 있다.

19 ②

W Good morning. May I help you?

M Yes. I want this coat dry-cleaned.

W All right.

M When can I pick it up? I have to wear it this Friday.

W Don't worry about it. This will be ready on Thursday.

M Okay. How much will it cost?

W It's ten dollars.

M Oh, that's not so expensive. Do I have to pay now?

W _____

W 안녕하세요. 도와드릴까요?

M 예. 이 코트를 드라이 클리닝하고 싶은데요.

W 알겠어요.

M 그것을 언제 찾아갈 수 있을까요? 이번 금요일에 그것을 입어야 해서요.

W 걱정 마세요. 목요일에는 준비해 놓을 게요.

M 좋아요. 얼마죠?

W 10달러예요.

M 오, 그렇게 비싸지는 않네요. 지금 돈을 지불해야 하나요?

W 아니요. 나중에 내셔도 돼요.

① 그래요. 그 때 봐요.

③ 10달러가 더 들 거예요.

④ 고마워요. 목요일에 다시 올게요.

⑤ 내일 제 셔츠를 주세요.

만점 솔루션 세탁비를 지금 지불해야 하느냐는 남자의 말에 알맞은 여자의 응답으로는 지불 시점을 말하는 것이 가장 자연스럽다.

20 ①

[Telephone rings.]

W Hello, is Frank there?

M Speaking.

W Hi, Frank. This is Susie. Guess what?

M What? Did something special happen?

W I just got my own cell phone.

M Great. Christine got a cell phone, too. Have you tried sending a text message?

W _____

[전화벨이 울린다.]

W 여보세요, Frank 있나요?

M 전데요.

W 안녕, Frank. 나 Susie야. 무슨 일인지 맞춰 볼래?

M 뭔데? 특별한 일이라도 생겼니?

W 나 막 휴대 전화를 샀어.

M 대단한데. Christine도 휴대 전화를 샀는데. 넌 문자 메시지 보내는 것을 해 봤니?

W ① 아니, 그건 안 해 봤어.

② 응, 네 문자 메시지를 받았어.

③ 응, 좀 더 편안하게 느껴질 거야.

④ 아니, 메시지를 남기고 싶어.

⑤ 그래, 그녀는 통화 중이야.

01 ③	02 ⑤	03 ④	04 ④	05 ①
06 ④	07 ③	08 ②	09 ⑤	10 ④
11 ②, ⊕②	12 ⑤	13 ④	14 ①, ⊕⑤	15 ③
16 ④	17 ③	18 ②	19 ②	20 ①

01 ③

① W May I open the windows, please?

　M Certainly. It's hot in here!

② W Hey! Look at the birds in the sky.

　M Oh, yeah! It's a very lovely day.

③ W Why can't you get up by yourself?

　M I have a terrible headache this morning.

④ W How long are you going to stay?

　M I'd like to stay for three days.

⑤ W How much is the bed over there?

　M Sorry, ma'am. It's not for sale.

① W 제가 창문을 열어도 될까요?

　M 물론이죠. 이 안은 더워요!

② W 이봐! 하늘에 새들을 봐.

　M 오, 정말! 아주 화창한 날이야.

③ W 왜 혼자서 일어날 수 없니?

　M 오늘 아침에 두통이 심해요.

④ W 얼마나 오랫동안 머무실 건가요?

　M 3일 동안 묵고 싶습니다.

⑤ W 저기에 있는 침대는 얼마입니까?

　M 죄송합니다. 손님. 그것은 판매용이 아닙니다.

02 ⑤

M I need a shirt for my new suit.

W For your black suit?

M Yeah. How about this shirt with small dots?

W I think it would probably look weird.

M Then, would this thick striped shirt be good?

W It might, if the stripes are very thin.

M How about this shirt? It looks like what you suggested.

W Yep, that is what I meant.

M OK. I will get this. Thanks.

M 내 새 양복에 맞는 셔츠가 필요해.

W 네 검정색 양복 말이니?

M 응. 이 작은 점무늬 셔츠는 어때?

W 이상해 보일 것 같아.

M 그럼. 이 두꺼운 줄무늬 셔츠가 어울릴까?

W 그럴지도, 만약 줄무늬가 아주 얇다면.

M 이 셔츠는 어때? 네가 제안한 것과 비슷해 보이는데.

W 응, 내가 말한 게 바로 그거야.

M 좋아. 이것을 사야겠다. 고마워.

만점 솔루션 남자는 여자가 말한 대로 얇은 줄무늬 셔츠를 사기로 했다.

03 ④

M Tired of your old clothes, but can't afford new ones? <u>Try changing them</u>. The easiest way is to <u>dye your clothes</u>. This works best on light-colored clothes. Use special paints or stickers to decorate dark clothes. Another option is to cut them. For example, an old pair of pants <u>becomes new shorts by cutting them</u>.

M 당신의 오래된 옷에 싫증이 났지만, 새 옷을 살 여유는 없나요? 그것들을 한번 바꿔 보세요. 가장 쉬운 방법은 당신의 옷들을 염색하는 것입니다. 이 방법은 밝은 색 옷에 가장 효과가 있습니다. 진한 색 옷을 장식하기 위해서는 특별한 물감이나 스티커를 이용하세요. 또 다른 선택은 그것들을 자르는 것입니다. 예를 들면, 오래된 바지는 그것을 잘라서 새로운 반바지가 됩니다.

만점 솔루션 염색, 물감이나 스티커 부착 또는 잘라서 헌 옷을 새로운 옷으로 만드는 방법을 소개하는 내용의 담화이다.

04 ④

M It's so hot. Why can't we <u>turn on the air conditioner</u>?

W The school wants to save money.

M That's ridiculous. I can't study in this heat.

W We could open the window.

M That won't help. I wish <u>we had a fan</u>.

W There's <u>a small one in the other room</u> we can use.

M Well, it seems that is all we've got.

M 정말 덥다. 왜 에어컨을 틀 수 없는 거야?

W 학교가 돈을 절약하고 싶어 해.

M 말도 안 돼. 이 더위에서는 공부를 할 수가 없어.

W 우리는 창문을 열 수 있어.

M 그건 도움이 안 될 거야. 선풍기가 있으면 좋을 텐데.

W 다른 교실에 우리가 사용할 수 있는 작은 선풍기가 하나 있어.

M 음, 그게 우리가 가진 유일한 방법인 것 같다.

05 ①

① **M** Excuse me, you're not allowed to <u>feed the animals</u> here.

   W Oops, I'm sorry. I didn't see the sign.

② **M** I really like rabbits. They are so cute.

   W So do I. I like how they eat the grass.

③ **M** Mom, can we get a dog, please?

   W I wish we could, but you're allergic to fur.

④ **M** It was a really good idea to <u>come out and get</u> <u>fresh air</u>.

W Yes, indeed, thank you for asking me.

⑤ **M** What is your favorite thing to do on the weekend?

   W I like going to the zoo and watching the animals.

① **M** 실례합니다. 여기 동물에게 음식을 주시면 안됩니다.

   W 이런, 죄송해요. 표지판을 못 봤어요.

② **M** 난 토끼가 정말 좋아. 정말 귀여워.

   W 나도 그래. 토끼들이 풀을 먹을 때 모습이 좋아.

③ **M** 엄마, 우리 개 기르면 안되나요?

   W 기르면 좋겠지만 네가 털에 알레르기가 있잖니.

④ **M** 밖에 나와서 신선한 공기를 마시는 건 정말 좋은 생각이었어.

   W 그래, 진짜, 함께 가자고 해줘서 고마워.

⑤ **M** 주말에 무엇을 하는 걸 가장 좋아해?

   W 동물원에 가서 동물들을 보는 것을 좋아해.

06 ④

W What are you doing here, David?

M I'm watering the garden. The flowers are dry.

W Take care of yourself. You should <u>stay in bed and rest</u>.

M But it's so boring.

W If you don't rest more, you <u>won't be well</u> enough to go to school tomorrow.

M Mom, I'm well enough to water the flowers.

W David, you <u>can do it later</u>.

M Yes, Mom.

W 여기서 무엇을 하고 있니, David?

M 정원에 물을 주고 있어요. 꽃들이 말랐어요.

W 네 몸을 돌봐야지. 너는 침대에서 휴식을 취해야 해.

M 하지만 너무 지루해요.

W 좀 더 쉬지 않으면, 너는 내일 학교에 갈 수 있을 만큼 충분히 회복되지 못할 거야.

M 엄마, 저는 꽃에 물을 줄 정도로 충분히 건강해요.

W David, 나중에 그것을 할 수 있어.

M 알겠어요, 엄마.

만점 솔루션 아픈 아들이 침대에 누워 있는 것이 지루하다며 정원의 꽃들에 물을 주고 있자 엄마가 내일 학교에 가려면 좀 더 휴식을 취해야 한다고 말하고 있는 상황이다.

07 ③

M Is everything all right? Do you need anything?

W Yes, actually, could we <u>have some water</u>, please?

M Sure, would you like it cold or warm?

W Cold would be great. Thank you. And we'd like to <u>order another dish</u>. Could you bring us the menu again?

M Of course, I'll be right back with your water and the menu.

W Thanks, oh, and this salad is delicious. What dressing is this?

M In fact, it's our chef's secret dressing, so I can't tell you. But I'm glad you like it.

M 다 괜찮으신가요? 필요한 게 있으신가요?

W 네, 물 좀 가져다 주시겠어요?

M 물론이죠, 차가운 것과 따뜻한 것 중 무엇이 좋으시나요?

W 차가운 물이 좋겠네요. 감사합니다. 그리고 다른 음식을 주문하고 싶어요. 메뉴를 다시 가져다 주시겠어요?

M 물론이죠, 물과 메뉴를 바로 갖다 드리겠습니다.

W 감사합니다. 아, 그리고 이 샐러드 맛있네요. 드레싱이 뭔가요?

M 사실, 저의 주방장의 비밀 드레싱이라고 말할 수 없습니다. 하지만 좋아하시니 기쁘네요.

08 ②

W How do you want to rearrange your office?

M Let's move the desk closer to the window.

W And your file cabinet?

M That should go by the door.

W Do you want the sofa by the file cabinet?

M Sure, and the table in the middle of the room.

W Won't it be crowded?

M Maybe. Let's put it against the wall.

W 네 사무실을 어떻게 재배치하고 싶니?

M 책상을 창문에 더 가깝게 옮기자.

W 그리고 네 서류함은?

M 그건 문 옆으로 가야 해.

W 소파가 서류함 옆에 있었으면 해?

M 물론이지, 그리고 탁자는 방 가운데 있었으면 해.

W 너무 복잡하지 않을까?

M 그럴지도. 그건 벽에 붙여서 놓자.

만점 솔루션 남자는 책상을 창문에 더 가깝게 옮기고 싶어 한다.

09 ⑤

[Telephone rings.]

W Hello, Global Tour. This is Yuna Lee.

M Hello, this is Chris Baker.

W Hello, Chris Baker. How can I help you?

M Well, I'm calling about the advertisement in yesterday's newspaper.

W Do you mean the ad for a bus driver?

M Yes. That's right.

W I'm sorry. The position has already been filled.

M I see. Thank you anyway.

[전화벨이 울린다.]

W 안녕하세요, Global 관광입니다. 저는 이유나입니다.

M 안녕하세요, 저는 Chris Baker입니다.

W 안녕하세요, Chris Baker 씨. 무엇을 도와드릴까요?

M 저, 어제 신문에 난 광고에 대해서 전화드리고 있습니다.

W 버스 기사를 찾는 광고 말씀이세요?

M 예. 그렇습니다.

W 미안합니다. 그 자리는 이미 충원되었습니다.

M 알겠습니다. 어쨌든 고맙습니다.

만점 솔루션 여자의 말 Do you mean the ad for a bus driver?에서 남자가 전화를 건 목적을 알 수 있다.

10 ④

W Kevin, are you going to stay home this afternoon?

M I'm not sure. I need to work on the science project with Sungho.

W Then, why not invite him here? I'm leaving right now, so you can work in silence.

M That sounds good. Can we have some food if we get hungry?

W Oh, there's not much food now. Actually, I ordered some groceries, and they'll be delivered soon. Can you make sure you get them?

M Sure, what time is the delivery guy supposed to come?

W 케빈, 오늘 오후에 집에 있을 거야?

M 잘 모르겠어. 성호랑 과학 프로젝트를 해야 해.

W 그럼, 성호를 여기로 초대하는 거 어때? 나 지금 나갈 거라 조용히 작업할 수 있을 거야.

M 좋은 생각이야. 배고프면 음식을 먹어도 돼?

W 아, 지금 음식이 충분히 없는데. 사실, 식료품을 주문해서 곧 배달될 거야. 그것 좀 확실하게 받아줄래?

M 물론, 배달원이 언제 오기로 되어 있어?

11 ② | ➕ ②

M Is supper ready? I'm hungry.

W Almost ready. Could you set the table?

M Okay. What are we having?

W We'll have salad to start and the steak.

M I'll have my steak well-done, please. By the way, don't we have soup tonight?

W I didn't prepare any, but we have some juice to drink and some ice cream for dessert.

M That sounds fine. Thanks.

M 저녁 준비되었어요? 배가 고파요.

W 거의 준비되었어요. 식탁 좀 차려 줄래요?

M 알았어요. 오늘 우리는 무엇을 먹나요?

W 샐러드로 시작해서 스테이크를 먹을 거예요.

M 스테이크는 완전히 익혀 줘요. 그런데, 오늘 밤에 수프는 없나요?

W 하나도 준비하지 않았는데, 하지만 마실 약간의 주스와 후식으로 아이스크림이 약간 있어요.

M 그거면 좋아요. 고마워요.

12 ⑤

W Hi, Adam, how are you? I heard you were sick a couple of days ago.

M I'm feeling better now, thanks.

W Did you have a cold?

M I don't know, but probably. I had a bad headache and felt very weak.

W Didn't you go to see a doctor?

M No, I just rested at home. I drank a lot of orange juice and slept a lot.

W Well, I'm glad you're better. But maybe you should go to the doctor and get checked out.

W 안녕. 아담. 잘 지냈어? 이틀 전에 아팠다고 들었어.

M 지금 괜찮아졌어. 고마워.

W 감기였어?

M 모르겠지만, 아마도. 두통이 진짜 심했고 힘이 없었어.

W 병원에 안 갔어?

M 그냥 집에서 쉬었어. 오렌지 주스를 많이 마시고 많이 잤어.

W 네가 나아졌다니 다행이야. 하지만 병원에 가서 검사를 받아보는 게 좋겠어.

13 ④

W May I help you?

M Yes, I'd like a cheese sandwich. How much is it?

W It's two dollars and fifty cents. Do you want anything to drink with that?

M Yes, I'll have a glass of orange juice.

W It's one dollar.

M Here you are.

W Thank you. Your food will be ready in a moment.

M Thank you.

W 도와드릴까요?

M 예, 치즈 샌드위치 한 개 주세요. 얼마죠?

W 2달러 50센트입니다. 그것과 함께 마실 것을 원하세요?

M 예, 오렌지 주스 한 잔 주세요.

W 1달러입니다.

M 여기 있습니다.

W 감사합니다. 음식은 곧 준비될 거예요.

M 감사합니다.

만점 솔루션 남자는 치즈 샌드위치($2.50)와 오렌지 주스($1.00)를 주문했으므로, 총 3.5달러를 지불해야 한다.

14 ① | ➕ ⑤

M Sorry I'm late. How is it going?

W Sit down. I saved a seat for you. You've missed a really exciting part.

M Really? What's the score now?

W Three to nothing.

M Who has three?

W The Korean team. They hit a three-run home run in the bottom of the third inning.

M Oh, that's too bad I missed it.

W Look out! The ball is flying towards us!

M 늦어서 미안해. 어떻게 진행되고 있니?

W 앉아. 너를 위해 자리를 잡아 두었어. 넌 정말로 흥미진진한 부분을 놓쳤어.

M 정말? 지금 점수가 어떤데?

W 3대 0이야.

M 누가 3점이니?

W 한국 팀. 한국 팀이 3회 말에 3점 홈런을 쳤어.

M 오, 그것을 놓쳐서 정말 유감이다.

W 조심해! 공이 우리 쪽으로 날아오고 있어!

15 ③

W Hurry up. The store's closing soon.

M Don't worry. I saw the sign telling closing times.

W But they usually close the store at eight.

M Right. But today they are going to close at nine.

W Are you sure?

M Of course. Before I came here I saw the sign clearly.

W Then, we have an hour more.

M So, take it easy.

W 서둘러. 곧 가게가 문을 닫아.

M 걱정 마. 내가 폐점 시간을 알리는 표지판을 봤어.

W 하지만 보통은 8시에 가게 문을 닫잖아.

M 맞아. 그런데 오늘은 9시에 문을 닫을 거야.

W 확실해?

M 물론이야. 내가 이곳에 오기 전에 분명히 그 표지판을 봤어.

W 그럼, 1시간이 더 있어.

M 그래, 천천히 해.

16 ④

W Hello, everyone. Today we have a new member, Bill Smith, in our PET club. He is an animal doctor from Canada. He is very interested in helping lost and deserted dogs so he is joining our club. He has three children, a daughter and two sons. Let's welcome our new member, Bill Smith. Thank you.

W 안녕하세요, 여러분. 오늘 우리 PET 동아리에 Bill Smith라는 새로운 회원이 옵니다. 그는 캐나다 출신의 수의사입니다. 그는 잃어버리고 버려진 개들을 돕는 데 매우 관심이 있어서 우리 동아리에 가입하려고 합니다. 그에게는 딸 한 명과 아들 두 명의 세 명의 자녀가 있습니다. 우리의 새 회원 Bill Smith 씨를 환영합시다. 감사합니다.

17 ③

W ① The purpose of the concert is to help poor children.

② The concert will be on October 12th.

③ The concert will last for three hours.

④ The concert will be held in the school gym.

⑤ They will give a free T-shirt to every student who pays for the concert.

W ① 음악회의 목적은 가난한 아이들을 돕는 것이다.
② 음악회는 10월 12일에 열릴 것이다.
③ 음악회는 3시간 동안 계속될 것이다.
④ 음악회는 학교 체육관에서 열릴 것이다.
⑤ 음악회 비용을 지불한 모든 학생들에게 무료로 티셔츠를 줄 것이다.

만점 솔루션 음악회는 5시부터 7시까지 2시간 동안 계속될 것이므로 ③이 일치하지 않는다.

18 ②

M Hurry up, Sally! You're on the stage in 20 minutes.
W Where is my dress? I'm sure I hung it here.
M Maybe it's in the other room. Some kids were looking at it this afternoon.
W Oh, here it is. Look! It's very dirty.
M You're right. It has a lot of spots on it.
W How could this happen? I won't forgive those kids.

M 서둘러, Sally! 20분 후에 무대 위에 올라가야 해.
W 내 드레스가 어디에 있지? 내가 분명히 이곳에 걸어두었는데.
M 아마 다른 방에 있을지도 몰라. 오늘 오후에 몇몇 아이들이 그것을 보고 있었어.
W 오, 여기 있네. 봐! 그것은 너무 더러워.
M 네 말이 맞아. 드레스에 얼룩이 많이 있어.
W 어떻게 이런 일이 일어날 수 있지? 그 아이들을 용서하지 않을 거야.

만점 솔루션 20분 후에 무대에 올라야 하는 여자는 드레스가 아이들에 의해 더러워진 것을 발견하고 화가 난 상황이다.

19 ②

M Did you hear that Ron is in the hospital?
W Oh, really? What's the matter with him?
M He's very ill. Probably he's got swine flu.
W Swine flu! How did he get that?
M He's just come back from Mexico. It is certain that he got it while he was there.
W _____

M Ron이 병원에 있다는 말을 들었니?
W 오, 정말? 그에게 무슨 문제가 있니?
M 그는 매우 아파. 아마도 돼지 독감에 걸렸나 봐.
W 돼지 독감! 그는 어떻게 하다 그게 걸렸데?
M 그는 멕시코에서 방금 돌아왔어. 분명히 그가 그곳에 있는 동안 걸렸을 거야.
W 정말 너무 안됐다.

① 너는 곧 좋아질 거야.
③ 나는 집에 가 봐야 해.
④ 오, 너는 정말 친절하구나.
⑤ 모든 일이 잘되기를 바라.

20 ①

M Did you take this picture?
W Yes, on my last vacation.
M It's good. Do you take a lot of pictures?
W Sometimes. Just for fun at special occasions and things.
M You mean birthdays and graduations?
W Yeah, it's something to do on the side.
M Did you take photography classes?
W Actually, when I was at university, photography was my minor.
M Wow, I didn't know that. Why didn't you become a professional photographer?
W _____

M 이 사진을 네가 찍었어?
W 응, 지난 번 휴가 때.
M 좋은데. 너는 사진을 많이 찍니?
W 가끔. 특별한 행사나 일이 있을 때 그냥 재미로 찍어.
M 생일이나 졸업식 같은 것을 말하는 거야?
W 그래, 부업으로 하는 일이야.
M 넌 사진 수업을 들었니?
W 사실. 난 대학에 다닐 때. 사진이 내 부전공이었어.
M 와, 그건 몰랐네. 그런데 왜 전문 사진작가가 되지 않았니?
W 난 내 지금 일이 더 좋아.

② 불행히도, 난 수업을 들어야 해.
③ 난 네가 직업을 바꾼 것을 몰랐어.
④ 그들은 보통 고용하는 데 돈이 많이 들어.
⑤ 난 특별한 행사에서 종종 사진을 찍어.

01 ⑤	**02** ⑤	**03** ②	**04** ⑤	**05** ③
06 ②	**07** ④	**08** ⑤	**09** ⑤, ✚②	**10** ⑤
11 ①	**12** ①	**13** ⑤	**14** ⑤	**15** ②, ✚③
16 ⑤	**17** ①	**18** ③	**19** ①	**20** ⑤

01 ⑤

W Good morning. This is the KBC weather forecast. It will be sunny tomorrow for all parts of Korea. It will be cloudy on Saturday morning and it will begin to rain Saturday afternoon for most parts of the nation. A storm will come in from the South Sea. You can see clear skies again on Sunday. The weather on Sunday will be perfect for outdoor activities all day long.

W 안녕하세요. KBC 일기 예보입니다. 한국 전 지역은 내일 맑을 것입니다. 토요일 아침에는 흐릴 것이고 토요일 오후에는 국내 대부분의 지역에서 비가 오기 시작할 것입니다. 폭풍이 남해에서 올 것입니다. 일요일에는 다시 맑은 하늘을 볼 수 있습니다. 일요일 날씨는 하루 종일 야외 활동에 적합할 것입니다.

02 ⑤

W Who am I supposed to meet at the airport?
M Jim Thacker. He's a guest speaker.
W What does he look like?
M He's quite tall and has dark hair and a mustache.
W Will he be wearing a suit?
M No, he said he'll wear jeans and a vest.
W And where should I wait for him?
M Outside Gate 7B.
W All right. Tell him I'll pick him up.

W 내가 공항에서 만나야 할 사람이 누구죠?
M Jim Thacker에요. 그는 초청 연설자에요.
W 그는 어떻게 생겼나요?
M 꽤 키가 크고, 짙은색 머리와 콧수염이 있어요.
W 정장을 입고 있을까요?
M 아니요, 청바지와 조끼를 입을 거라고 말했어요.
W 그리고 내가 그를 어디서 기다려야 해요?
M 7B 출구 밖에서요.
W 알겠어요. 그에게 제가 모시러 간다고 말해 주세요.

만점 솔루션 Jim Thacker는 꽤 키가 크고, 짙은색 머리에 콧수염이 있으며, 청바지와 조끼를 입고 있을 것이라고 했다.

03 ②

W Thank you for inviting me.

M Don't mention it. I'm glad you can visit my home.
W You have a very nice home.
W Thanks. We have lived here for a long time.
W When will everyone else arrive?
M They'll arrive in a few minutes. Would you like a drink?
W Yes, please. I'd like a glass of orange juice.
M OK, hold on. Make yourself at home.

W 저를 초대해 주셔서 감사합니다.
M 별 말씀을요. 당신이 우리 집을 방문해 주셔서 기뻐요.
W 당신은 아주 멋진 집을 가졌네요.
M 고맙습니다. 우리는 오랫동안 여기서 살아왔어요.
W 다른 모든 사람들은 언제 도착하죠?
M 몇 분 후면 도착할 거예요. 마실 것 좀 드실래요?
W 예, 오렌지 주스 한 잔 주세요.
M 알겠습니다. 잠시만 기다리세요. 편하게 계세요.

04 ⑤

W Did you bring anything to sell at the bazaar today?
M Yes, I brought some cookies.
W Really? Did you make them yourself?
M No, my mom did. But I decorated them.
W They look better than my pictures.
M You put them in frames. You made them in art class, didn't you?
W Yes, but I only have two that are good enough to sell.

W 오늘 바자회에서 팔 것을 가져왔어?
M 응, 쿠키를 조금 가져왔어.
W 정말? 그것들을 네가 직접 만든 거야?
M 아니, 우리 엄마가 만드셨어. 하지만 내가 그것들을 장식했어.
W 내 그림보다 더 좋아 보인다.
M 그림들을 액자에 넣었네. 네가 그것들을 미술 시간에 만든 거지, 그렇지 않니?
W 응, 하지만 팔 수 있을 정도로 좋은 건 2개 밖에 없어.

만점 솔루션 남자는 엄마가 만드신 쿠키에 장식만 했다고 했다.

05 ③

W Good evening, ladies and gentlemen! Thank you for shopping at K-mart. Our store will close in thirty minutes. Shopping hours are from 11 a.m. to 9 p.m. on weekdays, and from 11 a.m. to 6 p.m. on weekends. I hope you will visit again at 11 a.m. tomorrow morning. Thank you. Good-bye.

W 안녕하세요, 신사, 숙녀 여러분! K-마트에 쇼핑 오신 것을 환영합니다. 우리 가게는 30분 후면 문을 닫을 것입니다. 쇼핑 시간은 주중에는 오전 11시에서 오후 9시이고, 주말에는 오전 11시에서 오후 6시입니다. 내일 아침 11시에 다시 방문해 주시기 바랍니다. 감사합니다. 안녕히 가세요.

06 ②

W What are you going to do this weekend, Alex?
M Well, my friend is going to have a party. I will go there.
W Sounds great!
M How about you? Can you come with me?
W Thank you, but I can't.
M Why not? Do you have any plans?
W Nothing special. The reason is I'm not invited to the party.

W Alex, 이번 주말에 무엇을 할 거니?
M 글쎄, 내 친구가 파티를 열 예정인데, 거기 갈까 해.
W 좋겠다!
M 너는 어떠니? 나와 같이 갈 수 있어?
W 고맙지만, 갈 수 없어.
M 왜 안 되는데? 무슨 계획이 있니?
W 특별한 건 없어. 내가 그 파티에 초대받지 않았기 때문이야.

07 ④

M Excuse me, is it okay if I take some pictures?
W Yes, but you can't take any pictures in the special exhibition room.
M The special exhibition room? Where is it?
W It's in the right wing of the building. Currently, the exhibition "Realistic Paintings of Our Time" is on display there.
M I see, thank you.
W Oh, and one more thing. Please don't use your flash because it can disturb other visitors.
M Okay, no problem.

M 실례합니다, 사진을 찍어도 되나요?
W 네, 하지만 특별 전시실에서는 어떤 사진도 찍을 수 없습니다.
M 특별 전시실이요? 어디에 있나요?
W 건물의 오른쪽에 있습니다. 지금 그곳에선 "우리 시간의 현실주의 그림"이 전시 중입니다.
M 알겠습니다, 감사해요.
W 아, 그리고 한가지 더요. 다른 방문객들에게 방해가 될 수 있으니 플래시는 터트리지 마세요.
M 네, 걱정 마세요.

08 ⑤

M I wonder if you can go out to see a movie tonight.
W Probably not. I don't have time for a movie.
M You have to do your homework or something?
W Actually not. I've done already.
M Then, how about going for dinner instead?
W Sorry, I really can't. My parents are calling me at home.
M We could go to the nice restaurant after the phone call.
W The problem is, I'm not sure when they'll call me.
M I see. You have to wait for a while then.

M 네가 오늘 밤에 영화 보러 나갈 수 있을지 궁금해.
W 아마도 안 될 거야. 난 영화 볼 시간이 없어.
M 숙제라도 해야 하는 거야?
W 사실 아냐. 이미 했어.
M 그럼, 대신에 저녁 먹으러 가는 건 어때?
W 미안, 정말 안 돼. 부모님께서 내게 집으로 전화하실 거야.
M 우린 전화를 받은 후에 멋진 식당에 갈 수 있어.
W 문제는, 언제 그분들이 내게 전화하실지 확실하지 않다는 거야.
M 알았어. 그럼 넌 한동안 기다려야 하겠구나.

> **만점 솔루션** 남자가 영화를 보거나 저녁 식사를 하자고 제안하지만 여자는 부모님의 전화를 받아야 해서 나갈 수 없다고 말하고 있다.

09 ⑤ | ➕ ②

M Where have you been? You're late.
W I'm sorry. I couldn't leave work on time.
M Were you working on something?
W Kind of. We had a meeting, which lasted forever.
M Why didn't you call?
W My phone battery went dead. It's my mistake. I should have charged it in advance.
M That's all right. The dinner is on you.

M 어디 있었어? 늦었잖아.
W 미안해. 제 때 직장에서 나올 수가 없었어.
M 일하고 있는 것이 있었어?
W 비슷해. 회의가 있었는데, 시간이 연장이 되었어.
M 왜 전화를 안 했니?
W 내 전화기 배터리가 나갔어. 내 실수야. 미리 그것을 충전했어야 했는데.
M 괜찮아. 저녁 식사는 네가 내.

> **만점 솔루션** 여자는 미리 전화기를 충전하지 않은 것을 후회하고 있다. 「should have p.p.」는 과거에 하지 않은 일에 대한 후회를 나타내는 표현이다.

10 ⑤

M Don't touch me. My arm is killing me.
W Is there anything wrong with your arm?
M Yeah, I have muscle pain in my arm and shoulder.
W What did you do?
M I played baseball yesterday. I pitched a long game.
W You are a pitcher? Oh, I didn't know that.
M I threw the baseball too many times.
W Be careful. If you throw the ball too much, you'll hurt yourself.

M 만지지 마. 팔이 아파 죽겠어.
W 팔에 무슨 문제가 있니?
M 응, 팔과 어깨에 근육통이 있어.
W 무슨 일을 했는데?
M 어제 야구를 했는데 경기 내내 던졌어.
W 너 투수니? 오, 몰랐는걸.
M 나는 야구공을 너무 많이 던졌어.
W 조심해. 너무 많이 공을 던지면, 다칠 거야.

11 ①

M What did you do during this summer vacation?

W My family went to the beach.

M Were there a lot of people at the beach?

W No, we found a quiet beach. We <u>played beach volleyball</u> and <u>swam in the sea.</u>

M What else did you do?

W We <u>visited a beautiful temple</u> and <u>a small art museum</u> on the way home. How about you?

M I just stayed home and watched TV.

M 너는 이번 여름 방학 동안 뭐 했니?

W 우리 가족은 해변에 갔었어.

M 해변에는 사람이 많았니?

W 아니, 우리는 조용한 해변을 발견했어. 우리는 비치발리볼을 했고 바다에서 수영을 했어.

M 그 밖에 또 뭐 했니?

W 우리는 집으로 오는 길에 아름다운 사원과 작은 미술관을 방문했어. 너는 어땠어?

M 나는 그냥 집에서 TV를 봤어.

12 ①

[Telephone rings.]

W Hello, Yunjin Electronics. May I help you?

M Hello. I <u>bought a LCD monitor</u> there yesterday.

W Yes, is this Mr. Harrison?

M Yes, speaking.

W What's wrong with it?

M When I opened the package, I found the LCD panel <u>broken.</u> Can you <u>exchange it</u>?

W I'm sorry it was broken. I'll send a new one right now. Please <u>send the broken one</u> back to us.

M That's great. Thank you.

[전화벨이 울린다.]

W 여보세요. 윤진 전자입니다. 무엇을 도와드릴까요?

M 여보세요. 저는 어제 거기에서 LCD 모니터를 샀는데요.

W 예, Harrison 씨입니까?

M 예, 그렇습니다.

W 무슨 문제죠?

M 제가 포장을 열었을 때, LCD 판이 깨진 것을 발견했어요. 그것을 교환해 주실 수 있나요?

W 그것이 깨져서 미안합니다. 바로 지금 새것으로 보내드리겠습니다. 깨진 것을 저희에게 다시 보내 주세요.

M 좋습니다. 감사합니다.

13 ⑤

M I'm glad we have a long holiday.

W Me too. <u>I'm looking forward to</u> seeing my family.

M Are you going to your hometown?

W Yes, my parents still live there. How about you?

M I'm going to stay in Seoul. I live with my parents.

W <u>I can't wait for</u> this holiday to begin.

M But next year's Chusok is on Sunday. That means next year's Chusok holiday <u>will be shorter.</u>

W Oh, that sounds sad. I won't be able to go to my hometown next year.

M 긴 휴가를 갖게 되어 기뻐.

W 나도 그래. 나는 가족들을 보는 것이 기대가 돼.

M 너는 고향에 갈 거니?

W 응, 부모님들이 아직도 거기에 계셔. 너는 어떠니?

M 나는 서울에 머물 예정이야. 나는 부모님과 함께 살거든.

W 나는 이 휴가가 시작되는 것을 기다릴 수 없어.

M 하지만 내년 추석은 일요일이야. 그 말은 내년 추석 명절은 더 짧아질 거라는 거지.

W 오, 그건 슬프다. 내년에는 고향에 갈 수 없겠네.

14 ⑤

W ① The store sells electronic devices like TVs and computers.

② The store has <u>the cheapest prices.</u>

③ The store closes at 8 p.m. on Fridays.

④ The store opens at 10 a.m. on Saturdays.

⑤ The store <u>closes at 6 p.m.</u> on Sundays.

W ① 그 가게는 TV와 컴퓨터 같은 전자기기를 판다.

② 그 가게는 가장 싼 가격으로 판다.

③ 그 가게는 금요일에 오후 8시에 문을 닫는다.

④ 그 가게는 토요일에 오전 10시에 문을 연다.

⑤ 그 가게는 일요일에 오후 6시에 문을 닫는다.

만점 솔루션 가게는 일요일에는 문을 열지 않으므로, ⑤가 일치하지 않는다.

15 ② | ➕ ③

W What time does the plane take off?

M It <u>takes off at 3:20.</u>

W Really? We've been here for an hour! Do we have to <u>wait another hour</u>?

M I'm really sorry. <u>The flight is delayed an hour</u> because of the rain.

W This is terrible. I'm going to be late for tonight's meeting.

M I'm very sorry, ma'am.

W That's all right. There is no other way.

W 비행기는 몇 시에 이륙합니까?

M 3시 20분에 이륙합니다.

W 정말입니까? 우리는 여기서 한 시간을 기다려 왔습니다! 한 시간을 더 기다려야 한다는 말입니까?

M 정말로 죄송합니다. 비 때문에 항공편이 한 시간 지연되었습니다.

W 심각하군요. 오늘 밤 모임에 늦을 것 같은데요.

M 정말 죄송합니다. 손님.

W 괜찮습니다. 다른 방법이 없군요.

비행기는 3시 20분에 이륙할 예정인데, 앞으로 한 시간을 더 기다려야 한다고 했으므로, 현재 시각은 2시 20분이 된다.

16 ⑤

M I'm getting tired. Can we have a little break?

W Sure. I was actually getting hungry. Why don't we <u>have a bite</u> to eat?

M Great idea. The food court is just around the corner.

W That's convenient. What do you feel like?

M I'll have a hamburger and French fries. What about you?

W I'm not sure. Could you go get us a table? I want to <u>take a quick look around</u> the different restaurants first.

M Sounds like a plan.

M 피곤하다. 잠깐 쉬었다 할 수 없을까?

W 물론. 사실 배가 고파졌어. 뭐 먹을래?

M 좋은 생각이야. 푸드코트는 모퉁이를 돌면 돼.

W 편리하네. 뭐 먹고 싶어?

M 햄버거랑 감자튀김. 너는?

W 잘 모르겠어. 가서 자리 좀 잡아줄래? 우선 다른 식당을 빨리 둘러보고 싶어.

M 좋은 계획이네.

17 ①

W Congratulations, Dan. You did a wonderful job.

M It's all thanks to you, Ms. Tailor. Even entering this speech competition was all your idea. If it weren't for you, I never would have joined.

W Not at all. You always <u>do well in</u> my <u>class</u>.

M Thank you, but I still have a long way to go.

W Don't be so humble, Dan. You're allowed to feel proud today. <u>I can't wait to</u> share this good news with our school.

M Neither can I.

W 축하한다, 댄. 정말 훌륭한 일을 했어.

M 테일러 선생님 덕분입니다. 이 웅변 대회에 나가는 것도 선생님 생각이었어요. 선생님이 없었다면 전 참가조차 못했을 거예요.

W 아니야. 넌 언제나 학교생활을 잘 했어.

M 감사합니다. 하지만 아직 갈 길이 멀어요.

W 너무 겸손하지 말렴, 댄. 오늘은 자부심을 느껴도 된단다. 이 좋은 소식을 학교에 빨리 전하고 싶구나.

M 저도요.

18 ③

① W Can I talk to the manager, please?

　 M He is not in today. Can I help you with anything?

② W I think I've <u>lost my cellphone</u>. I can't find it in my bag.

　 M Do you want me to call your number?

③ W Okay, I found these. Is one of them yours?

　 M Yes, the blue jacket is mine. My ID card is in the pocket.

④ W I bought this new jacket. What do you think of it?

　 M It's really cool. Where did you buy it?

⑤ W Can you <u>leave your name</u> and contact information?

　 M Yes, sure. Please let me know if you find it.

① W 매니저와 이야기할 수 있을까요?

　 M 오늘 자리에 없습니다. 제가 도와드릴 수 있을까요?

② W 핸드폰을 잃어버린 거 같아. 가방 안에서 찾을 수가 없어.

　 M 네 번호로 전화해 볼까?

③ W 네, 이것들을 찾았습니다. 이 중에 당신 것이 있나요?

　 M 네, 파란 재킷이 제 거예요. 주머니에 제 신분증이 들어있어요.

④ W 이 새 재킷을 샀어. 어떻게 생각해?

　 M 진짜 멋지다. 어디서 샀어?

⑤ W 이름과 연락처를 남겨주시겠어요?

　 M 네, 물론입니다. 찾으면 알려주세요.

19 ①

W Did you put gas in the car yesterday?

M I'm sorry, I forgot.

W What? You said you would put gas. Hmm.... Then let's stop for gas before we go to dinner.

M It's fine. There's <u>enough in the tank</u>.

W I don't want to take a risk.

M OK. If we hurry up and leave now, we will have time to stop and get some gas.

W I wish you <u>had filled it up</u> yesterday like you said you would.

M _____

W 어제 차에 기름을 넣었어?

M 미안, 잊어버렸어.

W 뭐라고? 어제 넣겠다고 말했잖아. 흠…. 그럼 저녁 먹으러 가기 전에 들러서 기름을 넣자.

M 괜찮아. 기름은 통에 충분히 있어.

W 난 위험을 감수하고 싶지 않아.

M 알겠어. 서둘러서 지금 떠나면, 들러서 기름을 좀 넣을 시간이 있을 거야.

W 네가 말했던 대로 어제 기름을 가득 채워 두었으면 좋았잖아.

M <u>미안해. 다음 번에는 기억할게.</u>

② 좋아, 네가 충분할 거라고 생각한다면.

③ 좋은 생각이야. 내일 해도 돼.

④ 고마워. 네가 그것을 해 줘서 고마워.

⑤ 괜찮아. 모든 사람이 실수를 해.

20 ⑤

W Tom, you'd better go to bed early.

M I have a big test tomorrow, Mom. I have to <u>do well on the</u>

test tomorrow.

W I'm sure you'll <u>get good results</u> this time.

M I hope so, Mom.

W Do you want something to drink?

M Could I have some coffee?

W Coffee is not good for you. I'll <u>get you orange juice</u>.

M _____

W Tom, 너는 일찍 자는 것이 좋겠다.

M 저는 내일 중요한 시험이 있어요, 엄마. 저는 내일 시험을 잘 봐야 해요.

W 이번에는 네가 좋은 결과를 얻을 거라 확신해.

M 그러기를 바라요, 엄마.

W 너 뭐 마시고 싶니?

M 커피 좀 갖다 주실래요?

W 커피는 너에게 좋지 않아. 오렌지 주스를 갖다주마.

M <u>오, 엄마! 저는 잠을 깨기 위해 커피가 좀 필요해요.</u>

① 새 상품인 것 같아요.

② 나중에 그것에 관해 알려 드릴게요.

③ 엄마! 엄마는 제가 무엇을 하기를 바라세요?

④ 오, 제가 할 수 있는 선택이 너무 많이 있어요.

---

01 ③	02 ③	03 ④	04 ②, ➊②	05 ②
06 ③	07 ④	08 ⑤	09 ④	10 ①
11 ④, ➊①	12 ②	13 ⑤	14 ⑤	15 ③
16 ②	17 ③	18 ④	19 ③	20 ④

01 ③

M Excuse me. Can you tell me <u>where the pharmacy is</u>?

W Go straight two blocks, and turn right. It's <u>on your right</u>.

M Is there any big building near there?

W Yes, there is a department store <u>across the street</u> from it.

M What's the name of it?

W It's Hankuk Department Store.

M Thank you very much.

M 실례합니다. 이 근처 약국이 어디 있어요?

W 두 블록을 죽 가셔서 오른쪽으로 도세요. 그러면 오른편에 있습니다.

M 그 근처에 큰 건물이 있나요?

W 예, 그곳 맞은편에 백화점이 있습니다.

M 그 백화점 이름이 뭐죠?

W 한국 백화점입니다.

M 대단히 감사합니다.

02 ③

M I'm looking for a birthday present for my three-year-old son.

W We have many nice toys. How about a train, a plane or a car?

M I bought all of those for him last year.

W <u>Maybe a tricycle</u>, then?

M I guess he might be too young for that.

W No, a three-year-old boy can <u>easily ride one</u>. It's really fun.

M Okay. My son will love it. <u>I'll take it</u>.

M 3살짜리 아들을 위한 생일 선물을 찾고 있어요.

W 저희에게는 좋은 장난감들이 많이 있어요. 기차, 비행기, 자동차는 어때요?

M 그것들은 모두 작년에 그 애에게 사줬어요.

W 그럼 세발자전거는요?

M 그것을 하기에는 그 애가 너무 어린 것 같아요.

W 아니에요, 3살짜리 사내아이라면 쉽게 탈 수 있어요. 정말로 재미있고요.

M 좋아요. 제 아들이 그걸 좋아할 거예요. 그걸로 살게요.

03 ④

W There are some rules you have to follow at school, Steve.

M What are they, Mrs. Kim?

W First of all, you should not be late for class.

M Okay. I won't be late for class again.

W Next, you can't chew gum, and you're not allowed to run in the halls.

M Okay. I promise to follow those rules.

W Finally, you must raise your hand to ask me a question in class.

M I will, Mrs. Kim.

W Steve, 학교에서는 지켜야 할 몇 가지 규칙들이 있어.

M 그게 뭐예요, 김 선생님?

W 먼저, 수업 시간에 지각하지 말아야 해.

M 알겠습니다. 다시는 수업 시간에 지각하지 않을 게요.

W 다음으로, 껌을 씹을 수 없고 복도에서 뛰는 것이 허용되지 않아.

M 알겠습니다. 그러한 규칙들을 따를 것을 약속할 게요.

W 마지막으로, 수업 시간에 질문을 하려면 손을 들어야 해.

M 그럴게요. 김 선생님.

① 수업 시간에 지각하지 마라.
② 껌을 씹지 마라.
③ 복도에서 뛰지 마라.
④ 도서관의 책들을 잘 돌봐라.
⑤ 수업 시간에 질문을 하려면 손을 들어라.

04 ② | ➕ ②

M Wow, Christmas is coming!

W Yeah. I can't wait for Christmas holidays. I'm going to Phuket in Thailand.

M What made you choose that place? Was it because Phuket is good for tanning? Or, are prices low?

W Do you want to know? The most attractive thing about it is the distance from here.

M How long does it take to get there by plane?

W It takes only three hours. Imagine! In three hours, I can be on an emerald beach.

M 와, 크리스마스가 다가오고 있어!

W 그래. 나는 크리스마스 휴가를 기다릴 수가 없어. 나는 태국에 있는 푸켓에 갈 예정이야.

M 어떻게 해서 그곳을 선택하게 됐는데? 푸켓이 일광욕을 하기에 좋아서 그랬니? 아니면 가격이 싸서?

W 알고 싶니? 그것에 대해 가장 매력적인 것은 여기서부터의 거리야.

M 비행기로 거기에 가는 데 얼마나 걸리는데?

W 3시간밖에 안 걸려. 상상해봐! 3시간 후에 내가 에메랄드 색 해변에 있다고.

05 ②

W This is the first time I've lived on campus, but I enjoy campus life. I can make more friends here and discuss with them the problems in my studies. So, I enjoy living here. Here it's more convenient for me to use the library,

the sports center, and all the other facilities.

W 제가 캠퍼스에서 생활하는 것은 이번이 처음이지만, 저는 캠퍼스 생활이 즐겁습니다. 저는 여기에서 더 많은 친구들을 사귈 수 있고, 저의 공부에 대한 문제에 대해 그들과 토론할 수도 있습니다. 그래서 저는 이곳에서의 생활이 즐겁습니다. 여기에서는 제가 도서관, 스포츠 센터, 그리고 다른 모든 시설들을 이용하는 것이 좀 더 편리합니다.

06 ③

M Here's an ad. Let's take a look at it.

W Let's see.... It's a nice job.

M It is. You finished college three years ago, right?

W Yes, and I've worked in several companies since then.

M What's the most important for you in finding jobs? Money?

W No. I'm tired of part-time work. I really want a full-time job.

M Then, this is a good job for you.

M 여기 광고가 있어. 그걸 한 번 보자.

W 어디 보자…. 좋은 일자리인데.

M 그러게. 너는 3년 전에 대학을 마쳤지, 그렇지?

W 응, 그리고 그 이후로 여러 회사에서 일을 했어.

M 일자리를 찾는 데 있어서 너에게 가장 중요한 게 뭐니? 돈이니?

W 아니. 나는 시간제 일에 질렸어. 나는 정말로 전임제 일자리를 원해.

M 그럼, 이게 너한테 좋은 일자리야.

07 ④

M I'm looking for a book, but I can't find it.

W What's the title of the book?

M I'm sorry I forgot it. It is about President Lincoln's religious life.

W Oh, I know what you are looking for.

M Do you have a copy here?

W No, go downstairs, you can find one.

M Thanks a lot, ma'am.

M 책을 찾고 있는데요 찾을 수가 없어요.

W 책 제목이 뭐니?

M 죄송하지만, 잊었어요. 링컨 대통령의 종교생활에 관한 것이에요.

W 아, 무슨 책인지 알겠네.

M 여기에 책이 있나요?

W 여기에는 없고 아랫층으로 내려가면 찾을 수 있어.

M 감사합니다. 선생님.

만점 솔루션 할 일을 고르는 문제는 대화의 맨 마지막 부분에 정답의 실마리가 있다.

08 ⑤

① **M** What time does the concert begin?

　W It begins at eight. We still have some time.

② **M** The concert was really good, wasn't it?

W　I don't know. I thought it was a little boring.

③ M　Can I get two tickets for the 7 o'clock show?

W　Sure, that will be $40.

④ M　These are great seats. Thank you.

W　You're welcome. I got them as soon as the ticket sales opened.

⑤ M　Excuse me, but I think you're in my seat.

W　Oh, really? I'm so sorry. Isn't this 10D?

① M　콘서트 언제 시작해?

W　8시에 시작해. 아직 시간이 있어.

② M　콘서트 진짜 좋았어, 그치?

W　모르겠어. 난 조금 지루했어.

③ M　7시 쇼 표 두 장 구할 수 있을까요?

W　물론이죠, 40달러입니다.

④ M　진짜 좋은 자리다. 고마워.

W　천만에. 표 판매가 시작 되자마자 구했어.

⑤ M　실례합니다만 제 자리에 앉으신 거 같은데요.

W　아, 정말요? 죄송합니다. 10D가 아닌가요?

09 ④

M　Are you free this Friday night?

W　Sure, I am. What date is it?

M　It's May 27th.

W　Oh, it's Susan's birthday!

M　It is. Come to Pirate Ship Restaurant at 7 : 30 in the evening.

W　OK. I'll be there.

M　Here's the invitation card. See you then.

M　이번 주 금요일 밤에 시간 있니?

W　응, 괜찮아. 그날이 몇 일이지?

M　5월 27일이야.

W　아, Susan의 생일이구나!

M　그래. 그날 저녁 7시 30분에 해적선 식당으로 와.

W　알았어. 갈게

M　여기 초청장이 있어. 그럼 그때 보자.

만점 솔루션　숫자나 시각에 유의해서 듣는다.

10 ①

M　Today has been a long day.

W　Are you tired?

M　Yes. I have to do the same thing every day.

W　I understand you, but....

M　Look at those people. They seem to be tired of the same thing every day, too.

W　Hey, David. Look on the bright side of life.

M　I don't know. I'm not interested in this work any more.

M　오늘은 긴 하루였어.

W　피곤하니?

M　응. 매일 똑같은 일을 해야 하잖아.

W　이해해, 하지만….

M　저 사람들을 봐. 그들도 매일 똑같은 일에 싫증난 것처럼 보여.

W　이봐, David. 인생의 밝은 면을 봐.

M　모르겠어. 나는 더 이상 이 일에 흥미가 없어.

11 ④ | ❶ ①

M　Ms. Lee, I want to become a doctor. What should I do?

W　It is not easy to become a doctor. It takes many years.

M　Tell me about it in detail.

W　You need to major in biology or chemistry when you go to university. It takes four years, followed by four years of medical school and four years of medical practice.

M　It takes too long. I don't think I will be able to do it.

W　Haven't you heard of the saying, "No pain, no gain?"

M　I know, ma'am, but I'd rather become a pharmacist.

M　이 선생님, 저는 의사가 되고 싶은데요. 어떻게 해야 하죠?

W　의사가 되는 것은 쉽지 않단다. 오랜 세월이 걸리지.

M　구체적으로 말씀해 주세요.

W　우선 대학에 들어가서 생물학이나 화학을 전공하는 것이 좋다. 물론 4년이란 세월이 걸리지. 그리고 의학대학원 4년이 이어지고 4년 동안 의학실습을 받아야 한단다.

M　너무 긴 세월이에요. 그렇게 하는 게 가능할 것 같지 않아요.

W　이런 말 못 들었니? "노력하지 않고서는 얻는 것이 없다."

M　알아요, 선생님. 그런데 차라리 약사가 되는 게 낫겠어요.

만점 솔루션　남자가 마지막 부분에서 자기의 생각을 바꾼 것에 유의한다.

12 ②

[Telephone rings.]

W　Good morning. This is Julia Miller speaking. How can I help you?

M　I've been trying to call my house, but I can't get through.

W　You can't get through?

M　Yes. The phone line is dead. I've tried it at least ten times already.

W　What's your home phone number, sir?

M　It's 765-3876.

W　Hold on, please. *[pause]* It seems like we're having problems in your area. Our engineers are fixing it now. It'll be fixed soon.

M　Thank you.

[전화벨이 울린다.]

W　안녕하세요. Julia Miller입니다. 무엇을 도와드릴까요?

M　제가 저희 집에 전화를 걸려고 시도하는데, 연결이 안 되네요.

W　연결이 안 된다고요?

M　네. 전화가 불통이에요. 벌써 적어도 열 번은 시도했거든요.

W　손님, 집 전화번호가 어떻게 되나요?

M　765-3876이에요.

W 잠시만요. *[잠시 후]* 당신의 지역에 문제가 있는 것 같아요. 저희 기사들
이 지금 수리 중이거든요. 곧 수리될 겁니다.

M 고마워요.

13 ⑤

[Telephone rings.]

W Micro Electronics. May I help you?

M I haven't received my order yet. It's been already five days!

W We're really sorry. There must be a mistake. Can you tell me your name and address?

M My name is Bill Smith, 614 Maple Street, Pittsburgh, Pennsylvania.

W The address you told us was 410 Presley.

M Oh, I'm sorry, I made a mistake. It is my old address.

W Don't worry. I will send another item to your new address.

M Thank you.

[전화벨이 울린다.]

W 마이크로 전자입니다. 도와드릴까요?

M 제가 주문한 것을 아직 받지 못했어요. 벌써 5일이나 됐다구요.

W 죄송합니다. 착오가 있는 것 같아요. 이름과 주소가 어떻게 되죠?

M 제 이름은 Bill Smith이고, 펜실베이나 주 피츠버그 메이플 가 614번지
입니다.

W 당신이 신청하셨던 주소는 프레슬리 410번지입니다.

M 아, 죄송합니다. 제가 실수했군요. 그것은 제 옛날 주소예요.

W 염려 마세요. 새 주소로 물품을 보내드리겠습니다.

M 감사합니다.

14 ⑤

W Hi, Tom! Welcome home! How was your trip?

M It was fantastic, mom!

W How did you get to Mt. Halla?

M After I arrived at the airport, I took a taxi to the bus terminal. Then I took a bus and arrived at the mountain.

W Then you walked?

M Yes. I walked to the top of the mountain.

W No bike?

M No, no bike. I just walked, mom.

W 안녕, Tom! 집에 잘 왔다! 여행은 어땠니?

M 환상적이었어요, 엄마!

W 한라산에는 어떻게 갔는데?

M 공항에 도착한 후, 버스 터미널까지 택시를 탔어요. 그 다음에 버스를
타고 산에 도착했어요.

W 그 다음에는 걸었니?

M 네. 산 정상까지 걸었어요.

W 자전거는 안 타고?

M 네, 자전거는 타지 않았어요. 그냥 걸었어요, 엄마.

15 ③

W Can I help you?

M Yes. I want to book a table on Friday evening.

W This coming Friday?

M Yes. Friday 7 p.m. Is that possible?

W Sure. How many people are in your party?

M Eight.

W Okay, party of eight, this Friday at 7 p.m. Anything else?

M Some of them will arrive here at around 6:30. Is it okay?

W Oh, that's no problem.

W 도와드릴까요?

M 네. 금요일 저녁에 자리를 예약하고 싶은데요.

W 다가오는 금요일에요?

M 네. 금요일 저녁 7시예요. 가능할까요?

W 물론이죠. 일행은 몇 분이나 되시나요?

M 8명이요.

W 알겠습니다. 일행은 8명이고, 이번 금요일 저녁 7시요. 또 다른 것 있으
세요?

M 그들 중 몇 명은 6시 30분쯤에 여기에 도착할 거예요. 괜찮겠죠?

W 아, 괜찮습니다.

16 ②

M Hello, Mrs. Miller. What seems to be the problem?

W When I went to bed yesterday, I had chest pain and dizzy spells.

M Did you have dinner yesterday?

W Yes, I ate raw fish. After that, I felt sick in my stomach and my heart began to hurt.

M I think you have an upset stomach. Stomachache can go with a chest pain. I'll prescribe the medicine.

W Thank you, sir.

M 안녕하세요. Miller 여사님. 어디가 아프시죠?

W 어젯밤 잠을 자는데 가슴이 아프고 머리가 어지럽더라고요.

M 어제 저녁 식사는 드셨어요?

W 예, 회를 먹었어요. 그 후로 속이 메스껍고 제 심장이 아프기 시작했어
요.

M 제가 볼 때는 체하신 것 같아요. 위통은 가슴 통증과 같이 올 수 있어요.
약을 처방해 드릴게요.

W 감사합니다. 선생님

만점 솔루션 pain, stomach, prescribe the medicine 등의 표현에서 장
소를 파악할 수 있다.

17 ③

W Excuse me. We are going to city hall, right?

M No, I'm afraid not. This goes in the Marine Aquarium direction.

W Oh, I have to get off then. I'm sorry, but could you tell me which number I should take?

M You should take 970 or 971. I think 970 takes the quicker route.

W And can I take it from the stop when I can get off?

M No, you should cross to the other side. City hall is in the opposite direction.

W I see. Thank you very much!

W 실례합니다. 시청으로 가고 있는 거 맞나요?

M 아닙니다. 이건 해양 수족관 방향으로 가고 있습니다.

W 아, 그럼 내려야겠군요. 죄송합니다만 몇 번을 타야 하나요?

M 970번이나 971번을 타야 합니다. 970번이 더 빨리 갈 겁니다.

W 제가 내리는 역에서 그 버스를 탈 수 있나요?

M 아니요, 반대 쪽으로 건너가야 합니다. 시청은 반대 방향에 있어요.

W 알겠습니다, 감사합니다!

18 ④

W Andy, what are you doing? Are you looking for something?

M Yes, I need some things to sell at the school flea market.

W What kind of things do you need?

M Anything still useful, like books, clothes, bags, sneakers...

W Oh, what about your white sneakers? They're almost new, but you can't wear them because they're too small now.

M That's a good idea! But can you wash them, please? There's a little stain on one of them.

W Sure, when do you need them by?

W 앤디, 뭐라고 있어? 무언가 찾고 있어?

M 응, 학교 벼룩시장에서 팔 물건이 필요해.

W 어떤 종류의 물건이 필요해?

M 아무거나 아직 쓸 수 있는 거, 책, 옷, 가방, 운동화...

W 아, 네 하얀 운동화 어때? 거의 새 거잖아.

M 좋은 생각이야! 그런데 빨아줄 수 있어? 한 쪽에 작은 자국이 있어.

W 물론, 신발이 언제 필요해?

19 ③

M Can I exchange this shirt, please?

W What's wrong with it? Is there something wrong with it?

M No, but I think it's too large for me. Do you have something smaller?

W Of course, but do you have the receipt?

M Yes, here it is.

W Okay. This one is a smaller size. Why don't you try it on?

M _____

M 이 셔츠를 교환할 수 있을까요?

W 뭐가 문제인가요? 뭐 잘못된 게 있나요?

M 아니요, 하지만 제게 너무 큰 것 같아요. 좀 더 작은 것으로 있나요?

W 물론이지요, 하지만 영수증은 있으세요?

M 네, 여기 있어요.

W 좋아요. 이게 좀 더 작은 거예요. 입어 보시는 게 어때요?

M 알겠어요, 탈의실이 어디죠?

① 뭘 사려고 하는데요?

② 이름이 어떻게 되세요?

④ 케이크 좀 가져오시겠어요?

⑤ 예약을 하고 싶으세요?

만점 솔루션 입어 보는 게 어떻겠느냐는 여자의 마지막 말에 대한 남자의 알맞은 응답으로는 ③ '알겠어요, 탈의실이 어디죠?'가 가장 적절하다.

20 ④

M How was everything, ma'am?

W The sandwich and pasta were good, but the soup was a bit salty.

M Oh, I'm sorry about that. Do you want me to bring you your bill?

W Yes, please. [pause]

M Here you are.

W Let's see.... This can't be our bill. I'm sure you made a mistake.

M _____

M 모든 게 어땠는지요, 손님?

W 샌드위치와 파스타는 좋았는데, 수프는 약간 짰어요.

M 아, 그 점에 대해서는 죄송합니다. 계산서를 가져다 드릴까요?

W 네, 그렇게 해 주세요. [잠시 후]

M 여기 있습니다.

W 어디 봅시다…. 이것은 저희 계산서일 리가 없어요. 분명히 실수하셨어요.

M 그렇다면 죄송합니다. 확인해 볼게요.

① 물론이죠. 찬 음료가 있습니다.

② 네. 저는 스테이크로 하겠어요.

③ 아니오. 생선은 신선한 맛이 나지 않네요.

⑤ 네. 뭔가 다른 걸 시도해 보고 싶네요.

만점 솔루션 식사를 하고 나서 계산서가 잘못된 것을 말하는 여자에게 종업원인 남자가 할 수 있는 응답으로는 ④ '그렇다면 죄송합니다. 확인해 볼게요.'가 알맞다.

01 ⑤	02 ③	03 ⑤, ➕①	04 ③, ➕⑤	05 ⑤
06 ②	07 ④	08 ③	09 ②	10 ①
11 ①	12 ⑤	13 ⑤	14 ④	15 ①
16 ⑤	17 ③	18 ②	19 ①	20 ④

01 ⑤

M Jenny, how about making a cushion for mom as a birthday present?

W Sounds great. What kind of cushion do you have in mind?

M I'd like a square one with a heart in the middle of it.

W Well, how about a heart-shaped one with the words, "Love Mom" on it?

M Great! That would be better than the square one.

W Okay. Let's make it.

M Jenny, 엄마를 위한 생일 선물로 방석을 만드는 게 어때?

W 좋은 생각이야. 어떤 종류의 방석을 생각하고 있는데?

M 가운데에 하트 모양이 들어간 네모난 것을 원해.

W 글쎄, "Love Mom"이라는 글자가 들어간 하트 모양의 것은 어때?

M 멋져! 그것이 네모난 것보다 더 좋을 거야.

W 좋았어. 그것을 만들자.

02 ③

W Would you fasten your seatbelt?

M No, I don't want to.

W Well, put it on please.

M Why do I have to? You never drive fast.

W I know I don't drive fast, but it's much safer with your seatbelt on.

M Okay, I'll put it on.

W I hate this road. It's a very dangerous road. There are a lot of curves.

M I believe you drive very safely.

W 안전벨트를 착용하시겠어요?

M 아니오, 하고 싶지 않습니다.

W 글쎄요, 착용해 주세요.

M 제가 왜 해야 하나요? 당신은 절대 빨리 운전하지 않는데요.

W 제가 운전을 빨리 하지 않는 것은 알지만, 안전벨트를 착용하는 것이 훨씬 더 안전해요.

M 알겠어요, 착용하겠습니다.

W 저는 이 도로가 싫어요. 너무 위험한 도로예요. 커브 길이 많아요.

M 저는 당신이 매우 안전하게 운전한다는 것을 믿습니다.

03 ⑤ | ➕①

M Did you see the Champions league semi-final?

W Sure, I did. In fact, I supported Barcelona, but the result disappointed me a lot.

M As for me, I can't tell how excited I was to see that match. It was fantastic.

W Frankly speaking, Munich players were more energetic and powerful than those of Barcelona.

M I couldn't agree more.

M 너 챔피언스 리그 준결승 경기 봤니?

W 물론 봤지. 나는 바르셀로나 팀을 응원했는데, 실망이었어.

M 내 경우엔 그 경기를 보고 얼마나 흥분했는지 몰라. 환상적이었어.

W 솔직히 뮌헨 선수들이 바르셀로나 선수들보다 훨씬 활력 있고 힘이 있다고 생각해.

M 네 말에 전적으로 동의해.

만점 솔루션 남자와 여자의 심정이 다르다는 점에 유의한다.

04 ③ | ➕⑤

W What are you reading, Allan?

M A sports magazine.

W You like sports?

M Sure. Almost every man likes sports.

W What are your favorite sports?

M Basketball, soccer, and baseball, I'd say.

W Are you good at them?

M I'm pretty good at basketball. As for soccer and baseball, I just like watching games. How about you?

W Well! I don't like rough sports, so I like to go bowling.

W 무엇을 읽고 있니, Allan?

M 스포츠 잡지.

W 너는 운동을 좋아하니?

M 물론이지. 거의 모든 남자가 운동을 좋아해.

W 어떤 운동들을 좋아하니?

M 농구, 축구, 그리고 야구라고 말하고 싶어.

W 그것들을 잘하니?

M 농구는 아주 잘해. 축구와 야구에 대해서는 경기를 보는 것을 좋아할 뿐이야. 너는 어때?

W 글쎄! 나는 거친 운동은 좋아하지 않아서 볼링하러 가는 것을 좋아해.

만점 솔루션 'I'm pretty good at basketball.'에서 남자가 잘하는 운동이 농구임을 알 수 있다. 축구와 야구는 경기를 보는 것만 좋아한다고 했고, 볼링은 여자가 좋아하는 운동이다.

05 ⑤

M Now, Miss Baker. Look at the shoes on the table.

W Yes, they're the same shoes the man was wearing.

M And the bag?

W Yes, I saw him carrying it when he was coming out of the bank.

M And do you remember anything else?
W Hmm... Ah! He was wearing a white hat.
M Thank you for your help.
W I hope you can catch the man as soon as possible.

M 이제, Baker 양. 탁자 위에 있는 구두를 보세요.
W 예, 그 남자가 신고 있었던 것과 같은 구두예요.
M 그리고 가방은요?
W 예, 그가 은행 밖으로 나오고 있을 때 가지고 있는 것을 보았어요.
M 그리고 그밖의 다른 것을 기억하세요?
W 음… 아! 그 사람은 흰 모자를 쓰고 있었어요.
M 도움을 주셔서 고마워요.
W 가능한 한 빨리 그 남자를 잡을 수 있기를 바랍니다.

06 ②

M Is this your first time here?
W Yes. I'm a freshman. I'm looking for books about computers.
M Come over here, please.
W May I borrow this book?
M Yes, you may. Please fill out this card.
W I beg your pardon?
M Write your name and student ID number on this card.

M 이곳에 처음이세요?
W 네. 저는 신입생이에요. 컴퓨터에 관한 책을 찾고 있어요.
M 이쪽으로 오세요.
W 이 책을 빌릴 수 있나요?
M 네, 빌릴 수 있어요. 이 카드를 작성해 주세요.
W 다시 한 번 말씀해 주시겠어요?
M 이 카드에 이름과 학생증 번호를 쓰세요.

07 ④

① W How did you get here? Did you take the train?
  M No, I came here by plane. It's a lot faster.
② W I'll send you something nice for your birthday.
  M Really? Thank you. That's so nice of you.
③ W How much is it for two people to go to Seoul?
  M It is 50,000 won, but if you buy the tickets online, it's cheaper.
④ W How would you like to send this package to Canada?
  M How much would it cost by air?
⑤ W I have a package to deliver to you. Are you home now?
  M Yes, I am. What time are you coming?

① W 여기 어떻게 왔어? 기차 탔어?
  M 아니, 비행기 타고 왔어. 훨씬 빨라.
② W 네 생일이라 멋진 무언가를 보낼 거야.
  M 진짜? 고마워. 정말 친절하다.
③ W 서울행 두 사람이면 얼마야?
  M 5만원인데, 온라인으로 표를 사면 더 싸.

④ W 캐나다에 이 소포를 어떻게 보내실 건가요?
  M 항공으로 보내는 건 얼마인가요?
⑤ W 당신에게 배달할 소포가 하나 있습니다. 지금 집인가요?
  M 네. 몇 시에 오시나요?

08 ③

W Look at the crowd. Do you think we'll still be able to get tickets?
M Come on! We're already here. Besides, I want to see this movie.
W All right! When does the movie start?
M Five-thirty.
W Five-thirty? There's only twenty minutes left. But look at the long line and it's moving so slowly.
M Let's see the next movie.
W Sorry, but I have to be home before nine.

W 저 사람들 좀 봐. 너는 아직도 우리가 표를 구할 수 있을 거라고 생각하니?
M 진정해! 우리는 이미 이곳에 왔어. 게다가, 나는 이 영화를 보고 싶어.
W 좋아! 영화가 언제 시작하지?
M 5시 30분에.
W 5시 30분이라고? 겨우 20분밖에 안 남았어. 그런데 저 긴 줄을 봐. 너무 천천히 움직이고 있어.
M 다음 영화를 보자.
W 미안하지만, 나는 9시 전에는 집에 들어가야 해.

09 ②

M Do you live around here?
W No. Actually, I'm from Montreal, Canada.
M Were you born there?
W Well, I was born in Spain, but my family moved to Canada when I was eight.
M Can you speak Spanish?
W Sure, how about you? Are you American?
M No, I'm Australian, from Sydney.

M 너는 이 근처에 사니?
W 아니. 사실은, 나는 캐나다 몬트리올에서 왔어.
M 그곳에서 태어났니?
W 음, 스페인에서 태어났지만, 내가 여덟 살 때 가족이 캐나다로 이주했어.
M 너는 스페인 어를 말할 수 있니?
W 물론, 너는 어때? 너는 미국 사람이니?
M 아니, 나는 시드니 출신의 호주 사람이야.

만점 솔루션 여자는 캐나다에서 왔지만, 태어난 곳은 스페인이라고 하였다.

10 ①

W Welcome to JB Music Store. Today we have a special event for you. Win your chance of $1,000 worth of CDs here. If you just buy any two CDs, your name will go into competition. <u>Choose your own prize</u> from many different kinds of rock, pop, jazz, and classical music. Good luck to you. Thank you.

W JB 음악 상점에 오신 것을 환영합니다. 오늘 우리는 여러분을 위한 특별행사를 합니다. 이곳에 있는 1,000달러 상당의 CD들을 탈 기회를 잡으세요. 만약 어떤 CD라도 두 장을 사면, 여러분의 이름이 경쟁에 참여하게 됩니다. 많은 종류의 록, 팝, 재즈 그리고 클래식 음악에서 상품을 고르세요. 행운을 빕니다. 감사합니다.

11 ①

M What's wrong with you? You look upset.
W I'm upset with what you have said to me.
M What did I say?
W You belittled me.
M I don't know what you are talking about.
W Yesterday when you told me to email you the file, <u>I was so embarrassed</u> because I didn't know how to do that. Then, you said shouting on the phone, "You don't even know that?"
M I'm sorry I <u>hurt your feeling</u>. I won't do so next time.

M 무슨 일이니? 기분이 안 좋아 보이는 걸.
W 난 네가 한 말을 듣고 당황스러워.
M 내가 무슨 말을 했는데?
W 네가 나를 무시했잖아.
M 도대체 무슨 말을 하는지 모르겠네.
W 어제 네가 그 파일을 이메일로 보내달라고 말했을 때 나는 어떻게 그것을 해야 할지 몰라서 몹시 당황했었어. 그때 너는 전화에서 "너는 그것도 모르니?"라고 소리치며 말했잖아.
M 마음을 상하게 해서 미안해. 다음에는 그러지 않을게.

만점 솔루션 대화의 마지막 부분에서 여자가 화가 난 이유를 알 수 있다.

12 ⑤

[Someone knocks the door.]
M Hello. Does Mr. Raymond live here?
W Yes. He's my husband.
M I'm Jimmy Douglas at SMS Taxi Company. How do you do?
W How do you do? Is there a problem?
M Your husband <u>left his bag in my taxi</u> this morning.
W Oh, thank you! This is very nice of you.
M Don't mention it. This is only <u>one of my duties</u>.

[누군가 문을 두드린다.]
M 안녕하세요. Raymond 씨가 이곳에 사시나요?
W 예. 제 남편입니다.
M 저는 SMS 택시회사의 Jimmy Douglas입니다. 처음 뵙겠습니다.
W 처음 뵙겠습니다. 무슨 문제라도 있나요?
M 남편께서 오늘 아침 제 택시에 가방을 놓고 내리셨습니다.
W 아, 감사합니다! 정말 고맙습니다.
M 천만에요. 제 임무들 중 하나일 뿐인데요.

13 ⑤

M Hello, what problem do you have?
W For about six months, whenever I work on the computer, I've been feeling pain on the back.
M How long do you work on the computer every day?
W All day long. <u>I can't help</u> it because of my job.
M From now on, you have to exercise every day <u>according to the instruction</u> on the leaflet I will give you. See you at 9 next Wednesday.
W Sorry, I can't. How about Thursday afternoon?
M OK. I can make it by 4.
W Thank you. I'll see you then.

M 안녕하세요. 어디가 아프세요?
W 대략 6개월 동안 컴퓨터를 할 때마다 허리에 통증이 있어요.
M 하루에 얼마나 컴퓨터를 하는데요?
W 하루 종일 해요. 직업상 어쩔 수 없어요.
M 이제부터는 제가 드리는 안내서에 따라 매일 운동을 하셔야 합니다. 다음 주 수요일 9시에 봅시다.
W 죄송합니다만, 안 되겠는데요. 목요일 오후는 안 될까요?
M 좋아요. 4시는 괜찮네요.
W 감사합니다. 그때 뵐게요.

만점 솔루션 대화의 마지막 부분의 시각과 요일에 주의해서 듣도록 한다.

14 ④

M Who is that girl over there?
W Oh, that's Sarah. <u>Isn't she beautiful and tall</u>?
M Yes, she is. What does she do?
W She is <u>a nurse</u>. She works at the Grand Central Hospital in New York City.
M Um. She is young, isn't she?
W Yeah. She looks very young, but <u>she's 28 years old</u>. And she went to high school with me.

M 저기에 있는 저 여자는 누구니?
W 아, 저 여자는 Sarah야. 예쁘고 키가 크지 않니?
M 응. 그녀는 직업이 무엇이니?
W 간호사야. 그녀는 뉴욕시의 Grand Central 병원에서 근무해.
M 음. 그녀는 젊지, 그렇지 않니?
W 그래. 매우 젊어 보이는데, 28살이야. 그리고 그녀는 나와 함께 고등학교를 다녔어.

15 ①

M Oh, you bought a new laptop! It <u>looks sleek and light</u>.
W This is the latest model. Now, I can use the Internet <u>wherever they offer</u> free wireless Internet access, like coffee shops and libraries.
M Just so you know, you need to be careful when you use the Internet in free public Wifi areas. Hackers can easily <u>look into everything</u> such as your passwords, your bank

accounts.

W Really?

M Yes, I'm serious. It is not safe to use the Internet like here at the cafe. But I think it will be okay to check your mails, or surf the web.

W Thanks for your advice.

M 너 새로운 노트북을 샀네! 얇고 가벼워 보이는걸.

W 이거 최신 모델이야. 이제는 나도 커피숍이나 도서관 같은 무선 인터넷이 무료로 되는 곳이면 어디서든 인터넷에 접속해서 쓸 수 있어.

M 너도 알다시피 공공장소에서 무선 인터넷을 쓰는 것을 조심할 필요가 있어. 해커들이 너의 패스워드부터 은행 계좌까지 접근할 수 있다고.

W 정말?

M 응, 정말이야. 이런 카페에서 인터넷을 쓰는 것은 그다지 안전하지 않아. 공공장소에서는 그냥 간단하게 이메일을 확인하거나 웹서핑 같은 것만 사용하는 게 좋아.

W 알려줘서 고마워.

만점 솔루션 기술용어가 많이 나오지만 남자의 충고의 말을 집중해서 듣도록 한다.

16 ⑤

[Telephone rings.]

M Hello. May I speak to Mr. Parker?

W I'm afraid he isn't here right now. Can I take a message?

M Yes. This is Dean Martin from the BMB car repair shop.

W Dean Martin from the repair shop?

M Yes. I'm calling to tell him his car will be ready at five this afternoon. The charge is 130 dollars.

W Okay. I'll give him the message.

M Thanks.

[전화벨이 울린다.]

M 여보세요. Parker 씨를 바꿔주시겠습니까?

W 그는 지금 이곳에 없습니다. 메시지를 남기시겠어요?

M 예. 저는 BMB 자동차 수리점의 Dean Martin입니다.

W 자동차 수리점의 Dean Martin 씨요?

M 예. Parker 씨의 차가 오늘 오후 5시에 수리가 끝날 거라고 말하려고 전화드립니다. 수리비는 130달러입니다.

W 알겠습니다. 그에게 메시지를 전해 드리겠습니다.

M 감사합니다.

만점 솔루션 ⑤ 수리비는 130달러이다.

17 ③

[Telephone rings.]

W Napoli Bistro, how may I help you?

M Hi, my name is Nick, and I made a reservation for tonight.

W Hold on. Yes, here it is. Your reservation is for four people at seven, right?

M Yes, that's correct. But I'd like to make a change.

W What would you like to change?

M Can I add two more people? Is there a table for six?

W Let me check, please. *[pause]* Yes, luckily, there is one available.

M Awesome, thanks.

W Great, I'll see you at seven this evening then.

[전화벨이 울린다.]

W 나폴리 비스트로입니다. 무엇을 도와드릴까요?

M 안녕하세요. 제 이름은 닉이고 오늘 밤 예약 했습니다.

W 잠시만요. 네, 있네요. 일곱시에 4명 예약 맞나요?

M 네, 맞습니다. 하지만 변경을 하고 싶습니다.

W 어떻게 변경하길 원하시나요?

M 두 명을 추가할 수 있나요? 6명으로요.

W 확인해 보겠습니다. *[멈춤]* 네, 다행히, 가능한 자리가 있습니다.

M 잘됐네요, 감사합니다.

W 그럼 오늘 저녁 7시에 뵙도록 하겠습니다.

18 ②

W Hi, Mr. Jackson, can I ask you for some advice?

M Of course, what is it about?

W It's about my new project. You know, I'm researching the history of our town, but I can't get much information after the 1970s.

M Why don't you check out the library? They keep all the old newspapers there.

W That's a great idea. Why didn't I think of that?

M Maybe you depend too much on the Internet?

W That's true. Thank you. I think I'll go check right away.

W 안녕하세요, 잭슨 선생님, 조언을 구할 수 있을까요?

M 물론, 무엇에 관해서죠?

W 제 새로운 프로젝트에 관한 겁니다. 아시겠지만, 제가 우리 마을의 역사에 대해 연구하고 있습니다. 그런데 1970년대 이후 정보가 별로 없어요.

M 도서관에 가보는 거 어때요? 거기엔 옛날 신문들을 모두 보관하고 있잖아요.

W 좋은 생각이네요. 왜 그 생각을 못했지.

M 인터넷에 너무 많이 의존한 거 아닌가요?

W 맞아요. 감사합니다. 지금 바로 확인해봐야겠어요.

19 ①

W I haven't seen Clark in class for a few days.

M I heard he's sick in bed with the flu.

W Really? Should we drop in and see how he is?

M Okay. When do you want to go?

W How about today, after school?

M _____

W 며칠 동안 수업에서 Clark를 본 적이 없어.

M 나는 그가 독감으로 아파서 침대에 누워 있다고 들었어.

W 정말? 잠깐 들러서 그가 어떤지 볼래?

M 좋아. 언제 가기를 원하니?

W 오늘 어때, 방과 후에?

M 난 괜찮아.

② 늦어서 미안해.

③ 즐겁게 보낼 거야.

④ 너는 그것을 제시간에 끝낼 수 있어.

⑤ 오래 걸리지 않아.

만점 솔루션 독감으로 누워 있는 친구의 병문안을 가기로 하고 여자는 남자에게 시간을 제안하고 있다.

20 ④

M It's not so easy for me to work on the project together with Jane.

W Is that so?

M I don't know what she is so busy with. I can't even get to see her easily.

W But there's no other way. You guys might not get along, but you still have to work together to finish the project before the deadline.

W She isn't answering my phone, so that drives me crazy.

W Still, you need to calm down and ask her for help with smile.

M _____

M 나는 Jane하고 공동으로 작업하는 것이 쉽지 않아.

W 그러니?

M 그 애는 뭐가 그렇게 바쁜지 모르겠어. 쉽게 만나지도 못해.

W 하지만 어떻게 하겠어. 너희 남자 아이들도 서로 잘 지내지 않을 수 있고, 이 연구 과제를 기일 전에 끝내기 위해서 너희들은 서로 협력해야 해.

M 그녀가 내 전화를 받지 않으니 정말 돌아버리겠어.

W 우선, 진정하고 웃으면서 그녀에게 도움을 청해.

M 그게 말은 쉽지.

① 아마도 다음 번에

② 네 기분을 알아.

③ 친구 좋다는 게 뭐니?

⑤ 너에게 행운을 빌어줄게.

만점 솔루션 문장 전체의 흐름 속에서 답을 선택하도록 한다.

영어듣기능력평가 **13**회

01 ②	02 ②	03 ④	04 ⑤	05 ③, ➊①
06 ③	07 ②	08 ⑤	09 ⑤	10 ①
11 ②, ➊④	12 ②	13 ④	14 ⑤	15 ④
16 ①	17 ③	18 ③	19 ⑤	20 ⑤

01 ②

① **M** Do you see her?

　W Oh, yes.... She's sitting at the table at the back of the coffee shop.

② **M** We can't park here. Look at the sign.

　W No problem. I'll be back in a moment.

③ **M** Are there any coffee shops around here?

　W Oh, yeah, lots. There's one right over there.

④ **M** Can you show me how?

　W Sure. Look at me. You place your hands behind your back.

⑤ **M** You shouldn't move the table by yourself.

　W Maybe you're right. My back seems to hurt a little.

① **M** 그녀가 보이니?

　W 오, 보이네요…. 그녀는 커피숍 뒤쪽 테이블에 앉아 있어요.

② **M** 우리는 여기에 주차할 수 없어. 저 표지판을 봐.

　W 괜찮아. 금방 돌아올 거야.

③ **M** 여기 주위에 커피숍이 있어요?

　W 예, 많이 있어요. 저기 저쪽에 하나 있어요.

④ **M** 어떻게 하는 건지 보여 줄 수 있니?

　W 물론이지. 나를 봐. 손을 등 뒤로 놓아.

⑤ **M** 너는 혼자서 그 테이블을 옮겨서는 안 돼.

　W 네 말이 맞는 것 같아. 허리가 약간 아픈 것 같아.

02 ②

W I'd like to rearrange this room. Can you give me a hand?

M Sure. What can I do for you?

W OK. Put the sofa next to the door.

M Next to the door?

W Yes, please.

M And where do you want the desk?

W I'd like it in front of the window.

M Are you sure?

W Yeah. That looks good.

W 이 방을 재배치하고 싶어. 도와줄래?

M 물론이지. 어떻게 하지?

W 좋아. 소파를 문 옆에 놔줘.

M 문 옆이라고?

W 응, 그렇게 해줘.

M 그리고 책상은 어디에 놓길 원하니?

W 창문 앞에 놓고 싶어.

M 정말?

W 그래. 보기 좋다.

만점 솔루션 여자는 문 옆에 소파를, 창문 앞에 책상을 놓기를 원한다.

03 ④

M Wow! This is the largest indoor theme park in the world.

W Really? It would be terrific! I really enjoy riding a roller-coaster and balloons.

M In addition to the rides here, we can ice-skate in the center field.

W Why don't we go ice-skating first? After that, let's ride the most exciting thing—roller-coaster! OK?

M Sure. I don't mind either way.

M 와! 여기가 세계에서 가장 큰 실내 테마 공원이야.

W 정말? 정말 신나겠다! 나는 정말 롤러코스터랑 풍선을 타고 싶어.

M 여기서 놀이기구를 타는 것뿐만 아니라 광장 가운데에서 스케이트도 탈 수 있어.

W 먼저 스케이트를 타는 게 어때? 그 후에 가장 신나는 것, 롤러코스터를 타는 거야! 괜찮지?

M 그래. 난 아무래도 좋아.

만점 솔루션 대화 중 여러 가지 할 만한 것들이 언급되어 있으나 마지막 부분을 집중해서 듣는다.

04 ⑤

M Excuse me. I'm looking for a sweater.

W What size do you want?

M Medium.

W I don't think medium would fit you.

M Okay, give me large one.

W And what color do you want? We have white, black, and red.

M Black is good. How much is it?

W It's 9 dollars.

M Here's a ten-dollar bill.

W Here's your change. Thank you.

M 실례합니다. 스웨터를 찾고 있어요.

W 어느 사이즈를 원하세요?

M 중간 사이즈요.

W 중간 사이즈가 당신에게 맞지 않을 것 같은데요.

M 좋아요, 큰 사이즈로 주세요.

W 어느 색깔을 원하세요? 우리는 흰색, 검정색, 그리고 빨간색이 있어요.

M 검정색이 좋겠네요. 얼마죠?

W 9달러입니다.

M 여기 10달러가 있습니다.

W 잔돈 여기 있습니다. 감사합니다.

만점 솔루션 ⑤ 스웨터가 9달러인데 여자가 10달러를 계산했으므로 잔돈으로 1달러를 받아야 한다.

05 ③ | ➕ ①

W Excuse me, how long does it take to go from here to the National Museum?

M Oh, it's too far to walk. You'd better take a bus at this stop.

W OK. What number bus do I have to take?

M Take bus number 150. It will take 15 minutes.

W Is there a subway station near here?

M There's one two blocks away. That will take longer.

W I'm a stranger here in Korea. So using the subway is more convenient for me.

W 실례합니다만, 여기서 국립박물관까지 얼마나 걸리죠?

M 오, 걸어가기에는 너무 멀어요. 이 정류장에서 버스를 타는 것이 좋겠네요.

W 알겠습니다. 몇 번 버스를 타야 하죠?

M 150번 버스를 타세요. 15분 걸릴 거예요.

W 이 근처에 지하철역은 없나요?

M 2블록 떨어진 곳에 있습니다. 시간이 더 걸릴 거예요.

W 저는 한국이 처음이거든요. 그래서 지하철을 이용하는 것이 제게는 더 편합니다.

06 ③

W What seems to be the problem?

M I'm afraid we are about to run out of gas. We need to get some.

W We're in a remote village. We can't get gas around here. How much further can we go in the car?

M Around 25 kilometers. Look at the sign!

W Oh, we're lucky to find one in this remote place.

W 무슨 문제인 것 같니?

M 기름이 떨어질 것 같아. 기름을 좀 넣어야겠어.

W 우리는 외딴 마을에 있잖아. 이 근처에서는 기름을 얻을 수 없어. 우리는 차를 타고 얼마나 더 멀리 가야 하지?

M 25킬로 정도. 저 표지판을 봐!

W 오, 이 외딴 지역에 한 군데 있다니 다행이다.

07 ②

M Hi, do you need any help?

W No, thanks. *[pause]* Actually, it would be nice if you can help me.

M Sure, what are you looking for?

W I'm going to Thailand, and I want to buy a book to plan the trip.

M What about this one? This series is very popular nowadays.

W I already checked it, but I want something with more maps and detailed information.

M Oh, then, I think this one is perfect for you. The writer is known to be very thorough.

M 안녕하세요. 도와드릴까요?

W 아니요, 괜찮습니다. [멈춤] 사실, 도와주면 좋겠네요.

M 물론입니다. 무엇을 찾으세요?

W 태국에 가는데 여행 계획을 위한 책을 사고 싶어요.

M 이건 어때요? 이 시리즈가 요즘 아주 인기가 많아요.

W 이미 확인했는데 더 많은 지도와 자세한 정보가 있는 걸 원해요.

M 아, 그럼, 이게 딱 맞을 겁니다. 작가가 아주 꼼꼼해요.

08 ⑤

W Will you take a look at my car, please?

M What's the problem?

W Well, I'm not sure. But it's not running very well. It is making a lot of noises.

M I'll check the engine for you and find out what the trouble is.

W When will the work be finished?

M Let me see, the day after tomorrow.

W 제 차 좀 봐 주시겠어요?

M 무슨 문제가 있나요?

W 글쎄요, 잘 모르겠어요. 제 차가 잘 나가지 않아요. 소리가 많이 나요.

M 엔진을 점검해서 무엇이 문제인지 찾아 볼게요.

W 그 일이 언제 끝나죠?

M 잠깐만요, 모레가 되어야겠어요.

09 ⑤

M Hello, students! Our earth is getting more and more crowded, and many people aren't taking good care of it. If we keep going like this, it will be hard to protect our planet. Do you want to help? First, recycling is good, but there is a step you can do before that. See if you can use those things again first. Second, don't waste resources. When you aren't using water or electricity, turn them off. Please remember that little things can make a big difference.

M 안녕하세요, 학생 여러분! 우리 지구에 점점 사람이 많아지고 있고 많은 사람들이 지구를 소중히 여기지 않고 있습니다. 계속 이렇게 할 경우, 우리 지구를 보호하기 힘들어 질 것입니다. 돕고 싶습니까? 우선, 재활용도 좋지만 그 전에 여러분이 할 수 있는 것이 있습니다. 우선 그런 것들을 다시 쓸 수 있는지 봅시다. 두번째로, 자원을 낭비하지 맙시다. 물이나 전기를 사용하지 않을 때, 끄도록 합시다. 작은 것들이 큰 차이를 만들 수 있다는 것을 기억하세요.

10 ①

M How are you today?

W My whole body aches. Yesterday I played badminton. It was really fun.

M Why don't you join the badminton club I belong to? I bet lots of boys will happily help you out.

W Don't be kidding! I heard you get shoulder and back injuries playing badminton.

M It could happen. So you need to do enough warm-up beforehand.

W How could I relieve my sore muscles?

M You can just sit in the hot tub for a little while. That helps you feel better.

W That sounds good.

M 오늘 어떠니?

W 온 몸이 쑤셔. 어제 배드민턴을 했거든. 정말로 재미있었어.

M 내가 소속된 배드민턴 클럽에 가입하는 게 어때? 많은 남자들이 널 도와 주려고 서로 달려들 걸.

W 농담하지 마! 네가 배드민턴을 치다가 허리와 어깨에 부상을 당했다고 들었어.

M 그럴 수 있어. 그러니까 준비운동을 충분히 해야 해.

W 내 근육통을 어떻게 완화시킬 수 있니?

M 잠깐 동안 뜨거운 욕조에 앉아 있을 수 있어. 기분이 나아지는 데 도움이 될 거야.

W 좋은 생각이야.

만점 솔루션 마지막 남자의 말에서 통증완화를 위한 방법을 제시하고 있다.

11 ② | ➕ ④

W Hi, Dad. I'm home.

M Hi, Minyoung. Did you have a good day at school?

W Yes, it was a busy day. But I feel good because we won the volleyball game.

M That's great news. I know how hard you practiced. You must be very tired, though.

W Yes, and I'm very hungry. Is there anything to eat?

M Hmm, is a sandwich okay? I don't have time to cook, but I can quickly make you a sandwich.

W That's just what I want, thanks! I want to have dinner later, too!

W 안녕하세요, 아빠. 저 집에 왔어요.

M 안녕, 민영. 학교에서 좋은 시간 보냈니?

W 네, 바쁜 하루였어요. 하지만 배구 시합에서 이겼기 때문에 기분이 좋아요.

M 좋은 소식이구나. 네가 얼마나 열심히 연습했는지 알고 있다. 하지만 아주 지쳤겠구나.

W 네, 그리고 아주 배고파요. 뭐 먹을 거 있나요?

M 흠, 샌드위치 괜찮니? 요리할 시간이 없지만 샌드위치는 빨리 만들어 줄 수 있단다.

W 그게 제가 원하는 거예요. 고마워요! 나중에 저녁도 먹고 싶어요.

12 ②

W What's up, Tom?

M I know the report is due today. But I'd like to ask you if I can hand it in until tomorrow.

W Is there any problem with you?

M I'd like to have enough time to get a better report. So could you extend the due date?

W It wouldn't be fair if I gave you more time than other students. I suggest you finish up your assignment and hand it in today.

M I see. Thank you.

W 무슨 일이니, Tom?

M 보고서 제출 마감이 오늘이라는 걸 알아요. 하지만 내일 제출할 수 있을까 여쭤보려고요.

W 무슨 일이 있니?

M 충분한 시간을 갖고 더 좋은 보고서를 써보고 싶어서요. 마감 날짜를 연기해 주실 수 있나요?

W 내가 자네에게 다른 학생들보다 더 많은 시간을 주는 것은 불공평한 일이지. 과제를 끝내서 오늘까지 제출하라고 권하는 바이네.

M 알겠습니다. 감사합니다.

만점 솔루션 목적을 묻는 유형은 대부분 대화의 첫 부분을 주의해서 들으면 쉽게 해결할 수 있다.

13 ④

M What does Mr. Lee do, Susan?

W He works for the National Opera Company.

M Does he travel a lot?

W Yes. He does travel a lot for his work.

M What does he like to do when he's not working?

W He likes spending time with his friends. He loves cooking and he likes to make dinner for his friends. He often invites me to dinner.

M Does he live next door?

W Yes, he does. He sometimes visits my house with big gifts.

M Susan, 이 선생님은 무슨 일을 하시니?

W 그는 국립 오페라단에서 일해.

M 그는 여행을 많이 하겠네?

W 응. 그는 일로 정말 많은 곳을 여행하지.

M 그는 일하지 않을 때는 뭘 하는 것을 좋아하니?

W 그는 친구들과 함께 시간 보내는 것을 좋아해. 그는 요리를 좋아해서 친구들을 위해 저녁 식사를 요리하는 것을 좋아해. 그는 종종 나를 저녁 식사에 초대해.

M 그가 너의 옆집에 살지?

W 맞아. 그는 때때로 큰 선물을 가지고 우리 집을 찾아와.

14 ⑤

M Oh, you look like you've lost weight.

W I exercise as often as I can. And I don't eat anything at night.

M I often do exercise, but I like eating snacks at night. It's difficult to keep from eating them.

W What time do you go to bed?

M I go to bed very late. I do a lot of things late at night.

W You should go to bed early. That's the best way to lose weight.

M What do you think of taking diet medicine?

W Well, I'm against taking diet medicine. It is not good for your health.

M 오, 너 살이 좀 빠진 것 같다.

W 나는 할 수 있는 한 자주 운동을 해. 그리고 밤에 아무것도 먹지 않아.

M 나도 자주 운동을 해. 하지만 밤에 간식을 먹는 것을 좋아해. 간식을 끊는 것은 쉽지 않아.

W 너는 몇 시에 자는데?

M 나는 늦게 자. 밤 늦게 할 일이 많거든.

W 너는 일찍 잠자리에 들어야 해. 그것이 살을 빼는 가장 좋은 방법이야.

M 다이어트 약을 먹는 것은 어떻게 생각하니?

W 글쎄, 나는 다이어트 약을 먹는 것을 반대해. 그것은 건강에 안 좋거든.

만점 솔루션 여자의 마지막 말 'I'm against ~.'에서 남자의 의견에 반대하고 있음을 알 수 있다.

15 ④

M Do you collect stamps, Sarah?

W No, I collect postcards. I have many pen pals around the world. They send them to me.

M Wow! Amazing! How many pen pals do you have?

W Around 10.

M That's great! When do you usually write letters?

W I usually write on weekends. I write in English and French.

M Do you speak French, too?

W Yes, a little bit. I've been learning it for two years.

M Sarah, 너는 우표를 수집하니?

W 아니, 나는 우편엽서를 수집해. 나는 전 세계에 많은 펜팔 친구들이 있어. 그들이 나에게 그것들을 보내줘.

M 와! 놀라운 걸! 너는 펜팔 친구가 몇 명이 있니?

W 약 10명 정도.

M 근사한데! 너는 보통 언제 편지를 쓰니?

W 나는 주말마다 써. 나는 영어와 불어로 써.

M 너도 불어를 할 줄 알아?

W 응, 조금. 나는 2년간 불어를 배워왔어.

① Sarah는 약 10명의 펜팔 친구들이 있다.

② Sarah는 주말마다 편지를 쓴다.

③ Sarah는 영어와 불어로 편지를 쓴다.

④ Sarah는 프랑스에 갔다온 적이 있다.

⑤ Sarah는 2년 동안 불어를 배워왔다.

만점 솔루션 불어로 편지를 쓰고 불어를 배우고 있다는 내용은 언급되어 있지만 ④ '프랑스에 갔다온 적이 있다.'는 내용은 나와 있지 않다.

16 ①

M Have you heard the news?

W What news?

M The city is planning to build tall apartment buildings near the river.

W How awful! The river is beautiful now.

M I agree. If apartments are built, water pollution will get worse.

W How are the citizens feeling about it?

M Some of them are in favor of the city's plan, and others are against it.

W I don't understand those who are in favor of it.

M Neither do I.

M 너 그 소식 들었니?

W 무슨 소식?

M 시에서 강 근처에 고층 아파트 건물을 지을 계획이래.

W 심각하네! 강은 지금이 아름다운데.

M 나도 동감이야. 만약 아파트가 지어진다면 수질 오염은 더 악화될 거야.

W 시민들은 그것에 대해 어떻게 느끼는데?

M 그들 중 일부는 시의 계획에 찬성하지만 다른 사람들은 그것에 반대해.

W 나는 그것에 찬성하는 사람들을 이해할 수 없어.

M 나도 그래.

17 ③

W The movie starts at three. How about meeting around lunch time and having lunch before the movie?

M I don't think I can make it then. I have to go grocery shopping at lunch time with my mom.

W Anyway, you will have lunch, won't you?

M Right. I'm going to have lunch with my mom at a fast food restaurant. Can you make it at two?

W Sure. See you then. Let's meet at the subway station.

W 영화가 3시에 시작해. 점심시간 정도에 만나서 영화를 보기 전에 점심을 먹는 것이 어때?

M 나는 그때 시간을 낼 수 없을 것 같아. 나는 엄마와 점심 때 장을 보러 가야 하거든.

W 어쨌든, 너는 점심을 먹을 거지?

M 맞아. 나는 패스트 푸드점에서 엄마랑 점심을 먹을 거야. 2시에 만날 수 있을까?

W 물론. 그때 보자. 지하철역에서 만나자.

18 ③

W Hi, Jamie. Did you have a good weekend?

M Yes, I did. I'm a little tired, but that's OK.

W Why are you tired? There was no homework on the weekend. I thought you'd get some rest.

M I know, but my parents invited some neighbors over, and I helped them to prepare.

W What did you do?

M I cleaned the house with my dad, while my mom was cooking.

W What about your sister?

M Oh, she helped mom with the cooking and washed the dishes.

W 안녕, 제이미. 주말 잘 보냈니?

M 응. 조금 지쳤지만 괜찮아.

W 왜 지쳤어? 주말동안 숙제도 없었잖아. 네가 쉬었다고 생각했어.

M 알아, 하지만 부모님이 이웃을 초대해서 준비하는 걸 도왔어.

W 뭘 했어?

M 엄마가 요리하는 동안 아빠랑 집을 청소했어.

W 네 여동생은?

M 여동생은 엄마가 요리하는 걸 돕고 설거지를 했어.

19 ⑤

W I've decided to throw away this sofa.

M How long have you had it?

W I have had it for five years.

M That's not a long time. Why do you want to throw it away?

W Tom gave me a better sofa. Could you give me a hand? I'd like to move this outdoors.

M _____

W 나는 이 소파를 버리기로 했어.

M 너는 그것을 얼마 동안이나 사용했니?

W 5년간 사용했어.

M 긴 시간이 아니구나. 너는 왜 그것을 버리려고 하니?

W Tom이 나에게 더 좋은 소파를 주었어. 도와줄래? 나는 이것을 밖으로 옮기고 싶은데.

M 물론이지. 나는 혼자서도 그것을 들어올릴 만큼 힘이 세거든.

① 하나만 남았다고 생각해.

② 그것은 비쌀 것 같아.

③ 나는 네가 좋은 시간을 보내기를 바라.

④ 서둘러, 그렇지 않으면 늦을 거야.

만점 솔루션 여자는 Tom이 더 좋은 소파를 줘서 예전 것을 버리려고 남자에게 도움을 요청하고 있다. 이에 알맞은 응답으로는 부탁에 대한 승낙이나 거절의 말이 와야 한다.

20 ⑤

M It's raining again.

W Again? I hate this weather. It was sunny about half an hour ago. I can't stand this weather.

M Don't you have an umbrella?

W No, I don't. I'll have to get one at the grocery store.

M You have to keep an umbrella with you all the time in this type of weather.

W OK, I will. Oh, it's getting cold. I'm afraid I am catching a cold now.

M _____

M 다시 비가 오고 있어.

W 다시? 나는 이 날씨가 싫어. 30분 전에는 날씨가 맑았는데. 나는 이 날씨를 참을 수 없어.

M 너는 우산이 없니?

W 아니, 없어. 가게에서 하나 사야 할 것 같아.

M 너는 이런 날씨에는 항상 우산을 가지고 다녀야 해.

W 알았어, 그렇게. 오, 날씨가 점점 더 추워지네. 나는 지금 감기에 걸린 것 같아.

M 그러지 않길 바라. 조심해.

① 그냥 농담이야.

② 곧 거기에 갈게.

③ 나 역시 이곳이 처음이야.

④ 미안하지만, 같이 갈 수 없어.

만점 솔루션 감기에 걸린 것 같다는 여자의 말에 이어질 응답으로는 몸조심하라는 말이나 그러지 않기를 바란다는 말이 와야 적절하다.

영어듣기능력평가 **14**회

01 ②	02 ②	03 ③	04 ①	05 ④, ➊⑤
06 ③	07 ②	08 ④	09 ②	10 ⑤
11 ③	12 ①, ➊⑤	13 ③	14 ②	15 ⑤
16 ④	17 ③	18 ⑤	19 ④	20 ⑤

01 ②

W When you play this, you need a racket and a light ball. You can't play this alone. You need a partner. You and your partner play this game on a hard table, and it is divided by a net. The ball must bounce on your side only once. Then you hit it and return it to the other opposite side.

W 이것을 할 때는 라켓과 가벼운 공이 필요합니다. 이것은 혼자서 할 수 없습니다. 상대가 필요합니다. 당신과 당신의 상대는 딱딱한 탁자 위에서 이 경기를 하고, 그 탁자는 네트로 나뉘어져 있습니다. 공은 당신 쪽에서 한 번 튀겨져야 합니다. 그 다음에 당신은 그 공을 쳐서 맞은편으로 넘겨야 합니다.

02 ②

M I can't read books these days. My vision gets blurry.

W Oh, dad. It proves that you are getting older. You must be far-sighted. You need to go to the eyeglasses store.

M That's what I need to do.

W I know one of the stores. It's not far from our house.

M OK. Let's go there together.

M 요즈음 책을 읽을 수 없구나. 시야가 흐려 보여.

W 오, 아빠. 이제 아버지도 나이가 드시는군요. 분명히 원시일 거예요. 안경점에 가셔야겠어요.

M 그래야겠구나.

W 제가 한 군데 알아요. 우리집에서 가까워요.

M 그래. 함께 그곳에 가보자.

03 ③

① M Do you go to the movies very often?
　 W Yes. I go to the movies every weekend.

② M Could you give me a copy of this photo?
　 W Okay. Do you want it in the same size?

③ M Would you suggest some interesting places in this city?
　 W Sure. First of all, don't miss Seoul Tower.

④ M Did you buy this tour guide book?
　 W Yes, I bought it in ABC Bookstore yesterday.

⑤ M Would you please take a picture for me?
　 W Sure. Where would you like to stand?

① M 너는 영화를 아주 자주 보러 가니?

W 응. 나는 매주 영화를 보러 가.
② M 이 사진을 한 장 복사해 주시겠어요?
　 W 알았어요. 같은 크기로 원하시나요?
③ M 이 도시에서 흥미로운 장소 좀 추천해 주시겠어요?
　 W 물론이죠. 먼저 서울 타워는 놓치지 마세요.
④ M 이 여행안내 책자를 샀니?
　 W 응, 어제 ABC 서점에서 샀어.
⑤ M 제 사진을 좀 찍어 주시겠어요?
　 W 그러죠. 어디에 서시겠어요?

만점 솔루션 관광 안내소(TOURIST INFORMATION)에서 나눌 수 있는 대화로는 ③이 가장 적절하다.

04 ①

M Okay, let me see. Open your mouth, please.
W Sure. *[pause]* Do I have any cavities?
M I'm afraid so. There's one. You will have to get it treated.
W Is it bad? I didn't know, because it didn't hurt.
M No, it's not too bad, but we should take care of it as soon as possible.
W What about today? I have time.
M Today, you will just get your teeth cleaned. I'll take care of the cavity on your next visit.
W Oh, okay. I will make another appointment.

M 한번 봅시다. 입을 벌려주시겠어요?
W 네. *[멈춤]* 충치가 있나요?
M 그렇네요. 하나 있습니다. 치료해야 해야만 합니다.
W 그렇게 나쁜가요? 아프지 않아서 몰랐어요.
M 아뇨, 그렇게 나쁘지는 않지만 가능한한 빨리 치료해야 해서요.
W 오늘 어떤가요? 저는 시간이 됩니다.
M 오늘, 그냥 스케일링만 하겠습니다. 받으러 오셨으니 충치는 다음에 치료하겠습니다.
W 아, 알겠습니다. 예약을 해 놓겠습니다.

05 ④ | ✚ ⑤

M What's wrong? You look angry.
W Jessica really makes me angry in the office. She sometimes uses my Cellphone without my permission.
M Really? If I were you, I would tell her to stop.
W I've tried that, but she just keeps doing it.
M Why don't you talk to your boss about her?
W I'm not sure I have to do that.
M Maybe that's the only way to change her bad behavior.
W Okay. I'll do that right now.

M 뭐가 잘못됐니? 화가 나 보이는데.
W Jessica가 정말로 사무실에서 나를 화나게 만들어. 그녀는 가끔 내 허락도 없이 내 휴대 전화를 사용하거든.
M 정말? 내가 너라면 그녀에게 그만하라고 말하겠는데.

W 그렇게 했지, 그런데 계속해서 그러는 거야.
M 그녀에 대해서 사장님께 말씀드려 보는 건 어때?
W 내가 그렇게까지 해야 하는지 모르겠어.
M 아마도 그게 그녀의 나쁜 행동을 고칠 수 있는 유일한 방법일 거야.
W 알았어. 지금 바로 그렇게 할 게.

06 ③

W Could you please help me move this picture?
M Sure I can. Are you going to put it over your desk?
W I don't know. It would disturb my concentration on my study. I thought I'd hang it above the door.
M Who likes putting such a picture above the door? And the picture is too big.
W Then where do you think is the right place for it?
M I think it would be nice to put it over the desk. There is no other space for it.
W Ok. Let's do that.

W 이 그림 좀 옮기는 것을 도와줄 수 있겠니?
M 물론이지. 책상 위에 걸어 놓을 거니?
W 잘 모르겠어. 공부에 집중하는 것을 방해할 것 같아. 나는 문 위에 걸어 놓으려고 생각했는데.
M 세상에 그림을 문 위에 걸어 놓는 사람이 어디 있니? 그리고 그림이 너무 커.
W 그럼 어디가 적절한 장소라고 생각하니?
M 아무래도 책상 위에 걸어 놓는 것이 좋을 것 같다. 거기밖에 공간이 없잖아.
W 그래. 그렇게 하자.

만점 솔루션 대화의 마지막 부분에서 책상 위에 걸기로 한 것을 알 수 있다.

07 ②

W You've changed a lot. You look very slim.
M I've lost ten kilograms in the last three months.
W How did you lose that much weight? Did you eat only vegetables?
M No, but I had lots of them, especially beans. And I drank green tea whenever I felt hungry.
W Did you stop eating meat?
M No, but I ate only chicken, not pork.
W What about ice cream?
M I ate only a sugar-free ice cream. That's okay.

W 너 많이 변했다. 아주 날씬해 보이는데.
M 나는 지난 세 달 동안 10킬로그램을 뺐어.
W 그렇게 많은 체중을 어떻게 뺐니? 그저 야채만 먹었니?
M 아니, 하지만 그것들을 많이 먹었지, 특히 콩을. 그리고 배가 고플 때마다 녹차를 마셨어.
W 고기 먹는 건 그만뒀니?
M 아니, 하지만 닭고기만 먹었지, 돼지고기는 안 먹었어.
W 아이스크림은 어때?

M 무가당 아이스크림만 먹었어. 그거면 되거든.

08 ④

[Telephone rings.]

W Hello.

M Hello. Could I speak to Jane, please?

W I'm afraid she isn't here right now. Can I take a message?

M Yes, please. This is Richard.

W Oh, hello, Richard. This is Jane's mother.

M I was invited to her party this Saturday. But tell her that I'm very sorry I can't come. I have to get a physical exam that day.

W Oh, that's too bad. I'll give her the message.

M Thank you. Good-bye.

[전화벨이 울린다.]

W 여보세요.

M 여보세요. Jane과 통화할 수 있나요?

W 그녀는 지금 여기에 없는 것 같은데요. 전하실 말씀 있으세요?

M 네. 저는 Richard예요.

W 아, 안녕, Richard. 나는 Jane의 엄마란다.

M 제가 이번 토요일에 그녀의 파티에 초대받았거든요. 그런데 제가 갈 수 없어서 너무 미안하다고 그녀에게 좀 전해 주세요. 그날 건강검진을 받아야 하거든요.

W 오, 안 됐구나. 그녀에게 메시지를 전해 줄게.

M 감사합니다. 안녕히 계세요.

09 ②

W Hi, George. How are you doing?

M I'm fine. How about getting together tonight, Laura?

W Good. I'm free tonight.

M I'll be at the office until 7 in the evening.

W Let's meet at the restaurant in front of your office. How about 7:30?

M Could we meet a little earlier?

W No problem. Then, how about 7:10?

M Great. See you then at the restaurant.

W 안녕, George. 어떻게 지내니?

M 잘 지내. 오늘 밤에 만나는 게 어때, Laura?

W 좋아. 오늘 밤에는 시간이 있어.

M 나는 저녁 7시까지 사무실에 있을 거야.

W 너희 사무실 앞에 있는 음식점에서 만나자. 7시 30분이 어때?

M 조금 더 일찍 만날 수 있을까?

W 문제없어. 그럼 7시 10분은 어때?

M 좋았어. 그때 음식점에서 보자.

10 ⑤

W ① Tony Smith called.

② Tony Smith lives at 10 Maple Street.

③ Tony Smith's phone number is 576-3849.

④ Somebody will visit Tony at 3 o'clock this afternoon.

⑤ Tony Smith's computer makes a noise.

W ① Tony Smith가 전화했다.

② Tony Smith는 Maple 가의 10번지에 살고 있다.

③ Tony Smith의 전화번호는 576-38490다.

④ 누군가 오늘 오후 3시에 Tony를 방문할 것이다.

⑤ Tony Smith의 컴퓨터에서는 소음이 난다.

만점 솔루션 ⑤ 컴퓨터가 켜지지 않는다고 했지 소음이 난다고 한 것은 아니다.

11 ③

M I'm an animal trainer, Michael Taylor. Our zoo is in Redwood Forest. I usually get up at five in the morning every day. I have to feed the animals their breakfast at around six o'clock. After that, I visit all of the animals and check if they're in good health. In the afternoon, I spend about four hours training animals.

M 저는 동물 조련사인 Michael Taylor입니다. 저희 동물원은 Redwood Forest에 있습니다. 저는 보통 매일 아침 5시에 일어납니다. 저는 6시경에 동물들에게 아침 식사를 먹여야 합니다. 그러고 나서 저는 동물들을 찾아다니면서 그들의 건강 상태가 양호한지 점검합니다. 오후에 저는 동물들을 조련시키는 데 4시간 정도를 보냅니다.

만점 솔루션 동물원의 위치가 Redwood Forest에 있다는 것이지, 이것을 동물원의 이름으로 착각해서는 안 된다.

12 ① | ✚ ⑤

M What's the weather forecast for this afternoon?

W It'll rain, so we can't go to the beach this afternoon.

M That's too bad. How about tomorrow?

W The weather forecast said it would be cloudy in the morning and sunny in the afternoon.

M Then, let's go to the beach tomorrow afternoon.

W Sounds good.

M 오늘 오후에 일기 예보가 어때?

W 비가 올 거야. 그래서 오늘 오후에는 해변에 갈 수 없어.

M 정말 안 됐는걸. 내일은 어때?

W 일기 예보에 따르면 오전에는 구름이 끼고, 오후에는 맑을 거라고 했어.

M 그럼, 내일 오후에 해변에 가자.

W 좋아.

13 ③

M How's your diet these days, Rachel?

W Fine. I've already lost three kilograms.

M No kidding? That's great!

W Yeah, my clothes are starting to feel loose.

M How much do you want to lose?

W Seven kilograms more.

M Then how much do you weigh now, Rachel?

W I weigh seventy kilograms now.

M 요즘 다이어트는 어때, Rachel?

W 좋아. 벌써 3킬로그램이나 뺐어.

M 농담 아니지? 대단한 걸!

W 그래. 내 옷들이 헐거워지기 시작하고 있어.

M 얼마나 빼고 싶은데?

W 7킬로그램 더.

M 그럼 지금 체중은 얼마나 나가니, Rachel?

W 지금은 70킬로그램 나가.

만점 솔루션 현재 체중이 70kg인데 지금보다 7kg을 더 빼고 싶다고 했으므로, 여자가 목표로 하고 있는 체중은 63kg임을 알 수 있다.

14 ②

M Good evening. Do you have a reservation?

W Yes. My name is Jennifer Williams.

M Ah, yes, Miss Williams. You reserved a table for three at seven o'clock.

W That's right.

M Your table is ready now. Please come this way.

W All right. *[pause]* Could we have the menu, please?

M Here you are, ma'am.

M 안녕하세요. 예약은 하셨나요?

W 네. 제 이름은 Jennifer Williams입니다.

M 아, 네, Williams 씨. 7시에 3인용 테이블을 예약하셨네요.

W 맞아요.

M 테이블이 지금 준비되어 있습니다. 이쪽으로 오세요.

W 알겠어요. [잠시 후] 메뉴판 좀 주시겠어요?

M 여기 있습니다, 손님.

15 ⑤

W Hi, John. Long time no see.

M Beth! It's been so long since we last saw each other.

W You're right. I'm at home for the summer vacation. Would you like to get together this afternoon?

M I'd love to.

W Well, I'm going to be at the library at half past 4. I'll borrow some books for my report.

M I need some books, too. We can meet at the library.

W Great. See you there.

W 안녕, John. 오랜만이야.

M Beth! 우리가 지난번에 서로 만난 이후로 정말 오랜만이네.

W 맞아. 나는 여름방학 동안 집에 있거든. 오늘 오후에 만날래?

M 그러고 싶은데.

W 그럼, 4시 반에 나는 도서관에 있을 거야. 보고서 때문에 책을 좀 빌릴 거야.

M 나도 책이 좀 필요해. 도서관에서 만나면 되겠네.

W 잘 됐다. 거기서 보자.

16 ④

W Hello, listeners! Welcome back to Your Health Partner. I'm Dolly Sharp. A few months ago, I didn't sleep much because I was very busy. I got a lot of work done, so I thought I was being productive. But more research is saying that doing that is very bad for our health and brain activity. We need to sleep at least seven hours a day to work well the next day. And for young students, it's even more important. Let's talk about it today.

W 안녕하세요, 청취자 여러분! 당신의 '건강 파트너'에 돌아오신 것을 환영합니다. 저는 돌리 샵입니다. 몇 달 전, 저는 너무 바빠서 잠을 충분히 자지 못했습니다. 많은 일을 했기 때문에 내가 생산적이라고 생각했습니다. 하지만 많은 연구가 그렇게 하는 것이 우리 건강과 뇌활동에 아주 나쁘다는 것을 말해주고 있습니다. 우리는 다음 날 일을 잘 하기 위해 하루에 최소 일곱 시간을 자야 합니다. 그리고 젊은 학생들은 그것이 더욱 중요합니다. 오늘 그것에 대해 이야기해봅시다.

17 ③

M Wow, there are so many people here.

W Oh, look over there! That's Mark, the famous singer.

M Which one are you talking about?

W The man holding a glass of orange juice. He's wearing glasses.

M The man near the piano? He's got long hair?

W Yes. He's wearing a white suit. Let's go say hello.

M Really? Do you know him?

W Yes. He's one of my friends.

M 와, 여기 사람들이 아주 많네.

W 아, 저기를 봐! 저건 유명한 가수인 Mark야.

M 어떤 사람에 대해 이야기하고 있는 거니?

W 오렌지 주스 한 잔을 들고 있는 남자 말이야. 그는 안경을 쓰고 있어.

M 피아노 옆에 있는 남자 말이니? 그는 긴 머리를 하고 있니?

W 응. 그는 흰색 양복을 입고 있어. 인사하러 가자.

M 정말? 네가 그를 알고 있니?

W 응. 그는 내 친구들 중의 한 명이야.

만점 솔루션 ③ 피아노 옆에 있다고 했지 피아노를 치고 있는 것은 아니다.

18 ⑤

M Do you believe there are flying monsters in the lake?

W No, I don't. Look at it. It's so peaceful. Why are you asking me?

M I saw something flying last night. I'm really serious.

W Go ahead.

M As I was walking by the lake, I noticed something flying straight up into the air from behind the trees by the lake. It spread its wings and flew east.

W Wasn't it a bird?

M It was not a bird. It was just too big. I'd say it was about 10 ft long and had wings like a bat.

W I think you mistook a bat for a flying monster. Take it easy.

M 너는 저 호수에 날아다니는 괴물이 있다고 믿니?

W 아니. 봐. 저 호수는 참으로 평화로운데. 왜 묻는 거니?

M 어젯밤 뭔가 날아가는 것을 봤어. 진심이야.

W 계속 해봐.

M 내가 호수 주변을 따라 걷고 있었는데 뭔가가 호숫가 나무 뒤에서 하늘로 곧장 날아가는 것을 목격했어. 그것은 날개를 펴더니 동쪽으로 날아갔어.

W 새가 아니었을까?

M 그것은 새가 아니었어. 너무 컸어. 길이가 10피트 정도 되는 데다가 박쥐와 같은 날개가 있었어.

W 나는 네가 박쥐를 날아다니는 괴물로 착각한 것 같아. 진정해.

19 ④

M Have some French fries. Aren't you eating at all?

W No, thank you. I'm on a diet.

M Oh, come on. You can eat a few.

W No, thank you. I'd really like to lose some weight.

M Well, then what else do you do to lose weight?

W _____

M 감자튀김 좀 먹어. 아예 안 먹을 생각이니?

W 안 먹을래. 다이어트 중이야.

M 그러지 말고. 몇 개만 먹어.

W 아니야, 됐어. 정말 몸무게를 줄이고 싶어.

M 그러면 몸무게를 줄이기 위해 또 무엇을 하고 있니?

W 매일 저녁 공원에서 뛰고 있어.

① 그만둘 거야.
② 그래야만 하니까.
③ 명심할게.
⑤ 몸무게를 줄이는 것은 결코 쉽지 않아.

20 ⑤

W What should we cook for today's dinner party?

M I think I'm going to make the Indian chicken we had on Jane's birthday.

W Sounds good. Is that called 'Tandoori Chicken'?

M Right. That's the food we had at the Indian restaurant.

W Do you have the recipe for it?

M Of course. I asked the chef for the recipe that day.

W But Linda doesn't eat chicken, does she?

M Linda? Oh, my Gosh! I forgot to invite her! She'll be mad at me. It just slipped my mind.

W _____

W 오늘 만찬을 위해 무엇을 요리하지?

M 우리가 지난 번 Jane의 생일 때 먹었던 인도식 치킨을 만들까 생각 중이야.

W 좋지. 그게 '탄두리 치킨'이라고 하니?

M 맞아. 우리 지난 번 인도 식당에서 먹었잖아.

W 레시피를 알고 있니?

M 물론이지. 그날 내가 요리사에게 레시피를 물어봤어.

W 하지만 Linda가 치킨을 안 먹지 않니?

M Linda라고? 오 이런! 그녀를 초대하는 것을 잊었네. 그녀가 나에게 화를 낼 거야. 깜빡했어.

W 걱정하지마. 아직 너무 늦지 않았어.

① 난 괜찮아.
② 내가 나이들어 가는 것 같아.
③ 조언해 줘서 고마워.
④ 말보다 행동이 더 강하다.

만점 솔루션 깜빡 잊은 사실에 대해 위로하는 말이 온다

영어듣기능력평가 **15**회

01 ③	02 ④	03 ②, ➕①	04 ③	05 ③
06 ④	07 ②	08 ⑤, ➕②	09 ③	10 ②
11 ⑤	12 ⑤	13 ②	14 ④	15 ⑤
16 ③	17 ①	18 ④	19 ③	20 ①

01 ③

W ① Two students are crossing the road.
② Two students are answering quizzes.
③ Two students are singing on the stage.
④ Two students are helping an old woman.
⑤ Two students are making a model airplane.

W ① 두 학생이 도로를 건너고 있다.
② 두 학생이 퀴즈에 답하고 있다.
③ 두 학생이 무대 위에서 노래를 하고 있다.
④ 두 학생이 노부인을 돕고 있다.
⑤ 두 학생이 모형 비행기를 만들고 있다.

02 ④

M Good morning. This is Peter Lee. Here is a radio report of the weather for some big cities in the world. Let's start with Seoul. It will be warm and sunny in Seoul, so today will be a perfect time for outdoor activities. Beijing will be very foggy all day, but Tokyo will be windy. There will be snow in Moscow with a low temperature. New York is going to have heavy rain today. That's all. Thank you.

M 좋은 아침입니다. 저는 Peter Lee입니다. 세계의 일부 대도시의 라디오 일기 예보입니다. 서울부터 시작합니다. 서울은 따뜻하고 화창할 것이므로, 오늘은 야외 활동을 위한 완벽한 시간일 것입니다. 베이징은 하루 종일 안개가 가득하지만, 동경은 바람이 불 것입니다. 모스크바에는 눈이 오고 기온이 낮을 것입니다. 뉴욕은 오늘 많은 비가 내릴 것입니다. 이상입니다. 감사합니다.

만점 솔루션 ④ 모스크바는 눈이 오고 기온이 낮을 것이라고 했다.

03 ② | ➕①

W Do you have any special plans this weekend?
M Not really. How about you?
W I'm going hiking with my friends. Would you like to come with us?
M I'd like to, but I have to help my father paint my room.
W But you helped your mother clean the house last weekend, right?
M Yes. We have just moved to a new house, you know. We have a lot of work to do.
W 이번 주말에 특별한 계획을 가지고 있니?
M 그렇지도 않아. 너는 어때?
W 친구들과 함께 하이킹을 갈 예정이야. 우리와 같이 갈래?
M 가고 싶지만, 아버지가 내 방 페인트칠 하는 걸 도와드려야 해.
W 하지만 너는 지난 주말에 어머니가 집안 청소하는 걸 도와드렸잖아, 맞지?
M 그래. 너도 알다시피, 우리가 새 집으로 이사했잖아. 우리는 해야 할 일이 많아.

04 ③

M May I have your attention, please? I'm sorry to bother you again. As you know, our building is very old, and so is the elevator. Unfortunately, the elevator is out of order again. Our repairmen are trying to fix it, but it will take about an hour. Please take the stairs. Thank you for your understanding.

M 안내 말씀드리겠습니다. 다시 여러분들에게 폐를 끼치게 되어 죄송합니다. 아시다시피, 우리 건물은 매우 낡았고 또한 엘리베이터도 그렇습니다. 불행하게도, 엘리베이터가 또 다시 고장이 났습니다. 수리공들이 고치려고 노력하고 있지만, 대략 1시간 정도 걸릴 것입니다. 계단을 이용해 주시기 바랍니다. 이해해 주셔서 감사합니다.

05 ③

W Could I have something for a cough? I think I'm coming down with a cold.
M Well, I suggest a box of this cough syrup.
W Thank you. And what do you suggest for dry skin?
M Try this new lotion. It's very moisturizing.
W OK. And one more thing. My husband has no energy these days. Can you suggest anything?
M He should try taking multivitamins. They're excellent.
W And could you suggest something good for my frequent headaches as well?
M How about omega 3 pills? It helps blood circulation.
W Great! May I have three large bottles of multivitamins and one bottle of omega 3, please?
M Sure. I'll be right back with you.

W 기침에 좋은 것 있어요? 감기에 걸린 것 같아요.
M 글쎄요, 이 기침 물약 한 상자를 권해 드릴게요.
W 감사합니다. 그리고 건조한 피부에 좋은 것 있어요?
M 이 새로운 로션을 발라 보세요. 매우 보습력이 좋습니다.
W 좋아요. 그리고 한 가지 더요. 제 남편이 요즈음 기력이 없어요. 권해 주실 만한 것이 있나요?
M 복합 비타민을 드셔야 합니다. 정말 좋아요.
W 그리고 저의 잦은 두통에 좋은 것도 권해 주실래요?
M 오메가 3 정제는 어때요? 혈액 순환을 도와줍니다.
W 좋아요! 복합 비타민 3병과 오메가 3 한 병을 주시겠어요?
M 알겠습니다. 곧 돌아올 게요.

06 ④

W We finally got here. The traffic was so bad.

M I know, I've never experienced anything like that. Anyway, we really <u>need to hurry</u>.

W What time is our boarding time?

M I think it'll be 12:45 p.m., as our flight time is 1:15 p.m.

W Oh, no, then we have only an hour and a half.

M Yes, so we can't waste any time. Let's find the check-in counter, first. Then we need to go straight to the security check.

W I hope the line is <u>not too long</u>.

W 드디어 왔다. 교통이 정말 나빴어.

M 알아, 그런 건 처음 경험했어. 아무튼, 서둘러야 해.

W 우리 탑승 시간이 몇 시지?

M 비행 시간이 1시 15분이니까, 12시 45분일 거야.

W 안돼, 1시간 30분밖에 안 남았어.

M 그래, 그래서 시간을 낭비해서는 안돼. 우선 탑승 수속 창구부터 찾자. 그리고 바로 보안 검사대로 가야 해.

W 줄이 너무 길지 않았으면 좋겠다.

07 ②

M You were here when the accident happened. Could you tell me about it?

W It happened very fast, so I <u>didn't see everything</u>. But there was something wrong with the driver of the white car.

M What do you mean?

W Well, the driver was switching lanes a lot and then he <u>suddenly went faster</u> before he hit the blue car.

M Maybe he had a medical emergency. Can I use this interview on TV? It will help viewers understand what happened.

W Will I be on the news? Yes, you can use it.

M 사고가 났을 때 여기 계셨죠. 그 때 일을 말씀해 주시겠어요?

W 너무 빨리 일어나서 다 보지는 못했어요. 하지만 하얀색 차 운전자에게 무언가 문제가 있었어요.

M 무슨 뜻인가요?

W 운전자가 차선을 많이 바꿨고 파란색 차를 박기 전에 갑자기 더 빠르게 달렸어요.

M 긴급 상황이었을 수도 있겠네요. 이 인터뷰를 TV에 내보내도 될까요? 무슨 일이 일어났는지 시청자가 이해하는데 도움을 줄 거예요.

W 제가 뉴스에 나온다고요? 네, 괜찮습니다.

08 ⑤ | ➕ ②

[Telephone rings.]

M Hello, Cathy. This is Mark.

W Hi, Mark. What happened? Your voice sounds strange.

M I've <u>fallen off my bike</u>.

W Are you hurt?

M Yes. I've hurt my leg. I can't walk any more, so can you <u>take me to my house</u>?

W Oh, heavens! Why don't you call your mom?

M I did, but she <u>didn't answer the phone</u>.

W Wait! I'll come and take you home.

[전화벨이 울린다.]

M 여보세요, Cathy. 나 Mark야.

W 안녕, Mark. 무슨 일이야? 네 목소리가 이상하게 들린다.

M 자전거에서 떨어졌어.

W 너 다쳤니?

M 응. 다리를 다쳤어. 더 이상 걸을 수가 없는데, 나를 집으로 데려다 줄 수 있니?

W 어머, 이런! 엄마에게 전화하지 그래?

M 전화했지. 그런데 엄마가 전화를 받지 않았어.

W 기다려! 내가 가서 너를 집에 데려다 줄게.

09 ③

M Mom, you look tired. Are you okay?

W I'm just very tired. I've been so busy at work lately, and there's so much housework to do.

M I can help you with the housework. What can I do?

W <u>That's very nice of you</u>. The bathroom really needs cleaning.

M Sure, I can do that. Do you want me to do that now?

W No, I need to <u>buy</u> some <u>cleaning products</u> first. How about tomorrow?

M No problem.

M 엄마, 지쳐 보여요. 괜찮아요?

W 그냥 매우 지쳤단다. 요즘 일하느라 너무 바빴고 집안일도 너무 많았어.

M 집안일을 도와드릴 수 있어요. 뭘 할까요?

W 정말 착하구나. 화장실을 청소해야 해.

M 알겠어요, 할 수 있어요. 지금 할까요?

W 아니, 우선 청소용품을 사야해. 내일 하는 게 어떠니?

M 문제 없어요.

10 ②

W I need somebody to come over and fix my Internet connection.

M What's wrong with it?

W For some reason I <u>can't get access to</u> the site I want.

M Well, the Internet isn't down, so <u>there must be something wrong</u> with the site.

W What should I do? I need to download a file right now.

M The fastest solution is <u>making a phone call</u> to the site.

W I don't know the phone number.

M Why don't you call 114?

W Oh, that's it. I didn't think of that.

W 누군가 와서 내 인터넷 접속을 고쳐 줬으면 좋겠는데.

M 인터넷에 무슨 문제가 있는데.

W 어떤 이유에선지 내가 가고자 하는 사이트에 접속이 안 돼.

M 글쎄, 인터넷이 다운된 건 아니고, 그 사이트에 뭔가 문제가 있는 게 틀림없어.

W 어떻게 해야 하지? 당장 그곳으로부터 파일을 다운 받아야 하는데.

M 제일 빠른 방법은 그 사이트에 전화하는 거야.

W 거기 전화번호를 모르는데.

M 114에 전화하면 되잖아.

W 아, 그렇지. 그런 생각을 못했어.

만점 솔루션 마지막 부분에 남자가 Why don't you ~?라고 하면서 권하는 말을 잘 듣도록 한다.

11 ⑤

① **W** Would you like something to drink?

　M Yes, please. Can I have some water, please?

② **W** So... <u>what do you think of</u> this place?

　M I think it's very nice. We should take it.

③ **W** Are you ready to order now?

　M No, sorry, can I have some more time, please?

④ **W** Excuse me, sir, can I see your ticket, please?

　M Sure, I have it in my bag. <u>Hold on a second.</u>

⑤ **W** Excuse me, if you're not using this chair would you mind if I take it?

　M Not at all. Take it if you need it.

① **W** 마실 것을 드릴까요?

　M 네. 물 좀 마실 수 있을까요?

② **W** 이 장소 어떻게 생각하세요?

　M 아주 좋네요. 이 곳으로 할게요.

③ **W** 주문하시겠습니까?

　M 아니요, 시간을 조금 더 주시겠어요?

④ **W** 실례합니다. 표를 볼 수 있을까요?

　M 네, 가방 안에 있습니다. 잠시만요.

⑤ **W** 실례합니다. 이 의자를 사용하는게 아니라면 가져가도 될까요?

　M 네, 가져가세요.

12 ⑤

W I'm so glad that you've chosen chemistry. Now I'd like to talk about lab rules to you. First, you can't bring any food or drinks into the lab. Second, <u>don't enter the lab</u> without a teacher. Third, please <u>don't touch anything</u> on the shelves. Fourth, never taste anything in the bottles. Lastly, when doing experiments, <u>listen to your teacher</u> attentively. Thank you for listening to me.

W 저는 여러분이 화학을 선택해 주셔서 기쁩니다. 이제 여러분에게 실험실 규칙에 대해서 말하고자 합니다. 첫 번째, 실험실 안으로 먹을 것이나 마실 것을 가져올 수 없습니다. 두 번째, 선생님이 없으면 실험실에 들어오지 마십시오. 세 번째, 선반에 있는 것은 절대 만지지 마십시오. 네 번째, 절대 병 속에 있는 것을 맛보지 마십시오. 마지막으로 실험을 할 때, 선생님의 말씀을 집중해서 들으십시오. 제 말을 들어주어서 감사합니다.

만점 솔루션 ⑤ 실험 후 도구 정리를 잘하는 것에 대한 언급은 없다.

13 ②

W Here's a letter for you, Alex.

M Thanks. *[opens it]* <u>I can't believe it!</u>

W Why?

M This letter says I <u>won a free trip!</u>

W Really? To where?

M The letter says <u>I can go anywhere</u> in Europe or Asia.

W Are you sure the trip is really free?

M That's what it says. Here, you can read it.

W 여기 너에게 온 편지가 있어, Alex.

M 고마워. *[봉투를 연다]* 믿을 수 없어!

W 왜?

M 이 편지에 내가 공짜 여행에 당첨됐다고 쓰여 있어.

W 정말이야? 어디로?

M 편지에 내가 유럽이나 아시아 어디든지 갈 수 있다고 쓰여 있어.

W 그 여행이 정말 공짜라고 확신하니?

M 편지에 그렇게 쓰여 있어. 여기, 너도 읽어 볼 수 있어.

14 ④

W ① People can eat Italian food at Library Bistro.

　② Library Bistro is at 92 Madison Street, Seattle.

　③ Library Bistro opens every day at 10 a.m.

　④ Library Bistro <u>closes every day at 11 p.m.</u>

　⑤ People can <u>make a reservation</u> at 624-3646.

W ① 사람들은 Library Bistro에서 이탈리아 음식을 먹을 수 있다.

　② Library Bistro는 시애틀 Madison 거리 92번지에 있다.

　③ Library Bistro는 매일 오전 10시에 문을 연다.

　④ Library Bistro는 매일 밤 11시에 문을 닫는다.

　⑤ 사람들은 624-3646번으로 예약을 할 수 있다.

만점 솔루션 ④ 토요일과 일요일에는 자정에 문을 닫는다.

15 ⑤

W Jim, I'm sorry to have kept you waiting for so long.

M Oh, I don't mind. <u>It's only 6.</u>

W Thank you for saying so. When does the musical start?

M We've <u>still got 50 minutes.</u>

W But, we must enter the concert hall 10 minutes before the musical starts.

M Yes, but don't worry. It takes only 20 minutes to walk there.

W Okay. Let's go.

W Jim, 너무 오랫동안 기다리게 해서 미안해.

M 아, 나는 상관없어. 여섯 시밖에 안 되었는데.

W 그렇게 말해 주니 고마워. 뮤지컬은 언제 시작하니?

M 아직 50분이나 남았어.

W 하지만 뮤지컬이 시작되기 10분 전에 음악회장에 들어가야 해.

M 그래, 하지만 걱정 마. 그곳까지 걸어가는데 20분밖에 안 걸려.

W 좋아. 가자.

16 ③

W Hi, Jason.

M Hi, Carol. What's up?

W You want to do some volunteer work, don't you?

M Yes, I do. I want to help people in need.

W Well, Central Hospital needs volunteers. How about going together?

M Sounds interesting. When do they need volunteers?

W Anytime. But mostly on the weekends.

M Good. That's perfect for me.

W 안녕, Jason.

M 안녕, Carol. 무슨 일이야?

W 너는 자원봉사 일을 원하지, 그렇지 않니?

M 그래, 원해. 나는 어려운 사람들을 돕고 싶어.

W 그래, Central 병원에서 자원봉사자들을 필요로 해. 함께 가는 게 어때?

M 흥미로운데. 언제 자원봉사자들을 필요로 한데?

W 언제나. 하지만 대부분 주말에.

M 좋아. 나에게는 더할 나위 없어.

17 ①

M Youngmi, what are you doing tonight?

W Nothing much. Why?

M Would you like to go to a concert? I have free tickets.

W Really? It sounds interesting. What time is it?

M It starts at 7 p.m. Maybe, we can meet and have dinner before the concert.

W What kind of concert is it?

M It's classical music. They're going to play Mozart and Mendelssohn.

W Oh, well..., I'm not a big fan of that kind of music. Thanks for inviting me, but I'll pass.

M 영미, 오늘 저녁 뭐해?

W 별 거 없어. 왜?

M 콘서트 가지 않을래? 나 무료 표가 있어.

W 진짜? 재미있겠다. 몇 시야?

M 7시에 시작해. 콘서트전에 만나서 저녁을 먹을 수도 있어.

W 무슨 콘서트야?

M 고전 음악. 모짜르트와 멘델스존을 연주할 거야.

W 아... 난 그런 음악을 그렇게 좋아하지 않아. 초대해줘서 고맙지만 사양할게.

18 ④

[Cellphone rings.]

W Hello?

M Hello. This is Comfy Furniture. May I speak to Ms. Kim?

W Speaking.

M Hi, we'd like to deliver your sofa this week. Is it okay?

W Yes, I've been waiting. Hmm..., today is July 15. How about tomorrow?

M Sorry, we're booked with deliveries for tomorrow. But we can deliver it any day from Tuesday, July 17.

W I'll be away for the day this Tuesday. So, it'll have to be the next day.

M Sure, no problem. Do you prefer any particular time?

W No, anytime in the afternoon is fine.

[휴대 전화가 울린다.]

W 여보세요?

M 여보세요. 컴피 가구입니다. 김 씨와 통화할 수 있을까요?

W 접니다.

M 안녕하세요, 이번 주에 소파를 배달해 드리려고 합니다. 괜찮으세요?

W 네, 기다리고 있었어요. 흠... 오늘이 7월 15일이네요. 내일 어떤가요?

M 죄송합니다. 내일은 배달이 다 예약되었어요. 하지만 7월 17일 화요일부터는 아무 날이나 배달 할 수 있습니다.

W 이번주 화요일은 자리를 비울 거라 그 다음날이 좋겠네요.

M 알겠습니다. 원하시는 특별한 시간대가 있나요?

W 아니요, 오후 아무 때나 괜찮습니다.

19 ③

M I have a reservation. My name is John Stevens.

W Okay. You're in room 507. It's a single queen-size bed, spacious.

M Is that a smoking room?

W I'm sorry, but every room here is non-smoking.

M Okay. Thank you. And does that overlook the beach?

W Yes, it does.

M It sounds like everything I expected.

W ＿＿＿＿＿＿＿＿＿＿

M 예약을 했는데요. 제 이름은 Jahn Stevens입니다.

W 좋습니다. 당신이 예약하신 방은 507호실인데요, 싱글 퀸 사이즈 침대에 넓은 공간입니다.

M 담배를 피울 수 있는 방인가요?

W 죄송합니다만, 모든 객실이 비흡연 구역입니다.

M 알겠어요. 감사합니다. 그런데 바다가 보이는 방입니까?

W 예, 그렇습니다.

M 모든 것이 제가 예상했던 대로네요.

W 여기 열쇠 있습니다, 손님.

① 이상하게 들리네요.

② 시간 낭비였어요.

④ 그런 생각을 해 보지 않았어요.

⑤ 그것은 전혀 문제되지 않아요.

만점 솔루션 호텔 관계자가 체크인하는 과정의 마지막 단계에 하는 말을 선택하도록 한다.

20 ①

W I really enjoyed the movie. How about you?

M I liked it too. The last part was really exciting.

W Yes, it was. And now I'm really hungry. Let's have something to eat.

M Okay. What do you want to eat?

W Anything is okay with me. Do you like Chinese food?

M Sure, but do you know a Chinese food restaurant around here?

W _____

W 정말 그 영화 재미있었어. 너는 어땠니?

M 나도 좋았어. 마지막 부분이 정말 흥미진진했어.

W 그래, 그랬지. 그리고 지금 나 정말 배고파. 뭐 좀 먹자.

M 좋아. 무엇을 먹고 싶니?

W 나는 뭐든 좋아. 너 중국 음식 좋아하니?

M 물론이지, 하지만 이 부근에 중국 음식점을 알고 있니?

W 그래. 이 근처에 한 곳 있어.

② 그래. 여기서 너를 기다릴게.

③ 응. 네가 주문한 것은 오래 걸리지 않아.

④ 아니. 오늘은 외식하기 싫어.

⑤ 아니. 이 음식을 먹고 싶지 않아.

만점 솔루션 영화를 보고 배가 고파서 함께 식사를 하자는 상황에서 근처에 음식점을 알고 있냐는 남자의 말에 대한 응답으로는 알고 있는지의 여부를 말하는 ①이 가장 적절하다.

영어듣기능력평가 **16** 회

01 ③	**02** ③	**03** ④	**04** ①	**05** ④, ➕①
06 ②	**07** ①, ➕③	**08** ④	**09** ①	**10** ⑤
11 ⑤	**12** ④	**13** ③	**14** ④	**15** ②
16 ⑤	**17** ④	**18** ⑤	**19** ①	**20** ④

01 ③

M Did you come here alone?

W No, I came here with my friend Cathy.

M Where is she?

W She's sitting on the grass.

M You mean the one with long hair?

W No, she has short hair. She's wearing jeans and a T-shirt.

M Oh, I see, the one with glasses.

W That's right.

M 너는 혼자서 여기에 왔니?

W 아니, 내 친구 Cathy와 함께 여기에 왔어.

M 그녀는 어디에 있는데?

W 그녀는 잔디밭에 앉아 있어.

M 긴 머리의 소녀를 말하는 거니?

W 아니, 그녀는 짧은 머리야. 그녀는 청바지와 티셔츠를 입고 있어.

M 오, 알겠군. 안경 쓴 사람 말하는 거지.

W 맞아.

만점 솔루션 Cathy는 짧은 머리에 청바지와 티셔츠를 입고 있으며, 안경을 쓰고 있다.

02 ③

M Oh, it's raining!

W Why does it rain every weekend? We were supposed to go on a picnic today.

M The weather forecast said it would be sunny this weekend. So I was looking forward to the picnic.

W Sometimes weather forecasts are wrong.

M But most forecasts are right. I think this rain will stop soon.

W Oh, it's stopped raining. As you said, it was a shower.

M The weather forecast was right. It says tomorrow it will be sunny, too.

W Let's go on a picnic after lunch.

M 오, 비가 오고 있네!

W 왜 주말마다 비가 오지? 우리는 오늘 소풍을 갈 예정이었는데.

M 일기 예보에 의하면 이번 주말은 맑을 거라고 했어. 그래서 나는 소풍을 기대하고 있었는데.

W 때때로 일기 예보가 틀리기도 해.

M 하지만 대부분의 예보는 맞아. 이번 비는 곧 그칠 거라고 생각해.

W 오, 정말 비가 그쳤네. 네가 말한 대로 소나기였어.
M 일기 예보가 맞았어. 내일도 역시 맑을 거라고 해.
W 점심 먹고 소풍가자.

03 ④

W Did you get our tickets?
M No, tickets are sold out.
W Really? Then what are we going to do? That's the movie we didn't want to miss.
M That's right. We came a long way to see this movie. So we have to do something else.
W Let's make a reservation for tomorrow evening first and then have dinner.
M OK, sounds good.

W 표를 구했니?
M 아니, 표가 매진되었어.
W 정말? 그러면 우리 뭘 하지? 그것은 우리가 놓치고 싶지 않았던 영화인데.
M 맞아. 우리는 이 영화를 보러 먼 길을 왔는데. 그러니까 우리는 뭔가를 해야 해.
W 먼저 내일 저녁 예약을 하자. 그러고 나서 저녁 식사를 하자.
M 알았어. 그거 좋은데.

만점 솔루션 영화를 보려고 했지만 표가 매진되어서 저녁을 먹기로 하였다.

04 ①

W May I help you, sir?
M Yes, I made a reservation here. My name is Kim Chiwon.
W Just moment, please. OK, your room number is 702 on the 7th floor.
M Does the room have a view of the sea?
W I'm sorry, it doesn't.
M OK, I see.
W Take the elevator to your right, and you'll easily get to your room.
M Thank you very much.

W 도와드릴까요?
M 예, 여기에 예약을 했는데요. 제 이름은 김치원입니다.
W 잠깐만 기다리세요. 좋아요, 당신의 방 번호는 7층의 702호입니다.
M 그 방은 바다 경치가 보이나요?
W 미안하지만, 보이지 않습니다.
M 알겠습니다.
W 오른쪽의 엘리베이터를 타세요. 그러면 쉽게 방에 도착할 것입니다.
M 대단히 감사합니다.

만점 솔루션 ① 남자는 이미 호텔에 예약을 하고는 체크인을 하고 있다.

05 ④ | ➕ ①

M Hi. Can I help you?
W Yes, please. I'd like to go scuba diving. How much does it cost?

M It's $70 per person.
W I see. And what time does the boat leave?
M It leaves each morning at 8.
W Oh, that's quite early. How do I get here from my hotel?
M Just take the shuttle bus. It will stop in front of the hotel. The buses drop by here.
W OK, great. I'd like to book a trip for tomorrow morning.

M 안녕하세요. 도와드릴까요?
W 예. 스쿠버 다이빙을 가고 싶어요. 비용이 얼마나 되나요?
M 개인당 70달러합니다.
W 알겠습니다. 배는 몇 시에 떠나지요?
M 매일 아침 8시에 떠납니다.
W 오, 매우 이르군요. 어떻게 호텔에서 여기에 올 수 있나요?
M 셔틀버스를 타세요. 그것은 호텔 앞에 정차할 겁니다. 그 버스는 여기를 들르지요.
W 좋습니다. 내일 아침으로 여행을 예약하지요.

06 ②

① W Wow, look at that. What a nice view!
　 M You're right. It's really nice. Let's take a picture!
② W Excuse me, could you please take a picture of us?
　 M Sure, which button should I press?
③ W Is that a new Cellphone? It looks really nice!
　 M Yes, I bought it last week because it was on sale.
④ W How should we go back home from here?
　 M We can take the bus, can't we?
⑤ W Excuse me, you're not allowed to take pictures here.
　 M Oh, I'm sorry. I'll put the camera back in my bag.

① W 와, 저거 봐. 전망이 좋다!
　 M 맞아. 진짜 좋다. 사진 찍자!
② W 죄송합니다, 저희 사진 좀 찍어주실 수 있나요?
　 M 네, 어느 버튼을 눌러야 하나요?
③ W 저거 새 휴대폰이야? 진짜 멋지다!
　 M 응, 세일하길래 저번 주에 샀어.
④ W 여기서 집까지 어떻게 가야해?
　 M 버스 타고 갈 수 있어, 그치?
⑤ W 죄송합니다, 여기서는 사진을 찍으시면 안됩니다.
　 M 죄송해요. 카메라를 가방에 두고 올게요.

07 ① | ➕ ③

M Would you like to go to the movies this Saturday?
W Don't you know that's the day we go on the field trip?
M Really? Is it next Saturday?
W No, it isn't. We're supposed to go this Saturday.
M Oh, I'm sorry, I forgot. Then let's go to the movies next Saturday.
W What date is it next Saturday?
M It's May 8th.

W That's fine with me.

M 이번 토요일에 영화 보러 갈래?

W 너는 그 날이 현장학습 하러 가는 날인줄 모르니?

M 정말? 다음 주 토요일이 아니니?

W 아니야. 우리는 이번 주 토요일에 가기로 되어 있어.

M 오, 미안해. 잊었어. 그러면 다음 주 토요일에 영화 보러 가자.

W 다음 주 토요일이 며칠이지?

M 5월 8일이야.

W 좋아.

08 ④

W Would you like insurance on the car?

M How much is the insurance?

W It's $15 a day. Who is going to be the driver?

M My wife and me.

W Can I see your driver's license?

M Sure. Here you are.

W Thank you. OK. Now I will tell you some rules. The gas tank is full. You should fill it up before you return the car. Otherwise, we charge $3 a gallon. You can pick up your car downstairs.

M Thank you.

W 차에 보험을 드시겠어요?

M 보험이 얼마죠?

W 하루에 15달러입니다. 누가 운전을 할 거죠?

M 제 아내와 제가 할 겁니다.

W 운전면허증 좀 보여 주시겠어요?

M 물론이죠. 여기 있습니다.

W 고맙습니다. 좋아요. 이제 몇 가지 규칙을 설명해 드리겠습니다. 연료 탱크는 가득 채워져 있습니다. 차를 반납하시기 전에 가득 채워 주셔야 합니다. 그렇지 않으면 갤런 당 3달러의 요금이 부과됩니다. 아래층으로 내려가셔서 차를 인수받으세요.

M 감사합니다.

> **만점 솔루션** 대화의 마지막 부분에서 여자가 말하는 규칙을 잘 듣도록 한다.

09 ①

W Mr. Smith, I have difficulty speaking in English. What should I do?

M If you want to become fluent in English, you should try to learn English without studying the grammar.

W I don't understand what you are saying.

M Studying grammar will slow you down and confuse you. You will think about the rules when creating sentences.

W It makes sense. I'm worried too much about making grammatical mistakes when speaking English.

M So I want you to focus on what you want to express. Enjoy communication.

W Thank you for good advice.

W Smith 선생님, 저는 영어 말하기가 어려워요. 어떻게 해야 할까요?

M 유창한 영어를 하고 싶다면 문법을 공부하지 않고 영어를 배우도록 해야 한다.

W 도저히 이해가 가지 않는데요.

M 문법을 공부하는 것은 속도를 늦추게 하고 혼란스럽게 한단다. 문장을 만들어 낼 때마다 규칙을 생각하는 거지.

W 이해가 가요. 제가 말할 때 문법적인 실수를 하는 게 아닌지 무척 걱정이 되요.

M 그러니까 문법 자체에 집중하지 말고 표현하고 싶은 것에 집중하기를 바란다. 의사소통을 즐겨.

W 좋은 말씀을 해 주셔서 감사합니다.

10 ⑤

M What's up?

W Nothing special. My parents are away on vacation for about a month to celebrate their 20th wedding anniversary.

M Do you have any brothers or sisters?

W I have an older brother. He is a university student, so he stays in the dorm. So I'm home alone after school.

M What do you do in the evening?

W I read books for an hour or two until it gets dark. Then I turn on TV, watch it for a while, and fall asleep on the couch.

M I know how you feel.

W I'm just waiting for my parents to come back.

M 무슨 일 있니?

W 별 문제 없어요. 부모님이 결혼 20주년을 기념하려고 한 달 간 여행 중이시거든요.

M 형제나 자매는 없니?

W 오빠가 한 명이 있는데, 대학생이라 기숙사에 있어요. 그래서 방과 후에는 저 혼자예요.

M 주로 저녁 시간에 뭐 하니?

W 날이 어두워질 때까지 한 두 시간 정도 책을 읽어요. 그러고 나서 텔레비전을 켜고 좀 보다가 소파에서 잠이 들어요.

M 네 기분을 알겠다.

W 그저 빨리 부모님이 오시기만 기다리고 있어요.

> **만점 솔루션** 부모님이 한 달간 휴가를 가셔서 여자가 혼자 지내고 있는 상황을 파악한다.

11 ⑤

W Are you looking for tour guides?

M Yes, we need people to lead groups and explain each piece of art.

W Well, I was a history teacher. I retired last year. I'm looking for some ways to spend a few hours volunteering as a tour guide.

M Then you're the person we've been looking for.

W Great! When do I start?

M Can you come next Monday, please?

W 관광안내원을 찾고 계십니까?

M 예, 우리는 단체 관광객을 인도하여 각 예술작품을 설명할 사람이 요합니다.

W 음, 저는 역사교사였습니다. 작년에 은퇴하였습니다. 관광안내원으로 몇 시간 정도 자원봉사할 방법을 찾고 있답니다.

M 그렇다면 우리가 찾고자 하는 분이시네요.

W 좋습니다! 언제 시작할까요?

M 다음 월요일에 오실 수 있겠어요?

12 ④

[Telephone rings.]

W Thank you for calling Maple Dental Clinic. How can I help you?

M It's John Woods calling. How are you today?

W I'm fine, Mr. Woods. How are you?

M Well, actually, I have a toothache. I was hoping Dr. Morris would have some time to see me.

W OK. I can put you in for 2 p.m. tomorrow. How does that sound?

M That would be great.

W I'll have to give you the new address of our new office.

M Oh, you moved.

W Yes, we moved across the road from the Business Bank.

M I think I know where it is. I'll see you tomorrow.

W Okay. Thanks for calling. See you then.

[전화벨이 울린다.]

W 메이플 치과에 전화해 주셔서 감사합니다. 뭘 도와드릴까요?

M 저는 John Woods입니다. 잘 지내세요?

W 잘 지내요, Woods 씨. 어떻게 지내세요?

M 글쎄요, 사실은 이가 좀 아파서요. Morris 선생님이 절 진료할 시간이 있는지 모르겠네요.

W 알겠습니다. 내일 오후 2시로 예약해 드리겠습니다. 괜찮겠어요?

M 괜찮습니다.

W 우리 치과의 새 주소를 가르쳐 드려야 할 것 같아요.

M 오, 이사가셨군요.

W 예, 비즈니스 은행 건너편으로 이사했어요.

M 거기가 어딘 줄 알겠네요. 내일 뵙겠습니다.

W 예. 전화해 주셔서 감사합니다. 그때 뵙죠.

만점 솔루션 목적을 묻는 문제는 대화의 앞부분에서 답을 찾을 수 있다.

13 ③

W Hi, John.

M Hi, Jane. Did you have a nice vacation?

W It was wonderful. I went to Japan.

M Japan? How was your trip?

W It was fantastic! I stayed in a small town. It was very quiet, and the sights were so beautiful. People were very nice to me and the food was great, too.

M What was the weather like?

W It rained most days. But I like rainy weather. The foggy scenes looked like paintings.

W 안녕, John.

M 안녕, Jane. 방학은 잘 보냈니?

W 좋았어. 나는 일본에 갔었어.

M 일본이라고? 여행은 어땠어?

W 환상적이었어! 나는 작은 마을에 머물렀어. 매우 조용했고 경치도 아름다웠어. 사람들은 나에게 매우 친절했고 음식도 좋았어.

M 날씨는 어땠니?

W 대부분 비가 왔어. 하지만 나는 비오는 날을 좋아해. 안개가 낀 풍경은 그림과 같았어.

14 ④

[On the telephone.]

W John, why aren't you home from school yet?

M Soccer practice was longer than usual. I'm leaving now.

W I'm going to make soup and sandwiches for dinner. Can you buy some onions, ham and tomatoes on the way home?

M OK. Is there anything to drink?

W Yes, we have plenty of orange juice. And pick up some oranges for me.

M OK, mom.

[전화상에서]

W John, 너는 아직 학교에서 집에 안 오니?

M 축구 연습이 평소보다 더 길었어요. 지금 떠나요.

W 저녁 식사로 수프와 샌드위치를 만들려고 하는데. 집으로 오는 길에 양파, 햄 그리고 토마토 좀 사올래?

M 알겠어요. 마실 것은 있나요?

W 그래, 오렌지 주스는 많이 있어. 그리고 오렌지 좀 사와라.

M 알았어요, 엄마.

15 ②

M I'd like to buy this watch.

W OK. That's twenty dollars.

M Excuse me, but isn't this watch on sale this week?

W Oh, I'm sorry. You're right. It's thirty percent off.

M That's okay.

W That'll be fourteen dollars.

M Here's fourteen dollars.

W Thanks.

M 이 시계를 사고 싶은데요.

W 알겠습니다. 그것은 20달러예요.

M 죄송하지만, 이 시계는 이번 주에 세일 중이지 않나요?

W 오, 죄송해요. 맞아요. 그것은 30% 할인해요.

M 괜찮아요.

W 그것은 14달러입니다.

M 여기 14달러 있습니다.

W 감사합니다.

16 ⑤

[Telephone rings.]

W Hello. Can I speak to Mr. Adams?

M This is he speaking. Who's speaking, please?

W This is Jenny's mother. I want to know <u>how my daughter is doing</u> in school.

M She's doing fine. Her behavior is excellent, and she <u>likes her school life</u>. But her spelling is not good.

W I already know that. Can you help her <u>with her spelling</u>?

M Yes, I can. And I want you to help her at home, too.

W OK, I will.

W 여보세요. Adams 선생님과 통화할 수 있나요?

M 바로 전데요. 누구시죠?

W 저는 Jenny의 엄마입니다. 제 딸이 학교에서 어떻게 생활하는지 알고 싶어서요.

M 그녀는 잘 지내고 있어요. 그녀의 행동은 너무 좋고요, 학교생활을 좋아하고 있답니다. 하지만 그녀의 맞춤법은 좋지 못합니다.

W 이미 그것을 알고 있습니다. 그녀의 맞춤법을 도와주시겠어요?

M 예, 알겠습니다. 그리고 집에서도 역시 그녀를 도와주시기를 바랍니다.

W 알겠습니다.

17 ④

W Good afternoon, ladies and gentlemen. This is for <u>passengers waiting</u> for the 5 o'clock train to Busan. The 5 o'clock train to Busan <u>is delayed</u> because of heavy snow. <u>The train will leave</u> here at 7 o'clock. The train will arrive in Busan at 10:20. We're very sorry for the delay. Thank you for your patience.

W 안녕하세요, 신사 숙녀 여러분. 부산행 5시 열차를 기다리고 계신 승객들에게 말씀드리겠습니다. 부산행 5시 열차가 폭설로 인해 지연되었습니다. 기차는 7시에 출발할 예정입니다. 그 기차는 10시 20분에 부산에 도착할 예정입니다. 지연된 것에 대해 사과의 말씀을 드립니다. 경청해 주셔서 감사합니다.

만점 솔루션 부산행 열차가 폭설로 인해 출발 시각이 지연되었음을 안내하는 방송이다.

18 ⑤

W Hi, Matt. How was the exam?

M Don't ask. It was bad.

W But you <u>studied really hard</u>. I was sure you'd do well.

M Well, I hoped so, too. But maybe, my studying style wasn't right.

W That's too bad. Why don't you use the school's tutoring program? They find a senior student who can help you.

M Maybe... but you're <u>very good at</u> science, too. Why don't you be my tutor?

W I can, but do you really think I can help you?

M Of course!

W 안녕, 맷. 시험 어땠어?

M 묻지 마. 망했어.

W 하지만 진짜 열심히 공부했잖아. 시험을 잘 볼 줄 알았는데.

M 나도 그러길 바랐지. 그런데 아마, 내 공부 방식이 맞지 않았나봐.

W 안됐다. 학교 과외 프로그램을 이용하는 거 어때? 널 도와줄 수 있는 상급생을 찾아줘.

M 하지만 너도 과학을 잘 하잖아. 네가 내 과외선생님이 되는 거 어때?

W 할 수 있지만 정말로 내가 널 도울 수 있을 거라고 생각해?

M 물론이지!

19 ①

W Where can I find a toy?

M Come this way, please. This is <u>a toy section</u>. Is there anything you want?

W These are not the toys I'm looking for. Do you have anything bigger?

M How about this section? Here are some <u>more expensive ones</u>.

W How much is this?

M The robot is 90 dollars.

W I'll take it. Here's <u>a 100-dollar bill</u>.

M _____

W 어디에서 장난감을 찾을 수 있어요?

M 이쪽으로 오세요. 여기가 장난감 구역입니다. 원하는 것이 있나요?

W 이것들은 제가 찾는 장난감이 아닙니다. 더 큰 게 있나요?

M 이 구역은 어떻습니까? 여기 더 비싼 것들이 있습니다.

W 이것은 얼마예요?

M 그 로봇은 90달러입니다.

W 그것으로 사겠습니다. 여기 100달러가 있습니다.

M <u>여기 잔돈이 있습니다.</u>

② 시간이 얼마나 걸립니까?

③ 미안합니다만, 내일 할게요.

④ 당신은 그것을 하는데 더 많은 시간이 필요합니다.

⑤ 즐거운 시간을 보내셨으면 합니다.

만점 솔루션 사고자 하는 로봇이 90달러인데 여자의 마지막 말에서 여자가 100달러를 지불했음을 알 수 있다. 그러므로 다음에는 잔돈에 관한 말이 오는 것이 자연스럽다.

20 ④

W What would you like to order?

M I'd <u>like an order of</u> *galbi*.

W All right. And what would you like with that, rice or <u>a baked potato</u>?

M I'd like a baked potato.

W And would you like <u>anything to drink</u>?

M _____

W 무엇을 주문하시겠어요?

M 갈비 1인분 주세요.

W 좋습니다. 그리고 갈비와 함께 밥을 드시겠어요, 구운 감자를 드시겠어요?

M 저는 구운 감자를 주세요.

W 마실 것을 드시겠어요?

M <u>어디 봅시다. 우유 한 잔 주세요.</u>

① 훨씬 좋습니다. 감사합니다.

② 이것을 선택하는 것이 더 나아요.

③ 그것을 가지고 곧 돌아오겠습니다.

⑤ 좀 더 큰 게 있나요?

만점 솔루션 마실 것을 묻는 여자의 마지막 말에 남자의 알맞은 응답으로는 마실 것을 주문하는 말인 ④가 알맞다.

영어듣기능력평가 **17**회

01 ⑤	02 ①	03 ⑤	04 ⑤	05 ②, ➕④
06 ②	07 ③	08 ④, ➕⑤	09 ①	10 ⑤
11 ③	12 ③	13 ②	14 ②	15 ①
16 ②	17 ②	18 ④	19 ⑤	20 ④

01 ⑤

W Yeah. These characters are so cute. Did you make them all?

M Sure. Choose one, and I'll give it to you.

W Really? Hmm... I'll <u>choose the tiger</u>.

M You mean the one with a ball on his head?

W Well, no. The one <u>kicking the ball</u>.

M But I think the teddy bear playing the guitar is better.

W I <u>still want the tiger</u>.

W 그래. 이 캐릭터들 너무 귀엽다. 네가 그것들 모두를 만들었니?

M 물론이지. 하나 선택해. 그러면 너에게 그것을 줄게.

W 정말? 음… 나는 호랑이를 선택할래.

M 머리에 공을 얹고 있는 걸 말하니?

W 그게, 아니야. 공을 차고 있는 것 말이야.

M 하지만 나는 기타를 치고 있는 곰 인형이 더 좋은데.

W 그래도 나는 그 호랑이가 좋아.

만점 솔루션 처음에 여자가 공을 차고 있는 호랑이 캐릭터를 고른 후 남자가 다른 것을 고르라고 해도 마지막에 'I still want the tiger.'라고 하였으므로, 여자가 선택한 캐릭터는 ⑤가 맞다.

02 ①

W ① The boy is holding a receiver to his ear.

② The man is <u>climbing up</u> the ladder to fix the light.

③ The curtains have been pulled shut.

④ Boxes are stacked in the room.

⑤ Some tools <u>are scattered</u> on the floor.

W ① 남자아이가 전화기를 귀에 대고 있다.

② 남자가 전등을 고치기 위해 사다리를 오르고 있다.

③ 커튼이 닫혀 있다.

④ 상자가 방에 쌓여 있다.

⑤ 연장들이 방바닥에 흩어져 있다.

03 ⑤

W An old woman was walking down a street at night carrying two bags full of potatoes. One man <u>came up from behind</u>. She had <u>a big amount of cash</u> in her handbag. No one else was around and it looked like she was going <u>to be robbed</u>.

Suddenly she had an idea that she would give up her two bags of potatoes and run. She dropped them on the ground and started to run. Then the man said, "Mom, it's me! Your son, Tommy. What's wrong with you?" The man picked the bags up, and walked towards his mom.

W 한 나이든 아주머니가 감자가 가득 담긴 봉지를 두 개 들고 밤에 거리를 걷고 있었다. 한 남자가 뒤에서 다가오고 있었다. 그녀는 핸드백에 많은 현금이 있었다. 아무도 그 주변에 없었고 그녀는 강도를 당할 것만 같았다. 갑자기 두 봉지의 감자를 포기하고 달아나야겠다는 생각이 들었다. 그녀는 봉지를 땅에 떨어뜨리고는 달리기 시작했다. 그때 그 남자가 말했다. "엄마, 저예요. 아들 Tommy예요. 무슨 일이 있어요?" 그 남자는 봉지를 집어 들고는 엄마를 향해 걸어갔다.

04 ⑤

M Which do you think are smarter, dogs or cats?
W I think dogs are smarter. I think dogs have bigger brains. And dogs are more social than cats.
M Then I am smarter than you, because I have a bigger head than you.
W You are kidding. That doesn't make sense.
M Right. Most scientists still question whether the size of the brain is directly related to the intelligence level.
W That means cats might possibly be smarter than dogs.
M They might possibly be indeed.

M 너는 개와 고양이 중에서 누가 더 영리하다고 생각하니?
W 나는 개가 더 영리하다고 생각해. 개의 두뇌가 더 큰 것 같아. 그리고 개는 고양이보다 더 사회성이 있잖아.
M 그러면 나는 너보다 더 영리하겠네. 내가 너보다 머리가 더 크니까.
W 농담하지마. 말도 안 돼.
M 맞아. 대부분의 과학자들은 아직도 두뇌의 크기가 지능의 정도와 직접적인 관련이 있는지 의문을 가지고 있어.
W 그 말은 고양이가 개보다도 더 영리할 수도 있다는 말이네.
M 정말 그럴지도 모르지.

05 ② | ➕④

M Hi, Ann. How's it going? How is your new apartment?
W That's what I'm talking to you. I'm looking for a new place.
M Why? What's the problem with your apartment? I thought you liked the apartment.
W I liked it because it's cheap and spacious, but the problem is that it is too far from the school. It takes too long to get there.
M Well, I know there's an apartment complex around the corner near my place. I'll drop by there on my way to class today.
W Thanks a lot.

M 안녕, Ann. 어떻게 지냈니? 새 아파트는 괜찮니?
W 그걸 말하려고 해. 나는 새로운 곳을 찾고 있어.

M 왜? 너의 아파트에 무슨 문제가 있어? 나는 네가 그 아파트를 마음에 들어 한다고 생각했는데.
W 가격도 싸고 넓어서 좋은데 문제는 학교에서 거리가 너무 멀어. 학교 가는 데 시간이 너무 오래 걸려.
M 음, 내가 사는 곳 근처에 아파트 단지가 하나 있어. 오늘 수업 가는 길에 거기에 들러 볼게.
W 너무 고마워.

만점 솔루션 여자는 학교에서 거리가 먼 곳에 살고 있어 불편을 겪고 있다.

06 ②

W Look at this poster, Dad. The birds are so beautiful.
M Yeah. They are all from Africa.
W Look around and see the animals.
M Janet, I'm very hungry. Let's eat something before going around.
W After lunch, I'd like to watch the dolphin show, too. The third show starts at 2 o'clock.
M Wait a moment. I'll go to buy the tickets and some food.

W 아빠, 이 포스터 좀 보세요. 새들이 너무 아름다워요.
M 그래. 그 새들 모두가 아프리카에서 왔구나.
W 돌아보면서 동물들을 구경해요.
M Janet, 나는 배가 몹시 고프구나. 돌아보기 전에 뭐 좀 먹자.
W 점심 먹고, 돌고래 쇼도 보고 싶어요. 세 번째 쇼가 두 시에 시작해요.
M 잠깐 기다려라. 내가 가서 표와 먹을 것을 살게.

07 ③

M Hello, how can I help you?
W I think I'm getting a cold.
M Well, we have many over-the-counter medicines.
W Could I have something for a runny nose?
M Yes. This works for a runny nose or cough.
W Thank you. And what do you have for dry skin?
M Try some of this new lotion. It's very good.
W Okay. Thanks a lot.

M 안녕하세요, 어떻게 도와드릴까요?
W 감기에 걸리려고 해요.
M 그래요. 우리에게 의사의 처방 없이 복용할 수 있는 약이 많이 있습니다.
W 콧물을 흘리는 것을 위한 것을 살 수 있나요?
M 예. 이것은 콧물이나 기침에 효과가 좋습니다.
W 고맙습니다. 그리고 건성 피부를 위한 것으로 무엇이 있나요?
M 이 새로운 바르는 물약을 약간 써 보세요. 아주 좋습니다.
W 좋아요. 감사합니다.

08 ④ | ➕⑤

W David, can I ask a favor?
M What is it?
W Could you give me a ride to the Express Bus Terminal this afternoon?

M I think so. What time do you need to be there?

W Well, my plan is to take the 5:40 bus to Vancouver.

M Then, I'll pick you up at 5:00. It takes only 30 minutes to the terminal.

W Good. Thank you.

W David, 부탁 하나 해도 될까요?

M 뭔데요?

W 오늘 오후에 고속버스 터미널까지 차를 태워줄 수 있어요?

M 그렇게 할 수 있을 것 같아요. 그곳에 몇 시에 가야 해요?

W 그게, 내 계획은 밴쿠버로 가는 5시 40분 차를 타는 거예요.

M 그럼, 내가 오후 5시에 차로 태우러 갈게요. 터미널까지 30분밖에 안 걸려요.

W 좋아요. 고마워요

09 ①

W Do you like eating garlic?

M Actually I don't like it. It smells bad and tastes strong.

W That's the reason people don't like it. But it is very good for health.

M I know. Garlic doesn't smell good, but it helps food taste better. What is garlic good for?

W It prevents many different diseases. It helps lower blood pressure and prevent heart attack.

M That is why people in the world are more interested in Kimchi.

W That's right. Kimchi has been popular in the world these days. They know Kimchi has lots of garlic, so it is healthy food.

W 너 마늘 좋아하니?

M 사실 난 별로 좋아하지 않아. 독하고 나쁜 냄새가 나.

W 그래서 사람들이 싫어하지. 하지만 마늘은 건강에 매우 좋은 음식이야.

M 나도 알아. 마늘은 냄새가 좋지 않지만 음식을 더 맛있게 하거든. 마늘이 무엇에 좋지?

W 마늘은 여러 가지 질병을 예방해 줘. 혈압을 낮추는 데 도움을 주고 심장마비를 예방해 줘.

M 그래서 세상 사람들이 김치에 관심을 갖는 이유구나.

W 맞아. 요즈음 김치가 세계적으로 인기가 있지. 김치에 마늘이 많이 들어 있어 건강에 좋은 음식이라는 걸 알거든.

10 ⑤

[Telephone rings.]

M Hello, I'd like to speak to Cara.

W Oh, hi, Bill. What's up?

M Did you ever see the advertisement in the school newspaper?

W Which one do you mean?

M I mean the ad about the singing contest.

W No, I haven't seen it. When is it?

M November the 20th. Why don't we enter it together?

W That sounds great.

[전화벨이 울린다.]

M 여보세요, Cara와 통화하고 싶습니다.

W 오, 안녕, Bill. 무슨 일이야?

M 너 학교 신문에 난 광고 보았니?

W 어느 것을 말하는데?

M 노래 부르기 경연 대회에 관한 광고 말이야.

W 아니, 보지 못했어. 그것이 언제지?

M 11월 20일. 우리 함께 참여하는 것이 어때?

W 그거 좋지.

만점 솔루션 남자는 학교 신문에 난 노래 부르기 경연 대회에 함께 참가하자고 여자에게 전화했다.

11 ③

① **W** You look nice. Is that a new jacket?

M Yes, my parents bought it for me for my birthday.

② **W** I will take this jacket and this pair of pants.

M Great. How would you like to pay?

③ **W** What do you think? Does it fit you?

M I think it's too big. Can I try on a smaller size, please?

④ **W** What do you think of my new jacket?

M I like it, especially the pattern on the shoulders.

⑤ **W** Where can I try on these clothes?

M The fitting room is over there, around the corner.

① **W** 너 멋져 보인다. 그거 새 재킷이야?

M 응. 부모님이 생일에 사주셨어.

② **W** 이 재킷이랑 이 바지 주세요.

M 어떻게 계산하시겠어요?

③ **W** 어떻게 생각하세요? 잘 맞나요?

M 너무 큰 거 같아요. 더 작은 사이즈를 입어봐도 될까요?

④ **W** 내 새 재킷 어떻게 생각해?

M 마음에 들어. 특히 어깨에 있는 패턴이.

⑤ **W** 이 옷들은 어디서 입어볼 수 있나요?

M 탈의실은 저기 모퉁이를 돌면 있습니다.

12 ③

M I've lost my backpack in the waiting room. Could you help me find it?

W Of course. Could you tell me what it looks like?

M Let me see. It's a small cloth backpack.

W What color is it?

M Black. And my name is printed on the top.

W Oh, yes. What's your name then?

M Bill Jones.

W All right.

M 대합실에서 제 배낭을 잃어버렸습니다. 찾는 것을 도와주실 수 있나요?

W 물론이죠. 그것이 어떻게 생겼는지 말씀해 주시겠습니까?

M 글쎄요. 천으로 된 작은 배낭입니다.

W 무슨 색이죠?

M 검정색입니다. 그리고 제 이름이 위에 인쇄되어 있습니다.

M 검정색입니다. 그리고 제 이름이 위에 인쇄되어 있습니다.

W 아, 그래요. 그럼 이름이 무엇입니까?

M Bill Jones입니다.

W 됐습니다.

만점 솔루션 ③ 남자는 천으로 된 배낭을 잃어버렸다.

13 ②

W It's Lily's birthday tomorrow.

M Well, let me see. Should we buy her a present?

W Certainly. What should we buy her?

M How about a box of chocolates? She likes it very much.

W I hear she's on a diet. How about flowers? Most girls like flowers.

M But Peter will send her lots of flowers.

W Yeah. What about a purse? Hers doesn't look good.

M That's a good idea.

W 내일이 Lily의 생일이야.

M 음, 어디 보자. 우리가 그녀에게 선물 사 줘야 하니?

W 물론이야. 그녀에게 무엇을 사 줘야 하지?

M 초콜릿 한 상자 어때? 그녀는 초콜릿을 매우 좋아해.

W 나는 그녀가 다이어트 중이라고 들었는데. 꽃은 어때? 대부분의 소녀들은 꽃을 좋아해.

M 그러나 Peter가 그녀에게 많은 꽃을 보낼 거야.

W 그래. 지갑은 어때? 그녀의 것이 좋아 보이지 않아.

M 좋은 생각이야.

14 ②

M Thanks for coming, Joanna.

W Don't mention it. I'm glad to be here.

M We all know that you are in your mid-forties and you have two children. Do you exercise a lot?

W Yes, I go to a gym regularly.

M How often do you go there?

W Almost every day, except when I have to visit my mother.

M How long do you usually work out for each day?

W About two hours a day.

M 와 주셔서 감사합니다. Joanna.

W 천만에요. 이곳에 온 것이 기쁩니다.

M 우리 모두는 당신이 40대 중반이고 두 자녀를 두고 있다는 것을 알고 있습니다. 운동을 많이 하십니까?

W 예, 저는 규칙적으로 체육관에 갑니다.

M 얼마나 자주 그곳에 갑니까?

W 제가 어머니를 방문해야 할 때를 제외하고는 거의 매일요.

M 하루에 보통 얼마나 오래 운동을 하십니까?

W 하루에 약 두 시간이요.

15 ①

M Honey, I'm going to work. Don't be late for today's

meeting.

W Okay, but I don't know how to go there fast.

M You'd better not use your car. You don't know the way.

W Then should I go there by taxi?

M No. It is rush hour at that time. And it's too expensive.

W But there is no subway station around it.

M You'd better use a bus. There is a bus-only lane to the hotel.

W Okay. That's good.

M 여보, 나 출근할 거예요. 오늘 모임에 늦지 말아요.

W 알았어요. 하지만 그곳에 빨리 가는 방법을 몰라요.

M 당신의 차를 사용하지 않는 것이 좋아요. 길을 모르잖아요.

W 그럼 택시로 가야 하나요?

M 아니요. 그 때는 러시아워 시간이에요. 그리고 그것은 너무 비싸요.

W 하지만 그 주변에는 지하철역이 없잖아요.

M 버스를 이용하는 것이 좋겠어요. 그 호텔까지 버스 전용차로가 있어요.

W 알았어요. 좋아요.

16 ②

M Hi, Linda. How are you today?

W Fine. You look very good. What's new with you?

M Well, I'm going to San Francisco tomorrow.

W Going to San Francisco? What for?

M Yeah, I have an aunt there and she invited me. I'll stay there for about a month.

W That's great. Have a good time there.

M Thank you.

M 안녕, Linda. 오늘 어떠니?

W 좋아. 너 얼굴 매우 좋아 보인다. 뭐 새로운 일 있어?

M 그래. 나 내일 샌프란시스코에 갈 거야.

W 샌프란시스코에 갈 거라고? 무엇 때문에?

M 그래. 그곳에 이모 한 분 계시는데 그분이 나를 초대하셨어. 그곳에 약 한 달 동안 머물 거야.

W 그거 좋겠다. 그곳에서 좋은 시간 보내.

M 고마워.

17 ②

M Hi, Jenny, I heard you're performing a play in the school festival. How's it going?

W To be honest, we're in trouble. We need a new actor.

M Why? What happened?

W Jaehun dropped out suddenly. He didn't like his role.

M That's too bad. What's the role?

W It's a police officer role. *[pause]* Wait, are you interested, Woobin?

M Maybe. I've always wanted to try acting.

W Really? Can you do it, please? I think you'll be good at it.

M Hmm... okay. I'll give it a try.

M 안녕, 제니, 학교 축제에서 연극을 공연한다고 들었어. 어떻게 되어가?

W 솔직히, 큰일 났어. 새로운 배우가 한 명 필요해.

M 왜? 무슨 일이야?

W 재훈이 갑자기 중도하차했어. 자기 역할을 좋아하지 않았어.

M 안됐다. 그 역할이 뭔데?

W 경찰 역할이었어. *[멈춤]* 잠깐, 너 관심있니, 우빈?

M 아마도, 항상 연기를 해보고 싶었어.

W 진짜? 해 줄 수 있어? 네가 정말 잘 할 거 같아.

M 흠... 알겠어. 한 번 해볼게.

18 ④

W Hi, Minho, did you do anything interesting over the summer vacation?

M Well, I wanted to learn how to swim, but I didn't get the chance.

W Oh, no. Were you too busy with your soccer practice?

M No, I couldn't find a good swimming pool in my neighborhood.

W That's too bad. I heard a new gym will open soon. I hope they will have a pool there.

M Yes, but it's okay. I learned yoga instead, and I really liked it.

W Wow, really? Tell me more about it.

W 안녕, 민호, 여름 방학동안 뭐 재미있는 일 했어?

M 수영하는 법을 배우고 싶었는데 기회가 없었어.

W 이런. 축구 연습 때문에 너무 바빴니?

M 아니, 집 가까이에 괜찮은 수영장을 찾지 못했어.

W 안됐다. 새로운 체육관이 곧 개관한다고 들었어. 거기에 수영장이 있었으면 좋겠다.

M 그래, 하지만 괜찮아. 대신 요가를 배웠거든. 진짜 좋았어.

W 와, 진짜? 더 말해 봐.

19 ⑤

W Hello. I'm Mrs. Carter, David's mother.

M Oh! Mrs. Carter! I'm pleased to meet you.

W I'm glad to meet you, too. Please tell me, how is David doing in math this year?

M He's doing very well. He works very hard, and his grades are excellent. He's already a top student in my class.

W I'm glad to hear that.

M _____

W 안녕하세요. 저는 David의 엄마 Carter 부인입니다.

M 오! Carter 부인! 만나서 기쁩니다.

W 저도 만나서 반갑습니다. 올해 David가 수학에서 어떻게 하고 있는지를 말씀해 주시겠어요?

M 아주 잘하고 있습니다. 매우 열심히 공부해서 성적들이 우수합니다. 이미 우리 반에서 최고의 학생입니다.

W 그 얘기를 들으니 기쁘네요.

M 당신은 그를 매우 자랑스럽게 여겨야 합니다.

① 우리는 수학을 더 많이 공부해야 합니다.

② 그것을 비밀로 할 것을 약속합니다.

③ 나중에 그에게 전화하는 것이 좋겠다.

④ 좋아요, 당신에게 저녁을 사주고 싶어요.

만점 솔루션 엄마가 아들의 수학 성적이 우수하다는 선생님의 말을 듣고 기뻐하므로 이에 선생님이 할 수 있는 응답은 ⑤가 가장 적절하다.

20 ④

W How do you like my new dress? I bought it yesterday.

M It looks very fashionable.

W Thank you. I'm going to wear it to my friend's party tomorrow. What do you think?

M Not a bad idea. But I don't think the flower in the left matches the dress.

W I don't like it, either. I'll take it off.

M _____

W 내 새 드레스를 어떻게 생각하니? 어제 그것을 샀어.

M 아주 최신 유행처럼 보인다.

W 고마워. 내일 친구의 파티에 이것을 입고 갈 예정이야. 어떻게 생각해?

M 나쁜 생각은 아니야. 하지만 왼쪽의 꽃이 드레스와 어울리지 않는 것 같아.

W 나도 그 꽃이 싫어. 떼어 버릴 거야.

M 그렇게 하면 더 좋아 보일 거야.

① 내가 꽃을 좀 살 게.

② 그것은 전혀 문제가 아니야.

③ 나는 그것을 더 이상 사용하지 않을 거야.

⑤ 그러고 싶지만, 나는 너무 바빠.

만점 솔루션 꽃이 드레스와 어울리지 않는다는 말에 여자가 드레스에서 꽃을 떼어버릴 거라고 말했을 때 남자의 응답으로는 ④가 가장 적절하다.

영어듣기능력평가 **18**회

01 ⑤	02 ③	03 ④	04 ②, ✚①	05 ①
06 ④	07 ①	08 ②	09 ⑤	10 ④
11 ④	12 ②	13 ③	14 ③	15 ④
16 ①, ✚②	17 ③	18 ③	19 ⑤	20 ⑤

01 ⑤

M Can I use your computer for a moment, Susie?
W Sure, but is it okay if I ask why?
M I need to check some information about a dance club.
W Oh, I didn't know you're interested in dance.
M I heard that you're a member of the school band, right?
W Yes, I was last year, but I changed clubs this year.
M You're interested in painting. So, you joined the painting club?
W That's right.

M 잠시 동안 네 컴퓨터 좀 사용할 수 있을까, Susie?
W 물론이지, 하지만 이유를 물어봐도 되겠니?
M 댄스 동아리에 대한 몇 가지 정보 좀 확인할 필요가 있어서.
W 아, 나는 네가 댄스에 관심이 있는 줄은 몰랐는데.
M 나는 네가 학교 밴드부원이라고 들었는데, 맞니?
W 응, 작년에는 그랬는데, 올해 동아리를 바꿨어.
M 너는 그림에 관심이 있잖아. 그래서 미술부에 가입했니?
W 맞아.

02 ③

① M I'm looking for some flowers.
   W How about these?
② M Do you have a boyfriend?
   W Yes. His name is Richard.
③ M Happy birthday, Nancy. This is for you.
   W Oh, I'm really happy. Thank you.
④ M I'm sorry. I'm too cold.
   W Really? Then I'll close the window.
⑤ M The room was filled with the smell of roses.
   W Yeah, they smell good.

① M 저는 꽃을 좀 찾고 있어요.
   W 이것들은 어때요?
② M 남자 친구가 있니?
   W 응, 그의 이름은 Richard야.
③ M 생일 축하해, Nancy. 이건 널 위한 거야.
   W 아, 나는 정말로 행복해. 고마워.
④ M 미안해요. 제가 너무 추워서요.
   W 그래요? 그럼 창문을 닫을게요.
⑤ M 방 안이 장미꽃 냄새로 가득 찼어요.

03 ④

M Mom! Can I watch the basketball game on TV now?
W No, you can't. I want you to clean the living room now.
M Oh, mom! I'll do it tomorrow morning. I promise.
W Mr. and Mrs. Conway are coming over for dinner.
M But the basketball game starts now. Please, mom.
W No. I'm going shopping now and I need you to help out. So, please clean the living room now.
M Oh, alright.

M 엄마! 지금 TV에서 농구 경기를 볼 수 있을까요?
W 아니, 그럴 수 없어. 나는 네가 지금 거실을 청소했으면 해.
M 아, 엄마! 그건 내일 아침에 할 게요. 약속해요.
W Conway 씨 부부께서 저녁 식사를 하러 오실 거야.
M 하지만 농구 경기는 지금 시작하거든요. 제발요, 엄마.
W 안 돼. 나는 지금 쇼핑하러 갈 거고, 네가 도와줘야 해. 그러니까 지금 거실을 청소하렴.
M 아, 알았어요.

04 ② | ✚①

M Can I help you?
W Yes, how much is that skirt?
M It's $40.
W Can I try it on?
M Yes, you can. The changing room is over there.
W It feels like it's a bit small for me and I don't like the color. How much is that pink skirt?
M It was 60 dollars, but it's on sale for fifty percent off.
W I like it. It looks luxurious and high-quality. Is that size 11?
M Yes, it will perfectly fit you.
W OK. I'll take it.

M 도와드릴까요?
W 예, 저 치마는 얼마예요?
M 40달러입니다.
W 입어봐도 될까요?
M 예, 그러시죠. 갈아입는 곳은 저기 있습니다.
W 좀 작은 느낌이고 색깔도 마음에 들지 않네요. 저 분홍색 치마는 얼마예요?
M 60달러였는데 50% 세일을 하고 있습니다.
W 그게 마음에 드네요. 고급스럽고 재질이 좋아보이네요. 저거 11 사이즈인가요?
M 예, 손님에게 딱 맞을 거예요.
W 좋아요, 그걸로 주세요.

만점 솔루션 여자는 두 번째 고른 옷을 50% 할인된 가격에 산다

05 ①

M It's a quarter past six. The movie starts at 7:00. We should hurry.

W How should we get there?

M Let's take the subway. The subway is always the fastest way.

W But this isn't rush hour. How about taking a taxi? A taxi will be faster than the subway now.

M How about going by bus? They use the Bus Only Zone, and it's not so easy to catch a taxi here.

W I guess you're right. Oh, there comes the bus.

M Okay.

M 6시 15분이야. 영화가 7시에 시작하잖아. 서둘러야 해.

W 거기에 어떻게 가야 하지?

M 지하철을 타자. 지하철이 항상 가장 빠른 방법이야.

W 하지만 지금은 러시아워가 아니야. 택시를 타는 건 어때? 지금은 택시가 지하철보다 더 빠를 거야.

M 버스로 가는 건 어때? 버스는 버스 전용차선을 이용하잖아. 그리고 여기서 택시를 잡는 게 그렇게 쉽지는 않아.

W 네 말이 맞는 것 같다. 아, 저기 버스가 온다.

M 알았어.

06 ④

M You look upset. Is there anything wrong?

W My best friend won't talk to me.

M What happened?

W I don't know, but she doesn't even look at me.

M Maybe you can send a letter to her. Then she will like you again.

W Send a letter to her? That's a good idea. I'll write a letter right now.

M That's good. I'm sure your friendship will be fine again.

W Thank you, Jason.

M 속상해 보이는데. 뭐가 잘못됐니?

W 나의 가장 친한 친구가 나에게 말을 하지 않으려고 해.

M 무슨 일인데?

W 모르겠어. 그런데 그녀는 나를 쳐다보려고 하지도 않아.

M 아마도 너는 그녀에게 편지를 쓸 수도 있잖아. 그러면 그녀가 널 다시 좋아할 거야.

W 그녀에게 편지를 쓰라고? 그거 좋은 생각인데. 지금 바로 편지를 써야겠다.

M 좋지. 너희들의 우정이 다시 좋아질 거라고 확신해.

W 고마워, Jason.

만점 솔루션 친구와 문제를 겪고 있는 여자에게 조언해 주고 있다.

07 ①

W Hi, Andy! You've got a suntan!

M Yes, I have been to Thailand on holiday.

W I'm sure you saw many beautiful things.

M Well, Bangkok is really beautiful.

W I heard the city is like a great, big museum.

M Sure. There are many palaces and Buddhist temples.

W What is the most interesting thing you saw in Thailand?

M I enjoyed visiting an elephant farm, but the Royal palace in Bangkok is the most interesting thing I saw.

W 안녕, Andy! 햇볕에 탔구나!

M 그래. 휴가차 태국에 다녀왔어.

W 아름다운 것들을 많이 보았겠구나.

M 그래. 방콕은 정말 아름다워.

W 그 도시는 커다란 박물관 같다고 들었어.

M 물론이야. 많은 궁전들과 불교사원들이 있어.

W 태국에서 네가 본 것 중 가장 흥미로웠던 것은 무엇이니?

M 코끼리 농장을 방문한 것이 재미있었지만, 방콕에 있는 왕궁이 내가 본 것 중 가장 흥미로웠어.

08 ②

M You can't turn here.

W Oh, I'm so sorry. Can I park over there near the subway station?

M No, you can't. There's a police officer in front of the drugstore.

W But there's no sign about parking.

M There it is. You see that sign over there?

W Where? Oh, thanks for telling me. I had better not park here.

M Sure. You had better find a parking lot over there.

M 여기서 돌리면 안 돼요.

W 아, 정말 미안해요. 저쪽 지하철역 곁에 주차할 수 있나요?

M 아니오, 할 수 없어요. 약국 앞에 경찰관이 있어요.

W 하지만 주차에 관한 안내문은 없잖아요.

M 저기 있어요. 저쪽에 저 안내문 보이시죠?

W 어디요? 아, 말씀해 주셔서 감사해요. 여기에는 주차하지 않는 게 좋겠네요.

M 물론이죠. 저쪽에서 주차장을 찾아보는 게 좋겠어요.

만점 솔루션 'no sign about parking, not park here' 등의 표현을 통해 두 사람이 '주차 금지(NO PARKING)' 안내문에 관해 얘기하고 있음을 알 수 있다.

09 ⑤

W What are you going to do after you graduate?

M I'm planning to get a job as a designer.

W Good for you. I know that you're really gifted in that area.

M Thanks. I wanted to be a painter when I was young, but now I want to be one of the best designers.

W I'd like to be a teacher.

M Oh, really?

W Yeah, I want to teach at a primary school.

M I'm sure you'll be a great teacher.

W 졸업하고서 뭘 할 거니?

M 디자이너로서의 일자리를 얻을 계획이야.

W 잘했어. 네가 정말로 그 분야에 재능을 타고 난 걸 알고 있지.

M 고마워. 어렸을 때는 화가가 되고 싶었는데, 이제는 최고의 디자이너 중의 한 명이 되고 싶어.

W 나는 선생님이 되고 싶은데.

M 아, 정말?

W 응, 나는 초등학교에서 가르치고 싶어.

M 너는 훌륭한 선생님이 될 거라고 확신해.

10 ④

[Telephone rings.]

W Hi, Harry. It's Sally. How's it going?

M Good. How about you?

W I'm fine, too. By the way, did you hear that Mr. Baker from our elementary school <u>has been in the hospital</u> for three months?

M You mean <u>our homeroom teacher</u> when we were elementary school students?

W Yes. I'm going to see him this Saturday. Do you want to go with me?

M Okay. How about <u>meeting at the front gate</u> of our school at 9:30 Saturday morning?

W All right. See you then.

[전화벨이 울린다.]

W 안녕, Harry. 나 Sally야. 어떻게 지내니?

M 잘 지내. 너는?

W 나도 잘 지내. 그런데, 우리 초등학교 때의 Baker 선생님께서 3개월째 병원에 입원해 계신다는 걸 들었니?

M 우리가 초등학생일 때 우리 담임선생님을 말하는 거니?

W 그래. 이번 토요일에 그 분을 뵈러 갈까해. 나와 같이 갈래?

M 좋아. 토요일 아침 9시 30분에 학교 정문에서 만나는 게 어때?

W 좋아. 그때 보자.

만점 솔루션 ④ 초등학교 때 담임선생님이 현재 병원에 입원한 것이지, Sally가 3개월 동안 병원에 입원한 것은 아니다.

11 ④

M It's already two o'clock. We have to hurry to the airport.

W Yeah, but we should check we have packed everything we need.

M Okay, let's check. Do you <u>have the list</u>?

W Yes, I do. I'll read the list. You check. First of all, our <u>passports and airplane tickets</u>.

M Yes, they're here.

W Next, <u>swimming suits and sunglasses</u>.

M Perfect! And <u>guide books and maps</u> are here too.

W That's good.

M 벌써 두 시야. 공항으로 서둘러서 가야 해.

W 그래, 하지만 우리가 필요로 하는 모든 것을 꾸렸는지 점검해 봐야 해.

M 좋아, 점검하자. 목록을 가지고 있니?

W 그래, 가지고 있어. 내가 목록을 읽을 게. 네가 점검해. 먼저 여권과 비행기 표.

M 응, 여기 모두 있어.

W 다음, 수영복과 선글라스.

M 완벽해! 그리고 안내 책자와 지도도 여기에 있어.

W 좋아.

12 ②

[Telephone rings.]

W Good morning. May I help you?

M Yes. My father and I are planning to go camping tomorrow. Could you <u>tell me the weather</u> for tomorrow?

W Sure. It's going to rain tomorrow across the country.

M What? Are you sure it's going to <u>rain tomorrow</u>?

W Yes, I'm sure. Actually, <u>it's going to pour</u> tomorrow.

M Oh, no! I was looking forward to going camping tomorrow.

W That's too bad.

W 안녕하세요. 도와드릴까요?

M 네. 아빠와 제가 내일 캠핑을 갈 계획이거든요. 내일 날씨 좀 말씀해 주실 수 있나요?

W 물론이죠. 내일은 전국적으로 비가 올 예정입니다.

M 뭐라고요? 내일 비가 올 거라는 걸 확신하세요?

W 네, 확신해요. 사실 내일은 비가 퍼부을 거예요.

M 아, 저런! 저는 내일 캠핑 가는 걸 학수고대해 왔거든요.

W 정말 안 됐군요.

13 ③

M Who is taking a shower now? Isn't it Rebecca?

W I'll <u>go and check</u>. *[pause]* It isn't Rebecca. I think somebody else is taking a shower upstairs.

M I'll go upstairs and warn them. They are <u>not supposed to</u> take a shower after 10.p.m.

W Calm down now. If you tell them now, you will hurt their feelings. I'll talk to them about it later. The noise will stop before long.

M Even a little noise wakes me up at night. I think I'm sensitive to noise.

M 지금 누가 샤워를 하고 있지요? Rebeca 아니에요?

W 가서 확인해 볼게요. *[잠시 후]* Rebeca가 아닌데요. 윗층에서 다른 누군가가 샤워하고 있는 것 같아요.

M 내가 윗층에 올라가서 경고해야겠어요. 밤 10시 이후에는 샤워하지 못하게 되어 있는데요.

W 참으세요. 지금 얘기하면 그들의 감정을 상하게 할 것 같아요. 제가 나중에 잘 얘기해 볼게요. 소리가 곧 그칠 거예요.

M 밤에는 조그만 소리에도 잠이 깨요. 나는 소리에 민감한가봐요.

만점 솔루션 아파트의 층간 소음문제를 다루고 있다.

14 ③

W Do you <u>have a library card</u>?

M No, I don't. I just moved here last week.

W Then do you live around here?

M Yes, I do. I live on Maple Street.

W If you live in this town, you can <u>borrow books here</u>. But you have to have a library card. Let's see.... Here's a form for you to <u>fill out</u>.

M Thank you very much.

W 도서관 카드가 있으세요?

M 아니오, 없어요. 지난주에 이곳으로 막 이사 왔거든요.

W 그럼 이 근처에 사세요?

M 네, 그래요. Maple 가에 살아요.

W 이 마을에 사시면 여기서 책을 빌릴 수 있어요. 하지만 도서관 카드를 소지하셔야 해요. 어디 봐요⋯. 여기 당신이 작성할 양식이 있어요.

M 대단히 감사합니다.

15 ④

W Thank you for waiting. <u>Please be seated</u>. Is this your first time here?

M Yes, I just moved here.

W Really? Welcome. So, what can I do for you?

M I'd like to open a new account.

W Sure, do you have any ID with you? We need two different photo IDs.

M I have my passport. And..., will my student ID card be okay?

W Yes, it will. Which would you like to open, a savings account or a checking account?

M I'm sorry, but could you <u>explain the difference</u>, please?

W 기다려 주셔서 감사합니다. 앉으세요. 여기는 처음 오셨나요?

M 네, 여기서 막 이사왔어요.

W 정말요? 환영합니다. 무엇을 도와드릴까요?

M 새로운 계좌를 만들고 싶어요.

W 신분증 있으신가요? 두 개의 다른 사진이 있는 신분증이 필요합니다.

M 여권이 있습니다. 그리고... 학생증도 괜찮나요?

W 네. 저축예금계좌와 당좌예금계좌 중 어떤 걸 만들기 원하시나요?

M 죄송하지만 차이점을 설명해주실 수 있나요?

16 ① | ➕ ②

W Hanguk Airline. How can I help you?

M I want to <u>reconfirm my reservation</u>.

W Your membership number, please.

M It's 321475.

W Please, wait a moment. *[keyboard sound]* I'm sorry, but we have no reservation <u>under that number</u>.

M No way! I reserved it on the Internet a month ago.

W May I have your name and ID number?

M My name is Grey Waston, and my ID number CL23986.

W Wait a moment. *[keyboard sound]]* You <u>reserved two seats</u> for the flight for Singapore at 15:10 on June 27.

W Oh, that's right. I'm relieved to hear that.

W 한국항공사입니다. 뭘 도와드릴까요?

M 예약을 확인하려고 하는데요.

W 회원번호가 어떻게 되죠?

M 321475입니다.

W 잠깐만 기다려 주세요. *[키보드 치는 소리]* 미안합니다만, 그 번호로 예약되어 있지 않네요.

M 말도 안 돼요! 제가 한 달 전에 인터넷으로 예약을 했는데요.

W 성함과 신분증 번호를 말씀해 주시겠어요?

M 제 이름은 Grey Waston이고요, 신분증 번호는 CL23986입니다.

W 잠깐만요. *[키보드 치는 소리]* 고객님께서는 6월 27일 오후 3시 10분 싱가포르행 비행기로 두 좌석을 예약하셨네요.

M 네, 맞습니다. 그 말을 들으니 다행이네요.

만점 솔루션 항공기 예약 확인 과정에서 착오가 있었다가 문제가 해결되었다.

17 ③

W Hello, students! Are you all excited about our camping trip? I'd like to remind you of a few important things. First, we'll meet here at school at 8 o'clock tomorrow morning. Please <u>don't be late</u>, because our buses will leave on time. Second, don't forget to bring warm clothes. It'll be quite cold at night. Lastly, safety comes first. Don't leave your group without telling other members, and <u>look after each other</u>.

W 안녕하세요, 학생 여러분! 캠핑 여행으로 모두 신났나요? 여러분에게 몇 가지 중요한 점을 상기시켜주고 싶습니다. 우선, 내일 아침 8시에 이곳 학교에서 만날 겁니다. 버스는 정각에 떠나지 늦지 마세요. 둘째로, 따뜻한 옷을 가져오는 것을 잊지 마세요. 저녁에는 꽤 추울 겁니다. 마지막으로, 안전이 우선입니다. 다른 구성원에게 말하지 않고 무리를 벗어나지 말고, 서로를 돌봅시다.

18 ③

W Monday will be a good day for all you winter holiday skiers. It'll be snowy in the morning and then cloudy in the afternoon. Temperatures will be around two degrees Celsius. But <u>on Tuesday</u>, we'll have <u>some rain all day long</u> and it'll be warmer than today. We can expect another wonderful snowy day for the skiers Wednesday morning. But Wednesday afternoon, it'll rain again.

W 월요일은 겨울철 휴일에 스키를 타는 여러분 모두에게 좋은 날이 될 것입니다. 오전에는 눈이 올 것이고, 오후에는 구름이 낄 것입니다. 기온은 섭씨 2도 정도가 될 것입니다. 하지만 화요일에는 하루 종일 약간의 비가 올 것이고, 오늘보다 더 따뜻할 것입니다. 수요일 오전에는 스키를

타는 사람들에게 또 다른 멋진 날이 될 것입니다. 하지만 수요일 오후에는 다시 비가 오겠습니다.

만점 솔루션 ③ 화요일에는 하루 종일 비가 온다고 했다.

19 ⑤

M I heard that Koreans eat *kimchi* every day.
W That's right. This is cabbage *kimchi*. Why don't you try a bit?
M Is it hot?
W Yes, it's a bit hot, but if you try it once, you'll like it.
M [pause] Oh, it's not so hot.
W How do you like it?
M _____

M 한국 사람들은 매일 김치를 먹는다고 들었는데요.
W 맞아요. 이것은 배추김치예요. 조금 드셔 보실래요?
M 맵죠?
W 네, 약간 맵긴 하지만, 한 번 드셔 보시면 좋아하실 거예요.
M [잠시 후] 아, 그렇게 맵지는 않네요.
W 어때요?
M 좋은데요. 좀 더 먹어보고 싶어요.

① 내 뜻은 당신을 정말로 사랑한다는 거예요.
② 부탁 하나 들어 주실래요?
③ 뭐라고요? 제가 뭘 잘못 했다고요?
④ 그것들을 보고 싶으세요?

만점 솔루션 배추김치를 먹어본 남자에게 여자가 어떠냐고 물었으니 이에 알맞은 응답으로는 ⑤가 가장 자연스럽다.

20 ⑤

M Hello, Mary. You look tired. What's wrong with you?
W I have a terrible cold.
M Oh, how long have you had it?
W Since the day before yesterday. I got it from my brother.
M Really? I think you should go see the doctor.
W It's a good idea. I will go right now.
M _____

M 안녕, Mary. 너 피곤해 보인다. 무슨 일이 있니?
W 독감에 걸렸어.
M 오, 얼마나 됐는데?
W 그저께부터 걸린 것 같아. 내 남동생에게 옮았어.
M 정말? 병원에 가는 게 좋겠어.
W 좋은 생각이야. 지금 바로 갈게.
M 좋아. 몸 조심해.

① 농담하지마.
② 천만에.
③ 그곳 방문을 즐겨
④ 나에겐 괜찮아.

만점 솔루션 여자가 독감에 걸려 몸이 안 좋은 상태이다.

01 ④	02 ②	03 ②	04 ③	05 ⑤
06 ④, ❶②	07 ①, ❶⑤	08 ⑤	09 ③	10 ⑤
11 ⑤	12 ④	13 ⑤	14 ①	15 ③
16 ⑤	17 ⑤	18 ②	19 ④	20 ①

01 ④

W Can you show me your album?
M Sure. I was about to show it to you. This is the photo taken when I was in high school.
W Where are you in the photo? I can't tell who you are. You must have had curly hair. Oh, here, this boy with short hair in the front and long hair in the back, right?
M You got it.
W Then you were the tallest among them, and you were chubby. And you didn't wear glasses like you are now.
M At that time I had good eyesight.
W Anyway, you are quite different now.
M Yes, I am.

W 네 사진 앨범 좀 보여줄래?
M 물론이지. 그걸 네게 보여주려던 참이었어. 이건 내가 고등학교 때 찍은 사진이야.
W 이 사진에서 너는 누구지? 누가 너인지 알아볼 수가 없네. 분명 곱슬머리일 테고. 오, 여기. 여기 앞부분이 짧고 뒷부분이 긴 머리를 가진 아이, 맞지?
M 맞아.
W 그런데 네가 키가 제일 크고 포동포동하게 살쪘네. 그리고 지금은 썼는데 그때는 안경을 쓰지 않았구나.
M 그때는 눈이 좋았거든.
W 어쨌든, 지금 완전히 딴판이다.
M 그런 것 같아.

02 ②

M Look at the bear. It is telling us something.
W I think it's asking us for food.
M Do we have anything to feed? Oh, I have a piece of leftover bread.
W Look, it's coming towards us. Hey, It has a funny way of walking, doesn't it?
M Wait, look at that sign. It says, "Don't feed animals."
W Right. I heard that feeding animals is harmful. That causes many kinds of diseases.
M Let's just go.
W The bear keeps giving a sign to us for food.
M Let's go for the animal's health.

M 저 곰 좀 봐. 우리에게 뭐라고 말하는 것 같은데.

W 먹을 것을 좀 달라는 것 같아.

M 뭐 좀 줄 게 있니? 아, 먹다 남은 빵 조각이 있어.

W 봐, 곰이 우리쪽으로 오네. 야, 걷는 것이 우스꽝스럽지 않아?

M 잠깐, 여기 표지판 좀 봐. 동물들에게 먹을 것을 주지 말라고 되어 있네.

W 그렇군. 동물들한테 먹을 것을 주는 것은 해롭다고 들었어. 그것이 여러 가지 질병의 원인이 된다.

M 그냥 가자.

W 곰이 계속 먹을 것을 달라고 신호를 주는데.

M 동물의 건강을 생각해서 그냥 가자.

03 ②

M What's the weather like in winter in your country?

W It is hot in the day but turns very cold at night.

M You must live near the desert.

W Exactly. It never snows and is <u>windy</u> throughout the winter. Besides, there are <u>few cloudy days</u>.

M Does it rain much?

W It rains just a little, so <u>it is so dry</u>.

M 당신 나라의 겨울 날씨는 어떻습니까?

W 낮에는 언제나 덥고 밤에는 매우 추워집니다.

M 사막 주변에 살고 있군요.

W 맞아요. 눈은 절대 내리지 않고 연중 바람이 불어요. 게다가 흐린 날이 거의 없어요.

M 비는 많이 내리나요?

W 비는 조금만 내려서 몹시 건조해요.

만점 솔루션 ② 흐린 날이 거의 없다고 하였다. (there are few cloudy days)

04 ③

W You look very excited. Did you play soccer?

M No. Actually, I have a <u>special plan for tomorrow</u>.

W What is it? Do you have a date with your girl friend?

M I had a date with her yesterday. We went to a museum.

W Then what's the special plan?

M I'm going to the <u>Wonder Girls' concert</u>.

W How did you get the ticket?

M I <u>won the ticket</u> through a fan club website.

W 신나는 일이 있는 것 같아. 축구했었니?

M 아니야. 사실 내일 특별한 계획이 하나 있어.

W 무슨 일이야? 내일 여자 친구와 데이트가 있니?

M 어제 여자 친구와 데이트를 했어. 우리는 박물관에 갔었어.

W 그럼 특별한 계획이 뭐니?

M 나는 Wonder Girls 콘서트에 갈 거야.

W 티켓을 어떻게 구했니?

M 며칠 전 팬클럽 사이트를 통해 티켓을 구했어.

05 ⑤

[Telephone rings.]

M Hello.

W Hello. This is Yuna Lee from the ABC company. May I speak to Andrew, please?

M Oh, I'm sorry he is not here. He is in the boss's room.

W Could you take a message for him then?

M Yes, I could. Please go ahead. <u>What's the message</u>?

W Tomorrow's business meeting with the ABC company <u>is cancelled</u>.

M Okay. I will <u>give him the message</u>.

[전화벨이 울린다.]

M 여보세요.

W 여보세요. 저는 ABC 회사의 Yuna Lee입니다. Andrew 씨와 통화할 수 있습니까?

M 오, 죄송하지만 지금 이곳에 안 계십니다. 사장님 방에 계십니다.

W 그럼 그를 위해서 메시지를 받아주실 수 있나요?

M 예, 할 수 있습니다. 말씀하세요. 메시지가 무엇이죠?

W 내일 ABC 회사와의 업무 회의가 취소되었습니다.

M 알겠습니다. 메시지를 그에게 전해 드리겠습니다.

06 ④ | ➕ ②

M Excuse me, but what's the best way to get to the National Museum?

W You can take a bus, a subway, or a taxi.

M Then, how long does it take to walk there?

W Oh, it's about a thirty-minute walk. But are you a tourist?

M Yes, I'm from Canada.

W Well, you <u>can borrow a bike</u> for free in front of any subway station in this city.

M Good! I'd like to borrow one. Where is the nearest subway station?

W Look over there. <u>Around the corner</u>.

M Thanks for <u>the tip</u>.

M 실례합니다만, 국립박물관으로 가는 가장 좋은 방법이 무엇입니까?

W 버스, 지하철 또는 택시를 탈 수 있습니다.

M 그러면 그곳에 걸어가는 데 얼마나 걸립니까?

W 아, 대략 30분 걸어가는 거리입니다. 그런데 관광객이세요?

M 예, 캐나다에서 왔습니다.

W 그럼, 이 도시의 어느 지하철역 앞에서든 무료로 자전거를 빌릴 수 있습니다.

M 좋아요! 저는 자전거를 빌리고 싶어요. 가장 가까이 있는 역이 어디 있죠?

W 저기를 보세요. 길모퉁이를 돌아서요.

M 조언을 해 주셔서 감사합니다.

07 ① | ➕ ⑤

M Hi, ma'am. May I help you?

W I'd like to see <u>middle-sized used cars</u>.

M OK. This way. I think this would <u>fit your need</u>.

W How old is it?

M Well, it's only three years old.

W And what's the mileage?

M Uh, let me check. Oh yes. 75,000 miles.

W What's the price?

M You see, it's $16,000.

W Can you give me <u>a discount</u>? How about $14,000?

M Sorry, we can't.

W OK, I think I'll just keep looking around.

M 안녕하세요, 손님. 뭘 도와드릴까요?

W 저는 중형 중고차를 보고 싶은데요.

M 좋아요, 이리 오세요. 이게 당신의 요구 사항에 꼭 맞는 것 같군요.

W 몇 년 되었어요?

M 겨우 3년밖에 안 되었어요.

W 주행거리는 얼마나 되죠?

M 어, 잠깐 보겠습니다. 예, 7만 5천 마일이네요.

W 가격이 얼마죠?

M 보시다시피, 16,000달러입니다.

W 좀 깎아 주시겠어요? 14,000달러는 어때요?

M 미안합니다만, 그렇게 할 수 없네요.

W 좋아요. 계속 구경할게요.

만점 솔루션 대화의 앞부분에 I'd like to see ~ 다음에 나오는 말을 주의깊게 듣도록 한다.

08 ⑤

M Welcome to Antonius'. *[pause]* Are you ready to order?

W I'd like the seafood spaghetti and a grilled salmon, today's special.

M Would you like <u>anything to drink</u>?

W I'll have a coke, please.

M OK. That's one seafood spaghetti, one grilled salmon, and one coke. It will take five minutes.

M 안토니우스 식당에 오신 걸 환영합니다. *[잠시 후]* 주문하시겠어요?

W 저는 해물 스파게티와 오늘의 특별 요리인 구운 연어를 주세요.

M 마실 것을 드릴까요?

W 콜라 한 잔 주세요.

M 좋습니다. 그러니까, 해물 스파게티 하나, 구운 연어 하나, 그리고 콜라 한 잔이시죠. 5분 정도 걸릴 것입니다.

09 ③

W I'm glad to attend this camp with you.

M Me too. <u>What are your hobbies</u>?

W I am into music, drama, and painting.

M Really? You must be artistic. And then what is your major?

W My major is mass media studies.

M <u>What kind of job</u> do you want after you graduate?

W I want to be <u>a writer for TV dramas</u>. It is very difficult, but I'll keep trying.

M I'll keep my fingers crossed for you.

W 이 캠프에 당신과 함께 참석할 수 있게 되어서 기뻐요.

M 저도 좋아요. 취미가 뭐가요?

W 저는 음악, 드라마, 그리고 그림에 관심이 있어요.

M 그래요? 당신은 예술적인가 봐요. 그러면 당신의 전공은 무엇입니까?

W 제 전공은 미디어 학문입니다.

M 졸업 후에는 어떤 일을 하기를 원하세요?

W TV 드라마 작가가 되고 싶어요. 그것은 매우 힘들지만, 저는 계속해서 시도해 볼 거예요.

M 제가 당신을 위해 행운을 빌어 줄게요.

10 ⑤

M Who is next?

W You are. Are you ready to sing your song?

M Ye....s, I guess so. How much time do I have?

W You have to <u>go on stage</u> in five minutes.

M You know, this is my <u>first time</u> singing in front of an audience.

W Don't worry. I'm sure you'll do well. Just relax.

M That's easy to say, but <u>I cannot relax</u>!

M 다음은 누구죠?

W 너야. 노래 부를 준비는 되어 있니?

M 예…, 그런 것 같아요. 시간이 얼마나 남았죠?

W 5분 뒤에 무대에 올라가야 해.

M 알다시피, 저는 관객 앞에서 노래 부르는 것이 처음이에요.

W 걱정하지 마. 네가 잘할 거라고 확신해. 긴장을 풀어.

M 말하기는 쉽지만, 긴장을 풀 수 없어요!

만점 솔루션 남자는 관객 앞에서 처음으로 노래를 부른다며 긴장을 풀 수 없다고 하였다.

11 ⑤

M I visited my new house today. I'll move there soon.

W Is the house near the school?

M It is between our school and ABC Shopping Center.

W It is so near, but it may be noisy because of the large shopping center.

M It may be, but <u>the rental fee</u> is so cheap!

W Is there a washing machine, a dryer and a dishwasher?

M Of course, but <u>the problem is keeping pets</u>.

W You <u>can't raise pets</u> in most apartments!

M 오늘 새집을 방문했었어. 조만간 그곳으로 이사할 거야.

W 집이 학교 근처에 있니?

M 학교와 ABC 쇼핑센터 사이에 있어.

W 참 가깝구나. 하지만 대형 쇼핑센터 때문에 시끄러울 수 있을 거야.

M 그럴지도, 하지만 집세가 너무 싸!

W 그곳에 세탁기와 드라이어, 식기세척기는 있니?
M 물론이야, 문제는 애완동물을 기르는 거야.
W 대부분의 아파트에서는 애완동물을 기를 수 없어!

① 학교 근처에 있다.
② 시끄러울 것 같다.
③ 집세가 매우 싸다.
④ 식기세척기가 있다.
⑤ 애완동물을 기를 수 있다.

12 ④

W I'm hungry. Did you bring any food?
M No, I thought we could get something at the snack bar.
W Is there a snack bar? That's cool. Which car is it in?
M I think it's car number 4. Shall we go together?
W No, I'll go alone. I want to use the restroom on the way, and I don't want to leave our bags unattended.
M Okay, can you get me something as well?
W Sure, how long do we have until our destination?
M We just passed Daegu Station, so maybe an hour.

W 나 배고파. 음식 갖고 있는 거 있어?
M 아니, 난 우리가 매점에서 먹을 줄 알았어.
W 매점이 있어? 잘됐다. 어느 차 안에 있어?
M 4번 차일 거야. 같이 갈래?
W 아니, 혼자 갈래. 가는 길에 화장실도 가야하고 우리 가방을 주인없이 놔두고 싶지 않아.
M 알겠어, 내가 먹을 것도 갖고 와 줄래?
W 물론, 우리 목적지까지 얼마나 걸려?
M 대구역을 막 지났으니까 한 시간 정도.

13 ⑤

M Would you print this file for me? My printer broke down.
W How many pages is that?
M That'll be about 150 pages.
W 150 pages? That's not going to be possible. That's a really huge ask.
M I know. But I must have it right away.
W I'm sorry, but I think you'd better go to a print shop.
M I went to the shop first, but it's already been closed. If you let me print it, I'll pay for a new ink cartridge.
W Really? OK. Which file is it?

M 이 파일 좀 프린트 해 줄래? 내 프린터가 고장이 나서 그래.
W 몇 장이나 되는데?
M 약 150 페이지 정도 돼.
W 150페이지라고? 불가능할 것 같아. 너는 엄청난 요구를 하고 있잖아.
M 나도 알아. 하지만 당장 그것이 필요해.
W 미안하지만, 프린트 가게에 가 보는 게 좋겠어.

M 물론 먼저 갔었는데, 문이 닫혔어. 네가 프린트 해 주면 새 잉크 카트리지를 사 줄게.
W 정말? 알았어. 어느 파일이야?

14 ①

W Attention, please. Our Book Club was formed five years ago. Through your love and help, our club has progressed. Especially, our club's president, John, has worked hard for us. But he has decided to retire because of his business matters. So there will be an election for a new club president next Thursday night. We hope many members want to be president of our club. Please read our website for more information.

W 주목해 주세요. 우리 독서클럽은 5년 전에 결성되었습니다. 여러분들의 사랑과 도움 덕택에 우리 클럽이 발전했습니다. 특별히 우리 클럽의 회장인 John은 우리를 위해 열심히 활동하였습니다. 하지만 그는 사업상의 문제로 사직을 결심하셨습니다. 그래서 다음 목요일 밤에 새로운 클럽 회장 선출을 위한 선거가 있습니다. 많은 회원들이 우리 클럽의 회장이 되는 것을 원하길 희망합니다. 좀 더 많은 정보는 우리 홈페이지를 읽어 주시길 바랍니다.

15 ③

W John, I'd like to give you some science quizzes and guess the answers, OK?
M Fine. I'm quite good at science. Go ahead.
W How fast does light travel? Number 1, 30,000 km per second, Number 2, 300,000 km per second.
M The answer is number 1.
W Wow, you are great! Next question. How long does it take for light to travel from the Sun to the Earth? Number 1, 7½ minutes, Number 2, 8½ minutes.
M Number 1, 7½ minutes.
W This time you have the wrong answer. The answer is Number 2, 8½ minutes.
M I was confused. I'm not good at numbers.

W John, 내가 오늘 과학퀴즈를 내볼 테니 네가 답을 맞춰봐, 됐어?
M 좋아. 나도 과학은 좀 잘하지. 해봐.
W 빛은 얼마나 빠른 속도로 갈까? 1번. 초당 30,000킬로, 2번, 초당 300,000킬로.
M 정답은 1번
W 와, 대단한데! 다음 질문. 그러면 태양에서 지구로 빛이 오는 데 얼마나 걸리지? 1번, 7분 30초, 2번 8분 30초.
M 1번 7분 30초.
W 이번에 틀렸어. 정답은 2번 8분 30초야.
M 헷갈렸어. 나는 숫자에 약하단 말이야.

16 ⑤

M What's the matter, Jane? You're crying.

W It's okay. I'll be all right.

M Why? Did <u>something bad happen</u>?

W My dog, Charlie, died this morning. I loved my Charlie very much.

M I'm sorry to hear that. Was it an accident?

W No, it wasn't. He was a very old dog. And he hadn't eaten recently.

M Don't be so sad. Let's <u>go out to see a movie</u>.

W Thank you, David, but <u>I'd like to stay home</u> right now.

M 무슨 일이야, Jane? 울고 있잖아.

W 괜찮아. 괜찮아질 거야.

M 왜? 안 좋은 일이라도 생겼니?

W 내 개 Charlie가 오늘 아침에 죽었어. 나는 Charlie를 매우 많이 사랑했어.

M 그렇다니 안 됐는데. 사고였니?

W 아니, 그렇지 않아. 그 녀석은 나이가 아주 많은 개였어. 그리고 최근에는 먹지를 않았거든.

M 너무 슬퍼하지 마. 나가서 영화를 보자.

W 고마워, David, 하지만 지금은 집에 있고 싶어.

① 그녀는 지금 울고 있다.

② 그녀의 개가 오늘 아침에 죽었다.

③ 그녀는 자신의 개를 무척 사랑했다.

④ 그녀의 개는 나이를 매우 많이 먹었다.

⑤ 그녀는 지금 영화를 보러 갈 것이다.

만점 솔루션 ⑤ 영화를 보러 가자는 남자의 말에 Jane은 집에 있고 싶다며 거절하였다.

17 ⑤

① **M** Can you tell me when your birthday is?

　W Sure, my birthday is October 13.

② **M** How was the party? Did you enjoy it?

　W Yes, a lot of people <u>came to celebrate</u>, and it was fun.

③ **M** Which do you think is better?

　W I think this one is better. I like the blue color.

④ **M** What do you want for Christmas, Susie?

　W I'd love to have the new comic book series, Dad.

⑤ **M** Happy birthday, Sarah! <u>This is for you</u>.

　W Thank you so much! Can I open it now?

① **M** 네 생일이 언제인지 알려줄래?

　W 물론, 내 생일은 10월 13일이야.

② **M** 파티는 어땠어? 재미 있었어?

　W 응, 많은 사람들이 축하하러 왔고 재미있었어.

③ **M** 뭐가 더 나은 거 같아?

　W 나는 이게 더 좋은 거 같아. 파란 색이 좋아.

④ **M** 크리스마스에 무엇이 갖고 싶니, 수지?

　W 새로운 만화책 시리즈를 갖고 싶어요, 아빠.

⑤ **M** 생일 축하해! 사라! 이거 널 위한 거야.

　W 고마워! 지금 열어봐도 돼?

18 ②

M Mom, what time are we leaving tomorrow?

W If we want to avoid the rush hour, we should <u>leave early</u>. Probably at 7 a.m.?

M Wow, that's early. I should go to bed now, then.

W Yes, that's a good idea.

M I set the alarm, but can you still wake me up tomorrow morning? I'm afraid I won't <u>hear the alarm</u>.

W Sure, I will wake you up at 6.

M It takes only 30 minutes for me to get ready, so 6:30 would be fine.

W Okay. Good night, son.

M 엄마, 우리 내일 몇 시에 떠나요?

W 혼잡한 시간대를 피하고 싶다면 일찍 떠나야 해. 아마 오전 7시?

M 와, 이른 시간이네요. 지금 자야겠어요.

W 그래, 좋은 생각이구나.

M 알람을 맞추었지만 내일 아침 깨워줄 수 있어요? 알람을 못 들을까 겁나요.

W 물론, 6시에 깨울게.

M 준비하는데 30분이면 되니까 6시 30분에 깨워 주세요.

W 그래. 잘 자렴, 아들.

19 ④

W Have you ever been to Halla Mountain?

M No, I haven't. How about you?

W Neither have I. I really want to <u>go up to the top</u> of Halla Mountain. Shall we go to Mt. Halla during the Chusok holidays?

M That sounds fun.

W How is the weather going to be during the holidays?

M I heard that it's going <u>to be warm and sunny</u>.

W It's going to be perfect weather for climbing, isn't it?

M I believe so. But you know that the weather in Jeju-do is unpredictable.

W You're right. One minute it's sunny, and then the next minute it's rainy.

M _____

W 너 한라산 정상에 가 본 적이 있니?

M 아니, 못 가 봤어. 너는?

W 나도 못 가 봤어. 나는 정말로 한라산 꼭대기에 올라가고 싶어. 이번 추석 연휴에 한라산에 가 볼래?

M 좋지.

W 이번 추석 연휴의 날씨는 어떻대?

M 따뜻하고 맑을 것이라고 들었어.

W 등반하는 데 최고의 날씨가 되겠네, 그렇지 않니?

M 그랬으면 좋겠어. 하지만 알다시피 제주도의 날씨는 예측하기가 불가능해.

W 맞아. 잠깐 맑았다가도 그 다음에는 비가 오고 하잖아.

M 나는 날씨가 그냥 똑같은 상태에 머물렀으면 좋겠어.

① 아마도 그때는 너무 늦을 거야.

② 너는 나보다 그를 더 잘 알잖아.

③ 더운 곳에 그렇게 오래 머무를 수 없어.

⑤ 그 일을 하느라 늦게까지 있지 않는 게 좋겠어.

만점 솔루션 제주도의 변화가 많은 날씨에 대해 휴가 때 만큼은 날씨가 일정했으면 하는 희망의 표현이 이어지는 게 적절하다.

20 ①

W Andrew, will you do me a favor?

M Sure, what is it?

W Can you drive Jane and me to the hospital on Monday?

M I think so. I'll mark it on my calendar so I don't forget.

W It's really kind of you. But I'm sorry to bother you.

M Don't worry about that.

W Thanks. I haven't forgotten your helping me several times.

M _____

W Andrew, 부탁 하나 들어 줄래?

M 물론이지. 뭔데?

W 월요일에 Jane과 나를 병원에 태워다 줄 수 있니?

M 가능할 것 같아. 잊지 않도록 달력에 표시해 둘게.

W 정말 고마워. 하지만 너를 귀찮게 해서 미안해.

M 그 점에 대해서 걱정하지 마.

W 고마워. 네가 여러 번 나를 도와준 것을 잊지 않고 있어.

M 친구 좋다는 게 뭐니?

② 그런데, Kate가 누구니?

③ 조심해서 운전해야 해.

④ 미안하지만 나는 월요일에 바빠.

⑤ 운전할 줄 몰라서 미안해.

만점 솔루션 전에 도와준 것도 잊지 않고 있다면서 고맙다고 말하는 여자의 마지막 말에 알맞은 남자의 응답으로는 ①이 가장 자연스럽다.

---

01 ③	**02** ③	**03** ②	**04** ①	**05** ③
06 ①	**07** ④	**08** ②, ✚⑤	**09** ⑤, ✚①	**10** ③
11 ⑤	**12** ④	**13** ⑤	**14** ③	**15** ④
16 ④	**17** ④	**18** ②	**19** ②	**20** ⑤

01 ③

M I lost my dog. Have you seen a dog around here?

W Oh, yes. I saw a large, white dog on the farm.

M Really? It may be my dog. Is there anything that you can remember about it?

W Yes. I'm certain it had a short tail.

M Really? How about its ears? Were they short?

W Yes, they were short.

M Oh, it must be mine. Where was it?

W Just over there.

M 제 개를 잃어버렸어요. 이 근처에서 개를 보셨나요?

W 아, 네. 농장에서 크고 흰 개를 봤어요.

M 정말요? 그게 제 개일지도 몰라요. 그 개에 대해 기억하실 수 있는 게 있나요?

W 네. 꼬리가 짧았던 게 확실해요.

M 정말요? 귀는 어땠어요? 짧았나요?

W 네. 귀가 짧았어요.

M 아, 그게 제 개임에 틀림없어요. 그게 어디 있었어요?

W 저쪽에요.

만점 솔루션 남자가 찾고 있는 개는 크고, 흰색이며, 꼬리와 귀가 짧다.

02 ③

W ① It is raining cats and dogs.
② The car is damaged by the tree.
③ The big tree is fallen across the road.
④ The car is passing by the fallen tree.
⑤ The rescuers are pulling the injured driver from the car.

W ① 비가 억수같이 오고 있는 중이다.
② 자동차가 큰 나무에 의해 훼손되었다.
③ 큰 나무가 도로를 가로질러 쓰러져 있다.
④ 자동차가 쓰러진 나무 곁을 지나가고 있는 중이다.
⑤ 구조대원들이 자동차에서 부상당한 운전자를 구조하고 있다.

03 ②

W Wake up! It's four o'clock.

M Let's hurry up, or we'll miss the sunrise.

W Don't forget to take your camera.

M OK. Oh! I'm looking forward to taking pictures of the

---

beautiful sunrise.

W Me, too. Is it going to be sunny?

M Of course, I've already checked the <u>weather forecast</u>.

[After a while]

M Uh, the sky was filled with thick rain clouds.

W It's very foggy everywhere. Our hope is completely gone.

M It's been the second time we failed to take photos of a sunrise.

W Let's go to other places. There are lots of things we can take pictures of.

W 일어나! 새벽 4시야.

M 서두르자. 그렇지 않으면 일출을 놓치겠다.

W 카메라 가져가는 것은 잊지 말고.

M 알았어. 아! 아름다운 일출 장면을 사진에 담을 것이 기대가 돼.

W 나도 그래. 오늘 날씨가 맑다고 했지?

M 물론이지. 이미 일기 예보를 점검했지.

[잠시 후]

M 어, 하늘에 잔뜩 비구름이 끼었네.

W 안개도 모든 곳에 짙게 깔려 있고. 우리의 희망이 완전히 사라졌어.

M 일출 사진 찍는 것에 실패한 게 벌써 두 번째야.

W 다른 곳으로 가자. 일출이 아니어도 사진 찍을 것은 많아.

① 언짢은 → 안심한
② 흥분된 → 실망한
③ 놀라운 → 두려운
④ 화난 → 흥미 있는
⑤ 감사한 → 화난

만점 솔루션 일출 장면을 촬영하려고 기대에 부풀었다가 안개로 인해 실패한다.

04 ①

M Jessica, what classes are you planning to take?

W History, biology, and geography. How about you?

M I'm planning to take music, math, physical education, and chemistry.

W Do you like physical education?

M Of course. <u>Music and physical education</u> are my two <u>favorite subjects</u>.

W I took physical education last year. I really had a hard time in the class.

M My physical education teacher is <u>really nice to me</u>.

M Jessica, 어떤 수업을 들을 계획이니?

W 역사, 생물 그리고 지리. 너는?

M 나는 음악, 수학, 체육 그리고 화학을 들을 계획이야.

W 너는 체육을 좋아하니?

M 물론이지. 음악과 체육이 내가 가장 좋아하는 두 과목이지.

W 나는 작년에 체육을 들었어. 그 수업은 정말로 힘이 들었어.

M 체육 선생님은 나한테 아주 잘해 주셔.

05 ③

① **M** How long will it take to get to Seoul?

W I don't know exactly, but it usually takes two hours.

② **M** I'd like to buy two tickets. <u>How much is it?</u>

W Sure, it will be $20 in total.

③ **M** Can I check your ticket, please?

W Sure, here are tickets for both of us.

④ **M** I'm so excited about this trip.

W So am I. We'll see a lot of new things, and it'll be so fun.

⑤ **M** <u>Have you ever been to</u> Jeju Island?

W Yes, once. I went there with my family.

① **M** 서울까지 얼마나 걸릴까?

W 잘 모르겠지만 보통 2시간 걸려.

② **M** 표 2장 사고 싶어요. 얼마인가요?

W 총 20달러입니다.

③ **M** 표를 확인할 수 있을까요?

W 네, 여기 우리 두 명 표입니다.

④ **M** 이번 여행 엄청 기대된다.

W 나도 그래. 우리는 많은 새로운 걸 볼 거고 아주 재미있을 거야.

⑤ **M** 제주도에 가봤어?

W 응, 한번. 가족들이랑 갔었어.

06 ①

M Listen to that song! Do you know that song?

W Umm, it sounds familiar. Ah, it's "Memory."

M Right. It's a really beautiful song. Someday I want to see the musical "Cats."

W Anyway, <u>what are you having</u>, Kevin? Lobster? Steak?

M I can't decide yet. Why aren't they <u>taking our orders</u>?

W The waiters <u>look very busy</u> tonight.

M Yeah. It's very crowded here tonight.

M 저 노래를 들어봐! 저 노래를 알고 있니?

W 음, 많이 들어본 건데. 아, 그건 'Memory'지.

M 맞아. 정말 아름다운 노래야. 언젠가 나는 뮤지컬 'Cats'를 보고 싶어.

W 아무튼 너는 뭘 먹을 거니, Kevin? 바닷가재? 스테이크?

M 아직 결정을 못 하겠어. 왜 우리 주문을 받지 않는 거지?

W 종업원들이 오늘 밤에 아주 바쁜 것 같아.

M 그래. 오늘 밤에 여기 정말로 붐비네.

07 ④

W Do you have any <u>work experience</u>?

M Yes. I had a part-time job at a department store when I was a high school student.

W Why did you <u>apply for this job</u>?

M I'm interested in fashion.

W Are you interested in working <u>full-time or part-time</u>?

M I'd like to work part-time. As you know, I'm still a college student.

W Good.

W 경력이 있으신가요?

M 네. 고등학교 학생 때 백화점에서 아르바이트 일을 했어요.

W 왜 이 일자리에 지원하셨죠?

M 패션에 관심이 있어서요.

W 전임제로 일하는 것에 관심이 있나요 아니면 아르바이트로 일하는 것에 관심이 있나요?

M 저는 아르바이트로 일하고 싶어요. 아시다시피, 저는 아직 대학생이잖아요.

W 좋아요.

08 ② | ➕ ⑤

W Honey, what time does your train leave?

M At 7:30. Why do you ask?

W You have an appointment with Mr. Evans at 5 o'clock, remember?

M Oh, that's right! I nearly forgot about it. Thanks.

W What time are you <u>leaving the house</u>?

M About 4 o'clock, I guess.

W All right. <u>At around 3:50</u>, I'll call a taxi. It'll <u>take about ten minutes</u> for a taxi to get here.

M Okay. Thanks, honey.

W 여보, 당신이 탈 기차가 몇 시에 떠나죠?

M 7시 30분예요. 왜 물어봐요?

W 5시에 Evans 씨와 약속이 있잖아요, 기억하시죠?

M 아, 맞아요! 하마터면 그것에 대해 잊을 뻔했네요. 고마워요.

W 집에서는 몇 시에 나가실 거예요?

M 4시쯤이 될 것 같아요.

W 좋아요. 3시 50분경에 제가 택시를 부를게요. 택시가 여기 오는데 약 10분 정도 걸릴 거예요.

M 알았어요. 고마워요, 여보.

09 ⑤ | ➕ ①

M My office is far from where I live. Driving all those hours is just killing me.

W Yeah, I know what you mean. I <u>used to drive</u> two hours to work each day. But now I walk to work. It's great.

M Did you move?

W No, I got a new job near my apartment.

M Well, I don't think I can change my job, but I am thinking about moving.

W How about moving to my apartment building? There is one empty apartment for rent. And I'm sure it <u>would be closer</u> to your work than you are now.

M Really? Isn't it expensive?

W No, it isn't. It is new and big.

M That sounds great. I'd love to see it.

M 사무실이 내가 사는 곳에서 너무 멀어. 여러 시간을 운전하는 것이 너무 싫어.

W 그래, 무슨 말인지 알겠어. 나도 예전에 매일 여러 시간 운전해서 출근하곤 했었어. 하지만 지금은 걸어서 다녀. 정말 좋아.

M 너 이사했니?

W 아니, 집 근처에 새 직장을 얻었어.

M 글쎄, 나는 직장을 바꿀 수 없을 것 같아. 하지만 이사가려고 생각하고 있어.

W 우리 아파트로 이사오는 게 어때? 마침 임대하는 빈 집이 있어. 그러면 지금 있는 곳보다 직장이 더 가까울 것으로 확신해.

M 정말? 비싸지 않아?

W 그렇지 않아. 새 집이고 큰 편이야.

M 좋은데. 한 번 보고 싶어.

만점 솔루션 대화의 뒷부분에 여자가 권유하는 나오는 표현에 집중해서 듣도록 한다.

10 ③

W Attention, please, shoppers! Thank you for shopping at Super Mart. We're having <u>a big sale</u> this week. Our beef is only $8.99 a pound. That's right, shoppers, only $8.99 a pound. We're also offering chicken on sale. Our chicken is only $2.99 a pound. This sale is <u>for today only</u>. Enjoy your shopping today here!

W 쇼핑객 여러분께 알려 드리겠습니다! Super 마트에서 쇼핑해 주셔서 감사드립니다. 저희는 금주에 대 할인 판매를 실시하고 있습니다. 저희 쇠고기는 1파운드에 8달러 99센트밖에 안 합니다. 맞습니다, 쇼핑객 여러분. 1파운드에 8달러 99센트밖에 안 합니다. 저희는 또한 닭고기도 세일 중입니다. 저희 닭고기는 1파운드에 2달러 99센트 밖에 안 합니다. 할인 판매는 단지 오늘만 하는 것입니다. 오늘 이곳에서 쇼핑을 즐기시기 바랍니다!

11 ⑤

W We've finally finished all of the preparation work.

M Yes, but now is the real challenge. I hope we will <u>do well on</u> our presentation.

W Don't worry. We will do just fine. How long do we have before the class?

M About an hour. I'll <u>do the final check</u> to make sure our projector works with the computer.

W Thanks. What should I do meanwhile?

M Can you go photocopy these handouts?

W Sure, I can manage that. How many copies do we need?

M I think 40 will be enough.

W 드디어 준비 작업이 다 끝났어.

M 그래, 하지만 이제 진짜 도전이야. 우리가 발표를 잘 했으면 좋겠어.

W 걱정 마. 우리는 잘 할 거야. 수업시간까지 얼마나 남았지?

M 한 시간 정도. 우리 영사기가 컴퓨터에 잘 연결되는지 마지막으로 확인해 볼게.

W 고마워. 그동안 나는 뭐 할까?

M 이 발표 자료를 복사해줄래?

W 물론, 그 정도는 할 수 있어. 얼마나 많이 필요해?

M 40장이면 충분할 거 같아.

12 ④

[Telephone rings.]

W Hello, can I speak to Susan, please?

M She's not in now. Who's calling, please?

W This is her mother Jane Brown from Los Angeles.

M Oh, Mrs. Brown. May I take a message?

W Yes, please. Tell her that her grandmother <u>had an accident</u> this morning.

M Oh, no!

W She <u>fell down</u> in the bathroom. It's not serious, but she <u>wants to call</u> Susan.

M Oh, that's too bad. I'll give her the message.

[전화벨이 울린다.]

W 여보세요, Susan과 통화 좀 할 수 있을까요?

M 그녀는 지금 없는데요. 누구시죠?

W 저는 그녀의 엄마인, 로스앤젤레스에 사는 Jane Brown이에요.

M 아, Brown 여사님. 전하실 말씀 있으세요?

W 네, 있어요. 할머니께서 오늘 아침에 사고를 당하셨다고 그녀에게 좀 전해 주세요.

M 아, 저런!

W 화장실에서 쓰러지셨어요. 심각하지는 않지만, 할머니께서는 Susan과 통화하고 싶어 하세요.

M 아, 참 안 됐군요. 그녀에게 메시지를 전해 줄게요.

13 ⑤

W Tomorrow is my boyfriend's birthday, but I don't know what I should get for him.

M Boys like game CDs.

W He doesn't like computer games, so I don't want to give him that kind of present.

M Then, how about a watch or a digital camera?

W Those are too expensive.

M <u>What about a sweater</u>? It will <u>keep him warm</u>.

W Good idea. I'll <u>buy it for him</u>.

W 내일이 내 남자 친구의 생일인데, 그에게 뭘 사줘야 할지 모르겠어.

M 남자 아이들은 게임 CD를 좋아하잖아.

W 그는 컴퓨터 게임을 싫어해서, 그에게 그런 종류의 선물을 사주고 싶지는 않아.

M 그럼 시계나 디지털 카메라는 어때?

W 그것들은 너무 비싸.

M 스웨터는 어때? 그건 그를 따뜻하게 해 줄 거야.

W 좋은 생각이야. 그에게 그걸 사줘야겠어.

14 ③

M Laura, I'd like to introduce my brother to your sister.

W That's a good idea! My sister doesn't have a boyfriend.

M My brother is <u>tall and handsome</u>. He <u>works for a travel agency</u>.

W How old is he?

M He's 28 years old, but he looks very young.

W What are his hobbies?

M He <u>likes sports</u>, and he plays tennis very well.

W Wow, my sister also plays tennis. I think they'll like each other.

M Laura, 나는 우리 형을 너희 언니에게 소개하고 싶어.

W 그거 좋은 생각인데! 우리 언니한테는 남자 친구가 없거든.

M 우리 형은 키가 크고 잘 생겼어. 여행사에 근무하거든.

W 몇 살인데?

M 28세이지만, 아주 어려 보여.

W 그의 취미는 뭔데?

M 그는 스포츠를 좋아하고, 테니스를 아주 잘 쳐.

W 와, 우리 언니도 테니스를 치는데. 그들은 서로 좋아할 것 같아.

15 ④

W I want to go to Charlotte International Airport. How can I get there?

M You can take the express bus, but the bus stop is far from here.

W Oh, no! I have heavy bags, so I can't <u>walk a long way</u>.

M Then you can take a taxi, but it'll cost a lot. Umm, I have an idea.

W What is it?

M You can go to Hudson Airport <u>by subway</u>. From there you can <u>take a bus</u> to Charlotte International Airport.

W Okay. I'll do that.

W Charlotte 국제공항에 가려고 합니다. 어떻게 갈 수 있을까요?

M 급행 버스를 타실 수 있는데, 버스 정류장이 여기에서 멀어요.

W 아, 저런! 저에게는 무거운 가방들이 있어서, 먼 거리를 걸을 수는 없어요.

M 그럼 택시를 타실 수는 있지만, 비용이 많이 들 거예요. 음, 제게 생각이 하나 있어요.

W 그게 뭔데요?

M Hudson 공항까지 지하철로 가실 수 있어요. 거기에서 Charlotte 국제공항에 가는 버스를 타실 수 있어요.

W 알았어요. 그렇게 할 게요.

만점 솔루션 여자는 Hudson 공항까지 지하철을 타고 가서, 거기에서 Charlotte 국제공항에 가는 버스를 타기로 했다.

16 ④

M Rachel! How are you doing?

W I'm fine. What have you been up to lately?

M Nothing much. Oh, can you go bicycling this Saturday? Many of our friends are going.

W Where are you going bicycling?

M We're going to ride along the river.

W Sounds great, but I'm afraid I can't. I have to go to meet my grandma at the airport with my Mom. Maybe next time.

M Okay.

M Rachel! 어떻게 지내니?

W 잘 지내. 너는 최근에 어떻게 지냈니?

M 별일 없었어. 아, 이번 토요일에 자전거를 타러 갈 수 있니? 우리 친구들 중에서 많은 아이들이 갈 거야.

W 어디로 자전거를 타러 갈 건데?

M 강을 따라서 타려고 해.

W 멋진데, 하지만 나는 그럴 수 없어. 엄마와 함께 공항으로 할머니를 마중 나가야 하거든. 아마 다음에는 할 수 있을 거야.

M 알았어.

17 ④

M Sumin, you're late. The baseball game has already started.

W I'm so sorry. The traffic was really bad on the way back from the airport.

M The airport? Why did you go to the airport?

W Oh, you know my Aunt Sally was visiting us from Australia. She left today, and I went to see her off with my parents.

M I see. But you could have texted or called me, you know.

W I know, sorry. I forgot while talking to my parents. I promise I'll call next time.

M 수민, 늦었잖아. 야구 경기가 이미 시작했어.

W 진짜 미안. 공항에서 오는 길에 차가 많이 막혔어.

M 공항? 왜 공항에서 왔어?

W 아, 우리 이모 샐리가 호주에서 우리를 방문한 거 알지. 이모가 오늘 떠났거든 그래서 부모님과 이모를 배웅해주러 갔어.

M 알겠다. 그래도 나에게 문자나 전화를 할 수 있었잖아.

W 알아. 미안. 부모님과 대화하느라 까먹었어. 다음에는 전화한다고 약속할게.

18 ②

M So, what did you think of the movie?

W Hmm... I don't know. I have mixed feelings.

M What do you mean? I thought it was awesome.

W I thought it was good at first. The scenes were very colorful and unique, and the acting was pretty good.

M Then, what changed your mind?

W Well, the story was too boring, don't you think? It was a simple plot, and there weren't any surprises. The ending was very predictable.

M Yeah, you certainly have a point there.

M 영화에 대해 어떻게 생각해?

W 흠... 모르겠어. 복잡한 감정이야.

M 무슨 의미야? 난 멋졌다고 생각했는데.

W 나도 처음에는 좋았다고 생각했어. 장면이 아주 다채롭고 독특하고 연기도 아주 좋았어.

M 그럼, 뭣 때문에 마음이 바뀐 거야?

W 이야기가 너무 지루했어, 그렇게 생각하지 않아? 너무 단순한 구성에다가 놀랄 만한 게 없었어. 결말도 너무 예상 가능했어.

M 맞아, 네 말에 일리가 있어.

19 ②

M Hello. Is anyone here?

W Yes, can I help you?

M I saw your door open and I just wanted to make sure everything was okay. Are you moving out?

W Yes, I am. I'm only moving about a mile from here to another apartment.

M Oh, so you're not moving out of the area.

W No, I'm not.

M Can I help you take apart your furniture?

W Really? Are you sure you are able to do that?

M Sure. Hand me those tools and I'll have it done in no time.

W _____

M 여보세요. 여기 누구 없어요?

W 예, 뭘 도와드릴까요?

M 저는 그저 문이 열려 있어서 모든 것이 괜찮은지 확인하려고 했어요. 이사 가세요?

W 예, 여기서 약 1마일 떨어진 다른 아파트로 이사 가는 거예요.

M 오, 그러면 이 지역을 벗어나는 것은 아니군요.

W 예, 그렇답니다.

M 제가 가구를 분해하는 것을 좀 도와드릴까요?

W 정말입니까? 그렇게 하실 수 있어요?

M 물론이죠. 도구를 주세요, 그러면 즉시 해 드리겠습니다.

W 제가 문을 열어 놓은 게 잘한 것 같네요.

① 예, 그는 정말 좋아 보여요.

③ 그 때 그에게 이야기하는 게 좋겠어요.

④ 천만에요. 안전한 여행 하세요.

⑤ 곧 당신을 뵙기 바랍니다.

만점 솔루션 여자의 아파트 문이 열려 있어서 남자가 들여다 봄으로 대화가 시작되었다.

20 ⑤

M What happened to you, Judy?

W I can't believe this.

M What's that?

W I got my math test back this afternoon.

M And?

W I thought I would fail, but I didn't fail after all. In fact, I made only three mistakes.

M That's great!

W _____

M 무슨 일이라도 있니, Judy?

W 나는 이걸 믿을 수가 없어.

M 그게 뭔데?

W 오늘 오후에 수학 시험지를 되돌려 받았거든.

M 그런데?

W 낙제할 거라고 생각했었는데, 결국 낙제는 안 했어. 사실 실수는 세 개 밖에 안 했어.

M 대단한데!

W <u>나는 겨우 실수 세 개 가지고 걱정했던 거야.</u>

① 너는 지금 공부하는 게 어때?

② 나는 이 질문에 답변할 수가 없어.

③ 학교에서는 어떻게 지내니?

④ 나는 매일 영어 공부를 열심히 해.

만점 솔루션 낙제할 거라고 걱정했던 수학 시험에서 실수를 세 개밖에 하지 않은 여자에게 남자가 '대단한데!'라고 말했을 때, 여자가 할 수 있는 응답을 찾는다.

고난도 영어듣기능력평가

01 ①	**02** ④	**03** ③	**04** ④	**05** ⑤
06 ②	**07** ①	**08** ⑤, ➕④	**09** ③	**10** ②
11 ③	**12** ④	**13** ③, ➕②	**14** ⑤	**15** ②
16 ①	**17** ④	**18** ②	**19** ①	**20** ⑤

01 ①

W Good morning! Are you all enjoying the recent good weather? Do you wonder if this weather will continue? Here's the weather forecast for this week. We'll start the week <u>on a good note</u>. It'll be sunny and nice on Monday, just like today. But we'll have some clouds on Tuesday. These clouds will stay with us all day Tuesday. On Wednesday and Thursday, we'll <u>have heavy rain</u>. On Friday, the sunny weather will return, but the temperature will drop, and it might even snow.

W 안녕하세요! 최근 좋은 날씨를 다들 즐기고 계신가요? 이런 날씨가 계속될지 궁금하신가요? 여기 이번 주 일기 예보입니다. 한 주의 시작은 좋습니다. 월요일은 오늘처럼 맑고 좋을 예정입니다. 하지만 화요일에 약간의 구름이 있습니다. 화요일 내내 구름이 끼겠습니다. 수요일과 목요일은 폭우가 내리겠습니다. 금요일은, 맑은 날씨로 돌아오겠지만 온도는 떨어져 눈이 올 수도 있습니다.

02 ④

M Good afternoon, may I help you?

W Yes, please. I'd like to <u>buy a birthday cake</u> for my friend.

M Do you want a message on the cake?

W Yes, I want "Happy Birthday!" on the cake.

M Okay. What about this dark chocolate cake? It's very popular.

W I don't think she likes chocolate. She loves cakes with fresh fruit.

M Then, we have strawberries, cherries, and blueberries.

W Oh, she likes strawberries. Do you have one with lots of strawberries?

M Sure, what about this one? It's <u>covered with</u> lots of strawberries.

W Yes! That's the one.

M 안녕하세요, 도와드릴까요?

W 네. 친구의 생일 케이크를 사려고요.

M 케이크 위에 메시지를 원하시나요?

W 네, "생일 축하해!"라고 있었으면 좋겠네요.

M 알겠습니다. 이 다크 초콜릿 케이크 어떠세요? 아주 인기가 많습니다.

W 친구가 초콜릿을 좋아할지 모르겠네요. 친구는 신선한 과일을 들어간 케이크를 좋아해요.

M 그렇다면, 딸기, 체리, 블루베리가 있습니다.

W 아, 친구가 딸기를 좋아해요. 딸기가 많이 들어간 케이크가 있나요?

M 물론이죠, 이건 어떠세요? 많은 딸기로 덮여 있습니다.

W 네! 그걸로 주세요.

03 ③

W Hi, Minsu, I heard you're busy lately.

M Yes, I'm organizing the food competition for the school festival.

W That sounds amazing. Are you cooking something, too?

M No, I'm just organizing the event. I'd need to set up the tents and arrange the chairs.

W Tents? Is it an outdoor event?

M Yeah, but I'm not so sure anymore.

W What do you mean?

M They are calling for rain that day. So now I have to find an indoor place, but it's not going well.

W What about the auditorium? It would be perfect.

M It would be good, but it's already fully booked. I don't know what to do.

W 안녕, 민수. 요즘 바쁘다고 들었어.

M 응, 학교 축제를 위한 요리 대회를 준비하고 있어.

W 굉장하다. 요리를 하기도 하는 거야?

M 아니. 난 그냥 행사 준비만 하고 있어. 텐트를 설치하고 의자를 배열해야 해.

W 텐트? 야외 행사야?

M 응, 하지만 더 이상 확실히 모르겠어.

W 무슨 의미야?

M 그날 비가 온대. 그래서 지금 실내 장소를 찾아야 하는데, 잘 안되네.

W 강당은 어때? 완벽하잖아.

M 좋겠지만 이미 예약이 다 찼대. 어떻게 해야 할지 모르겠다.

만점 솔루션 학교 행사를 준비하는 남자가 야외에서 실내로 장소가 변경되었지만 행사에 쓸 만한 실내 장소를 찾지 못하고 있는 상황이다.

04 ④

M Hi, Yerin! Did you have a good weekend?

W Yes, I went to an outlet mall with my family.

M An outlet mall? Did you buy many new things?

W No, I didn't have time for shopping.

M Really? Then what did you go there for?

W Oh, there's a lot to do at this mall. There's a movie theater, a swimming pool, a bowling alley, and even a skating rink.

M Wow, that's cool. I know you like skating.

W Yeah, but this time we all went bowling together. It was

really fun!

M Cool! Let's see a movie there one day.

M 안녕, 예린! 주말 잘 보냈니?

W 응, 가족과 아울렛 몰에 갔어.

M 아울렛 몰? 많은 새로운 것들을 샀니?

W 아니, 쇼핑할 시간이 별로 없었어.

M 진짜? 그럼 거기는 왜 갔어?

W 아, 이 몰에는 많은 것들이 있어. 영화관, 수영장, 볼링장, 그리고 심지어 스케이트장까지.

M 와, 멋지다. 너 스케이트타는 거 좋아하잖아.

W 그래, 하지만 이번에는 다같이 볼링을 치러 갔어. 진짜 재미있었어!

M 좋다! 나중에 거기서 영화 보자.

05 ⑤

W Hi, how may I help you?

M I'd like to return these books.

W Okay, let me check. *[pause]* Oh, they are two days late. That means that you can't borrow any other books for four days.

M Yes, I know. But there's a book I really need today. Isn't there any way I can borrow it today?

W You can pay the late fee instead. It's 50 cents per book for each day. Would you like to do that?

M Yes, please. Here's $2.

W Okay, now you can borrow the book you want.

W 안녕하세요, 무엇을 도와드릴까요?

M 이 책들을 반납하고 싶어요.

W 네, 확인해 보죠. *[멈춤]* 아, 이틀 연체되었네요. 즉, 나흘간 다른 어떤 책도 대출할 수 없습니다.

M 네, 알아요. 하지만 오늘 진짜 필요한 책이 한 권 있어요. 오늘 그 책을 대출할 수 있는 방법이 없을까요?

W 대신 연체료를 내야 합니다. 하루에 한 권당 50센트입니다. 그렇게 하시겠어요?

M 네, 부탁드려요. 여기 2달러요.

W 알겠습니다. 이제 원하는 책을 대출하실 수 있어요.

06 ②

M Hi, Cathy, happy birthday!

W Thank you, Dan. You remembered!

M Of course. I also remember your birthday party last year. It was great.

W You're right. It was a really good party, but it was so hard to clean up afterwards.

M Oh, really? I'm sorry to hear that.

W Don't worry. It wasn't your fault.

M So, what about this year? When are you having the party?

W Actually, there's no party this year. I decided to have a quiet birthday this year.

M Oh, that's too bad. I was looking forward to it.

M 안녕, 캐시, 생일축하해!

W 고마워, 댄. 기억하고 있었구나!

M 당연하지. 작년 네 생일파티도 기억해. 정말 멋졌어.

W 맞아. 정말 멋진 파티였지. 하지만 그 후에 청소하는 게 너무 힘들었어.

M 아 진짜? 그런 소리를 들으니 유감이다.

W 걱정 마. 네 잘못이 아니니까.

M 그래서, 이번에는 어때? 언제 파티를 할 거야?

W 사실, 이번에는 파티가 없어. 이번에는 생일을 조용히 보내기로 했어.

M 아, 참 아쉽다. 기대하고 있었는데.

07 ①

M You did so well. I'm so proud of you, Jihye.

W Thanks, Dad. I'm glad I didn't make any mistakes this time.

M Are you still thinking about the last concert? You should forget about it.

W Yes, I know. But I was so afraid it would happen again.

M You were a beginner with the violin at that time. You are much better at it now.

W Yes, that's true. I feel a lot better with my violin ability.

M So, you play the piano and the violin so far. What's the next instrument?

W Actually, I'd like to try the drums.

M 잘했어. 네가 자랑스럽단다, 지혜.

W 고마워요 아빠. 이번에는 실수를 안 해서 기뻐요.

M 지난번 콘서트를 아직도 생각하고 있니? 그건 잊어야 해.

W 네, 알아요. 하지만 똑같은 일이 일어날까 두려워요.

M 그때는 바이올린 초보자였을 때야. 지금은 훨씬 잘하잖아.

W 네, 사실예요. 제 바이올린 능력이 훨씬 나아졌다고 느껴요.

M 지금까지 피아노와 바이올린을 연주했지. 다음 악기는 뭐니?

W 사실, 드럼을 연주해보고 싶어요.

08 ⑤ | ➕ ④

M It is so hot. I should study for my exams, but I can't concentrate.

W Why don't you go to the library?

M If I go to the library and see my friends, I'll end up hanging out with them.

W Hmm, what about a coffee shop?

M I can't study there either. It's too noisy.

W Well, then you have no other choice. You'll have to study in your room.

M But the air is too hot and stuffy in my room.

W You can take this fan to your room if you want.

M Thanks, I'll do that.

M 너무 덥다. 시험 공부 해야 하는데, 집중할 수가 없어.

W 도서관에 가는 거 어때?

M 도서관에 가면 친구들을 볼 텐데, 그럼 친구들과 놀다가 끝날 거야.

W 흠, 커피숍은 어때?

M 거기서도 공부할 수 없어. 너무 시끄러워.

W 그럼 다른 방법이 없어. 네 방에서 공부해야 해.

M 하지만 내 방은 공기가 너무 뜨겁고 답답해.

W 네가 원하면 이 선풍기를 네 방에 가져가도 돼.

M 고마워, 가져가야겠다.

만점 솔루션 둘의 대화에서 보기와 일치하는 표현들(go to the library, see my friends, coffee shop)이 지문에 등장하지만, 여자의 제안들을 남자가 거절을 하면서 결국 대화의 마지막에 답이 등장한다.

09 ③

W Hi, is this your first time to our swimming pool?

M Yes, I just moved to this city.

W Welcome. I'll just go over a few rules first.

M Sure. Let me guess. I can't take any food into the pool area.

W Right. And you can't take your Cellphone, either. Please leave it in your locker.

M Oh, okay. Anything else?

W You must wear a swimming cap when you swim. And you should take a 10-minute break after swimming for 50 minutes.

M I see. Luckily, I brought my swimming cap today.

W 안녕하세요, 저희 수영장은 처음이신가요?

M 네, 이 도시로 막 이사왔어요.

W 환영합니다. 우선 몇 가지 규칙을 알려드릴게요.

M 맞춰 볼게요. 수영장에서 음식을 갖고 올 수 없다.

W 네. 그리고 휴대 전화도 갖고 올 수 없습니다. 보관함에 넣어두세요.

M 아, 알겠습니다. 다른 거는요?

W 수영을 할 때는 수영모를 반드시 써야 합니다. 그리고 50분 수영 후에는 10분 휴식을 취해야 합니다.

M 알겠습니다. 다행히 오늘 수영모를 가져왔어요.

10 ②

W Welcome to Citizen's Park. This park is for everyone, but please let me remind you of some important rules to follow in our park. First, please don't litter in the park. Take any garbage back with you when you leave. Second, don't feed the animals. People food isn't good for animals, and it poses lots of problems. Last, if you're walking your dog, keep your dog on a leash at all times. Respect that some people are scared of dogs. Thank you.

W 시민공원에 오신 것을 환영합니다. 이 공원은 모두를 위한 곳입니다. 하지만 우리 공원에서 따라야 하는 몇가지 중요한 규칙을 알려드리겠습니다. 첫째, 공원에 쓰레기를 버리지 마세요. 공원을 떠날 때 쓰레기를 가져가세요. 둘째, 동물들에게 음식을 주지 마세요. 사람들의 음식은 동물들에게 좋지 않고 많은 문제를 일으킵니다. 마지막으로, 개를 산책 시킬 때는 항상 목줄을 해주세요. 개를 무서워하는 사람들을 존중하세요. 감사합니다.

11 ③

M Hello, everyone. This is Chris from Movie World. I'm going to talk about the movie *The Tree House* that was released two weeks ago. It was the most watched movie last weekend, and it's receiving a lot of good reviews from critics. This movie was made in France, and it's a story about a family who moved to a little town in the countryside. Many strange things happen to them, but they work hard and solve the mystery.

M 안녕하세요, 여러분. 무비 월드의 크리스입니다. 2주 전에 개봉한 '더 트리 하우스'라는 영화에 대해 이야기하려고 합니다. 지난 주말 가장 인기 있는 영화였는데요 평론가들에게 많은 호평을 받고 있습니다. 이 영화는 프랑스에서 만들어졌고 시골 지역의 작은 마을로 이사를 가게 된 한 가족에 대한 이야기입니다. 많은 이상한 일들이 그들에게 생기지만 노력해서 그 미스터리를 풀어냅니다.

12 ④

[Telephone rings.]

W Hello, Hugh Dentist Clinic. How may I help you?

M Hi, I'd like to make an appointment.

W Okay, sure. Is it your first visit to our clinic?

M Ah, no. It's my second time. I was there six months ago.

W Then we should have your record. Could you give me your name, please?

M It's David Kim. I'd like to go on a Saturday, if possible.

W Hold on, Mr. Kim. *[pause]* Ah, here's your record. This Saturday is not possible, but next Saturday at 2 o'clock is open.

M You said 2 p.m., right? That should work.

[전화벨이 울린다.]

W 안녕하세요, 휴 치과입니다. 무엇을 도와드릴까요?

M 안녕하세요. 예약을 하고싶습니다.

W 네. 저희 병원은 처음이신가요?

M 아니요. 두번째입니다. 5개월 전에 갔었습니다.

W 그러면 기록이 있겠네요. 이름을 알려주시겠어요?

M 데이비드 김입니다. 가능하면 토요일에 가고 싶습니다.

W 기다리세요, 김 씨. *[멈춤]* 아, 여기 기록이 있네요. 이번주 토요일은 불가능하지만 다음주 토요일 2시는 가능합니다.

M 2시라고 하신 거 맞죠? 그 날로 할게요.

13 ③ | ➕ ②

[Telephone rings.]

W Hello?

M Hello, this is Hana Delivery Service. May I speak to Mina Park?

W This is she speaking.

M Hi, will you be home today? I have a package for you.

W Can you come in the morning? I'm leaving around 12.

M Sorry, but I can't get there in the morning. What time will you be back? I'm working until 6 today.

W Oh, I won't be back until after 7, but actually my mom will be home at 5. Can you leave it with her?

M Sure, I can do that.

[전화벨이 울린다.]

W 여보세요?

M 안녕하세요, 하나 택배 회사입니다. 미나 박씨와 통화할 수 있을까요?

W 접니다.

M 안녕하세요, 오늘 집에 계시나요? 보내 드릴 소포가 있습니다.

W 오전에 오실 수 있나요? 12시쯤에 집에서 나가서요.

M 죄송하지만 오전에는 갈 수 없습니다. 언제 돌아오시나요? 오늘은 6시까지 일합니다.

W 아, 7시 이후 전까지는 돌아오지 못합니다. 하지만 엄마가 5시에 집에 있을 거예요. 엄마에게 전해주시겠어요?

M 네, 알겠습니다.

14 ⑤

M Hi, how may I help you?

W I was wondering if you sell express train tickets here.

M Yes, we do. Where are you going?

W I want to go to Amsterdam next Thursday, preferably before 8 a.m. How much will that be?

M Hold on, please. *[pause]* Okay, for the 7:40 train, it's €82 for 2nd class, and €117 for 1st class.

W I'll take 2nd class.

M Okay. Do you need any help with hotel reservations or a car rental? We also have many great sightseeing programs.

W No, that's okay, thanks. I'm staying at a friend's place.

M 안녕하세요, 무엇을 도와드릴까요?

W 여기서 급행열차 표를 파는지 궁금하네요.

M 네. 팝니다. 어디로 가시나요?

W 다음주 목요일에 암스테르담에 가고 싶습니다. 가능하면 오전 8시 전에. 얼마인가요?

M 잠시만요. *[멈춤]* 네, 7시 40분 기차로 이등실은 82유로, 일등석은 117유로입니다.

W 이등실로 주세요.

M 네. 호텔 예약이나 자동차 대여 같은 도움이 필요하신가요? 저희는 많은 좋은 관광 프로그램을 가지고 있습니다.

W 아니요, 괜찮아요, 감사합니다. 친구네 집에서 머물 거예요.

15 ②

W Whew, I think we're finally done. What time is it?

M It's 5:30. Mom and Dad will be back in 30 minutes.

W Okay, let's do one more final check. The house is clean, and the food is ready to serve for dinner.

M And our presents are wrapped. I can't wait to see them surprised!

W Neither can I. Now, we need to set the table. Can you do that while I heat up the food?

M Sure. Is there anything else we need to do?

W I don't think so. We have to take out the garbage, but we can do that after dinner.

W 휴, 마침내 끝난 거 같네. 몇시야?

M 5시 30분. 엄마랑 아빠는 30분 후에 올 거야.

W 좋아, 마지막 확인을 한번 더 하자. 집은 깨끗하고 저녁을 위한 음식도 준비됐지.

M 그리고 우리 선물 포장도 끝났어. 엄마 아빠가 놀라는 모습을 빨리 보고 싶어!

W 나도. 이제 식탁을 차려야 해. 내가 음식을 데우는 동안 해 줄래?

M 물론이야. 우리가 더 해야 할 거 없나?

W 없을 거야. 쓰레기를 내 놔야 하지만 그건 저녁 먹고 할 수 있어.

16 ①

M Thank you, Mrs. Brown. The dinner was delicious.

W I'm glad you liked it, Jason. Now, would you like some walnut pie for dessert?

M I'd like to, but I can't.

W Oh, are you allergic to nuts?

M Ah, no, actually, I'm just too full. I ate too much.

W Then, would you like to take some with you? I can wrap it up for you.

M Really? That's very nice of you. I usually don't like sweet things, but it looks very good.

W Thanks. I'll give you enough so that you can share it with your family.

M 감사합니다, 브라운 씨. 저녁 맛있었어요.

W 좋았다니 기쁘네요. 이제, 월넛 파이를 후식으로 먹을래요?

M 그러고 싶지만 먹을 수 없어요.

W 아, 견과류에 알레르기가 있나요?

M 아뇨, 사실 너무 배가 불러요. 너무 많이 먹었어요.

W 그럼, 좀 가져갈래요? 싸줄게요.

M 정말요? 친절하시네요. 보통 단 음식을 좋아하지 않지만 정말 맛있어 보이네요.

W 고마워요. 가족들과 나눠 먹을 수 있도록 충분히 드릴게요.

만점 솔루션 둘의 대화에서 보기와 일치하는 표현들(allergic to nuts, don't like sweet things)이 지문에 등장하지만, 남자의 대사 'I'm just too full. I ate too much.'에서 답을 찾을 수 있다. 'be full'이 '배가 부르다'라는 의미라는 것을 몰라도 뒤에 나오는 문장으로 답을 유추할 수 있다.

17 ④

① W Hi, long time no see! Is this your dog? It's so cute!

M Thanks. His name is Baily. I'm just walking him. He likes this park.

② W Where did you get the hat? It looks really good on you.

M Thank you, Sandy. I actually borrowed it from my dad.

③ W Which scene did you like the best in the movie?

M I liked the scene when all the people ran across the beach at the same time.

④ W Excuse me, you're not allowed to go in there. Step out, please.

M Oh, I'm so sorry. I didn't know that.

⑤ W Can I have a look at those pictures, too?

M Sure, take a look. I think you look really good in this one.

① W 안녕, 오랜만이다! 이거 네 강아지야? 정말 귀엽다!

M 고미워. 강아지 이름은 베일리야. 산책하고 있었어. 베일리가 이 공원을 좋아해.

② W 그 모자 어디서 샀어? 진짜 잘 어울린다.

M 고마워, 샌디. 아빠한테 빌렸어.

③ W 영화에서 어떤 장면이 가장 좋았어?

M 사람들이 동시에 해변가를 가로질러 달리는 장면이 좋았어.

④ W 실례합니다. 거기 들어가시면 안됩니다. 나오세요.

M 정말 죄송합니다. 몰랐어요.

⑤ W 그 사진들을 봐도 될까?

M 응. 봐. 이 사진에서 너 정말 잘 나온 거 같아.

18 ②

W Let me tell you today's schedule first. It will take us three hours to get to today's main attraction, Blue Aquarium, and we'll stop at two places on the way. The first is the lavender field, where you can take pictures with beautiful flowers. We'll have lunch at noon at a famous local restaurant. After lunch, we'll take a short tour of the local village. When we finally arrive at the aquarium, it'll be 2:30, and you'll have two hours to spend there.

W 우선 오늘 스케줄을 알려드리겠습니다. 오늘의 주요 명소인 블루 수족관에 가는 데 3시간이 걸릴 겁니다. 그리고 가는 길에 두 장소에서 멈출 것입니다. 첫 번째는 아름다운 꽃과 사진을 찍을 수 있는 라벤더 밭입니

다. 우리는 유명한 지역 식당에서 정오에 점심을 먹을 것입니다. 점심을 먹은 후, 지역 마을을 짧게 돌아볼 것입니다. 수족관에 도착하면 2시 30분일 겁니다. 거기서 2시간을 보낼 겁니다.

19 ①

M Hi, Areum, are you okay? You look worried.

W Hi, Brad, I was just thinking what I should do to lose weight.

M What do you mean? You're <u>not fat at all</u>.

W Okay, maybe it's not about losing weight. This summer, I promised to <u>go to the water park</u> with my cousins. I want to look healthier in my swimsuit.

M If that's the case, tennis is a very good sport.

W Really? Do you play?

M Yes, I do. Would you like to give it a try?

W _____

M 안녕, 아름, 괜찮니? 걱정스러워 보여.

W 안녕, 브래드, 몸무게를 줄이기 위해 무엇을 해야 하나 생각 중이었어.

M 무슨 의미야? 넌 전혀 뚱뚱하지 않아.

W 그래, 어쩌면 살을 빼려는 게 아니야. 이번 여름, 사촌들이랑 워터파크에 가기로 약속했거든. 내가 수영복을 입었을 때 더 건강해 보였으면 좋겠어.

M 그런 경우라면, 테니스가 정말 좋은 운동이야.

W 진짜? 너 테니스 해?

M 응. 한번 해 볼래?

W <u>응, 해 보고 싶어.</u>

② 유감이다.

③ 축하해!

④ 많이 드세요.

⑤ 걱정 마. 넌 할 수 있어.

20 ⑤

W What are you reading, Dan?

M I'm <u>reading a book</u> about technology. It's really interesting.

W Can you give me one example?

M It says if cars had been developed as fast as computers, we'd have flying cars now.

W Wow, that is interesting. That means computers were developed very fast, right?

M Yes, exactly. My mom said she didn't have a computer when she was a child.

W Yeah, my dad said the same thing. He didn't have a Cellphone, either.

M It's crazy. Can you imagine <u>life without computers</u> or smartphones?

W _____

W 뭘 읽고 있어, 댄?

M 기술에 관한 책을 읽고 있어. 진짜 재미있어.

W 예를 하나 들어 줄 수 있니?

M 책에서 차가 컴퓨터만큼 빨리 발전했다면 지금 우리는 날아다니는 차를 가지고 있을 거래.

W 와, 재미있다. 그 말은 컴퓨터가 굉장히 빨리 발전했다는 거잖아, 맞지?

M 정확해. 엄마가 어렸을 때는 컴퓨터를 가지고 있지 않았다고 했어.

W 응, 우리 아빠도 똑같은 말을 했어. 휴대 전화도 없었대.

M 정말 미쳤어. 컴퓨터나 스마트폰이 없는 생활을 상상할 수 있어?

W <u>말도 안돼. 그럼 진짜 불편할 거야.</u>

① 난 상상력이 풍부한 사람이 되고 싶어.

② 응, 우리 아빠랑 얘기 해 봐.

③ 그치? 그것들은 너무 오래 되었고 지루해.

④ 글쎄, 난 컴퓨터를 매우 잘 다뤄.

만점 솔루션 둘은 컴퓨터나 휴대 전화가 없던 과거의 이야기를 하면서 믿을 수 없다는 반응을 보이고 있다. 그런 상황에서 남자가 컴퓨터나 스마트폰이 없는 삶을 상상할 수 있냐며 질문을 던지고 있으므로 여자가 할 수 있는 알맞은 응답은 '상상할 수 없다'의 방향이 될 것이다.

듣기는
실전이다

중학 2

Plus Book

24회

디딤돌

Step 1 우리말 보면서 영어 듣기

		1회	2회	3회
1	지난 주말에 무엇을 했니?	☐	☐	☐
2	그는 긴팔 셔츠를 입고 있어.	☐	☐	☐
3	이것은 작지만 강력한 모터를 가지고 있어서, 아주 빨리 움직일 수 있습니다.	☐	☐	☐
4	나는 자전거 타는 것을 매우 좋아해.	☐	☐	☐
5	그렇게 짧은 시간에 점심을 먹는 것이 저는 어려워요.	☐	☐	☐
6	거기까지 걸어가는 데 시간이 얼마나 걸리나요?	☐	☐	☐
7	잠깐 주목해 주시겠습니까?	☐	☐	☐
8	뭔가 바쁜 일이 있었어?	☐	☐	☐
9	난 내 오래된 책을 좀 팔고 싶어.	☐	☐	☐
10	내 전화기가 작동이 안 돼!	☐	☐	☐
11	넌 친절하구나!	☐	☐	☐
12	언제 출발하시죠?	☐	☐	☐
13	뭘 도와드릴까요?	☐	☐	☐
14	테니스를 칠 때는 오른손을 사용하지만 야구는 아니에요.	☐	☐	☐
15	좀 더 늦게 시작하는 영화가 있니?	☐	☐	☐
16	예약하셨어요?	☐	☐	☐
17	그것을 발견하면 연락 드리겠습니다.	☐	☐	☐
18	가기 전에 설거지를 하려고 했거든.	☐	☐	☐
19	그림 그리기는 내가 가장 좋아하는 취미 중 하나야.	☐	☐	☐
20	누구세요?	☐	☐	☐

Step 2 듣고 따라 말하기

		1회	2회	3회
1	What did you do last weekend?	☐	☐	☐
2	He's wearing a long shirt.	☐	☐	☐
3	It has a small but strong motor, so you can move very fast.	☐	☐	☐
4	I like riding a bike very much.	☐	☐	☐
5	It's hard for me to have lunch in such short time.	☐	☐	☐
6	How long does it take to walk there?	☐	☐	☐
7	May I have your attention, please?	☐	☐	☐
8	Were you busy with something?	☐	☐	☐
9	I want to sell some of my old books.	☐	☐	☐
10	My phone isn't working!	☐	☐	☐
11	It's kind of you!	☐	☐	☐
12	When are you going to leave?	☐	☐	☐
13	What can I do for you?	☐	☐	☐
14	I use my right hand for playing tennis, but not baseball.	☐	☐	☐
15	Is there a movie that starts a little later?	☐	☐	☐
16	Do you have a reservation?	☐	☐	☐
17	I'll give you a call if it turns up.	☐	☐	☐
18	I was going to do the dishes before I go.	☐	☐	☐
19	Painting is one of my favorite hobbies.	☐	☐	☐
20	Who's calling, please?	☐	☐	☐

Step 1 우리말 보면서 영어 듣기

		1회	2회	3회
1	그것을 포장해 주시면 좋겠어요. 선물이거든요.	☐	☐	☐
2	조깅과 수영은 지겨워.	☐	☐	☐
3	하와이행 여행을 즐기렴.	☐	☐	☐
4	오늘 누구를 데려와야 하는 거지?	☐	☐	☐
5	귀하의 아이디어가 저희에게 큰 힘이 될 것입니다.	☐	☐	☐
6	출구 옆의 창구에서 지불하시면 됩니다.	☐	☐	☐
7	요즘 열심히 노력하고 있습니다.	☐	☐	☐
8	호텔 객실을 하나 예약하고 싶은데요.	☐	☐	☐
9	일요일에 비가 올 거야.	☐	☐	☐
10	그들은 꽤 작았고 곤충을 먹고 살았습니다.	☐	☐	☐
11	거기 날씨는 어땠나요?	☐	☐	☐
12	그녀가 돌아오는 대로 저에게 전화를 좀 해 달라고 전해 주시겠어요?	☐	☐	☐
13	당신을 위해 그 책을 주문해 드릴 수는 있어요.	☐	☐	☐
14	누군가의 집에서 저녁 식사를 할 때는 그런 종류의 선물을 가져갈 수 있어요.	☐	☐	☐
15	어떤 영화가 가장 좋아?	☐	☐	☐
16	내가 너한테 지하철을 타라고 말했잖아.	☐	☐	☐
17	내가 좋아하는 가수가 나오는 새로운 오락쇼야.	☐	☐	☐
18	정말 이걸 네가 만들었니?	☐	☐	☐
19	여기 공항이 아주 붐비는군요.	☐	☐	☐
20	얼마나 오랫동안 그것을 배우고 있는 거야?	☐	☐	☐

Step 2 듣고 따라 말하기

		1회	2회	3회
1	I'd like you to wrap it.	☐	☐	☐
2	I'm tired of jogging and swimming.	☐	☐	☐
3	Enjoy your trip to Hawaii.	☐	☐	☐
4	Who do we have to pick up today?	☐	☐	☐
5	Your ideas may help us greatly.	☐	☐	☐
6	You can pay it at the window by the exit.	☐	☐	☐
7	I'm trying hard these days.	☐	☐	☐
8	I'd like to book a room at your hotel.	☐	☐	☐
9	It's supposed to rain on Sunday.	☐	☐	☐
10	They were quite small and fed on insects.	☐	☐	☐
11	What about the weather there?	☐	☐	☐
12	Could you please ask her to give me a call as soon as she comes back?	☐	☐	☐
13	We can order the book for you.	☐	☐	☐
14	We can bring those types of gifts when we have dinner at someone's house.	☐	☐	☐
15	What kind of movies do you like best?	☐	☐	☐
16	I told you to take the subway.	☐	☐	☐
17	It's a new entertainment show with my favorite singer.	☐	☐	☐
18	Did you really make this yourself?	☐	☐	☐
19	It's very crowded here in the airport.	☐	☐	☐
20	How long have you been learning it?	☐	☐	☐

Step 1 우리말 보면서 영어 듣기

		1회	2회	3회
1	이번에는 내가 널 이길 수 있어.	☐	☐	☐
2	그것을 부엌 식탁 위에 두었어?	☐	☐	☐
3	뭐가 문제인 거 같나요?	☐	☐	☐
4	젊은 층에게 매우 인기가 있어요.	☐	☐	☐
5	기차로 갈 것인지 버스로 갈 것인지 결정해야 해.	☐	☐	☐
6	연체료는 얼마인가요?	☐	☐	☐
7	걸으면서 스마트폰을 사용하지 말아주세요.	☐	☐	☐
8	네가 원하면 나는 너랑 다시 갈 수 있어.	☐	☐	☐
9	저쪽에 있는 표지판 보지 못했어?	☐	☐	☐
10	당신이 산을 좋아한다고 생각했는데요.	☐	☐	☐
11	내가 다음 학기에 너의 학교 선생님이 될 예정이거든.	☐	☐	☐
12	너는 장래에 뭐가 되고 싶니?	☐	☐	☐
13	내 컴퓨터에 문제가 있어.	☐	☐	☐
14	오늘은 외출하고 싶지 않아요.	☐	☐	☐
15	시험에 통과하지 못할까 봐 두려워.	☐	☐	☐
16	몇 시에 출발할까?	☐	☐	☐
17	방금 안 좋은 소식을 들었어.	☐	☐	☐
18	네 차에 무슨 문제가 있니?	☐	☐	☐
19	내 여동생이 마침내 그 시험에 합격한 것이 놀랍지?	☐	☐	☐
20	가구를 옮기는 데 네 도움이 필요해.	☐	☐	☐

Step 2 듣고 따라 말하기

		1회	2회	3회
1	I can beat you this time.	☐	☐	☐
2	Did you leave it on the kitchen table?	☐	☐	☐
3	What seems to be the problem?	☐	☐	☐
4	It's very popular with young adults.	☐	☐	☐
5	We have to decide whether to go by train or by bus.	☐	☐	☐
6	What's the overdue charge?	☐	☐	☐
7	Please don't use your smartphone while walking.	☐	☐	☐
8	I could go again with you if you want.	☐	☐	☐
9	Didn't you see the sign over there?	☐	☐	☐
10	I thought you liked the mountains.	☐	☐	☐
11	I'm going to be a teacher at your school next semester.	☐	☐	☐
12	What do you want to be in the future?	☐	☐	☐
13	There's something wrong with my computer.	☐	☐	☐
14	I don't feel like going out today.	☐	☐	☐
15	I'm afraid I won't pass the test.	☐	☐	☐
16	What time shall we leave?	☐	☐	☐
17	I've just heard some bad news.	☐	☐	☐
18	What's the matter with your car?	☐	☐	☐
19	Are you surprised that my sister has finally passed the test?	☐	☐	☐
20	I need your help to move furniture.	☐	☐	☐

Step 1 우리말 보면서 영어 듣기

		1회	2회	3회
1	저것은 내가 그린 그림이야.	☐	☐	☐
2	철물점이 어디 있지?	☐	☐	☐
3	하지 말았어야 할 말을 내가 방금 했어.	☐	☐	☐
4	너처럼 노란색보다는 빨간색을 더 좋아해.	☐	☐	☐
5	당신은 항상 무언가를 할 때 조심해야 합니다.	☐	☐	☐
6	당신은 약을 복용하고 있습니까?	☐	☐	☐
7	이 문제를 가진 지 얼마나 됐어요?	☐	☐	☐
8	병원에서 만나자.	☐	☐	☐
9	샌드위치는 몇 개가 필요하지?	☐	☐	☐
10	이미 그것을 신청한 학생들은 정시에 오시기 바랍니다.	☐	☐	☐
11	새로운 영어 선생님은 어디 출신인가요?	☐	☐	☐
12	얼마나 빨리 배달될 수 있죠?	☐	☐	☐
13	추천해 주실 만한 것이 있나요?	☐	☐	☐
14	엘리베이터를 타고 1층으로 가세요.	☐	☐	☐
15	개인적인 질문을 해도 될까요?	☐	☐	☐
16	내가 어렸을 때 갖고 있던 포스터야.	☐	☐	☐
17	이 문 앞에서 사진 좀 찍어줄 수 있을까요?	☐	☐	☐
18	오늘 오후에 축구 연습이 있어요.	☐	☐	☐
19	난 살을 좀 빼고 싶어.	☐	☐	☐
20	나는 오늘 더 이상 일할 수 없을 것 같아.	☐	☐	☐

Step 2 듣고 따라 말하기

		1회	2회	3회
1	That's the picture I painted.	☐	☐	☐
2	Where's the hardware store?	☐	☐	☐
3	I just said something I shouldn't have.	☐	☐	☐
4	I like red more than yellow, just like you.	☐	☐	☐
5	You should always be careful when you do something.	☐	☐	☐
6	Are you taking any medicine?	☐	☐	☐
7	How long have you had this problem?	☐	☐	☐
8	Let's meet at the hospital.	☐	☐	☐
9	How many sandwiches do we need?	☐	☐	☐
10	The students who have already applied for it should show up on time.	☐	☐	☐
11	Where is the new English teacher from?	☐	☐	☐
12	How soon can it be delivered?	☐	☐	☐
13	What would you recommend?	☐	☐	☐
14	Take the elevator to the first floor.	☐	☐	☐
15	Can I ask you a personal question?	☐	☐	☐
16	It's a poster I had when I was a kid.	☐	☐	☐
17	Could you take a picture of me in front of this door, please?	☐	☐	☐
18	I have soccer practice this afternoon.	☐	☐	☐
19	I want to lose some weight.	☐	☐	☐
20	I'm afraid I can't work anymore today.	☐	☐	☐

Step 1 우리말 보면서 영어 듣기

		1회	2회	3회
1	내일은 날씨가 맑을 거라고 들었어.	☐	☐	☐
2	그는 지금 샤워하고 있어요.	☐	☐	☐
3	이 현금 인출기 사용법을 말씀해 주시겠어요?	☐	☐	☐
4	나는 운동하는 것을 아주 좋아하지는 않아.	☐	☐	☐
5	여기 근처에 꽃집이 있나요?	☐	☐	☐
6	여기서 공항 가는 버스를 탈 수 있나요?	☐	☐	☐
7	당신은 의사에게 당신이 원하는 어떤 질문이든지 하실 수 있습니다.	☐	☐	☐
8	나는 무엇보다 음식을 즐겼지.	☐	☐	☐
9	프로그램에 등록하면 일주일 동안 거기에 머물 수 있어.	☐	☐	☐
10	그녀의 부모님이 여기 머무르시기로 결정하셨대!	☐	☐	☐
11	우리는 일주일에 두 번 방과 후에 모여서 다양한 운동을 해.	☐	☐	☐
12	나는 오늘 오후에 그를 보러 갈 거야.	☐	☐	☐
13	그냥 도서관에 가서 책을 읽자.	☐	☐	☐
14	네가 숙제를 못 끝내는 게 이해가 간다.	☐	☐	☐
15	입어 보실 수 있어요.	☐	☐	☐
16	어떤 종류의 빵을 원하세요?	☐	☐	☐
17	그냥 물 속에서 수영만 하고 싶어요.	☐	☐	☐
18	어딘가에서 서로 지나쳤을 수도 있겠다.	☐	☐	☐
19	내 보고서를 끝내지 못했어.	☐	☐	☐
20	바로 여기서 인터뷰를 하고 싶은데요.	☐	☐	☐

Step 2 듣고 따라 말하기

		1회	2회	3회
1	I heard it's going to be fine tomorrow.	☐	☐	☐
2	He's taking a shower now.	☐	☐	☐
3	Could you tell me how to use this cash machine?	☐	☐	☐
4	I don't like to play sports very much.	☐	☐	☐
5	Is there a flower shop near here?	☐	☐	☐
6	Can I take a bus to the airport from here?	☐	☐	☐
7	You can ask a doctor any question that you want.	☐	☐	☐
8	I enjoyed the food above all.	☐	☐	☐
9	If you sign up for the program, you can stay there for a week.	☐	☐	☐
10	Her parents decided to stay here!	☐	☐	☐
11	We get together twice a week after school and play various sports.	☐	☐	☐
12	I'm going to see him this afternoon.	☐	☐	☐
13	Let's just go to the library and read books.	☐	☐	☐
14	No wonder you can't finish your homework.	☐	☐	☐
15	You can try it on.	☐	☐	☐
16	What kind of bread do you want?	☐	☐	☐
17	I'd just like to swim in the water.	☐	☐	☐
18	We could have passed each other somewhere.	☐	☐	☐
19	I couldn't finish my report.	☐	☐	☐
20	I'd like to interview you right here.	☐	☐	☐

Step 1 우리말 보면서 영어 듣기

		1회	2회	3회
1	내일의 일기 예보 들었니?	☐	☐	☐
2	하나 사는 것이 어때요?	☐	☐	☐
3	자신에 대한 것을 말씀해 주시겠어요?	☐	☐	☐
4	이 책들을 반납하러 도서관에 가고 있어.	☐	☐	☐
5	때때로 밤에 강도 사건이 발생했어.	☐	☐	☐
6	이 시각에는 교통이 매우 혼잡해요.	☐	☐	☐
7	이 필름을 현상하고 싶습니다.	☐	☐	☐
8	난 겨울용으로 예쁘고 두꺼운 것을 원해.	☐	☐	☐
9	어제 공원에서 농구를 하다가 다리를 다쳤어.	☐	☐	☐
10	우리 엄마가 나를 위해 특별히 그것을 만드셨어.	☐	☐	☐
11	난 클래식 기타에 더 관심이 있어.	☐	☐	☐
12	네가 아직 자동차를 팔고 있는지 궁금해.	☐	☐	☐
13	난 그것 때문에 돈을 모아 왔어.	☐	☐	☐
14	실습실에 들어오기 전에 신발을 갈아 신으세요.	☐	☐	☐
15	거스름돈 여기 있습니다.	☐	☐	☐
16	우산 챙겼니?	☐	☐	☐
17	네 왼발이 오른발 앞에 있어야 해.	☐	☐	☐
18	주말내내 날씨가 정말 좋았어, 그렇지?	☐	☐	☐
19	십대들 사이에서 아주 인기 있는 색상이에요.	☐	☐	☐
20	나는 그 시각에 도서관에서 보고서를 작성하고 있었어.	☐	☐	☐

Step 2 듣고 따라 말하기

		1회	2회	3회
1	Did you hear tomorrow's weather report?	☐	☐	☐
2	How about buying one?	☐	☐	☐
3	Can you tell us something about yourself?	☐	☐	☐
4	I'm going to the library to return these books.	☐	☐	☐
5	Sometimes robberies happened at night.	☐	☐	☐
6	The traffic is very heavy at this hour.	☐	☐	☐
7	I'd like to have this film developed.	☐	☐	☐
8	I'd like a nice thick one for the winter.	☐	☐	☐
9	I hurt my leg while I was playing basketball in the park yesterday.		☐	☐
10	My mom made it especially for me.	☐	☐	☐
11	I'm more interested in the classic guitar.	☐	☐	☐
12	I wonder if you're still selling your car.	☐	☐	☐
13	I've been saving up for it.	☐	☐	☐
14	Change your shoes before you enter the lab.	☐	☐	☐
15	Here is your change.	☐	☐	☐
16	Do you have an umbrella with you?	☐	☐	☐
17	Your left foot must be in front of your right one.	☐	☐	☐
18	The weather was really nice over the weekend, wasn't it?	☐	☐	☐
19	It's a very popular color among teens.	☐	☐	☐
20	I was writing a report at the library at that time.	☐	☐	☐

Step 1 우리말 보면서 영어 듣기

		1회	2회	3회
1	너는 어젯밤에 천둥 소리를 들었니?	☐	☐	☐
2	나의 남동생은 팔짱을 낀 채로 자전거에 앉아 있다.	☐	☐	☐
3	콧물은 나지 않지만 기침을 합니다.	☐	☐	☐
4	걱정되는 일들이 많이 있어요.	☐	☐	☐
5	저는 그 이야기에 관한 글을 쓸 거예요.	☐	☐	☐
6	운동을 하기 전에는 항상 준비 운동을 해야 해.	☐	☐	☐
7	넌 언젠가 전문 피아노 연주자가 될 거라고 확신해.	☐	☐	☐
8	그녀에게 오늘 모임이 취소되었다고 말씀해 주시겠어요?	☐	☐	☐
9	넌 인터넷을 통한 음성 통화를 이용할 수 있어.	☐	☐	☐
10	당신이 작업한 것을 저장했나요?	☐	☐	☐
11	예약을 하고 싶은데요.	☐	☐	☐
12	결혼식은 무슨 요일입니까?	☐	☐	☐
13	거기에 어떻게 가는지 말씀해 주실 수 있나요?	☐	☐	☐
14	한 대의 버스에 몇 명이 탈 수 있죠?	☐	☐	☐
15	공항으로 가는 버스는 몇 시에 출발하죠?	☐	☐	☐
16	어디서 그것을 잃어버렸니?	☐	☐	☐
17	주문하시겠어요?	☐	☐	☐
18	그는 나에게 빌려간 돈을 절대 갚지 않아요.	☐	☐	☐
19	한 가족이 길 건너 집으로 이사 올 예정이라고 해요.	☐	☐	☐
20	오늘 비가 올 거래?	☐	☐	☐

Step 2 듣고 따라 말하기

		1회	2회	3회
1	Did you hear the thunder last night?	☐	☐	☐
2	My little brother is sitting on a bicycle with his arms folded.	☐	☐	☐
3	I don't have a runny nose, but I have a cough.	☐	☐	☐
4	I have many things to worry about.	☐	☐	☐
5	I'm going to write an essay about the story.	☐	☐	☐
6	You should always warm up before playing sports.	☐	☐	☐
7	I bet you will become a professional piano player someday.	☐	☐	☐
8	Can you tell her today's meeting has been canceled?	☐	☐	☐
9	You can use voice calls over the Internet.	☐	☐	☐
10	Did you save what you had done?	☐	☐	☐
11	I'd like to make a reservation.	☐	☐	☐
12	What day is the wedding ceremony?	☐	☐	☐
13	Can you tell me how to get there?	☐	☐	☐
14	How many people can fit in one bus?	☐	☐	☐
15	What time does the bus leave for the airport?	☐	☐	☐
16	Where did you lose it?	☐	☐	☐
17	May I take your order?	☐	☐	☐
18	He never pays back the money he borrows from me.	☐	☐	☐
19	A family is moving into the house across the street.	☐	☐	☐
20	Is it going to rain today?	☐	☐	☐

Step 1 우리말 보면서 영어 듣기

		1회	2회	3회
1	설거지하는 것은 정말 싫어.	☐	☐	☐
2	당신은 거의 모든 종류의 신발과 함께 나를 신을 수 있습니다.	☐	☐	☐
3	이번 주말에 어떤 계획이라도 있니?	☐	☐	☐
4	난 그 결과를 봤을 때 충격을 받았어.	☐	☐	☐
5	도와드릴까요?	☐	☐	☐
6	여기서 얼마나 먼가요?	☐	☐	☐
7	이 계좌에서 돈을 인출하세요.	☐	☐	☐
8	방법을 보여 줄 수 있니?	☐	☐	☐
9	그에게 문자 메시지를 보내는 게 어때?	☐	☐	☐
10	나 우체국이랑 매우 가까운 곳에 살고 있어.	☐	☐	☐
11	그는 아마도 우리와 함께 축구 경기를 보러 갈 수도 있을 거야.	☐	☐	☐
12	나는 우리 학교 밴드부에서 드럼 연주자가 되고 싶어.	☐	☐	☐
13	네 창문이 열려 있는 것을 봤어.	☐	☐	☐
14	나는 그가 훌륭한 화가가 될 거라고 생각해.	☐	☐	☐
15	요즘 밤에 잠을 푹 잘 수가 없어.	☐	☐	☐
16	30분 일찍 만나는 것은 어때?	☐	☐	☐
17	우리 어젯밤 별을 관찰하러 갔어.	☐	☐	☐
18	우리는 모든 동물들을 보호하기 위해 더 많은 것을 해야 합니다.	☐	☐	☐
19	지금 돈을 지불해야 하나요?	☐	☐	☐
20	넌 문자 메시지 보내는 것을 해 봤니?	☐	☐	☐

Step 2 듣고 따라 말하기

		1회	2회	3회
1	I hate washing the dishes.	☐	☐	☐
2	You can wear me with almost any other kind of footwear.	☐	☐	☐
3	Do you have any plans this weekend?	☐	☐	☐
4	I was shocked when I saw the result.	☐	☐	☐
5	Do you need any help?	☐	☐	☐
6	How far is it from here?	☐	☐	☐
7	Please take the money out of this account.	☐	☐	☐
8	Can you show me how?	☐	☐	☐
9	Why don't you send him a text message?	☐	☐	☐
10	I live very close to the post office.	☐	☐	☐
11	Maybe he could go with us to watch a soccer game.	☐	☐	☐
12	I want to be a drummer in our school band.	☐	☐	☐
13	I saw your window is open.	☐	☐	☐
14	I think he's going to be a great artist.	☐	☐	☐
15	I can't sleep well at night these days.	☐	☐	☐
16	How about meeting half an hour earlier?	☐	☐	☐
17	We went to observe the stars last night.	☐	☐	☐
18	We must do more to protect all animals.	☐	☐	☐
19	Do I have to pay now?	☐	☐	☐
20	Have you tried sending a text message?	☐	☐	☐

Step 1 우리말 보면서 영어 듣기

		1회	2회	3회
1	오늘 아침에 두통이 심해요.	☐	☐	☐
2	내 새 양복에 맞는 셔츠가 필요해.	☐	☐	☐
3	가장 쉬운 방법은 당신의 옷들을 염색하는 것입니다.	☐	☐	☐
4	학교가 돈을 절약하고 싶어 해.	☐	☐	☐
5	여기 동물에게 음식을 주시면 안됩니다.	☐	☐	☐
6	너는 침대에서 휴식을 취해야 해.	☐	☐	☐
7	물 좀 가져다 주시겠어요?	☐	☐	☐
8	그건 벽에 붙여서 놓자.	☐	☐	☐
9	버스 기사를 찾는 광고 말씀이세요?	☐	☐	☐
10	배고프면 음식을 먹어도 돼?	☐	☐	☐
11	식탁 좀 차려 줄래요?	☐	☐	☐
12	두통이 진짜 심했고 힘이 없었어.	☐	☐	☐
13	오렌지 주스 한 잔 주세요.	☐	☐	☐
14	넌 정말로 흥미진진한 부분을 놓쳤어.	☐	☐	☐
15	내가 이곳에 오기 전에 분명히 그 표지판을 봤어.	☐	☐	☐
16	그는 캐나다 출신의 수의사입니다.	☐	☐	☐
17	음악회의 목적은 가난한 아이들을 돕는 것이다.	☐	☐	☐
18	오늘 오후에 몇몇 아이들이 그것을 보고 있었어.	☐	☐	☐
19	멕시코에서 방금 돌아왔어.	☐	☐	☐
20	왜 전문 사진작가가 되지 않았니?	☐	☐	☐

Step 2 듣고 따라 말하기

		1회	2회	3회
1	I have a terrible headache this morning.	☐	☐	☐
2	I need a shirt for my new suit.	☐	☐	☐
3	The easiest way is to dye your clothes.	☐	☐	☐
4	The school wants to save money.	☐	☐	☐
5	You're not allowed to feed the animals here.	☐	☐	☐
6	You should stay in bed and rest.	☐	☐	☐
7	Could we have some water, please?	☐	☐	☐
8	Let's put it against the wall.	☐	☐	☐
9	Do you mean the ad for a bus driver?	☐	☐	☐
10	Can we have some food if we get hungry?	☐	☐	☐
11	Could you set the table?	☐	☐	☐
12	I had a bad headache and felt very weak.	☐	☐	☐
13	I'll have a glass of orange juice.	☐	☐	☐
14	You've missed a really exciting part.	☐	☐	☐
15	Before I came here I saw the sign clearly.	☐	☐	☐
16	He is an animal doctor from Canada.	☐	☐	☐
17	The purpose of the concert is to help poor children.	☐	☐	☐
18	Some kids were looking at it this afternoon.	☐	☐	☐
19	He's just come back from Mexico.	☐	☐	☐
20	Why didn't you become a professional photographer?	☐	☐	☐

Step 1 우리말 보면서 영어 듣기

		1회	2회	3회
1	일요일에는 다시 맑은 하늘을 볼 수 있습니다.	☐	☐	☐
2	그는 어떻게 생겼나요?	☐	☐	☐
3	우리는 오랫동안 여기서 살아왔어요.	☐	☐	☐
4	그것들을 네가 직접 만든 거야?	☐	☐	☐
5	우리 가게는 30분 후면 문을 닫을 것입니다.	☐	☐	☐
6	무슨 계획이 있니?	☐	☐	☐
7	사진을 찍어도 되나요?	☐	☐	☐
8	네가 오늘 밤에 영화 보러 나갈 수 있을지 궁금해.	☐	☐	☐
9	미리 그것을 충전했어야 했는데.	☐	☐	☐
10	나는 야구공을 너무 많이 던졌어.	☐	☐	☐
11	너는 이번 여름 방학 동안 뭐 했니?	☐	☐	☐
12	바로 지금 새것으로 보내드리겠습니다.	☐	☐	☐
13	나는 가족들을 보는 것이 기대가 돼.	☐	☐	☐
14	그 가게는 가장 싼 가격으로 판다.	☐	☐	☐
15	비행기는 몇 시에 이륙합니까?	☐	☐	☐
16	가서 자리 좀 잡아줄래?	☐	☐	☐
17	이 좋은 소식을 학교에 빨리 전하고 싶구나.	☐	☐	☐
18	이름과 연락처를 남겨주시겠어요?	☐	☐	☐
19	네가 말했던 대로 어제 기름을 가득 채워 두었으면 좋았잖아.	☐	☐	☐
20	커피 좀 갖다 주실래요?	☐	☐	☐

Step 2 듣고 따라 말하기

		1회	2회	3회
1	You can see clear skies again on Sunday.	☐	☐	☐
2	What does he look like?	☐	☐	☐
3	We have lived here for a long time.	☐	☐	☐
4	Did you make them yourself?	☐	☐	☐
5	Our store will close in thirty minutes.	☐	☐	☐
6	Do you have any plans?	☐	☐	☐
7	Is it okay if I take some pictures?	☐	☐	☐
8	I wonder if you can go out to see a movie tonight.	☐	☐	☐
9	I should have charged it in advance.	☐	☐	☐
10	I threw the baseball too many times.	☐	☐	☐
11	What did you do during this summer vacation?	☐	☐	☐
12	I'll send a new one right now.	☐	☐	☐
13	I'm looking forward to seeing my family.	☐	☐	☐
14	The store has the cheapest prices.	☐	☐	☐
15	What time does the plane take off?	☐	☐	☐
16	Could you go get us a table?	☐	☐	☐
17	I can't wait to share this good news with our school.	☐	☐	☐
18	Can you leave your name and contact information?	☐	☐	☐
19	I wish you had filled it up yesterday like you said you would.	☐	☐	☐
20	Could I have some coffee?	☐	☐	☐

Step 1 우리말 보면서 영어 듣기

		1회	2회	3회
1	그 근처에 큰 건물이 있나요?	☐	☐	☐
2	3살짜리 사내아이라면 쉽게 탈 수 있어요.	☐	☐	☐
3	복도에서 뛰는 것이 허용되지 않아.	☐	☐	☐
4	비행기로 거기에 가는 데 얼마나 걸리는데?	☐	☐	☐
5	저는 저의 공부에 대한 문제에 대해 그들과 토론할 수 있습니다.	☐	☐	☐
6	일자리를 찾는 데 있어서 너에게 가장 중요한 게 뭐니?	☐	☐	☐
7	책을 찾고 있는데요 찾을 수가 없어요.	☐	☐	☐
8	콘서트 언제 시작해?	☐	☐	☐
9	이번 주 금요일 밤에 시간 있니?	☐	☐	☐
10	나는 더 이상 이 일에 흥미가 없어.	☐	☐	☐
11	의사가 되는 것은 쉽지 않단다.	☐	☐	☐
12	당신의 지역에 문제가 있는 것 같아요.	☐	☐	☐
13	이름과 주소가 어떻게 되죠?	☐	☐	☐
14	버스를 타고 산에 도착했어요.	☐	☐	☐
15	금요일 저녁에 자리를 예약하고 싶은데요.	☐	☐	☐
16	속이 메스껍고 제 심장이 아프기 시작했어요.	☐	☐	☐
17	반대 쪽으로 건너가야 합니다.	☐	☐	☐
18	어떤 종류의 물건이 필요해?	☐	☐	☐
19	입어 보시는 게 어때요?	☐	☐	☐
20	계산서를 가져다 드릴까요?	☐	☐	☐

Step 2 듣고 따라 말하기

		1회	2회	3회
1	Is there any big building near there?	☐	☐	☐
2	A three-year-old boy can easily ride one.	☐	☐	☐
3	You're not allowed to run in the halls.	☐	☐	☐
4	How long does it take to get there by plane?	☐	☐	☐
5	I can discuss with them the problems in my studies.	☐	☐	☐
6	What's the most important for you in finding jobs?	☐	☐	☐
7	I'm looking for a book, but I can't find it.	☐	☐	☐
8	What time does the concert begin?	☐	☐	☐
9	Are you free this Friday night?	☐	☐	☐
10	I'm not interested in this work any more.	☐	☐	☐
11	It is not easy to become a doctor.	☐	☐	☐
12	It seems like we're having problems in your area.	☐	☐	☐
13	Can you tell me your name and address?	☐	☐	☐
14	I took a bus and arrived at the mountain.	☐	☐	☐
15	I want to book a table on Friday evening.	☐	☐	☐
16	I felt sick in my stomach and my heart began to hurt.	☐	☐	☐
17	You should cross to the other side.	☐	☐	☐
18	What kind of things do you need?	☐	☐	☐
19	Why don't you try it on?	☐	☐	☐
20	Do you want me to bring you your bill?	☐	☐	☐

Step 1 우리말 보면서 영어 듣기

		1회	2회	3회
1	어떤 종류의 방석을 생각하고 있는데?	☐	☐	☐
2	안전벨트를 착용하시겠어요?	☐	☐	☐
3	네 말에 전적으로 동의해.	☐	☐	☐
4	나는 거친 운동은 좋아하지 않아서 볼링하러 가는 것을 좋아해.	☐	☐	☐
5	그 남자가 신고 있었던 것과 같은 구두예요.	☐	☐	☐
6	컴퓨터에 관한 책을 찾고 있어요.	☐	☐	☐
7	온라인으로 표를 사면 더 싸.	☐	☐	☐
8	나는 9시 전에는 집에 들어가야 해.	☐	☐	☐
9	내가 여덟 살 때 가족이 캐나다로 이주했어.	☐	☐	☐
10	만약 어떤 CD라도 두 장을 사면, 여러분의 이름이 경쟁에 참여하게 됩니다.	☐	☐	☐
11	도대체 무슨 말을 하는지 모르겠네.	☐	☐	☐
12	남편께서 오늘 아침 제 택시에 가방을 놓고 내리셨습니다.	☐	☐	☐
13	직업상 어쩔 수 없어요.	☐	☐	☐
14	그녀는 나와 함께 고등학교를 다녔어.	☐	☐	☐
15	이런 카페에서 인터넷을 쓰는 것은 그다지 안전하지 않아.	☐	☐	☐
16	그는 지금 이곳에 없습니다.	☐	☐	☐
17	어떻게 변경하길 원하시나요?	☐	☐	☐
18	도서관에 가보는 거 어때요?	☐	☐	☐
19	나는 그가 독감으로 아파서 침대에 누워 있다고 들었어.	☐	☐	☐
20	진정하고 웃으면서 그녀에게 도움을 청해.	☐	☐	☐

Step 2 듣고 따라 말하기

		1회	2회	3회
1	What kind of cushion do you have in mind?	☐	☐	☐
2	Would you fasten your seatbelt?	☐	☐	☐
3	I couldn't agree more.	☐	☐	☐
4	I don't like rough sports, so I like to go bowling.	☐	☐	☐
5	They're the same shoes the man was wearing.	☐	☐	☐
6	I'm looking for books about computers.	☐	☐	☐
7	If you buy the tickets online, it's cheaper.	☐	☐	☐
8	I have to be home before nine.	☐	☐	☐
9	My family moved to Canada when I was eight.	☐	☐	☐
10	If you just buy any two CDs, your name will go into competition.	☐	☐	☐
11	I don't know what you are talking about.	☐	☐	☐
12	Your husband left his bag in my taxi this morning.	☐	☐	☐
13	I can't help it because of my job.	☐	☐	☐
14	She went to high school with me.	☐	☐	☐
15	It is not safe to use the Internet like here at the cafe.	☐	☐	☐
16	I'm afraid he isn't here right now.	☐	☐	☐
17	What would you like to change?	☐	☐	☐
18	Why don't you check out the library?	☐	☐	☐
19	I heard he's sick in bed with the flu.	☐	☐	☐
20	You need to calm down and ask her for help with smile.	☐	☐	☐

Step 1 우리말 보면서 영어 듣기

		1회	2회	3회
1	허리가 약간 아픈 것 같아.	☐	☐	☐
2	이 방을 재배치하고 싶어.	☐	☐	☐
3	여기가 세계에서 가장 큰 실내 테마 공원이야.	☐	☐	☐
4	중간 사이즈가 당신에게 맞지 않을 것 같은데요.	☐	☐	☐
5	몇 번 버스를 타야 하죠?	☐	☐	☐
6	우리는 차를 타고 얼마나 더 멀리 가야 하지?	☐	☐	☐
7	더 많은 지도와 자세한 정보가 있는 걸 원해요.	☐	☐	☐
8	그 일이 언제 끝나죠?	☐	☐	☐
9	작은 것들이 큰 차이를 만들 수 있다는 것을 기억하세요.	☐	☐	☐
10	내 근육통을 어떻게 완화시킬 수 있니?	☐	☐	☐
11	배구 시합에서 이겼기 때문에 기분이 좋아요.	☐	☐	☐
12	보고서 제출 마감이 오늘이라는 걸 알아요.	☐	☐	☐
13	그는 일하지 않을 때는 뭘 하는 것을 좋아하니?	☐	☐	☐
14	그것이 살을 빼는 가장 좋은 방법이야.	☐	☐	☐
15	너는 보통 언제 편지를 쓰니?	☐	☐	☐
16	너 그 소식 들었니?	☐	☐	☐
17	지하철역에서 만나자.	☐	☐	☐
18	엄마가 요리하는 동안 아빠랑 집을 청소했어.	☐	☐	☐
19	너는 왜 그것을 버리려고 하니?	☐	☐	☐
20	너는 우산이 없니?	☐	☐	☐

Step 2 듣고 따라 말하기

		1회	2회	3회
1	My back seems to hurt a little.	☐	☐	☐
2	I'd like to rearrange this room.	☐	☐	☐
3	This is the largest indoor theme park in the world.	☐	☐	☐
4	I don't think medium would fit you.	☐	☐	☐
5	What number bus do I have to take?	☐	☐	☐
6	How much further can we go in the car?	☐	☐	☐
7	I want something with more maps and detailed information.	☐	☐	☐
8	When will the work be finished?	☐	☐	☐
9	Please remember that little things can make a big difference.	☐	☐	☐
10	How could I relieve my sore muscles?	☐	☐	☐
11	I feel good because we won the volleyball game.	☐	☐	☐
12	I know the report is due today.	☐	☐	☐
13	What does he like to do when he's not working?	☐	☐	☐
14	That's the best way to lose weight.	☐	☐	☐
15	When do you usually write letters?	☐	☐	☐
16	Have you heard the news?	☐	☐	☐
17	Let's meet at the subway station.	☐	☐	☐
18	I cleaned the house with my dad, while my mom was cooking.	☐	☐	☐
19	Why do you want to throw it away?	☐	☐	☐
20	Don't you have an umbrella?	☐	☐	☐

영어듣기능력평가 **14**회

만점 듣기 표현

Step 1 우리말 보면서 영어 듣기

		1회	2회	3회
1	이것을 할 때는 라켓과 가벼운 공이 필요합니다.	☐	☐	☐
2	안경점에 가셔야겠어요.	☐	☐	☐
3	이 사진을 한 장 복사해 주시겠어요?	☐	☐	☐
4	입을 벌려주시겠어요?	☐	☐	☐
5	내가 너라면 그녀에게 그만하라고 말하겠는데.	☐	☐	☐
6	이 그림 좀 옮기는 것을 도와줄 수 있겠니?	☐	☐	☐
7	그렇게 많은 체중을 어떻게 뺐니?	☐	☐	☐
8	그녀에게 메시지를 전해 줄게.	☐	☐	☐
9	너희 사무실 앞에 있는 음식점에서 만나자.	☐	☐	☐
10	누군가 오늘 오후 3시에 Tony를 방문할 것이다.	☐	☐	☐
11	오후에 저는 동물들을 조련시키는 데 4시간 정도를 보냅니다.	☐	☐	☐
12	내일 오후에 해변에 가자.	☐	☐	☐
13	벌써 3킬로그램이나 뺐어.	☐	☐	☐
14	메뉴판 좀 주시겠어요?	☐	☐	☐
15	보고서 때문에 책을 좀 빌릴 거야.	☐	☐	☐
16	저는 너무 바빠서 잠을 충분히 자지 못했습니다.	☐	☐	☐
17	그는 안경을 쓰고 있어.	☐	☐	☐
18	어젯밤 뭔가 날아가는 것을 봤어.	☐	☐	☐
19	아예 안 먹을 생각이니?	☐	☐	☐
20	그날 내가 요리사에게 레시피를 물어봤어.	☐	☐	☐

Step 2 듣고 따라 말하기

		1회	2회	3회
1	When you play this, you need a racket and a light ball.	☐	☐	☐
2	You need to go to the eyeglasses store.	☐	☐	☐
3	Could you give me a copy of this photo?	☐	☐	☐
4	Open your mouth, please.	☐	☐	☐
5	If I were you, I would tell her to stop.	☐	☐	☐
6	Could you please help me move this picture?	☐	☐	☐
7	How did you lose that much weight?	☐	☐	☐
8	I'll give her the message.	☐	☐	☐
9	Let's meet at the restaurant in front of your office.	☐	☐	☐
10	Somebody will visit Tony at 3 o'clock this afternoon.	☐	☐	☐
11	In the afternoon, I spend about four hours training animals.	☐	☐	☐
12	Let's go to the beach tomorrow afternoon.	☐	☐	☐
13	I've already lost three kilograms.	☐	☐	☐
14	Could we have the menu, please?	☐	☐	☐
15	I'll borrow some books for my report.	☐	☐	☐
16	I didn't sleep much because I was very busy.	☐	☐	☐
17	He's wearing glasses.	☐	☐	☐
18	I saw something flying last night.	☐	☐	☐
19	Aren't you eating at all?	☐	☐	☐
20	I asked the chef for the recipe that day.	☐	☐	☐

Step 1 우리말 보면서 영어 듣기

		1회	2회	3회
1	두 학생이 도로를 건너고 있다.	☐	☐	☐
2	오늘은 야외 활동을 위한 완벽한 시간일 것입니다.	☐	☐	☐
3	너도 알다시피, 우리가 새 집으로 이사했잖아.	☐	☐	☐
4	불행하게도, 엘리베이터가 또 다시 고장이 났습니다.	☐	☐	☐
5	건조한 피부에 좋은 것 있어요?	☐	☐	☐
6	1시간 30분밖에 안 남았어.	☐	☐	☐
7	이 인터뷰를 TV에 내보내도 될까요?	☐	☐	☐
8	나를 집으로 데려다 줄 수 있니?	☐	☐	☐
9	집안일을 도와드릴 수 있어요.	☐	☐	☐
10	내가 가고자 하는 사이트에 접속이 안 돼.	☐	☐	☐
11	시간을 조금 더 주시겠어요?	☐	☐	☐
12	선반에 있는 것은 절대 만지지 마십시오.	☐	☐	☐
13	이 편지에 내가 공짜 여행에 당첨됐다고 쓰여 있어!	☐	☐	☐
14	사람들은 624-3646번으로 예약을 할 수 있다.	☐	☐	☐
15	너무 오랫동안 기다리게 해서 미안해.	☐	☐	☐
16	나는 어려운 사람들을 돕고 싶어.	☐	☐	☐
17	콘서트 가지 않을래?	☐	☐	☐
18	원하시는 특별한 시간대가 있나요?	☐	☐	☐
19	모든 것이 제가 예상했던 대로네요.	☐	☐	☐
20	뭐 좀 먹자.	☐	☐	☐

Step 2 듣고 따라 말하기

		1회	2회	3회
1	Two students are crossing the road.	☐	☐	☐
2	Today will be a perfect time for outdoor activities.	☐	☐	☐
3	We have just moved to a new house, you know.	☐	☐	☐
4	Unfortunately, the elevator is out of order again.	☐	☐	☐
5	What do you suggest for dry skin?	☐	☐	☐
6	We have only an hour and a half.	☐	☐	☐
7	Can I use this interview on TV?	☐	☐	☐
8	Can you take me to my house?	☐	☐	☐
9	I can help you with the housework.	☐	☐	☐
10	I can't get access the site I want.	☐	☐	☐
11	Can I have some more time, please?	☐	☐	☐
12	Plase don't touch anything on the shelves.	☐	☐	☐
13	This letter says I won a free trip!	☐	☐	☐
14	People can make a reservation at 624-3646.	☐	☐	☐
15	I'm sorry to have kept you waiting for so long.	☐	☐	☐
16	I want to help people in need.	☐	☐	☐
17	Would you like to go to a concert?	☐	☐	☐
18	Do you prefer any particular time?	☐	☐	☐
19	It sounds like everything I expected.	☐	☐	☐
20	Let's have something to eat.	☐	☐	☐

영어듣기능력평가 **16**회

만점 듣기 표현

Step 1 우리말 보면서 영어 듣기

		1회	2회	3회
1	그녀는 청바지와 티셔츠를 입고 있어.	☐	☐	☐
2	일기 예보에 의하면 이번 주말은 맑을 거라고 했어.	☐	☐	☐
3	그것은 우리가 놓치고 싶지 않았던 영화인데.	☐	☐	☐
4	그 방은 바다 경치가 보이나요?	☐	☐	☐
5	내일 아침으로 여행을 예약하지요.	☐	☐	☐
6	어느 버튼을 눌러야 하나요?	☐	☐	☐
7	다음 주 토요일에 영화 보러 가자.	☐	☐	☐
8	아래층으로 내려가셔서 차를 인수받으세요.	☐	☐	☐
9	문장을 만들어 낼 때마다 규칙을 생각하는 거지.	☐	☐	☐
10	날이 어두워질 때까지 한 두 시간 정도 책을 읽어요.	☐	☐	☐
11	우리가 찾고자 하는 분이시네요.	☐	☐	☐
12	비즈니스 은행 건너편으로 이사했어요.	☐	☐	☐
13	안개가 낀 풍경은 그림과 같았어.	☐	☐	☐
14	축구 연습이 평소보다 더 길었어요.	☐	☐	☐
15	이 시계는 이번 주에 세일 중이지 않나요?	☐	☐	☐
16	누구시죠?	☐	☐	☐
17	기차는 7시에 출발할 예정입니다.	☐	☐	☐
18	정말로 내가 널 도울 수 있을 거라고 생각해?	☐	☐	☐
19	여기 더 비싼 것들이 있습니다.	☐	☐	☐
20	무엇을 주문하시겠어요?	☐	☐	☐

Step 2 듣고 따라 말하기

		1회	2회	3회
1	She's wearing jeans and a T-shirt.	☐	☐	☐
2	The weather forecast said it would be sunny this weekend.	☐	☐	☐
3	That's the movie we didn't want to miss.	☐	☐	☐
4	Does the room have a view of the sea?	☐	☐	☐
5	I'd like to book a trip for tomorrow morning.	☐	☐	☐
6	Which button should I press?	☐	☐	☐
7	Let's go to the movies next Saturday.	☐	☐	☐
8	You can pick up your car downstairs.	☐	☐	☐
9	You will think about the rules when creating sentences.	☐	☐	☐
10	I read books for an hour or two until it gets dark.	☐	☐	☐
11	You're the person we've been looking for.	☐	☐	☐
12	We moved across the road from the Business Bank.	☐	☐	☐
13	The foggy scenes looked like paintings.	☐	☐	☐
14	Soccer practice was longer than usual.	☐	☐	☐
15	Isn't this watch on sale this week?	☐	☐	☐
16	Who's speaking, please?	☐	☐	☐
17	The train will leave here at 7 o'clock.	☐	☐	☐
18	Do you really think I can help you?	☐	☐	☐
19	Here are some more expensive ones.	☐	☐	☐
20	What would you like to order?	☐	☐	☐

Step 1 우리말 보면서 영어 듣기

		1회	2회	3회
1	나는 기타를 치고 있는 곰 인형이 더 좋은데.	☐	☐	☐
2	남자아이가 전화기를 귀에 대고 있다.	☐	☐	☐
3	그 남자는 봉지를 집어 들고는 엄마를 향해 걸어갔다.	☐	☐	☐
4	그 말은 고양이가 개보다도 더 영리할 수도 있다는 말이네.	☐	☐	☐
5	오늘 수업 가는 길에 거기에 들러 볼게.	☐	☐	☐
6	돌아보기 전에 뭐 좀 먹자.	☐	☐	☐
7	이것은 콧물이나 기침에 효과가 좋습니다.	☐	☐	☐
8	그곳에 몇 시에 가야 해요?	☐	☐	☐
9	혈압을 낮추는 데 도움을 주고 심장마비를 예방해 줘.	☐	☐	☐
10	우리 함께 참여하는 것이 어때?	☐	☐	☐
11	이 옷들은 어디서 입어볼 수 있나요?	☐	☐	☐
12	그것이 어떻게 생겼는지 말씀해 주시겠습니까?	☐	☐	☐
13	초콜릿 한 상자 어때?	☐	☐	☐
14	하루에 보통 얼마나 오래 운동을 하십니까?	☐	☐	☐
15	그곳에 빨리 가는 방법을 몰라요.	☐	☐	☐
16	그곳에 약 한 달 동안 머물 거야.	☐	☐	☐
17	항상 연기를 해보고 싶었어.	☐	☐	☐
18	축구 연습 때문에 너무 바빴니?	☐	☐	☐
19	이미 우리 반에서 최고의 학생입니다.	☐	☐	☐
20	내 새 드레스를 어떻게 생각하니?	☐	☐	☐

Step 2 듣고 따라 말하기

		1회	2회	3회
1	I think the teddy bear playing the guitar is better.	☐	☐	☐
2	The boy is holding a receiver to his ear.	☐	☐	☐
3	The man picked the bags up, and walked towards his mom.	☐	☐	☐
4	That means cats might possibly be smarter than dogs.	☐	☐	☐
5	I'll drop by there on my way to class today.	☐	☐	☐
6	Let's eat something before going around.	☐	☐	☐
7	This works for a runny nose or cough.	☐	☐	☐
8	What time do you need to be there?	☐	☐	☐
9	It helps lower blood pressure and prevent heart attack.	☐	☐	☐
10	Why don't we enter it together?	☐	☐	☐
11	Where can I try on these clothes?	☐	☐	☐
12	Could you tell me what it looks like?	☐	☐	☐
13	How about a box of chocolates?	☐	☐	☐
14	How long do you usually work out for each day?	☐	☐	☐
15	I don't know how to go there fast.	☐	☐	☐
16	I'll stay there for about a month.	☐	☐	☐
17	I've always wanted to try acting.	☐	☐	☐
18	Were you too busy with your soccer practice?	☐	☐	☐
19	He's already a top student in my class.	☐	☐	☐
20	How do you like my new dress?	☐	☐	☐

Step 1 우리말 보면서 영어 듣기

		1회	2회	3회
1	나는 네가 댄스에 관심이 있는 줄은 몰랐는데.	☐	☐	☐
2	방 안이 장미꽃 냄새로 가득 찼어요.	☐	☐	☐
3	지금 TV에서 농구 경기를 볼 수 있을까요?	☐	☐	☐
4	저에게 좀 작은 느낌이고 색깔도 마음에 들지 않네요.	☐	☐	☐
5	지하철이 항상 가장 빠른 방법이야.	☐	☐	☐
6	너희들의 우정이 다시 좋아질 거라고 확신해.	☐	☐	☐
7	아름다운 것들을 많이 보았겠구나.	☐	☐	☐
8	저쪽에서 주차장을 찾아보는 게 좋겠어요.	☐	☐	☐
9	네가 정말로 그 분야에 재능을 타고 난 걸 알고 있지.	☐	☐	☐
10	이번 토요일에 그 분을 뵈러 갈까해.	☐	☐	☐
11	우리가 필요로 하는 모든 것을 꾸렸는지 점검해 봐야 해.	☐	☐	☐
12	내일 날씨 좀 말씀해 주실 수 있나요?	☐	☐	☐
13	밤에는 조그만 소리에도 잠이 깨요.	☐	☐	☐
14	이 마을에 사시면 여기서 책을 빌릴 수 있어요.	☐	☐	☐
15	새로운 계좌를 만들고 싶어요.	☐	☐	☐
16	예약을 확인하려고 하는데요.	☐	☐	☐
17	여러분에게 몇가지 중요한 점을 상기시켜주고 싶습니다.	☐	☐	☐
18	오전에는 눈이 올 것이고, 오후에는 구름이 낄 것입니다.	☐	☐	☐
19	조금 드셔 보실래요	☐	☐	☐
20	병원에 가는 게 좋겠어.	☐	☐	☐

Step 2 듣고 따라 말하기

		1회	2회	3회
1	I didn't know you're interested in dance.	☐	☐	☐
2	The room was filled with the smell of roses.	☐	☐	☐
3	Can I watch the basketball game on TV now?	☐	☐	☐
4	It feels like it's a bit small for me and I don't like the color.	☐	☐	☐
5	The subway is always the fastest way.	☐	☐	☐
6	I'm sure your friendship will be fine again.	☐	☐	☐
7	I'm sure you saw many beautiful things.	☐	☐	☐
8	You had better find a parking lot over there.	☐	☐	☐
9	I know that you're really gifted in that area.	☐	☐	☐
10	I'm going to see him this Saturday.	☐	☐	☐
11	We should check we have packed everything we need.	☐	☐	☐
12	Could you tell me the weather for tomorrow?	☐	☐	☐
13	Even a little noise wakes me up at night.	☐	☐	☐
14	If you live in this town, you can borrow books here.	☐	☐	☐
15	I'd like to open a new account.	☐	☐	☐
16	I want to reconfirm my reservation.	☐	☐	☐
17	I'd like to remind you of a few important things.	☐	☐	☐
18	It'll be snowy in the morning and then cloudy in the afternoon.	☐	☐	☐
19	Why don't you try a bit?	☐	☐	☐
20	I think you should go see the doctor.	☐	☐	☐

Step 1 우리말 보면서 영어 듣기

		1회	2회	3회
1	이건 내가 고등학교 때 찍은 사진이야.	☐	☐	☐
2	동물들한테 먹을 것을 주는 것은 해롭다고 들었어.	☐	☐	☐
3	낮에는 언제나 덥고 밤에는 매우 추워집니다.	☐	☐	☐
4	티켓을 어떻게 구했니?	☐	☐	☐
5	메시지를 그에게 전해 드리겠습니다.	☐	☐	☐
6	그곳에 걸어가는 데 얼마나 걸립니까?	☐	☐	☐
7	이게 당신의 요구 사항에 꼭 맞는 것 같군요.	☐	☐	☐
8	마실 것을 드릴까요?	☐	☐	☐
9	제가 당신을 위해 행운을 빌어 줄게요.	☐	☐	☐
10	네가 잘할 거라고 확신해.	☐	☐	☐
11	대부분의 아파트에서는 애완동물을 기를 수 없어.	☐	☐	☐
12	우리 목적지까지 얼마나 걸려?	☐	☐	☐
13	이 파일 좀 프린트 해 줄래?	☐	☐	☐
14	여러분들의 사랑과 도움 덕택에 우리 클럽이 발전했습니다.	☐	☐	☐
15	태양에서 지구로 빛이 오는 데 얼마나 걸리지?	☐	☐	☐
16	안 좋은 일이라도 생겼니?	☐	☐	☐
17	네 생일이 언제인지 알려줄래?	☐	☐	☐
18	우리 내일 몇 시에 떠나요?	☐	☐	☐
19	따뜻하고 맑을 것이라고 들었어.	☐	☐	☐
20	네가 여러 번 나를 도와준 것을 잊지 않고 있어.	☐	☐	☐

Step 2 듣고 따라 말하기

		1회	2회	3회
1	This is the photo taken when I was in high school.	☐	☐	☐
2	I heard that feeding animals is harmful.	☐	☐	☐
3	It is hot in the day but turns very cold at night.	☐	☐	☐
4	How did you get the ticket?	☐	☐	☐
5	I will give him the message.	☐	☐	☐
6	How long does it take to walk there?	☐	☐	☐
7	I think this would fit your need.	☐	☐	☐
8	Would you like anything to drink?	☐	☐	☐
9	I'll keep my fingers crossed for you.	☐	☐	☐
10	I'm sure you'll do well.	☐	☐	☐
11	You can't raise pets in most apartments!	☐	☐	☐
12	How long do we have until our destination?	☐	☐	☐
13	Would you print this file for me?	☐	☐	☐
14	Through your love and help, out club has progressed.	☐	☐	☐
15	How long does it take for light to travel from the Sun to the Earth?	☐	☐	☐
16	Did something bad happen?	☐	☐	☐
17	Can you tell me when your birthday is?	☐	☐	☐
18	What time are we leaving tomorrow?	☐	☐	☐
19	I heard that it's going to be warm and sunny.	☐	☐	☐
20	I haven't forgotten your helping me several times.	☐	☐	☐

Step 1 우리말 보면서 영어 듣기

		1회	2회	3회
1	이 근처에서 개를 보셨나요?	☐	☐	☐
2	자동차가 쓰러진 나무 곁을 지나가고 있는 중이다.	☐	☐	☐
3	이미 일기 예보를 점검했지.	☐	☐	☐
4	음악과 체육이 내가 가장 좋아하는 두 과목이지.	☐	☐	☐
5	표를 확인할 수 있을까요?	☐	☐	☐
6	종업원들이 오늘 밤에 아주 바쁜 것 같아.	☐	☐	☐
7	왜 이 일자리에 지원하셨죠?	☐	☐	☐
8	집에서는 몇 시에 나가실 거예요?	☐	☐	☐
9	지금 있는 곳보다 직장이 더 가까울 것으로 확신해.	☐	☐	☐
10	저희는 금주에 대 할인 판매를 실시하고 있습니다.	☐	☐	☐
11	이 발표 자료를 복사해줄래?	☐	☐	☐
12	할머니께서 오늘 아침에 사고를 당하셨다고 그녀에게 좀 전해 주세요.	☐	☐	☐
13	그에게 그런 종류의 선물을 사주고 싶지는 않아.	☐	☐	☐
14	나는 우리 형을 너희 언니에게 소개하고 싶어.	☐	☐	☐
15	택시를 타실 수는 있지만, 비용이 많이 들 거예요.	☐	☐	☐
16	최근에 어떻게 지냈니?	☐	☐	☐
17	공항에서 오는 길에 차가 많이 막혔어.	☐	☐	☐
18	장면이 아주 다채롭고 독특하고 연기도 아주 좋았어.	☐	☐	☐
19	그렇게 하실 수 있어요?	☐	☐	☐
20	낙제할 거라고 생각했었는데, 결국 낙제는 안 했어.	☐	☐	☐

Step 2 듣고 따라 말하기

		1회	2회	3회
1	Have you seen a dog around here?	☐	☐	☐
2	The car is passing by the fallen tree.	☐	☐	☐
3	I've already checked the weather forecast.	☐	☐	☐
4	Music and physical education are my two favorite subjects.	☐	☐	☐
5	Can I check your ticket, please?	☐	☐	☐
6	The waiters look very busy tonight.	☐	☐	☐
7	Why did you apply for this job?	☐	☐	☐
8	What time are you leaving the house?	☐	☐	☐
9	I'm sure it would be closer to your work than you are now.	☐	☐	☐
10	We're having a big sale this week.	☐	☐	☐
11	Can you go photocopy these handouts?	☐	☐	☐
12	Tell her that her grandmother had an accident this morning.	☐	☐	☐
13	I don't want to give him that kind of present.	☐	☐	☐
14	I'd like to introduce my brother to your sister.	☐	☐	☐
15	You can take a taxi, but it'll cost a lot.	☐	☐	☐
16	What have you been up to lately?	☐	☐	☐
17	The traffic was really bad on the way back from the airport.	☐	☐	☐
18	The scenes were very colorful and unique, and the acting was pretty good.	☐	☐	☐
19	Are you sure you are able to do that?	☐	☐	☐
20	I thought I would fail, but I didn't fail after all.	☐	☐	☐

Step 1 우리말 보면서 영어 듣기

		1회	2회	3회
1	이런 날씨가 계속될지 궁금하신가요?	☐	☐	☐
2	이 다크 초콜릿 케이크 어떠세요?	☐	☐	☐
3	텐트를 설치하고 의자를 배열해야 해.	☐	☐	☐
4	주말 잘 보냈니?	☐	☐	☐
5	이 책들을 반납하고 싶어요.	☐	☐	☐
6	언제 파티를 할 거야?	☐	☐	☐
7	드럼을 연주해보고 싶어요.	☐	☐	☐
8	도서관에 가는 거 어때?	☐	☐	☐
9	수영을 할 때는 수영모를 반드시 써야합니다.	☐	☐	☐
10	개를 무서워하는 사람들을 존중하세요.	☐	☐	☐
11	시골 지역의 작은 마을로 이사를 가게 된 한 가족에 대한 이야기입니다.	☐	☐	☐
12	저희 병원은 처음이신가요?	☐	☐	☐
13	언제 돌아오시나요?	☐	☐	☐
14	여기서 급행열차 표를 파는지 궁금하네요.	☐	☐	☐
15	우리가 더 해야 할 거 없나?	☐	☐	☐
16	좀 가져갈래요?	☐	☐	☐
17	거기 들어가시면 안됩니다.	☐	☐	☐
18	우리는 유명한 지역 식당에서 정오에 점심을 먹을 것입니다.	☐	☐	☐
19	한번 해 볼래?	☐	☐	☐
20	엄마가 어렸을 때는 컴퓨터를 가지고 있지 않았다고 했어.	☐	☐	☐

Step 2 듣고 따라 말하기

		1회	2회	3회
1	Do you wonder if this weather will continue?	☐	☐	☐
2	What about this dark chocolate cake?	☐	☐	☐
3	I'd need to set up the tents and arrange the chairs.	☐	☐	☐
4	Did you have a good weekend?	☐	☐	☐
5	I'd like to return these books.	☐	☐	☐
6	When are you having the party?	☐	☐	☐
7	I'd like to try the drums.	☐	☐	☐
8	Why don't you go to the library?	☐	☐	☐
9	You must wear a swimming cap when you swim.	☐	☐	☐
10	Respect that some people are scared of dogs.	☐	☐	☐
11	It's a story about a family who moved to a little town in the countryside.	☐	☐	☐
12	Is it your first visit to our clinic?	☐	☐	☐
13	What time will you be back?	☐	☐	☐
14	I was wondering if you sell express train tickets here.	☐	☐	☐
15	Is there anything else we need to do?	☐	☐	☐
16	Would you like to take some with you?	☐	☐	☐
17	You're not allowed to go in there.	☐	☐	☐
18	We'll have lunch at noon at a famous local restaurant.	☐	☐	☐
19	Would you like to give it a try?	☐	☐	☐
20	My mom said she didn't have a computer when she was a child.	☐	☐	☐

중요 어휘 및 표현

듣기는
실전이다

중학 2

Plus Book

24회

디딤돌

영어듣기능력평가 **01** 회

01

□ really	정말로
□ look like	~처럼 생기다
□ long	긴
□ hair	머리카락, (동물의) 털
□ small	작은
□ big	큰
□ spot	점
□ back	등
□ cute	귀여운

02

□ beside	~의 옆에
□ striped shirt	줄무늬 셔츠
□ thin	마른
□ tall	키가 큰

03

□ travel	여행하다, 이동하다
□ distance	거리
□ motor	모터
□ loud	시끄러운
□ move	움직이다
□ ride	타다 (-rode-ridden)
□ dangerous	위험한
□ That is why ~.	그것이 ~한 이유이다.

04

□ free	한가한
□ special	특별한
□ go boating	보트 타러 가다
□ get motion-sickness	멀미하다
□ instead	대신에
□ go bicycling	자전거를 타러 가다
□ ride a bike	자전거를 타다
□ I'd like to, but ~.	그러고 싶지만, ~.

05

□ more than	~ 이상
□ cafeteria	구내식당
□ slow-eater	천천히 먹는 사람
□ such	그러한, 그렇게
□ bring	가져오다
□ own	자신의

06

□ around	~주변에
□ far	멀리, 먼
□ How long does it take to ~?	~하는 데 (시간이) 얼마나 걸리나요?

07

□ attention	주의, 주목
□ land	착륙하다, 도착하다
□ international	국제의
□ remain	계속 ~이다, 남다
□ seat belt	안전벨트
□ complete	완전한, 완벽한
□ turn off	~을 끄다 (↔ turn on)
□ enter	들어가다
□ make sure	확인하다
□ valuables	귀중품
□ forget	잊다 (↔ remember)
□ passport	여권
□ get off	내리다 (↔ get on)

08

□ essay	에세이, 글
□ busy with	~로 바쁜
□ babysit	돌보다
□ stay up late	늦게까지 자지 않다
□ toy	장난감

09

□ sell	팔다
□ kind	종류
□ novel	소설
□ get rid of	처리하다
□ textbook	교과서
□ travel	여행

10	
□ work	작동하다
□ make phone calls	전화를 걸다
□ get ~ fixed	~을 수리하다
□ return	반납하다
□ terrible	최악의

11	
□ worried	걱정스러운, 걱정하는
□ present	선물
□ enough	충분한
□ bake	(빵을) 굽다

12	
□ book	예약하다
□ flight	항공기
□ available	이용할 수 있는
□ make a reservation	예약하다

13	
□ expensive	비싼 (↔ cheap)
□ be pleased with	~에 기쁘다
□ don't have to	~할 필요가 없다 (= need not)
□ pay for	~에 대해 값을 지불하다
□ That's all right.	괜찮습니다.

14	
□ left-handed	왼손잡이의
□ draw	(그림을) 그리다
□ either	(둘 중) 어느 하나의
□ fork	포크
□ chopstick	젓가락
□ knife	칼, 나이프

15	
□ sound	~하게 들리다
□ a little	조금
□ later	나중에
□ possible	가능한
□ bus station	버스 정류장
□ Shall we ~?	우리 ~할까요?

16	
□ check in	입실하다 (↔ check out)
□ reservation	예약
□ sign	서명하다
□ form	양식, 서식
□ stay	숙박, 체류; 머무르다

17	
□ report	신고하다
□ realize	알다
□ fill in	작성하다
□ form	양식
□ contact number	연락가능한 번호
□ turn up	나타나다[찾게 되다]

18	
□ day off	쉬는 날
□ get	도착하다
□ leave	떠나다

19	
□ lovely	멋진
□ I can't believe it.	믿을 수 없어.
□ painting	그림, 그림 그리기
□ work	작품

20	
□ classmate	학급 친구
□ leave a message	메시지를 남기다
□ call back	다시 전화하다

01

□ wrap	포장하다
□ gift	선물
□ wrapping paper	포장지
□ kitten	새끼고양이
□ puppy	강아지
□ ribbon	리본
□ cute	귀여운
□ skirt	치마

02

□ get exercise	운동을 하다
□ regularly	규칙적으로
□ be tired of	~이 지겹다, 싫증이 나다
□ something else	그 밖의 다른 것
□ badminton	배드민턴

03

□ win	이기다, 타다, 얻다
□ amazing	놀라운
□ summer vacation	여름 휴가
□ envy	부러워하다

04

□ pick up	데려오다
□ street	도로
□ move	이사하다
□ near	가까이에
□ somewhere	어딘가에

05

□ invite	초대하다
□ research	연구, 조사
□ project	프로젝트, 계획
□ greatly	대단히, 크게
□ provide A with B	A에게 B를 제공하다
□ work-related	일과 관련된
□ support	지원, 지지
□ accept	받아 주다, 수락하다
□ invitation	초대

□ opportunity	기회
□ contact	연락하다
□ by email	이메일로

06

□ fill out	(양식을) 기입하다
□ vase	꽃병
□ overseas	해외에서
□ duty	관세
□ How much do I owe you?	얼마를 지불해야 하죠?
□ window	창구
□ exit	출구

07

□ take a class	수업을 받다
□ honestly	솔직히
□ difficult	어려운
□ fast	빠른
□ keep -ing	계속 ~하다
□ try	노력하다

08

□ book	예약하다
□ double room	2인실
□ per night	하룻밤에
□ arrive	도착하다

09

□ fellow student	동창
□ be supposed to	~하기로 되어 있다
□ class reunion	동창회 모임
□ change	변경하다
□ school auditorium	학교 강당
□ available	이용 가능한

10

□ dinosaur	공룡
□ advantage	이점
□ creature	생명체
□ feed on	~을 먹고 살다

□ insect	곤충	□ police officer	경찰관
□ amazing	놀라운	□ take the subway	지하철을 타다
□ access	접근하다	□ first of all	무엇보다도, 우선
		□ careful	조심하는, 주의 깊은

11

□ trip	여행	**17**	
□ coast	해안	□ turn off	끄다
□ scenery	풍경, 경치	□ fall asleep	잠들다
□ along	~을 따라		
□ fantastic	환상적인	**18**	
□ tax	세금	□ field trip	현장 학습
□ whenever	~할 때마다	□ pottery	도자기
		□ talent	재능

12

□ Can I leave a message?	메시지를 남길 수 있을까요?	**19**	
□ give ~ a call	~에게 전화하다	□ Spanish	스페인 사람(말)의; 스페인 사람(어)
□ as soon as	~하자마자	□ by the way	그런데 (화제 전환)
□ come back	돌아오다(가다)	□ crowded	붐비는
		□ luggage	(여행용) 짐

13

□ check	확인하다	□ carry	운반하다, 나르다
□ in stock	비축되어, 재고로		
□ order	주문하다; 주문	**20**	
□ Go ahead.	그렇게 하세요.	□ lately	최근(에), 요즈음
		□ What have you been up to lately?	요즈음 뭐 하고 지냈니?

14

□ housewarming party	집들이	□ after-school class	방과 후 수업
□ toilet paper	화장지	□ How interesting!	흥미로운데!
□ practical	실용적인	□ How's it going?	잘 되어가니?
□ common	보통의, 일반적인		
□ gift	선물		
□ move	이사하다		
□ decide	결정하다		

15

□ science fiction	과학 공상
□ get a snack	간식을 먹다

16

□ get a ticket	교통 위반 딱지를 받다
□ on the way	도중에
□ run a red light	정지 신호에서 달리다

01

□ lift	들어 올리다
□ stone	돌
□ alone	혼자
□ tank	수족관
□ rod	낚싯대
□ feel like	~처럼 느끼다
□ hop	깡충깡충 뛰다
□ deep	깊은
□ race	경주하다
□ beat	이기다

02

□ deliver	배달하다
□ inside	~ 안으로 (↔ outside)
□ leave	놓다 (–left–left)
□ refrigerator	냉장고
□ floor	바닥
□ side table	협탁
□ next to	~ 옆에
□ coat rack	옷걸이

03

□ throw up	토하다
□ unusual	특이한, 이상한
□ possible	있을 수 있는

04

□ a pair of shoes	구두 한 켤레
□ How do you like ~?	~을 어떻게 생각하나요?
□ young adult	젊은층, 청소년

05

□ lots of fun	매우 재미있는
□ excited	신나는, 흥분한
□ whether A or B	A인지 B인지
□ by train	기차로
□ travel	여행하다
□ by bus	버스로
□ online	온라인으로 (↔ off-line)

□ right now	지금 당장

06

□ look for	~을 찾다
□ run through	빠르게 살펴보다
□ allow	허락하다
□ semester	학기
□ overdue charge	연체료
□ due date	마감 일자

07

□ public service announcement	공익 광고
□ accident	사고
□ subway station	지하철역
□ prevent	예방하다
□ while	~동안
□ rush	급히 움직이다
□ serious harm	심각한 해
□ cooperation	협조

08

□ exhibition	전시회
□ gladly	기쁘다
□ take up on	~을 채택하다

09

□ quiet	조용한
□ flow	흐르다
□ quietly	조용히
□ scenery	경치
□ feel like -ing	~하고 싶다
□ perfect	완벽한, 완전한
□ sign	표지판, 간판
□ over there	저쪽에
□ What a disappointment!	정말 실망이야!

10

□ vacation	휴가
□ clean up	청소하다
□ time off	여유 시간
□ to tell you the truth	사실

□ all-inclusive	전부를 포함하는

11

□ principal	교장선생님
□ You're kidding!	설마!(강한 놀람을 표현)
□ grade	학년

12

□ singer	가수
□ painter	화가
□ in the future	미래에, 장래에
□ What do you want to be in the future?	너는 장래에 뭐가 되고 싶니?
□ nurse	간호사
□ take care of	~을 돌보다
□ sick	아픈

13

□ May I speak to ~?	~와 통화할 수 있나요?
□ What's up?	무슨 일이야? (= What's the matter?)
□ give ~ a hand	~를 도와주다
□ at the moment	바로 지금

14

□ go shopping	쇼핑 가다
□ feel like -ing	~하고 싶다
□ paint	페인트를 칠하다
□ fence	담장, 울타리
□ a lot of work	큰 일
□ need a hand	도움이 필요하다
□ brush	솔, 붓

15

□ answer	대답, 답; 대답하다
□ question	질문; 질문하다
□ forget	잊다 (↔ remember)
□ pass the test	시험에 통과하다
□ too ~ to ...	너무 ~해서 …할 수 없는
□ worry about	~에 대해 걱정하다

16

□ art gallery	미술 화랑, 미술관

□ entrance	입구, 문
□ library	도서관
□ exactly	정확히

17

□ pass away	돌아가시다
□ I am truly sorry for your loss.	삼가 고인의 명복을 빕니다.
□ close	가까운
□ spend	(시간을) 보내다

18

□ Speaking.	(전화상에서) 전데요. (= This is speaking.)
□ That's too bad.	그거 안 됐구나. (= I'm sorry to hear that.)
□ What's the matter with ~?	~에 무슨 문제가 있니?
□ engine	엔진
□ take a look at	~을 보다(= look at)
□ in a minute	금방, 곧
□ in front of	~의 앞에

19

□ surprised	놀란
□ finally	마침내
□ succeed	성공하다
□ fail	실패하다
□ twice	두 번

20

□ move	옮기다
□ polish	닦다
□ What should I do?	어떻게 해야 할까요? (충고를 할 때)
□ later	나중에
□ suggest	제안하다
□ right away	바로

01

□ exhibition	전시회
□ statue	동상
□ in the middle of	~의 가운데에
□ national flag	국기
□ fly	휘날리다
□ pole	막대기, 기둥
□ on the top of	~의 꼭대기에

02

□ light bulb	전구
□ hardware store	철물점
□ main street	시내 중심가
□ pharmacy	약국
□ grocery store	식료품점
□ department store	백화점
□ around	주변에
□ area	지역

03

□ congratulate	축하하다
□ academic award	성적 우수상
□ honest	정직한
□ mistake	실수

04

□ plant	식물
□ bloom	꽃이 피다
□ favorite	가장 좋아하는
□ better	더 좋은

05

□ accident	사고
□ happen	일어나다, 발생하다
□ electricity	전기
□ comfortable	편안한
□ socket	소켓
□ shock	충격을 주다
□ scissors	가위
□ cut	베다, 자르다

□ careful	조심하는, 주의 깊은

06

□ take medicine	약을 복용하다
□ vitamin	비타민
□ multivitamin	종합비타민
□ prescription	처방(전)
□ fill a prescription	처방전 대로 조제하다
□ across from	~의 맞은편에

07

□ What's the matter?	무슨 일이니?
□ lift up	들어올리다
□ headache	두통
□ heartbeat	심장 박동

08

□ What's up?	무슨 일이니?
□ in front of	~의 앞에
□ in hospital	입원해 있는
□ broken	부러진
□ How awful!	저런!
□ get out of	~에서 나오다

09

□ field trip	현장 학습
□ each	각각
□ cost	비용이 들다

10

□ attention	주목
□ competition	경시대회
□ felt pen	사인펜
□ correction	수정
□ apply for	~에 응시하다, 지원하다
□ show up	나타나다
□ on time	정각에

11

□ nationality	국적
□ major	전공
□ graduate from	~을 졸업하다

□ university	대학
□ early	초반의
□ information	정보
12	
□ product	상품
□ deliver	배달하다
□ charge	(요금을) 내다
□ delivery	배달
□ free	무료의
□ make it	약속을 잡다
□ possible	가능한
13	
□ recommend	추천하다
□ special	특별 메뉴
□ Caesar salad	시저 샐러드(양상추 · 안초비 (anchovy)) · 치즈 가루 등으로 만듦)
□ popular	인기 있는
□ order	주문하다
14	
□ pool	수영장
□ work out	운동하다
□ fitness center	헬스클럽
□ floor	층
□ gift	선물
□ cash machine	현금 인출기
15	
□ personal	개인적인
□ Go ahead.	어서 하세요.
□ most	가장
□ get married	결혼하다
□ reservation	예약
16	
□ kid	아이
□ still	여전히
□ remind A of B	A에게 B를 떠올리게 해 주다
□ childhood	유년기

□ frame	액자에 넣다
□ No way.	안 돼.
17	
□ get	도착하다
□ in front of ~	앞에
18	
□ return	반납하다
□ remind	상기시키다
□ favor	호의, 친절
19	
□ go out for	~하러 외출하다
□ lose	잃다
□ weight	몸무게
□ be supposed to	~하기로 되어 있다
□ exercise	운동
□ forget to	~하는 것을 잊다
20	
□ sneeze	재채기하다
□ direction	방향
□ catch a cold	감기에 걸리다
□ distance	거리
□ dizzy	어지러운
□ work	효과가 있다
□ give one's regards to	~에게 안부를 전하다
□ until	~할 때까지

01

□ be going to	~할 예정이다
□ by the way	그런데 (화제 전환)
□ these days	요즘
□ rainy season	장마철, 우기
□ at least	적어도
□ Look on the bright side.	밝은 면을 봐., 긍정적으로 생각해.

02

□ May I ask who's calling?	누구시죠?
□ cell phone	휴대전화
□ take a shower	샤워하다
□ promise	약속하다
□ take a walk	산책하다
□ keep one's promise	약속을 지키다
□ call back	나중에 다시 전화하다
□ anyway	어쨌든, 아무튼

03

□ cash machine	현금 인출기
□ press	(버튼 등을) 누르다
□ put A into B	A를 B에 투입하다(집어넣다)
□ slot	가늘고 긴 구멍
□ select	선택하다
□ enter	입력하다
□ account number	은행 계좌 번호
□ password	비밀번호, 암호
□ Wait a minute.	잠깐만 기다리세요.

04

□ play basketball	농구를 하다
□ to be honest	솔직하게 말하면
□ go to a movie	영화 보러 가다
□ How about ~?	~은 어때?
□ That's a good idea.	좋은 생각이야.

05

□ wild flower	야생화
□ field	들판

□ I'm a stranger here.	저도 여기가 처음이에요.

06

□ take a bus	버스를 타다
□ fast	빠른
□ get to	~에 도착하다
□ airport	공항
□ as soon as possible	가능한 빨리
□ directly	곧장, 즉시
□ have to	~해야 한다

07

□ wonder	궁금하다, 궁금해 하다
□ whether	~인지 아닌지
□ healthy	건강한
□ anytime	언제든지
□ email	이메일; 이메일을 보내다
□ turn on	~을 켜다 (↔ turn off)
□ address	주소
□ website	웹사이트

08

□ above all	무엇보다
□ Like what?	예를 들면?
□ crepe	크레페
□ scenery	풍경
□ amazing	놀라운
□ favorite	가장 좋아하는 것

09

□ sign up	등록하다
□ practice	익히다
□ brochure	책자

10

□ cheerful	기분이 좋은
□ down	기분이 좋지 않은
□ turn out	판명 나다
□ after all	결국

11

□ decide	결정하다

□ join	가입하다	□ baseball bat	야구 방망이
□ photo club	사진반	□ delicious	맛있는
□ drama club	연극반	□ inner	안의, 내부의, 속의
□ get together	모이다, 만나다	□ This way, please.	이쪽으로 오세요.
□ twice a week	일주일에 두 번	**17**	
□ after school	방과 후에	□ be afraid of	～을 두려워하다
□ various	다양한	□ kid	아이, 청소년
□ Why don't you ~?	～하는 게 어때요?	□ board	갑판, 다이빙대
□ would like to	～하고 싶다	□ dive	다이빙하다
□ photographer	사진사, 사진작가	□ have fun	재미있게 놀다
12		□ practice	연습하다
□ How's it going?	어떻게 지내니?	□ butterfly stroke	접영(나비 모양으로 수영하는 것)
□ classmate	급우, 반 친구	**18**	
□ be in the hospital	입원해 있다	□ go bowling	볼링 치러 가다
□ in front of	～의 앞에	□ watch a movie	영화를 보다
□ library	도서관	□ pass	지나치다
13		□ somewhere	어딘가에서
□ amusement park	놀이 공원	**19**	
□ hate	몹시 싫어하다	□ worry	걱정하다
□ crowded	(사람들이) 붐비는, 복잡한	□ lately	최근에
□ inside	～ 안으로, 안에 (↔ outside)	□ due	마감인
14		□ help out	돕다
□ part-time job	아르바이트 일	□ lie	거짓말하다
□ No wonder ~.	～은 조금도 놀랍지(기이하지) 않다.	**20**	
		□ lose	지다 (−lost−lost)
□ quit	그만두다	□ score	득점, 스코어, 점수
□ fall behind	뒤처지다	□ pitch	～을 던지다
15			
□ sweater	스웨터		
□ fit	꼭 맞다		
□ discount	할인		
□ expensive	비싼 (↔ cheap)		
16			
□ bread	빵		
□ remember	기억하다 (↔ forget)		
□ look like	～처럼 보이다		

01
□ weather report	일기예보
□ sunny	화창한, 햇빛 밝은
□ warm	따뜻한
□ heavy rain	폭우

02
□ need	필요로 하다
□ dining table	식탁
□ be broken	망가지다
□ fix	고치다, 수리하다
□ look around	둘러보다

03
□ hairdresser	미용사
□ champion	챔피언, 선수권 대회 우승자
□ ride alone	혼자서 타다
□ coach	(스포츠 팀의) 코치
□ racing bicycle	경주용 자전거
□ win the championship	선수권 대회에서 우승하다

04
□ library	도서관
□ return	돌려주다, 반납하다
□ special plan	특별한 계획
□ dance festival	춤 축제

05
□ How did you like ~?	~은 어땠니?
□ exciting	신나는, 활기찬
□ always	항상, 늘
□ unkind	불친절한
□ foreigner	외국인
□ robbery	강도 (사건)
□ happen	일어나다, 발생하다

06
□ drive	운전하다
□ concert hall	연주회장
□ traffic	교통
□ far from	~에서 멀리
□ station	역, 정류장
□ in front of	~의 앞에

07
□ I'm full.	배가 부르다.
□ feel better	더 나아진 느낌이다
□ What can I do for you?	무엇을 도와드릴까요?
□ develop	현상하다

08
□ blanket	담요
□ thick	두꺼운 (↔ thin)
□ enough	충분히
□ a bit	약간
□ fit	잘 맞다
□ bright	밝은

09
□ hurt one's leg	다리를 다치다
□ much better	훨씬 더 나은(건강한)
□ nurse	간호사
□ a lot	많이
□ stay	머무르다

10
□ wear	(옷·모자 등을) 입고(쓰고) 있다
□ especially	특히
□ be proud of	~을 자랑스러워하다
□ I'm sure ~.	~을 확신한다.

11
□ invention	발명
□ be interested in	~에 관심이(흥미가) 있다
□ classic	고전의, 전통적인
□ guitar	기타
□ the other day	요전날
□ fantastic	환상적인, 멋진

12
□ What's up?	무슨 일이니?
□ sell	팔다
□ check ~ out	~을 보다, 확인하다

□ test-drive	시승하다	□ get a tan	햇볕에 태우다
□ If possible.	가능하면.	□ plant	심다
		□ environment	환경
13		**19**	
□ catalogue	카탈로그, 목록	□ What do you think?	어떻게 생각하세요? (= How do you like?)
□ a lot	훨씬		
□ save up for	~을 위해 저축하다	□ perfect	완벽한, 완전한
□ on sale	할인 판매하는	□ popular	인기 있는
□ online	온라인으로 (↔ off-line)	□ among	~중(사이)에
14		□ teen	십 대 (=teenager)
□ language lab	어학 실습실 (lab=laboratory)	□ look on	~에게 어울리다
□ change one's shoes	신발을 갈아 신다	□ funny	우스운, 웃기는
□ enter	들어가다(오다)	**20**	
□ except	~을 제외하고	□ get off	~에서 내리다 (↔ get on)
□ textbook	교과서	□ subway	지하철
□ turn off	~을 끄다 (↔ turn on)	□ write a report	보고서를 작성하다
□ machine	기계	□ usually	보통, 대개
□ one by one	한 명씩	□ make a mistake	실수를 하다, 착각하다
15			
□ each	각각(각자)(의)		
□ watermelon	수박		
□ anything else	(부정문이나 의문문에서) 그 밖의 다른 것		
□ change	거스름돈, 잔돈		
16			
□ What's up?	무슨 일이야?		
□ weather forecast	일기 예보		
□ wrong	틀린		
□ bus stop	버스 정류장		
17			
□ throw	던지다		
□ wrong	틀린, 잘못된		
□ foot	발		
□ fast	빠른		
□ learner	학습자		
□ bat	공을 치다; 방망이		
18			

01

□ thunder	천둥
□ heavy rain	폭우
□ awful	끔찍스러운
□ forecast	예보, 예측
□ stop -ing	~하는 것을 멈추다

02

□ microphone	마이크
□ smile	미소짓다
□ hold one's hands up	손을 위로 치켜세우다
□ with one's arms folded	팔짱을 낀 채로
□ giraffe	기린
□ face	얼굴
□ point	가리키다

03

□ headache	두통
□ dizzy	어지러운
□ take one's temperature	체온을 재다
□ fever	열
□ take a pill	약을 먹다 (=take medicine)
□ meal	식사
□ visit	방문하다
□ in two days	이틀 후에

04

□ look tired	피곤해 보이다
□ soundly	깊이(곤히)
□ these days	요즘
□ worry about	~에 대해 걱정하다
□ get some exercise	운동하다
□ You've got a point.	좋은 지적이에요.
□ knee	무릎
□ What should I do?	어떻게 해야 할까요? (충고를 구할 때)
□ be good for	~에 좋다
□ had better	~하는 게 낫다
□ go swimming	수영하러 가다

05

□ turn off	~을 끄다 (↔ turn on)
□ do one's homework	숙제를 하다
□ essay	에세이, 과제물, 글
□ pollution	오염, 공해
□ cartoon	만화
□ water pollution	수질오염
□ lie	거짓말을 하다
□ write an essay	글을 쓰다

06

□ go bowling	볼링을 치러 가다
□ shoulder	어깨
□ get hurt	부상을 당하다 (=be injured, be wounded)
□ warm up	준비 운동을 하다
□ forget	잊다 (↔ remember)
□ get better	더 좋아지다

07

□ nervous	초조한
□ piano recital	피아노 연주회
□ audience	청중
□ frighten	겁나게 하다
□ perform	연주하다
□ I bet ~.	~을 확신한다.
□ someday	(미래의) 언젠가

08

□ be back	돌아오다
□ leave a message	메모를 남기다
□ be canceled	취소되다

09

□ waste	낭비하다
□ cell phone bill	휴대전화 요금
□ chat	채팅하다
□ video chat	비디오 채팅
□ guess	추측하다
□ voice call	음성 통화

□ over the Internet	인터넷을 통해	□ on the way to	~로 가는 길에
10		□ by subway	지하철로
□ (It's) My pleasure.	(도와드릴 수 있어) 저도 기뻐요.	□ lost and found office	분실물 보관소
□ type a letter	타자를 치다	**17**	
□ stop working	작동이 멈추다	□ this way	이쪽으로
□ save	저장하다	□ perfect	완벽한
□ restore	복구(복원)하다	□ take an order	주문을 받다
□ try	시도하다, 노력하다	□ two orders	2인분
11		**18**	
□ make a reservation	예약하다	□ anymore	더 이상
□ leave	떠나다	□ pay back	갚다
□ flight	항공편	□ crazy	화가 난
12		□ frankly	솔직하게
□ get married	결혼하다	□ lend	빌려 주다
□ take place	일어나다(=be held, happen)	□ from now on	지금부터는
□ ceremony	식, 의식	**19**	
□ finish	끝나다	□ move	이사하다
13		□ empty	빈
□ sign	표지판	□ for a long time	오랫동안
□ take the train	기차를 타다	□ be from	~출신이다
14		□ the same A as B	B와 같은 A
□ field trip	현장 학습	□ take A to B	A를 B로 데려가다
□ adult	성인	□ get along with	~와 잘 지내다
□ book	예약하다	**20**	
□ enough	충분한	□ weather report	일기예보
□ count in	셈에 넣다	□ rain coat	우비
15		□ sweat	땀을 흘리다
□ check out	퇴실하다 (↔ check in)	□ stop at	~에 들르다
□ be in room	~호실에서 묵다		
□ make a phone call	전화하다		
□ international phone call	국제 전화		
□ charge	요금		
□ leave for	~을 향해 출발하다		
16			
□ quarrel with	~와 말다툼하다		
□ lose	잃어버리다 (-lost-lost)		

01
□ notebook	노트
□ look for	~을 찾다
□ a pair of pants	바지 한 벌
□ dictionary	사전
□ wash the dishes	설거지하다

02
□ especially	특히
□ That's because ~.	그것은 ~이기 때문이다.
□ wet	젖은 (↔ dry)
□ footwear	신발
□ protect	보호하다
□ rub	문지르다

03
□ airport	공항
□ go bowling	볼링을 치러 가다
□ go to the movies	영화 보러 가다
□ play tennis	테니스를 치다

04
□ fail	떨어지다
□ shock	충격을 주다
□ result	결과
□ upset	화가 난
□ mistake	실수
□ write down	적다
□ in fact	사실

05
□ colorful	화려한
□ as well	또한, 역시

06
□ get to	~에 도착하다
□ rainbow	무지개
□ department store	백화점
□ either A or B	A나 B 둘 중의 하나
□ take the subway	지하철을 타다
□ shuttle bus	셔틀 버스

□ in front of	~의 앞에

07
□ What can I do for you?	무엇을 도와드릴까요?
□ in cash	현금으로
□ take the money out of this account	이 계좌에서 돈을 인출하다
□ passport	여권

08
□ cook	요리하다
□ fried rice	볶음밥
□ I can't wait to ~.	~을 몹시 기대하다

09
□ Teacher's Day	스승의 날
□ graduate from	~을 졸업하다
□ middle school	중학교
□ take care of	~을 돌보다
□ science report	과학 보고서
□ Why don't you ~?	~하는 게 어때?
□ text message	문자 메시지
□ right now	지금 바로

10
□ close	가까운
□ package	소포
□ owe	빚지고 있다

11
□ good-looking	잘생긴
□ work for	~에서 근무하다
□ maybe	아마도
□ play the piano	피아노를 치다
□ for years	수년 동안

12
□ play the guitar	기타를 치다
□ elementary school	초등학교
□ play the violin	바이올린을 연주하다
□ take a drum lesson	드럼 레슨을 받다
□ special	특별한

□ drummer	드럼을 치는 사람
□ school band	학교 밴드부

13

□ open	열린 (↔ close)
□ Any time.	천만에.
□ screen	방충망
□ keep ~ out	~을 못 들어오게 하다
□ bug	벌레

14

□ get the first prize	1등상을 타다
□ national	국가적인, 전국적인
□ painting	그림, 그림 그리기
□ contest	경연대회
□ amazing	놀라운
□ artist	예술가, 화가
□ congratulation	축하, (~s) 축하의 말

15

□ recommend	권하다, 추천하다
□ maintain	유지하다
□ regular	규칙적인
□ lifestyle	생활방식
□ first of all	무엇보다도, 우선
□ wake up	일어나다
□ stay up late	늦게까지 깨어있다
□ exercise	운동하다
□ daily	매일의, 나날의
□ jogging	조깅

16

□ cinema	영화, 영화관
□ How about ~?	~하는 게 어때?
□ half an hour earlier	30분 일찍

17

□ worth	~의 가치가 있는
□ observe	관찰하다
□ astronomy	천문학
□ falling star	유성

18

□ protect	보호하다
□ focus on	초점을 맞추다
□ mainly	주로
□ endangered	위험에 처한, 멸종 위기에 처한
□ common animal	일반 동물
□ treat	대우하다
□ company	회사
□ cosmetics	화장품
□ medication	약품
□ suffer	고통받다
□ deserve	자격이 있다

19

□ dry-clean	드라이 클리닝하다
□ pick up	(물건을) 가지러 가다
□ cost	비용이 들다

20

□ Guess what?	무슨 일인지 맞춰볼래?
□ happen	일어나다, 발생하다
□ send a text message	문자 메시지를 보내다

01

☐ Certainly.	그럼요., 물론이지요.
☐ lovely day	화창한 날
☐ by oneself	혼자서, 홀로
☐ terrible	끔찍한, 심한
☐ headache	두통
☐ over there	저쪽에
☐ not for sale	비매품인, 판매용이 아닌

02

☐ suit	정장
☐ dot	점
☐ weird	이상한
☐ striped	줄무늬의
☐ thin	얇은 (↔ thick)

03

☐ tired of	~에 싫증이 난
☐ can't afford	~할 여유가 없다
☐ dye	염색하다
☐ light-colored	밝은 색의
☐ decorate	장식하다
☐ option	선택
☐ cut	자르다 (-cut-cut)
☐ a pair of	한 벌의 ~

04

☐ turn on	~을 켜다 (↔ turn off)
☐ air conditioner	에어컨
☐ save	절약하다
☐ That's ridiculous.	말도 안 돼.
☐ fan	선풍기

05

☐ feed	먹이다
☐ sign	표지판
☐ allergic	알레르기가 있는
☐ fur	털
☐ indeed	정말, 진짜

06

☐ water	물; 물을 주다
☐ rest	휴식하다, 쉬다
☐ boring	따분한, 지루한
☐ be well	회복되다
☐ enough to	~하기에 충분한

07

☐ dish	음식
☐ secret	비밀의

08

☐ rearrange	재배치하다
☐ move	옮기다
☐ file cabinet	서류함
☐ crowded	혼잡한
☐ in the middle of	~의 가운데에
☐ against the wall	벽에 기대어

09

☐ tour	관광
☐ advertisement	광고 (= ad)
☐ bus driver	버스 운전사
☐ position	지위, 위치
☐ be filled	차다, 충원되다
☐ anyway	어쨌든, 여하튼

10

☐ silence	고요, 적막
☐ groceries	식료품류
☐ be supposed to do	~하기로 되어 있다

11

☐ ready	준비된
☐ set the table	식탁(상)을 차리다
☐ well-done	완전히 익힌
☐ by the way	그런데(화제 전환)
☐ prepare	준비하다
☐ dessert	후식

12

☐ have a cold	감기에 걸리다

□ headache	두통		**18**	
13			□ hang	걸다, 매달다 (−hung−hung)
□ anything to drink	마실 것		□ spot	얼룩, 점
□ a glass of	한 잔의 ~		□ forgive	용서하다
□ be ready	준비되다, 완료되다		**19**	
□ in a moment	곧, 순식간에		□ be in the hospital	입원하다
14			□ swine flu	돼지 독감
□ save a seat	자리를 맡다		□ while	~하는 동안
□ miss	놓치다		□ get well	회복되다
□ score	점수		**20**	
□ nothing	영, 무(無), 공		□ for fun	재미로
□ a three-run home run	3점 홈런		□ special	특별한
□ the bottom of the third inning	(야구의) 3회 말		□ occasion	행사
□ Look out!	조심해!		□ graduation	졸업식
□ towards	~으로, ~을 향하여		□ on the side	부업으로
15			□ minor	부전공
□ hurry up	서두르다		□ professional	전문의
□ sign	표지판, 게시판		□ photographer	사진작가
□ clearly	분명히			
□ an hour more	한 시간 더			
□ Take it easy.	천천히 해라.			
16				
□ member	회원, 구성원			
□ animal doctor	수의사			
□ help	돕다			
□ lost	잃어버린			
□ deserted	버려진			
17				
□ poor	가난한			
□ last	계속되다, 진행되다			
□ be held	개최되다			
□ gym	체육관			
□ free	무료의			
□ pay for	~의 값을 치르다			

01

□ weather forecast	일기예보
□ nation	나라, 국가
□ storm	폭풍우
□ clear	맑은
□ perfect	완벽한
□ outdoor	야외의
□ activity	활동
□ all day long	하루 종일

02

□ be supposed to	~하기로 되어 있다
□ guest speaker	초청 연설자
□ mustache	콧수염
□ vest	조끼
□ outside	~ 밖에서 (↔ inside)

03

□ Don't mention it.	별 말씀을요.
□ for a long time	오랫동안
□ else	그밖에
□ arrive	도착하다
□ drink	마실 것, 음료
□ a glass of	한 잔의 ~
□ hold on	기다리다
□ make oneself at home	마음을 편히 갖다

04

□ bazaar	바자회
□ by oneself	직접
□ decorate	장식하다
□ frame	액자에 넣다
□ art class	미술 시간
□ enough	충분한
□ sell	팔다

05

□ close	문을 닫다 (↔ open)
□ on weekdays	주중에는
□ on weekends	주말에는

06

□ plan	계획
□ special	특별한
□ reason	이유
□ invite	초대하다

07

□ exhibition room	전시실
□ currently	현재, 지금
□ on display	전시된
□ disturb	방해하다

08

□ already	이미, 벌써
□ instead	대신에
□ for a while	얼마 동안은

09

□ on time	제 때에
□ last	계속되다
□ charge	충전하다
□ in advance	미리
□ The dinner is on you.	저녁은 네가 사.

10

□ muscle	근육
□ pain	통증
□ shoulder	어깨
□ pitch	~을 던지다
□ pitcher	투수
□ throw	던지다
□ careful	조심하는, 주의 깊은
□ hurt oneself	다치다

11

□ beach	해변
□ quiet	조용한
□ beach volleyball	비치발리볼
□ temple	절, 사원
□ art museum	미술관
□ on the way	도중에

12	
☐ electronics	전자제품
☐ monitor	모니터
☐ package	포장
☐ panel	판, 패널
☐ broken	망가진, 깨진
☐ exchange	교환하다
☐ send	보내다

13	
☐ holiday	휴가, 방학
☐ look forward to -ing	~하기를 고대하다, 기대하다
☐ hometown	고향
☐ wait for	~을 기다리다
☐ begin	시작하다

14	
☐ sell	팔다
☐ cheap	값싼 (↔ expensive)
☐ electronic device	전자제품
☐ price	가격

15	
☐ take off	이륙하다
☐ wait	기다리다
☐ flight	항공편
☐ delay	연기하다
☐ because of	~ 때문에
☐ terrible	끔찍한, 심한, 극심한

16	
☐ convenient	편리한
☐ What do you feel like?	뭐 먹고 싶어?

17	
☐ speech competition	웅변 대회
☐ humble	겸손한
☐ feel proud	자부심을 느끼다

18	
☐ ID card	신분증
☐ leave	남기다

19	
☐ gas	기름
☐ forget	잊다 (↔ remember)
☐ take a risk	위험을 무릅쓰다
☐ hurry up	서두르다
☐ fill up	채우다

20	
☐ You'd better ~.	~하는 게 좋겠다.
☐ do well on	~을 잘하다
☐ result	결과

01
□ pharmacy	약국
□ straight	곧장
□ on one's right	~의 오른편에
□ across ~ from	~ 건너편에

02
□ present	선물
□ tricycle	세발자전거
□ ride	타다

03
□ rule	규칙
□ have to	~해야 한다
□ follow	따르다
□ first of all	먼저, 우선
□ be late for class	수업 시간에 지각하다
□ chew	(껌을) 씹다
□ gum	껌
□ be allowed to ~	~하도록 허락받다
□ hall	복도
□ promise	약속하다
□ raise	(위로) 들어올리다

04
□ holiday	휴가, 방학
□ Thailand	태국
□ choose	고르다, 선택하다
□ place	장소, 곳
□ tanning	햇볕에 탐
□ price	값, 가격
□ attractive	매력적인
□ distance	거리
□ imagine	상상하다
□ emerald	에메랄드색(선녹색)(의)

05
□ discuss	토론하다
□ convenient	편리한
□ facility	시설

06
□ ad	광고(＝advertisement)
□ take a look at	~을 보다
□ several	몇몇의, 여러 가지의
□ company	회사
□ be tired of	~에 질리다, 싫증나다
□ part-time work	아르바이트
□ full-time job	전업

07
□ religious	종교적인
□ downstairs	아래층으로

08
□ get	얻다, 구하다
□ seat	자리

09
□ free	시간이 있는
□ What date is it?	몇 일이에요?
□ pirate ship	해적선
□ invitation card	초청장

10
□ Look on the bright side of life.	인생의 밝은 면을 보라.
□ be interested in	~에 관심이 있다
□ not ~ any more	더 이상 ~아닌

11
□ in detail	구체적으로
□ major in ~	~을 전공하다
□ biology	생물학
□ chemistry	화학
□ followed by ~	~이 뒤따른
□ medical school	의학대학원
□ be able to ~	~할 수 있다
□ No pain, no gain.	노력하지 않고서는 얻는 것이 없다.
□ pharmacist	약사

12
□ get through	전화가 연결되다

□ The phone line is dead.	전화가 불통이다.	**18**	
□ at least	적어도	□ flea market	벼룩시장
□ already	이미, 벌써	□ wash	빨다
□ engineer	기사, 기술자	□ stain	얼룩
□ fix	고치다, 수리하다	**19**	
□ Hold on.	(전화를) 끊지 않고 기다리다.	□ exchange	교환하다
13		□ receipt	영수증
□ order	주문, 주문한 것	□ try on	~을 입어보다
□ There must be ~.	~가 있음에 틀림없다.	□ fitting room	탈의실
□ address	주소	**20**	
□ mistake	실수	□ pasta	파스타
□ item	물건, 품목	□ soup	수프
14		□ salty	짠
□ fantastic	환상적인	□ bill	계산서
□ get to	~에 도착하다		
□ take a taxi	택시를 타다		
□ bus terminal	버스 터미널		
□ arrive at	~에 이르다, 도착하다		
□ bike	자전거		
15			
□ book a table	테이블(식사할 자리)을 예약하다		
□ coming	다가오는		
□ possible	가능한		
□ party	일행		
16			
□ seem to ~	~인 것 같다		
□ chest pain	가슴 통증		
□ dizzy	어지러운		
□ raw fish	회		
□ feel sick	메스껍다		
□ have an upset stomach	체하다		
□ prescribe	처방하다		
17			
□ get off	내리다		
□ route	길[경로]		
□ opposite direction	반대 방향		

01

□ cushion	방석
□ have ~ in mind	~을 마음속에 두다, 생각하다
□ square	정사각형(의)
□ in the middle of	~의 가운데에
□ heart-shaped	하트 모양의

02

□ fasten one's seatbelt	안전띠를 착용하다
□ put on	~을 입다, 착용하다
□ drive	운전하다
□ safe	안전한
□ hate	싫어하다, 미워하다
□ road	도로, 길
□ dangerous	위험한
□ curve	굴곡, 굽음, 커브
□ believe	믿다
□ safely	안전하게

03

□ league	(경기) 리그
□ semi-final	준결승
□ support	응원하다, 지지하다
□ result	결과
□ disappoint	실망시키다
□ frankly	솔직히
□ energetic	활력이 있는
□ powerful	힘이 있는
□ I couldn't agree more.	네 말에 전적으로 동의해

04

□ magazine	잡지
□ favorite	매우 좋아하는
□ be good at	~을 잘하다
□ like watching	보는 것을 좋아하다
□ rough	거친, 격한
□ go bowling	볼링을 하러 가다

05

□ wear	(옷 등을) 입고 있다
□ carry	들고 있다, 가지고 다니다
□ come out of	~ 밖으로 나오다
□ remember	기억하다
□ catch	잡다, 붙잡다
□ hope	희망하다, 바라다
□ as soon as possible	가능한 한 빨리

06

□ freshman	신입생, 1학년생
□ look for	~을 찾다
□ borrow	빌리다
□ fill out	(서식 · 문서 등의) 빈 곳을 채우다, ~에 써 넣다
□ student ID number	학생증 번호

07

□ by plane	비행기로
□ by air	항공으로
□ cost	비용이 들다

08

□ crowd	사람들, 군중, 무리
□ still	아직도
□ be able to	~ 할 수 있다(=can)
□ already	이미, 벌써
□ besides	게다가
□ slowly	천천히, 서서히

09

□ around	~ 주위에
□ be born	태어나다
□ move	이사하다, 이주하다
□ Spanish	스페인 어

10

□ special event	특별행사
□ worth	가치
□ competition	경쟁
□ prize	상, 상품
□ classical	고전적인

11	
□ upset	기분이 언짢은
□ belittle	무시하다
□ embarrassed	당황한
12	
□ husband	남편
□ leave	남기다
□ This is very nice(kind) of you.	매우 고맙습니다.
□ Don't mention it.	천만에요., 별 말씀을요.
□ duty	의무, 임무
13	
□ work on ~	～의 작업을 하다
□ pain	통증
□ can't help it	어쩔 수 없다
□ because of ~	～ 때문에
□ instruction	지시사항
□ according to ~	～에 의하면
□ leaflet	리플릿, 인쇄물
14	
□ over there	저기에, 저 너머에
□ What does she do?	그녀는 직업이 뭐니?
□ go to school with ~	～와 학교를 같이 다니다
15	
□ sleek	얇은
□ light	가벼운
□ latest	최근의
□ wherever ~	～하는 곳은 어디든지
□ offer	제공하다
□ wireless	무선의
□ access	접근
□ public	공공의
□ look into ~	～을 들여다 보다
□ password	비밀번호
□ bank account	은행계좌
□ serious	진지한

□ surf	(인터넷을) 검색하다
16	
□ take a message	메시지를 받아 두다
□ car repair shop	자동차 수리점
□ be ready	완료되다, 준비되다
□ charge	비용, 요금
17	
□ make a reservation	예약을 하다
□ make a change	변경을 하다
□ available	이용할 수 있는
18	
□ advice	조언
□ research	연구하다
□ keep	보관하다
□ depend on	～에 의존하다
19	
□ for a few days	며칠 동안
□ be sick in bed	아파서 누워 있다
□ drop in	잠깐 들르다
□ after school	방과 후에
20	
□ project	과업, 프로젝트
□ get along	잘 지내다
□ deadline	마감시한
□ calm down	침착하다
□ ask ~ for	～에게 …을 부탁하다

01	
□ at the back of	~의 뒤에
□ park	주차하다
□ sign	표지, 간판, 게시
□ in a moment	곧, 바로
□ place	놓다
□ behind	뒤에
□ by oneself	혼자서
□ move	이동하다, 옮기다
□ a little	약간
02	
□ rearrange	재배열하다, 재배치하다
□ give ~ a hand	~을 도와주다
□ next to	~ 옆에
□ sure	확신하는
03	
□ indoor	실내의(↔ outdoor)
□ theme park	테마공원
□ roller-coaster	롤러코스터
□ balloon	풍선
04	
□ medium	중간 크기
□ fit	~에게 맞다
□ bill	지폐
□ change	잔돈
05	
□ national	국립의
□ far	먼
□ stop	정류장, 정거장
□ block	블록
□ stranger	낯선 사람, 처음 본 사람
□ convenient	편안한
06	
□ run out of	~을 다 써버리다, ~이 떨어지다
□ remote	외딴, 멀리 떨어진
□ village	마을

□ lucky	행운의, 운이 좋은
07	
□ plan	계획하다
□ nowadays	요즈음
□ detailed	자세한
□ thorough	빈틈없는
08	
□ take a look at	~을 보다
□ run	움직이다, 작동하다
□ check	점검하다
□ find out	~을 찾아내다, 발견해내다
□ the day after tomorrow	모레
09	
□ protect	보호하다
□ recycling	재활용
□ step	움직임[조치]
□ electricity	전기
10	
□ whole	전체의
□ ache	아프다; 통증
□ Why don't you ~?	~하는 것이 어때?
□ belong to ~	~에 속하다
□ bet	생각하다
□ Don't be kidding!	농담하지 마!
□ injury	상처
□ It could happen.	그럴 수 있어.
□ warm-up	준비운동
□ beforehand	이전에, 미리
□ relieve	덜어주다
□ tub	목욕통
□ for a little while	잠시 동안
11	
□ hard	열심히 하는
□ have dinner	저녁을 먹다
12	
□ extend	(기한을) 늘리다

□ due date	마감날짜	□ lift	들다
□ hand ~ in	~을 제출하다	**20**	
□ assignment	숙제	□ hate	미워하다, 싫어하다
13		□ half an hour	30분
□ company	(함께 일하거나 공연하는) 단체	□ stand	참다, 견디다
□ next door	옆집	□ grocery store	식료품점, 슈퍼마켓
14		□ type	형(태), 유형, 종류
□ weight	몸무게	□ catch a cold	감기에 걸리다
□ exercise	운동하다	□ joke	농담하다
□ keep ~ from -ing	~이 …하지 못하게 하다	□ join	~와 함께 하다
□ against	반대하다	□ take care	몸조심하다
15			
□ collect	모으다, 수집하다		
□ stamp	우표		
□ postcard	우편엽서		
□ amazing	놀라운		
□ a little bit	약간		
16			
□ awful	끔찍한		
□ pollution	오염		
□ get worse	더 나빠지다		
□ citizen	시민		
□ in favor of	~에 찬성하여		
□ against	~에 반대하여		
17			
□ make it	시간을 정하다		
□ go grocery shopping	(생필품 등을) 쇼핑하다		
18			
□ get some rest	휴식을 취하다		
□ prepare	준비하다		
□ wash the dishes	설거지를 하다		
19			
□ decide	결정하다, 결심하다		
□ throw away	버리다		
□ outdoors	야외에서		
□ hurry up	서두르다		

01	
☐ racket	라켓
☐ light	가벼운
☐ alone	혼자서
☐ partner	상대, 파트
☐ divide	나누다
☐ net	네트
☐ bounce	(공 따위가) 바운드하다, 되튀다
☐ hit	(공을) 치다
☐ return	(공을) 받아 치다(넘기다)
☐ opposite	맞은편의
02	
☐ these days	요즈음
☐ vision	시야, 시력
☐ blurry	흐릿한, 희미한
☐ prove	입증하다
☐ far-sighted	원시의
☐ far from	~로부터 멀리 떨어진
03	
☐ copy	복사(본), 복제(본)
☐ photo	사진(=photograph)
☐ suggest	제안하다, 권하다
☐ interesting	흥미로운, 재미있는
☐ place	장소, 곳
☐ miss	(빠뜨리고) 보지 못하다, 놓치다
☐ tour guide book	여행 안내 책자
☐ bookstore	서점
☐ take a picture	사진을 찍다
☐ stand	서다, 서 있다
04	
☐ cavity	충치
☐ treat	치료하다
☐ make an appointment	예약을 하다
05	
☐ sometimes	가끔, 때때로
☐ permission	허락

☐ keep -ing	계속해서 ~하다
☐ boss	우두머리, 고용주, 사장
☐ maybe	아마도
☐ behavior	행동
☐ right now	지금 바로
06	
☐ move	옮기다
☐ disturb	혼란스럽게 하다
☐ concentration	집중
☐ right	적절한
07	
☐ slim	날씬한
☐ weight	무게, 체중
☐ vegetable	야채
☐ especially	특히
☐ bean	콩
☐ green tea	녹차
☐ whenever	~할 때마다
☐ hungry	배고픈
☐ meat	고기, 육류
☐ pork	돼지고기
☐ sugar-free ice cream	무가당 아이스크림
08	
☐ Can I take a message?	전하실 말씀 있으세요?
☐ invite	초대하다
☐ get a physical exam	건강검진을 받다
09	
☐ How about ~?	~은 어때?
☐ get together	모이다, 만나다
☐ free	한가한
☐ tonight	오늘 밤(에)
10	
☐ make a noise	소음이 나다
☐ telephone message	전화 메시지
☐ caller	전화 건 사람
☐ visiting time	방문 시간

11	
□ animal trainer	동물 조련사
□ feed	(음식을) 먹이다
□ check	점검하다
□ health	건강
□ spend+시간+-ing	~하는 데 (시간이) …걸리다
□ train	교육(훈련)시키다

12	
□ weather forecast	일기 예보
□ beach	해변

13	
□ these days	요즈음
□ loose	헐거운
□ weigh	무게가 ~이다(나가다)

14	
□ have a reservation	예약하다
□ reserve	예약하다
□ be ready	준비되다

15	
□ each other	서로
□ summer vacation	여름 방학
□ get together	모이다, 만나다
□ at half past 4	4시 30분에
□ borrow	빌리다
□ report	보고서

16	
□ productive	생산적인
□ research	연구
□ brain activity	뇌활동

17	
□ famous	유명한
□ singer	가수
□ hold	잡고(들고) 있다
□ a glass of	한 잔의 ~
□ wear glasses	안경을 쓰다
□ near	가까이

□ suit	정장
□ go say hello	인사말을 건네러 가다

18	
□ flying	날아다니는
□ monster	괴물
□ peaceful	평화로운
□ serious	심각한
□ notice	보다
□ into the air	공중으로
□ from behind ~	~의 뒤에서
□ by the lake	호수 옆에
□ spread	펼치다
□ wing	날개
□ mistake A for B	A를 B로 착각하다
□ take it easy	진정하다

19	
□ not at all	전혀 ~하지 않다
□ be on a diet	식이요법을 하다
□ a few	약간, 조금
□ lose weight	몸무게를 줄이다
□ what else	다른 어떤 것

20	
□ recipe	조리법
□ chef	요리사
□ be mat at ~	~에게 화를 내다
□ It slips one's mind.	깜빡하다.

01

□ cross the road	도로를 건너다
□ answer	대답하다
□ quiz	퀴즈, 시험
□ on the stage	무대 위에서
□ model airplane	모형 비행기

02

□ perfect	완벽한
□ outdoor activity	야외 활동
□ foggy	안개 낀
□ temperature	온도
□ heavy rain	폭우

03

□ Not really.	그렇지도 않아.
□ go hiking	하이킹 가다
□ paint	페인트를 칠하다
□ clean	청소하다
□ have a lot of work to do	해야 할 일이 많이 있다

04

□ attention	주목
□ bother	폐를 끼치다, 괴롭히다
□ elevator	엘리베이터
□ unfortunately	불행하게도
□ out of order	고장 나다
□ repairman	수리공
□ fix	고치다, 수리하다
□ stair	계단

05

□ cough	기침
□ syrup	물약
□ dry	마른
□ moisturizing	(피부를) 촉촉하게 해 주는
□ multivitamins	종합비타민
□ excellent	아주 좋은
□ frequent	잦은
□ circulation	순환

06

□ traffic	교통
□ experience	경험하다
□ boarding time	탑승 시간
□ security check	보안 검사대

07

□ accident	사고
□ happened	발생하다
□ switch	바꾸다
□ lane	차선
□ emergency	비상, 위급

08

□ What happened?	무슨 일이니?
□ sound	~처럼 들리다
□ strange	이상한
□ fall off	~에서 떨어지다
□ not ~ any more	더 이상 ~ 않다
□ answer the phone	전화를 받다

09

□ lately	최근에
□ housework	집안일
□ product	상품

10

□ come over	오다
□ fix	고치다
□ connection	연결, 접속
□ for some reason	어떤 이유에선지
□ get access to ~	~에 접속하다
□ site	(인터넷) 사이트
□ down	작동이 안 되는
□ download	내려받기하다
□ solution	해결책
□ make a phone call to ~	~에게 전화하다

11

□ Hold on a second.	잠시만요.
□ Would you mind if~?	~해도 괜찮을까요?

12	
□ choose	선택하다
□ chemistry	화학
□ lab	실험실(＝laboratory)
□ rule	규칙
□ touch	만지다, (손 등을) 대다
□ shelf	선반
□ taste	맛보다, 먹다
□ bottle	병
□ lastly	마지막으로, 끝으로
□ experiment	실험
□ attentively	귀를 기울이게
13	
□ I can't believe it.	믿을 수 없어. ('놀랄 만한 일이야.'라고 해석하기도 한다.)
□ say	～라고 쓰여 있다
□ free trip	공짜 여행
□ anywhere	어디에라도, 어디에나
14	
□ make a reservation	예약을 하다
□ midnight	자정, 한밤중
15	
□ keep -ing	계속 ～하다
□ I don't mind.	나는 상관없어.
□ musical	뮤지컬
□ have got	가지고 있다, 소유하다
□ enter	～에 들어가다
□ concert hall	음악당, 콘서트 홀
16	
□ volunteer	자원봉사(자)
□ in need	어려운 처지에 있는
□ mostly	대부분
17	
□ classical music	고전 음악
□ play	연주하다
□ I'll pass.	사양할게.

18	
□ book	예약하다
□ be away	부재중이다
□ particular	특별한, 특정한
19	
□ single	단 하나의
□ queen-size	퀸사이즈의
□ spacious	공간이 넓은
□ non-smoking	금연
□ overlook	～이 내려다 보이다
□ It sounds like ~.	～처럼 들리다.
20	
□ the last part	마지막 부분
□ Anything is okay.	어느 것이든 좋다.

01

□ alone	혼자서
□ grass	잔디, 풀
□ mean	의미하다, 뜻하다
□ glasses	안경

02

□ be supposed to	~하기로 되어 있다
□ picnic	소풍
□ forecast	예보
□ look forward to	~을 고대하다, 기대하다
□ shower	소나기

03

□ sold out	표가 매진된
□ miss	놓치다
□ else	그밖에

04

□ reservation	예약
□ moment	잠깐, 잠시
□ floor	층
□ view	풍경, 전경

05

□ scuba diving	스쿠버 다이빙
□ cost	(비용이) 들다
□ per	~당(마다)
□ person	사람, 개인
□ shuttle bus	셔틀버스
□ in front of	~ 앞에
□ drop by	~에 들르다
□ book	예약하다

06

□ view	전망
□ on sale	세일 중인
□ allowed	허용된

07

□ field trip	현장학습
□ date	날짜

08

□ insurance	보험
□ driver's license	운전면허증
□ gas tank	연료통
□ full	가득찬
□ fill up	(기름을) 가득 채우다
□ return	반납하다
□ otherwise	그렇지 않으면
□ charge	(요금을) 부과하다
□ pick up	인수하다
□ downstairs	아래층에서

09

□ have difficulty -ing	~하는 데 어려움을 겪다
□ fluent	유창한
□ without -ing	~하지 않고
□ grammar	문법
□ slow ~ down	~을 느리게 하다
□ confuse	혼란케 하다
□ rule	규칙
□ create	만들다
□ grammatical	문법적인
□ focus on ~	~에 초점을 맞추다
□ express	표현하다
□ communication	의사소통

10

□ be away on vacation	멀리 휴가를 가 있다
□ celebrate	축하하다
□ wedding anniversary	결혼 기념일
□ dorm	기숙사
□ get dark	어두워지다
□ fall asleep	잠에 빠지다
□ couch	소파, 안락의자
□ come back	되돌아오다

11

□ tour	여행
□ guide	안내원

□ lead	인도하다	□ heavy snow	폭설
□ explain	설명하다	□ leave	떠나다(↔ arrive 도착하다)
□ piece	(미술·음악 등의 작품) 한 점(하나)	□ patience	인내
□ art	예술품	**18**	
□ retire	은퇴하다	□ exam	시험
□ volunteer	자원봉사하다	□ tutor	가르치다; 개인 지도 교사
12		**19**	
□ dental clinic	치과	□ Come this way.	이쪽으로 오세요.
□ actually	사실	□ section	구역, 부분
□ put ~ in	~을 …에 끼워 넣다	□ expensive	비싼
13		□ bill	지폐
□ wonderful	놀랄 만한, 훌륭한, 멋진	□ change	잔돈
□ fantastic	환상적인	□ have a good time	즐거운 시간을 보내다
□ quiet	조용한	**20**	
□ sight	경치	□ order	주문, (1인분의) 주문 요리
□ foggy	안개 낀	□ baked	구운
□ scene	경치, 풍경	□ had better	~하는 것이 낫다
□ painting	그림, 그림 그리기	□ choose	선택하다
14		□ a glass of	한 잔의
□ yet	아직		
□ than usual	평상시보다		
□ onion	양파		
□ on the way	~로 가는 중에		
□ plenty of	많은 ~		
15			
□ on sale	할인 중인		
16			
□ behavior	행동		
□ excellent	훌륭한, 우수한		
□ spelling	철자법, 맞춤법		
□ already	이미, 벌써		
17			
□ passenger	승객		
□ delay	연기하다; 연기		
□ because of	~때문에		

01

□ character	캐릭터, 등장인물
□ cute	귀여운
□ choose	선택하다, 고르다
□ kick	(발로) 차다
□ teddy bear	테디 베어, 곰 인형

02

□ receiver	전화기
□ climb up	올라가다
□ ladder	사다리
□ fix	고치다
□ be pulled shut	잡아당겨 닫다
□ be stacked	쌓여 있다
□ tool	연장
□ scatter	흩어져 있다
□ floor	바닥

03

□ walk down ~	~로 곧장 걷다
□ full of ~	~로 가득 찬
□ from behind	뒤에서
□ a big amount of	~ 많은 분량의
□ cash	현금
□ be robbed	강도를 당하다
□ suddenly	갑자기
□ give up	포기하다
□ ground	땅
□ towards	~을 향하여

04

□ smart	영리한, 똑똑한
□ brain	두뇌
□ social	사교적인
□ make sense	일리가 있다
□ question	의문을 갖다
□ whether	~인지 아닌지
□ directly	직접적으로
□ be related to ~	~와 관련이 있다

□ intelligence level	지적 수준
□ might possibly	아마도 ~할 것이다
□ indeed	참으로, 정말로

05

□ spacious	넓은
□ complex	단지
□ around the corner	모퉁이를 돌아
□ drop by	들르다
□ on one's way to ~	~로 가는 도중

06

□ poster	포스터
□ look around	둘러보다, ~을 찾아 돌아다니다
□ animal	동물
□ go around	돌아다니다
□ Wait a moment.	잠깐 기다리세요.

07

□ over-the-counter medicine	의사의 처방 없이 복용할 수 있는 약
□ runny nose	콧물이 흐르는
□ cough	기침
□ dry skin	건성 피부
□ lotion	바르는 물약, 로션

08

□ ask a favor	부탁을 하다
□ give ~ a ride	~를 태워주다
□ plan	계획
□ pick up	~를 도중에서 차로 태우다

09

□ garlic	마늘
□ reason	이유
□ prevent ~ from ...	~을 …로부터 예방하다
□ disease	질병
□ lower	낮추다
□ blood pressure	혈압
□ heart attack	심장마비
□ popular	인기 있는

10	
□ advertisement	광고, 선전, 공시
□ school newspaper	학교 신문
□ enter	~에 들어가다, 참가하다

11	
□ fit	맞다
□ especially	특히
□ try on	~을 입어보다

12	
□ backpack	배낭
□ waiting room	(역·병원 등의) 대합실
□ look like	~처럼 보이다
□ cloth	천, 옷감
□ be printed	인쇄되다
□ leather	가죽

13	
□ Certainly.	물론이야., 그렇고 말고요.
□ a box of chocolates	초콜릿 한 상자
□ be on a diet	다이어트 중이다
□ lots of	많은(=a lot of)
□ purse	지갑

14	
□ in one's mid-forties	40대 중반에
□ gym	체육관
□ regularly	규칙적으로, 정기적으로
□ except	~을 제외하고
□ work out	운동하다

15	
□ be late for	~에 늦다, 지각하다
□ meeting	모임, 회의
□ by taxi	택시로
□ rush hour	붐비는 시간, 러시아워
□ bus-only lane	버스전용 차로

16	
□ What's new with you?	뭐 새로운 일 있어?
□ What for?	무엇 때문에?

□ aunt	아주머니, 고모, 이모
□ invite	초대하다
□ stay	머무르다, 남다
□ have a good time	재미있게 보내다

17	
□ perform	공연하다
□ drop out	(참여하던 것에서) 빠지다
□ role	역할

18	
□ learn	배우다
□ get a chance	기회를 얻다

19	
□ be pleased to	~해서 기쁘다(만족하다)
□ work very hard	매우 열심히 공부하다
□ grade	성적
□ excellent	우수한, 훌륭한
□ keep ~ a secret	~을 비밀로 지키다
□ be proud of	~을 자랑스러워하다

20	
□ fashionable	최신 유행의, 유행하는
□ match	~와 어울리다
□ take off	~을 떼어내다
□ not ~ any more	더 이상 ~ 않다(=no more)

01

□ for a moment	잠시 동안
□ check	확인하다, 점검하다
□ information	정보
□ be interested in	~에 관심이 있다
□ member	회원, 구성원
□ school band	학교 밴드부
□ painting club	미술부

02

□ be filled with	~로 가득 차다
□ smell	냄새(가 나다)

03

□ clean	청소하다
□ living room	거실
□ promise	약속하다
□ come over for dinner	저녁 식사하러 오다
□ go shopping	쇼핑하러 가다
□ help out	도와주다
□ alright	알았어, 좋아(=all right)

04

□ try ~ on	~을 입어보다
□ changing room	탈의실
□ it feels like ~	~인 것 같다
□ a bit	약간
□ on sale	판매 중인
□ ~ off	~을 할인하여
□ fit	~에게 어울리다

05

□ hurry	서두르다
□ take the subway	지하철을 타다
□ rush hour	(출퇴근) 혼잡 시간대, 러시아워
□ by bus	버스로
□ Bus Only Zone	버스 전용차선
□ catch a taxi	택시를 잡다

06

□ upset	속상한, 마음이 상한

□ look at	~을 쳐다보다
□ send a letter	편지를 보내다
□ friendship	우정

07

□ suntan	햇볕에 탐
□ have been to	~에 다녀오다
□ Buddhist temple	불교 사원
□ royal palace	왕궁

08

□ turn	돌리다, 회전시키다
□ park	주차하다
□ subway station	지하철역
□ police officer	경찰관
□ in front of	~의 앞에
□ drugstore	약국
□ sign	표지판
□ parking	주차
□ had better	~하는 게 낫다
□ parking lot	주차장

09

□ graduate	졸업하다
□ be planning to	~할 계획이다
□ get a job	일자리를 얻다
□ designer	디자이너
□ Good for you.	잘했어.
□ gift	(재능을) 부여하다
□ area	분야, 지역
□ painter	화가
□ primary school	초등학교

10

□ How's it going?	어떻게 지내니?
□ by the way	그런데(화제를 바꿀 때)
□ homeroom teacher	담임선생님
□ front gate	정문

11

□ check	점검하다, 확인하다

pack	짐을 싸다, 꾸리다	reservation	예약
list	목록	membership	회원
first of all	먼저, 우선	seat	좌석
passport	여권	flight	항공기
swimming suit	수영복	**17**	
perfect	완벽한	remind	상기시키다
guide book	안내책자	on time	정각에
map	지도	quite	꽤
12		look after	돌보다
go camping	캠핑하러 가다	**18**	
across the country	전국적으로	skier	스키를 타는 사람
pour	퍼붓다	temperature	기온
look forward to -ing	~하기를 고대하다, 기대하다	degree	(온도·각도의) 도
13		Celsius	섭씨
take a shower	샤워를 하다	all day long	하루 종일
upstairs	윗층에서	expect	기대하다, 예상하다
warn	경고하다	**19**	
calm down	진정하다	cabbage kimchi	배추김치
hurt	상하게 하다	try	먹어보다, 마셔보다
feeling	감정	a bit	약간, 조금
later	나중에	hot	매운
noise	소음, 소리	**20**	
before long	오래지 않아	terrible	끔찍한
wake ~ up	~을 깨우다	the day before yesterday	그저께
sensitive	신경이 예민한		
14			
library card	도서관 카드		
live around here	이 근처에 살다		
form	양식		
fill out	기입하다		
15			
Please be seated.	앉으세요.		
open an account	계좌를 만들다		
16			
airline	항공사		
reconfirm	재확인하다		

01

□ curly	곱슬머리의
□ in the back	뒤에
□ among ~	~ 중에서
□ chubby	포동포동한
□ eyesight	시력
□ anyway	어쨌든
□ quite	매우

02

□ feed	먹이를 주다
□ a piece of ~	한 조각의 ~
□ leftover	남은
□ way of walking	걷는 방식
□ sign	표지판
□ harmful	해로운
□ cause	일으키다
□ disease	질병
□ give a sign to ~	~에게 표시하다

03

□ in the day	낮에는
□ turn	변하다
□ desert	사막
□ exactly	정확하게
□ throughout the winter	겨울 내내

04

□ actually	사실은
□ special	특별한
□ have a date with	~와 데이트를 하다
□ website	웹사이트

05

□ boss	사장
□ take a message	메시지를 받아 두다
□ business	사업, 일, 업무
□ cancel	취소하다

06

□ How long does it take ~?	시간이 얼마나 걸리는가?

□ tourist	관광객
□ borrow	빌리다
□ for free	무료로
□ around the corner	길모퉁이를 돈 곳에
□ tip	정보, 조언

07

□ middle-sized	중간 크기의
□ used car	중고차
□ this way	이쪽으로
□ fit	어울리다
□ mileage	주행거리
□ price	가격
□ discount	할인
□ look around	둘러보다

08

□ order	주문, 주문하다
□ seafood	해산물
□ grilled	구운
□ salmon	연어
□ take	(시간이) 걸리다

09

□ attend	참석하다
□ be into	~에 몰두하다, 열중하다
□ artistic	예술적인
□ major	전공(과목)
□ mass media	매스 미디어
□ keep trying	계속해서 시도하다
□ keep one's fingers crossed	행운을 빌어주다

10

□ stage	무대
□ audience	관객, 청중
□ relax	긴장을 풀다, 마음을 풀다

11

□ noisy	시끄러운
□ rental fee	집세, 임대료

☐ cheap	값싼		☐ accident	사고
☐ washing machine	세탁기		☐ recently	최근에
☐ dryer	건조기, 드라이어		☐ go out	나가다, 외출하다
☐ dishwasher	식기세척기		**17**	
☐ pet	애완동물		☐ a lot of	많은
☐ raise	～을 기르다, 키우다		☐ celebrate	축하하다
☐ allow	허락하다		**18**	
12			☐ avoid	피하다
☐ bring	가져오다		☐ rush hour	혼잡한 시간대
☐ snack bar	매점		☐ wake up	깨우다
☐ unattended	지켜보는 사람이 없는		**19**	
☐ destination	목적지		☐ have been to ～	～에 간 적이 있다
13			☐ neither	또한 ～하지 않다
☐ break down	고장 나다		☐ top	꼭대기
☐ possible	가능한		☐ holiday	휴일
☐ huge	거대한		☐ perfect	완벽한
☐ let	허락하다		☐ climbing	등산
☐ cartridge	카트리지		**20**	
14			☐ mark	표시하다
☐ form	형성하다		☐ calendar	달력
☐ through	～을 통해서		☐ forget	잊다
☐ progress	전진하다		☐ bother	～를 성가시게 하다
☐ president	회장, 의장		☐ several times	몇 번, 여러 번
☐ retire	은퇴하다			
☐ matter	문제			
☐ election	선거			
15				
☐ Go ahead.	해 봐.			
☐ light	빛			
☐ travel	여행하다			
☐ per second	초당			
☐ confused	헷갈린			
☐ be good at	～을 잘하다			
16				
☐ cry	울다			
☐ die	죽다 (die－died－died)			

01
□ farm	농장
□ I'm certain ~.	나는 ~을 확신한다.
□ tail	꼬리

02
□ cats and dogs	억수로
□ damage	상하게 하다
□ fall across ~	~을 가로질러 넘어지다
□ fallen	쓰러진
□ rescuer	구조원
□ injured	다친

03
□ wake up	일어나다
□ hurry up	서두르다
□ sunrise	해돋이
□ look forward to -ing	~할 것을 기대하다
□ take pictures of ~	~의 사진을 찍다
□ weather forecast	일기예보
□ thick	짙은
□ completely	완전히
□ fail to ~	~하지 못하다

04
□ history	역사(학)
□ biology	생물학
□ geography	지리학
□ physical education	체육
□ chemistry	화학
□ subject	과목

05
□ usually	보통
□ check	확인하다

06
□ listen to	~을 듣다
□ familiar	익숙한, 친근한
□ someday	언젠가
□ musical	뮤지컬

□ anyway	아무튼
□ lobster	바닷가재
□ steak	스테이크
□ crowded	붐비는

07
□ work experience	경력
□ part-time job	아르바이트
□ department store	백화점
□ apply for	~에 지원하다, 신청하다
□ be interested in	~에 관심이 있다
□ work full-time	전임으로 일하다
□ college student	대학생

08
□ appointment	약속
□ nearly	거의

09
□ office	사무실
□ kill me	나를 힘들게 하다
□ each day	매일
□ move	이사하다
□ empty	텅 빈
□ rent	집세
□ expensive	비싼

10
□ Attention, please.	여러분께 알려 드리겠습니다.
□ shopper	쇼핑객
□ a big sale	대폭 할인 판매
□ beef	쇠고기
□ pound	파운드(무게 단위)
□ offer	제공하다
□ on sale	세일 중인

11
□ challenge	도전
□ presentation	발표
□ meanwhile	그 동안에
□ photocopy	복사

□ handout	유인물, 인쇄물		□ see off	배웅하다
12			□ text	문자를 보내다
□ Who's calling?	누구세요?(전화 대화에서 상대방이 누구인지 물을 때)		**18**	
			□ awesome	멋진
□ accident	사고		□ unique	독특한
□ fall down	쓰러지다		□ pretty	꽤
□ serious	심각한		□ plot	구성[줄거리]
13			□ surprise	놀라움
□ boyfriend	남자 친구		□ predictable	예측할 수 있는
□ kind	종류		**19**	
□ present	선물		□ make sure	확인하다
□ sweater	스웨터		□ move out	이사가다
14			□ out of ~	~로부터
□ introduce	소개하다		□ take apart	분해하다
□ handsome	잘생긴		□ furniture	가구
□ work for	~에서 근무하다		□ hand	건네주다
□ travel agency	여행사		□ tool	연장
□ hobby	취미		□ in no time	즉시
□ each other	서로		**20**	
15			□ fail	(시험에) 떨어지다, 낙제하다
□ international	국제적인		□ in fact	사실
□ express bus	급행 버스		□ mistake	실수
□ bus stop	버스 정류장		□ be worried about	~에 대해 걱정하다
□ far from	~에서 먼			
□ heavy	무거운			
□ cost	비용이 들다			
□ by subway	지하철로			
16				
□ What have you been up to lately?	최근에 어떻게 지냈니?			
□ nothing much	(양 · 중요성 · 가치가) 별로 없는			
□ go bicycling	자전거 타러 가다			
□ ride	타다			
□ along the river	강을 따라서			
□ grandma	할머니			
17				
□ traffic	교통			

01
☐ recent	최근에
☐ continue	계속되다
☐ weather forecast	일기 예보
☐ temperature	온도
☐ drop	떨어지다

02
☐ popular	인기 있는
☐ fresh	신선한
☐ lots of	많은

03
☐ lately	최근에
☐ organize	준비하다
☐ competition	대회
☐ set up	설치하다
☐ arrange	배열하다
☐ outdoor	야외의
☐ indoor	실내의
☐ fully	완전히
☐ book	예약하다

04
☐ bowling alley	볼링장
☐ go bowling	볼링 치러 가다
☐ see a movie	영화를 보다

05
☐ return	반납하다
☐ borrow	대출하다
☐ late fee	연체료

06
☐ clean up	청소하다

☐ afterwards	그 뒤에
☐ fault	잘못
☐ decide	결정하다
☐ look forward to	~를 기대하다

07
☐ proud of	~를 자랑으로 여기는
☐ beginner	초보자
☐ ability	능력
☐ instrument	악기
☐ try	시도하다

08
☐ concentrate	집중하다
☐ end up	결국 ~이 되다
☐ hang out	어울리다
☐ noisy	시끄러운
☐ choice	선택
☐ stuffy	답답한

09
☐ move	이사하다
☐ rule	규칙
☐ area	구역
☐ lock	보관함
☐ take a break	휴식을 취하다

10
☐ remind	상기시키다
☐ follow	따르다
☐ litter	쓰레기를 버리다
☐ pose	문제를 제기하다
☐ leash	목줄
☐ respect	존중하다

11	
□ release	개봉하다
□ receive	받다
□ good review	좋은 평
□ critic	비평가
□ countryside	시골 지역
12	
□ make an appointment	예약을 하다
□ clinic	병원
□ record	기록
13	
□ May I speak to ~?	~와 통화할 수 있나요?
□ package	소포
□ leave	떠나다; ~을 두고 가다
14	
□ express train	급행열차
□ preferably	가급적이면
□ car rental	자동차 대여
□ sightseeing	관광
15	
□ serve	(음식을) 내다
□ wrap	포장하다
□ set the table	식탁을 차리다
□ heat up	~을 데우다
□ take out	내놓다
□ garbage	쓰레기
16	
□ Would you like some ~?	~드실래요?
□ allergic	알레르기가 있는
□ full	배가 부른

□ wrap	싸다
□ That's very nice of you.	아주 친절하시네요.
□ share	나누다
17	
□ Long time no see!	오랜만이다!
□ walk	산책하다
□ borrow	빌리다
□ scene	장면
□ allow	허락[허가]하다
18	
□ attraction	명소
□ take pictures	사진을 찍다
□ have lunch	점심을 먹다
□ local	지역의
□ aquarium	수족관
19	
□ lose weight	몸무게를 줄이다
□ give it a try	한번 해보다
20	
□ technology	기술
□ example	예
□ develop	발전하다
□ imagine	상상하다